Johann Georg Keyssler

Travels Through Germany, Bohemia, Hungary, Switzerland, Italy, and Lorrain

Giving a true and just description of the present state of those countries. Vol. 3

Johann Georg Keyssler

Travels Through Germany, Bohemia, Hungary, Switzerland, Italy, and Lorrain
Giving a true and just description of the present state of those countries. Vol. 3

ISBN/EAN: 9783337344979

Printed in Europe, USA, Canada, Australia, Japan

Cover: Foto ©Andreas Hilbeck / pixelio.de

More available books at **www.hansebooks.com**

TRAVELS

THROUGH

GERMANY, ITALY, SWITZERLAND, &c.

LETTER LVI.

Journey from ROME to NAPLES.

SIR,

THE gates of Rome are never shut, so that at any hour by day or night a traveller may go out or come into the city without any difficulty. In travelling from Rome to Naples it is very inconvenient to go with the Vetturini; for though the road they take lies over Monte Cassino, and consequently gives one an opportunity of seeing the celebrated Benedictine monastery on that hill; yet it is attended with the mortification of being five days on the road, and paying the Vetturini an extraordinary price for their loss of time. The abbey of Monte Cassino stands on a high mountain, the ascent to which is near two German miles. The fathers are very courteous and hospitable; the prospect from this abbey is charming, the library well kept, and the revenues very considerable: but what gains it an un-

Abbey on Monte Cassino.

common

common veneration among the Roman-catholics, is, that here St. Benedict, the patriarch of the monks among the western Christians, first instituted his order, which has produced so many eminent personages. For in the year 1688, the registers of this order contained four emperors, twelve empresses, forty popes, one and forty queens, forty-six kings, fifty patriarchs, two hundred cardinals, sixteen hundred archbishops, four thousand six hundred bishops, and three thousand six hundred canonized saints.

Velletri. In the road from Rome to Torre di mezza via, which is the first stage, are to be seen the noble ruins of some ancient aqueducts. Velletri lies at the distance of three posts or stages from Rome, on a hill, and is celebrated by Pliny, lib. xiv. c. 6. for the excellency of its wine; but at present it is much degenerated, being so rough as to be hardly drinkable, unless it be boiled. The vineyards or mountains near Setia, not far from Casa Nuova, have degenerated in the same manner; for they are now almost barren, whereas they produced a great quantity of generous wine, for which Setia is celebrated by Martial, Strabo, Athenæus, Statius, Juvenal, and Pliny. The author last mentioned says, ' That Augustus preferred the Setia wine to any other.' The princi-

Ginetti palace. pal, and indeed, the only palace now in Velletri, is that which formerly belonged to the family of Ginetti, and since devolved to prince Lancellotti. It was built by cardinal Ginetti, from a design of the famous architect Lunghi, and is said to have cost five hundred thousand *scudi*, or crowns. The great stair-case is built with white marble, and is so magnificent and well-contrived, that it passes for the finest in all Italy. In the aparments are a great number of fine statues, busto's *basso-relievo's*, and paintings. The most remarkable among the first are, a Venus with Cupid, and the fable of the unfortunate Dirce in little, after the manner of the Toro Farnese. The prospect from the gardens is extremely beautiful: they are also ornamented with fine pieces of sculpture, particularly four pillars, which were brought hither from the temple of Mars at Velletri, and several antique *sarcophagi*, dug up in that neighbourhood; one of which, from the naval ornaments carved on it, is thought to have belonged to a sea-officer. Plates of these antiques are to be seen in cardinal Corradini's Vetus Latium profanum & sacrum, continued by Vulpi, a learned Jesuit.

Among the antiquities collected by the Borgia family in their house at Velletri, the busto's of a philosopher, and the emperor Pertinax, are worth observing.

In

From ROME to NAPLES.

In the market-place, near the Ginetti palace, is a superb bronze statue of Urban VIII. who is represented in his pontifical habit pronouncing the benediction: this statue was designed by Bernini. It stands on a marble pedestal, and, as appears by the inscription, was erected in 1637.

Misson, relying on the authority of Suetonius, affirms that Augustus was born at Rome, and that Velletri has no claim to the honor of being the place of his birth; but from the same historian (chap. v. and xciv. of his life of Augustus) and from the beginning of the 55th book of Dio Cassius, it appears, that this emperor's family was of Velletri, and that he himself was educated at a seat in the neighbourhood of that town. [*Whether the emperor Augustus was born at Velletri.*]

About three Italian miles from Velletri, towards Nettuno, at a place called le Cento Colonne, are the remains of an ancient reservoir, or fishpond; and not far from Velletri, towards Cintiano, are to be seen the ruins of a magnificent palace, which is thought to have been the residence of the emperor Otho, as the hill on which it stood is still called Colle Ottone. Copper-plates of some lofty vaulted rooms still remaining, and of the above-mentioned reservoir, are to be seen in *Corradini's Vetus Latium continuatum*, tom. IV. tab. iii. and ix. [*Remains of Otho's palace.*]

On the left hand, near Cisterna, which is the fourth stage from Rome, stands a noble palace belonging to prince Caserta. Sermoneta lies in a marshy unhealthful soil. The name of this country, in Pliny's time, was Palus Pomptina; but instead of twenty-three towns which stood there in his time, only a few houses scattered through the country are now to be seen *. It appears indeed from Strabo (*Geogr. lib.* v.) that the air of this country was reckoned very unhealthy in ancient times, and Silius Italicus terms it Campus Pomptinus pestifer: but at present it is more noxious than ever, as the extent of the fens and stagnating waters, which were the causes of its insalubrity, is now increased. The woods about Cisterna and Sermoneta, especially those to the south of the former, intercept a great part of the infectious exhalations, which otherwise the southerly winds must have carried towards Rome, where they naturally would be attended with very pernicious consequences. For this reason,

---
* Plin. Hist. Nat. lib. iii. c. 5. vide Corradini Latium, tom. II.

From ROME to NAPLES.

In 1714, the pope would not permit the duke di Sermoneta, who could have made it turn to a very great account, to cut down those woods at once: for a commiffion of feveral cardinals was appointed to examine the affair, and Lancifi, the pope's phyfician (a very competent judge of fuch matters) being confulted, laid before them a weighty remonftrance, fetting forth the evils that would refult to the city of Rome by cutting down this wood, unlefs it was done gradually by certain parcels and divifions. Accordingly a proper regard was paid to his opinion, and the wood was cut down in fuch a manner, as to allow one part of it time to grow before another part was touched.

Sermoneta.

Sermoneta lies on the left of the road from Rome to Naples; it is fituated on an eminence well planted with olive-trees. The road as far as Cafa Nuova is along a flat country, and being interfperfed with ancient ruins, is not unpleafant;

St. Paul's three taverns.

among which, thofe on the left, called Tre-Taverna, is faid to be the place mentioned in the twenty-eighth chapter of the Acts of the Apoftles. Beyond Cafa Nuova the road bears to the left into a delightful valley, from which to Piperno is a continual afcent; thefe parts alfo abound with olive plantations. Thofe who are fond of natural curiofities may meet with fome entertainment in the various petrefactions to be found there. From Piperno the road lies through a large wood of cork-trees, the bark of which is thick, and being ftripped off for ufe, grows again in two years time. This tree is an ever-green, with leaves refembling thofe of a pear or plumb-tree, and bears a kind of maft *. This tree is to be met with on the other fide of Piperno, and likewife in Spain, and the fouthern parts of France.

Terracina.

Terracina, by the ancients called Anxur, lies on a hill, and is the laft town in the papal dominions. The country in this neighbourhood, excepting fome moraffes, is very fruitful, and produces good wines. It exhibits feveral delightful gardens, and is interfperfed with little groves of orange-trees which grow in the open fields. Both here and further on towards Naples, are to be feen great quantities of a kind of fruit called *coroba*, or *corobola*, refembling large bean-fhells. The whole country hereabouts has the appearance of a delicious garden, fo that it is not at all furprifing that the antient pagan inhabitants (as appears from the images of that deity

---

* It is a kind of ever-green oak, and bears acorns, as I obferved in France; fo that the author's defcription of it is not very accurate.

carved

From ROME to NAPLES.

carved in numberless places) should pay divine honors to Priapus, the god or patron of gardens *.

Just beyond Terracina are to be seen the ruins of the temple of Janus, the palaces of Julius Cæsar, Adrian, and other remains of antiquity; particularly the Via Appia, which here reaches from Mola to the river Garigliano. This famous road derives its name from Appius Claudius the censor, who made it at his own expence, from Rome to Capua. From Tacitus's annals, Strabo, and Horace, it appears, that it extended as far as Brundusium in their time; yet they make no mention of the person by whom it was continued. As there are other roads to Brundisi, and this is in some places extremely damaged, passengers do not always keep the Via Appia: however, by the constant and durable repairs bestowed on it, it may be travelled hereabouts without any considerable inconveniency. The stones of this pavement are about a foot and a half square, and so hard and firmly cemented, as to have stood the continued frictions of carriages, &c. for above two thousand years. This causey is twenty *palmi* broad, and affords sufficient room for two carriages to go abreast. From Terracina there is a fine view of the sea to the right, which is so near the road, that at the distance of an Italian mile from that town, there was a necessity of breaking down a piece of a rock to clear the way, which there runs close by the sea. Three miles further on this road is the frontier wall of the kingdom of Naples, called Portello, which extends itself, according to some, from the hill to the sea, or at least to a fort, where, in war time, the Neapolitans keep a garrison. On that side of the gate which looks towards Naples is the following inscription: *Remains of antiquity.* *Inscription at the Neapolitan frontiers.*

> * *Sinum lactis, & hæc te liba, Priape, quotannis*
> *Exspectare sat est: custos es pauperis horti.*
> *Nunc te marmoreum pro tempore fecimus: at tu,*
> *Si fœtura gregem suppleverit, aureus esto.*
> VIRG. Ecl. vii. v. 33.
>
> ‘ This bowl of milk, these cakes, our country fare,
> ‘ For thee, Priapus, yearly we prepare,
> ‘ Because a little garden is thy care.
> ‘ But if the falling lambs increase my fold,
> ‘ Thy marble statue shall be turn'd to gold.’
> DRYDEN.

From ROME to NAPLES.

Philippo II. Rege Catholico
Peraf, Alcalæ Duce pro-Rege.
Hospes, hic sunt fines Regni Neapolitani.
Si amicus advenis, pacata omnia invenies
&, malis moribus pulsis, bonas leges.
Anno Domini MDLXVIII.

'Stranger, these are the frontiers of the kingdom of Na-
'ples. If thou comest as a friend, thou shalt meet with
'humane treatment; vice and diforders being here fuppreffed
'by the happy influence of falutary laws. This infcription
'was put up in the reign of Philip II. king of Spain, the
'duke of Alcala being vice-roy of Naples, and in the year
'of Chrift 1568.'

<small>Difference betwixt the papal and Neapolitan dominions.</small> In going from Rome to Naples it is requifite to have a pafs-port which is given gratis by the imperial minifter, or the cardinal-agent; and in returning from Naples to Rome another pafs-port muft be procured from the vice-roy. In both of them is fpecified the time of their continuing in force; however it was not till we came to Mola that any pafs-port was required of our company: at Terracina, and even at the fort we were not afked to produce it. The ecclefiaftical ftate and the kingdom of Naples are diftinguifhed by giving the appellation of *La Campagna* to the former, and *Il Regno* to the latter: but the difference between them is very vifible, the kingdom of Naples being much more populous and better cultivated than the papal territories.

It is with pleafure I recall the idea of the fine profpect all the way from Fondi to Iteri: the country to the right produces grofs, flax, and wheat, interfperfed by double rows of vines, the upper branches of which are interwoven in a beautiful manner. This profpect terminates with a view of the fea, which diverfifies this charming fcene, by the vaft number of tartans and other veffels continually failing on it. On the left-hand the profpect is not inferior to it, being variegated with vines, olive and mulberry trees, lofty, cypreffes, and orange-groves, terminated by a diftant range of hills; nor is the country beyond Mola lefs beautiful or fertile. In the neighbourhood of the Gargliano the foil alters for the worfe, but upon croffing the river, the road lies through a level and moft delicious country.

The

From ROME to NAPLES.

The firſt town in the Neapolitan dominions on this ſide *Fondi.* is Fondi. In 1534 it ſuffered extremely by the attempt of *Story of Hariaden Barbaroſſa* to carry off Julia Gonzaga, counteſs of *Julia Gonzaga.* Fondi, a celebrated beauty, with a view of preſenting her to the grand Signior. However, her virtue or modeſty was of the ſavage kind, if the ſtory be true, that a gentleman who reſcued her in her ſhift with the utmoſt hazard of his life, was afterwards aſſaſſinated by her order, merely becauſe he had ſeen her in ſuch a plight. If this execrable murder had been perpetrated by her huſband Veſpaſiano Colonna in a fit of jealouſy, which is almoſt natural to an Italian huſband, it would in ſome meaſure have exculpated the lady; but Julia's unheard of villany and ingratitude admits of no excuſe. Brantome in his *Les Vies des Dames illuſtres*, or Lives of illuſtrious Ladies, and from him Varillas in his hiſtory of Francis I. give a particular account of the whole tranſaction. They tell us, that Julia being awakened by the outcries at the approach of the Turks, leaped out of a window in her ſhift, and eſcaped to the neighbouring mountains. There is not a word in theſe authors of a cavalier aſſiſting her in making her eſcape. On the contrary it is added, that ſhe fell into the hands of the Banditti; and though Julia afterwards proteſted upon oath, that as ſoon as they knew who ſhe was, they obſerved all the diſtant reſpect due to her dignity, few people could be brought to belive that ſo tempting an object had ſuffered no indignity or indecency among a troop of ſuch lawleſs and brutal people. This little agrees with the account above of the gallantry and ſubſequent murder of the ſuppoſed cavalier. But Brantome and Varillas are both miſtaken in giving the name of Livia to the counteſs, and of Aſcanius to Veſpaſiano Colonna her huſband. Barbaroſſa being diſappointed of his prize, vented his rage by deſtroying and pillaging the town, not ſparing ſo much as the tombs of two dukes of Colonna; and beſides exerciſing other cruelties, carried away many of the inhabitants into ſlavery.

Mola is ſituated near the ſea, where the emperor has a *Mola.* cuſtom-houſe and a ſmall garriſon which is relieved every week from Gaëta. Here is a garden very well kept, with fine walks and abundance of orange-trees. Near Mola are to be ſeen the ruins of a palace, which, according to ſome inſcriptions ſaid to be found in it, belonged to Cicero; but the grotto's and ſubterraneous vaults were very much damaged in the preſent century by the imperialiſts, who when they laid ſiege to Gaëta, made this place their magazine. It

From ROME to NAPLES.

Death of Cicero. was on a journey from hence to some other place that Cicero was assassinated by that ungrateful wretch Popilus Lænas. At Mola the two unfortunate German princes Frederic of Austria, and Conrad of Suabia, were discovered and sent to Naples, where they were beheaded. These remarkable events have caused Mola to make some figure in history, though they are such transactions as cannot be thought of without regret. However, it is the opinion of some men of learning, that Cicero's last place of residence was Astura, and not Mola *.

Gaëta. The fortress of Gaëta lies three Italian miles from Mola, and by water is an hour's passage. As Gaëta is supposed to have derived its name from Cajeta, Æneas's nurse, who, as Virgil tells us, died and was buried here, the people, according to the common practice in Italy, might have found some ruin or other to have shewn to strangers for her monument; but nothing of that kind is pretended: however, on a fortified eminence is to be seen Rolando's tower, as it is called, or rather an ancient mausoleum of Lucius Munatius Plancus, as appears by the following inscription:

> *L. Munatius. L. F. L. N. L. Pron.*
> *Plancus. Cos. Cens. Imp. Iter. VII. Vir.*
> *Epul. Triump. ex. Rætis. ædem. Saturni.*
> *Fecit. de. manibiis. agros. divisit. in. Italia.*
> *Beneventi. in. Gallia. colonias. deduxit.*
> *Lugdunum. & Rauricam.*

In

---

* Other writers place the last residence of this famous orator at Cajeta, where he had another *villa*. It must be owned, that Cicero's irresolution and fear towards the last scene of his life, is inconsistent with the firmness of a philosopher. One while his apprehensions hurry him to sea, then he hastens to get ashore; now he entertains a glimmering hope in the clemency of his enemies: this is succeeded by a whimsical thought of stealing privately into Augustus's house and there killing himself, from an idle notion, that his ghost would haunt that emperor. Amidst those fluctuations he is surprised by that parricide Popilius, whom his eloquence had saved from the gallows. His attendants, partly by force and partly by intreaties, got him into a litter and made towards the sea; but they were soon overtaken, and the greatest orator that Rome ever produced died obscurely, being beheaded in a place of no note. The insults of Fulvia offered to the head of this great man after his death, are still more shocking. *Dio Cass. (hist. lib. xlvii.)* says, *Caput Ciceronis arreptum insultans amarulentis verbis & conspuens genibus suis imposuit Fulvia, oreque ejus aperto linguam extractam acubus, quales secum comendi capitis caussâ mulieres ferunt, compunxit, additis crebris*

From ROME to NAPLES.

In the fourth line, I conceive Manibiis ſtands for Manubiis, and from the offices with which this Plancus, (who lived in Auguſtus's time, and had been a hearer of Cicero,) was inveſted, this work muſt have been erected about fifteen years before the birth of Chriſt. Some are for making this tower a temple of Saturn built by Munatius; but this conjecture is overthrown by the inſcription, from which it may be demonſtrated to have been his monument, tho' it wants the uſual preamble of Diis Manibus; and the enumeration of the high offices he had filled might in his life-time, and by his order, be placed on every edifice of his building. Suetonius in the life of Octavius Cæſar, ſays, that it was by the advice of this Plancus that the ſurname of Auguſtus was conferred on that emperor, preferably to that of Romulus. The city of Lugdunum or Lyons, mentioned in the inſcription, was totally conſumed by fire in Seneca's time, exactly two hundred years from the foundation thereof, as appears from the ninety-firſt letter of that philoſopher, *lib.* i. Seven years after, Nero (as Tacitus writes, *Annal* xvi. *c.* 13.) laid a plan for rebuilding it.

On the Monte della Trinità, the Benedictines have a church, near which is to be ſeen a rock with a large cleft, reaching from the ſummit of it down to the bottom of the ſea. That it was not originally ſo, appears from the cavities and convexities on the two oppoſite ſides, which if they could be brought into contact, would be found to correſpond exactly. But whether this diſruption of the rock happened miraculouſly at the time of our Saviour's paſſion, is another queſtion. This opinion is grounded only upon modern, and conſequently ſuſpicious, traditions, and is abſolutely contradicted by thoſe who confine the miracles which the Holy Scriptures mention to have accompanied the death of Chriſt to Judea; for they alledge, that in other parts of the world where people were ignorant of the matter in proof of which they were wrought, they would have carried neither conviction nor information *. But whenever the earthquake happened

[Fiſſure in a rock.]

---

crebris ac turpibus opprobriis. ' Fulvia furiouſly ſiezing Cicero's head, ' ſpit on it with the moſt bitter revilings; then ſetting it on her knees, and ' opening the mouth, drew out the tongue, and with a bodkin, ſuch as ' women ſtick in their hair, ſhe pierced it through and through, in the ' mean time pouring forth the ſevereſt reproaches againſt the orator.'

* This remarkable fiſſure is unqueſtionably to be attributed to an earthquake, tho' not to that which happened at the death of our Saviour. The

ſacred

pened the effect is surprising and worthy of observation. The rent is about four or five feet wide, and by a flight of steps you pass through it to a small chapel called Capello del Crocifisso, from which there is a fine view of the sea. The Benedictine church stands about fifty-nine paces from this chapel, fifty-one of which are taken up by the rock, of which the monks present strangers with some small fragments. To these fragments the grateful bigots shew a great veneration, and give the monks a small offering or alms, which they need not grudge, the fathers assuring them, that *Superstition concerning it.* they are now possessed of a sovereign preservative against the head-ach, falling-sickness, &c. Tartans and other vessels, as they pass by the lower chapel, usually salute it with a gun, and lying upon their oars, perform a devotional office with music, or send ashore to the convent a pecuniary offering, at least, equal to the expence of a salute. But what is more extraordinary the infidel Corsairs, have frequently sent a sum of money to the monks in acknowledgment of their preservation in bad weather, upon addressing their devotions to this chapel.

Franciscan convent. The Franciscan convent here boasts of having been the residence of the founder of that seraphic order, as it is stiled; *Place where St. Francis preached to the fishes.* and by the sea-side, without the Porta di Ferro, is shewn the place where St. Francis stood when he preached with such power, that the very fishes raised themselves above the surface of the water, listening to his voice.

Consecrated standard. In the choir of the cathedral hangs the consecrated standard presented by pope Pius V. to Don John, on his going to sea to fight against the Turks as commander in chief of the united fleets of the Christian powers: in the middle of this flag is represented our Saviour on the cross, and St. Peter and St. Paul, with this motto:

In hoc signo vinces.

'This is the standard by which thou shalt conquer.'

The people never fail to pay their devout adorations to this standard.

sacred historians make mention of many miracles and prodigies which happened at that time, but without particularly specifying the places. Phlegon Trallian indeed speaks of a similar earthquake in Bithynia; but the date being in the 4th year of the 202d Olympiad, it cannot be reconciled with the time of Christ's passion. See Bayle on the word Phlegon.

The

From ROME to NAPLES.

The *basso-relievo*'s on the marble font exhibit Fauns and **Remarkable** satyrs dancing, and Mercury delivering Bacchus to Ino **font.** to be nursed. The workmanship is exquisite, and, as appears by the following inscription, was done by Salpion an Athenian:

ΣΑΛΠΙΩΝ
ΑΘΗΝΑΙΟΣ
ΕΠΟΙΗΣΕ.

'Salpion, an Athenian, carved it.

This vase, supported by four lions of marble, was brought from the ruins of Formia to Gaëta, and probably belonged to a temple of Bacchus. The statue of Æsculapius, facing the altar of the holy sacrament, has been described by Misson, tom. II. p. 23. Besides this, there is another small pagan idol also fixed in the church-wall. On a pillar near eighteen feet high, is a curious piece of sculpture, representing the martyrdom of St. Erasmus, whose body, deposited in this church, is to be seen. A subterraneous chapel under this cathedral is painted by Brandi. The altar and the balustrade before it are of beautiful inlaid marble; here are also six statues of cast silver, as big as the life. The tower is said to have been built by Frederic Barbarossa, by way of attonement for his sins.

Near the door of the castle, which stands upon a hill, is **Remains of** shewn the remains of the famous Charles of Bourbon, with **the famous** a wooden lower-jaw inserted to supply the place of the na- **Charles de** tural one, long since decayed. This nobleman was shot in **Bourbon.** storming Rome, and thus dying under the pope's excommunication, and being openly in arms against the holy see, he could not be allowed a burial-place in consecrated ground; and to leave him unburied, or lay him among the vulgar, did not seem compatible either with his dignity, or the regard due to his eminent services. The Spaniards, therefore, had recourse to another expedient, for they dried his corps like a mummy, and set it up here. He stands in a closet, being properly cloathed; his boots are yellow, with red facings; and the stockings, which come but a little above the boots, have a border of fine lace. In 1719 general Prampero, governor of the city, had this memorable skeleton new cloathed in blue trimmed with silver, and furnished it with a sword, cane, and hat and feather. Over the closet-door are these lines in Spanish:

Francia

*Francia me diò la leche, Espanna fuerza y ventura.
Roma me diò la muerte, y Gaëta la sepultura.*

'France gave me birth, Spain strength and honours gave,
'Rome my death's wound, and Gaëta a grave.'

Ciacconi, in his life of Clement VII. p. 465, gives us the following epitaph on this famous warrior:

*Aucto Imperio, Gallo victo,
Superatâ Italiâ, Pontifice obsesso,
Româ captâ,
Carolus Borbonius in victoriâ cæsus
Hic jacet.*

' Here lies Charles de Bourbon, who after enlarging the
' empire, defeating the French, conquering Italy, besieg-
' ing the Pope, and taking Rome, lost his life in the midst
' of a victory.'

However, it is a known story, that a Spaniard, in whose house the duke had taken up his quarters, set fire to it the very next day, to efface the infamy of its having harboured a traitor; and indeed all the epitaphs written on this hero are far from running in the same strain.

On each side of the skeleton is an inscription, one in Italian, the other in French; both of which are to the same purpose. The latter, which has been incorrectly printed before, is as follows:

Au Charles Duc de Bourbon de la Maison Royale de France, Grand Connetable du Royaume, clair par sa naissance, plus clair par sa fortune, qui perfecuté de son Roy, protegé de l' Empereur Cing, fait son Capitain General de l Armée, glorieux par ses exploits & par les victoires emportées sur les trouppes du même Roy, qu'il fit prisonnier en Pavie, s'acheminant à la ville de Rome, ou chacun croyoit, qu'il alla triompher, comme un Heros de l'Antiquité, il y fut tué pendant le siege 1527. *Son corps enbaumé fût transporté à Gaëta & Monf. le General Comte de Prampero, Gouverneur de cette place & de son chateau pour donner un admirable exemple aux autres Ministres de trés juste Impereur Charles Six, restaura le tombeau* 1719.

' To Charles duke of Bourbon, of the blood-royal of
' France, constable of the kingdom, illustrious by his birth,
and

' and yet more so by his personal merit, who being persecuted
' by his sovereign, was protected by the emperor Charle V.
' and made captain-general of his army, in which quality he
' acquired immortal honour by his glorious exploits, having
' several times defeated the troops of that king by whom he
' had been injured, and taken him prisoner at Pavia; from
' thence he directed his march to Rome, into which it was
' expected he would have entered in triumph, like the heroes
' of antiquity; but he was killed in an assault during the
' siege of that city, in 1527. His body was embalmed and
' sent to Gaëta, where, by the generosity of the count de
' Prampero, governor of that town and castle, to set a
' worthy example to the other officers of the most gracious
' emperor Charles VI. this monument was repaired in the
' year 1719.'

Formerly the officers of this garrison, when in their cups, *Drinking out of a skull.* on any public rejoicings, used to take off the duke's skull, and fill it with liquor, in order to drink healths out of it; but this savage custom frequently occasioning quarrels, some of which had unhappy consequences, has been forbidden *.

The garrison of Gaëta at present consists of a thousand men. *Siege of Gaëta in 1707.* In 1707 this place was taken sword in hand by the Imperialists, under Count Daun, after a siege which greatly redounded to the honour both of the besieged and assailants; the Spanish garrison having fired fifteen thousand cannot shot, and four thousand bombs; which, on the part of the Germans, were returned with twenty thousand of the former, and fourteen thousand of the latter. The marquis de Vigliena, afterwards vice-roy of Naples, who commanded in the fort, with two thousand Spaniards surrendered themselves prisoners of war. The ten colours and standards, taken on that occasion were, pursuant to a vow made to St. Januarius, hung up in the Capella del Tesoro at Naples, where they are still to be seen †.

About eight Italian miles from Mola is a ruinous aqueduct, which begins at Trajetto, a little town two miles to the left

* This savage custom of drinking out of the enemies skulls was of a very ancient date, and very common among the Scythians, Germans, and northern nations, as appears from Herodotus, Diodorus Siculus, and Livy.

† In 1734, Gaëta was recovered by the Spaniards, and without any considerable loss.

of

Minturna. of the road, on a pleasant eminence, and some ruins of the ancient Minturna. Near it runs the Garigliano, antiently **Garigliano.** called the Liris, which was the boundary of Latium. The village of the same name, which lies along the river, belongs to the Caraffa family, who also have the profits arising from the ferry. The author of the Voyage Historique d'Italie, lately published, talks of crossing the Garigliano over a bridge (tom. II. p. 196.) but either his memory has strangely failed him, or, as I am more inclined to suspect from several other particulars in that work, he never set a foot in these parts. After crossing this river, the road lies through a luxuriant country as far as Capua, and on the left lies the **Falernum.** district of Falernum, which formerly extended from Sinuessa to the Vulturnus, and produced the famous Falernian wine.

Sessa. On a hill to the left near St. Agatha, stands the small town of Sessa. In the church is to be seen some ancient mosaic-work, which, however, will not bear a comparison with the modern. The artist himself, conscious of its defects, has illustrated the imagery by placing the name under every figure, in mosaic. This was one of the chief towns of the ancient Volsci, under the names of Aurunca and Suessa Pometia.

New Capua. In the area before the cathedral at New Capua are several large antient *sarcophagi*, adorned with fine *basso-relievo*'s representing sacrifices and religious ceremonies; and in the church is a fine picture of the Annunciation.

On the town wall is the following inscription:

Philippo IV. Rege,
Romano quondam pacem imperio,
Lumen columenque Campaniæ;
Marte, Opibus, Copiis diu florentem
C A P V A M
Vicissitudine collapsam deterrimâ,
Cassam munimentis, nudatam subinde muris,
Hostesque propè insultantes contemplatus
Emanuel Fonseca & Zunica Com. Mont. Reg. VII.
consilia antevertens belli,
Suoque, futuroque præcavens ævo,
Refectis mœnibus, structisque propugnaculis,
Si minus pristinæ magnitudini,
Pristinæ restituit munitioni.
Anno Salutis hum. M.DCXXXVI.

‘ Capua

From ROME to NAPLES.

'Capua, to which formerly the Roman empire owed its safety, the glory and defence of Campania, long celebrated for opulence and strength, being by various accidents and viciffitudes brought to a defencelefs ftate, its fortifications and walls being fo ruined, that it became expofed to the continued infults of the enemy, was reftored to its antient ftrength, though not to its former extent, by Emanuel Fonfeca and Zunica the feventh count of Montreal, who, to defend it from hoftile attacks, and for its prefervation in his own and future ages, repaired the walls and towers, with the addition of feveral new works, in the reign of Philip IV. and in the year of our redemption 1636.'

A ftatue of king Charles II. of Spain is erected in the market-place, with a long infcription under it, full of adulation, &c.

The ancient Capua, which enervated Hannibal's army, *Old Capua.* lies two Italian miles from New Capua, on the right-hand towards Naples. Little is to be feen of its antient fplendor, except the ruins of an amphitheatre; it having fucceffively felt the favage fury of the Vandals, Oftrogoths, and Longohardians. The diftance from new Capua to Naples is fixteen miles; the road lies through as fine a country as eye ever beheld. The caufey, though of a much later date than the Via Appia, is not at all inferior to it; and in many parts, the rows of trees planted on each fide of it form a fine vifta of above a mile in length. The country on each fide is diverfified with corn-fields, gardens, and vineyards; and the vines climbing up the lofty trees, and interwoven with their luxuriant branches, form a kind of natural feftoons.

In the months of February and March a perfon muft be very expeditious to travel feven ftages in a poft-chaife from fung-rifing to fun-fet; but in fummer the feventeen ftages and a half between Rome and Naples are eafily performed in two days. For the two chaife-horfes at every ftage within the Neapolitan territories, one pays eleven Carlini *, and half as much for the chaife, if wanted. The goodnefs of the roads, the fertility of the country, and the vigour and ftrength of the horfes, make travelling extremely pleafant in the Neapolitan dominions. However, one cannot be too careful that the *Louis d'or*, or Spanifh piftoles, that a travel- *Caution about money.* ler brings into this country be of the juft weight; for both

* Three fhillings and eight-pence fterling.

at Naples and on the road all gold coins are weighed with more cunning than equity, and needless cavils raised to make them appear to be under weight. I remember a waiter who belonged to an inn at Mola, a place infamous for knavery and cheats of all kinds, peremptorily insisted that a pistole, which he had only weighed in his hand, was too light; but, upon trial, it was found to be something above weight.

Naples, March 8, 1730.   I am, &c.

LETTER LVII.

Of natural Curiosities in the Kingdom of NAPLES.

SIR,

Manna. Saffron.

IT is not without reason that the kingdom of Naples is termed a paradise, as it abounds with all kinds of grain, fruit, herbage, flax, oil, and wine, in the highest perfection. Calabria is famous for its manna; and produces saffron equal to the oriental, which likewise grows in other parts of the kingdom *.

The kingdom of Naples also produces alum, vitriol, sulphur, rock-crystal, marble, and several sorts of minerals. The wool of this country is excellent both for strength and fineness; and it yields silk in such plenty, that vast quantities of it are annually exported. As for wines, it rivals those of the richest climates. Here are to be seen the finest flocks and herds in the world; and Neapolitan horses are so much esteemed, that to mention them is enough. The exportation of these products, together with great quantities of snuff and soap, are very considerable funds of wealth to this kingdom. I must not omit a particular manufacture, which is chiefly carried on at Tarento and Rheggio, where waistcoats, caps, stockings, and gloves, are knit with a kind of hairy filaments growing on a species of shell-fish. In soft-

Manufacture of filaments in shell-fish.

---

* Saffron also grows in the southern parts of Germany, and also in Normandy, Languedoc, Provence, and the principality of Orange in France. [The English saffron is the best of any in the world, but is not mentioned by the author.

ness

Kingdom of NAPLES.

ness and fineness this stuff yields indeed to silk; but it retains a particular gloss to the last. The natural colour of these filaments is a kind of an olive-green, and the shell on which they grow is also commonly found about Malta, Corsica, and Sardinia: I have met with some of these shells even in the Adriatic, which afford but few of these useful filaments, which yield a comfortable subsistence to the industrious.

Among the natural curiosities of the kingdom of Naples may be also reckoned the *Lapis Phrygius* *, or *Pietra fungifera*, as it is commonly called; which, when laid in shady or damp places, within a few days yields two, three, or more *fungi* or mushrooms, according to the largeness of the stone. These are eaten by the Neapolitans; but it is a mistake to imagine that the vegetable proceeds simply from a real stone. This *Lapis Phrygius* is only a hard congeries of earth, rotten box-wood, and sprays of several shrubs and herbs, together with the mushroom-seeds, which are so very small, as not to be distinguished from dust, but by the help of a very good microscope. That these seemingly strange *fungi* issue from homogeneous seeds is manifest from hence, that if a mushroom be not left to ripen on the stone till it drops its seeds, the stone loses its virtue; or, to speak more properly, the seeds being taken away before they come to maturity, the vegetation ceases. Warm water poured on the stone is found considerably to forward the growth of these *fungi*, as it penetrates into the closest interstices, and dilates the pores of the stone, causing a fermentation in the confined sap, and fomenting the seeds to a speedy vegetation. The natural season for these stones, when they lie in the earth, to produce mushrooms, is the spring; but by putting them in pots filled with moist earth, they yield them all the year round. Possibly many other seeds are contained in this mass; though, for want of a proper cultivation, &c. their growth may be checked. The *fungi*, when the stone is duly prepared, generally appear on the third or fourth day, and on the sixth attain to their full maturity. They grow to the height of a span above the stone, and are of different figures. The outside of them is of a brownish red; but within they are very white. These fungiferous stones are chiefly found on eminences, but seldom in valleys and low grounds. They

Lapis Phrygius, or Pietra fungifera.

---

* Here is another sort of *Lapis Phrygius*, not unlike the English fuller's-earth, which is described by Pliny, *lib.* xxxvi. *c.* 20.

are

are to be met with in great plenty, and of all sizes, in the southern parts of the Ecclesiastical State, and near Fondi, Gaeta, Itri, about Naples, and in other parts of this kingdom. This mass, which has neither the hardness of a stone, nor the properties of earth, by its fecundity becomes gradually more porous, and decreases in weight. Paolo Boccone, botanist to the great duke of Tuscany, afterwards a Cistertian monk under the name of Silvio Boccone, and Michael Mercati, in his *Metallotheca*, published in folio at Rome in 1717 by Lancisi, whom I have frequently mentioned with the honour due to his great abilities, have made some remarks on this *Lapis Phrygius*. The heat of the climate, and the fatness of the soil of Italy, is very proper, with suitable moisture, for producing truffles, morels, mushrooms, &c. of an extraordinary size. On an estate called Guadagnola, about twenty miles from Rome, belonging to the Conti family, a very palatable sort of mushrooms are produced, some of which have weighed twenty pounds; but unless they are carefully watched, the birds are apt to peck them to pieces. The duke of Poli presented queen Christina of Sweden with one of those mushrooms, which weighed thirty pounds; of which, on account of its extraordinary size, Kircher has given an accurate description.

Mushrooms of an extraordinary weight.

Mount Vesuvio often fills the neighbouring country with terror; but few things in nature are so absolutely noxious and hurtful, as not to be productive of some good. Even this raging vulcano, by its sulphureous and nitrous manure, and the heat of its subterraneous fires, contributes not a little to the uncommon fertility of the country about it, and the profusion of fruit, herbage, &c. with which it is every-where covered. The same happy effect from the same cause is visible about mount Ætna in Sicily; where the general produce of grain is thirty-six fold, and in one part, when well cultivated, fifty fold. Those are observed to be the most fertile spots which abound in sulphur, salt-petre, &c. If such igneous and inflammable substances were pent up, their fermentation and ebullition would be productive of the most calamitous effects; whereas they find a vent through these vulcano's, and make frequent discharges. Experience shews, that earthquakes, after any continued eruptions of Vesuvio, are not so frequent, and less fatal in their effects than at other times. The inhabitants are far from being alarmed at this mountain's vernal eruptions, when they are not very violent; and the air is so far from being rendered unhealthful by them, that

Mount Vesuvio.

that Barra, a village at the foot of Vesuvio near the sea, is remarkable for its healthfulness.

The ancient fertility of this mountain is celebrated by Martial in the following lines:

Hic est pampineis viridis Vesuvius umbris,
   Presserat hic madidos nobilis uva lacus.
Hæc juga, quàm Nisæ colles, plùs Bacchus amavit,
   Hoc nuper Satyri Monte dedere choros.
Hæc Veneris sedes, Lacedæmone gratior illi;
   Hic locus Herculeo nomine clarus erat.
Cuncta jacent flammis, & tristi mersa favillâ,
   Nec superi vellent hoc licuisse sibi.   Lib. ii. Epig. 105.

' Vesuvio, cover'd with the fruitful vine,
' Here flourish'd once, and ran with floods of wine;
' Here Bacchus oft to the cool shades retir'd,
' And his own native Nisa less admir'd;
' Oft to the mountain's airy tops advanc'd,
' The frisking satyrs on the summits danc'd;
' Alcides here, here Venus grac'd the shore,
' Nor lov'd her fav'rite Lacedæmon more:
' Now piles of ashes, spreading all around,
' In undistinguish'd heaps deform the ground.
' The gods themselves the ruin'd seats bemoan,
' And blame the mischiefs that themselves have done.'
                                        ADDISON.

Though the upper part of mount Vesuvio be covered with cinders, ashes, &c. the lower parts yield three sorts of exquisite wine, namely, the *Vino Greco*, white muscadel, and a wine called *Lacrymæ Christi*; the second has the advantage in flavour, but will not bear any distant exportation. At Pietrabianca this wine is sold for a carlino and a half * per bottle. The *Vino Greco* was originally made from the produce of some vines transplanted hither from Greece †, which have succeeded to admiration.

Wines of the growth of mount Vesuvio.

The

---

* About six-pence.
† The transplanting of vines, &c. has often turned to the great improvement of them. From the vines growing near the Rhine, transplanted to another climate, the celebrated Canary was first produced; and from this same vine, and that of Burgundy, we have that delicious wine brought from the cape of Good-Hope. The China oranges, of such advantage to
                                        Portugal,

Wine why called Lacrymæ Christi. The *Lacrymæ Christi* is so called from the drops of juice ousing from the grapes when fully ripe.

This year, so early as the close of February, mount Vesuvio began to issue flames; and the smoke was to be seen from Naples rising to a considerable height, in a large black column, till it was broke and dissipated by the wind: this happens in three or four minutes, and then one has a clear sight of the top of the mountain, till another eruption comes on in a few minutes, and throws up cinders, smoke, and stones. Amidst the variety of agitations into which the wind blows the smoke, some fanciful persons have imagined that they discerned many sorts of frightful figures. According to Dion Cassius, *lib.* xvi, in Vespasian's time the country was terrified with the imaginary representation of a troop of fuliginous giants issuing from the mouth of Vesuvio. The smoke is not immediately dissipated when blown from the mountain, but expands itself in thick clouds. At night, after every explosion, the mountain was observed to discharge a short fiery column, which was seen to shoot upwards, but was extinguished before it fell. Probably, this only proceeded from the ignited stones thrown up in a perpendicular direc-

---

Portugal, were transplanted thither from China, and from thence to Naples, where they also thrive. The same frequently holds good with regard to animals. The wool of Andalusia is known to surpass all other; and yet that kind of sheep on which it grows were originally natives of England, where the wool, though preferable to any other country in Europe, is inferior to the Spanish. The Spanish horses, though in some parts of the West-Indies they degenerate, in Chili they become far preferable to their progenitors. The origin and descent of nations is copiously set forth in history; and an account of the transmigrations and settlements in the animal and vegetable kingdoms would be no less entertaining. The first pheasants were aborigines of the country about the river Phasis (which issues from the mountains of Armenia, and runs through Mingrelia) and are said to have been first brought into Greece by the Argonauts; red-legged partridges are natives of Numidia; the first of the turkey fowls, as they are commonly called, came from Mexico, and were served up at the nuptial feast of Charles IX, king of France, in 1570. That the difference of air, diet, &c. considerably influences the melioration or degeneracy consequential to these changes of climate is manifest in the human species; the issue of negro parents, when born in Europe, gradually acquire the fair complexion of Europeans; and the descendants of the Portuguese colonists settled on the western coast of Africa, are known to have contracted not only the African complexion of the natives, but the woolly hair, the flat nose, and thick lips, yet still retaining the names of their European ancestors. It is remarkable that the milk of the European women, on their coming to Batavia in the East-Indies, becomes so brackish, that their children refuse the breast, and must be suckled by female negro slaves.

tion,

Kingdom of NAPLES.

tion, of which the greatest part, especially in still weather, drop again into the caverns from whence they issued. After a week's expectation that Vesuvio would return to a state of tranquillity, at the end of which, on the contrary, an increase of its violence was apprehended by the inhabitants, or at least that it would continue longer than my purposed stay at Naples; on the fourteenth of March I resolved that its commotion should not deter me from visiting this extraordinary mountain. The parties for this expedition can never be very numerous; hackney horses being scarce at Naples, and the peasants on the mountain (whose assistance is absolutely necessary) being too few in number to attend on a large company. The distance from Naples to the foot of Vesuvio (here commonly called *Monti di Somma*, either from *sommità*, a summit*, or from *somma*, an adjacent estate) is five Italian miles, including the circuit round the bay; and from the foot of the mountain to the summit it is near three miles further. By an inscription at Capua, mentioned by Parini, Vesuvio seems to have been consecrated to Jupiter Tonans: Jupiter Vesuvius.

Jovi Vesuvio
Sacrum
D.D.

‘ Sacred to Jupiter of Vesuvius.’

Mount Vesuvio, like Parnassus, consists properly of two heads, or summits, though at present only that on the right-hand as you come from Naples, emits fire and smoke. The valley betwixt those hills is about a mile long, and extremely fertile. The height of the burning summit (which is the lower of the two) is computed to be eleven hundred fathoms above the surface of the sea. This mountain by a sudden eruption in the year 1631, laid waste all the neighbouring country; and an earnest admonition to posterity in Latin was cut in stone, and set up in Resina, a village within three miles of Naples, to advise the inhabitants to fly in time, when they are threatened with an eruption of Vesuvio.

At Torre del Greco, a village situated on the sea-coast, three miles from this mountain, are two other inscriptions, giving an account of the destruction of three convents and

---

* As Ætna is now called *Monte Gibello*; for the Saracens, when they were masters of Sicily, gave it the name of *Gibel*, which has the same signification with the German word *Giebel* or *Gipfel*, the summit of a hill.

other buildings thereabouts by the same terrible eruption in 1631, &c.

From Resina the acclivity of the mountain increases, yet so that one may ride still on horse-back. Here are seen several large stones half calcined, scattered in different places, which are left as memorials of former devastations; the greatest part having been cleared away by the peasants living on the mountain, and used for inclosing their vineyards. It is astonishing to think of the impetuosity by which huge masses of four or five hundred weight have been thrown to the distance of several Italian miles. At last the steepness of the ascent, especially as it is all over covered with ashes and cinders, will not admit of riding, and the horses are left to be taken care of by the servants. It is adviseable also both for ease and expedition in climbing among the ashes, &c. to

Hermitage on mount Vesuvius. change boots for shoes. Hereabouts a hermit has built a dwelling, but of a meanness entirely correspondent to the character of self-denial; and such is his fortitude, that Vesuvio must rage with uncommon vehemence before he removes his quarters; as travellers are apt to be fatigued with climbing up this uncommon ascent, he stands ready with some wine to refresh them at their return; and as the rules of his order do not prohibit him from fingering money, he thankfully receives any little acknowledgment made for his seasonable civility.

Character of the peasants. At this hermitage the attendance of the peasants who follow travellers from the neighbouring villages, becomes necessary; but if there happen to be more than can be employed, they are apt to quarrel with one another; this is sometimes attended with bloodshed, and proves of ill consequence to the strangers whom they are so eager to serve. A traveller should by all means carry fire-arms with him on these occasions; those people being trained up to rob and murder, and accustomed to wear at their sides large couteaux. Besides, they are so void of all shame as to make a jest of their detestable practices among one another, when they are laid down to rest. Whilst we were about the skirts of the mountain they talked big, and boasted that they would carry us up to the *bocca* or mouth on the summit of it; but in advancing upwards their note was changed; and at every little blaze they called upon the virgin Mary and St. Januarius, telling us of the great danger we were exposing ourselves to; so that we ourselves were obliged to be upon the chearful strain, in order to keep our guides in heart. All the service they

Kingdom of NAPLES. 23

they do is to go before with leathern belts round their waifts, Their ſer‑
by which travellers hold, that they may climb up with grea‑ vice.
ter eaſe. If the two peaſants that go before every traveller
are not ſufficient, others help by ſhoving him behind. Be‑
fore a perſon puts himſelf in their power, an agreement
muſt be made; and at diſmiſſing them it is beſt to add a
ſmall gratuity, as they have been known to proceed to rude‑
neſs without it, and indeed are ſeldom ſatisfied with the bare
wages agreed upon.

The mountain being very ſteep and moſtly covered with
black aſhes, the aſcent is very difficult; the aſhes giving way
cauſes a man to ſlide ſeveral ſteps downwards, and in places
free from the aſhes, the ruggedneſs of the melted matter puts
you to no leſs trouble. That ſulphur lies here a foot deep,
as a certain writer takes upon him to advance, is what I ſaw
nothing of; but among theſe droſſy clods I met with ſome
red and yellow ſtony ſubſtances, containing a great deal of
ſulphur: neither is there any neceſſity of treading in the
guide's ſteps; for, very often, it cannot be done, the aſhes
inſtantly filling up the impreſſion of his feet. From this
Vulcano has been too often known to iſſue a *lava* or mixed
floods of melted ſulphur, metallic ore and roſin, to the inex‑
preſſible damage of the neighbouring country. The *ſcoria*
of this ejected matter ſtill lies ſtratum upon ſtratum with
large ſtones projecting from them, which, in their courſe
along the ſulphureous ſtream, were ſtopped by their inequali‑
ties; and fixed as the melted matter gradually hardened;
whereas had the ſtream been entirely fluid, it would have
cooled and ſettled in a more even and uniform ſurface. In
the year 1694, the country was viſited with one of thoſe
fiery *lava's*; and the burnt ſtones, though forced under the
melted matter with poles, immediately emerged again.
Theſe ſtreams or currents are not thrown up from the moun‑
tain like the ſtones, but pour down as from an inclined veſ‑
fel; ſo that it ſeems as if ſuch an effuſion could proceed
from no other cauſe but the fulneſs of the whole cavity and
all the receſſes of the mountain of melted ſubſtances. Some
pretend to have computed, that, during the eruption in the
year 1694, ſo great a quantity of *lava* was diſcharged, that
in ſome places it hardened at the height of ſixty ells above the
ſurface of the ground; and that, if it had been accumulated
into one maſs, it would have equalled in bulk the mountain
from the bowels of which it had iſſued. If this be true,
what muſt we think of the abyſs to which this vaſt moun‑
tain

tain is, as it were, the spiracle. The matter thrown up by mount Ætna, in 1669, is said to have amounted to 93,838,750 cubic feet *. I here searched very narrowly for pumice-stones, but could not see a single stone of that kind all over the mountain. In the *scoriæ* are scattered up and down several burnt stones that are very porous; but, on account of their weight and dark adust colour, they differ very much from the genuine pumice-stones found about Baiæ and its neighbourhood. By chemical experiments it appears, that the stones ejected by Vesuvio contain pitch, sulphur, vitriol, alum, antimony, marcassite, arsenic, &c. The differences of the *scoriæ* in colour and substance have therefore nothing strange in them; as, from the various mixtures of such bodies with earth and stone, there must result a great diversity in the alterations they undergo by such a vehement and lasting fusion or ignition. Small quantities of gold, silver, copper, tin, lead, and other minerals have also been extracted from them, which give a light into the constitution of the adjacent strata. I pulverised one of these stones of a red and yellow colour, and applied the magnet to it, but I could observe no attraction or even adhesion; which unquestionably was owing to the prevalency of the remaining sulphur. I was sensible the magnet has no effect upon iron ore, however abounding with metal, till by a strong fire the sulphur mixt with it be expelled; and hereupon repeating the trial with a black clod which had been thoroughly burned, the adhesion was very strong. I shall not animadvert on what some persons have said of their finding in these cinders sparks of rubies and other gems: vitreous substances I myself saw; but these may have been caused by the fusion of a fine sand, salt, and marcassite. As I was standing at one of the former mouths or apertures of Vesuvio, a stone of a greenish yellow, ejected from the mountain, fell close by me. Upon taking it up when it had cooled, I found it to be covered with a kind of glossy varnish, and to contain several bits of glass; but, at my return, I

No pumice-stones on mount Vesuvio.

Minerals in the stones.

Experiment by the magnet.

---

* This is the computation of Dr. Burnet in his Theory of the Earth. Virgil says,

Vidimus undantem ruptis fornacibus Ætnam,
Flammarumque globos, liquefactaque volvere saxa.

‘ What rocks did Ætna's bellowing mouth expire
‘ From her torn entrails! and what floods of fire!

DRYDEN.

found

found its beauty very much diminished by rubbing against some other stones in my pocket, which I had picked up. I made use of water for cleaning it, which rather penetrated the stone, and dissolved its texture, so that a greenish liquor was continually oosing from it, and I was obliged to use proper means for drying it.

Near to the summit of the mountain we met with stones, at least of a hundred weight, glowing hot, and when broken exactly resembling red-hot iron, or the slag just taken out of a smith's forge. These ejected stones immediately set paper on fire; and, if our guides may be relied on, they had been but just ejected from the abyss. I saw about fifteen of these, but not one thrown in the air or in motion. As we still advanced, our ears were frequently assaulted with a horrid noise like that of the explosion of a whole battery of cannon; and under our feet we were surprised with a continued noise, not unlike the boiling of a large cauldron. Upon making a hole with a stick in the ashes but a few inches deep, a heat was immediately felt in it, which in some places was hotter than a man's hand could bear. We perceived the smoke to issue out as it were in several places through small fissures. I was for a long time at a loss what to make of great numbers of little round holes about half an inch diameter in this part of the hill, till I found them to be avenues to the nests of wasps and hornets, which retreated hither on account of the heat; the cold at this time of the year, and especially in the night, being too severe for them at the foot of the hill. We found a scorched acorn among the ashes, a considerable way up the hill, but it is no easy matter to form a probable conjecture from whence it came; not a single tree or shrub being to be seen on all that part of the mountain, which is covered with ashes and stones; and birds, which might have carried such a thing by a way of food, are never known to visit this dreary region.

At length, after many weary steps, we came to the place where formerly the largest mouth or aperture of the mountain was; but this has undergone such changes by the frequent eruptions, that at present it is not only choaked up, but covered by a round hill of ashes and cinders. In Addison's and Misson's time there was a plain of near three hundred paces to cross before they came to the skirts of this round hill or new mountain; but such great eruptions have so enlarged the circumference of the hill, that this interval in most places is now no more than a kind of trench seven

Red-hot stones.

Heat of the soil.

Former mouth of Vesuvio.

or

or eight feet deep, and about thirty paces wide. It is not improbable but in a few years this vacuity may be filled up, and thus the two mountains form but one. The lower or old mountain is of such a height that the trench is not perceived at the foot of it. Here we felt a very sensible increase of heat; and especially at every explosion of the mountain, which made the ashes fly against our faces, so that some of the company were obliged to cover their eyes. The ground also was almost insupportably hot under our feet; for the embers or slag burnt the very soles of our shoes. Here indeed we were not terrified with the horrid noises we had heard below; but every discharge was attended with a whizzing like that of a great number of rockets flying up at once. The multitude of stones and other matter ejected, together with the clouds of smoke with which the sky is totally obscured, resemble the springing of a mine. Most of the stones, especially the largest, the weight of which has not been much diminished by burning, return perpendicularly into the abyss from whence they were thrown up; and this possibly is several times repeated till their weight decreases, or a violent eruption happens, and then they are thrown beyond the verge of the aperture. Great quantities, however, fall on the sides of the hill, and the noise they make in rolling down is indeed something terrible. As the wind generally drives the ashes, smoke, &c. one particular way, it gives the spectator an opportunity of chusing the most favourable station; yet if the eruptions happen to be violent, there is danger of approaching on any side. It being a very bright day, we could perceive no flame at the mouth of the hill; and the great increase of the heat felt at every discharge might proceed from the melted matter and ignited stones thrown into the air, which in the night appear like red-hot bullets. The phænomena exhibited by vulcano's are not constantly alike; for they differ according to the violence or moderation of the eruptions. This has been observed so long ago as Virgil's time, who gives this description of Ætna:

- - - - *Horrificis juxtà tonat Ætna ruinis:*
Interdumque atram prorumpit ad æthera nubem,
Turbine fumantem piceo, & candente favillâ;
Attollitque globos flammarum, & sidera lambit.
Interdum scopulos avulsaque viscera montis
Erigit eructans, liquefactaque saxa sub auras
Cum gemitu glomerat, fundoque exæstuat imo.

VIRG. Æneid. III. v. 571.

- - - - - ' And

Kingdom of NAPLES.

>   — — — — 'And secure from wind,
> Is to the foot of thund'ring Ætna join'd.
> By turns a pitchy cloud she rolls on high,
> By turns hot embers from her entrails fly;
> And flakes of mounting flames that lick the sky.
> Oft from her bowels massy rocks are thrown,
> And shiver'd by the force come piece-meal down.
> Oft liquid lakes of burning sulphur flow,
> Fed from the fiery springs that boil below.'
>
> DRYDEN.

Sarnelli, bishop of Bisceglia, informs us, that the upper or new mountain first appeared on the 26th of September, 1685. We had still about eight hundred paces to ascend among hot stones and ashes; but the eruptions followed so thick upon one another, that before we could have reached the summit we must have stood at least eight shocks more; and as the danger every minute became manifestly greater, and our faint-hearted guides grew excessively out of humour, we all agreed to return. After all, it is very probable, that, had we ventured to the aperture or mouth of Vesuvio, a thick smoke would have been all we could have seen, which would not have rewarded our pains and hazard. I wonder some travellers who affect great courage and intrepidity should pretend that they had been on the summit of the hill during an eruption, and that looking down the aperture they saw the vast hollow all on fire and full of sulphur, pitch, and metal boiling with prodigious vehemence; whereas several curious persons of undoubted veracity, who have been more than once on the top, when the mountain was still, assured me, that, by reason of the smoke, it is very seldom they could get a sight of the bottom of the cavity; which is also subject to great variations: for it is sometimes of a vast depth, and at other times but a little more than two hundred feet, according to the height of the melted matter, at the last eruption, which by hardening gradually forms this bottom. Some have ventured a considerable way down the cavity; but this is a temerity from which no real advantage or glory can accrue. Such rashness about two years since unhappily proved fatal to an English gentleman of a very good character, both for his learning and morals. If a stone be rolled down the aperture; within a short time after, an eruption, followed by a hollow sound and a cloud of smoke, happens. The ascent

ascent to the summit takes up two hours; but the descent takes less, and is much easier: for the ashes often carry one several paces downwards at one slide. Some days after this excursion, I observed from Naples, in the evening, that the mountain continually ejected stones, &c. and over it appeared a pale gleam, which, at first, I took to be flame: it continued a long time gradually ascending, and at length I discovered it to be the refraction of the beams of the setting sun through the fuliginous exhalations issuing from the aperture. As the sun gradually descended towards the horizon, this phænomenon insensibly diminished; when it was set, it totally disappeared. A strong party of us (for otherwise it is very dangerous to walk the streets of Naples in the night) used most evenings to go to the great area near the vice-roy's palace, to observe the changes in the appearance of Vesuvio. On the 17th of March, to the left of the place where we had taken our station on the mountain there was a continual fire; and from the upper aperture, every four or five minutes, issued ignited columns, in appearance about four feet high, and near a foot and a half in diameter. On the 18th, that part near the old *bocca* or mouth of Vesuvio was all in glowing fire, but without any considerable blaze; whilst the upper, or new mountain, emitted towering flames without intermission; and vast clouds of smoke appeared above the summit of the mountain. On the 19th there was a general fire spread all over the upper mountain, and in the city of Naples were heard subterraneous rumblings and concussions like the discharge of cannon at a distance. On the 20th, and likewise on the 1st day of April, the fire was visible at Gaëta, which is six stages from Vesuvio; and as abundance of ashes was driven by the wind to Naples, recourse was had to processions, and the invocation of St. Januarius, in whom, in all public calamities, the Neapolitans place a great confidence; but of late, to make matters sure, the archangel Michael has been added as a collegue to that saint. It must be owned their devotion is very well grounded if what they tell us be true, namely, that upon the saint's head being exposed, and proper supplications made to him, the wind has immediately shifted, and sometimes the eruptions of Vesuvio

Medal of St. Januarius. have been suppressed; and so powerful a protector well deserved the honour of a large medal, which the governor of the treasury-chapel, where the saint's reliques are kept, had struck. On one side is the effigies of this saint, with these words round it:

D. JAN.

Kingdom of NAPLES.

**D. JAN. LIBERATORI. VRBIS.
FVNDATORI. QVIETIS.**

' To St. Januarius, the deliverer of the city, author of
' its security.'

On the reverse are two phials, representing those in which his miraculous blood is kept; under them is a garland, with this legend:

**POSTQVAM. COLLAPSI. CINERES.
ET. FLAMMA. QVIEVIT. CIVES
NEAPOLITANI. INCOLVMES.
A. D. MDCCVII.**

'.The ashes subsided, the eruption suspended, and the
' citizens of Naples preserved in the year 1707.'

In commemoration of this same miracle of the year 1707, a marble statue of the saint, with the following inscription, has been erected on the spot near the church of S. Caterina à Formello, where the saint's head, attended by numerous procession, was placed on an altar which faces Vesuvio, as it were to keep it in awe:

Thankgiving monument.

*DIVO JANUARIO,
Urbis Neap. Indigetum Principi,
Quòd Montis Vesuvii
Anno MDCCVII.
Cum Maxima ignis eruptione
Facta, dies complures magìs
Magisque ferociret,
Jam ut certissimum Urbi
Totique Campaniæ
Incendium minaretur,
Sacri ostensu capitis
In arâ hic exstructâ
Excidiosos impetus
Extemplò oppresserit,
Et omnia serenârit,
Neapolitani
Ejus divini Beneficii
Uti & innumerorum aliorum
Quibus à Bello, Fame,
Pestilentia, Terræ motu,*

Urb. m,

Urbem, Civitatemque
Liberavit memores
P. P.

'To St. Januarius, the chief of the Neapolitan saints,
' by the exposure of whose sacred head on an altar erected
' on this spot, a most dreadful eruption of mount Vesuvio in
' 1707, which had raged several days with increasing vio-
' lence, so as to threaten the city and the whole country
' with an unavoidable conflagration, was instantaneously
' suppressed, and fair prosperous weather succeeded, the
' Neapolitans, in acknowledgment of this, and innumera-
' ble other signal deliverances from war, pestilence, famine,
' and earthquakes, have erected this monument.'

Aurelius Victor, and other historians, who relate that it was in the reign of Vespasian when fiery eruptions from this vulcano were first perceived, are easily confuted from Strabo, who lived in Augustus's time. It is also far from being true that Pliny the elder lost his life on this mountain; for it appears from the younger Pliny's account of his uncle's death *, that he was at a considerable distance from Vesuvio; and being very fat and asthmatic, the air then saturated with sulphureous particles, obstructed his respiration.

Since the Christian Æra above twenty remarkable eruptions of Vesuvio are recorded by historians; but it is very probable that in so many centuries the number must have been greater. It is certain, however, that one of the most violent eruptions of this vulcano, was that which happened in Titus's reign, by which Herculaneum, or Heraclea †, and Pompeii, two towns near Naples, were destroyed ‡.

Destruction of Herculaneum and Pompeii.

Accord-

---

* Pliny's words are, *Innixus servis duobus adsurrexit & statim concidit, ut ego conjecto, crassiore caligine spiritu obstructo, clausoque stomacho, qui illi naturâ invalidus & angustus & frequenter interæstuans erat. Ubi dies redditus, corpus inventum est integrum, illæsum opertumque, ut fuerat indutus: habitus corporis quiescenti quam defuncto similior.*

† The remains of Heraclea, discovered in our days, have for some years exercised the pens of the most learned antiquarians.

‡ This country has, by earthquakes and eruptions of Vesuvio, undergone so many changes, that the situation of these towns cannot be exactly determined. In the like destiny Thaurania, Cora, or Thora, and Stabia have been involved. The damages which Pompeii and Herculaneum sustained by an earthquake in Seneca's time, are related at large in the vith book of his Natural Questions, and likewise in Tacitus's Annals, *lib.* xv. Probably it is to that earthquake, and not to an eruption of Vesuvio, that

Dion

Kingdom of NAPLES.

According to Dio Cassius, the ashes, during that eruption, were driven as far as Africa, Syria, and Egypt; and at Rome the sun was totally obscured by them *.

It might be supposed that the manifest danger continually hanging over the heads of the inhabitants of this country from earthquakes and the irruptions of Vesuvio should make some happy impression on their minds, and dispose them to lead pious and moral lives; but it is far otherwise: for the generality of these people are like sailors, and never think of heaven or hell but in imminent danger; and, as soon as that is over, eagerly return to their former wicked practices. Of this there was a striking instance in the year 1707, when the people flocking out of the city to see the fiery torrent from the mountain, which began to harden, gave themselves up to all sorts of debaucheries.

The variety of mineral and other substances ejected by Vesuvio, sufficiently indicate the nature of the vast hollow within the mountain, and the cause of its fiery eruptions; for quick sulphur and the filings of iron being kneaded together into a kind of dough, is not only violently heated, but even kindled into a flame, by the addition of a little cold water. Lemery, in his garden at Paris, once made an artificial volcano of this sort, which took fire spontaneously; and later chemists instantly produce flame from the mixture of two different liquids properly prepared. That the strata under Vesuvio and other volcano's, contain abundance of sulphur and iron †, appears evident both by the cinders ejected and the chalybeate springs issuing from the root of this mountain towards the sea-coast. The proximity of the main sea not on-

Inside of Vesuvio.

Artificial vulcano.

Dion Cassius, *lib.* lxvi, alludes, when he speaks of the sudden fall of a theatre when crouded with the inhabitants of these two cities: for the ravages caused by the eruption of Vesuvio, as appears from Pliny, were not caused on a sudden, but the fire gradually increased; and self-preservation would naturally have prompted the people to hurry out of the theatre at the first appearance of danger.

* The eruption of Vesuvio in 473, according to Marcellinus Comes, covered all Europe with ashes: *Vesuvius, mons Campaniæ torridus, intestinis ignibus æstuans exusta vomuit viscera, nocturnisque in die tenebris omnem Europæ faciem minuto contexit pulvere. Hujus metuendi memoriam cineris Bizantii annuè celebrant* viii. *Idus Novembris.* c Vesuvius, a volcano in Campania, ejected from its inflamed bowels such prodigious quantities of matter as obscured day-light, and covered all Europe with ashes. The anniversary of this devastation is observed at Constantinople on the 6th of November.' This day of humiliation is likewise mentioned by Procopius *de Bello Goth. lib.* ii. c. 4.

† The soil about Viterbo, Pozzuolo, Sienna, and the islands of Stromboli, Lepari, Sicily, &c. is of the same nature.

ly supplies water for the aliment of the inflammable substances, but likewise salt and pitch, which it washes away from their subterraneous beds; and from these also proceeds the saline acridity of the sea-water: for oil of sea-coal (which has a great deal of pitch in it) mixed with common salt and water, gives it a taste like that of sea-water. In a calm the fishermen about Resina and Torre, two villages on the sea-coast near Vesuvio, look out for Pretoleum, a fragrant kind of oil which floats on the surface of the sea, and take it off with pieces of spunge: this they sell for a good price to the apothecaries. It is plain that Vesuvio has a communication with the sea, not only from the waters being surprisingly absorbed in 1631 as an immediate prelude to the eruption of the mountain, so that several vessels, afloat before, were left dry; but also by what happened in 1698, for in that year the sea suddenly ebbed twelve paces, and the mountain disembogued a vast torrent of pitch and other combustibles; and on the return of the sea to its former height, and the cessation of the igneous discharge, great quantities of shells, &c. were found along the shore near the mountain, which were half burnt, and emitted a sulphureous smell. Parrini and Boccone farther affirm, that, in a violent eruption of Vesuvio, hot sea-water, fishes, shells, and sea-weeds have been ejected by that mountain.

Communication betwixt Vesuvio and the sea.

This vulcano, however, affords several fresh springs, of which some are conveyed to Naples by a beautiful aqueduct, to the great conveniency of the inhabitants. These waters have not the least heat in them; and, what one could less expect, a very cold wind is felt to blow from several fissures or chasms in the side of the mountain.

Fresh water in the mountain.

I shall add, that tho' a new mountain has risen on the summit of Vesuvio over its former aperture, yet it wants something of its ancient height. Of this there is ocular demonstration likewise with regard to mount Ætna in Sicily; the top of which, within these sixty years, might be seen from Furnari and other places thereabouts, but cannot be discerned from thence at present.

The height diminished.

Such is the climate of Naples, and the south part of this kingdom, that little or no winter is known there. Garden-vegetables are in season there all the year round. Ice is seldom seen in the level country, and snow fell but twice during these last five years; and then it dissolved as soon as it touched the ground. Among the inhabitants of the mountains it is a branch of trade to gather snow, and send it to Naples,

Temperature of the air.

Naples, where it supplies the want of ice for cooling liquors *, &c. The extreme summer heats, however, never fail of being tempered by cool evenings, which are spent in taking the air, after being confined within-doors during the sultry heat of the day. Of the fertility and wealth of this country, some idea may be formed by considering how long it has been under a foreign government, which by contributions, troops, wars, and other circumstances, must necessarily have drained it of vast sums. Yet this country is still in a much better condition than many of the states of Italy, and capable by proper measures of affording new sources of wealth. The tobacco-farms alone in this kingdom produce near thirty thousand ducats annually. *Fruitfulness of the country.*

But amidst its fertility and other natural advantages, the kingdom of Naples is not without many inconveniencies. Besides the frequent calamities this country is subject to from the neighbourhood of mount Vesuvio, it suffers extremely by earthquakes; particularly the south part of the kingdom, all over which are to be seen the melancholy remains of cities, once famous in history, but now almost without a name †. *Inconveniencies in the kingdom of Naples. Earthquakes.*

Another disagreeable circumstance, but common to most other parts of Italy, is the swarms of lizards, especially of the green kind. In spring hundreds of these little animals are seen basking themselves on the flat roofs, and as they crawl up and down the walls, if a window or door be left open, they make their way into the houses. The green lizards are very nimble, and have a fine glossy skin and very beautiful eyes; but they are quite harmless. About Fondi, Capua, and Gaëta, there is a noxious species of lizards, *Lizards.*

---

* The climate of Sicily is so hot, that even in January the shade is agreeable, and not a chimney is to be seen all over the island. In March some cold piercing winds may happen to set in for a few days; but this inconveniency is relieved by a very small coal fire. The use of ice and snow in liquor, I suppose, was first introduced to gratify the palate; but now it has the sanction of the faculty: and since its coming into general vogue, the fatal rage of fevers is said to be considerably abated. Plempius, in his treatise de *Valetudine Togatorum tuenda*, affirms, that since the use of snow has obtained in Messina, the burials of that city are decreased a thousand every year; and that this custom has been attended with the same success in Spain, appears from Ludov. Nonnius, *de re cibaria*, lib. iv. cap. 5.

[The author takes no notice of the frequency of pleurisies in those countries where this custom has been introduced, particularly in France.]

† Sicily, which formerly made one continent with the kingdom of Naples, is, in this respect, not less unfortunate, having, in January 1693, by one single earthquake lost forty-nine towns and villages, nine hundred and twenty-two churches, colleges and convents, with ninety-three thousand persons buried in the ruins.

commonly but improperly called *tarantula*, whose bite is attended with danger; these are brown, larger than the green sort, and, when the tail is cut off, resemble a toad.

Scorpions. The scorpion is a much greater nuisance, which harbours not only in old buildings and under large stones, but infests the houses in this country; so that in some places it is not unusual to make the bed-steads of polished iron, and to place them at some distance from the wall, to prevent these vermin from getting into the beds. It is true, they seldom hurt, unless they are first assaulted or accidentally injured; which may easily happen only by a man's turning himself or moving a leg or an arm in a bed where these noxious animals harbour themselves. The surest remedy against the sting of a scorpion is to bruise that animal and bind it fast on the wound; or if that cannot be done, the best way is to foment it with oil-olive, in which dead scorpions have been steeped, applying warm bandages to the part, and to give the patient warm draughts of theriaca mixed up with a generous wine to promote perspiration. This oil, Boccone (*Observ. Phys.* xviii.) says, is a sovereign remedy against the

Where most dangerous. sting of the spider called *solifuga*. In the northern parts of Italy this creature has little or nothing of that rage and venom which appears in those of hotter climates, as Malta and Africa. The venom or poison of vipers has also the like gradations according to the proximity of the country to the equator. Scorpions yield a salt and oil which are a part of the *materia medica*. They are caught in great numbers among ruins or in stony places, and being taken hold of with a pair of pincers, are dropped into a narrow-necked glass vessel which is too slippery for them to climb out of.

Whether they kill themselves. A late naturalist says, that the scorpion, when hemmed in with live coals, or any kind of fire, upon its being moved nearer to him, and finding no way to escape, plants itself in the middle of the circle, turns up his tail and stings himself in the head. This observation at first sight had appeared to me very suspicious, and made me imagine that this pretended suicide was no more than a natural motion of the animal on such an occasion. Being at Naples I was determined to bring this vulgar error to the test of repeated experiments, which proved it to be no other. Some of the scorpions, instead of going round to look out for a passage to escape, ran directly into the fire, where they were soon consumed; others, upon feeling the heat of the fire, drew back and fell into a kind of convulsions, but never offered to dart their

sting

Kingdom of NAPLES.

sting into their heads; others again lay quite still, and, as if they made a virtue of necessity, quietly submitted to be burnt to death. As groundless is the notion, that a scorpion when thrown into oil, destroys itself in the same manner, whereas some will live in it twenty-four hours, and when they expire do not exhibit the least appearance of stinging themselves to death.

Another plague almost peculiar to the kingdom of Naples, especially the southern parts, is the tarantula; so called from the city of Tarento, in the neighbourhood of which they abound, and are the largest and most venomous. This is the *Phalangius* and *Phalenges* of Pliny and other ancient naturalists. The persons bit by this insect, by the Italians are called *Tarantolati*; and their extravagant vicissitudes of shrieking, sobbing, laughing, dancing, &c. are pretty well known. Very few of such unhappy persons can bear the sight of black or blue, but seem delighted with red and green objects. They are also seized with an aversion to eating fruit or vegetables. A melancholy silence and a fixed eye are the first symptoms by which the bite of the tarantula discovers itself; and then music is immediately called in to the assistance of the patient to rouse him to a violent motion, and by that means to promote perspiration and a copious sweat. But neither the same tunes nor the same instruments answer this end with regard to different patients; several trials are therefore made, and chiefly with the guitar, hautboy, trumpet, volin, and Sicilian kettle-drum. The tunes that usually have the best effect in these disorders are *la Pastorale* and *la Tarantella*. In some parts of the kingdom of Naples, particularly in Apulia, the venom of the scorpions is so subtle, that their sting produces the like effects as the bite of the tarantula; and though the two before-mentioned tunes have a proper effect on these patients also, yet they require softer instruments, as the flute, &c. but accompanied with a brisk beat of the drum. The country people, who are more or less skilled in all these instruments, inforce the operation of their music with grimaces and odd gesticulations. The *Tarantolati* on their side vigorously exert themselves, regulating their motions according to the music till the venom is quite expelled; this exercise and cure sometimes takes up five or six days. It is not to be supposed that they are kept continually dancing for so many days: when nature seems to be exhausted the music is suspended, and the patient put to bed well covered, and a sudorific cordial given him to promote perspira-

Tarantula.

perspiration. It is remarkable, that the patient on his recovery remembers nothing of what passed during his disorder. If the cure be not perfectly effected, and the poison entirely expelled, the same symptoms fail not to appear again the succeeding year, especially during the summer heats; and some have laboured under this terrible disorder at intervals for ten, twenty, and thirty years, and others during their lives. Instances are not wanting of such persons who merely from a sense of their incurable state, or from the melancholy effects of the venom, have drowned themselves. If the tarantula be killed immediately after the bite, the venom with its effects is in a way of being expelled the first year by vigorous dancing; or if with the same exercise, previous to a fomentation, an incision be made in the part affected, and Venice-treacle, or in want of that, mithridate, orvietan, or a clove of garlic bruised be applied, the same success may be expected: but in case these two precautions be neglected, it is seldom that any remedies administered afterwards, can preserve the unhappy patient from a long continuance of the usual ill consequences attending such a misfortune, as melancholy, lassitude, loss of appetite and indigestion. If the patient uses no means for cure, a few days infallibly carry him off. The petticoats of women are apt to harbour these vermin, and consequently they are more liable to be bitten by them than men. The bite of a tarantula at first occasions only a small red tumour like that occasioned by the sting of a wasp; and there are above eight species of them differing in size, colour, and form, but producing the same mischievous effects by their venom. In the dog-days and during the violent heats, the tarantula is most dangerous; especially on the plains, as if these creatures were incited to greater rage by the heat of the sun: for those of Tuscany never occasion such deplorable disorders as the malignant kind found in Apulia; and even in these, when carried to the northern parts of the kingdom of Naples, or to Rome, the venom is rendered less noxious, so that their bite is attended there only with a slight transitory pain *.

In the island of Corsica there are neither wolves not vipers; but its tarantulas and scorpions are extremely venomous.†

* *Vide* Boccone, *Observ. Phys.* XVII.

† One kind of the Corsican spiders bite like the Apulian tarantulas, another stings; but the beneficent Creator has checked their increase by means of a species of wasps which make terrible havock among them. *Boccone Obs.* I.

The

Kingdom of NAPLES. 37

The tarantula's chief haunts are holes in the earth, old walls and hollow trees, and the cobweb it makes is stronger and coarser than that of a common spider. The poison is contained in two small vesicules within the gums near two fangs, with which they are armed besides lesser teeth. *Its haunts.*

But, according to some, a greater evil still remains; and the worst creatures in this delicious country, say they, are the inhabitants themselves, who, besides their execrable and unnatural lusts, are of a vindictive, treacherous, bloody disposition. *The people wicked.*

Though national charges generally imply ignorance, narrowness of soul, and uncharitableness, it is certain, however, that the history of Naples, almost beyond any other, abounds in sad instances of the excessive depravity of human nature. Tophana the noted female poisoner, who first invented the *Aqua Tophania* is still living in prison here, and few foreigners leave Naples without seeing this infernal hag. She is a little old woman who had entered into a kind of religious sisterhood; and on this account, if not on a worse, her life has been hitherto spared. She is said to have poisoned some hundreds of people, and was remarkably liberal of her drops, which she gave by way of alms, to wives who, from several intimations, she knew would not be inconsolable for the death of their husbands. Five or six drops of this liquid it seems answer the purpose, and may be lowered or tempered so as to take effect in any determinate time. This water continues still to be privately made at Naples under the appellation of *Acquetta di Napoli*, and not many years since a small cask of it was according to orders sent to a certain country. But since lemon-juice has been found to be a sort of antidote against it, this vile composition is fallen into some disrepute. The humane Dr. Branchaletti wrote a book expresly on the remedies or antidotes against these Stygian drops; but all the inventions to counterwork this poison presuppose the fatal potion to be very recently administered, or previously guarded against, upon any suspicion, by such preservatives. *Poisoning.*

The inhabitants of this country have in all ages been remarkable for a voluptuous manner of living; the luxury of Capua and Atella is well known, and Naples is, by Ovid, stiled,

- - *in otia natam*
Parthenopen - -

' Naples of luxury the native seat.'

It

It must be owned that in no great city in Europe the prostitutes are so numerous and so abandoned: these *Donne libere*, as they are called, amount to eighteen thousand in this city, and in one particular part of it is a receptacle for two thousand of them; and yet it is no uncommon thing for ecclesiastics to lodge in those infamous parts of the town. This totally corrupts all the youth; and the clergy being exempt from the civil jurisdiction, and connived at by their superiors that the sacred order may not be disgraced by punishments, set the worst of examples. Any complaints against the latter from laymen are looked upon as the height of insolence; it is not for them to scrutinize the actions of those, to whose superior lights they owe an implicit submission.

Sloth

The peasants in this country are so slothful, as to prefer beggary or robbing to labour and industry; but in the city of Naples there is something of an industrious spirit, and several flourishing manufactures are carried on there. It is a phrase here, that a vice-roy, to keep the people quiet, must provide three F's, namely, *feste*, *farine*, *forche*, i. e. 'festivity, flour, and gibbets;' the people being excessively fond of public diversions, clamorous upon the dearth of corn, and seditious unless they are intimidated by severity. Among their public entertainments, one of the most remarkable is the procession with four triumphal cars on the four Sundays immediately preceding Lent, the first loaded with bread, the second with flesh, the third with vegetables, and the fourth with fish. These provisions are piled up very high, with musicians placed at the top, and guarded by armed men till they are given up to be pillaged by the populace. But that which draws the greatest concourse at Naples is the Cocagna, or castle, built according to the rules of fortification, and faced all over with pieces of beef, bacon, hams, geese, turkeys, and other provisions, with which the imaginary country of Cocagna is said to abound; where the very trunks or branches of trees are supposed to be Bologna sausages. This welcome spectacle is exhibited once a year, and on each side of the castle is a fountain running with wine during the whole day. A party of soldiers is posted to restrain the ardour of the populace till the vice-roy appears in his balcony, which is the signal for the assault.

Neapolitan nobility.

It is usual for the Neapolitan nobility to spend some years in a parsimonious retirement on their estates in the country, that they may cut a figure for a while in the city, and live in a profuse a profuse magnificence; so that the generality of them are ever running into extremes, but their fortunes are not very considerable. This is the consequence of the disproportion of their great number to the small extent of the kingdom; for there are in the kingdom of Naples a hundred and nineteen princes, a hundred and fifty-six dukes, a hundred and seventy-three marquisses, forty-two counts, and four hundred and forty-five barons, all vassals of the crown. Many a spot of land not worth above fifty dollars a year gives the title of marquis to the owners; so that they are in general very poor.

The standing forces throughout the kingdom do not exceed fourteen thousand men, a number very insufficient for keeping the inhabitants in awe on the approach of an enemy. The vice-roy's ordinary income is eighteen thousand *scudi*, or crowns, a month; and the several officers of his court, which is very splendid, have stated salaries from funds appropriated to those services; so that here is no room left for savings out of the pay of the guard, the chapel, the band of music, company of comedians, and the like attendants on a court, but every thing continues on its original footing. The vice-roy's post is only triennial; but, at the expiration of such a term, the commission is renewable *.

Army.

As to the currency of money, a Spanish pistole, or old louis-d'or, is here equal to forty-five *carlini*. The papal money also goes at the rate of four *carlini* for three *paoli*. By a ducat is here meant an imaginary piece, equal to ten *carlini* †.

Current coins.

LETTER LVIII.
Of the City of NAPLES in general, and its public Buildings.

SIR,

THE city of Naples lies in forty-one degrees and twenty minutes north latitude: its walls are mostly faced with a hard black stone, called *piperno*, and are nine Italian miles

---

* The reader will naturally suppose that the court and government have undergone great alterations within these few years, since a prince of Spain of the Bourbon family ascended the throne of Naples and Sicily, and resides in the capital of the former.

† Three shillings and four-pence sterling.

NAPLES.

Buildings. in circuit; but there are near twenty suburbs included. If Naples has not such magnificent palaces as are to be seen at Rome and Genoa, it has also very few of those mean houses, which, in other cities, disgrace their finest streets. The roofs of the houses here are flat, and surrounded with elegant balustrades: the streets also are very well paved, and most of them with very large square stones; but the fault is, that they have no slope or gutters to carry off water, &c. The finest street for length, breadth, &c. is that called *la Strada di Toledo*, and yet not one eminent palace is to be seen in it; the breadth is about twenty-three common paces; and, after running in a direct line of fifteen hundred paces, it is continued some hundreds more in an easy curve line. It seems an inexcusable neglect that the streets of Naples are not lighted at night, as the lamps would not only be an ornament to the city, but would also prove a considerable security for persons who walk the streets; for few cities are more dangerous after dark.

Harbour. The harbour of Naples is very spacious, and has a grand light-house, with a mole near five hundred paces in length, which separates the Porto della Città, or main harbour, from the Darsena, or bason. The latter lies behind the Castello Nuovo, and has generally in it four galleys, the crews of which, both rowers and soldiers, are obliged every Lent to come to a formal confession, and to receive the sacrament.

Annual communion on board the galleys. The devotions of the first galley are followed by a day of rest, the second by a like interval, and so on. In the evening, at the close of the procession usual on such solemnities, the host is exposed, and all the galleys honour it with a salute.

Number of inhabitants at Naples. The number of inhabitants at Naples cannot be less than three hundred thousand; and as its commerce occasions a great stir and bustle, Rome, in comparison of this city, has by some travellers been looked upon as a kind of desart. The

Fountains. great number of fountains in Naples are very elegant ornaments to the city, though in most of them the water is none of the best. Of these fountains the finest is that of Medina, facing Castello Nuovo, or the new castle; the upper bason is supported by the three graces, and on the top stands a superb Neptune, attended by several other figures, all ejecting water, which make a very grand appearance. The inscription is as follows:

CAROLO

NAPLES.

CAROLO II. REGNANTE
Hic ubi pulvereo squalebat Olympia tractu,
Nunc hilarant fontes stratque saxa viam,
Quam Ducis adjuta auspiciis opibusque dicavit
Medina Cæli nomine Parthenope,
Excell. Dom. D. Ludovico de Cerda,
Cæli Duce, Prerege
Cavitas Neapolis Anno
M. DC. XCVII.

' In this place, which was formerly a dusty waste, Naples, under the auspices of the duke of Medina Cœli, has caused this refreshing fountain, which, in gratitude to his munificence, bears his title, and a noble pavement to be made, in the reign of his catholic majesty Charles II. his excellency don Lewis de Cerda, duke of Medina Cœli, being vice-roy. 1697, &c.'

There is a long inscription on a fountain in the great market-place, and on most of the other fountains in the city, which are full of flattery to their vice-roys.

The fountain in St. Lucia, by Giovanni di Nola, an eminent architect, with that in the street near St. Lucia, by Cosmo Faniego, are both of an elegant architecture, and adorned by good pieces of sculpture. Not far from the Darsena is another fountain, adorned with a spread eagle.

A very fine aqueduct supplies the city with a vast quantity of water from the foot of mount Vesuvio, by means of which, Alphonso II, in 1442, made himself master of the city of Naples. The place where formerly was the greatest reservoir of these waters, is at present known by the name of *Seggio di Nido*, or *di Nilo*; where there is an antique statue of the river Nile, represented under the figure of an old man sitting on a crocodile, with boys playing about him; the head is modern, as appears by an inscription under it. {Aqueduct from Vesuvio. Statue of the river Nile.}

The statue of *Jupiter Terminalis*, another antique, stands near the arsenal: it was dug up at Puzzuolo, and erected in this place by the duke of Segovia, when vice-roy.

Of all the palaces in Naples, that of the vice-roy is, agreeably to the dignity of the owner, unquestionably the most magnificent. As to its beauty, it is sufficient to say that it is the work of the famous *cavaliere Fontana*. The great *per-* {Vice-roy's palace.}

ron

ron is divided into two flights of steps, and is of white marble. It is eleven common paces in breadth, and a superb work. At the foot of the steps on each side is the statue of a river; that on the left-hand representing the Tagus, and that on the right the Ebro, with inscriptions under them.

The eye of a connoisseur, at entering the palace on this side, must be immediately offended at the disproportionate narrowness of the court to such a large and superb *perron*. In the audience-room are finely painted the most remarkable actions of the Spanish nation, among which it has been thought fit to place the expulsion of the Jews out of Spain. The *Sala Regia*, where the carnival entertainments are given, is hung with the pictures of all the vice-roys at full length. A particular gallery is taken up with the exploits of the duke d'Alva. In another saloon is represented the war carried on by Charles V. with John Frederic elector of Saxony. Indeed all the apartments abound in fine paintings, and beautiful tapestry.

In the palace-chapel are surprising quantities of plate; and behind the altar stands a most exquisite white marble statue of the virgin Mary. This palace has a subterraneous communication with the Castello Nuovo, which, in case of an insurrection, is a very necessary resource to the vice-roy and courtiers.

Castello Nuovo.

Castello Nuovo on one side joins to the sea, and is always well garrisoned; forty-two pieces of ordnance are mounted on the walls and bastions, among which are nine pieces taken by Charles V. from the elector of Saxony at the battle of Muhlberg.

An inscription informs us, that on the bastion del San Spirito formerly stood a large piece, called *Magdalena*, weighing twenty-one thousand pounds, which carried balls weighing a hundred and twenty pounds. This destructive engine was cast in the time of the emperor Maximilian I, and brought hither by Charles V.

Near the entrance of the castle stands a triumphal-arch, adorned with sculpture, and the two following inscriptions:

Alphonsus Regum Princeps hanc condidit arcem.

' This castle was built by Alphonso, the best of princes.'

Alphensus Rex Hispanus, Siculus, Italicus, Pius, Clemens, Invictus.

' Alphonso

NAPLES.

'Alphonso king of Spain, Sicily, and Italy, the pious, the merciful, and the invincible.'

The place where this arch was erected is something too narrow: the gate near it is adorned with some fine sculpture in stone. Further on is a brass gate, decorated with fine basso-relievo's, representing some of the atchievements of the kings of Arragon. The castle-church is handsomely decorated with gilding and stucco-work; and a *Pietà*, in a room adjoining to it, is greatly admired. Facing the armory, which, according to Parrini, can compleatly furnish fifty thousand men, stands a marble antique statue of a young soldier [*], or, according to some, of the emperor Nero; as likewise that of brass in the *facade* of St. Barbara's church in this castle is said to be. In the church dell' Assunto is a picture of the wise men of the East, two of which represent Alphonso and Ferdinand, kings of Spain. Vasari says, this piece was the first work of Giov. da Bruggia in oil-colours: some, however, attribute it to the celebrated Zingaro, with this addition, that the heads of the three wise men are copied from the portraits of Charles king of Naples, and his sons the prince of Salerno and the duke of Calabria. The castle-hall is so constructed, that a whisper on one side is distinctly heard at the other.

Castello del Uovo, i. e. Egg-castle, so called from its oval figure, stands in the sea, on a rock, which is joined to the continent by a bridge of two hundred and twenty paces long. This castle is said to have been anciently Lucullus's palace, and not originally situated on an island, but altered to its present state and form by the Norman kings, on which account it was, for a long time, called the Norman castle. Over the entrance are these words:

Philippus Secundus Rex Hispaniarum Pontem a continenti ad Lucullanas arces, olim Austri fluctibus conquassatum, nunc saxeis obicibus restauravit, firmumque reddidit, D. Joanne Zunica Pro-Rege, Anno MDLXXXXV.

---

[*] Cœlestin tells us, that this soldier was a native of France, and maintained a post so bravely against a hundred men of the enemy, that he laid forty of them dead at his feet; but the Roman habit little agrees with the first part of this account.

'The

'The bridge from the continent to Lucullus's palace, hav-
' ing been broken down by the violence of the sea and
' storms, is now, by order of Philip II. king of Spain, re-
' paired with greater strength, and secured by a mole of huge
' stones, in the year 1595, &c.'

This castle is supplied with fresh water by means of a stone conduit embellished with marble figures of all kinds of animals: it conveys the water from the city under the bridge to the castle, where are two reservoirs, near a marble lion, with an inscription in honour of Charles II. and the vice-roy.

Invention of mines. The memory of Pedro Navarro is loaded with execrations at Naples, for his first making use of mines in sieges: he was not, however, the inventor, but first conducted them so as to take effect. In the year 1487, an officer in the Genoese army, then in the field against the Florentines, and besieging Serezanella, had contrived a mine, and sprung it; but not answering the great expectations conceived of it, the inventor lost all his credit, and such projects were looked upon as chimerical. Pedro Navarro, at that time only a private centinel, having attentively considered the invention, thought the want of success to be rather owing to mismanagement, than to the impracticability of the thing itself; and, in the year 1503, the siege of the castle of Naples gave him an opportunity of putting his conjecture to the trial; which he did so effectually both to the damage and terror of the besieged, that in a few days the Spaniards saw themselves masters of the place.

St. Elmo castle. The third check upon the city of Naples is the castle of St. Elmo, or St. Eramo, so called from a church dedicated to that saint, formerly standing on this spot. It is situated on an eminence towards the west, and the plan is in the form of a star, with six rays. As its fortifications were chiefly built by Charles V, this inscription is placed over the gate:

Imperatoris Caroli V. Aug. Cæsaris jussu, ac Petri Toleti Villæ Franchæ Marchionis justiss. Proregis auspiciis, Pyrrhus Aloysius Serina Valentinus, D. Joannis Eques, Cæsareusque militum Præfectus, pro suo bellicis in rebus experimento F. curavit. MDXXXVIII.

' This

'This castle was fortified by order of his imperial and august majesty Charles V. under the auspices of our excellent vice-roy Don Pedro de Toledo, marquis of Villa Franca, and from a plan of that excellent engineer Pyrrho Aloysio Serena Valentini, knight of St. John, and colonel in the imperial service. 1538.'

The subterraneous works are very spacious, and hewn out of the rock to such a depth as to be bomb-proof, on which account a great quantity of military stores are kept here. This castle can likewise be supplied with provisions from Castello Nuovo by means of a subterraneous communication, at present walled up. In the upper part of St. Elmo's castle are seven cisterns for water; and under the vaults and mines is a reservoir large enough for two galleys to sail on. The water which is always extremely cold, is drawn from it by a bucket through a kind of aperture or well. *Cisterns.*

The arms of Naples are a horse; and formerly near the church di Santa Restituta, stood a brass one of such an enormous size, that the commonalty have a notion that it was cast by Virgil, by the help of magic, whom they imagine to have been a sorcerer. It was also the object of a most gross superstition, being accounted of such efficacy against all distempers incident to horses, that they were brought hither from all parts, and led round this all-healing statue. At last, in the year 1322, Maria Caraffa, archbishop of Naples, to abolish a practice which reflected disgrace on human nature, had it demolished and cast into a large bell for the cathedral. The head being reserved for a memorial, is still to be seen in the court of the Caraffa palace, among a collection of statues and basso-relievo's. Charles king of Naples having made himself master of the city, after an eight-months siege, ordered a bit to be put in the mouth of this horse, whose attitude expressed its impatience of controul, as an emblematical representation of his having tamed the Neapolitans. *City arms. Superstition concerning a brass horse.*

In the above-mentioned court is also to be seen, on a pillar, a small equestrian statue of Alphonso the Second.

Poggio Reale, formerly a magnificent royal palace without the city, is now so fallen to decay as not to be worth seeing. Among the ruins is shewn a steep place, from whence queen Joanna used to have those whom she wanted out of the way to be privately thrown down headlong. *Poggio Reale.*

In

Il Palagio degli Spiriti, or the haunted palace.   In returning from the last mentioned place to the city, on the left are the ruins of an old castle, commonly called *il Palagio degli Spiriti*, from a vulgar fancy, that this palace was deserted by the owners, on account of its being haunted. At present there is nothing worth observing to be seen here, though it seems once to have been a charming retreat.

Bats cave.   On the right hand, in returning from Poggio Reale lies the *Grotta degli Sportiglioni*, or the bats cave, which is an Italian mile and a half in length, very broad and high. About the middle it divides, forming two vaults, one of which extends itself towards Poggio Reale, but has been walled in since the year 1656, when it was made a repository for the bodies of above fifty thousand persons who died of the pestilence. The hill over this cavity is extremely pleasant, and called *Monte del Trecco*, from the French General Lautrec, who, in 1528, besieging Naples, pitched his camp here; and not to damage a city of which he thought himself sure of being master, he broke up and ruined the aqueducts, in order to reduce it by distress. But the stagnation of the waters occasioned thereby, together with the summer heats, bred such a contagion, as swept away the greatest part of the army and Lautrec himself; and of those who survived the sickness, very few escaped the rage of the Italians. Lautrec's fatal oversight was, that, previously to the demolishing of the aqueducts, he had not cut a canal for carrying off the waters to the sea. It was also the fate of Henry VI, emperor of Germany, after closely besieging Naples for three months, to see his army dwindle away by epidemical distempers, so that he was obliged to raise the siege.

Noblemen's palaces.   The most remarkable palaces at Naples are those of the prince di S. Agata, the dukes di Gravina and Mataloni, and a few others, though indeed they will hardly bear seeing after those of Rome. The house of Ferdinando di S. Felice or Sanfelicius, as he is called in some inscriptions, not yet finished, will be very superb and elegant; he orders every thing himself, and is not only a judge in pictures, but no mean painter; having purely from inclination been a disciple of Solimene. Besides several fruit-pieces, here are some capital paintings of his, one of the massacre of the innocents, and another of Joseph's escape into Egypt. A half of this palace is to be entirely painted *in fresco* from designs of Solimene. One of the pleasantest parts of the city is the suburb, commonly called *Chiaia*, but more properly *Spiaggia*

or

or *Piaggia*, i. e. the Strand, from its proximity to the sea-shore. The coolness of the air, the agreeableness of the prospect, the extent of the area, and the freedom from dust, make it the evening resort of the quality; so that it is no uncommon thing to see some hundreds of coaches here; but on these occasions persons of different sexes never ride together in the same coach. Nothing can be more delightful than the gardens to the right-hand on the hill, adorned with walks of orange, cedar, and palm-trees, and a profusion of the most beautiful flowers,

At Pietra Bianca, situated about four Italian miles from Naples, at the foot of mount Vesuvio, is a country seat, originally built by Bernardino Martirano, secretary to Charles V, where the emperor was entertained on his return from Tunis in 1535, which, according to the inscription over the gate, has made this place for ever sacred:

Pietra Bianca.

> *Hospes,*
> *Etsi properas, ne sis impius,*
> *Præteriens hoc ædificium veneretur,*
> *Hic enim Carolus V. Rom. Imper.*
> *Debellatâ Aphricâ,*
> *Veniens triduum in liberali*
> *Leuco-Petræ gremio consumsit.*
> *Florem spargito, & vale.*
> *MDXXXV.*

' Stranger, how great soever thy haste may be, fail not,
' as thou wouldst avoid impiety, to pay the veneration due
' to this edifice; this is the place where, amidst the affluence
' and rural beauties of Pietra Bianca, Charles V. emperor of
' the Romans, returning from his African conquests, passed
' three days. Strew flowers here, and farewel! 1535.'

This palace has a very bad neighbour of mount Vesuvio; the effects of its eruptions being but too visible, notwithstanding all the expensive repairs and improvements continually made here.

LETTER

NAPLES.

LETTER LIX.

Churches, and other religious Edifices at NAPLES.

Attempts of the Neapolitan clergy. SUCH is the power and opulence which the Neapolitan clergy have attained to, and the veneration paid them, that more than once they have been ready to seize the civil power, and to arrogate to themselves a decisive authority in matters quite foreign to the pastoral care. Nor can they bear the least controul or censure on this account; one instance of which is their rancour against Pietro Giannone, a civilian, author of the *Iſtoria Civile del Regno di Napoli*. His freedom in aſſerting the civil rights againſt the incroachments of the clergy incenſed them to such a degree, that he found himſelf under a neceſſity of leaving Naples to avoid the fury of the populace, whom the clergy had ſpirited up againſt him. Naſo the printer of it was excommunicated; and had not the protection of the emperor, to whom the book was dedicated, checked the impetuoſity of pope Benedict XIII, the author would have fared no better: the effect, however, has been, that this valuable piece is become very ſcarce *. The firmneſs with which Riccardi, attorney-general to the Neapolitan government, had, according to the duty of his office, lately oppoſed the attempts of the court of Rome, drew upon him the ſame perſecuting ſpirit, till at Vienna he found a patron in Garelli, the emperor's phyſician and librarian; who making his ſervices and abilities known at court, ſet him above the malice of his enemies.

Toleration in ceremonies. As to external ceremonies, the devotion of the Roman catholics here is not ſo outrageous as in ſeveral provinces of of Germany. At the elevation of the hoſt in churches, or

---

* He fled to Vienna, but here that ambition which he had ſo juſtly expoſed, would not let him reſt; San Felice, a jeſuit, was employed to traduce him as a tool of Spain, and with too much ſucceſs, for Giannone ſaw himſelf deprived of a penſion of which he was but very lately poſſeſſed. This obliged him to remove to Venice with a view of publiſhing a ſecond edition of his hiſtory; but, on an advantageous overture from a bookſeller at Geneva, he went thither in the year 1735. He ſoon after fell into the hands of his enemies; for, a Piedmonteſe officer, who had pretended a mighty friendſhip for him, enticing him to spend a day at a country ſeat without the territories of the city, he was there ſeized and immediately hurried away to Chambery.

when

NAPLES.

when it is carried along the streets, no stranger is compelled to kneel; and so little difficulty is made about travellers eating flesh and fowls in Lent, that the inn-keeper's first question is, What the company will be pleased to eat; and in some parts eating *meagre*, *i. e.* fish, eggs, and vegetables, is not so acceptable to the host as an heretical meal, which makes the reckoning more considerable. Since the government came into the hands of the Austrian line of the house of Hapsburg, the statue of St. Nepomuk has been erected on several bridges; but the crosses are not very numerous in the streets, nor public processions, even in the capital itself, so frequent as in most other popish cities. The most common procession, which is exhibited almost every day, is not so much intended to excite devotion as to raise a fund for penitent prostitutes who have quitted their abandoned way of living for a convent. In order the more effectually to move the spectators to charity, the youngest and most beautiful of these penitents are selected, who are ordered to walk barefooted through the city, two a-breast: at some particular places they kneel down, acknowledge their past wickedness, and sing penitential hymns; the ecclesiastic and a lay-assistant who attend them in the mean time receiving the contributions of the public in a purse fastened to the end of a stick. Their habit on these occasions is a violet-coloured gown tied round the waist with a cord of the same colour. Their heads are shaved, but they wear a blue veil, which however is thin enough to give a sight of the charms of youth and beauty, as powerful incentives to a liberal contribution. *Procession of penitent prostitutes.*

The vivacity and penetration of the Neapolitans, (as they do not always meet with a satisfactory solution of religious scruples from their ecclesiastics, and want an opportunity of receiving better information by foreign books, or verbal instructions) too often carries them into wild systems of religion, and sometimes to downright atheism: and the necessity of concealing such notions makes them take the deeper root; so that it is with great difficulty any one of them is reclaimed. Molinos had a strong party in this city; and Ernest Ruthan (who had been amanuensis to M. Arnauld, and lately died at Brussels, where his burial met with no small opposition) assured me in 1715, that in Naples above half of those, who, disdaining the yoke of human ordinances, had been endeavouring to bring the established religion to some test, were, in their hearts, Jansenists. Perhaps it is owing to the apprehension of finding the delinquents too numerous, *The Neapolitans inclinable to atheism. Molinists and Jansenists.*

. VOL. III. E that

that prosecutions are not so indiscreetly carried on here as in many other places, and the punishments for such offences are tempered with so much lenity; which would not be the case if the ecclesiastics had a manifest superiority. At least Naples is the place of all Italy where booksellers are under the least restraint; for they openly sell *L'Enfant's Bibliotheque Germanique*, and other books written by protestants, even on religious and polemical subjects; whilst, in other popish cities, it would be dangerous to have such works in their houses.

Freedom of booksellers.

The roofs and *façades* of the churches of Naples are but ill contrived, and the monuments within them, in size and grandeur, are vastly inferior to those at Rome; but, in the beauty and richness of other ornaments, scarce any country can equal them; so that only the jewels and altar-plate in many of the churches amount to many millions of dollars. It must be acknowledged, that the clergy here are extremely civil to strangers, and freely bestow their time and trouble in gratifying their curiosity. To take a view of all the churches in Naples would be a work of time, there being no less than three hundred and four in all, conventual and parochial. I shall therefore only take notice of the most remarkable churches and convents, keeping to my usual alphabetical order.

Fault in the Neapolitan churches. Their beauty and richness.

Number.

S. Agnello is famous for a miraculous crucifix in the Capella de Monaci, which, upon a debtor's denying a debt in its presence, is said to have reproached his ingratitude, &c. The greatest altar is of white marble, adorned with exquisite basso-relievo's. The statue of St. Dorothea, by Giovanni da Nola, is a good piece: and in the wall opposite to it are several ancient basso-relievo's. In the Capella del Purgatorio, over the tomb of Antonia Capuana, is a superb marble basso-relievo representing the virgin Mary with the divine infant in her arms, shewing herself to the souls in purgatory *.

St. Agnello's miraculous crucifix.

In the adjoining convent is a monument of G. Battista Marino, a celebrated poet, with a brass bust of him erected pursuant to a clause in the will of his liberal Mæcenas the marquis di Villa, which formerly stood in that nobleman's house, from whence it was removed hither. The following inscription on the monument was drawn up by Cornelio:

Marino's tomb.

* Abundance of reliques, &c. are here omitted in the translation.

D. O. M.
Et Memoriæ
Equitis Joannis Baptiſtæ Marini,
Poëtæ incomparabilis,
Quem ob ſummam in condendo
Omnis generis carmine felicitatem
Reges & viri Principes cohoneſtârunt,
Omneſque Muſarum amici ſuſpexernt,
Joannes Baptiſta Manſus
Villæ Marchio,
Dum præclaris favet ingeniis,
Ut poſteros ad celebrandam illius
Immortalem gloriam excitaret,
Monumentum extruendum legavit,
Quod Montis Manſi Rectores
Ad præſcripti normam exegere.
Anno M. DC. LXXXIII.

' This monument, ſacred to God the greateſt and beſt of
' Beings, and the memory of John Baptiſta Marino, knight,
' an univerſal poet, whoſe incomparable verſes, admired by
' all lovers of the muſes, endeared him to ſeveral monarchs
' and other illuſtrious perſonages, was erected purſuant to a
' legacy left by John Baptiſta Manſi, marquis of Villa, &c.
' 1683.'

He died in 1625; and ſeveral other epitaphs were compoſed for him, one of which, together with a picture of him
on the wall, was ſet up by the academy of the Humoriſts,
of which he had been preſident.

This poet was a knight of the order of St. Lazarus and
St. Maurice, which honour was cônferred on him by Charles
Emanuel duke of Savoy. Several manuſcripts of his are
ſtill kept among the records of this church, where his remains are depoſited.

This church of S. Angelo à Segno is conſecrated to St.
Michael the archangel, and was built on the following occaſion: In 574 the Saracens had forced their way into the city
by the Porta Ventoſa; but, being on this ſpot vigorouſly attacked by Giacomo de Marra, were repulſed after a very ſharp
ſkirmiſh. How far theſe ravagers had penetrated is ſeen by
a braſs nail on a piece of white marble fixed in the wall of
this church.

S. Angelo
à Segno.
Irruption of
the Saracens.

S. Angelo à Nido. In the church of S. Angelo à Nido are several fine monuments, particularly one belonging to the Brancaccio family. Cardinal Francesco Maria Brancaccio has bequeathed a good library to this church. The great altar-piece, representing the archangel Michael, is a celebrated piece, by Marco da Siena.

SS. Apostoli. The church de' SS. Apostoli is almost covered with gilding and painting; so that, with a suitable façade, which it wants, it would be a beautiful edifice. Over the entrance is a piece of painting, by Lanfranco, representing the angel descending to stir the waters of the pool of Bethesda; and near it the same artist has so curiously drawn a crack or fissure, that the wall appears to be actually cleft: a similar deception is also to be seen in the refectory of the Theatines convent, to which this church belongs. The roof is beautifully painted by Lanfranco, and the cupola by Benaschi. The tabernacle on the great altar is said to have cost forty thousand *scudi*, or crowns, and is indeed a most admirable piece, consisting of eight pillars, and other decorations of amethysts, emeralds, *lapis lazuli*, agates of several colours, a topaz of the bigness of a walnut, and other gems. The altar is of *marmo fiorito*, or flowered marble, and the balustrade before it of red and white marble. On the two sides stand two brass gueridons nine *palmi* high, but much more valuable for the workmanship than the size. The basso-relievo represents the four beasts in Ezekiel's vision, which are generally supposed to be emblematical representations of the four evangelists; the designs were Finelli's, but they were cast by Bersotino, a Florentine. On the altar-piece is a fine painting of Christ's head with a crown of thorns. On the right **Capella del card. Filamarino.** side of the high altar is cardinal Ascanio Filamarino's chapel, where the greatest artists in the time of Urban VIII. have displayed their skill; and, though it be constructed of several pieces of white marble, no joinings are discernible. Its splendid appearance is greatly heightened by five mosaic pieces, by Giov. Battista Calandra da Vercelli: the noble altar-piece, representing the annunciation, together with the four Christian virtues, Faith, Hope, Charity, and Humility, on each side, were originally painted in oil-colours by Guido Rheni, but have since been altered into very beautiful mosaic pieces. The groupe of cherubim, seraphim, &c. in a marble basso-relievo is by Francesco Fiamingo, who, for sculpture, is accounted a second Michael Angelo. The two lions on which the altar rests, together with the intended sa-

crifice

crifice of Isaac in basso-relievo, are the workmanship of Giul. Finelli da Carrara.

This chapel has always the appearance of being new; the heirs of the founder being, by his will, obliged to have it twice a year carefully cleaned and beautified, under the penalty of two hundred ducats for every neglect, payable to the convent, to be laid out for the above-mentioned purposes.

The Capella de' Pignatelli, on the left-side of the high-altar, is equally worth seeing. Its altar is inlaid with gems, among which is an amethyst seven inches broad, and near ten spans in length. In the vestry are several good paintings, and a great quantity of very fine plate; particularly a very large silver lamp, valued at two thousand *scudi*, which was designed by Solimene. Here are also several golden chalices, set with rubies and diamonds; six silver flower-pots; a crucifix which cost fifty thousand *scudi*; and six chandeliers of coral set in gold. In the vaults belonging to this church are several bodies of both sexes wrapt up in linen, which have lain there several years undecayed.

Capella de' Pignatelli.

In the convent are three galleries over one another; but that on the ground floor is by much the finest. The staircase runs in a spiral line, and the steps, like those of St. Peter's at Rome, are very low, for the conveniency of asses carrying up corn to the granaries. The library is elegant, well furnished with books, and affords a delightful prospect. Near this convent is held a weekly meeting of the heads of a society, consisting of two hundred gentlemen of the law, to examine the private grievances of the poor; and in case any pauper is found to be oppressed, and that his complaint is well founded, a member of this society is nominated to undertake his cause: but neither this member, nor the society, are at any expence in such cases; the law-charges being defrayed by the Theatine convent, which has large endowments for this particular purpose. This is an institution which must give pleasure to every benevolent and humane person.

Convent.

In the church of S. Catarina à Formello are several monuments, of which the most remarkable are those of the Spinelli family. In the Capella di S. Domenico are several good pieces in painting and sculpture. Under the altar is the figure of a dog, with a horn in his mouth, in which is a flaming torch; on his back rests a globe, with these words on it:

S. Catarina à Formello.

E 3 *A seculo*

NAPLES.

A seculo usque ad seculum.
'From age to age.'

And under the hound:

Sustinet, inflammat *.
'It supports and inflames.'

This is the coat of arms belonging to the court of inquisition.

<small>Eastern magi.</small> The altar-piece, representing the arrival of the three eastern *magi* at Bethlehem, is by Silvester Buono. In the area before the church is erected a bust of St. Januarius, with an inscription. In the dispensary of the adjoining Dominican convent one is shewn a copy of the head of the famous rebel or patriot Masaniello. Here is also a cabinet of curiosities, with abundance of antique medals, urns, idols, minerals, petrifactions, large pieces of coral, &c.

<small>S. Chiaria.</small> S. Chiaria is one of the principal churches in Naples. Facing the high altar are two superb pillars of white marble, pretended to have belonged to Solomon's temple; two others nearer the altar, in appearance perfectly resembling the former, are only of wood incrusted with marble. The <small>Monument of Robert king of Sicily.</small> table of the high altar is a single piece of marble eighteen *palmi* in length; and behind it lies the brave and excellent founder of this church, king Robert, with this short inscription:

Cernite Robertum Regem virtute refertum.

'Behold king Robert, a prince endowed with every virtue.'

He died in 1343, after a reign of thirty-three years.
Near the high altar is the monument of Charles the illustrious, son of king Robert, and duke of Calabria.
In 1686 part of the roof of the vault happening to fall in, the body of this excellent prince was found without any visible decay.

<small>Of Mary of France, &c.</small> On the other side of the altar stands the marble tomb of Mary, sister of Joanna I, a posthumous child, and born in

---

* This motto is capable of various explanations.

1329;

NAPLES.

1329; she was first married to Charles duke of Durazzo, afterwards to Robert de Baux; her third husband was Philip II, prince of Tarento, when she bore the title of empress of Constantinople. Her statue has a crown on the head, and the drapery is enriched with gilded lilies, with this epitaph:

Hic jacet corpus Illustris Dominæ D. Mariæ de Francia Imperatricis Constantinopolitanæ, ac Ducissæ Duracii, quæ obiit anno Domini 1366. die 20. mensis Maji Ind. 4.

'Here lies the body of the illustrious Mary of France,
'empress of Constantinople, and duchess of Durazzo, who
'died on the 20th of May, in the year 1366, and of the in‑
'diction the fourth.'

In a chapel under the organ-loft lies a sister of this Mary, daughter to Charles duke of Calabria and Mary de Valois.

Near the vestry is the monument of queen Joanna I. who caused her first husband Andrew of Hungary to be strangled; and she herself met with the same fate, from king Charles, her second husband: these two circumstances are mentioned in the epitaph which is now scarce legible:

*Inclyta Parthenopes jacet hic Regina Joanna
Prima, prius felix, mox miseranda nimis;
Quam Carolo genitam mulctavit Carolus alter,
Quâ morte illa virum sustulit antè suum.
MCCCLXXXII. 22. Maji v. Indict.*

'Here lies Joanna the First, queen of Naples, whose pros‑
'perous life was terminated by a wretched exit. To one
'Charles she owed her being; another, justly severe, de‑
'prived her of it, by the same means that she had made use
'of to put an end to the life of her former husband. May
'22, 1382.'

Hic jacet is an impropriety in the epitaph; the body of this unhappy woman being in reality buried in the church di S. Francesco del Monte Gargano.

Near one of the doors of this church is to be seen a beautiful marble tomb, adorned with sculpture by Giovanni da Nola, on which is an admirable statue of a young lady, with the following epitaph by Antonio Epicuro, a Neapolitan poet:

E 4 *Nata,*

Nata, Eheu miserum! misero mihi nata parenti,
  Unicus ut fieres, unica nata, dolor.
Dum tibi namque virum, tedas, thalamumque parabam
  Funera & inferias anxius ecce paro.
Debuimus tecum poni Materque Paterque,
  Ut tribus hæc miseris urna parata foret.
At nos perpetui gemitus, tu nata sepulchri
  Esto hæres, ubi sic impia fata volunt.

Antoniæ filiæ chariss. quæ Hieronymo Granatæ Juveni ornatiss. destinata uxor Ann. nondum XIIII. impleverat, Joannes Gaudinus & Heliodora Bossa Parentes infeliciss. pos. raptæ ex eorum complexib. ann. sal. MDXXX. Prid. Kal. Jan.

' My only child, alas, my only grief!
' With silent raptures of paternal love
' For thee the bridal robe and nuptial bed
' I late prepar'd, which now, alas, are chang'd
' To death's black trophies and funereal rites.
' O that one grave the wretched parents held
' With thee, whom from their arms relentless fate
' Has snatch'd in all the pride of blooming youth;
' And left them to lament, but all in vain,
' With endless sighs and tears thy early doom.'

' To their dear daughter Antonia, who was betrothed to
' Gieronimo Granata, a youth of the finest accomplishments,
' and snatched from their embraces on the last day of the
' year 1530, by a premature death, before she had compleated her fourteenth year, John Guadiano and Heliodora Bossa, her disconsolate parents, have erected this monument.'

In this church lies also the author of this epitaph: a monument, with the following inscription, was erected to him by a person to whom his poetical talent had endeared him:

ANTONIO EPICVRO, Musarum Alumno, Bernardinus Rota, primis in annis studiorum socio posuit. Moritur octuagenarius, unico sepulto filio. I nunc & diu vivere miser cura. MDLV.

' To Anthonio Epicuro, a favourite of the muses, who,
' after burying his only son, died in his eightieth year, this
' monument

'monument was erected by Bernard Rota, his *quondam*
'school-fellow. 1555.

'Go now, vain man, and covet length of days.'

All the monuments in this church are of white marble, and some are embellished with masterly basso-relievo's. In the convent adjoining, none but women of the noblest families are admitted; and as the rules are not very strict, the number of nuns, exclusive of maid-servants and other attendants, exceeds three hundred and fifty. The church is served by the Franciscans, who also are the spiritual guides of this beautiful flock, unquestionably the most numerous of the kind in the Christian world.

The Jesuits college, as usual, is one of the finest structures in the city: the refectory, the library, the great staircase, the dispensary, and the church belonging to this college, will afford entertainment to a traveller of taste. Most of the buildings belonging to this aspiring order are generally embellished with the most sumptuous ornaments, of which the church della Concezzione, adjoining to which the fathers have their seminary, is an instance. The front is built with large cubic stones of *pietra pipernina*. The most remarkable altars in this church are those of St. Ignatius, St. Francis Xavier, and *l'Altare Maggiore*, or high altar, which, though it be not quite finished, is adorned with six Corinthian pillars of a carnation marble, four statues, &c. The cupola, which is exquisitely painted by Lanfranco, was damaged by an earthquake in 1688; so that the only remains of that eminent pencil are the evangelists on one side of it, the rest being painted since by Paolo de Mattheis, a Neapolitan. St. Ignatius's chapel is particularly remarkable for two statues, by Cosmo Fonsago; one of David with Goliah's head at his feet, the other of Jeremiah bewailing the calamities of his country. Here is also a porphyry tomb of Nicolas Sanseverini, the last prince of Bisignano.

In the church are also to be seen two curious holy-water basons of a yellow and brown marble. In the vestry, which is finely gilded, are three pictures of the Virgin, one by Annibal Caracci, and two others by Raphael. The silver tissue in the treasury, valued by the weight of the silver, amounts to a hundred and fifty thousand *scudi*. Here are also several statues and busts; St. Cyr, as big as the life, of silver, enriched with emeralds; several chalices, a curious altar covering,

Il Collegio del Giesu.

Chiesa della Concezzione.

ing, cast in silver by Gennaro Monte, and many other things of immense value.

The Jesuits also, besides other churches, are in possession of that of S. Giuseppe; of which, in its proper place, I shall give a full description.

S. Domenico Maggiore. S. Domenico Maggiore belongs to the Dominican monks; and contiguous to it is a convent, where there are generally a hundred and forty monks. The church was built by king Charles II. whose heart is kept here embalmed in a small ivory urn, with this inscription:

Conditorium hoc est cordis Caroli II. Illustrissimi Regis, Fundatoris Conventus. Ann. Domini MCCCIX.

' The repository of the heart of the most illustrious prince, ' Charles II. founder of this convent. 1309.'

Crucifix which spoke to Thomas d'Aquino. In the Capella del Santissimo Crocefisso is the crucifix which condescended to express its approbation of the writings of the celebrated Thómas d'Aquino, or Aquinas, concerning the real presence of the body and blood of Christ in the sacrament in these words: *Bene scripsisti de me, Thoma, quam ergo mercedem accipies?* ' Thomas, thou hast written well con- ' cerning me; what reward shall I give thee thee on that ' account?' To which the doctor is said to have answered: *Non aliam nisi te ipsum.* I'll have no other recompence but ' thyself *.' On certain days of the year this crucifix is with great pomp exposed to public view; but, at all other times, is not to be seen; seven persons having in their custody as many different keys of the shrine in which it is kept. Over the crucifix is an admirable picture of the descent from the cross, by Zingaro. On a monument in the chapel belonging to the Caraffa family is the following epitaph:

Huic
Virtus gloriam,
Gloria immortalitatem
Comparavit.
M. CCCC. LXX.

' By virtue he acquired glory, and glory gained him im- ' mortality. 1470.'

* At Salerno this crucifix is accounted an imposture, the right one being, as they say, in their possession.

In

NAPLES.

In the duke d'Acerenza's chapel is an highly-esteemed annunciation-piece, by Titian. The monument of Bernardini Rota, in St. John the Baptist's chapel, is worth seeing, both on account of his statue, and those of the Tiber and the Arno, with which it is adorned.

In the Capella di Stigliano is an exquisite image of the virgin Mary, by Giov. da Nola; and in that of St. Joseph are two fine pictures, by Guido. The vestry is very lofty, and finely painted by Solimene. In the gallery lie seven coffins richly covered, in which are the remains of the kings and queens of Naples, and other great personages. Of these the first in order is Antonio Petruccio, secretary to the emperor Ferdinand. The lid can be taken off, to give a sight of his body, which is in a full dress, and so far undecayed, that all the teeth are still found, and in their proper arrangement. He lost his life in the conspiracy of the barons, being strangled, and not beheaded, as is manifest from the cord which still remains about his neck. Misson gives some of the inscriptions on the coffins; but the present coverings, which are of crimson velvet and silk damask, would not admit my comparing his copies with the originals.

The riches of this church in plate, &c. is very considerable. Some of the *palliotti*, or altar-coverings, are of cast silver, and one for the high altar cost fourteen thousand *scudi*. In the vestry is an admirable busto of pope Pius V. Near the gate of the college which was formerly appropriated to the study of divinity, stands a statue of Thomas Aquinas, with this remarkable inscription:

Statue of Thomas Aquinas.

Viator, huc ingrediens, siste gradum, atque venerare hanc imaginem & Cathedram, in qua sedens Mag. ille Thomas de Aquino de Neap. cum frequente, ut par erat, Auditorum concursu, & illius seculi felicitate, cæterosque quam plurimos admirabili doctrinâ Theologiam docebat, accersito jam a Rege Carolo I. constitutâ illa mercede unius unciæ auri per singulos menses, R. F. V. C. in anno 1272. *D. SS. F. F.*

' Traveller, at thy entrance here, stop and reverence this
' statue, and the chair, in which the great Thomas de
' Aquino a Neapolitan, in happy times, taught theology
' with admirable skill, attended by a numerous audience,
' worthy of such a doctor; who being invited hither by king
' Charles I, had a pension of an ounce of gold *per* month,
' settled on him by that monarch, &c.

NAPLES.

Dispute about his body.

The Dominicans at Toulouse affirm, that they have the entire body of Thomas Aquinas, the right arm only excepted, which they made a present of to Lewis XIII, who committed it to the custody of the Dominicans in the rüe S. Jacques at Paris; but at Naples they also shew his right arm, the cell he lived in, and his professional chair, which is respected to such an absurd degree, that no person must presume to sit down in it. His manuscript notes on Dionysius's book, *de Cœlesti Hierarchia,* is kept with all the care and veneration of a relique: but at the beginning of this century Philip king of Spain coming to Naples, expressed a desire to have some leaves of so precious a piece, and it was not thought proper to oppose his devotion.

In the area before the lesser door of the convent stands an elegant pyramid with the statue of St. Dominic on the top of it.

The cathedral.

Il Duomo, or the cathedral, is dedicated to the assumption of the virgin Mary. The foundation was laid by Charles I, king of Naples and Sicily, to whom a monument is erected near the great door, with this inscription:

Carolo I. Andegavensi, Templi hujus extructori, Carolo Martello Hungariæ Regi & Clementiæ ejus uxori, Rodulphi I. Cæsaris F. ne Regis Neapolitani ejusque Nepotis, & Austriaci sanguinis Reginæ debito sine honore jacerent ossa, Henricus Gusmannus, Olivarensium Comes, Philippi III. Austriaci Regias in hoc Regno Vices gerens, pietatis ergô posuit. Anno Domini M.D.C.IC.

' To Charles I, of Anjou, the founder of this church,
' and to Charles Martel king of Hungary, and Clementia
' his consort, daughter of the emperor Randolph, Henry
' Gusman count of Olivares, vice-roy of Naples under
' Philip III. of Austria, erected this monument, that the
' king of Naples and his grandson, also a king, and a
' princess of the house of Austria might not want the due
' honours of a tomb.'

Charles's original epitaph was the following:

*Conditur hac parva Carolus Rex Primus in urna
Parthenopes, Galli sanguinis altus honos:
Cui sceptrum & vitam sors abstulit invida, quando
Illius famam perdere non potuit.*

' In

NAPLES.

'In this small tomb lies Charles I, the glory of France, and king of Naples: his fame was beyond the reach of envious fate, which deprived him of his life and scepter.'

The steps up the ascent to the high altar are of white marble and adorned on the sides with curious basso-relievo's. Fronting the altar are two pillars of red jasper, twelve feet high without the pedestals which are of *verde antico*. Near the latter is a monument erected by cardinal Cantelmo to pope Innocent XII, whilst living, with an inscription full of the grossest flattery.

Not far from this is the fine tomb of cardinal Alphonso Caraffa, who died in the year 1561, and opposite to it that of cardinal Cesvaldi.

On the high altar-piece is the assumption of the virgin Mary by Pietro Perugino, a painter, who lived in the 15th century, and was Raphael's master.

In the chapel under the high altar, built in 1506, by cardinal Oliverio Caraffa, are some curious works in marble, as festoons, foliages, birds, children, angels, &c. which are by some attributed to Michael Angelo, who also cut the transparent alabaster statue of the noble founder, placed behind the altar. The pavement is inlaid with *verde antico*, jasper, *giallo antico*, and porphyry. The remains of St. Januarius have been removed from the church dedicated to that saint without the walls, to this subterraneous chapel, where they are still kept. The present emperor offered at his shrine twelve silver eagles: in the crowns on the heads of these eagles twelve lamps are continually burning, and one hundred *scudi* a year are appropriated for supplying them with oil. Here is also a fine Madonna with her divine infant painted on wood by the cavalier Massa. In a side chapel are the portraits of several of the Caraffa family, who were eminent benefactors to this church; and likewise a very curious wooden crucifix. In the church is a font made in 1621, which, as it cost eleven thousand five hundred *scudi*, may be supposed to be something extraordinary. The pedestal is of porphyry, and the bason of touch-stone. On the right hand near the high altar is another beautiful altar of Florentine work; and its tabernacle is set with the finest gems. Not far from this is the monument of Innocent IV. who honoured the cardinal with the red hat; likewise that of the unfortunate

Chapel under the high altar.

unfortunate king Andrea, who was strangled by the contrivance of his queen Joanna, as the epitaph specifies.

Andreæ, Caroli Uberti Pannoniæ Regis F. Neapolitanɔrum Regis; Joannæ uxoris dolo & laqueo necato: ne Regis corpus insepultum, sepultumve facinus posteris remaneret, Franciscus Berardi F. Capycius sepulcrum, titulum nomenque P. mortuo annor. XIX. 1345. XIV. KL. Octob.

‘ That the body of Andrew king of Naples, the son of
‘ Charles Hubert king of Hungary, who was strangled by
‘ the intrigues of his queen Joanna, might not be unburied,
‘ and that her guilt might not be buried in oblivion, Francis
‘ Capycio, &c. erected this monument and inscription.
‘ At the time of this horrid murder, which was on the 18th
‘ of September, 1345, this unhappy prince was but nineteen
‘ years of age.’

Not far from this monument is a most beautiful white marble basso-relievo of John the Baptist.

Fine chapel. The most remarkable thing in this cathedral is the chapel on the right hand at entering the church, called *il Tesoro*, the architecture of which is extremely beautiful. In it are the statues of St. Peter and St. Paul, finely executed by Finelli, and two pillars of black marble most beautifully spotted; the door is of brass, curiously wrought with festoons and foliages, which cost thirty-six thousand *scudi*. The chapel is of a round figure, and contains seven altars of the finest marble, and forty-two pillars of Broccatello. Round the upper part of the wall stand twenty-one large bronze images of saints, each valued at four thousand *scudi*; and under them are sixty silver busts of so many saints. Most of these bronzes are by Finelli. The cupola was painted by Lanfranco, Domenichini, and Permeggiano; but these noble pieces have very much suffered by earthquakes that damaged the cupola. Behind the high altar, which is detached from the wall and entirely of red porphyry, is the shrine with St. Januarius's head and blood. silver doors, where are kept St. Januarius's head, and two crystal phials containing some of that saint's blood, said to have been gathered up by a woman at the time of his martyrdom. Besides the three stated times in the year for exposing these reliques to the public view, the like is done with the deepest humiliations, on account of famine, pestilence, earthquakes, or any public calamity which is supposed to require

quire St. Januarius's interposition. The pretended lique- Liquefaction
faction of the coagulated blood in the phials when placed of the blood.
near the head is known to all the world. This farce is acted
the first Sunday in May, and on the success or failure of this
miracle the prosperity or calamity of the succeeding year is
supposed to depend. As the former occasions great public
rejoicings, so if the blood remains coagulated recourse is had
to processions, public flagellations, &c. that the impending
dangers may be averted.

The substance in the phial is of a brownish red, and looks
like balsam of Peru, which may be very easy liquefied. On
the day when this miracle is to be exhibited, the phial containing the blood stands surrounded with a great number of
lights: it is about three inches long, and is applied to the
mouths and foreheads of an innumerable multitude of people, who throng to partake of such a blessing: the priest all
the while turning it every way, so that by the continual agitation, the warmth of his hand, the heat from the lights,
the effluvia from such crowds, the sultriness of the weather,
&c. it is not unreasonable to suppose a condensed fluid may
be gradually restored to its liquidity. At last, however, the
priests cry out, *Il miraculo e fatto.* 'The miracle is done;'
which is immediately answered by a *Te Deum* amidst the ac-
clamations of the people and a discharge of cannon *. But
this miracle is not peculiar to St. Januarius's blood; that of
St. John the Baptist, St. Stephen, St. Pantaleon, St. Vitus,
and St. Patricia, exhibiting the like spectacle in other
churches at Naples, where such reliques are kept, and generally on the days dedicated to those saints. Over the entrance within the old vestry formerly belonging to the Capella del Tesoro is a bust of St. Januarius of touch-stone,
with two small phials full of a red liquor standing before it.
The silver images, chandeliers, lamps, altar-coverings, &c.
with which the new chapel is crowded, are valued at a hundred thousand *scudi.*

---

* In 1733, Mr. Neuman a celebrated chemist at Berlin invented a method by which the liquefaction of blood so much boasted of with regard
to Januarius is easily and at any time imitated; and it is to be hoped,
that he will lay it open to the world. Dr. Cassebom, professor of physic
at Hall, is said to be possessed of a like secret. Besides, it bears very
hard upon the Austrian party here, that, at the late unjust irruption of the
Spaniards into the kingdom of Naples, St. Januarius shifted sides, and
by the speedy liquefaction of his blood declared for Don Carlos.

Opposite

Oppofite to the Teforo, is the entrance into St. Reftituta's church, which was formerly the cathedral. Many of the pillars of this church are faid to be the remains of a temple of Neptune. On the wall is the virgin Mary in mofaic, given out to be the firft image, not of Naples only, but of all Italy, to which adoration was paid; but its apparent antiquity, however, little agrees with the opinion of thofe who place the building of this church fo far back as the age of St. Peter and his difciple St. Afpreno, whom they alfo are pleafed to make bifhop of Naples.

In the area between the cathedral and the Strada Capuana ftands a fine marble obelifk by Cofmo Fonfeca, on which is erected a brafs ftatue of St. Januarius by Finelli; with this infcription:

*Divo Januario Patriæ Regnique
præfentiffimo Tutelari
Grata Neapolis Civ. optimè merito.*

'Erected by the city of Naples out of gratitude to St. Ja-
'nuarius, the ever propitious and powerful protector of his
'native city and the whole kingdom.'

This obelifk is illuminated annually on the 19th of September with a fplendor hardly to be conceived; while a numerous band of mufic play by it, and all the guns in the feveral forts are fired on the occafion.

Church of S. Francefco di Paola.

The church of S. Francefco di Paola which faces the viceroy's palace is remarkable for a beautiful pavement, a roof finely gilt and carved, and feveral marble ornaments, efpecially at the high altar. The tabernacle is embellifhed with eight incomparable pillars, two of *lapis lazuli*, and the other fix of green jafper. In the middle of this altar is an excellent piece of perfpective in enamel. Befides very large pieces of agate, it is profufely enriched with gems, one of which is an intaglio, faid not only to be the work of nature without any human fkill, but by it defigned to reprefent St. Francis, to whom the church is dedicated. The painting about the altar and of the whole choir is by Luca Giordano. Among its reliques are two fmall phials full of the virgin Mary's milk, as is pretended, which is dried to a refemblance of white *terræ figillatæ*, but liquefies on the feftivals of the virgin Mary. In the adjoining cloifter formerly refided S. Francis de Paola; and to the reputation of his fanctity

Remarkable intaglio.

Virgin Mary's milk.

tity it owes the best part of its present opulence. Among the silver ornaments in the chapel contiguous to the dispensatory, is a statue of St. Michael near three feet high, glittering with jewels, which is valued at twelve thousand ducats. In the dispensatory, not to mention the curiosities in coral and gems, and the water-works, a person cannot forbear being extremely pleased with the elegancy and most judicious oeconomy of it. Some continue to call this church by its ancient name of S. Luigi detto di Palazzo.

St. Gaëtano's church is entirely new and worth seeing, both for its architecture and marble ornaments. The vestments are shewn here which cardinal Orsini, afterwards Benedict XIII, had on at the time of his providential deliverance in an earthquake.

S. Gaëtano.

S. Gennaro extra moenia is also called *ad fores,* and *ad corpus,* the body of St. Januarius having been first interred there. The church formerly belonged to the Benedictines, but at present to an adjoining hospital. On an eminence to the right of this church stands St. Severus's chapel, and near it is the entrance into St. Gennaro's catacombs; of the four hitherto discovered in Naples these are both of the greatest extent and kept in the best order. The vulgar opinion that these subterraneous vaults were the work of the primitive Christians, and served them as retreats in times of persecution, is entirely confuted by taking a view of the Neapolitan catacombs; which are hewn out of a solid rock, and could not have been accomplished clandestinely, or without immense charges; and consequently could never be the work of the Christians either of Rome or Naples during the superiority of the pagans. The sandy soil at Rome, perhaps, would not admit of making the subterraneous galleries wider; but here, where the work was carried on through a solid rock, the galleries or passages are lofty, and generally arched, and so broad, that six persons may walk in them a-breast. That the Romans buried their dead long before the establishment of Christianity is out of dispute; besides, the Christians wanted no such spacious repositories for their dead. The bodies in these catacombs were deposited in cavities on both sides of the vaults, four or five one upon another; and the cavity, when full, was closed up with a marble slab, or with tiles: but as most of these are taken away, the pagan monumental inscriptions do not occur so frequently here as in the catacombs at Rome, where many of these cavities still remain closed up. The pretended bones of the primitive Christians,

Catacombs.

VOL. III.   F   possibly

NAPLES.

possibly to inhance the respect paid to them, or to attract curiosity, have been removed into churches and consecrated vaults; but the bones now to be seen here lying in heaps are chiefly the remains of those who were swept away by the terrible pestilence in 1656. Instead of consecrated tapers, as at Rome, the guides here use common flambeaux. At the entrance of the first vault in St. Gennaro's catacombs is to be seen a marble basso-relievo of St. Januarius, in a reclining posture, indicating the spot where he had lain buried some centuries. Behind it is St. Severus's marble seat, close by the grave wherein he was first deposited, and near it this distich:

Saxum, quod cernis, supplex venerare, viator,
Hic divi quondam jacuerunt ossa Severi.

' Traveller, devoutly venerate this stone, for St. Severus's
' remains were formerly interred here.'

At a little distance from this are the tombs of St. Agrippino, Lorenzo, and other saints; and likewise a mosaic altar in a small cavity within the wall. The guides tell us, that in most places there are three galleries over one another. The passages branching out on each side are very narrow; and in many parts, where they are said to extend several Italian miles, are walled up; robberies, &c. having been committed by banditti, who used to lurk in these vaults. Here is one particular vault, or grotto, of such a height, that the roof cannot be discerned by the light of the flambeaux. In another large empty vault, which our guide told us was the cathedral in the primitive times, are three huge pillars, which seem to support an arch hewn out of the rock; and near it is shewn a baptistery, with the mark annexed on the wall near it:

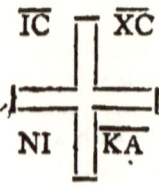

These, with several other paintings and characters, many of which are disfigured by the plaster falling off, though they

they are unquestionably the work of Christians, the Gothic letters, &c. shew them to be of no great antiquity.

S. Giacomo degli Spagnuoli was built by Don Pedro de Toledo, vice-roy of Naples; whose tomb, by Giov. di Nola, is a great ornament to the church, being one of the finest pieces of sculpture in all Naples. *S. Giacomo degli Spagnuoli.*

The sculpture and inlaid work at the high altar make a very noble appearance. The clock of this church strikes the hours after the French and German method of computation; and indeed in Naples there are more French clocks, as they are called, than in any other city in Italy.

S. Giovanni à Carbonara, so called from the Carbonara family, who were once proprietors of a considerable estate in this part of the city, or from the charcoal said to have been formerly burnt near it, is famous for being the burying-place of Ladislaus king of Naples, Sicily, and Hungary, and lord of Rome, whose military glory was sullied by an inglorious death. For a physician, whose daughter was the king's mistress, being bribed by the Florentines, poisoned him. This poison was administered under colour of a philtre, which the daughter was persuaded to give the king, in order to raise his love to the highest pitch, and to fix it unalterably on her. Some, indeed, give a different account of this affair, affirming that Ladislaus besieging Florence, offered the city very favourable terms, upon delivering up to him the daughter of a physician, the report of whose beauty had inflamed his desires. All private concerns being obliged to give way to the public welfare, the father could not refuse his consent; but by his artful management the concession proved fatal both to the inamoured monarch, and his beautiful mistress, as is related by a Latin historian: *Et ità nova Venus ad maritum suum egrediebatur, cui amore deflagranti cum se permitteret, ex domestico mandato incalescentes carnes sudariolo perfricat; quâ re venenum in utriusque corpus eâ penetravit vehementiâ, ut mox inter mutuos amplexus ambo expirarent.* *S. Giovanni à Carbonara. Inglorious death of a martial prince.*

This unhappy end of Ladislaus, which happened in 1414, little agrees with the title of *divus*, or saint, given him in his epitaph. His monument, though of Gothic architecture, is a grand piece; and his epitaph, in Latin verse, is full of the grossest flattery.

Behind the high altar, which is of a most beautiful white marble, is to be seen the tomb of Caracciolo, the favourite of king Ladiflaus, whofe abilities were of fingular fervice to queen Joanna the Second; but, by the wicked inftigation of the duchefs of Seffa, he was affaffinated in his bed on the night of the 25th of Auguft, 1438, as appears by his epitaph.

The chapel de Vico. The chapel of the marquiffes de Vico, of the Caracciola Roffa family, abounds in moft exquifite marble ftatues and baffo-relievo's; thofe of St. John the Baptift, St. Sebaftian, St. Luke, St. Mark, and St. George, are by Pietro di Piata, a Spaniard; the reft by Giov. da Nola; Santa Croce, and Caccavello. In the chapel of the Mirabella family are feven white marble ftatues, and two lions; all curious pieces. Scipio di Somma, the great favourite of Charles V, has a noble monument in the chapel of that name. In another chapel is an admirable crucifixion, by Vafari; and in the church a ftatue of St. Monica, in a black habit. The hiftory pieces painted on wood in the veftry, are by Vafari.

A curious paffion. There is alfo to be feen the paffion of Chrift in feven exquifite marble baffo-relievo's, which fold up like a fcreen, and were a part of king Ladiflaus's baggage in all his expeditions, and placed on the altar when mafs was performed before him *.

S. Giovanni Vangelifta del Pontano. The Auguftine monaftery near S. Giovanni Batt. Carbonara has a fine library, furnifhed with a great many Latin and Greek manufcripts, which were the gift of cardinal Seripando.

The church di S. Giovanni Vangelifta del Pontano derives the laft name from its noble founder Giovanni Pontano. On the walls both without and within this church are feveral moral maxims compofed in Latin by Pontano.

Miffon has publifhed four epitaphs in this church, compofed by Pontano for himfelf and family, which are all accounted mafterpieces both in fentiment and expreffion. That on his daughter Lucia is as follows:

† *Tumulus Luciæ Filiæ.*
Liquifti patrem in tenebris, mea Lucia, poftquam
E luce in tenebras filia rapta mihi es.
Sed neque Tu in tenebras rapta es, quin ipfa tenebras
Liquifti, & medio lucida fole micas.

Cœle

---

* Here an account of miracles, &c. is omitted; whoever is defirous of fuch an entertainment, may confult the Jefuit Silvefter Pietrafanta's *Thaumafia*.

† The poet's playing fo much on the word *tenebræ*, is, I think, fomething

NAPLES.

Cœlo te natam aspicio, num Nata parentem
Aspicis ? an fingit hæc sibi vana Pater ?
Solamen mortis miseræ, Te, Nata, sepulchrum
Hoc tegit, haud cineri sensus inesse potest.
Si qua tamen de Te superat pars, Nata, fatere
Felicem quod Te prima juventa rapit.
At nos in tenebris vitam luctuque trahemus,
Hoc pretium Patri, Filia, quod genui.

Musæ, Filia, luxerunt Te in obitu, at lapide in hoc luget Te Pater tuus, quem liquisti in squalore, cruciatu, gemitu; heu! Filia, quod nec morienti Pater adfui, qui mortis cordolium tibi demerem; nec sorores ingemiscenti collachrymarentur misellæ; nec Frater singultiens, qui sitienti ministraret aquulam; nec Mater ipsa, quæ collo implicita, ore animulam acciperet infelicissima; hoc tamen felix, quod haud multos post annos revixit, tecumque nunc cubat. Ast ego felicior, qui brevi cum utraque edormiscam eodem in conditorio. Vale, Filia. Matri frigescenti cineres interim caleface, ut post etiam refocilles meos.

Joannes Jovianus Pontanus L. Martiæ Filiæ dulciss. P. quæ vixit Ann. XIIII. Men. VII. D. XII.

' My dearest Lucia, since thou from light was snatched
' into darkness, to thy father light is become darkness: no,
' thou art not in the regions of darkness; but being passed
' from darkness, thou now shinest in the plenitude of light.
' I behold thee amidst the celestial effulgence: dost thou, dear
' child, look down on thy father; or is all a pleasing illu-
' sion? It is some solace that after death thou liest in this
' tomb-----but, alas, thy dead remains are quite insensible.
' If any part of thee, once the joy of thy fond parent, sur-
' vives the grave, let it own thy early death a happiness,
' whilst a gloomy life of sorrow and grief is my portion; and
' the only solace I now have is that of having once been thy
' father.

' Thy death, my Lucia, the Muses have bewailed, which
' on this stone thy wretched father laments, whom thou
' hast left in anguish, sorrow, and continual sighs and tears.
' Alas, alas, my child, that thy father was not with thee in

thing puerile. I have omitted the other six epitaphs by Pontanus, (which the author has transcribed) and given this as a specimen.

'thy laſt moments, to alleviate the pangs of dying; nor thy
'unhappy ſiſters to echo back thy dying groans with their
'ſighs, nor thy ſympathiſing brother to allay thy thirſt with
'a few refreſhing drops of cold water; nor even thy diſcon-
'ſolate mother, who, with a fond embrace, would have re-
'ceived thy departing ſoul with a kiſs: who in this, how-
'ever, was happy, that, after few years, ſhe again enjoyed
'the ſight of thee, and now lies in the ſame grave; but
'greater ſtill will be my happineſs, who ſhortly ſhall ſleep
'with you both, and the ſame repoſitory ſhall hold us all
'three. Adieu, my child! cheriſh thy mother's cold aſhes,
'and hereafter perform the ſame kind office to thoſe of thy
'affectionate father.'

S. Giovanni Maggiore. The church of S. Giovanni Maggiore is ſuppoſed to have been originally a temple built by the emperor Adrian, in honour of his favourite Antinous; but, by Conſtantine the Great and his mother Helena, conſecrated to John the Baptiſt. They who derive the name *Parthenope*, which the city bore antecedently to that of Naples, from Parthenope, a Theſſalian princeſs, affirm that her tomb is ſtill to be ſeen in this church, being brought hither from ſome other place; but the following characters were all I could perceive on it:

From the word **EGE** or TEGE in the laſt line, this inſcription is ſuppoſed to be an epitaph; but I queſtion whether, in ſuch compoſitions, the laſt word *Fauſte* was ever uſed. Beſides, the favourers of the above-mentioned opinion muſt preſuppoſe the middle line, whether St. John or St. Januarius be meant, to have been done by modern Chriſtians; but that the other two lines are a Lombard or Gothic compoſition, or of earlier date, without any difference of characters. That this fabulous opinion is exploded in Naples itſelf, appears from an inſcription on the wall under the ſtone above deſcribed, which was put up by the Jeſuits in 1689 to undeceive the credulous.

The church of S. Giovanni Pappacodi derives its laſt name S. Giovanni from the founder, who being too haſtily buried whilſt in an Pappacodi. apoplectic fit, came to life again: for a relation of his, upon advice of his friend's death, coming poſt to town, ordered the coffin to be opened * three days after he was buried, and

---

* Such over-haſty interments, as we learn from Pliny, *Hiſt. Nat. l.* xxvi. *c.* 3, were not uncommon among the ancients. Was it not the deplorable

NAPLES.

and found that the deceased had bruised himself by struggling, and altered the posture in which he had been laid in the coffin.

Here also lie two excellent bishops of the same family; one of which declined the offer of the purple, and the other distinguished himself by his extraordinary diffusive charity. Their epitaphs are as follow:

Sigismundo Pappacudæ Franc. F. Tropejensium Præsuli, Viro Opt. & Jurisconsulto, qui cum in cœtum Cardinalium fuisset a Clemente VII. adscitus, maluit in patria Episcopus vivere. Hæredes pos. vixit ann. LXXX. M. VI. D. X. Obiit 1536.

' To Sigismund, son of Francis Páppacodi, bishop of
' Tropea, who to his noble endowments added a consum-
' mate knowledge of the law, and, being nominated cardinal
' by Clement VII, rather chose to remain a bishop in his
' own country, this monument is erected by his heirs. He
' lived fourscore years, six months, and ten days, and died
' in the year 1536.'

Angelo Pappacudæ Franc. Fil. Martoranensi Episcopo, viro ornatiss. qui in non magnis opibus magnum exercens animum, nulla magis in re, quam in aliorum levanda inopia suis bonis usus est. Hæredes B. M. Decessit ex mortalibus Ann. nat. LXVI. ab ortu mundi redivivi 1537.

' To Angelo, the son of Francis Páppacodi, bishop of
' Martorano, a person of great virtues and endowments,
' whose beneficent soul employed the best part of his mode-
' rate income in relieving the indigent, this monument was
' erected by his heirs. He departed this life in the sixty-
' sixth year of his age, and in the year of the Christian
' Æra 1537.'

The front of the church abounds with Gothic ornaments.

deplorable misfortune of Joh. Duns Scotus, distinguished by the appellation of *Doctor subtilis*, to be too soon put into the ground? Was not a person laid on the funeral pile soon restored to life by Asclepiades the physician? And who has not heard of the Norman lord, Louis de Cirille, who was more celebrated for having been buried three times, than for any heroic atchievements? It is matter of great concern that real narratives of this kind should be obscured and brought into disrepute by other absurd fictions.

In

In the church di S. Giuseppe, belonging to the Jesuits, are four Corinthian pillars, of a beautiful grey marble, which, though sixty *palmi* in height, and nine in circumference, are each of one block. Formerly, in the Tribuna hung a large picture of St. Joseph with the child Jesus in his arms, and a group of angels, by Francesco di Maria, a Neapolitan; but this is removed into the vestry, and its place supplied by one which far surpasses it, of our Saviour when an infant, and his parents, by Amato. On the righthand of the vestry is a grand altar-piece, which is glazed and covered with a curtain, representing St. Xavier in a very devout posture, by Luca Giordano; who also painted the other pieces in the chapel to which this superb altar belongs. Opposite to it is another altar-piece, likewise glazed, &c. painted by de Mattheis, exhibiting the virgin Mary and her divine infant; and, were it not for the incomparable beauty of the former, a connoisseur should not omit seeing this church. The pulpit is of marble, finely inlaid with precious stones.

 The church di S. Lorenzo de' Padri Minori has a lofty arched roof, and on its high altar the statues of St. Francis, St. Antony, and St. Laurence, finely executed by Giov. da Nola. The three basso-relievo's under them, and the virgin Mary amidst four angels over these three statues, are by other artists, whose names are not known. On one side of the altar is the chapel of S. Antonio di Padua, built from a design of Cosmo Fansago, which is worth seeing; but it is far exceeded by the chapel of the Rosary, in which are two pillars of *verde-antico*, and an altar of inlaid work of *lapis-lazuli,* topaz, agate, jasper, and other gems. At the sides of the chapel, on their respective monuments, stand the statues of its founders Camillo Cacace and his wife. These statues, according to the usual phrase, want only speech, and are the work of Bolgi da Carrara, a Roman.

In another chapel, from its foundress queen Margaretta V. consort to Charles III, called la Reina, lies Charles duke of Durazzo, beheaded in 1347, by Lewis king of Hungary, to revenge the death of his brother Andrew, who was strangled. Also Robert of Artois, with his wife Joanna dutchess of Durazzo (both poisoned by queen Margaret) together with a daughter of Charles III. Catharine a daughter of the emperor Albert I. and married to Charles duke of Calabria, and Lewis a son of Robert king of Naples, lie here.

First painting in oil colours.

 In the vestry is shewn a picture of St. Jerom, as the first piece painted in oil colours, being the work of Cola Antonio de Fiore, in 1436.

 The invention of oil colours, of which the Neapolitans claim the honour, is more justly attributed to John of Bruges, otherwise Van Eyck, a Fleming, who was both a chymist and painter; he was born in 1370, and died in 1441, at the age of seventy-one. The epocha of this noble invention was the beginning of the fifteenth century, about the year 1410, though Malvasia of Bologna, in order to attribute the honour of this invention to his countrymen, mentions some paintings in oil colours of a prior date, with the year and the painter's name annexed. However, a small difference in time is of no great importance, since it is certain that no other method but painting *à fresco*, as it is called by the Italians, was known before the fifteenth century.

 In a subterraneous chapel under the choir, the coronation of Robert, by his brother St. Lewis, is painted in colours by Simon of Cremona, who lived about the year 1353; and in the cloister of the convent is a tomb embellished with admirable basso-relievo's.

 In the refectory of this convent is a fine geographical piece of the twelve provinces of the kingdom of Naples, by the famous Sicilian painter Luigi Roderico, being a present to this convent from the count d'Olivares, when viceroy. Here the states of the kingdom annually meet to deliberate on the customary free-gift made to their sovereign, which has often exceeded a million and a half of *scudi*, or crowns.

Liberal free-gifts.

S. Maria Annunziata.
Its riches.

 S. Maria Annunziata is one of the finest churches in Naples; for the eye every-where meets with noble paintings, statues, monuments, basso-relievo's, &c. The gilding only of the high altar, and the chapel belonging to it, cost twenty-three thousand crowns; and the other ornaments, enriched with *lapis-lazuli*, cornelian, jasper, agate, and a profusion of other gems, eighteen thousand ducats more. In these computations, and in common discourse at Naples, a ducat is equal to ten *carlini* *. The plate in the vestry of this church a few years since weighed above twenty-one thousand marks. In the Tesoro is an admirable tomb of Alphonso Sancio de Luna, who died in 1564. To the left of the high altar when facing it, stands the statue of a lady, holding

---

* Three shillings and four-pence sterling.

a death's

a death's head in her hand, with her eyes fixed on it; and underneath is an encomium on her virtue and beauty.

Near the altar is the following epitaph on queen Joanna II.

JOANNÆ II. Hungariæ, Hierusalem, Siciliæ, Dalmatiæ, Croatiæ, Ramiæ*, Serviæ, Galatiæ, Lodomeriæ, Comaniæ, Bulgariæque Reginæ, Provinciæ & Folcalquerii ac Pedemontis Comitissæ, Anno Domini M.CCCC.XXXV. die II. Mensis Febr.

Regiis ossibus & memoriæ, sepulchrum, quod ipsa moriens humi delegerat, inanes in funere pompas exosa, Reginæ pietatem secuti, & meritorum non immemores Oeconomi restituendum & exornandum curaverunt, magnificentius posituri, si licuisset. Anno Domini M.DC.VI. Mens. Maji.

‘ To the memory of Joanna II. queen of Hungary, Jerusalem, Sicily, Dalmatia, Croatia, Ramia, Servia, Galatia, Lodomeria, Comania, Bulgaria; countess of Provence, Folcalquier, and Piedmont; this monument was erected the 2d day of February, 1435.

‘ This plain tomb, chosen by herself preferably to all the vain pomp of obsequies, the magistrates have, in conformity to her majesty's humble piety, and in regard to her merits, thus repaired without ornaments: and, had splendor and magnificence been permitted, they should not have been wanting. 1606.’

Near the church-door is a little statue, holding out a label, with these words:

*Purissimum Virginis templum
castè memento ingredi.*

‘ As thou art entering the pure temple of the Virgin, let
‘ thy thoughts be pure and chaste.’

The hospital called la Casa Santa, belonging to this church, was once the best endowed in the whole world; for its annual income in lands, tythes, imposts, endowments, interest of money, &c. amounted to two hundred thousand

La Casa Santa. Its wealth.

* Misson and others have it *Romæ*, but erroneously, as is evident from the titles of the ancient kings of Hungary.

ducats,

ducats, or, as some compute it, to a million of *scudi* *. On the other hand, the annual expences for the sick, poor, foundlings, and other charitable uses, were no less; so that the following lines over the main entrance say no more than what is strictly true:

> *Lac pueris, Dotem innuptis, Velumque pudicis,*
> *Datque medelam ægris hæc opulenta domus.*
> *Hinc meritò sacra est illi, quæ nupta, pudica,*
> *Et lactans; orbis vera medela fuit.*

' This wealthy house gives milk to babes, a portion to
' maids, a veil to nuns, and medicines to the sick; and is
' therefore justly dedicated to her who was a mother and gave
' suck, and yet was a pure Virgin, and brought redemption
' to heal the world.'

The children brought up here are generally about two thousand five hundred in number; it being no uncommon thing in one night for twenty infants to be put into the wheel or machine which stands open both day and night for the reception of them, and eight wet-nurses attend every day. The boys are brought up to handicraft trades, and some even to the church; they being, notwithstanding the uncertainty of their legitimacy, by a bull of pope Nicholas IV, declared capable of holy orders. The girls, as they grow up, according to their capacities or inclinations, do the necessary work of the hospital, are employed in the care and instruction of the children, entered into a convent, or married with a portion of a hundred or two hundred ducats; and this last article has formerly amounted to ten thousand ducats *per annum*, whilst that of the foundlings was seldom less than fifteen thousand. The young women married from this house, in case they are left widows in necessitous circumstances, or forsaken by their husbands; or if the marriage, without any fault of theirs, proves unfortunate; are intitled to a re-admission, and have a particular apartment allowed them, being distinguished by the name of *Ritornate*. The annual amount of the dowries to other women with which this house is charged by several ancient legacies and foundations, was at least eighteen thousand ducats; there being not a few noble families whose daughters at their marriage

* About 230,000 *l.* sterling.

received

received two or three thousand dollars from this hospital. The physicians, surgeons, apothecaries, servants &c. stood the house annually in fourteen thousand ducats. The dispensary belonging to it is extremely well worth seeing. To the Casa Santa belong four other hospitals, one of which is at Puzzuolo, whither, as also to Tritoli, great numbers of patients, about three hundred at a time, are sent thrice every summer to the warm baths and sudatories, and there provided with food, lodging, and necessary attendance; their stay at these baths is limited to seven days.

Such was the state of this hospital at the beginning of this century, when it proved bankrupt for above five millions of ducats; upon which its total ruin was apprehended. The affair, which for a long time had lain concealed like fire hidden under the ashes, in the year 1701 began to discover itself, and was at length brought before an imperial commission: which, till a total discharge of the debts, assigned over to the creditors so much of its income as to reserve only forty-two thousand ducats a year for the support of the hospital, the church, and the convent. This has reduced the girls portions from two hundred ducats to fifty, and the other expences have suffered a proportional diminution; even a great part of the silver ornaments of the church (which still does not want for splendor) has been disposed of, in order the sooner to emerge from these difficulties; which however must be a work of time. *Failure of the hospital.*

S. Maria del Carmine, from a small chapel, is become a magnificent church; the empress Elizabeth, mother to the unfortunate Conradine, having expended on it all the wealth which she had brought for the ransom of her son then a prisoner at Naples. *S. Maria del Carmine.*

Conradine duke of Swabia and Frederick of the house of Austria (in the inscription erroneously stiled Federico d'Asburg or Habsburg) lie on the right, near the entrance of the church, behind an altar; and on the wall are these words:

Qui giaccono Corradino di Stouffen, figlio dell' Imperatrice Margarita & di Corrado Rè di Napoli, ultimo de' Duchi dell' Imperial Casa di Suevia, & Federico d'Asburg ultimo de' Duchi d'Austria, anno MCCLXIX.

' Here lie Conradine of Stouffen son of the empress Mar-
' garet and of Conrade king of Naples, the last of the dukes

'of the imperial house of Swabia; and Frederick d'Asburg
'the last of the dukes of Austria, 1269.'

The name Margaret, by which Conradine's mother is here called, is a proof that this inscription has been since set up by monks unacquainted with the genealogy of these two illustrious persons: for the right name of Conradine's mother, who was a daughter of Otho the Great duke of Bavaria and count Palatine of the Rhine, was unquestionably Elizabeth. Her second husband was Maynhard the third count of Tirol; and she died in the year 1269. Not far from the great door of the church is a round cavity with an inscription, signifying that this was the place where a large cannon-ball, at the siege of the city, in 1439, by king Alphonso of Aragon, pierced through the cupola of the church, and carried away the crown of thorns from a crucifix; and it is added, that the head of the image would have gone with it, had not the crucifix, as the tradition goes, bowed its head, and thus avoided the blow. The ball still hangs by a chain before the high altar, and the crucifix is exposed to public view on the third day of the Christmas holidays, and every Friday in the month of March. In this story the question is, which carries most wonder with it, the fortunate prudence and foresight of this wooden image, or its fear and inability to save its crown and avoid such danger, otherwise than by stooping?

Crucifix bows its head to avoid a cannon-ball.

Here also, as appears from several inscriptions, are interred the bowels of a great many vice-roys; among which are Carpi and Gallas, the bodies standing in their respective coffins against the vestry-wall. The roof of this church is finely decorated; and in the cloister of the convent is to be seen the life of the prophet Elijah, painted *in fresco* by Balducci. Here also is the statue of the above-mentioned empress, improperly called Margaret, with this inscription:

Margaritæ

NAPLES.

Margaritæ Augustæ,
Quæ Conradino Filio & Friderico Nepoti captivis
Opitulatum opibus onusta Neapolim festinârat,
Cum Capite plexos reperisset,
Virili quidem animo non lachrymas pro illis,
Sed profusissima munera ad hoc templum exornandum profundens,
Ad aram hic maximam humandos curavit,
Familia Carmelitana ingentibus ab ea divitiis donata
Tam piæ benemeritæ semper ærumnam ploratura
Ac cælestem pro tantis principibus Imperatricem Oratura
P.
Anno Dom MCCLXIX.

' In remembrance of Margaret Augusta, who came to
' Naples with immense riches, to redeem her son Conrade
' and her nephew Frederick from captivity; and finding they
' had been beheaded, her exalted soul, above shedding tears,
' poured forth immense donations for the embellishment of
' this church; in return for such munificence the Carmelite
' monks caused the two princes to be buried at the high altar;
' and as they shall ever lament the loss sustained by their ge-
' nerous benefactress, so shall they never cease to offer
' prayers to the heavenly empress in behalf of the two vir-
' tuous unfortunate princes. 1269.'

That the Carmelites owe their establishment here to the empress Elizabeth's liberality, is shewn by Riccobaldi of Ferrara, *in Historia Imperatorum, p.* 1181; and it will be difficult to prove, that this order made any figure in Europe before the thirteenth century. But father Hardouin the Jesuit far overshot the mark in asserting *(in Antiquis Numismatibus Regum Francor. p. 645.)* that the Carmelites were not in being before the year 1300. It is strange, that a person of his orthodoxy should decry the supposed origin of these monks who pretend to deprive it from mount Carmel and the prophet Elijah; especially as his implicit devotion to the papal chair and its infallibility has led him into the most ridiculous and unwarrantable positions in support of it. Pope Innocent XII, on occasion of the disputes concerning the first institution of the Carmelite order, issued a mandate enjoining perpetual silence to both sides; which certainly according to the tenets of his church ought to have been a rule of conduct to father Hardouin, had he not construed this proceed-

Origin of the Carmelite order.

ing of the pope to be an indication, that both opinions seemed to him of equal weight. But from this time no devout Roman catholic will presume to combat the absurd opinion of the Carmelite order's being instituted by Elijah, as pope Benedict XIII. has now determined the affair in favour of that order.

Place where Massaniello was killed. In the above-mentioned cloister they also shew the place where Tomaso Aniello, commonly called Massaniello, the famous usurper, was shot in the year 1647; and the area which was as it were the theatre on which he acted his mock reign of eighteen days, is near this church, and at present a market for meat and vegetables. It is a pity that a grand area which might be so great an ornament to the city should be taken up with sheds for shops, &c. Almost in the centre of this market stands the Capella della Croce, on the spot where the two above-mentioned princes, Conradine and Frederick, were beheaded and buried, till the empress Elizabeth caused their bodies to be removed to St. Maria del Carmine. According to Parrino, Sarnelli, Misson, &c. the porphyry pillar above the altar has this distich inscribed on it:

Asturis ungue Leo pullum rapiens Aquilinum,
  Hic deplumavit acephalumque dedit.

' The Asturian lion seizing a young eagle, plucked off his
' feathers, and left him a headless trunk.'

But this also is manifestly false, the letters on that pillar indicating only the maker's name; and these words, *Hoc opus - - - Neapolitanus* are above all others distinctly legible. On the wall is an old piece of painting *in fresco* of the cruel execution of prince Conradine, &c. in which is a figure, with a hatchet lifted up, standing behind the judge, who sits on a chair of state pronouncing sentence on the princes; possibly alluding to what has been intimated by some historians, that Robert, earl of Flanders, from a detestation of such injustice immediately slew the judge who had pronounced the sentence. Riccobaldi of Ferrara, in his *Historia Imperatorum*, relates, that Conradine was playing at chess when the sentence was notified to him; and that some time (*modicum temporis*) was allowed him to prepare for his end. Some are for exculpating pope Clement IV, for having advised Charles of Anjou to put Conradine to death, by this laconic
way

way of reasoning, 'The life of Conradine is the death of Charles, the death of Conradine the life of Charles,' and affirm that pope died before the execution of the prince. But could it be shewn, that Clement IV. was actually dead before the execution, he might nevertheless have given such villainous and bloody advice immediately upon the imprisonment of Conradine, who, a few days after the loss of the battle on the 23d of August, fell into his enemies hands: and such an instigation is laid to the pope's charge by so many impartial writers, that, without the most solid proofs, it cannot with candour be questioned *.

The above-mentioned Carmelite church is by no means to be confounded with another called Madre di Dio, delli Scalzi Carmelitani, which for its stupendous altar, far surpassing any in all Naples, and valued at a hundred thousand *scudi*, deserves particular notice. There is scarce any gem to be named which is not to be seen there. On the fore part of it is a perspective view of a palace or temple with statues of gold and basso-relievo's placed alternately before it. The tabernacle is equally superb, with a flower-piece of *pietre commesse*, made at Florence, in the centre. The ten green and white pillars of jasper are very great ornaments to it. Every part abounds with *lapis-lazuli*, which in some places is the ground in, which other gems are inserted. The candlesticks, and all other ornaments of the altar, are likewise of inlaid gems set in gilt brass, as are also even the doors which open on each side into the choir. *Madre di Dio. Incomparable altar.*

On one of these doors is a reddish brown agate with white veins; so exactly representing the situation and plan of the city of Mantua, that the late duke of Mantua offered thirty thousand crowns for it. This brings to my mind the agate in the imperial museum at Vienna, on which is a natural representation of the city of Buda. Of king Pyrrhus's agate, on which Apollo and the nine muses were very plainly discernible, I shall speak on another occasion. Indeed, the infinite variety of stains and shades on agate and marble may well be supposed sometimes to form a faint resemblance of the works of nature or of art. But I return to the high altar of the Carmelites church, designed by Dionysio Lazari, and *Representation of the city of Mantua on an agate.*

---

* Smemonta and Spondanus are the historians of the greatest note who have undertaken to vindicate the pope; but of their impartiality Struv gives no advantageous idea, terming them, in his history of the German empire, (c. 21. §. 8.) 'court sycophants.'

Vol. III.   G   executed

executed by some Germans and Flemings. The pavement and the balustrade before it are of the most beatiful marble, and as beautifully inlaid. Behind the altar are three large pictures very well, worth seeing; one by Paolo di Matteis, representing the virgin Mary investing the devout Simon Stocc with the habit of the order. The other two, by a brother of the convent, called Lucas, are the adoration of the wise men of the East, and the shepherds, at the manger. On the right-hand in returning from the high altar is a very large painting of the battle of the White Mountain near Prague, by Giacomo del Pò, in which he has taken care not to omit father Domenico with his crucifix, mounted on a fiery steed. The memorable actions of the most eminent Carmelite monks are written on golden letters on large scrolls of paper which are hung up against the church wall. In the fine chapel of S. Teresa, a silver statue of that saint, six *palmi* in height, stands on the altar, with the ridiculous ornament of the golden fleece about the neck. The convent to which this church belongs is a fine structure; and its dispensary well worth seeing for its complete order and contrivance, and the elegancy of the gally-pots and vessels, which are all of fine porcelain.

S. Teresa with the golden fleece.

In the church of S. Maria della Concordia is interred Gaspar Benemerini, once king of Fez, who afterwards renounced Mahometism; he lived to the age of a hundred years, and died in 1641. All the inscription on his tombstone is,

S. Maria della Concordia.

Sepulchrum hoc Gasparis Benemerini Infantis de Fez, & ejus familiæ de Benemerino.

' This is the burying-place of Gaspar Benemerini prince
' of Fez, and of his family the Benemerini.'

Round his arms, which are the moon, a star, a sword, and a castle, are these words:

Laus Tibi Jesu! & Virgo Mater, quod de pagano Rege me Christianum fecisti.

' Praise be to thee, O Jesus, and thou virgin mother, by
' whom, of a pagan king, I was made a Christian.'

In

NAPLES.

In the banner hanging near it are the letters, *R. F.* [*Rex Fessanus,*] and under the banner a heart with these letters in it BVR and on the wall is the following epitaph:

D. O. M.   *B. M. V.*

Gaspar ex Serenissima Benemerina familia, vigesimus secundus in Africa Rex, dum contra Tyrannos à Catholico Rege arma rogat auxiliaria, liber effectus à Tyrannide Machometi, cujus impiam cum lacte hauserat legem, in Catholicam adscribitur; Numidiam proinde exosus pro Philippo III. Hispaniarum Monarcha, pro Rudolpho Cæsare, quibus carus, præclarè in hæreticos apud Belgas Pannonosque sæviit armatus. Sub Urbano VIII. Eques Commendator Inimaculatæ Conceptionis Deiparæ creatur, & Christianis, Heroicis, Regiisque virtutibus ad immortalitatem anhelans, centenarius hic mortale reliquit, & perpetuum censum cum penso quater in hebdomade incruentum Missæ sacrificium ad suam offerendi mentem. Anno Domini MDCXLI.

    ' To God the greatest and   ' To the blessed virgin
      ' best of beings.'   ' Mary.'

' To the memory of Gaspar, of the most noble family of
' the Benemerini, twenty-second king in Africa, who,
' whilst he was solliciting succours from the Catholic king
' against tyrants, was delivered from the tyranny of Maho-
' met, whose impious law he had sucked in with his milk;
' and admitted into the Catholic church; afterwards detest-
' ing Africa, he distinguished himself in the service of Philip
' III; king of Spain, and the emperor Rodolph, who both
' honoured him with particular favours, in the wars against
' the heretics in the Netherlands and Hungary. Under Ur-
' ban VIII, he obtained a commandery in the order of the
' immaculate conception of the mother of God; and, hav-
' ing passed forward towards a blessed immortality in an uni-
' form course of christian, heroic, and royal virtues, in the
' hundredth year of his age, he put off mortality, and left a
' perpetual revenue for four unbloody sacrifices of the mass to
' be performed weekly for the repose of his soul, 1641.'

The family of the Bellimerini, or Benemirini, which had been in possession of the throne of Fez and Morocco above three hundred years, within these two last centuries have seen themselves deprived of their power. Leo Africanus (*lib.* iii. *c.* 38.) praises the liberality and zeal shewn by them in their prosperity, for the improvement of arts and sciences.

S. Maria di Donna Reina.

S. Maria di Donna Reina was built by queen Mary, wife of Charles II, king of Naples, who also desired to be buried here; the epitaph on her tomb is modern, and begins *Corpus Mariæ, &c.* Among the best paintings in this church may be reckoned those of our Saviour's feeding five thousand men in the wilderness, and the marriage at Cana, both by Giordano, who has here also most naturally imitated a piece of iron work.

The high altar, on which are two silver statues as big as the life, is now just finished, as are also six masterly marble statues of saints, designed for the nave of the church, each of which cost twelve hundred *scudi*. In this church is a silver *pyx* richly set with rubies and emeralds. Here are also some very fine pieces of painting by Solimene. A large cleft, caused by an earthquake, runs the whole length of the roof of this church; and to the frequency of those concussions it may possibly be owing that so few churches with arched roofs are to be seen in this city.

S. Maria Donna Romita.

In the church di S. Maria Donna Romita are several fine pieces of painting; particularly the beheading of John the Baptist, near the high altar; and opposite to it Herodias's daughter delivering his head to her mother in a charger. The roof of the church is finely decorated with painting, sculpture, and gilding.

S. Maria delle Grazie.

In the church di S. Maria delle Grazie de' Padri Girolamitani are some excellent pieces in painting and sculpture. Among the latter is a most noble basso-relievo in the Giustiniani chapel, by Giovanni da Nola, representing the virgin Mary, St. John, and Mary Magdalen, lamenting over a dead Christ. On festivals, the high altar is covered with a silver *palliotto*, and other rich ornaments. On each side of it are seen the fine statues of S. Pietro Gambacurta di Pisa and St. Jerom, by Lorenzo Vaccaro. On the right-hand near the altar stands a wooden image of St. Onuphrius naked; but care is taken to lengthen his beard down to his knees. Among the many fine tombs, that of Fabricio Brancaccio is particularly worth seeing.

Under a basso-relievo of the annunciation, I read with some surprise the following verse:

Remarkable titles of the virgin Mary.

Nata, Soror, Conjux, eadem Genitrixque Tonantis.

' Daughter, sister, spouse, and mother of the Thunderer.'

In

NAPLES.

In the vestry are some good paintings *in fresco*; and the pavement is of very beautiful tiles of all colours.

The convent of S. Maria Maddalena delle Spagnuole was founded by Donna Isabella d'Alarcon, marchioness della Valle, for Spanish prostitutes inclined to forsake their debauched life. *Convent of S. Maria Maddalena delle Spagnuole for penitent prostitutes.*

The cieling of S. Maria Nuova is adorned with such fine paintings and gilding, that it passes for one of the most beautiful churches in Naples. In the chapel of the Madonna della Grazia, the *Pallioto* and almost all the ornaments of the altar are of silver. The robe in which the virgin is dressed is almost entirely covered with pearls, diamonds, rubies of a very extraordinary size, and other jewels. In the Capella di Graziano is an *Ecce Homo*, by Giovanni da Nola; it is cut in wood, but the sculpture is inimitable. The Capella del' Beato Giacobo della Marca is likewise worth observation: in it is a monument erected in honour of Urban VI, who was a Neapolitan; and likewise the tomb of Don Carlo d'Austria, (whose original name was Anida) a son of the king of Tunis, who was converted to Christianity. Without it is the tomb of Pedro Navarro, who rose by his merit through the several ranks, from a private man, to be commander in chief of the Spanish army; but, resenting the delay of the court of Spain to ransom him when taken prisoner, he renounced his natural sovereign, and entered the service of France. He accompanied Lautrec in his unfortunate expedition against Naples, where being again taken prisoner, he endeavoured to avoid the ignominy of being executed as a rebel by putting an end to his life. Others affirm that he was strangled in the night, when he was seventy-five years of age, after having survived that pestilence, which, a few weeks before, had made such dreadful havoc in Lautrec's army. The epitaph of this warlike person is as follows: *S. Maria Nuovo. Account of Pedro Navarro.*

Ossibus & memoriæ
PETRI NAVARRÆ CANTABRI,
Solerti, in expugnandis urbibus arte clarissimi,
Gonsalvus Ferdinandus Ludovici Filius,
Magni Gonsalvi Nepos, Sueffæ Princeps,
Ducem Gallorum partes secutum
Pio sepulchri munere honestavit,
Quum hoc in se habeat præclara virtus,
Ut vel in hoste sit admirabilis.

'Sacred to the remains and memory of Pedro Navarro, a
'Spaniard, excellently skilled in the attack of fortresses and
'the military art, Gonsalvo Ferdinand, &c. erected this
'monument, though he had deserted his country, and en-
'tered into the French service; for bravery and virtue,
'though in an enemy, cannot but raise our admiration.'

Opposite to it lies Lautrec himself, with this epitaph:

ODETTO FUXIO LAUTRECCO,
Gonsalvus Ferdinandus Ludovici Fil.
Cordub. Magni Gonsalvi Nepos,
Quum ejus ossa, quamvis hostis, in avito sacello,
Ut belli fortuna tulerat,
Sine honore jacere comperisset,
Humanarum miseriarum memor
Gallo Duci Hispanus Princeps P.

'To the memory of Odet Foulx de Lautrec, a French
'general, Gonsalvo Ferdinand, a Spanish prince, and grand-
'son of the great Gonsalvo of Cordova, hearing that his
'enemy's remains, by the fortune of war, lay in an obscure
'old chapel, and, being sensible of the vicissitudes of human
'life, erected this tomb.'

As Lautrec died of the pestilence, his body, like that of
a common soldier, was buried in the sand; but a Spaniard,
prompted by the hopes of a round sum of money for the ransom of it, dug it up, and brought it to Naples; where his
avidity, however, was disappointed, the guardians of Lautrec's children wisely refusing to diminish, in such an unavailing purchase, the little fortune the old general had left
behind him. It lay a long time unburied, till, as appears
by the epitaph, the duke di Sussa caused a tomb built at his
own expence for Lautrec's remains, which at the same time
is a monument of his own generosity and humanity.

Near the high altar lies buried a lady called Johanna, and
in her epitaph stiled the daughter of John king of Aragon, and
second wife of Ferdinand I, king of Jerusalem and Sicily,
who died in 1517.

S. Maria del Parto.

The church of S. Maria del Parto belongs to the suburb
Chiaja, in the Mergellina, which is said to be so called from
the multitudes of fishes to be seen here emerging out of the
water.

water. Frederic king of Naples beſtowed a parcel of lands near this place on Sannazario the poet, who at firſt had ſo mean an idea of the gift, that he compoſed the following lines:

Scribendi ſtudium mihi, Frederice, dediſti,
Ingenium ad laudes dum trahis omne tuas;
Ecce ſuburbanum rus & nova prædia donas
Feciſti Vatem, nunc facis Agricolam.

‘ Great Frederic, by thee I was firſt made a poet, and to
‘ thy praiſe were all my talents confined; but, by giving me
‘ theſe dirty acres, thou haſt reduced me from a poet to turn
‘ farmer.’

However, he afterwards became ſo inamoured with this rural retreat, that he not only built here a moſt elegant palace, but frequently mentions it in his poems with raptures, as in this paſſage:

O' lieta Piaggia, ò ſolitaria Valle
O' accolto Monticel, che mi difendi
D' ardente Sol, con le tue ombroſe ſpalle;
O' freſco, e chiaro rivo, che diſcendi
Nel verde prato trà fiorite ſponde,
E dolce ad aſcoltor mormorio rendi*, &c.

‘ O bliſsful ſolitude! delicious vale!
‘ O ever-verdant hill, whoſe tufted brow
‘ From noon-tide ſun with cool refreſhing ſhade
‘ Defends me wand'ring o'er the devious plain;
‘ Where thro' the verdant mead a cryſtal ſtream
‘ Runs murm'ring, and reflects each beauteous flow'r
‘ That crowns its banks, cooling the ambient air.’

Rupis o ſacræ Pelagique Cuſtos,
Villa Nympharum domus, & propinquæ
Doridis, Regum decus una quondam
Deliciæque.

‘ O ſweet retreat! the haunt of rural nymphs,
‘ Who guard the ſacred rock and neighb'ring main,

---

* *Vide Sarnelli Guida de' foreſtieri, p. 222.*

'Once the delight of kings, who in thy shades
'Forgot the toils of empire.'

The destruction of this *villa*, with all its rural improvements, by Philibert prince of Orange, general to Charles V, was very near to break Sannazario's heart *; and, by way of consolation, he afterwards built on the same spot a church, which he consecrated *al Santissimo parto della Gran Madre di Dio*; 'To the most holy parturition of the great mother 'of God:' and also composed three canto's on the same subject.

Sannazario, or, as he used to stile himself, *Actius Sincerus*, died in the year of Christ 1532, (not in 1530, as his epitaph says) and in the seventy-third of his age. He was buried here in a beautiful tomb of white marble, which is universally allowed to be a master-piece in sculpture. At the top Sannazario's bust is placed between two winged angels, or Cupids; and in the middle of the monument is an admirable basso-relievo, representing fauns, nymphs, and satyrs singing, and playing on all kinds of instruments. Neptune is also to be seen here; for Sannazario was the first who wrote piscatory and marine eclogues. On each side stand two large statues, one of Apollo, the other of Minerva: but offence having been taken at the introducing of pagan deities into churches, and the removal of these exquisite pieces being apprehended, they were saved by the artifice of making them pass for the images of David and Judith. The whole is the workmanship of Girolamo Santa Croce, a Neapolitan; but, by reason of his untimely death, the finishing hand was put to the statues of Apollo and Minerva, by Poggibonzo of Tuscany, who was a Servite monk in the convent. Under the bust of the poet are these words:

ACTIVS SINCERVS.

Above the basso-relievo are these letters:

D. O. M.

'To God the greatest and best of beings.'

* On hearing that this prince had lost his life in a battle, he said, with no little joy, *La Vendetta d'Apollo ha fatto Marte.* 'Well done, Mars, 'thou hast revenged Apollo's cause.'

And

And under it the following diftich by cardinal Bembo:

Da facro cineri flores; hic ille Maroni *
Sincerus, Musâ proximus, ut tumulo.
Vix Ann. LXXII. Obiit M. D. XXX.

' Here refts Sincerus, (ftrew the facred place
' With flow'rs!) who next in fame to Maro liv'd;
' And, dying, wifh'd his afhes might repofe
' Near that immortal bard, whofe mufe he lov'd.
' He lived to the age of feventy-two, and died in the year 1530.'

But the epitaph which he compofed for himfelf was as follows:

Actius hic fitus eft. Cineres gaudete fepulti,
Jam vaga poft obitus Umbra dolore vacat.

' Here Actius lies; his afhes here enjoy
' A calm repofe, whilft happily enlarg'd,
' His fleeting fpirit's free from every pain.'

His relations, however, though Actius's own writings bear fufficient teftimony of his religious fentiments, did not think proper that thefe ambiguous lines fhould be placed on the tomb of a Chriftian poet †.

In the above-mentioned church of S. Maria del Parto are likewife two ftatues of white marble of St. James the apoftle, and St. Nazario the martyr, both by father Poggibonzo. They are far from being defpicable pieces; but greatly inferior to the Apollo and Minerva at Sannazario's tomb. In the firft chapel on the right-hand of the entrance into the church is Michael the archangel, painted by Leonardo di Piftoja. The angel's face is faid to be copied from Don Diomede Caraffa, bifhop of Ariano; and the female features given to the dragon, which he tramples under foot, by the fame cardinal's direction, in order to difplay the triumph of his continency over the allurement of female charms, reprefents a lady who had a paffion for him; and, as her name was Victoria Venofa, the words *Fecit Victoriam, Allelujah,*

S. Maria del Parto.

---
* Virgil's grave is fhewn in the neighbourhood of this church.
† There is nothing in the fentiment that is inconfiftent with Chriftianity; but probably it was the Romifh doctrine of purgatory that caufed this epitaph to be rejected.

are

are said to allude to it. But the whole affair, if it be true, seems either the result of private revenge for a repulse the cardinal had met with, or of an idle ostentation, rather than any proof of rational piety and real virtue.

Near Michael and the dragon is an old piece of painting, representing the Lord's-supper, where Christ and his disciples are sitting on chairs, otherwise it is no bad piece. The encounter between a cat and a dog under the table would have better become some ludicrous piece, though one cannot help being pleased with the liveliness of the expression. Here are also several good pieces *in fresco*; most of which were done at the expence of a father of this convent, whose liberality hath been honoured with the following inscription:

Lautrec's epitaph.

Sacram hanc ædem
Actii Sinceri Sannazarii
Domicilio, Poësi, Tumulo
Illustrem
Elegantibus picturis ac pavimento
lithostrato
Pat. Mag. Angelus M. Nappi
Neapolitanus
Anno M. DCIC.
Quod propriis expensis illustriorem
Reddi curaverit,
Cæteri hujus Conventûs alumni
Fratri suo bene merenti PP.

' Father Maestro Angelo Maria Nappi, a native of Na-
' ples, having in the year 1609, at his own expence, to this
' church famous for the residence, poetry, and tomb of
' Actius Sincerus Sannazario, added the embellishments of fine
' paintings and a variegated marble pavement; the monks
' of this convent, in acknowledgment of the generosity of
' their brother, have erected this memorial.'

S. Maria di Piedigrotta. The church of S. Maria di Piedigrotto owes its name to the Pausilypean hole or cave, at the entrance of which it stands.

At the high altar of this church are six admirable pillars of black and white marble.

S. Maria de' Sangri. The church of S. Maria della Pietà de' Sangri wants a proper light; but otherwise makes a fine appearance, abounding

ing in statues and curious monuments belonging to the Sangro family.

At the great altar stand two beautiful pillars of porphyry.

In the church of S. Maria della Sanità, which belongs to the Dominicans, are thirteen small cupola's over so many altars, all finely ornamented with paintings. The eight pillars of the tabernacle on the high altar are of rock cryſtal, each a foot high, yet cut out of a single piece. It is also enriched with a great number of sapphires, and other precious stones. The pulpit is an exquisite inlaid work of marble and mother-of-pearl. In the vestry are twelve cryſtal candlesticks, made by Marino Converso, a monk of the convent, who being employed in a work of rock cryſtal, which was to fill the whole front of the great altar, was, a few years ago, prevented by death. Here also are shewn a crucifix and several pyramids of cryſtal, and nineteen large silver busts of saints, with their reliques inclosed in them; fourteen silver candlesticks, each above six feet high; a very small casket in the form of an altar, on one side of which is the passion of Chriſt, of such fine workmanſhip, that in the bosom of the virgin Mary, which opens with two folding doors, the crucifixion of our Saviour is to be seen within the compass of a silver two-pence; the whole is of wood. In the casket is also kept another representation of Chriſt's crucifixion on mount Calvary, composed of emeralds and other gems. On an *oſtenſorium* stands a little silver statue of Noah with a girdle of emeralds, and on his ſhoulders a model of the ark in gold set with diamonds. Over it is a silver dove, at whose wings hang two ear-rings with two sapphires in each, being the offering of a princeſs who devoutly took them from her ears, and preſented them to this church. On the *oſtenſorium*, where the confecrated wafer lies, the sun is finely reprefented with his golden beams, the radiancy of which is heightened by the blaze of diamonds, pearls, and rubies with which they are set. The church and the convent are built on an aſcent, so that a great part of the former, and even some pillars are hewn out of the rock. The outside of the roof is flat and paved with small ſtones. The proſpect from thence towards the sea and mount Vesuvio is extremely beautiful. Before the refectory is an orangery in the open air; and the trees are of an uncommon growth and size. When I viſited this convent, it was with some pleaſure

I saw

NAPLES.

I saw a hundred and ninety-six fathers and noviciates supping together with great decency and elegancy of behaviour. As it was a fast, the allowance was a slice of bread and three apples. But the superior or provincial and the prior had a larger portion of bread and six apples a-piece. The dispensary belonging to this convent is very large and well contrived: it is also furnished with several elaboratories and some gally-pots, said to be painted by Raphael. The general of the Dominicans has an annual income of eighteen thousand ducats, besides extraordinary presents, which, from the great regard paid him as president of the inquisition, even by cardinals, and the greatest officers of the papal court, must be no inconsiderable addition.

S. Martino. S. Martino belongs to the Carthusians, and stands in the highest part of the city, except the castle of St. Elmo; whence it may easily be conceived what a glorious prospect they enjoy over the neighbouring islands, the city, the port, the sea-coast, and the country towards Vesuvio and Pausilypo. Though no woman is permitted to enter into this place, a church stands open without the convent for that sex to perform their devotions in. The church which the monks frequent has few equals. The cieling is painted with historical pieces; and in the front of the choir is the crucifixion of Christ, and the twelve apostles, by Lanfranco, who, whilst he was employed by these fathers, had a salary of thirty *scudi* or crowns a-day, and was elegantly entertained at the expence of the convent. The *pietà* over the grand entrance is by the cavalier Massimo, and the twelve prophets painted in oil colours, with the busts of Moses and Elias, by the celebrated Giuseppe di Ribera, commonly called Lo Spagnoletto; who has signalized his skill in this convent by above a hundred pieces. On the cieling of the choir where the monks assemble at mass, Giusepino d'Arpino and Giov. Berardino a Sicilian, have, in conjunction, displayed the delicacy of their pencils. In this choir is also to be seen the celebrated Nativity of Christ by Guido, for which the fathers paid five thousand ducats, and have been more than once offered twelve thousand. But a society which boasts of having, during the life only of one superior, laid out five hundred thousand ducats in paintings, sculptures, and plate, seldom expose their curiosities to sale. Here are also four other master-pieces, all representing the Lord's-supper; one by the above-mentioned Ribera, another by Annibal Caracci,

Famous picture of Rheni.

Profuse expence.

Caracci*, the third by Paolo Veronese, and the fourth by the cavalier Maffimo. The other paintings in the church are also by several eminent masters whom we have already had occasion to mention, *viz.* Belisario, Fignoli, Giov. Batt. Caracci, the cavalier Calabrese, Domenichino, Vaccaro, Giordano, &c. The pavement is of beautiful figured marble, and the wall of *pietre commesse*. The high altar, though already above a hundred thousand *scudi* have been expended on it, is far from being finished; and, to judge by the model, it will be a work of incomparable beauty and magnificence. The steps near the vestry were designed by the cavalier Cosmo, the painted perspective by the cavalier Viviani, and the figures by the cavalier Maffimo. The closets in the vestry are worth seeing for their inlaid work in cane; some representing scriptural histories, others landscapes, &c. Giusepino d'Arpino has painted the crucifixion of Christ on the cieling; the perspective piece is by Viviani, and Peter's denial of his master by Caravaggio. The arch before the two *tesori*, or treasuries, is finely painted *in fresco* by Maffimo, and here a child is particularly admired, so boldly painted as hardly to be distinguished by the eye from a basso-relievo in a raised piece of sculpture. In the *tesoro vecchio* is likewise some excellent inlaid work of wood; and the pavement represents all kinds of figures in marble. The paintings *in fresco* are by Lanfranco, Maffimo, and Spadaro; and on the cieling are several extremely natural imitations of fissures and cracks. The riches shewn in these treasuries are hardly to be described. Among other things here are a globe of *lapis-lazuli* of the bigness of a child's head, an amethyst a span broad and a span and a half in length, and four turquoises on the convex side equal to a walnut; a great number of large silver busts, a silver statue of St. Martin with a ring on one of the fingers of the right-hand set with a ruby of the size of a large hazel-nut, which cannot be surpassed; four pearls and as many topazes of a very uncommon size; a silver statue of the virgin Mary standing on the moon with a dragon at her feet, almost as big as the life; two mother-of-pearl shells, as large as a small dish, most beautifully painted; gold and silver chalices, lamps, candlesticks, flower-pots, and the like, without number. But what particularly deserves notice is a little altar supported by silver pillars,

---

* In this piece Christ is represented standing, and the disciples kneeling round him.

NAPLES.

with a *pyx* reprefenting the fun refting on one pillar, the beams of which and the pillar are covered with fapphires, rubies, turquoifes, and other gems; fo that this piece alone coft forty thoufand *fcudi*. Here is alfo to be feen Spagnoletto's celebrated *pietà*, for which he received four thoufand ducats, but at prefent valued at ten thoufand. Amidft fuch fplendid objects the rotten bones and other reliques kept within glaffes with infcriptions fhewing to what faint each piece belongs, make but a very fcurvy appearance.

The convent has a grand fquare cloifter built under the infpection of the cavalier Cofmo Fonfago; it is adorned with fixty pillars of white Carrara marble: the pavement is of black and white marble difpofed in a variety of figures. Within the area of the cloifter is a burial-place for the monks, which is feen through a baluftrade ornamented with death's heads and other emblems of mortality cut in marble. The number of monks in this convent is only fix; and to each of them is affigned an apartment wainfcotted with cedar, very well furnifhed, and adorned with fine paintings; and alfo a garden with a marble fountain, planted with all kinds of efculent herbs, fruit, and flowers. The prior's apartment is very fpacious and magnificent, confifting of feveral rooms, embellifhed with a very valuable collection of paintings, defigns, and feveral geographical pieces. Here is a fmall picture on wood of the crucifixion of our Saviour, highly efteemed, and faid to be done by Michael Angelo. The piece is very fmall, and has nothing remarkable in it; but, contrary to nature, reprefents our Saviour's head quite upright, inftead of being reclined like that of a dying perfon. This, like that piece at the Borghefe palace at Rome, is faid to be done from the life, a perfon being put to death on the crofs for that purpofe; and with equal probability. The ftory of Parrhafius * putting a perfon to a death by tortures, that having fuch an object before him he might the more naturally paint a Prometheus, may poffibly have given rife to this groundlefs charge againft Michael Angelo; who was a man of no bad morals, and cannot be fuppofed to have been guilty of fuch a piece of barbarity; and, if he had, he would have copied it to greater advantage.

In the apartment of the prior of this convent is a very pretty marble groupe by Cofmo, of the virgin Mary with the child Jefus in her arms, and John the Baptift kiffing his feet.

* *Vide Junium de pictura veterum.*

Our

NAPLES.

Our Saviour is reprefented fmiling and laying his hand upon John's head, as if they were playing together; whilft the virgin mother's looks moft exquifitely exprefs her fweet complacency at their innocent fportivenefs. The library confifts of feleɛt books, to the value of fix thoufand ducats; the cieling is painted *in frefco* by Viviano, Rafaelino, and Spadaro. The convent's difpenfary is alfo well contrived, lofty, and painted *in frefco*; the pavement is of painted tiles, and all the medicines are kept in porcelain veffels. Here is alfo a beautiful collection of corals; and in the anti-chamber are four white marble bufts of the feafons.

The church and convent di Monte Oliveto are endowed with a yearly revenue of ten thoufand *fcudi*, the donation of a gentleman whofe name was Gurello Origlia, as is commemorated in the following infcription:

Church di Monte Oliveto.

D. O. M. Gurello Auriliæ Neapol. hujus Regni Logothetæ ac Protonotario, fummæ apud Ladiflaum Regem, ob fidem eximiam, auɛtoritatis, adeo feptem filios Comites viderit, fortunatiffimus, idemque pientiffimus, qui Ædes has conftruxit, patrimonio donato, Ordo Olivetanus Pietatis ergô F. C.

' Sacred to God the greateft and beft of beings, and to
' the memory of Gurello Origlia of Naples, recorder and
' prothonotary of the kingdom, who for his capacity and
' fidelity was in fuch high efteem with king Ladiflaus, that
' his feven fons were created counts, and (his profperity be-
' ing equal to his piety) built and endowed this church and
' convent, the order of Olivetans have in gratitude erected
' this infcription.'

Alphonfo the Second had fuch an affection for the monks of this convent, that he not only frequently took a repaft with them, and fometimes even waited at the fecond table where the lay-brothers eat; but, among other more fubftantial marks of his cordial affection, conferred on them the caftles of Teverona, Aprano, and Pepona, with their civil and criminal jurifdictions. Thefe benefactions are recorded in the infcriptions in the refectory and on his monument near the high altar.

In the Capella del Conte di Terranuova is a moft beautiful marble altar, the work of Benedetto da Majano, an eminent Florentine fculptor of the 15th century. Here alfo lies Mario Curiale, a youth in great favour with king Alphonfo I,

Capella del Conte di Terranuova.

who

who even honoured him with the following epitaph of his own compofition:

*Qui fuit Alfonfi quondam pars maxima Regis
Marius hâc modicâ nunc tumulatur humo.*

' Within this narrow tomb lies Marius, who once pofleſ-
' fed king Alphonfo's better part.'

In the Origlia chapel is a reprefentation of a dead Chriſt with feven perfons lamenting over the body, fome kneeling and others ſtanding, of *terra cotta*, or a kind of plaſter, painted in natural colours; it is the work of Moldavino da Modena, an ingenious ſculptor, who lived about the middle of the fifteenth century. The affiſtants reprefent feveral eminent men, then living: Nicodemus is perfonated by Giovanni Pontano, Jofeph of Arimathea by Giacomo Sannazario, and two others by Alphonfo II; king of Naples, and his fon Ferdinand.

On the right-hand near this chapel is an incomparable baſſo-relievo of the annunciation by the above-mentioned Benedetto di Majano. The countenance of the angel dawns with celeſtial joy and benevolence, and the virgin's attitude and looks expreſs a moſt amiable mixture of ferenity; humility, and a modeſt baſhfulneſs.

In the Tolofa chapel is to be feen an ingenious perfpective of *intarfiatura*, or inlaid wood, by Frà Giov. Angelo da Verona Olivetano, who excelled in this branch, and lived in Vafari's time, that is, about the middle of the fixteenth century.

The baſſo-relievo reprefenting the nativity of Chriſt in the duke of Amalfi's chapel, or, as it is now called, of Picolomini d'Aragona, is accounted a maſter-piece in ſculpture; and by fome attributed to the famous Donatello, and by others to Rofellino of Florence. The latter is, however, univerfally allowed to have defigned and executed the fuperb monument, in this chapel, of Maria of Aragon, a natural daughter of king Ferdinand, and duchefs of Amalfi.

In the fame chapel, which is remarkable for its pavement; is alfo this epitaph:

Conſtantia

NAPLES.

Conſtantia Davala & Beatrix Piccolominea Filia, redditis quæ ſunt cœli cœlo, & quæ ſunt terræ terræ, ut ſemper uno vixere animo, & ſic uno condi tumulo voluere. O beatam & mutui amoris conſtantiam!

' Here in one grave are depoſited the remains of Conſtan‐
' tia Davala and Beatrice Piccolomini her daughter, who,
' having rendered to heaven the things which were heaven's,
' and to the earth the things that were earth's, as they had
' but one ſoul while living, deſired to be united in death.
' Happy patterns of a conſtant and mutual affection!'

Each of the before-mentioned chapels has ſomething remarkable, and every-where affords ſome entertainment to the admirers of painting and ſculpture. In the veſtry, beſides the fine paintings by Vaſari, the ſhrines and cloſets repreſent caſtles, landſcapes, and other pieces of perſpective, ſo well executed in wood inlaid, as ſcarce to be paralleled.

The organ in this church is ſaid to have coſt four thouſand ſcudi, and is greatly cried up here; but as to this noble inſtrument, both for makers and performers on it, all nations muſt yield to Germany.

The convent library owes its foundation to Alphonſo II, who alſo enriched it with ſome good vellum manuſcripts, ſtill in being; of which the principal are, 1. The Bible, in a ſmall folio, written in 1476, by Matthias Moravius, finely illuminated, &c. 2. Another ancient manuſcript of the Bible, in two large volumes in folio. 3. St. Bernard's works. 4. St. Jerom's epiſtles, and his commentary on Iſaiah. 5. The lives of the ſaints in two volumes folio. 6. The hiſtory of the tranſlations of the bodies of St. Benedict and St. Scholaſtica, &c. On the front is this inſcription:

Piis ad Dei cultum ſtudiis nè vel hora fruſtra teratur, Bibliothecæ locus erectus.

' This library was erected for the improvement of reli‐
' gious ſtudies, that not an hour may be miſpent, but dedi‐
' cated to the ſervice of God.'

Nothing can be more delightful than the proſpect from the library and the upper ſtory of this convent. It is alſo
VOL. III.　　　　　　　H　　　　　　　　famous

NAPLES.

famous for making the best Neapolitan soap, which brings in a very considerable profit to the society.

Monte della Pietà. The revenue of the Sacro Monte della Pietà, which amounts to fifty thousand ducats, is, for the term of two years, lent in sums not exceeding ten ducats, on equivalent pledges, without interest; for many wealthy persons, who either want opportunity, or are not inclined to make purchases, or lend on interest or mortgages, place their fortunes here; partly for security, and partly for the advantage of the poor. The building was designed by the cavalier Fontana, and cost seventy thousand *scudi*. As for the marble statue of *Pietà*, or Charity, erected on the front of the chapel, it is a sufficient commendation of it to say, that it came from the hand of the celebrated Bernini.

S. Paolo Maggiore. S. Paolo Maggiore, by an inscription formerly on the *façade*, which, in 1688, was demolished by an earthquake, appears to have been originally a temple of Castor and Pollux, and built by Julius Tarsus, a freed man of Augustus, and procurator of the sea-coasts about Naples. Of this noble piece of antiquity there are still remaining two pillars, two fine statues, some pedestals, &c. several marble fragments having been used for the pavement of this church. The tradition, that, at the command of St. Peter, the statues of Pollux and Castor fell from the top of this structure, has given rise to the following distichs, which are to be seen on the left-hand of the entrance, near two mutilated statues:

Audit vel surdus Pollux cum Castore Petrum,
Nec mora præcipiti marmore uterque ruit.

' The deaf statues of Castor and Pollux heard Peter's
' voice, and immediately the idolized marble fell down head-
' long from the top of this edifice.'

And on the right:

Tyndaridas vox missa ferit, palma integra Petri est;
Dividit at tecum, Paule, trophæa libens.

' With one word Peter vanquishes the martial sons of
' Tyndaris; but thee, Paul, he willingly admits as his
' partner in this victory.'

The

NAPLES.

The sculpture about the high altar of this church is exquisite, and the tabernacle is of inlaid gems. On the altar of the chapel of the princes di S. Agato is a fine marble statue of the virgin Mary with her divine infant, and two persons in a posture of adoration, who represent Antonio Ferrao and his son Cæsar, both princes of S. Agata.

In the chapel of Santa Maria della Purità are four most beautiful statues of the cardinal virtues, among which Prudence is the best executed.

The walls of S. Gaëtano's chapel are almost entirely covered with votive pieces, and representations of the several parts of the body, which, by the intercession of that saint, have been delivered from pain, or restored to their natural functions. This church abounds in the finest paintings; for those pieces only in the anti-chamber of the vestry are valued at eighteen thousand *scudi*. The most admired among them are Pico della Mirandola, in the character of young Tobias, and cardinal Bembo in that of St. Jerom *.

This is an excellent copy from an original by Raphael, and the painting *in fresco* in the vestry is by the celebrated Solimene. In the area before this church stands a bronze statue of St. Gaëtano on a very lofty pedestal, with an inscription.

The church of S. Patrizia, though it be small, is exceeding splendid, near a hundred and forty thousand *scudi* having been expended on it. The tabernacle is of surprising rich-

S. Patrizia.

---

* Formerly it was usual, among celebrated painters, to introduce even in scripture-history pieces the portraits of their relations, most esteemed friends, or eminent personages of their time. At the altar of the parish-church of Wittenberg, is the baptism of Christ, by Luke Cranach, where the spectators consist of persons then very well known, and painted in an exact likeness; but Cranach's wife, who extremely importuned her husband, that she might be one, is drawn with her back to the spectator. The marriage of Cana, shewn at Venice, has in it the faces of the most celebrated Italian musicians of the time when it was painted. Albert archbishop of Mentz is accused of setting up in the cathedral a statue of his mistress to represent the virgin Mary; but these artifices are not a modern refinement: for Praxiteles, according to Posidippus, had the pleasure of seeing his mistress Cratina admired and worshipped in his supposed statue of Venus of Cnidos; and the beauty of the celebrated courtezan Phryne of Thebes induced most of the Grecian painters to make her sit for their pictures of the goddess of love. *Vid. Clement. Alexandr. in Protrept. ad gent. p. 22.* Cicero reproaches Clodius with having publicly consecrated the image of a prostitute under the title of the goddess of liberty, *Cic. pro Dom. c. 43.* *Hanc Deam quisquam violare audeat, imaginem meretricis?* 'And will any body dare to violate this goddess, or rather the image of a harlot?'

ness, and the *pallioti*, or coverings for the altar, are of silver. The vestry is finely painted, as the vestries of Naples generally are, being little inferior to the finest churches in other countries. This church, together with the adjoining convent, belongs to the Benedictine nuns; and behind the altar is a window which looks into their choir *.

S. Filippo Neri.

The church of S. Filippo Neri was built by the celebrated architect Dionysio Bartolomeo, and the front would have an uncommon air of grandeur, were the tower on the right built to correspond with that on the left side. The church is divided into three isles by two ranges of granate Corinthian pillars, each of which cost a thousand ducats, being cut out of one block, though twenty-four *palmi* high, and eleven in circumference. The roof, indeed, is not arched, but finely decorated with sculpture and gilding. At the high altar is a curious piece of Florentine work, and the front of the table is done on a ground of mother-of-pearl. There is scarce an altar in this church which is not adorned with the works of the most eminent sculptors and painters; so that it may be ranked among the greatest curiosities of Naples. The vestry exhibits several noble monuments of the admirable skill of Guido Rheni, Domenichino, Gioseppino, the two Bassani's, &c. The vestments, the silver and gold utensils, the chalices, the *pallioti*, the jewels, and variety of other things of value, that lie useless here, are not to be seen without astonishment and concern; but the most valuable piece is a silver *ciborio*, or *pyx*, weighing eight pounds, which is set with diamonds, rubies, and emeralds. Here is also a tabernacle made in the form of a canopy, supported by four angels, all of silver; but the *pyx* is of massy gold. In some of the chalices, gold is the least valuable part of them. In a silver *pallioto*, designed by Giordano, are ten detached figures, besides very bold and high-finished relievo's.

S. Pietro d' Ara.

The church of S. Pietro d' Ara is said to have been anciently a temple of Apollo; but that St. Peter caused an altar to be set up in it to the true God, and was pleased to officiate at it, as is intimated by this inscription:

Siste fidelis & priusquam Templum ingrediaris, Petrum sacrificantem venerare, hic enim primò, mox Romæ, filios per Evangelium genuit, paneque illo suavissimo cibavit.

* A long catalogue of reliques is here omitted.

' Stop,

NAPLES.

'Stop, devout Christian, and, before thou settest thy foot
'in this temple, revere St. Peter, who first performed mass
'here, and afterwards at Rome, and begot spiritual sons
'through the gospel, whom he fed with that bread which
'came down from heaven.'

The noble picture in the chapel of the Ricci family is by Leonardo da Vinci, who died in 1520.
In this church is the following short but comprehensive epitaph:

D. O. M.
FABRITIO FRANCIPANO, cui nec viventi Romana virtus, nec morienti vera pietas defuit, hæredd. ex Testam. B. M.

'Sacred to God the greatest and best of beings,
'And to the memory of Fabritio Francipani, who, while
'he lived, was endowed with all the virtues of a Roman,
'and died a pious and devout Christian, &c.'

The church of S. Pietro à Majella is also called St. Cata- S. Pietro à rina; the cieling is finely painted by the cavalier Calabrese, Majella. and adorned with gildings round the compartments. The espousals of Christ with St. Catharine of Sienna, over the altar, is by Caracci; though by some attributed to Criscuolo, a disciple of Andrea da Salerno. The most remarkable statue in this church is St. Sebastian bound to a tree, by Giovanni da Nola.

In the chapel of the Spinella family is a marble basso-re- Bust of Au-lievo, which was originally a head of Augustus; but, that guftus altered to that of no profane piece might remain in the church, it was altered, an angel. by the addition of a pair of wings, to an angel; an honour of which Augustus dreamed as little, as Cicero did of the prostitution of his name, which is bestowed on so many paltry antiquarians of this country.

In the church of S. Pietro Martire, behind the high altar, S. Pietro is the nativity of Christ, in *pietra cotta*, greatly esteemed; Martire. and the altar, with the tabernacle upon it, are of curious inlaid work.

In the choir lies queen Isabella, who died in 1465; and near her is interred the infant Don Pedro, brother of king Alphonso I. The following epitaph was set up by the Dominicans, to whom the adjoining convent belongs:

H 3 *Ossibus*

Offibus & Memoriæ Ifabellæ Clarimontiæ Neap. Reginæ, Ferdinandi Primi Conjugis, & Petri Aragonei Principis ſtrenui, Regis Alphonſi Senioris Fratris, qui, ni mors ei illuſtrem vitæ curſum interrupiſſet, fraternam gloriam facilè adæquaſſet. O fatum! quot bona parvulo ſaxo conduntur!

' For the remains and in memory of Iſabella de Clairmont
' queen of Naples, and conſort to Ferdinand I, and of the
' valiant prince Pedro of Aragon, who, had not death cut
' ſhort his glorious career, would unqueſtionably have e-
' qualled the reputation of king Alphonſo his brother. Hea-
' vens! what worth is concealed under this little ſtone!'

Here alſo is the tomb of Beatrix of Aragon, daughter to Ferdinand I, king of Naples, and queen conſort to Matthias Corvinus king of Hungary, who died in 1508, with the following ſhort panegyric:

Beatrix Aragonea, Pannoniæ Regina, Ferdinandi Primi Neap. Regis filia, de ſacro hoc Collegio opt. merita hic ſita eſt. Hæc religione & Munificentiâ ſeipſum vicit.

' Here reſts Beatrix of Aragon, queen of Hungary, daugh-
' ter of Ferdinand I, king of Naples, an illuſtrious bene-
' factreſs to this convent, who in munificence and devotion
' even excelled herſelf.'

The fine picture of Joſeph with the child Jeſus in his arms, is by del Po. Here are alſo ſeveral fine pieces by Solimene. In the veſtry are two admirable ſtatues of Prudence and Juſtice; the drapery of the latter cannot be exceeded. Between theſe ſtatues is a baſſo-relievo impiouſly repreſenting God the Father. Here alſo is ſhewn a ſilver *pallioto*, or altar-covering, the front leaf of which is in length fourteen ſpans and a half, and five in height; the candleſticks of the ſame metal belonging to it are nine feet high. In the refectory, which is very ſpacious and elegant, are ſome curious water-works.

S. Severino. Under the high altar of St. Severino's church, which belongs to the Benedictines, are depoſited the remains of the two ſaints Severinus and Soſius, as is expreſſed in this inſcription:

Hic

NAPLES:

Hic sua sanƈta simul divinaque corpora Patres
Socius unanimes & Severinus habent.

' Here with mutual complacency lie together the sacred
' bodies of the venerable fathers Sosius and Severinus.'

St. Benedict glorified in heaven, in the center of the choir, was painted by Belisario Cortensi, and likewise some other pieces near it; which so endeared this place to him, that, in his life-time, he prepared a sepulchre for himself in the chapel of the Maranta family, with this epitaph:

Belisarius Cortensius ex antiquo Arcadum genere, D. Georgii Eques, inter Regios stipendiarios Neapoli a pueris adscitus, depiƈto hoc Templo, sibi suisque locum quietis vivens paravit.
MDCXV.

' This place of rest Belisario Cortensi, descended from
' the ancient Arcadians, and knight of St. George, (who,
' when a boy, had a pension conferred on him by the king
' of Naples) prepared, whilst living, for himself and family
' in this church, which he had beautified with his paint-
' ings. 1615.'

The portraits on both sides of the church of the kings, popes, and other illustrious persons of the Benedictine order, are by Zingaro.

The stalls in the choir are so curiously inlaid with walnut-tree, that the work cost sixteen thousand ducats; the artists were Tortelli and Chiarini.

In the area under the cupola are four superb monuments belonging to the family of Mormile.

Near the vestry is the following epitaph of Giovanni Battista, of the Cicara family:

Liquisti gemitum miseræ lachrymasque Parenti
Pro quibus infelix hunc Tibi dat tumulum.

' Nothing but sighs and tears by thee bequeath'd
' To thy fond parent, who, in sad return,
' Erects (vain gift!) this monumental stone.'

NAPLES.

Not far from this lies Andrea Bonifacia, a child, with an exquisite monument by Pietro da Prata; and a suitable epitaph by the celebrated Sannazario:

> *Note, Patris Matrisque amor, & suprema voluptas,*
> *En Tibi, quæ nobis Te dare fors vetuit.*
> *Busta, Eheu, tristesque notas damus, invida quando*
> *Mors immaturo funere te rapuit.*
> *Andreæ filio, qui vixit annos VI. - - - parentes ob raram indolem - - -*

> ' To thee, thy parents short-liv'd joy, we raise
> ' A mournful bust; O unrelenting fate!
> ' To crop his youthful bloom with iron hand,
> ' Who should have clos'd his dying parents eyes.
> ' To Andrea their son, who lived but six years; his disconsolate parents - - - for his extraordinary endowments - - -'

The chapel of the Sanseverina family, besides its fine paintings, is remarkable for the tombs of three unfortunate brothers, whom their father's brother poisoned, in order to make his way to the estate; and also that of their mother, who desired to be buried near them; the sculpture by Giovanni da Nola is extremely fine, and one of the epitaphs is as follows:

> *Hic ossa quiescunt JACOBI SANSEVERINI Comitis Saponariæ, veneno miserè ob avaritiam necati, cum duobus miseris fratribus, eodem fato, eadem horâ commorientibus.*

> ' Here lie the remains of Giacomo Sanseverini, count of
> ' Saponara, barbarously poisoned through avarice, with his
> ' two unhappy brothers, who expired in the same manner,
> ' and at the same hour.'

On the mother's tomb is the following inscription:

> *Hospes, miserrimæ miserrimam defleas orbitatem. En illa HIPPOLYTA MONTIA post natas fœminas infelicissima, quæ Ugo Sanseverino conjugi tres maximæ expectationis filios peperi, qui venenatis poculis (vicit in familia, proh scelus! pietatem cupiditas, timorem audacia, & rationem amentia) unâ in miserorum complexibus Parentum miserabiliter illicò exspirârunt. Vir, ægritudine sensim obrepente, paucis post annis in his etiam manibus exspiravit. Ego tot superstes funeribus, cujus requies in tenebris, solamen in lachrymis, & cura omnis in morte collocatur. Quos vides separatim tumulos, ob æterni doloris argumentum, & in memoriam illorum illorum sempiternam. Anno M.D.XLVII.*

' Stranger,

' Stranger, lament my wretchedness, who was the happiest
' of women. Behold here the remains of Hippolyta Montia,
' who to my dear husband, Ugo Sanseverini, bore three sons,
' youths of promising hopes ; but, horrid guilt ! (so far did
' avarice overcome affection, boldness fear, and madness
' the reason of one of the same family) they were inhuman-
' ly poisoned, and immediately expired in the embraces of
' their distracted parents. My husband, by an insensible
' decay, also died, a few years after, in these arms. To
' me, the wretched survivor of so many relations, darkness
' was repose, tears administered relief, and the grave was
' my only solace. These several tombs remain as perpetual
' monuments of my grief, and my children's unhappy fate.
' 1547.'

From this church one descends by some steps into the old church, which wants neither light nor ornaments.

In the vestry, among other curiosities, is shewn the crucifix sent by Pius V. to Don John of Austria, to the miraculous assistance of which, the Christians, as is pretended, owe the famous naval victory of Lepanto. In the inscription the image is termed *Patibulati numinis effigies.*

The large Benedictine convent to which this church belongs, maintains eighty monks, and consists of four spacious courts, with cloisters round them. In one of these St. Benedict's life is painted, by Antonio Solario, a Venetian, commonly called Zingaro, who has painted his own portrait among the spectators.

The Palazzo degli Studii publici, or Novi, near the Constantinopolitan gate, will, when compleated, be the finest academy in all Italy, if not the whole world. Though the sums already laid out upon it amount to a hundred and fifty thousand *scudi*; yet it is not above half compleated. It was first intended for a riding-school ; but the want of water occasioned that design to be laid aside. The founder of it was the count de Lemos, when he was vice-roy ; who ordered a great number of beautiful statues, found in the duke d'Ossuna's time betwixt Pozzuoli and Cuma, to be brought hither to adorn this noble edifice. Betwixt every two windows a statue is erected ; and it is indeed a pity that so fine a structure, which was designed by the cavalier Fontana, is likely to remain unfinished. I have observed great neglect in keep-

Palazzo degli Studii Publici.

ing

ing several of the public buildings in repair at Naples, and this is one instance of it; for the grass grows in several of the windows, and the cieling of the great saloon already begins to decay. The antique building discovered near Cuma, and from which a great number of statues were brought hither, had this inscription on the front:

Lares Augustos
M. Agrippina refecit.

' The palace of Augustus repaired by M. Agrippina.'

In this academy, among others, is the following inscription:

Philippo III. Rege Catholico
Don Petrus Fernandez de Castro
Lemens. Comes, Prorex,
Composita pro voto re omni publica,
Legum opportunitate,
Delectu magistratuum,
Fori ac judiciorum emendatione,
Ærariorum ac Fisci
Præter spem præterque vacationem
Incremento,
Alta omnium Ordinum quiete,
Ubertate maxima
Exhaustis ad annonam paludibus,
Importata multiplicem ad usum oblectationemque
Aqua castria,
Quasi operum coronidem,
Gymnasium cum urbe natum,
Ulysse auditore inclytum,
A Tito restitutum,
A Frid. II. legibus munitum,
Auctum honorarius,
A Carolo II. Andigav. intra mœnia positum,
Ferdinandi Catholici tumultibus penè obrutum,
Ex humili angustoque loco
In amplissimum augustissimumque, juxta Urbem
Vetere Sapientum instituto,
Regis sumptu excitatum transtulit
Ann. Sal. Hum. MDCXVI.

NAPLES.

'In the reign of Philip III, Don Pedro Fernandes de Ca-
ſtro, count of Lemos, and vice-roy, having happily ſettled the ſtate of public affairs, reformed the tribunals of
juſtice by the choice of magiſtrates, and the equity of
laws, &c. to crown his noble actions, cauſed this college
(which is of equal antiquity with the city itſelf, and where
Ulyſſes was once a pupil) repaired by Titus, confirmed
with larger endowments by Frederic II, and afterwards
rebuilt by Charles II, of Anjou, within the walls, but
ſince almoſt totally demoliſhed in the tumults during the
reign of Ferdinand king of Spain, to be at his Catholic
Majeſty's expence rebuilt in a magnificent manner, and
according to the uſage of the ancient philoſophers, at a
ſmall diſtance from the buſtle and amuſements of the city,
in the year of our redemption 1616.'

This inſcription, of which P. Orfo the Jeſuit was the Whether U-
author, has been criticiſed by Lanſena, who ſeverely ex- lyſſes ſtudied
poſes him for aſſerting that this college is of equal anti- at Naples.
quity with the city, and that Ulyſſes was one of its members.

The univerſity of Naples appears from Petrus de Vineis,
lib. iii. *epiſt.* and *Ricard. de S. Germano ad ann.* 1224. *p.* 984,
to have been founded by the emperor Frederic II, whoſe
patent was confirmed by pope Innocent IV, in the year
1254.

The church della Santiſſima Trinità della Monache is Chieſa della
adorned with ſeveral pieces of painting and ſculpture, which Trinita.
are very well worth ſeeing. Among the former are a
great many pieces by Giov. Berardino Siciliano; the reſt
are by Luigi Siciliano, St. Girolamo del Ribera, and Giovanni Caracciolo, by ſome called Battiſtello. The taber- Rich tabernacle of the high altar is valued at ſixty thouſand *ſcudi*. nacle.
The nunnery to which this church belongs is very ſpacious
and magnificent; and the nuns are under the care of the
Franciſcans.

LETTER

LETTER LX.

Of the Antiquities and natural Curiosities near the City of NAPLES towards PUZZUOLO, BAIÆ, CUMA, MISENO, &c.

SIR,

A Foreigner who is desirous of reaping instruction and advantage from his travels in Italy, should not neglect spending some days in visiting the country about Puzzuolo, Cuma, &c. In going from the suburbs of Chiaja to the Grotto del Monte di Posilipo, &c. on an eminence to the left, in a garden, at present in the possession of Don Paolo Ruffo, are to seen the ruins of an ancient mausoleum. It was originally built in the form of a pyramid; but the lower part, which is all that now remains of it, is not unlike a large oven *. The way to it is not to be found without a guide; and on the side towards the cave of Pausilypo it is so narrow, and runs along such a high precipice, that it is something dangerous to persons subject to dizziness. This ancient ruin generally passes for the monument of the poet Virgil; but without any sufficient grounds for such a conjecture. In the wall within it are ten small niches or cavities, apparently designed for urns. According to Alphonso de Heredia, late bishop of Ariano, the marble urn, in which Virgil's ashes had been deposited, stood here on nine small marble pillars, of which, at present, there is not the least appearance; and what became of such a remarkable piece of antiquity is also a great mystery. Some pretend, that, at the earnest sollicitations of the inhabitants of Mantua, they were presented to that city; but others affirm, that the cardinal of Mantua found means to get them into his possession. The third opinion is, that the urn was transported to Genoa; but that the pillars were applied to some other use. This is certain, that at Mantua, where they pride themselves not a little on account of their city being the birth-place of that great poet †, they know nothing of the place

of

---

* Of all the copper-plates which I have seen of it, there is not one which doth not make this monument much higher than it really is.

† Possibly no writer of antiquity has been so idolized as Virgil: even

in

Near the City of NAPLES.
of his burial. Pietro di Steffano, in his account of the churches of Naples, says, that in his time, which was no longer ago than the year 1560, both the urn and the pillars were in being, with this distich, then legible, near them:

Mantua me genuit: Calabri rapuere: tenet nunc
Parthenope: cecini pascua, rura, duces.

' I sung, flocks, tillage, heroes; Mantua gave
' Me life, Brundusium death, Naples a grave.'
DRYDEN.

This inscription was set up again in 1684, by order of Gieronimo di Alessandra duke di Pescolanciano, to whom this garden then belonged. The mausoleum is now overgrown with shrubs and bushes, among which are a few laurel-trees, supposed by the credulous to grow again, though often rooted up. At present the only inscription in the whole mausoleum is the following:

Quæ cineris tumulo hæc vestigia? conditur olim
Ille hoc qui cecinit, pascua, rura, duces.

' What traces now remain within this tomb,
' Where once repos'd that sacred bard, who sung
' Of swains, of tillage, and heroic deeds?

That Silius Italicus, besides Cicero's *villa*, also purchased the land where Virgil's monument stood, appears from the following pretty compliment of Martial:

In the primitive times there were not wanting some divines, whose charity was so great as to make a Christian of him; and to this wild opinion they were so firmly attached, that they maintained the orator Marcellianus to have been converted to the Christian faith by reading Virgil's fourth Eclogue. Later ages have even improved upon the matter, by casually dipping into his poems, and accounting the verse which first struck the eye to be no less than a divine declaration. But what follows is still more extraordinary, *viz.* that Ignatius Loyola, the founder of the order of Jesuits, by repeating the 165th verse of the fourth Æneid, is said to have put the devil to flight. [As the verse mentioned here is quite foreign to the purpose, I imagine there is an error of the press in the German original; probably the author means some part of the sixth Æneid, or perhaps the following verse:

Non fugis hinc præceps; dum præcipitare potestas?
Æneid. iv. v. 565.]

Silius

Silius hæc Magni celebrat monumenta Maronis,
Jugera facundi qui Ciceronis habet.
Hæredem dominumque sui tumulique larisque
Non alium mallet nec Maro, nec Cicero.

'Silius inherits tuneful Maro's tomb,
'And Tully's *villa* whose mellifluous tongue
'Dropt nectar; but their gentle shades are pleas'd,
'As dubious where to find a worthier heir.

At Sorento, not far from mount Vesuvio, are shewn some laurel-trees growing spontaneously out of the ruins of the house in which Torquato Tasso is said to have been born; as if nature itself was disposed to crown the birth-place of such a poet, and to decide the hot contests betwixt Pergamo, Naples, Salerno, and Sorento (each of which laid claim to Tasso) in favour of the last. It is most adviseable for a traveller instead of taking Virgil's tomb in his way to Puzzuolo to visit it at the same time with the church of S. Maria del Parto, and the other curiosities of the suburb of Chiaja.

La Scuola di Virgilio. In going by water from Naples to Puzzuolo, not far from Cape Pausilypo one passes by a dome or cupola hewn out of the rock, supposed to be the remains of a temple of Venus, though vulgarly, but for what reason I know not, called la Scuola di Virgilio, or Virgil's school.

Mountain of Pausilypo. Formerly in going from Naples to Puzzuolo it was necessary to cross mount Pausilypo (which on account of its delightful appearance is said to have derived its name ἀπο της παυσεως της λυπης) but at present that trouble is spared, a broad subterraneous road being cut through the mountain. This passage is conducted for the most part through large rocks, and sometimes through *strata* of sand. It is at both ends betwixt ninety and a hundred feet high in order to throw in more light. Towards the middle where the top is lower, two large vent-holes for light and air are made through the roof of this grotto: however, the light is not sufficient, and travellers are extremely incommoded with dust in this subterraneous passage. The bottom of it, which in the time of Don Pedro de Toledo, vice-roy under Charles V, was paved with broad stones like the streets of Naples, is cleaned several times in a year, and then it is pretty free from dust; but, as it is a road extremely frequented, this convenience is of no long duration. The breadth is betwixt eighteen and twenty feet, so that there is sufficient room for two carriages to avoid each other: and, to prevent any inconveniency on this head, it is usual in the dark places to call out to any person coming the contrary way, to know on which side they intend to keep. When they answer *alla Montagna* it signifies the Naples side, which, to those coming from the city, is on the right hand; and *alla Marina* denotes the left-hand side.

The length of this subterraneous passage is about three hundred and forty-four *canne*, which is something more than half an Italian mile. On the left hand, near the middle of it is an oratory hewn out of the rock, with a lamp continually burning in it. This grotto is by the vulgar supposed to have been made by magic, and that Virgil * was the sorcerer who wrought it. The Neapolitan writers, after Strabo, affirm it to be the work of one Cocceius, of whom they can give no further account †. The next who mentions it after Strabo is Seneca, who in his fifty-seventh letter makes a lamentable complaint of the darkness, dust, &c. Possibly the cutting of a road through the mountain was at first not thought of; but the great quantities of stone being fetched out of it for the buildings in Naples and Puzzuolo might occasion such a deep excavation on both sides, that at last, for the conveniency of travelling, the government employed workmen to pull down and clear away the intermediate space; besides, it is not to be thought that the way at first was in such a good condition as it is at present. Seneca in the above-mentioned place says, *Nihil illo carcere longius, nihil illis faucibus obscurius*; i. e. ' This dungeon is of an in-
' tolerable length and extremely dark.' From whence it may be inferred, that the apertures thro' which, in Strabo's

---

* I heartily pity poor Virgil, who, without any fault of his, is thus classed among magicians. The poet, 'tis true, gives a description of the Cumean grotto; but this the learned populace apply to the grotto of Pausilypo; and, since Virgil has so particularly described an ancient sybil or prophetess, they conclude of course that he must have been a wizard.

† Strabo, after finishing his concatenation of fables, at length comes to acknowledge the singularities of this place. *Geogr. lib.* v. *p*. 375. *Omnia ista fabulas esse liquido adparuit, quum quidem Coccejus, qui cuniculum istum duxit, & alium à Puteolis ad Neapolin supra Bajas tendentem fere sequutus sit fabulam istam de Cimmeriis modò relatam*, i. e. ' All these things
' plainly appear to be no more than fables. Cocceius himself the maker
' of this subterraneous passage, and of another in Puzzuolo towards Na-
' ples, by the way of Bajæ, followed that fable just now related of the
' Cimmerians.'

time,

time, the light entered at the sides, were soon after stopped up, either by earthquakes or want of proper care.

The Neapolitan historians agree, that king Alphonso I, of the Aragon family, caused this passages to be considerably widened; and Don Pedro de Toledo vice-roy under the emperor Charles V. is known to have given orders for levelling and paving of the ground, as likewise the enlarging of two vent-holes which had been at first bored through by order of Alphonso I. That it was entirely wrought by art is unquestionable from the marks it bears of chizels and other tools used by stone-cutters. The earthquakes which have made such havoc among the numerous remains of antiquity in these parts, have hitherto spared this useful work. About fifty paces before you come to the entrance of this cavern in the road from Naples, the vice-roy Don Pedro Antonio d'Aragona, after the physicians Vincenzo Erisconio and Sebastiano Bartoli had, by his order, examined the warm baths of Puzzuolo, and the proper repairs had been made there at the charge of nine thousand *scudi*, caused an inscription on marble to be set up for the information of posterity, concerning the right method of using those baths, &c. It begins in the following manner:

Inscription touching the warm baths in Puzzuolo.

Quisquis es, vel indigena, vel advena, vel convena,
Ne insolitus prætereundo horribile hoc antrum
In Phlegræis Campaniæ campis naturæ obrigescas portentis,
Vel humanæ temeritatis obstupescas prodigiis;
Siste gradum, lege, nam stupori & admirationi assuesces
Neapolitanæ, Puteolanæ ac Bajanæ telluris balnea
Ad omnes fere morbos profligandos experta,
Apud omnes olim gentes, apud omnes ætates, celeberrima,
Hominum incuriâ, Medicorum invidiâ, temporum injuriâ,
Incendiorum eruptione, confusa, dispersa, diruta
Obrutaque hactenus adeo stetere,
Ut vix unius aut alterius dubia & incerta
Superessent vestigia,
Nunc Carolo II. regnante
Petri Antonii Aragonii Regni Proregis
Providentia, Charitas, Vigilantia, Industria
Investigavit, distinxit, reparavit, restituit.
Siste adhuc paulisper,
Et substrati lapidi in literas intuere
Balneorum enim nomina, loca ac virtutes habebis,
Ac lætior abibis,
P. P. A. D. M.DC.LXIIX.

Near the City of NAPLES.

'Whoe'er thou art, a native, foreigner, or sojourner, that in passing by this dreadful cave, thou mayest not be struck with terror at the prodigies of nature in the Phlegrean fields of Campania, nor with astonishment at the wonders of human temerity, stop and read; then well mayest thou admire that the baths of Naples, Puzzuolo, and Bajæ of such approved efficacy against almost all distempers, and so famous in all nations and all ages, should by the negligence of the people, the malice of the physicians, the injury of time, and the rage of fiery eruptions have been ruined and laid in such confusion, that scarce any traces of them remained: but now in the happy reign of Charles II. and by the wisdom, benevolence, vigilance, and activity of Pedro Antonio of Aragon, vice-roy of Naples, they have been cleared from a heap of ruins, cleansed, repaired and restored to their former state. Stay a little longer and cast thine eye upon the inscription placed underneath. It is worth thy while, as thou wilt find the names, the situation, and medical virtues of the several baths. 1668, &c.'

At coming out of the grotto of Pausilypo, you turn off on the right hand into a very pleasant road, which running betwixt five vine-yards, leads to the Lago d'Agnano, which is almost a perfect circle about an Italian mile in circumference. At high water in some parts of it is seen a strong ebullition: on approaching near it one is indeed sensible of the motion of the water, which possibly proceeds from the violent ascent of effluvia, which do not, however, convey any heat. The tenches and eels in this lake in winter are of a very good flavour; whereas in summer they are not eatable, which I impute in some measure to the great quantities of flax and hemp which are brought thither from all the neighbouring parts to be mellowed.

Lago d'Agnano.

Every waggon-load of flax that is laid in this lake pays six *carlini* *, which duty annually amounts to two thousand five hundred *scudi*, neat produce, three fourths of which the Jesuits are entitled to, and the rest goes to some private person.

Near this lake stand *i Sudatorii di S. Germano*, or Sudatories of St. Germano, which consist of several apartments built with stone, where the heat and sulphureous vapours issuing from the earth soon cause a profuse sweat; in some

Sudatories of St. Germano.

* Two shillings.

places the wall is too hot for the hand to bear it, and yet the heat is supportable in the hotteſt room, eſpecially if you ſtoop towards the ground: the ſame obſervation is made on the baths of Tritoli. The patients are put in rooms of different degrees of heat, according to the nature of their complaint; and in the ſudatories of St. Germano they never ſtay above a quarter of an hour at a time: they are ſaid to be very efficacious in the gout, debilities, inward hurts, &c.

Grotto del Cane. Within a hundred paces of theſe ſudatories is a ſmall natural cavity, known by the name of *Grotta del Cane*, or Dog's Grotto, that animal being generally choſen for the proof of the ſurpriſing effect of the vapour in this cavity. It is about twelve feet in length, five broad, and ſix high, and ſtands within twenty paces of the lake d'Agnano. The vapour which riſes in it is condenſed on the roof and ſides into very clear drops; unleſs, as this phænomenon is not conſtant, they rather proceed from the rain water collected on the little eminence over it, and ſoaking through the pores of the earth. This grotto is left always open, for there is no door nor incloſure to ſhut it up. In the way to the Lago d'Agnano there is a cottage where lives a man who makes it his buſineſs to keep dogs, in order to ſhew ſtrangers the ſurpriſing effects of this grotto, and is generally rewarded with five or ſix *carlini* *. The dogs, when they find that they are to undergo this experiment, become untractable and uſe their utmoſt efforts to make their eſcape.

The owner of the dog going into this cavern holds its noſe forcibly to the ground, when after a minute and a half, or two minutes, the creature falls into violent convulſions, and in about two minutes longer becomes quite motionleſs, as if he was dead. The man, during the operation, is almoſt on his knees; but throws his head back as far as poſſible, that the vapours in their aſcent may not affect him. The dog, having lain two or three minutes in all appearance dead, is thrown into a lake hard by, where within half a minute ſome ſigns of life are perceived in him. For a minute after he ſeems to be dizzy, and reels from ſide to ſide, when on a ſudden he preſently recovers and leaps upon his maſter with the greateſt joy and fondneſs. But if the dog, or any other animal, be left too long in the cave, it dies irrecoverably, ſo that the immerſion in the lake has no manner of effect on it. It is obſervable, that the ſpace during

* Two ſhillings.

which animals may remain in the cavity without the total loſs of life, is not the ſame in all ſpecies, and muſt not exceed the duration of the convulſions before they become motionleſs and apparently dead. A viper the firſt time bears the vapour from ſix to nine minutes before it becomes motionleſs; but, after recovering itſelf in the lake, it ſeems to have fortified itſelf with freſh vigour and laid up a proviſion of air. Accordingly it appears larger and inflated, and will undergo a much longer trial, even ſometimes an hour and a quarter before it dies irrecoverably. It is alſo the ſame with regard to frogs; and indeed the air-pump experiments ſhew, that the oftener an animal is rendered motionleſs by the rarefaction of the air, and afterwards releaſed to the free enjoyment of that element; the longer it will bear the want of a denſer air, and as it were become accuſtomed to that rarefied air which at firſt was near proving fatal to it in a ſhort time.

Charles VIII. king of France, when he made himſelf maſter of the kingdom of Naples, viſiting the curioſities of this place, ordered a trial of the Grotto del Cane to be made with an aſs; but it expired within a very ſhort time. Don Pedro de Toledo vice-roy of Naples made an experiment with two ſlaves under ſentence of death, who alſo were ſoon overcome by the noxious vapour. M. Villamont in his travels, publiſhed in the year 1609, relates, that, about fifteen or twenty years before, a French gentleman de' Tournon by name, having ſtooped only to take up a ſmall ſtone in the grotto, inſtantly fell down ſenſeleſs; and that, on being brought to the water, he in ſome meaſure came to himſelf, but ſoon after expired. *Experiment made with an aſs.*

Properly ſpeaking, it is not the water, or any particular virtue of the Lago d'Agnano which recovers theſe dogs, but the freſh air; in which alone, though much ſlower, they are found to come to themſelves. The effect of the water here is ſimilar to that on a perſon in a ſwoon; it invigorating the reſpiration of the animal, the total ſuppreſſion of which would otherwiſe be inevitably followed by death. It is the opinion of ſome that the earth in the grotto emits arſenical effluvia, and that it is this which ſo quickly deſtroys the animals: but, were it ſo, no kind of water could be of any ſervice againſt its effects. It is much more probable, that theſe exhalations, which float near the bottom of the grotto, without riſing higher than ten inches, by their ſubtil-

Antiquities and Natural Curiosities

ty * gradually stop the play of the lungs, and consequently the circulation of the blood: and this is also confirmed by the dissection of a frog which died in this cave, not the least air being perceivable in his lungs. From the same reason, and for want of denser air, or on account of the stagnation of it, a burning torch immediately goes out, when lowered from the upper part of the grotto, within the distance of ten inches from the bottom: and it not only extinguishes the flame, but even the snuff likewise; and the smoke, being pressed by the gravity of the air above, is observed to make its way out at the mouth of the cave, not in a vertical but an horizontal direction, within ten inches of the bottom of the grotto. This rarefaction of the air likewise is the cause that a loaded musket placed near the bottom of the grotto will not go off, nor the gun-powder so much as flash: this is, however, effected by a quantity of powder set on fire by means of a train laid on a board, part of which is immerged in the vapour, and part without it; for it will disperse the vapour at the bottom, and gradually expels it out of the grotto. Though the vapour hinders the powder in single grains from taking fire, yet it is not strong enough to obstruct the communication of the fire from the powder already kindled with that part of the train immerged in it. Now that the rarefaction of the air will produce such effects is evident from the experiments on the pneumatic engine; for a candle placed under the exhausted receiver immediately goes out, animals lose their respiration, and, without a re-admission of the air, their lives. That the sulphureous, unctuous, and hot effluvia, so copiously emitted from the adjacent *Sudatorii de S. Germano*, and the neighbouring country, contribute not a little to this, is a point not at all questioned by the inhabitants of those countries where wine is made. For, in autumn, when the cellars are full of new wine, the people who enter the vaults are not only so intoxicated by the effluvia, that they reel about as if they were drunk; but, if they are not careful to withdraw on the first symptoms, fall down senseless, and lose their lives unless they are carried with all possible speed into the fresh air. The vapour in these wine-vaults will likewise extinguish a lighted candle, like that of the Grotto del Cane. Some years since I observed that a pistol would not go off at the bottom of the

Effect of sulphureous vapours in wine cellars.

---

* Or rather their viscous or glewy quality, as Mr. Addison observes; whose hypothesis seems to account for all the phænomena of the grotto better than the author's.

deep

Near the City of NAPLES.

deep mines at Lauenstein, in the electorate of Brunswic-Lunenburg. To which may be added, that, in spring and autumn, the weather (as the miners call it) that is, the air is so noxious, that the workmen, though very hardy and vigorous, find their heads dizzy and much disordered. Mr. Addison makes it a doubt, whether there are any sulphureous effluvia in the Grotto del Cane, not the least sulphureous smell being perceived on the hand, or any thing dipped on the vapour; but, with submission to that great man, this proves no more than that those effluvia are not in such abundance as to effect the smell as in warm baths, where the sulphur is violently forced up in steam from the water by the heat.

The Pyrmont water, the virtue of which chiefly consists in a subtile, acrid, sulphureous spirit, and a mineral unctuousness, is yet without any sulphureous smell, even when it is boiled; nor is the colour of silver, and other metals, which are turned yellow or black by sulphureous steams, altered by it. Now from both these circumstances one would be apt to conclude, that sulphur is no ingredient in these mineral waters, which yet has been demonstrated by numberless chymical experiments.

Account of the Pyrmont springs.

' Some drops of spirit of sulphur put into a solution of
' iron by vitriol or spirit of sulphur, and mixed with a great
' quantity of common spring water; or some of the above-
' mentioned spirits, and Glauber's salts mixed with common
' water, will in smell and taste hardly be distinguishable
' from the real Pyrmont water *.'

The learned Dr. Seipp, physician to the prince of Waldeck, has observed, that the subtile sulphureous effluvia aris-

---

* As the author's recipe mentions no quantity, it is presumed the following method of imitating Pyrmont water, as it is delivered with more accuracy and precision, will not be unacceptable to the reader.

This medicinal water may be imitated very nicely by art in the following manner: take a quart of the purest and lightest water; add to it thirty drops of a strong solution of iron made in spirit of salt, a drachm of oil of tartar *per deliquium*, and thirty drops of spirit of vitriol, or a little more or less, as is found necessary, not to let the alcali of oil of tartar prevail too strongly, tho' it must prevail a little; shake all briskly together, and, on tasting, it will be found extremely to resemble the true Pyrmont water.

The basis on which this is founded, is the analysis and trial of the true Pyrmont water, by which it is found to contain a subtile aqueous fluid, a volatile iron, and a predominant calcali, all joined together into one brisk pungent spirituous water. The artificial Pyrmont water thus made, if the proportions are carefully minded, will extremely resemble the natural, and will have the same effects, as a medicine. Shaw's Lectures. See also the Supplement to Barrow's Universal Dictionary of Arts and Sciences.

ing from the Pyrmont springs, sometimes bring on very strong vertigo's, and dizziness in the heads of the waiters that attend them; and mostly when the water is drawn at the spring-head. It soon grows fatal to fishes and frogs. Ducks and young geese, when put into these springs, first become giddy, then very faint, and in a few minutes fall on their sides, and sink to the bottom. But this effect does not take place immediately, the ducks sometimes swimming about with great alacrity for near an hour, without any visible disorder. Possibly the effluvia are not at all times equally copious; or rise above the water only at certain times. These aquatic fowls, being taken out when they begin to sink, are not long in recovering their former strength and activity *.

In a stone quarry, about eight hundred common paces from the above-mentioned Pyrmont springs, is a hole, which, by the following observations Dr. Seipp favoured me with in a letter, has no little analogy with the Grotto del Cane:
' If a barometer or thermometer be put into it, no alteration
' is observed in either. Lighted straw, candles, or even
' torches, are put out; but soon recover their flame, unless
' totally extinguished, when drawn back into the open air.
' No fire-arms will go off, and any animal soon loses its
' respiration in it, and, if kept in a few minutes longer,
' dies irrecoverably. The time of the convulsions and deli-
' quium of animals in these sulphureous effluvia varies ac-
' cording to the season of the year, the weather, and the
' time of the day. In windy, moist, cloudy, and rainy
' weather, the effect is scarce perceivable, as if the vapour
' retired into the earth; but in clear weather, in winter as
' well as summer, it ascends very high, and with extreme
' violence. The effect is most sensible in summer, and then
' in the mornings and evenings; but towards noon, when
' the sun approaches to the meridian, the vapour subsides.
' Gunpowder explodes in this hole or cave, when set on fire
' by a train without it; but frequent trials must be made
' before it succeeds; the exhalation being gradually dispersed
' by the fire so often introduced into the cavity. Small
' birds, as robin-red-breasts, &c. often drop down dead on-
' ly by flying into a hole near the entrance of the cavity, to
' look for dead flies, butterflies, and worms: and to the
' frequent finding of dead birds about this cavity is owing

* Dr. Seipp's account of the Pyrmont waters.

the

'the discovery of its quality *. When the evaporation is
'copious, fowls, ducks, and geese immerged in it seem mo-
'tionless or dead in a few seconds. Quadrupeds hold out
'longer than the winged species, though the former seldom
'hold out above a minute, unless the animal be very large,
'or by the length of the neck can reach above the height to
'which the vapour ascends. An animal, when taken out
'of the cave, requires for its recovery sometimes five minutes
'or more; but, if it be delayed too long, the creature, after
'violent convulsions, dies irrecoverably, as in an exhausted
'receiver. The air alone, without the aid of water, will
'gradually restore an animal to life; but the recovery is con-
'siderably accelerated by pouring water on his head, in his
'mouth, or forcing it up his nostrils. The vapour in this
'cavity, in the year 1719, ascended to the height of a foot
'and a half or two feet above the ground: but since that
'time, the cave having been put in better order, and an
'arch built over it; before sun-rise and after sun-set, and
'especially in a long drought, or before thunder, the vapour
'has been seen to ascend five or six feet from the bottom,
'and with a proportional strength; so that, upon going down
'only a few steps, the greatest caution is required to pre-
'vent a fatal surprize by the unexpected emission of these in-
'visible effluvia. This is indeed an extraordinary case, the
'vapour generally keeping within a foot or two of the bot-
'tom. It sensibly discovers itself by a stimulative warmth,
'penetrating through the shoes, stockings, &c. of the per-
'son that approaches it. This heat, which is not unwhole-
'some, in a few minutes is followed by a sweat, and a pun-
'gent stimulation in the nose, like that caused by horse-ra-
'dish; but, when it is growing too strong to be borne, it is
'only drawing back into the open air, and every trouble-
'some sensation immediately ceases. Before an arch was
'built over the place, the vapour, especially on the south-
'side, was observed to ascend with a tremulous motion, and
'intermixed with coruscations; but nothing of that kind is
'now perceivable. The subtilty of this vapour is such, that
'it does not adhere to any thing, and not the least sulphu-
'reous smell remains in things which have been hung up
'for some time under the arch for trial. Oil of tartar *per*

* The like is seen in the springs of Pyrmont, so that in dry and still weather a bird, only by flying across them, immediately drops down dead; yet all the Pyrmont springs are cold.

'*deliquium*

'*deliquium* undergoes no kind of change in it, whereas, by the fume of lighted sulphur, it usually degenerates into a neutral salt. Silver, or polished iron, contracts no kind of specks or tarnish. Whilst a person stands upright, he is not sensible of any smell; but, upon stooping towards the ground, a very pungent smell of sulphur fills the nose, mouth, and throat; the eyes water, as at the smell of horse-radish, onion, or leek; some symptoms of a vertigo come on, and then it is high time to hasten into the open air.' The like sulphureous caverns are also shewn in many other places celebrated for mineral waters, especially at Ems and Schwalbach.

<small>Grotto del Cane known in Pliny's time.</small> Probably Pliny points at the Grotto del Cane, when in *lib.* ii. *c.* 93. he observes, that, about Sinuessa and Puteoli, *Spiracula vocant, alii Charoneas scrobes, mortiferum spiritum exhalantes*; 'Those spiracles by some called Charon's ditches, exhaled a noxious deadly vapour.' Seneca, *Nat. Quæst. lib.* vi. *cap.* 28, writes thus: *Quid, quod pluribus Italiæ locis per quædam foramina pestilens exhalatur vapor, quem non homini ducere, non feræ tutum est? aves quoque si in illum inciderint, antequam cœlo meliore leniatur, in ipso volatu cadunt, liventque corpora, & non aliter quam per vim elisæ fauces tument, &c.* 'Are there not in several places in Italy holes or chasms in the earth, exhaling a pestilential vapour, in which neither man nor beast can respire? The birds, if they happen to fly into it before it is tempered with a purer air, immediately drop down. Their bodies grow livid, and their throats swell, &c.' But what Rodiginus asserts in *lib.* xix. *c.* 12, *viz.* That in these cavities, or Charon's ditches, which prove fatal to all other animals, such as are castrated are not in the least hurt, is a most gross fable.

<small>Royal entertainment in the forest of Astruni.</small> About half an Italian mile from the Lago d'Agnano, in a circular valley six miles in circumference, is a delightful forest, and three small lakes. This charming spot is called Astruni, and here the vice-roys usually take the diversion of hunting. In the year 1452, king Alphonso d'Aragon entertained the emperor Frederic III, (who came to Naples to receive his bride Eleanora on her landing from Portugal) with a very splendid hunting-match in this valley, on which occasion three thousand persons were feasted, and fountains ran with several sorts of wines. On an eminence near this forest is a tower, which yields a most charming prospect.

<small>Nisida.</small> In returning from the Lago d'Agnano, on the left-hand, towards the sea-coast, one comes in sight of the island Nisida,

rising

Near the City of NAPLES.

rising above the surface of the sea like a mountain, with a tower on its summit. Sannazarius, in the twelfth Eclogue of his Arcadia, gives the following account of it:

Dimmi Nisida mia, così non sentano
Le rive tue giammai cruciata Dorida,
Nè Pausilippo in te venir consentano,
Non ti vidi io poc' anzi herbosa e florida
Habitata da lepri e da cunicoli?
Non ti veggo hor più ch'altra incolta, ed horrida
Non veggio i tuoi recessi, e i diverticoli
Tutti cangiati e freddi quegli scopuli
Dove temprava Amor suo' ardenti scipoli.

' Say, Nisida, so may th' enraged sea,
' And Pausilippo's noxious vapours spare
' Thy naked shores; did I not, late, behold
' Thy hills with od'rous flow'rs and herbage crown'd,
' And every bush or brake inhabited
' By timid hares? But now, alas, how chang'd!
' No traces left of grove or sweet recess;
' But barren, cold, uncultivated rocks,
' Lash'd by the boist'rous ocean, now are seen,
' Where love attemper'd once his fiery shafts.'

In the south part of this island is a small harbour, called Porto Pavone, and on one of the gates is this distich: *Porto Pavone.*

Navita siste ratem, temonem hic, velaque fige;
Meta laborum hæc est læta quies animo.

' Here wearied mariners their sails unbend,
' And all their toils here meet the wish'd-for end.'

At present a *lazaretto* has been built upon a rock near this place; this island being the place appointed for performing quarantine, on account of the salubrity of the air; whereas its noxious air anciently grew into a proverb; and Lucan, lib. vi, says of it: *Lazaretto.*

— — — *Tali spiramine Nesis*
Emittit Stygium nebulosis aëra saxis.

' Nesis'

'Nefis' high rocks such Stygian air produce,
'And the blue breathing pestilence in mists diffuse.'
ADDISON.

Caprea.   A little farther from the sea, and three Italian miles from the extremity of the main land, lies the island of Caprea, sufficiently known by Tiberius's infamous retreat thither:

— — *Quem rupes Caprearum tetra latebit*
Incesto possessa seni?   CLAUD. de IV. Conf. Hon.

'Who has not heard of Caprea's guilty shore,
'Polluted by the rank old emperor.'   ADDISON.

This island has its peculiar bishop, the greatest part of whose revenue arises from licences to hunt; and especially to *Quails here,* catch quails, turtle-doves, and other birds of passage, great *from whence* numbers of which, in spring and autumn, resort to Caprea. *they come.* These birds are generally supposed to come from Africa; and, after having propagated their species, to return thither. That, on their first arrival here, they are so lean as to require to be fed a considerable time before they are fit for the table is certain; but whether this be the consequence of a long voyage, and that they come from such a distant part as the coast of Africa, is much to be doubted; especially as the quail is neither strong nor light enough for flying so far, nor is he at all adapted for swimming: and it would be with great difficulty that such a bird, when its feathers are once thoroughly wet, could ever be able to raise itself on the wing again. At least it is pretty certain that the quails which in the spring appear in England in vast flights, and are extremely lean, have not crossed the seas, but passed the winter in the holes of clifts on the sea-shore. I know that storks *Winter-* are said, at the approach of our winter, to repair to some *quarters of* distant country, where the climate is milder. I am also in*the stork.* formed, that some years ago, in the dutchy of Mecklenburg, an old stork was shot, in the wing of which a piece of an arrow was stuck; from whence some inferred that it had been in a country where bows and arrows are commonly used: but even this does not prove that it had ever crossed the sea; especially as, according to what information I could get in England, no master of a ship ever pretended to have seen a stork at sea. I might here also add, that no stork was ever
known

Near the City of NAPLES.

known to crofs the narrow ftraits betwixt the coaft of France and England, though their diftance be fo fmall, that, in clear weather, one coaft is very plainly diftinguifhed from the other. But that no ftorks are found in England is not fo much to be attributed to any impoffibility of their flying acrofs the fea, as to fome quality in the air and foil of that ifland; for the ftorks which fome, out of curiofity, have tranfported from Holland to England, neither live long, nor propagate their fpecies.

Further on towards Puzzuolo, on the right-hand, lies Monte Secco, which is here and there covered with fmall shrubs, and a kind of broom. The fummit of this mountain, which is known to have been once in the form of a cone, is now funk into an oval cavity, about a thoufand feet in the fhorteft, and twelve hundred and forty-fix in the longeft diameter. This place Strabo, in his fifth book, calls *Forum Vulcani*, and it is at prefent known by the name of Solfatara, or rather Solfarata. Monte Secco.

A perfon who is fond of feeing natural curiofities cannot but meet here with the higheft entertainment, as without danger and much trouble he may behold Vefuvio in miniature. Though the Solfatara be upwards of two German miles diftant from Vefuvio, it is unqueftionable that both thefe volcano's have a communication with each other: for it is obferved that the fmoke, heat, and force of the fubterraneous fire is lefs violent in the Solfatara when Vefuvio rages, and gives a free vent through its mouth to the fulphureous vapours that have been pent up in it; whereas, on the other hand, the heat, &c. in the former increafes, when the latter is at reft. Several fiffures, or chafms, that emit fmoke, &c. are feen in this place, and their vehemence increafes, the more the fefiffures are widened; fo that at laft a man cannot approach them on account of the heat. A fword, or any other piece of iron, being held over one of thefe holes or fpiracles, a fweetifh kind of condenfed fteam drops from it; but a fheet of paper faftened to a ftick, fo as not to be blown away by the air iffuing from the aperture and held over it, receives not the leaft moifture; nor is it damaged by the heat, but becomes very dry and ftiff. The ftones which lie about thefe apertures feem to be in continual motion. And upon throwing a handful of fmall pebbles into thefe holes they are ejected to the height of about twelve feet, and fometimes thrown obliquely on the fides, as more ponderous maffes are from Vefuvio. In fome places Solfatara, Vefuvio in miniature.

the

the fand, by the force of the effluvia, fprings up and down near the vent-holes, like the fparkling of Champagne or cyder.

Sal Ammoniacum. The ftones that lie near thefe apertures are often incrufted with a yellow fubftance (not unlike the yolk of an egg boiled hard) with the white efflorefcence upon it, which paffes for *Sal Ammoniacum*; but whether it has the fame property with that brought from Egypt, which is made of foot, fea-falt, and urine of horfes, mules, or camels, I am, as yet, not certain *.

The furface and foil of the Solfatara are of a whitifh colour, as are the ftones alfo, which are very foft and impregnated with *fulphur vivum*, and when firft dug up they are quite hot; they retain their foftnefs when expofed to the air.

When I vifited Solfatara, fome workmen were employed upon a vein or *ftratum* of a greyifh kind of afhes, feveral feet in thicknefs: thefe afhes, among which lay feveral whitifh fulphur-ftones, were exactly like thofe on mount Vefuvio, which, in the extraordinary eruptions of that vulcano, have been known to cover the whole city of Naples five or fix inches deep. This Solfatara afh was at firft moift and cohefive; but the magnet had no power on it, which was poffibly owing to a mixture of fulphureous particles.

Vitriol. Befides fulphur, vitriol is alfo made here, of a fapphire colour, and efteemed better than that of Rome; and likewife alum to the greateft perfection. The large leaden kettles ufed in this operation are not heated by any fire of wood or coals, but only by the natural heat of holes in the ground over which they are placed. This diftrict produces alfo a good plafter; and of the earth itfelf are made cups and other veffels, which in feveral diftempers are reckoned to be very wholefome for fick people to drink out of. The produce of the Solfatara is yearly farmed at feven or eight hundred *fcudi*

---

* In Egypt, for want of wood, a great part of their fuel is the dung of animals mixt with ftraw, and dried; and the foot thereof, with the addition of fea-falt, is the principal ingredient in the Egyptian *Sal Ammoniacum*. This branch of commerce is chiefly carried on with Venice, where it is refined, and caft like fugar in large conical loaves. In its outward appearance it has very little affinity with the *Sal Ammoniacum* of Solfatara. Mr. Geoffroy at Paris makes his *Sal Armoniac* of human urine mixt with fea-falt, which is not at all inferior to that of the Levant. He alfo makes it of bone, horn, blood, &c. The Englifh falts, as they are called, are nothing but the volatile falt of the *Sal Ammoniacum* brought from the Levant.

or

Near the City of NAPLES.

or crowns. The greatest part of it belongs to the hospital of the Annunciata at Naples, and the remainder to the bishop of Puzzuolo. The steam or vapour issuing from these apertures of the Solfatara is said to be serviceable in a great many disorders. The soil hereabouts is so light and hollow that it is dangerous to use a horse in this excursion. Upon a spot betwixt the place where the sulphur-stones are dug and the alum-huts, I caused a hole to be dug to the depth of a foot and a half, and a stone of about fifteen or twenty pounds weight to be thrown into it. This was immediately attended with a rumbling noise under ground, like the explosion of cannon at a distance; and from the continuance of the noise and reverberations it might easily be inferred, that it passed through a great number of caverns. It is not seldom that the effluvia of the Solfatara reach as far as Naples to the great prejudice of marble and silver utensils. The ancients, misled by the fables of their poets, held that some rebellious giants were thrown into the abyss under the Solfatara, and that the fumes issuing from the earth are caused by their eructations. The historian Dio himself (*lib.* lxvi.) says, that these giants appeared in great numbers both by day and night, which was a presage of some terrible eruption of Vesuvio. Even the light of Christianity has not expelled these chimera's; only the giants are turned into spirits or ghosts, said often to appear in these parts making most dismal lamentations. These ridiculous stories are now current in both city and country; for the vulgar believe, that those apertures are spiracles, if not of hell, at least of purgatory; and these idle notions are carefully promoted by a Capuchin convent in the neighbourhood, the people being thereby rendered more tractable. The church of this convent is built on the place where St. Januarius is said to have been beheaded.

There is always a great heat felt in this church, which is principally emitted from some holes near the high altar. A good marble bust representing St. Januarius is to be seen here, which is said to be done by a pagan artist, only from the bare description given of the saint by those devout matrons who gathered up his blood; and this bust serves for an original to all painters and sculptors in making the statues and portraits of St. Januarius. In the year 1697, cardinal Giacomo Cantelmi decorated the high altar with a beautiful basso-relievo of the martyrdom of that saint.

marginalia: Capuchin convent and church. Bust of St. Januarius.

A great

Antiquities and Natural Curiosities

Salt-petre. A great quantity of salt-petre is to be seen on the walls of the vestry. That the monks may be provided with cool and wholsome water, their refervoir stands upon a pillar, inclosed within a wall, out of the reach of the warm and sulphureous exhalations; which are farther guarded against by a cavity underneath the ciftern, lined with stone and filled with water, which intercepts the warm vapours as they arise. The garden belonging to this convent is planted with beautiful hedges of myrtle; there is likewise shewn in it the entrance of a cave, which is said to reach from Puzzuolo to the Lago d'Agnano.

Il Colifeo. Near this church of St. Januarius is an amphitheatre, commonly called il Colifeo, and said to have stood formerly within the city of Puzzuolo, but is now near an Italian mile from it. This is a proof of the great decay of this town from its former extent and splendor. This amphitheatre is built with brick; the figure of it is oval, being a hundred and seventy-two feet in its longest, and eighty-eight feet in its shortest diameter. It has suffered very much from earthquakes; however, the two lowest galleries are still in pretty good condition. Here, it is said, St. Januarius and his companions were thrown to be devoured by wild beasts; but the latter were, it seems, not wanting in respect due to such holy personages, and never offered to lay a paw on them.

St. Januarius's prifon. At the entrance of St. Januarius's prison, now converted into a chapel, is an inscription, signifying that it was consecrated by the bishop of Puzzuolo in 1689, and promising an indulgence of forty days to those who devoutly visit that sacred spot in this amphitheatre.

St. James's church. Close by the Colifeo is a church dedicated to St. James, in which, according to Sarnelli, the following ancient inscription on marble was dug up:

Near the City of NAPLES.

Pro Salute
Imp. Cæsaris Titi Aelii
Hadriani Antonini Aug. Pii PP. &
M. Aelii Aurelii Cæsaris N.
Genio Coloniæ Puteolanorum
Chrysanthus Aug. Disp. a frumento
Puteolis & Ostis
L. D. Decurionum permissu.

†
Felicitati perpetuæ temporis
D. N. Valentiniani
Victoris ac Triumphatoris
Semper Aug.
Avianus Valentinianus
V. C. Consul Companiæ
Devotus Numini
Majestatique ejus.

Ancient inscription.

Within a small distance of the amphitheatre are a great number of subterraneous vaults running into each other which are commonly called a labyrinth; but by the learned supposed to have been a reservoir to serve the city of Puzzuolo with water. To every one of these apartments there are four doors, which makes the place extremely intricate; and, did not the almost total ruin of these subterraneous vaults obstruct the way, a person who would venture into them without a guide, would be in danger of losing himself among so many turnings and windings.

Ancient reservoir.

A little further, towards Puzzuolo is an arched vault, which likewise seems to have been a reservoir; it is supported by eleven pillars which are incrusted with tartar, and at present is a wine-cellar. About this spot a great many ancient tombs have been discovered, and likewise the remains of some pagan temples, supposed to have been dedicated to Diana and Neptune; but antiquarians are not agreed about it.

Puzzuolo is eight Italian miles distant from Naples, and takes its Latin name *Puteoli*, either from a sulphureous stench, or from the great number of *putei* or holes which are made here on account of the sulphur works, and by digging for sand, which in ancient times was found very serviceable for building, especially under water *. This city stands

Puzzuolo.

* Senec. Nat. Quæst. lib. iii, c. 20. Plin. lib. xxxv. c. 13. *Quis enim satis*

stands on an acclivity, and the great quantity of beautiful stones and gems cast up by the sea is a sufficient proof of its former splendor and magnificence. The greatest part indeed of these stones are of a blue or red cast, with several pieces of *verde-antico*, porphyry, &c. and seem to have been used in mosaic work; there are frequently found among them agate, cornelian, amethyst, jasper, onyx, beryl, *lapis-lazuli*, &c. and many of them cameos's or intaglio's. But whether antiquarians may with sufficient reason conclude from hence, that in the time of the ancient Romans a great number of goldsmiths and jewellers resided here, I will not take upon me to determine. This however is certain, that Cicero in his epistle to Atticus, *lib.* v. *ep.* 2, makes mention of the *Emporium Puteolanorum*. This city has been very much damaged by the ravages of war, inundations and earthquakes; particularly from an earthquake in 1538, as appears from an inscription over the garden gate belonging to the palace of Toledo:

Petrus Toletus Marchio Villæ Franciæ, Caroli V. *Imper. in Regno Neap. Vicarius, ut Puteolanos ob recentem agri conflagrationem palantes ad pristinas sedes revocaret, hortos, portus, & fontes marmoreos ex spoliis, quæ Garsia filius, partâ victoriâ Africanâ, reportaverat, otio genioque dicavit; ac, antiquorum restaurato purgatoque ductu, aquas sitientibus civibus suâ impensâ restituit. Anno a partu Virginis M.D.XL.*

' Don Pedro di Toledo, marquis of Villa Franca, vice-
' roy of Naples under the emperor Charles V, that he might
' restore to their former settlement the inhabitants of Puz-
' zuolo dispersed by the late conflagration of their country,
' dedicated to ease and pleasure the garden and havens of
' this city, together with the marble fountains, and the

satis miretur, pessimam ejus (terræ) partem ideoque pulverem appellatum in Puteolanis, collibus opponi maris fluctibus, mersumque protinus fieri lapidem inexpugnabilem undis, & fortiorem quotidie, utique si Cumano misceatur camento; i. e. ' Who can sufficiently admire, that the worst part
' of the soil in the mountains of Puteoli, which is therefore call-
' ed dust or sand, should be made into a bulwark against the sea; and
' when sunk under water should soon become a stone, impregnable by the
' waves, and every day grow stronger; especially if it be mixed with Cu-
' mean cement. Commonly this red sand is called Puzzuolano, and is
' also found in other places.'

' spoils

Near the City of NAPLES.

'spoils of his son Garsia's victory in Africa *; and, having
' repaired and cleansed the ancient aqueducts at his own
' expence, restored water to the distressed inhabitants.
' 1540.'

In the piazza di Don Pedro di Toledo is the following
inscription on marble relating to the Puzzuolo baths:

> Carolo II. Austriaco Regnante,
> Providentiâ
> Petri Antonii Aragonii Proregis,
> Neapoli
> Egenis hospitio,
> Naufragis portu,
> Hic
> Infirmis, restitutis thermis,
> Subvenit:
> Sic
> Una pietas
> Triplici flagello triumphat.
> Salubritatem sitientes,
> Ad has aquas trans Puteolos manantes accurrite;
> Quarum virtutes in substrato lapide contractè,
> In volumine Thermologiæ Aragoniæ,
> A Sebastiano Bartolo elucubrato,
> Et Neapoli impresso Ann. Dom. M. DC. LXIIX.
> Plenius legantur.

' In the reign of Charles II, of Austria, the bounty of
' Pedro Antonio of Aragon, vice-roy, provided an hospital
' for the poor, and a port for the shipwrecked of Naples;
' and here, by repairing the baths, relieved the sick; thus
' the stream of his benevolence flows in three branches to
' relieve the necessities of the inhabitants. Ye who thirst
' after health repair quickly to these waters that flow through
' Puzzuolo, the virtues of which, briefly exhibited in the
' stone underneath, may be read at large in the *Thermo-*
' *logia Aragonia* of Sebastiano Bartoli, printed at Naples in
' 1668.'

* These words particularly allude to a small pillar with an Arabic inscription which D. Garsia brought out of Egypt and set up in the garden
belonging to the Toledo palace.

VOL. III.   K   In

130   ANTIQUITIES and Natural CURIOSITIES

Antique statue. In this square is also a fountain adorned with a fine statue of St. Januarius, and an ancient Roman statue which was dug up without the city, behind the garden of the above-mentioned palace of Toledo in 1704. The last piece stands on a pedestal of five *palmi*, and is nine *palmi* high; it is of fine marble, and represents a Roman nobleman in a *Toga*. The following ancient inscription is to be seen under it:

Inscription.
Mavortii
Q. Flavio Mæsio Egnatio Lolliano C. V. Q. K. Prætori Urbano, Auguri Publico Populi Romani Quiritium Conf. Albei Tiberis & Cloacarum, Conf. Operum Public. Conf. Aquarum, Conf. Camp. Comiti Flaviali*, Comiti Orientis, Comiti primi ordinis & Proconsuli Provinciæ Africæ, collectus Decatresfemum Patrono dignissimo posuerunt.

A few days after this statue had been dug up in this piazza or area, was found another, representing a young man in a Roman *Toga*; it is only five *palmi* in height without the pedestal, on which is the following inscription:

Mavortii Jun.
Q. Flavio Maesio Cornelio
Egnatio Severo Lolliano
C. P. Q. K.
Decatrenses Clientes ejus
Patrono Præstantissimo
Posuerunt.

According to Parrini, several urns and old coins were likewise discovered near this piece of antiquity.

Monument of the emperor Tiberius. Near the house of Signior Magliarese in the above-mentioned Piazza di Toledo, was dug up, in 1693, a pedestal of white marble, seven *palmi* in breadth, and five and a half high. Upon it are fourteen figures in basso-relievo, which, according to the opinion of some learned men, represent so many cities in Asia Minor, to which the emperor Tiberius, as we are told by Suetonius, in the forty-eighth chapter of his life, sent very liberal supplies, when they were demolished by an earthquake. Under some of the figures are still legible the names Philadelphia, Tmolus, Cyme, Hierocæsarea, Mostene, Ephesus, Myrina, Cibyra, and Temnos;

* Puzzuolo was from its restorer also called *Colonia Flavia Vespasiana.*

the

Near the City of NAPLES.

the others muſt have been Ægæ, Cumæ, Apollonia, and Hircania. Euſebius, in his *Chronicon*, ſpeaks of thirteen cities that were deſtroyed, and ſpecifies the names of them, but very erroneouſly. Tacitus, *Ann.* ii. *c.* 47. Pliny, *lib.* ii. *c.* 84. and Seneca, *Nat. Quæſt. lib.* vi. *c.* 1. mention only twelve. Oroſius, and after him Cæſar Baronius, fix the time of this calamity at our Saviour's crucifixion. But the twelve cities were deſtroyed in the night, and, according to Tacitus, in the third year of the emperor Tiberius's reign, which was about fourteen years after the death of our Saviour. Upon one ſide of the pedeſtal is the following inſcription between two of the figures mentioned above:

> *Ti. Cæſari Divi*
> *Auguſti F. Divi*
> *Julii N. Auguſto*
> *Pontif. Maximo Coſ. IIII.*
> *Imp. VIII. Trib. poteſtat. XXXII.*
> *Auguſtales*
> *Republica*
> *Reſtituit.*

Probably the ſtatue of Tiberius, that ſtood on this pedeſtal, lies under or near ſignior Magliareſe's houſe. The diſcovery of theſe remains of antiquity was made by digging a ciſtern for keeping oil. Gronovius and Fabretti have communicated their explanations of this baſſo-relievo, &c. to the learned world; the former, in a particular treatiſe printed at Leyden, and the latter in his collection of inſcriptions.

A little way from the cathedral in the wall of a houſe occupied by one Calzola, there are four monumental inſcriptions of Turks or Saracens cut on marble in Arabic characters. The firſt died in the year of Chriſt 1079, the ſecond in 1181, the third in 1182, and the fourth in 1285. According to the learned Benedictine, Montfaucon, theſe prolix inſcriptions contain, beſides particulars of the perſons to whoſe memory they are erected, many ſentences out of the Alcoran, concerning death and a future ſtate.

Sepulchral inſcriptions of Turks.

The cathedral of Puzzuolo is built with large blocks of marble, and was converted from a pagan temple into a Chriſtian church. Over the frontiſpiece is the following ancient inſcription:

Cathedral.

Calphurnius L. F. Templum Auguſto cum ornamentis.

132   Antiquities and Natural Curiosities

Statue of St. Januarius. It is now dedicated to St. Proculus and St. Januarius, whose statues of marble stand in the middle of the church, with inscriptions. Under the statue of St. Januarius is the following:

> *Urbis Liberatori Patronoque amantissimo*
> *Divo Januario,*
> *Qui, postquam in eodem sui Martyrii loco*
> *Dicatum sibi Templum fuit,*
> *Publici memor obsequii,*
> *Suos Puteolos a sepulchralibus flammis*
> *Assiduisque telluris motibus*
> *Ardente adhuc Vesuvio M. DC. XXXI.*
> *Servavit immunes;*
> *Noluit enim, tremeret solum suo firmatum sanguine;*
> *Noluit flagraret Hospitium sui triumphi laureâ decoratum.*
> *Grati animi ergo*
> *Hoc in sua Cathed. monimentum erexit*
> *Idem D. Fr. Martinus de Leon & Cardenas,*
> *Summi Pontificis Assistens,*
> *Atque Catholicæ Majestatis a latere status Consiliarius,*
> *Secundâ hujus instauratione Basilicæ*
> *Idibus Octobris MDCXLVII.*

' To the deliverer of the city, and its most propitious
' patron, St. Januarius, who, after a church had been de-
' dicated to him on the very spot where he was martyred, in
' regard of that public mark of veneration, preserved his
' Puzzuolo from destructive flames and earthquakes during
' the dreadful inflammation of Vesuvio in 1631, being un-
' willing that the ground, which was rendered firm and
' stable by his blood, should tremble; or that a place deco-
' rated with the laurels of his triumph over death should be
' consumed with fire. Dr. Fr. Martini de Leon and Car-
' denas, &c. in gratitude for the saint's protection, erected
' this monument the 15th of October, 1647, &c.'

At the entrance of the church, on the left-hand, is a beautiful altar of inlaid work, with a very costly tabernacle, in which *lapis-lazuli* has not been spared. On the high altar the beheading of St. Januarius is extremely well painted. Puzzuolo, antiently Puteoli, values itself as having been honoured with the first Christian community in Italy;

St.

Near the City of NAPLES.

St. Paul *, in his journey to Rome, having found brethren there.

The harbour of Puzzuolo is very commodious, and is formed by fourteen piers, or pilasters, rising above the surface of the water, which were anciently joined together by arches. The nearest pilaster on the Puzzuolo side consists of large blocks of that sort of stone called *piperno*, but faced with brick-work; and the interstices are filled up with a very hard mortar or cement, which is, undoubtedly, mixed up with *Puzzuolano*, or the Puzzuolo sand. On the sides of these pilasters are vast stones, with holes in them, for fastening ships, &c. The force of the waves is very much broken against these piers; and many judge them better for securing a harbour than a continuous mole, as in the former the accumulation of sand is not to be apprehended, the waves washing it back again through the intervals between the pilasters. From the ruinous arch-work some have been induced to look upon these pilasters as the remains of a bridge; and the common people usually call it *il ponte di Caligola*, as if it were the ruins of the bridge built by that emperor from Puzzuolo to Bajæ. This error, which Burnet has given into, Suetonius *(in vit. Calig. c. 19.)* very plainly refutes; where he says, that what Caligula built was no more than a bridge of boats covered with earth, and reaching from Bajæ to the Puzzuolo mole; so that the piers in the sea before Puzzuolo is not only plainly distinguished by that author from the moveable bridge of Caligula, but he has likewise called it by the name of *moles*, which is even now applied to any congeries of rocks or stone that serves for the security of an harbour. That the pilasters in the sea before Puzzuolo did not belong to a bridge is likewise apparent from hence, that they are not placed in a straight line, but form a curve towards the north. Lastly, it is manifest, from the following inscription found entire in the sea, near this place, in the year 1575, that the above-mentioned pilasters are no remains of any of Caligula's follies:

_{Harbour of fourteen pilasters in the sea.}

* Acts, chap. xxviii. ver. 13, 14.

Imp. Cæsar. Divi. Hadriani. Fil.
Divi. Trajani. Parthici. Nepos.
Divi. Nervæ. Pronepos. T. Aelius.
Hadrianus. Antoninus. Aug. Pius.
Pont. Max. Trib. Pot. II. *Cos.* II.
Desig. III. *Opus Pilarum* VI. *

Now what necessity was there to repair (as the inscription intimates) at a vast expence, a work so far from being of any adequate advantage, that it only kept up the remembrance of the infamous Caligula's madness. This stone is at present fixed over the gate of Puzzuolo, with the following inscription superadded to it:

Quem lapidem Antoninus Imp. statuerat, vetustas dejecerat, mare atque arena obduxerant, Francifcus Murillus Regiæ Classis Curator suâ impensâ eductum Puteolanis municipibus pari studio restituit. A. D. MDLXXV.

' The stone erected by the emperor Antoninus time had
' thrown down, and the sea-water, sand, &c. covered, till
' Francesco Murillo, &c. caused it, at his own expence, to
' be removed and restored to the citizens of Puzzuolo in the
' year 1575.'

Mr. Addison, in his travels through Italy, quotes from Julius Capitolinus, *in vita Antonini Pii*, an inscription, in which the city of Puzzuolo celebrates this emperor, alledging, *Quòd super cætera beneficia ad hujus etiam tutelam portûs, Pilarum viginti molem cum sumptu fornicum reliquo ex ærario suo largitus est.* ' That, besides his other benefactions, he
' likewise bestowed money out of his treasury for building a
' mole of twenty pilasters with arches, for the security of
' this harbour. But probably Mr. Addison, trusting to Sarnelli's quotation, has ascribed to Capitolinus what is not to be found in his life of that emperor. This last-mentioned author only says, that Antoninus Pius assisted several cities with money, in order to build new public works, or to re-

---

* Seneca, *Epist.* 77, likewise calls them *pilæ*, or pilasters; and, according to his description, one might conveniently walk round them, and see all the ships coming in and going out of the harbour.

pair

Near the City of NAPLES,

pair such as had fallen to decay; and this is all that can be inferred from him concerning this work at Puzzuolo.

As to the above-mentioned inscription, it rests only on Pighi's credit; who, in his *Hercules Prodicius*, says, that he found here the following inperfect inscription, which had, probably, belonged to a triumphal arch:

```
.... AESARI. DIVI ....
...., IICI. NEPOTI. DIVI ....,
.... ONINO AVG. PIO ....
.... OLONIA. FLAVIA ....
.... VPER CETERA BEN....,
.... VS. PILARUM. VIG.....
.... QVO. ET. MVNITION....,
```

Which may be restored in the following manner:

Imp. cAESARI. DIVI. Hadriani. Filio. Divi. Trajani, PartHICI. NEPOTI. DIVI, Nervæ. Pron. T, Ael. Hadriano. AntONINO. AVG. PIO. Pont. Max. Trib. Pot. Coss. p. p. coLONIA. FLAVIA. Aug. Puteolanorum. Quod. sVPER. CETERA. BENeficia. ad, hujus. etiam, tut;lam. portVS,, PILARVM. VIGinti. molem. cum. sumptu. fornicum. reliQVO. ET. MVNITION. ex. ærario. suo. largitus. sit.

Formerly the pilasters that appeared above the surface of the water were twenty-five in number; but at present most of them do not appear above the water, and some have been totally demolished and washed away by the agitation of the waves.

The sea about Puzzuolo abounds in fish, especially of the testaceous kind. Here is also a fish called Cavallo Marino, which is not quite an inch in length, and is generally dried for keeping. The head of this little fish very much resembles that of a horse: it is often bruised with vinegar and honey, and applied by way of plaister to the part bitten by a mad dog; and the women eat them to procure a good breast of milk, and likewise apply them to the breast as an anodyne. This species of fish is also found on the other side of Italy, along the coast of the Adriatic; but not in such abundance as they are here.

The road on the right-hand, by the Grotto del Cane and Lago Agnano, is not the nearest way from the grotto of Pausilypo to Puzzuolo, but that which turns off on the left to-

Cavallo Marino.

Antiquities and Natural Curiosities

wards the sea, and runs along the coast: besides it is broader and pleasanter, as well as shorter than the other road. The barren mountain of Olivano lies on the right-hand of this road, and it is with a pleasing surprize a traveller sees a country, which was once only the dreary haunt of sea-fowls, &c. so greatly improved with a road extremely commodious for carriages and horses. The æra of this alteration was the year 1571, which is commemorated in an inscription erected on the road.

<small>Monte Olivano.</small>

There are several hot baths along the coast, impregnated with alum, copper, and iron. On a spot about five hundred paces from Puzzuolo, near the sea, persons labouring under the gout or rheumatism are laid in a hole, dug in the ground for that purpose, according to the size of the patient, and about two feet deep; where the whole body, especially the part affected, is covered with the sand which came out of the hole, and, when it is too hot, they cool it by pouring some sea-water on it. This method, if often repeated, seldom fails of abating the violence, if not totally expelling the disease.

<small>Hot baths.</small>

The remains of antiquity hitherto described in this letter should be seen the first day, and the following should be reserved for the journey to Cuma, and the other neighbouring places. Without an antiquarian for his guide, a foreigner would be at a loss; but they easily are to be met with in these parts. The first day is taken up with the grotto of Pausilypo, and the second spent in and about Puzzuolo. The usual gratification to an antiquarian for his trouble is from ten to fifteen *carlini* *.

Just without Puzzuolo are the ruins of an ancient structure, said to be the *villa* or *academia Ciceroniana*, where the body of the emperor Adrian was deposited till the senate of Rome built a temple at Puzzuolo for his interment †. According to Pliny, *Hist. Nat. lib.* xxxi. c. 2, this seat, remarkable for its fine portico and grove, stood near the sea, betwixt Puzzuolo and the Lago d'Averno. After Cicero's death it came into the possession of C. Antistius.

<small>Cicero's villa.</small>

At present this celebrated *academia* is converted into a cowhouse. Not far from it are some of the ruins of an old structure, which passes for Lentulus's seat.

---

* About four or five shillings.

† *Vid. Aelius Spartianus in vita Hadriani, ad finem.*

Near the City of NAPLES.

Gauri, a mountain in this neighbourhood, and in Juvenal, Sidonius Apollinaris, Galen, and Statius, highly celebrated for its wine, is at present a barren spot, and called il Monte Barbaro; but whether this proceeds from the degeneracy of the soil, or the long possession of the Saracens, is uncertain. However, the Franciscans have a convent upon this hill, which affords a glorious prospect. The vulgar here are possessed with a notion that immense treasures lie buried in this mountain; but guarded by evil spirits, whose favour not a few endeavour to procure by incantations, &c.

Mount Gauri.

Directly opposite to il Monte Barbaro, towards the west, lies il Monte Nuovo, or the new mountain, which rose instantaneously in the night between the nineteenth and twentieth of September, 1538, during an earthquake, which caused a terrible devastation in the neighbourhood. The subterraneous fire, after making a wide chasm in this place, ejected such a quantity of stones, ashes, sulphur, and sand, as within twenty-four hours formed this mountain; the perpendicular height of which is not less than four hundred rods, and the circumference is three Italian miles. Gieronimo Borgia, who saw the new mountain soon after its first appearance, and wrote a poem on it, dedicated to Paul III, says, that the height of it was thirty *stadia*. Several fields, houses, cattle, and men were destroyed by this earthquake and eruption; and even the sea was strongly impregnated with sulphur, and suddenly ebbed away above two hundred paces, and left the shore covered with dead fish. The edge or brink of the original chasm is still to be discerned on the mountain, though it be almost filled up; and its circuit could not be less than an Italian mile. No fire, sand, or stone, is known to have been ejected since the first formation of the mountain. Gassendi in his *Physica, sect.* iii. *membr.* i. *lib.* i. *c.* 6. *p.* 50. *Oper. tom.* ii, thinks it to have been the effects of an earthquake: his words are as follows:

Il Monte Nuovo.

Mirabilius videri potest, enasci ex opposito non modo in continentibus montes, sed etiam in medio mari insulas. Nam de montibus quidem facit fidem PVTEOLANVS ILLE, quem Simon Portius ita describit, ut fuerit unâ nocte ad plus quam M. Passuum altitudinem ex pumicibus cineribusque congestus, id nempe sub finem Septembris anno M. D. XXXVIII.

' It may seem still more wonderful, that not only mountains shoot up in the continent, but even islands in the
' middle

'middle of the sea. As to mountains, nothing can be more
'notorious than that of Puzzuolo, which, according to
'Simon Portio's account of it, was, in one night, towards
'the end of September 1538, formed by a congeries of
'pumice-stones and ashes to the height of above a thousand
'paces.'

But, though this alteration happened at the time of an earthquake, it was not caused by it; earthquakes indeed often overturn mountains, but never produce any; to do this, the eruption of a vulcano is required. The passage in Gassendi, quoted above, led Bernier in his *Abregè de la Philosophie de Gassendi*, tom. v. *p.* 127. edit. de Lion 1684, into a very pleasant mistake, where, of *Puteolanus* [*scilicet mons* *] he makes an author. Such errors, however ridiculous, are not uncommon in many authors. Coiffeteau, in book iii, chap, xviii. of his translation of L. Florus, makes the city of Corfinium a general of that name. Antony Pinet, in his French translation of Pliny, by a strange metamorphosis converts two kinds of marble, one of which was called *lapis Numidicus*, and the other *Sinandicus*, into two cavaliers. The French translator of Bongar's letters mistakes the Altorff academy for one monsieur Altorff; whereas he might easily have been better informed from Thuanus. Ludovicus à Santo Carolo in his *Bibliotheca Pontificia*, published at Lyons in 1643, takes *Articulus Smalcaldicus* to be a Lutheran author supposed to have written against the power and supremacy of the pope. Du Fer, the famous French geographer, has translated *Deserta Loca* in Witzen's map of Tartary by *Deserts des Loques*. A like sagacity gave its origin to the island of Uspiam in some French maps of America; the geographers mistaking the words of our historian, *Gallis detecta insula uspiam in America*. The learned Menken himself, in his preface to his ingenious book *de Charlataneria Eruditorum*, mentions Bayle's *Calendarium Carlananum* as a satire levelled against quackery, in French *Charlatanerie*; whereas it owes its name to Carla, a little town in the county of Foix, which was Bayle's native place. How often foreigners confound the dutchy of Wurtemberg with the town of Wittemberg in the electorate of Saxony is sufficiently known. Mallet places the county of Reuss in the dutchy of Mecklenberg. Ma-

Flagrant mistakes of authors.

* The author says, *Terræ Motus*, whereas *mons* is the word understood.

dame

Near the City of NAPLES.

dame Scuderi brings in a Turkish bashaw embarking at Constantinople, in order to sail to the Caspian sea within twenty days. Madame de Montmorency, in the year 1672, informs count Bussy Rabutin, that the Brandenburg forces were obliged to retreat; the Turks having made an irruption into the duchy of Prussia, and taken Kaminieck *.

But to return to my subject. It is farther to be observed, that by the eruption of this new mountain, besides the destruction of the suburbs and the hospital of Tripergola †, the greatest part also of the Lago Lucrino, or Lucrine lake, was filled up, so that at present it has scarce any water; whereas among the ancients it was in great repute for its fish, especially oysters ‡. Pliny, *Nat. Hist. lib.* ix. *c.* 8. *Solinus, cap.* 17. and others, relate a remarkable story of a dolphin, which in Augustus's time appeared in the Lucrine lake, and was made so tame by a boy, that he would sit upon him, and used frequently to cross the lake on the dolphin's back from Bajæ to Puteoli. Augustus, according to Suetonius, by means of a canal, joined the Averno and Lucrine lakes with the Tyrrhene sea, and made the Portus Julius near Bajæ (employing twenty thousand men in these works ‖) which are thus celebrated by Virgil:

Lacus Lu-
crinus.

Tame dolphin.

* *Lettres de Bussy, tom.* ii. *p.* 325. What is still more extraordinary, in the year 1683, the grand vizier loudly complained to the French ambassador at the Porte, that France had given the Poles free passage through their country to facilitate their junction with the Imperialists.
† On a dispute betwixt the city of Puzzuolo and the Casa Santa della Annunciata, about rebuilding this hospital a great number of eye-witnesses were heard concerning the particulars of the eruption of Monte Nuovo in 1538, which served to put the fact itself beyond all doubt. These records are to be found in the episcopal archives at Puzzuolo.
‡ *Senec. Epist.* lxxviii. *Horat. Epod. Od.* 2.

Non me Lucrina juverint conchylia.

' Not Lucrine oysters would my palate please.'

Plin. Hist. Nat. lib. ix. *c.* 54. *Sergius Orata - - primus optimum saporem ostreis Lucrinis adjudicavit,* ' Sergius Orata was the first who distinguished the delicate flavour of the oysters of the Lucrine lake.'
‖ In *Vit. Octav. cap.* 16. *viginti servorum millibus manumissis & ad remum datis portum Julium apud Bajas, immisso in Lucrinum & Avernum Lacunt mari, effecit.*

An

*An memorem portus, Lucrinoque addita clauſtra:
Atque indignatum magnis ſtridoribus æquor,
Julia qua ponto longe ſonat unda refuſo,
Tyrrheniſque fretis immittitur æſtus Avernis!*
VIRG. Georg. lib. ii. v. 161.

' Or ſhall I praiſe thy ports, or mention make
' Of the vaſt mound that binds the Lucrine lake,
' Or the diſdainful ſea that, ſhut from thence,
' Roars round the ſtructure and invades the fence.
' There, where ſecure, the Julian waters glide,
' Or where Avernus' jaws admit the Tyrrhene tide.'
DRYDEN.

Some think that theſe lines intimate, that Auguſtus only contracted the paſſage and checked the influx of the ſea into the Lucrine lake, in order to put a ſtop to the damages which the fiſhery ſuffered from its impetuoſity. The great change which happened in this neighbourhood in 1538, and by which the Monte Nuovo was produced, has alſo choaked up this canal; ſo that at preſent the lake is ſeparated from the ſea by a ſlip of land fifty or ſixty paces in breadth.

The way to Cuma lies betwixt Monte Barbaro and Monte Nuovo, the former being on the right, and the latter on the left hand. About half a mile from the Lucrine lake, on the left-hand, is the Lago Averno, which, like the mountain Gauri, is exceedingly altered, but much for the better. According to ancient hiſtorians, no fiſh could live in this lake; and its noxious vapours aſcended to ſuch a height, that birds flying over it dropt down dead. Hence it is ſaid to have been called ἄορνος. Lucret. *lib.* vi. ſpeaks thus of it:

*Principio, quod Averna vocant, non nomen id abs re
Impoſitum eſt; quia ſunt avibus contraria cunctis* *.

Lago Averno.

---

* See Silius Ital. *lib.* xii. Pliny and Varro. That nothing of this kind is now ſeen at Averno, is no proof that it never was ſo, as the ſulphureous or other noxious effluvia which produced ſuch effects in this lake may by earthquakes or other accidents have been obſtructed.

' Next

' Next of Averno sung, and whence the name,.
' And whence the rage and hurtful nature came;
' So call'd, becaufe the birds that cut the fky,
' If o'er thofe places they but chance to fly
' By noxious fteams opprefs'd, fall down and die.'
                                                    CREECH.

This lake is at prefent ftocked with variety of good fifh, and the birds not only fly over it unhurt, but wild ducks and other aquatic fowls are to be feen upon it; and the adjacent vine-yards produce a very good fort of wine. Servius *(ad Æneid.* iii. *v.* 442.) afcribes the noxious air about this lake in ancient times to the thick and lofty woods that then furrounded it, which hindered the difperfion of the effluvia; adding, that, Auguftus having ordered the wood to be cut down and extirpated, the country foon put on a chearful appearance. This lake in fome places is a hundred and eighty feet deep. Boccacio * tells us, that about three hundred years ago its water fuddenly became fo vitiated, poffibly from the burfting of a vein of fulphur, &c. that moft of the fifhes in it died. As for the ruinous temple of Mercury and Neptune near the fea, and alfo the entrance into the fibyl's cave, which lies on the other fide, I fhall take notice of them in the fequel, as it is moft convenient to vifit them in returning from Bajæ.

Nero was for making a broad and navigable canal from the lake Averno to Oftia, of which fome traces are ftill remaining; but it was never finifhed †.

Betwixt Averno and the city of Cuma is to be feen a part Arco Felice. of the Via Appia, where two hills are joined by means of a noble arch called Arco Felice, built with large bricks; its height is feventy, and its breadth fifty-five feet; the paffage under it is twenty feet four inches.

After paffing the Arco Felice, a narrow way leads to the The giant's remains of a temple, which, as the deity to whom it was temple.

---

* In his book *de Lacubus*.
† *Sueton. in vit. Neron. c.* 31. *Inchoavit - - - foffam ab Averno Oftiam ufque, ut navibus nec tamen mari iretur, longitudine per centum fexaginta millia: latitudinis, qua contrariæ quinqueremes commearent.* ' He began
' a canal from Averno to Oftia for a convenient water-paffage betwixt
' thofe places, without going by fea, a hundred and fixty miles in length,
' and of a breadth fufficient for gallies with five branches of oars to pafs by
' one another.' *Vide Tacit. Annal.* xv. *c.* 42. *Plin. lib.* xiv.

confecrated

consecrated is not known, is called il Tempio del Gigante. The arched roof of it is divided into small square compartments, like those in the temple of Peace at Rome, and plates of gold or silver, and other ornaments, seem to have been once fixed in them. This temple is thirty-six *palmi* in length, above thirty in breadth, and about forty in height. The colossus which stands at Naples, not far from the Darsena, called il Gigante di Palazzo, supposed to have been a Jupiter Terminalis, is said to have been dug up near the front of this temple.

Not far from this temple, on the left-hand, is an ancient edifice ninety-six *palmi* in length, and twenty-six in breadth, with an aperture in the roof to admit the light, which, from the many niches in the sides, where probably the urns with the ashes of the dead were set, is looked upon to have been a pagan sculpture.

This country affords several other remains of antiquity worth a traveller's notice; among which the antique statues, which contribute so much to the grandeur of the yet-unfinished university at Naples, are to be reckoned.

Cuma. The greatest part of the ancient city of Cuma, with its magnificent temple of Apollo, was situated on a hill which afforded a beautiful and extensive prospect. This city, celebrated in the times of the ancient Romans, is now reduced to a heap of ruins *.

The country still retains a luxuriant fertility, especially towards Torre di Patria, where it produces abundance of fig-trees of an uncommon size. The name of di Patria applied to this tower, is said to be derived from the second word in the following line, which Scipio Africanus ordered to be put upon his monument:

Scipio Africanus's tomb.

Ingrata Patria, ne quidem ossa mea habes.

'Ungrateful Rome, thou dost not possess so much as my bones.'

* That it was a very populous city in Lucan's time, appears from the following passage in that poet:

——— *Acidaliâ quæ condidit Alite muros*
Euboicam referens fœcunda Neapolis urbem.

'Where the fam'd walls of fruitful Naples lie,
'That may for multitudes with Cumæ vie.'

This

Near the City of NAPLES.

This place was anciently called Linternum; and, when it was besieged by the Vandals in 455, this tower was built on the spot where stood the great Scipio's tomb; and the word *patria* being all that was then legible on the monument, gave name to the new tower.

Near the city of Cuma is a very large reservoir, with a lofty arch over it, in which are several apertures, like wells, for drawing out the water. It is built of free-stone, and at present is quite empty. As far as can be conjectured from the sound caused by stamping with the foot against the bottom, there is another cavity under it.   *Reservoir.*

On the opposite side, towards the sea-coast, is the entrance of a cave, said formerly to have been the abode of the Cumæan Sibyl. If the antiquarians may be credited, this cave extends three Italian miles in length to the Lago Averno, where it has another entrance: but in several parts the passages have been ruined; and at the entrance near Cuma there is no possibility of advancing in it above two hundred paces. This part of it is cut out of a rock, and of a considerable height and breadth. A few years ago the imperial general Wezel caused an aperture with one-and-fifty steps to be cut in the side of the cave, for the conveniency of coming out of it; but the peasants have since stopped it up.   *Sibyl's cave.*

Betwixt Cuma and Miseno lies the lake Acheron, or Palus Acherusia, so well known among the ancients; and from its back water it is, by Virgil, termed *tenebrosa palus*, i. e. ' the gloomy lake.' Its name of Acheron some derive from the Greek ἄνευ χαρας, i. e. ' without joy.' For the increase of its fishery, a canal has been made from the main sea into this lake; by which means the waters of it have been greatly mended, and rendered fitter for fish to live in. Most of the fishermen live upon a little island in the middle of the lake; but the fish they catch are mostly eels and barbels. In the summer great quantities of hemp and flax are mellowed here, which brings in to the Neapolitan hospital of the Annunciata, to which it belongs, a yearly income of eight or nine hundred *scudi*, the sum for which it is usually farmed. At present it is generally called Lago della Coluccia, or del Fusaro.   *Acheron.*

In these parts, as our antiquaries told us, Servilius Vatia, who, under the tyrannical reign of Tiberius, retired from court and business, had a seat; in the ruins of which were found several good inscriptions, which Capaccio has preserved.   *Servilius Vatia's seat.*

preserved. Among others, he gives us the following fragment:

> *Hic est posita Albacia Blesilla*
> *- - - pari sine exemplo Fæmina*
> *Quæ vixit annos XXX. M. V. D. XIX.*
> *Dulcissimæ conjugi fecit - - -*

'Here lies Albacia Blesilla - - - a woman without an equal; who lived thirty years, five months, and nineteen days. Erected to his entirely-beloved spouse - - -'

Under the calamities of Tiberius's intolerable reign, Vatia, on account of the retirement he had chosen, was cried up as the happiest of the Romans; so that it was a common saying, *O Vatia, solus scis vivere;*' O Vatia, thou alone knowest 'how to live.' But Seneca seems to have been of another mind; for he says, in his fifty-fifth epistle: *At ille latere sciebat, non vivere. - - - Nunquam aliter hanc villam Vatia vivo præteribam, quam ut dicerem: Vatia hic situs est.* 'But he 'knew how to lie buried in retirement, rather than how to 'live. - - - I never used to pass by his house, whilst Vatia 'was alive, without saying, Here lies Vatia.'

According to Seneca's account, which is the only one extant, Vatia's seat could not stand on this spot; but must have been much nearer Baiæ, towards the west: *Occurrit Favonio & illum adeo excipit, ut Bajis neget.* 'It faces Favonius, 'so as to intercept it from Baiæ.' Now Pliny, *lib.* ii. *c.* 47, says, that Favonius blows from the *occasu equinoctiali*, or west point. However Seneca, on account of its advantageous situation, honours Vatia's seat so far, as to call it *villa totius anni*, or a pleasant retreat for all the year; whereas persons of quality among the Romans had different seats according to the different seasons: for they resorted to Baiæ only in the cold months, or the spring; but their summer retreats were at Tivoli and Frescati.

Piso's baths. From this place, a narrow road among rocks, and over a steep eminence where a continual guard is kept, leads to the ruins of Lucius Piso's warm baths; or according to others (though, I think, not with sufficient grounds, of a Bay of Baiæ. temple of Diana; and from thence to the delightful bay of Baiæ. In this bay, which is in the form of a crescent, the ships ride in perfect safety. On the sea-shore, facing Baiæ,

Near the City of NAPLES.

is an ancient temple of Mercury *, which may be looked upon as the Pantheon in miniature; for it is not above twenty-five common paces in diameter. It is quite round, with an aperture in the center of the roof for the admiſſion of light: two perſons directly oppoſite to each other, and whiſpering cloſe to the wall, may converſe with each other, without being over-heard by the company in the middle. Beſides the round aperture at the top, this temple has four windows. The pavement at the entrance lies a foot under water, and moſt of it is either overflowed, or covered with rubbiſh; there is alſo a large crack or fiſſure in the cupola.

Not far from this temple, and nearer Baiæ, is an octangular ſhell of a temple of Venus, which is ſeven *palmi* thick, with eight large windows; and its inward circuit is ſeventy-three paces. *Temple of Venus.*

Behind this temple is a dark apartment hewn in a rock, called *la Stanza di Venere*, or Venus's apartment, the roof of which is embelliſhed with baſſo-relievo's. Theſe pieces repreſent nothing obſcene or immodeſt, but only mythological ſtories and emblems, as a man purſuing a woman, a Cupid, ſeveral ſwans, fiſhes, feſtoons, &c. The marquis de Cellemare has ſtript this place of ſome of its beſt pieces, and a Centaur has been carried from hence to France; all theſe ſtatues will be totally disfigured with the ſmoke of the flambeaux which are neceſſarily uſed in ſuch dark receſſes. In a ſide chamber, to which one muſt creep through a hole, is the figure of a tree formed by a kind of ſpar; but by ſome erroneouſly ſuppoſed to be a petrified vegetable. This *Stanza di Venere* lies betwixt the above-mentioned temples of Venus and Mercury. *La Stanza di Venere.*

The voluptuous and licentious manners of the ancient inhabitants of this country are ſufficiently known by the deſcriptions given of them by Martial, Horace, and others †.

The

---

* This temple is alſo called Truglio, from *trullus*, or *trullum*, which ſignifies any building with a circular roof, as may be ſeen, p. 146. *Geſtis Innocentii III. Pontif.* For ſuch an apartment in the imperial palace at Conſtantinople, in which a council of the clergy was held, is known in hiſtory by the appellation of *Synodus Trullana*, or *in Trullo*.

† Seneca, *epiſt.* li, deſcribes it as *Regionem, quam ſapiens vir, aut ad ſapientiam tendens declinet, tanquam alienam bonis moribus --- Videre ebrios per litora errantes, & commeſſationes navigantium, & ſymphoniarum cantibus perſtrepentes lacus, & alia, quæ velut ſoluta legibus luxuria, non tantum peccat, ſed publicet, quid neceſſe eſt? --- Effœminat animos amœnitas nimia: nec dubie, aliquid ad corrumpendum vigorem poteſt regio.* ' A coun-

The monuments still remaining sufficiently shew the ancient splendor and delightfulness of the coast round this bay, where there is now scarce a single house to be seen. It must have once extended itself considerably farther into the sea, since from Baiæ all along to the Promontorium Penatæ, in clear still weather, one may discern under the water a large paved road, and the remains of several magnificent buildings, with grand portico's, &c. As for the city of Baiæ, which stood on this coast, there is not the least remains to be seen of it. The fort lately built here is called Baia, and stands upon a rock; but the air of it is so unwholesome, that the governor takes care every night to lie at Puzzuolo. Sometimes prisoners are brought to the fort of Baia, which is more dreaded than any other prison in Italy.

Baiæ.

After passing a precipice that projects over the sea, you descend again to the shore; where the remains of Hortensius's villa are to be seen. This celebrated orator Cicero jestingly calls Triton, because he had accustomed the fishes in his ponds at this villa, to come at his call, and fed them with his own hand.

Hortensius's villa.

Near Hortensius's villa is shewn an ancient ruin, said to have been the monument of Agrippina, who was put to death by Nero, her own son. Within it, on the left-hand, is an apartment, to which one ascends by a ladder, where are several relievo's of plaster, representing a sphynx, a griffin, and other imaginary animals. A figure of a woman about two feet high to be seen here, passes for Agrippina herself; and adjoining to this is a smaller apartment, where the antiquarians say that her remains were deposited: but with what truth, or even probability, is not easily determined. For Tacitus, *annal.* xiv. *c.* 9, affirms, that, even after the death

Agrippina's tomb.

' try which a man of any wisdom or prudence would avoid, as the bane
' of virtue, and destructive of good morals. - - - Where is the necessity
' or pleasure of seeing drunken people reeling along the shore, or the lake,
' echoing with effeminate music, with the noise of riotous persons sailing
' on it, and other disorders of an unbridled luxury, where they are so far
' from having any sense of shame, that they publish their own infamy?
' - - - Luxuriancy of soil effeminates the mind, and the climate unque-
' stionably conduces something to relax the vigour of the mind and body.'
Propertius calls the coast of Baiæ,

Littora quæ fuerant castis inimica puellis.

――― ' A licentious place
' To chaste and modest virgins dangerous.'

Near the City of NAPLES.

of her unnatural son, the tomb of Agrippina consisted only of an heap of earth thrown together, betwixt Misenum and a *villa* of Julius Cæsar. That this unfortunate princess had a seat in this neighbourhood is unquestionable, as appears from Tacitus; but the same writer points out its situation nearer the Lucrine lake.

Betwixt Baiæ and Cape Miseno are likewise several other remains of antiquity; but the explanations of them are mostly grounded upon uncertain conjectures. Amongst other pieces there has been dug up hereabouts the statue of Venus, twice as big as the life, holding a globe in one hand, and three golden apples in the other; from whence some antiquarians conclude, that Venus Genetrix must have had a temple in this neighbourhood; and, as Julius Cæsar had a country seat near Baiæ *, others still farther alledge, that he founded and built this temple.

On this coast there is likewise an ancient temple called Boalia, a Boaula, or Boalia, ascribed to Hercules, who, according to the ancient fable, brought safe hither the oxen which he had stolen in Spain. Even now a small district here bears the name of Baulo, or Baula, concerning which Silius Italicus says:

     -- *Herculeos videt ipso littore Baulos.*   Lib. xii.

     ' Herculean Bauli founded on that shore
     ' He view'd.'

The antiquarians are at a loss where to look for Bauli, or the *villa* whither Nero conducted his mother, after her coming from Antium. According to Tacitus it must have stood betwixt cape Miseno and the Lago Bajano. Those who distinguish it from Hortensius's *villa* are mistaken, and refuted by the following lines of Symmachus, who himself was afterwards the possessor of that *villa*:

---

* According to Seneca, *epist.* 51, where he also mentions the seats of Marius and Cn. Pompeius on this coast, and approves of their choice of such a delicious country, saying, These heroes, according to their art of war, had built their mansions, like watch-towers, on the tops of mountains. *Vide* Tacit. *Annal.* xiv. c. 9.

*Huc Deus Alcides stabulanda armenta coëgit
Eruta Geryonis de lare tergemini,
Inde recens ætas corrupta Boaulia Baulos
Nuncupat, occulto nominis indicio.
A Divo ad proceres dominos fortuna cucurrit,
Fama loci obscuros ne pateretur heros,
Hanc celebravit, opum felix Hortensius, aulam,
Contra Arpinatem qui stetit eloquio.*

'Hither the god Hercules drove the oxen he had stolen
'from the triple Geryon, to be kept in stalls. From thence
'modern ages, being ignorant of the derivation of the name,
'have erroneously called Boaulia Bauli. From the god it
'descended to illustrious princes, left the fame of the place
'should suffer from obscure possessors; for the powerful Hor-
'tensius, who stood in competition with Cicero for eloquence,
'made this seat famous.'

Elysian-fields.
That the Elysian-fields extend themselves towards the Dead-Sea, is taken for granted; but, as for the exact situation, some look for it about the district of Baula, where at present stands a mean village; and in the wall, built on both sides of the way, are several cavities, in which probably some urns were once deposited. Others place the Elysian-fields near the Mercato del Sabato, as it is called. Others again are positive that the Elysian-fields must have been in the neighbourhood of Cuma. All these spots, the fertility of the soil excepted, which produce delicious fruits and wine, exhibit nothing so beautiful and striking as to deserve the appellation of Elysian-fields.

Il Mercato del Sabato.
Il Mercato del Sabato does not seem to have been a market-place, where things were every Saturday exposed to sale; but rather a *circus* for public spectacles, exercises, &c.

Mare Mortuum.
The Mare Mortuum, or Dead-Sea, has a communication with the sea by a small canal, in which are several wire nets, &c. to prevent the fish, with which it abounds, from returning to the sea. This lake belongs to a private person, who farms it for five or six hundred *scudi* a year.

Promontory of Miseno.
On the other side of the Mare Mortuum, towards the left-hand, lies the promontory of Miseno, where is still to be seen the remains of an ancient *pharos*, or light-house. The isthmus at the extremity near the cape is about two hundred paces in breadth from sea to sea; but farther up, towards
the

Near the City of NAPLES.

the Dead-Sea, it is scarce fifty. Miseno is said to derive its name from a companion of Æneas, who was buried here, according to Virgil:

At pius Æneas ingenti mole sepulchrum
Imponit, suaque arma viro, remumque, tubamque,
Monte sub aërio: qui nunc Misenus ab illo
Dicitur, æternumque tenet per sæcula nomen.
Æneid. vi. v. 232.

' But good Æneas order'd on the shore
' A stately tomb, whose top a trumpet bore,
' A soldier's faulchion, and a seaman's oar.
' Thus was his friend interr'd, and deathless fame
' Still to the lofty cape consigns his name,' DRYDEN.

This promontory is almost entirely undermined, and the Grotta Traconaria, vulgarly called Dragonara, under it, is very well worth observing. It is divided by twelve large pilasters into five walks, or isles. The middle is the broadest, and (besides the entrance, which is sixty-eight feet) is a hundred and seventy-eight feet long; the rest being only a hundred and seventy. They are all of the same height which is twenty feet. The four passages which cut these walks at right angles are of an unequal length, from a hundred and eighty to two hundred and twenty-four feet. The breadth of the walks is about four feet, and the walls are of freestone. The use of such a building is not known with any certainty; but it is most probable that it served for a reservoir of fresh water; which was here the most necessary, part of the Roman fleet being stationed at Miseno †.

There are also many other ruins to be seen here, which shews that this promontory was once covered with magnificent buildings. In the year 1699, the pedestal of a pillar or statue, five feet high, and three in breadth, with the following inscription, was found here:

---
* *Tracones*, in the middle ages, signified subterraneous passages and caverns. *Vid.* Vossius, lib. iii. *de vitiis serm.* c. 53.

† *Vid. Plin. lib.* vi. *epist.* 16. & 20. but especially *Tacit. Hist. lib.* iii. c. 57, to which may be added the nearness of the Portus Julius.

Jussu
Jovis Optimi Maximi
Damasceni
Sacerdotes
M. Nemonio M. F. Pal.
Eutychiano
Sacerdoti honorato
Equo publico ab
Imp. Antonio Aug.
Pie P. P.
Adlecto in ordinem
Decurion. Puteolanor.
aedili
M. Nemonius Callistus P.
Sacerdos remissa
Collatione.

The city of Miseno was in the middle of the ninth century destroyed by the Saracens; so that at present no remains of it are to be seen. The distance from Cuma to this promontory is five Italian miles. Opposite to it are the islands of Procita and Ischia, both producing plenty of fruit and excellent wine, and affording several pleasant spots for hunting. Procita is something above six Italian miles in circumference, and contains about four thousand inhabitants.

Procita and Ischia.

Ischia anciently bore the name of Enaria or Pitecusa. Its circumference, including the windings of the coast, is eighteen Italian miles: it lies about two miles from Procita. Formerly it suffered frequent damages from vulcano's, and especially in the year 1301: but for these last two or three centuries no fiery eruptions have happened here; and the smoke seen here and there to issue from betwixt the rocks proceeds from the hot springs and baths, of which there are in this island above thirty still in vogue; not to mention several sudatories for which it is famous.

Piscina Mirabilis.

On this side the Mare Mortuum in returning from Miseno is the *Piscina Mirabilis*, to which one descends by forty steps, part of which are at present in a ruinous condition. It is a square vault supported by forty-eight pillars; its length is two hundred and fifty *palmi*, the breadth a hundred and sixty, and its height near forty. The pillars are disposed in four rows, making five walks or isles. This unquestionably was

a re-a refervoir; and the fquare apertures in the roof, of which there are thirteen, were made for drawing out the water. The pavement is made floping towards the center, that the fediment of the water, gathering there, might be the more conveniently removed when it was empty.

This water is impregnated with tartar, fo that the bottom and pillars, as high as the furface of the water ufed to rife, are incrufted with it: it is of fuch à hardnefs as fcarce to be feparated from the ftone with hammers. The cement on the upper part of the pillars and walls where the water has not reached, which is about five *palmi*, is far from being fo hard. This confutes the fuppofition, that the incruftation with which the lower parts of the work is covered, is a particular kind of mortar or cement compounded of the whites of eggs and pulverifed marble, faid to be ufed by the ancients.

It is much difputed by whom the *Pifcina Mirabilis*, or wonderful refervoir, was built. Some attribute it to Lucullus, who had a fuperb palace in the neighbourhood: others are of opinion, that Agrippa had it made for the conveniency of the Mifeno fleet, or for watering the gardens; and the chambers near it called *Cento Camerelle* feem to have been defigned for the fame purpofe. As for the opinion of their being prifons for the Chriftians under fentence of death in Nero's time, it has not the leaft probability on its fide. This work which very much refembles the labyrinths, as they are called, at Puzzuolo, is lofty and in pretty good condition; the galleries are long and narrow, and feveral of the doors are broken down.

In returning from Bajæ to Puzzuolo, there is a road clofe by the fea, hewn through a rock; and near it is the following infcription:

Semita

*Semitæ
In subjecti pelagi lubricitate
Furto ab Hercule aggeratæ,
Lucro à Cæsare Dictatore reparatæ,
Ostentationi ab Agrippa restitutæ,
Æstibus ejusdem pelagi disjectæ
Hanc
CAROLO II. REGE
In hujus montis firmitudine,
Hominum salubritati restitutis Thermis,
Petrus Antonius Aragonius
Substituit,
Quæ
Prudentiore excogitata Hercule,
Meliori destinata usui,
Nec Cæsares expectabit, nec Agrippas.
Per Aragoniam viam
Iter perge, viator, ad Bajas,
Eæ enim non luxui thermas
Sed saluti paratas exhibent,
Marmor quas suppositum docet.
P. P. A. D. M. DC. LXIIX.*

'Instead of the road raised for theft by Hercules amidst the fury of the waves, repaired by Cæsar, when dictator, for self-interest, and restored by Agrippa again for ostentation, and after all ruined by the violence of the sea, Pedro Antonio of Aragon, in the reign of Charles II, having, for the health of the public, put the baths in a good condition, has on the firmness of a rock substituted this road, contrived by a wiser Hercules, destined to a better purpose, and which will stand in no need of a Cæsar or an Agrippa. Traveller, go on chearfully along the Aragonian road to Bajæ, where, as the marble underneath informs thee, are noble baths, not subservient to luxury but conducive to health. 1668.'

Sudorii di Tritoli.

In returning from the remains of Julius Cæsar's palace, you pass through an arched way hewn through the rocks like a long cavern, at the end of which are the celebrated warm baths, or rather, as they are indeed commonly called, *i Sudatorii*, or sudatories of Tritoli. They have two entrances, but afterwards are divided into six long apartments, where the

Near the City of NAPLES.

the heat is fcarce fupportable, till cuftom has inured one to it. A ftranger fhould not go in without a guide and fome flambeaux, as one may without fuch precaution fall into dangerous holes. In fome parts of thefe fudatories are warm fprings, one of which, at the end of a long paffage of a hundred and twenty paces, is fo hot, that a man can fcarce bear a finger in the water of it, even after it has been carried out of the mouth of the cavern. Three times a year the hofpital of the Annunciata fends hither whole caravans of patients, and the women have feparate fudatories affigned them. This operation generally lafts feven days, and is begun about the 20th of June. Thefe paffages in the rocks, it is probable, were at firft made for difcovering the warm fprings, of which manifeft traces are to be perceived on the top of the mountain, and even in the adjacent fea. But probably, when thefe paffages were cut in the rock, the heat might not be fo intenfe as at prefent; for now, in a few minutes, a perfon ftript naked is put into a profufe fweat. This increafe of the heat may poffibly be owing to the admiffion of the external air. This place has fomething of the afpect of a mine, where the paffages are about feven or eight *palmi* high and four in breadth. It is not uncommon that, in fome places, the fulphureous exhalation kindles into a fmall flame, which, though it appears confiderable, is not to be approached without danger. On the road which has been pierced through the rocks, and before the entrance into thefe fudatories, are fix apartments, all hewn out of the rock; which alfo ferve for fudatories, as the heat iffuing from the paffages abovementioned can be communicated to them. Formerly on the walls of thefe apartments were feen paintings and infcriptions expreffing the diftempers for which every apartment was beft adapted; but nothing of thefe is now to be feen. This, as it is faid, is owing to the envy and avarice of the Salerno phyficians; the wonderful cures of thefe baths being a detriment to their profeffion. The prefent phyficians of Naples are fo far from looking on the Tritoli fudatories with an evil eye, that they not only prefcribe the ufe of them, but have publifhed a great number of infcriptions and Latin verfes, with directions for the right application of moft of the baths and fudatories in Naples.

The main fea wafhes againft the rocks in which the fudatories have been cut, and the fands at the depth of four or five inches under water are very warm. Spunge, pumice-

ftones,

Balle-ma-rine. stones, and *balle-marine*, are thrown up in great quantities along the shore: the last are large round balls, composed of filaments like hairs, and not very different from the balls found in the maws of young calves. The pumice-stone is supposed to be ejected by a vulcano, and that its porousness is owing to the dissolution of its saline particles by the sea-water. It must be owned, that they are found in great abundance in the Sicilian sea, near the islands of Stromboli, di Volcano, Ischia, and other parts near burning mountains; yet, without examining particularly how the pumice-stone is formed, a subterraneous fire, or a vulcano, is not necessary for that purpose; for great numbers of such stones are found in lakes far enough from any vulcano's. Bocconi, in his remarks, mentions a kind of red pumice-stone frequently met with in the mountains of Radicofani near Florence; they are also found in some rivers.

From Tritoli it is proper to return to the Lago Averno, to take a view of some antiquities on this side, and likewise Sibyl's cave. of the entrance into the sibyl's cave. From this entrance to the other near Cuma, already described, which is four Italian miles, there is said to have been in ancient times a lofty passage, which, according to Strabo, was discovered in Augustus's time. But time and earthquakes have caused such alterations here, that, to get to the entrance of the grotto, one is obliged to crawl ten or twelve paces along the ground; and to leave a servant without, in order to fetch proper assistance, in case, as it has sometimes happened, the entrance of the cave should be filled up by the falling in of the earth and stones. Within the grotto there is a large arched passage hewn out of the rock, near four hundred paces in length; you then descend on the right into another passage where the heat is greater, and overflowed with warm water; so that without boots there is no proceeding any further. Beyond this there is an apartment, in which is a kind of stone trough, by some antiquarians supposed to be the sibyl's bath, and by others her bed; on the walls are several figures made of small stones and shells of different colours curiously arranged. The pavement is also a mosaic work, but cannot be seen distinctly, as it is covered with water. Whether this cave was made for warm baths, or to provide stones for the great number of palaces which anciently stood in its neighbourhood; or whether it was designed for a refreshing cool retreat, or for some other more important use, probably, will never be ascertained. The pagan priests

Near the City of NAPLES.

priests finding such a place ready finished to their hands, it was no difficult matter for them to turn it to their advantage in their impostures and pretended oracles: but that such a spacious and expensive subterraneous structure was no more than the mansion of a sibyl is the more incredible, as all the stories of the ancients about sibyls, upon examination, are found to be entirely fabulous.

Here the Lago Averno is twenty-five fathoms deep, and almost entirely surrounded with a rising ground; so that a canal of communication with the sea, which need not be above the length of half an Italian mile, would make it one of the most commodious harbours in the world. *Depth of the Lago Averno.*

Near the banks of this lake are to be seen the ruins of a building, by some said to have been a temple of Mercury, and by others, of Neptune. Others again will have it to be the temple of Apollo described by Virgil; but nothing can be plainer, than that the poet is speaking of a temple standing on a hill *. This structure, whatever it was, is octangular without, but the inside is a perfect circle, about thirty-six *palmi* in diameter. The roof is fallen in. *Ancient temple.*

On the side of the Lucrine lake towards the sea is a hill with a deep rent on its summit; and the poor illiterate people are taught to believe that it was made at our Saviour's crucifixion, and was the passage through which he descended into the *Limbus Patrum*, in order to release the patriarchs; and to this the mountain owes the name of il Monte di Christo. *Passage into Limbus Patrum.*

All these curiosities, exclusive of the islands, take up a compass of thirty-five or forty Italian miles; which shews that a very superficial view of them can hardly be taken in one day, though some travellers pretend to have done it. The narrow stony roads in these parts are scarce practicable for carriages, and therefore a saddle-horse is best for this excursion, which may be hired for six *carlini* † a day.

---

* *At pius Æneas arces, quibus altus Apollo*
  Præsidet, horrendæque procul secreta sibyllæ
  Antrum immane petit.   *Æneid.* vi. v. 9.

' The pious prince ascends the sacred hill
' Where Phœbus is ador'd, and seeks the shade,
' Which hides from sight his venerable maid;
' Deep in a cave the sibyl makes abode.'   DRYDEN.

† Two shillings sterling.

LETTER LXI.
Journey from ROME to LORETTO.

SIR,

IN returning from Rome to Germany, you set out through the Porta Flumentana, formerly called Porta Flaminia; and on this road, at the distance of an Italian mile from Rome, lies the Ponte Molle, or Milvio, so called, but corruptly, from M. Æmilius Scaurus, who first built this bridge.

Il Ponte Molle.

That the space betwixt this city and the Ponte Molle, in the time of the ancient Romans, was not built upon; and that Rome did not then extend itself beyond the present walls is manifest both from its present appearance (for no traces of any ruins are to be seen here) and as it was the ground on which Constantine the Great drew up his army in order of battle against Maxentius. On crossing the Tiber over Ponte Molle, the road to Sienna and Florence (which was formerly called Via Cassia) turns off to the left; and the Via Flaminia on the right leads to Ariminum, or Rimini, and again crosses the Tiber by means of the Ponte Felice, where is to be seen the following inscription:

Via Cassia.
Via Flaminia.
Ponte Felice.

Sixtus V. Pont. Max.
Ut commeantes trajectionis molestiâ
Et vectigali sublevaret,
Pontem inchoavit
Ann. Sal. MDLXXXIX. Pontif. sui V.

' For easing travellers of the trouble and expence of fer-
' rying over, his holiness Sixtus V. began this bridge in the
' year 1589, and the fifth of his pontificate.'

This bridge was called Ponte Felice, from the name that pope assumed whilst a monk.

Opposite to the above inscription are these words:

Clemens VIII. Pontif. Max.
Pontem a Sixto V. Pont. Max. incœptum
Opere magnifico absolvit,
Alveo excavato Tiberim induxit,
Anno Sal. MDCIIII. Pontif. sui XIII.

' This

'This bridge, begun by pope Sixtus V, was magnificently compleated by pope Clement VIII, and the Tiber brought under it by a channel which he caufed to be made for it, in the year of our Lord 1604, and of his pontificate the thirteenth.'

Some hundred paces from thence, on the left-hand of the road, is a fquare large ftone, with this infcription:

VRBANVS VIII. PONT. -MAX.
Tiberim viâ publicâ everſâ
Veterem repetentem alveum,
Novi effoſſione
Ad dextram deductum,
Aggeris objectu
Validâque compact. lignorum
Sub ponte, quem declinabat,
Continuit,
Confervationi proſpiciens
Peninſulam adjacentem
Attribuit,
Anno Salutis MDCXXVIII.
Pontif. ſui ſexto.

'The Tiber having borne down the public road in its efforts to return to its ancient channel, was carried to the right, and, by a new channel and a bank ftrongly fenced with ftakes, kept to its courſe under the bridge, which it had left; and, for the preſervation of it, the adjacent peninſula was added: fuch are the effects of the liberality and paternal care of Urban VIII, *A. D.* 1628, and of his glorious pontificate the fixth.'

At this bridge is the fifth ftage, after having paſſed through Prima Porta, Caftel Nuovo, Rignano, Civita Caftellana, and Borghetto.

Betwixt Rignano and Civita Caftellana, on the righthand, lies the mountain of St. Orefte, which fome hermits have choſen for their retreat. It is alſo called Monte di S. Silveftro, from the convent built there by Charles the Great in honour of St. Silveſter; but its more ancient names were Mons Faliſcorum and Soracte. Poſſibly a period unjudiciouſly put after the firſt letter of the latter, made it S. Oracte,

St. Orefter

which

which at last gave rise to the imaginary saint, Orestе. In the same manner, according to the testimony of Mabillon himself, St. Viarus was very near increasing the number of saints, had it not been discovered that the letters *S. VIAR*, on which the sticklers for Viarus's saintship relied, were no more than the remains of the title *Præfectus VIARum* *, or surveyor of the high-ways.

An account of the remarkable annual offering of the Hirpii to Apollo on mount Soracte may be seen in Strabo, *lib.* v. *Servius ad Æneid. lib.* xi. *Plin. lib.* vii. *c.* 2. and Solinus, *c.* 8. Varro says, that the goats on this mountain leaped from one rock to another at the distance of sixty paces.

<small>Civita Castellana.</small> The village of Civita Castellana stands upon a steep hill, and is by Antonio Massa, who wrote a particular treatise <small>The ancient Fescennium.</small> *de origine Faliscorum*, thought to be the ancient Fescennium, or capital of the Falisci. Its distance from Rome is about thirty-seven or thirty-eight Italian miles; and the counrry about it is hilly, and not cultivated to the best advantage.

On the bridge towards Otricoli is the following inscription:

Clemens XI. P. M.
Oppositam agrorum partem
Ponte raræ magnitudinis excitato
Civitati conjunxit,
Viâque Flaminiâ intra muros perductâ
Ac longioris itineris incommodo sublato,
Civium non minus quam exterorum utilitati
Consuluit,
Josepho Renato Card. Imperiali
Cong. Bon. Reg. Præfecto
Curante
Anno Sal. MDCCXII. Pont. XII.

‘ This stately bridge, which opens a communication be‑
‘ tween the city and the opposite part of the country, was
‘ built by pope Clement XI, by whose munificence also the
‘ Flaminian way was brought within the walls, to the great

<small>* The Romish church histories abound with new saints, who owe their titles either to ignorance or fraud. Witness St. Longinus, St. Veronica, and the eleven thousand virgins. The author, in his Antiquities, wishes to see a treatise *de pia Pontificiorum vel fraude vel ignorantia in explicandis veterum inscriptionibus*; and he who will give himself the trouble of gratifying the public with such a work, will find sufficient materials in Baronius, Allatius, Mabillon, and other Romish historians.</small>

‘ conveniency

'conveniency of the public, the road being thereby confide-
'rably shortened, &c. 1712.'

On the left-hand, about an Italian mile from Otricoli, in the plain adjoining to the Tiber, are still to be seen the ruins of the old Sabine town Ocrea, or Ocriculum; but they will not answer the trouble of turning out of the road to see them. The modern Otricoli is a wretched village standing on a mountain. *Ruins of Ocrea.*

Five Italian miles beyond Otricoli towards Calvi, the soil near the Tiber is so deep and marshy, that the men who draw barges laden with oil for Rome (ten or fourteen of which often tug at one barge) are obliged to walk barefooted; and, if it happens to rain, such a thick fog is raised, that they are not able to keep their eyes open to pursue their journey, but are forced to come to an anchor. That the river Nera, which discharges itself into the Tiber above Otricoli, runs along a chalky bottom, is evident from the whiteness of its waters, which is taken notice of by Silius Italicus, *lib.* viii. and Martial; but it is remarkable the rain turns its water red *. *Remarkable chalky bottom near Calvi.*

In the front of the post-house at Otricoli is to be seen this old inscription in honour of Julia Lucilia, &c.

Juliæ. Luciliæ.
L. *Juli. Juliani. Fil.*
Patroni. Municipi
Cujus. Pater
Thermas. Ocricula-
nis. a. solo. extructas
Sua. pecunia. dona-
vit.
Dec. Aug. Plebs
L. D. D. D.

Betwixt this place and Narni the country exhibits some charming prospects, especially towards Porcaria, or Portaria (as it is termed on an inscription over the gate) which lies on the side of a hill. Near the Ponte Sanchonaro, a little be- *Porcaria.*

---

* Plin. *Hist. Nat. lib.* iii. *c.* 12. makes the water of the river Nar to be sulphureous; and Martial, *lib.* vii. agrees with him. Of the Vadimon lake, which lies in this neighbourhood, not far from the Tiber, mention has been already made, in describing the floating islands of Tivoli.

yond

yond it is an inscription on a stone, commemorating the liberality of Gregory XIII, by whom this road was repaired. From hence the road runs through a very stony and mountainous country, with very deep precipices on the left-hand; but it is broad, and kept in good repair. On the summit of a hill are some suppositious monuments of an ancient giant, called Orlando; and among them a huge stone said to be his chair, and a cavern in which he lived. The cavern is very mean, partly hewn out of a rock, and partly built of flint and mortar; and in some places the water drops through. It is also called *Antrum Sibyllæ*, or the Sibyl's cave. In the rock on one side of the cave is an impression, as is pretended, of a horse's foot, but done by a bungling carver. Near it is a deep hole in the earth, which in heavy rains is said to emit smoke, or steam.

Cavern of the giant Orlando, or of a Sibyl.

Narni is a very poor town; but, as it stands high, the prospect of the vale below, reaching as far as Terni, is extremely pleasant. The name of this town was formerly Nequinum, which was so called on account of the obstinacy of the inhabitants; who, being besieged, first killed their wives and children, to husband what provisions they had; and, when these were consumed, chose rather to lay violent hands on themselves than surrender. Others derive this name from the badness of the roads near this town. But, notwithstanding its present mean condition, it prides itself not a little in having been the birth-place of the emperor Nerva, pope John XIII, the Venetian general Gattamelata, cardinal Cesi, and other famous men. But cardinal Sacripanti does it no great honour. Here are some good springs, and a fine aqueduct, which conveys the water about fifteen Italian miles. In the episcopal church, the high altar and the stairs by which one descends into St. Juvenal's chapel are worth seeing.

Narni.

But, above all the rest, the ruins of the noble bridge built by Augustus over the Nera, deserves particular notice. It lies on the left-hand just below the city, and the only way to it is down a very difficult descent; but no person who has a taste for antiquity will grudge the trouble. By this bridge two mountains on the opposite sides of the river were joined, for the conveniency of making a road to Perugia. It was built with large square pieces of freestone inserted without cement or iron braces; the outsides of which are cut like diamonds. The piers, still to be seen in the water, give a very grand idea of the arches; which however were

Ancient bridge.

not

From ROME to LORETTO.

not all of an equal diameter. Near the foot of the bridge is a hole said to be of such a depth, that by means of a subterraneous passage under the Nera one might cross to the other side of the river. On the Narni side, and on dry ground, one entire arch, of a very extraordinary height, is still remaining, which is above forty paces wide. Martinelli in his *Descritione de' diversi ponti essistenti sopra il fiumi Nera e Tevere* has given a particular description of this bridge; and according to his computation the length of it was eight hundred and fifty *palmi*, or six hundred and thirty-seven Roman feet and a half*. The distance betwixt the piers of the first arch, which are still to be seen, is a hundred *palmi*; and the height of the arch is a hundred and fifty *palmi*. The distance betwixt the piers of the second arch was a hundred and eight *palmi*, that of the third a hundred and fifty, and the last arch on the other side of the Nera was a hundred and ninety *palmi*, or a hundred and forty-two Roman feet and a half. This arch, however, comes short of the Ponte Rialto, and other arches to be seen at present in Europe. Martial, *Epigr. lib.* vii, speaks of the bridge at Narni in the following manner:

Sed jam parce mihi, nec abutere, Narnia, Quinto,
  Perpetuo liceat sic tibi ponte frui!

' Preserve my Quintus, Narni, from all harm,
' So may thy noble bridge withstand the shock
' Of all-devouring time!'

The most convenient way for seeing this bridge is to let the carriage wait in the road to Terni, whilst one is getting down the steep descent mentioned above, which saves the trouble of climbing up the hill with the chaise. The Nera, which at a small distance from hence falls into the Tiber near Guastanello, abounds in tenches, mullets, eels, trouts, and other kinds of delicate fish. Terni lies seven Italian miles from Narni; and the road runs along a fine valley, especially that part of it betwixt Cessa and Colle Scipoli (a corruption of *Collis Scipionis*) is quite charming. The fields are planted with rows of trees, and very large and spreading vines interwoven with their branches. Amongst other kinds

Terni.

Collis Scipionis.

* The Roman foot, according to Montfaucon, is equal to eleven Paris inches.

VOL. III.   M   here

From Rome to Loretto.

Uva Paſſa. here is a sort of vine which bears small grapes without any stones in them. These are called *Uva Paſſa* *, or *Paſſarina*, and are much used in sauces. They are also fraudulently mixed with the currants of the Levant, which they very much resemble both in taste and appearance. These parts also abound in olive-trees and fig-trees. According to Pliny (*lib.* xviii. *c.* 28.) the meadows about Terni, even those which could not be watered, were mowed four times in a year: and, in the less fertile parts where they had three crops of hay, very rich pasture remained for the cattle. Turneps

Large turneps. are here of such an uncommon size as sometimes to weigh thirty or forty pounds †; they seem to thrive best in stony ground. The seeds of these turneps however do not produce such roots in other countries; nor even in the Milanese, where the soil is remarkably fertile. The melons, peaches, figs, and other fruits that grow about Narni are much larger than in other places; it being nothing uncommon here to see peaches weighing from fifteen to eighteen ounces.

Interamna. Terni was anciently called Interamna from its situation between the two channels of the Nera. It was the birthplace of Cornelius Tacitus the famous historian, and of the emperors Tacitus and Florianus. On one side of the market-place, near the entrance of the seminary, are some ancient inscriptions relating to the old Interamna. Over the market-clock is this moral verse:

Hora, dies, & vita fugit, manet unica Virtus.

' Hours, days, and ages fly away,
' Virtue alone knows no decay.'

On a small pyramid that stands over the fountain in the market-place, is the following inscription:

---

* The name of *Uva Paſſa* is not derived from *Patientia*, as Pliny would intimate, (*lib.* xiv. *c.* 1.) but rather from their dryness; for they seem to be, as it were, trodden together ατυθως, or a *pandendo*, *i. e.* being exposed to the air and sun, &c.

† What Pliny says (*Hiſt. Nat. lib.* viii. *c.* 13.) of his having seen turneps of above forty pounds weight, is therefore the less to be questioned.

Aquarum

*Aquarum delicias
Quas suo mirabatur in agro,
Et sitiebat in gremio
Interamna,
Inclytæ Patriæ commodis
Comes Antonius Manasse,
Eques Sancti Michaëlis,
De Dnis. Castri. Copparum Condnus
Terrar. Cœlestat. & Turris Ursinæ
Suo ære ingenioque adduxit,
Marco Butaglino Gubernat.
MDCLXXXIII.*

' These refreshing waters which Terni admired in its ter-
' ritory, and wished to receive within its bosom, were, to
' the infinite benefit of our illustrious country, and at the
' expence, and by the skill of count Antonio Manasse, knight
' of St. Michael, &c. brought hither under the inspection
' of Marco Butaglino in the year 1683.'

But the fountain on which this encomium was made does not yield any water, which gave occasion to the following verse:

*O voi, che qui trovare aqua pensate,
Se non piove dal Ciel, non l'aspettate.*

' Whoever hopes to find water here will be disappointed,
' unless Heaven be kindly pleased to send some rain.'

After the example of several other cities in Italy, pretending to a greater antiquity than Rome, the inhabitants of Terni are extremely infatuated with this frivolous pretension; which however is confuted by an inscription of their own. It is to be seen on the wall of the portico belonging to the seminary; where it is expressly said, that this city [Interamna] in the consulship of Cn. Domitianus Ænobarbus and M. Camillus Scribonianus (which was in the seven hundred and thirty-fourth year from the building of Rome) had existed seven hundred and four years. This ancient inscription is as follows:

Saluti perpetuæ Augustæ libertatique publicæ Populi Romani, Genio Municipii Anno post Interamnam conditam DCCIIII. ad Cn. Domitianum Ænobarbum ------ Coss. Providentiæ Tib. Cæsaris Augusti nati ad æternitatem Romani nominis sublato hoste perniciocissimo P. R. Faustus Titius Liberalis VI. Vir. Aug. iter. P. S. F. C. i. e. *iterum pecunia sua fieri curavit.*

This monument very probably was a flattering compliment paid to Tiberius, after he had got rid of Sejanus. To this may be added another inscription relating to the antiquity of this place, were there any certainty of its authenticity, or at least that it was not quite modern. It stands in the cathedral, and is expressed in the following words:

Interamna anno ante Christum DCLXXI. condita vivente Pompilio.

' Interamna was built in the year 671 before Christ, whilst
' Pompilius was living.'

Over the Spoletto gate are the following lines:

*Porta, quam, Viator, ingrederis, trium monumentorum dicta,
Ob proquinqua à fluminibus disjecta monumenta,
C. Cornelii Taciti Politicorum Principis,
Tacitique & Floriani Imperatorum hujus Urbis civium,
Nunc in honorem sacratissimæ Laureti domûs,
Quò revertentem te ducit, Lauretana nuncupata,
Aditum præbet spectanti Interamnam,
Præstantissimum Italiæ municipium,
Patriam illius Claudii Neronis, qui ad Metaurum fluvium,
Collatis cum Asdrubale signis,
Istius interneciones & exercitûs octoginta Pænorum millium
Annibalem ex Italiâ expulit,
Carthaginensem Rempublicam concussit,
Romanam periclitantem constabiliit,
Et plures Cæsares terrarum Orbi dedit,
Ad perennitatem gloriæ hujus municipii,
Tantorum Heroum progenitoris
Interamnenses Nahartes hanc memoriam ap poni curârunt
Anno Dñi. MDCLXXXIX.*

' Traveller,

'Traveller, the gate which thou entereſt, formerly called the gate of the three monuments (on account of the monuments of Cornelius Tacitus the prince of politicians, and the emperors Tacitus and Florianus natives of this town, that once ſtood near it) but long ſince ruined by inundations, now in honour of the holy houſe of Loretto, to which it directs thee as thou goeſt out of the town, is called the gate of Loretto, and opens an acceſs to thee coming towards Terni the moſt eminent free town of Italy, the native place of Claudius Nero, that illuſtrious warrior, who, in the battle with Aſdrubal near the river Metaro, flew him and defeated his army, conſiſting of eighty thouſand Carthaginians; drove Hannibal out of Italy, ſhook the Carthaginian ſtate, and retrieved the Roman commonwealth; from whom alſo deſcended ſeveral emperors. To perpetuate the glory of this borough, the nurſery of ſuch diſtinguiſhed heroes, the magiſtracy of Interamna or Terni have erected this monument in the year of Chriſt 1689.'

The greateſt trade of this place is in oil, and wine of a *Trade.* moſt delicious flavour.

A traveller ſhould not omit beſtowing three or four hours *Remarkable* to ſee the caſcade formed by the Velino, about four Italian *cataract of* miles eaſtward of Terni. As the road is impracticable for *the Velino.* carriages, this excurſion muſt be made on horſeback: four *paoli* * is the uſual hire for each horſe. The road is not only very bad up the acclivity of the mountain, but by its narrowneſs and the ſteep precipices on the left-hand is ſo dangerous, that in ſome places it is adviſeable to light and lead the horſe. The ſource of the river Velino lies among the Appenine mountains near Civita Reale, about fifteen or ſixteen miles from Terni; and this river, after paſſing by Anterdoco, Citta Ducale, and the Lago di Rieti, which has a communication with the Lago di Pie di Luco, empties itſelf into the Lago delle Marmore; the latter alſo joins with the Lago di Cor delle Fratte. Some are inclined to think that the Velino, after running through the Lago delle Marmore, formerly inclined its courſe more to the left than it does at preſent, and that its channel was in the valley below: but, as the caſcade extended itſelf ſo far as to be dangerous to

* About two ſhillings.

From ROME to LORETTO.

the inhabitants of Terni, there was a necessity of altering its course and carrying it on the right towards a steep precipice inclosed within rocks, where its violence would be more easily broken.

Ancient Lacus Velini. As to the ancient situation of the Lacus Velini, and the course of the river running from it, they cannot be traced out with any certainty. Cicero (*lib.* iv. *epist.* 15. *ad Atticum*) mentions a complaint of the Reatini against the Interamnates, who had diverted the course of this river. His words are, *Reatini me ad sua τέμπη duxerunt, ut agerem causam contra Interamnates apud Cos. & decem legatos, quòd lacus Velinus à M. Curio emissus, intercisò monte in Nar defluxit : ex quo est villa siccata, & humida tamen modicè rosea.* ' The Reatini led me
' to their τέμπη, or meadows, that I might plead their cause
' before the consuls and the ten commissioners against the
' Interamnates, because the Lacus Velinus had been diverted
' from its course by M. Curius, and, by piercing through a
' mountain, made to run into the Nar; so that their town
' labours under a scarcity of water, *&c.*' Varro also mentions this diverting the course of the river. On what the complaint against the Interamnates was grounded, I do not readily conceive; especially as Marcus Curius Dentatus, who had carried on bloody wars in those parts, was consul of Rome in the year 463 from the building of the city; so that this alteration must have been made above two hundred years before Cicero wrote this letter. Besides, Servius says, that the fertility of that country was greatly increased by altering the course of the Velino; and Virgil represents it as a very extraordinary improvement:

*Et quantum longis carpent armenta diebus
Exigua tantum gelidus ros nocte reponet.*
VIRG. *Georg.* ii. v. 201.

' For what the day devours, the nightly dew
' Shall to the morn in pearly drops renew.'
DRYDEN.

The last words of the passage of Cicero quoted above are something obscure. *Roseus* is often put for *roscidus*; and Servius says, that the country about Reate was called *Ager Rosulanus*. Virgil's *Rosea rura Velini*, *&c.* must also relate to these parts: but I do not think that Dentatus altered the course of the Velino; Cicero speaking only of the intersection

tion of a mountain, which has nothing to do with the fall of the Velino down a precipice into the valley. Besides, this work is so far from diverting the stream from the inhabitants of Terni, that it brought it nearer to them. It is farther to be considered, that (as Tacitus writes, *Annal. lib.* i. *c.* 79.) the Reatini petitioned Tiberius against damming up the influx of the lake Velino into the Nar, which was then under deliberation, as it would infallibly overflow all the adjacent country. Had this cascade, where the stream precipitates itself into the valley, been then stopt, no detriment could have happened to the high country of the Reatini from the obstruction of its communication with the Nar. On the contrary, the Interamnates, or inhabitants of Terni, towards which the stream, after falling down from the rock, prosecutes its course along a deep valley, must have been exposed to the impetuosity of the water, and consequently were filled with apprehensions at the projected alteration; but it seems all their follicitude was, that the Nar might not be divided into small streams, as their vale would, by that means, be more subject to inundations. Had this cascade, which is now viewed with such astonishment, existed in the days of Cicero, it must seem strange that no mention of such a cataract occurs in that author, or any other ancient writer. Pliny, *lib.* ii. *Hist. Nat. c.* 62, speaking of the particular qualities of the air in different climates, says, *roscidas æstate Africæ noctes; in Italia Locris & in lacu Velino nullo non die apparere arcus.* 'That the summer nights in Africa are attended 'with copious dews; and in Italy, at Locri and the lake 'Velino, a rainbow appears every day.' And though he takes notice here of the rainbow daily formed over the lake Velino, possibly by the exhalations, yet he is entirely silent throughout his works with regard to this remarkable cataract. The river Nar is not a great way from Velino; hence Virgil places them together:

Audiit & longè Trivia lacus audiit amnis
Sulphureâ Nar albus aquâ, fontesque Velini.
VIRG. Æn. vii. v. 516.

'The sacred lake of Trivia from afar,
'The Veline fountains, and sulphureous Nar,
'Shake at the baleful blast, the signal of the war.'
DRYDEN.

Claudian,

Claudian, in his poem on Honorius, when the emperor quits the common road to take a view of the river Nar, does not make the leaft mention of the fall of the Velino; though fuch a work deferved a monarch's attention, and naturally offered to the poet a very entertaining picture for the embellifhment of his poem. Some writers, indeed, imagine to have difcovered a defcription of this cafcade in the feventh *Æneid, v.* 563, where Virgil defcribes the gulf through which the fury Alecto, after fucceeding in her deteftable expedition, plunges into the infernal fhades:

> *Eft locus Italiæ in medio fub montibus altis,*
> *Nobilis, & fama multis memoratus in oris,*
> *Amfancti vailes: Denfis hinc frondibus atrum*
> *Urget utrumque latus nemoris, medioque fragofus*
> *Dat fonitum faxis, & torto vertice torrens. &c.*

> ‘ Amid fair Italy, renow'd by fame,
> ‘ Lies a deep vale, Amfanctus is the name.
> ‘ Its gloomy fides are fhaded with a grove,
> ‘ And a huge range of mountains tow'rs above:
> ‘ Fierce thro' the dufky vale the torrents pour,
> ‘ And o'er its rocky bed the whirlpools roar.'   PITT.

In fupport of this conjecture it is farther alledged, that, according to the teftimony of Solinus, Varro places the diftrict of Reate fo near the middle of Italy, that he ftiles it the *umbilicus,* or navel of it: but what Virgil adds in the following lines by no means agrees with the cafcade of Velino:

> *Hic fpecus horrendum, fævi fpiracula Ditis,*
> *Monftratur, ruptoque ingens Acheronte vorago*
> *Peftiferas aperit fauces - - -*

> ‘ There the black jaws of hell are open'd wide;
> ‘ There rolls dire Acheron his baleful tide;
> ‘ There lies the dark infernal cave, and there
> ‘ Pluto's abodes inhale refrefhing air.'   PITT.

The poet's defcription may, according to the opinion of Servius, in his notes on this paffage, be more juftly applied to a fpot near the Via Flaminia, not far from mount Soracte, where there are ponds of a fulphureous water, and a cavern which emits a very noxious vapour.

The

The mountain which the Velino crosses before it falls from the precipice is indeed, with regard to the country about Terni, exceeding high; but it is inclosed on both sides with rocks that are still higher. As the country hereabouts is upon the descent, the rapidity of the Velino is increased after it has passed the Lago delle Marmore. This cataract consists of three cascades, one above another, and the lowest seems to be near two hundred feet. Nature has, on the left of it, prepared a narrow place like a promontory, in the form of a crescent, where the spectators may have a full view of the principal cascade. I own I differ from those who affirm this cascade to be three hundred feet high; yet this is certain, that one cannot, without a kind of pleasing horror, hear * the roaring noise caused by the impetuous fall of the water, which immediately, even before it reaches the bottom, is converted into a white froth, and, dashing against the rocks at the bottom, causes a thick mist, like a cloud of smoke, to rise, which, in a clear sunshine, exhibits a most beautiful rainbow. What has induced some travellers to affirm, that this mist of watery particles ascends twice the height of the fall, I cannot say; nor shall I venture to determine whether the name of Lacus Velini, mentioned by Pliny and others, properly belongs to the Lago delle Marmore, or Lago di Cor delle Fratte, or Lago di Pie di Luco. According to the general opinion, the situation of the *Lucus*, or sacred grove, and of the temple of Velinia, corresponds with that of the little town of Pie di Luco, together with the lake of that name. This is also the opinion of Varro; but the cataract derives its name from the first mentioned lake, and is called Cascata delle Marmore.

In the year 1543, one Pietro Terrenatico had a very providential escape here. He was carried down the precipice by the force of the current, and yet was taken out without the least hurt. As he attributed his safety to the assistance of the holy virgin of Loretto, the story, with all its circumstances, Remarkable escape.

---

* Seneca writes thus of a cataract in the Nile, *Ubi scopulos verberavit, spumat: & illi non ex natura sua, sed ex injuria loci color est. Tandemque eluctatus obstantia, in vastam altitudinem subitò destitutus cadit cum ingenti circumjacentium regionum strepitu.* ' The water falls with such impetuo-
' sity against the rocks, that it raises a froth: but this colour is not na-
' tural, but owing to the cragginess of the rock. At last, having made
' its way through every impediment in its course, it is at once precipitated
' from such a vast height, that all the neighbouring country echoes with
' the noise of its fall.'

is

is transmitted to posterity, being inscribed on marble at Loretto in the following words:

Ego Petrus Terennaticus, Eques & Marescallus equitatûs Ducis Castrorum, & cæteri equites ex Piceno ad vicum Varronis proficiscentes, cum Nonis Martii MDXLIII. ad Velinum lacum pervenissemus, & duo alii milites, Tiberius ex Graviscis, & Antonius Cortonensis a cæteris equitibus discessimus, ut illum viseremus locum, quo se Velinus in Nar præcipitat. Ac non procul inde, cum equum adaquarem, ego unà cum equo in quasdam fluminis angustias incidi, ex quibus præcipitem altissimo casu, circiter videlicet centum cubitos altum, & Deiparæ Virginis Lauretanæ opem implorantem, quidam me scopulus excepit incolumem, & rei miraculo admirabundum atque attonitum. Quapropter illicò votum persolvi Beatissimæ Virgini, quam tum præsentem propitiamque sum expertus, testibus oculatis duobus Centurionibus Chiancio Urbevetano & Raimundo cum universa equitum ala.

'I Petro Terennatico, captain in the duke of Castro's regi-
' ment of horse, being on a march from Piceno to the town
' of Varro, came to the Velino on the 4th of March, 1543,
' with my troops: Tiberio Gravisi, Antonio da Cortona,
' and myself, leaving the rest of the regiment, went up to
' take a view of the place where the Velino falls down a high
' precipice into the Nar. But, as I was watering my horse at
' a small distance from the cascade, myself and horse, by the
' force of the current in a narrow part of the river, were
' carried down the precipice to the depth of a hundred cubits.
' In the extremity of my danger, as I implored the help of
' the virgin mother of God of Loretto, I fell without the
' least hurt upon a rock, quite astonished at my miraculous
' preservation. Wherefore, in gratitude to the propitious
' presence and protection of the most blessed Virgin, which
' I then experienced, I hereby discharge the vow I then
' made in the presence of the captains Chiancio Urbevetano
' and Raimundo, with the rest of the regiment.'

The Velino, after this fall from the rock, runs into the Nera or Nar near Terni, where it loses its name.

Il Mont-Eolo. Il Mont-Eolo lies on the other side of Terni, six or seven Italian miles from that town, and is noted for the cool air, which, in summer-time, proceeds from the clefts and cavities of this mountain. Misson tells us, that the inhabitants
of

of the little town of Ceffi convey the air through pipes into their houses and wine-cellars.

The road from Terni to Spoletto is extremely pleasant, being planted on both sides with olive and other fruit-trees, as far as the Monte di Somma, which in rainy or snowy weather is very slippery and difficult to be crossed.

Spoletto stands on a steep acclivity, and makes but a mean figure; yet, like other paultry towns in Italy, exhibits bombastic inscriptions concerning its antiquity, and many trivial occurrences which have happened there. *Spoletto.*

One of the gates of the town derives its name from Annibal, the Carthaginian general, and on it is the following inscription:

ANNIBAL   Inscriptions
Cæsis ad Thrasymenum Romanis   over the Porta d'Anni-
Urbem Romam infenso agmine petens,   bale.
Spoleto magnâ suorum clade repulsus,
Insigni fugâ portæ nomen fecit.

' Annibal, after defeating the Romans at Thrasymene,
' marching his army towards Rome, was driven from Spo-
' letto with great slaughter: and his flight on that occasion
' gave name to this gate.'

In the cathedral are some paintings by Filippo Lippi Ca- *Cathedral.* rini, which, after that artist had been poisoned out of envy in the year 1438, were finished by his assistant, one Diamante, a monk. He lies buried in the church, and has a marble bust and an epitaph erected to his memory.

Opposite to this bust is the monument of Giov. Francesco Ursini, adorned with beautiful basso-relievo's. And over the main entrance of the church is to be seen the virgin Mary, with some of the disciples, in ancient mosaic work.

The castle of Spoletto lies on an eminence, and is joined *Castle.* to the city by a bridge. From a mountain lying over-against the castle, which takes its name from St. Francis, the water is conveyed by an aqueduct into the town. The canal, or aqueduct, is a beautiful work, consisting of ten freestone arches, narrow indeed, but in the middle, on account of the depth of the valley, it is supported by a double arcade, the whole height of which is between four and five hundred feet; but Misson makes it still higher.

Round Spoletto, and also about Umbria, is found a fossile *Fossile wood.* wood, which is dug up in a chalky soil; it is porous like

other

other wood, and burns to a coal. This is entirely different from a wood growing in some parts of Italy, which is not consumed after being red-hot for several hours. The best burning-glasses, which cause a fusion even in iron and stone, make very little impression on this wood; nor does it lose either colour or weight in the fire. The grain of this wood is not unlike that of oak; but it is something softer, and of a reddish colour. It grows soft and brittle after having been often in the fire, and is specifically heavier than water, the smallest bits of it sinking to the bottom. Vitruvius, *lib*. ii. *c*. 9, attributes a like specific gravity and incombustibility to the *larix*, which grows about the Po and the Adriatic sea: and adds, that Julius Cæsar set on fire a town built of this wood on the Alps; which, however, was not consumed. Pliny *, who classes this tree among the species of pine and fir-trees, ascribes the like qualities to it. I shall enrich your collection of natural curiosities with a piece of this incombustible wood. Some of it has been found in Andalusia, near Seville †. The *linum asbestum* found in Transilvania and other parts, and of which incombustible paper and linen are made, is a stone, and differs specifically from the above-mentioned wood.

Fine country.

From Spoletto the road lies through a most delightful valley, much resembling the country between Pisa and Florence. There is a most enchanting prospect from the temple of Clitumnus, which lies two or three hundred paces from the first stage on this road, which is called la Vene. This temple has been converted into a Christian chapel, under the title of St. Salvadore. The front towards the plain makes a superb appearance, being adorned with six Corinthian pillars; two of which are covered with a foliage of laurel-leaves, two twisted, and the other two square and fluted. On the frize are these words:

Temple of Clitumnus.

† SCS *Deus Angelorum, qui fecit resurrectionem.*

' The most holy God, and king of angels, the author of
' the resurrection.'

---

* *Hist. Nat. lib.* xvi. *c.* 10. *Exceptâ larice, quæ nec ardet, nec carbonem facit, nec alio modo ignis vi consumitur, quam lapides.* ' Except the *larix*, which never flames, nor burns to a coal; nor is any more consumed
' by the force of the fire than stones are.'
† *Vide Clerc Bibliotheque Choisie, tom.* xii. *p.* 57.

From ROME to LORETTO.

On the right-hand, the architrave of the pillars with foliages exhibits this imperfect inscription:

$\overline{SCS}$ *DEVS APOSTO - - - - -*
- - - - - - SIONEM.

On the left-hand:

$\overline{SCS}$ *Deus Profetarum qui fecit redemptionem.*

'The most holy God of the prophets, the author of re-
'demption.'

This edifice is oblong, and on the roof are the following words cut in stone:

T. Septimus Plebeius.

On the side towards the road is a crucifix, with vine-branches twisted about it, in basso-relievo.
This edifice having so few marks of paganism, and on the contrary so many signs of Christianity, the most probable conjecture is, that this chapel was built out of the ruins of a pagan temple; but whether this temple was consecrated to Clitnmnus is another question, and not a little dubious: for Pliny [*] places that temple near the source of the river Clitumnus, just on the spot where the river became navigable; which is not the case here. This scruple is farther countenanced by what Suetonius says, chap. 43. in the life of Caligula, namely, that this emperor went to Mevania to see the temple of Clitumnus, and the consecrated grove. Now Mevania is unquestionably the present little town of Bevagna, situated on the west-side of the Tinia, or Timia, at the influx of the rivers Tacarena and Rucciano into the Clitum-

---

[*] *Lib. viii. ep. 8. Fons ad hæc, & jam amplissimum flumen atque etiam navium patiens, quas obvias quoque & contrario nisu in diversa tendentes, transmittit & perfert: adeo validus, ut illa, qua properat ipse, quanquam per solum planum, remis non adjuventur: idem ægerrime remis contisque superetur adversus.*——— *Rigor aquæ certaverit nivibus, nec color cedit.*
'Here it appears a fountain, and there immediately a very noble river,
'fit even to receive large vessels, that pass backwards and forwards, ac-
'cording as they are bound, one way or another: the current is so strong,
'that while the boat glides with the stream there is no necessity for oars;
'all is even as plain ground: but oars and poles are scarce sufficient in re-
'turning against the stream. ——— The water is as cold as snow, and
'the colour of it is as white.'

nus, which anciently might have retained that name as far as the Topino *. But one of the many small chapels which Pliny places in this neighbourhood may have stood on this spot; especially as but a few paces from it there is an excellent spring, which illustrates the passage of Pliny quoted in the note †. Observing an inscription on free-stone in the bottom of this little spring, I persuaded some of the peasants to take it up, and found on it these imperfect words:

T. TFGALL
X VIRO FE ‥ IEIS

Notions of the Italians concerning hidden treasures. No sooner had I read these words, than the peasants asked me where they should begin to dig; and, upon my enquiring of them the cause of such a question, they very eagerly answered, *Per trovare i denari*; i. e. 'To come at the pence;' for they expected that I was now thoroughly informed where the treasure, which they were persuaded lay buried in the old temple or near it, was to be searched for. The common people all over Italy are strongly possessed with the notion that treasures are concealed in every part of the country; and, if curiosity detains a stranger any considerable time among ancient buildings or ruins, they immediately suppose, that it is to get an account of hidden treasures. On such occasions some caution is necessary to be observed, left a person should bring himself into some disagreeable adventure

* *Vid. Lucan. lib. i. & Stat. lib. i. Sylv.*
† *Adjacet templum priscum & religiosum. Stat Clitumnus ipse amictus ornatusque prætextâ. Præsens numen atque etiam fatidicum indicant sortes. Sparsa sunt circà sacella complura, totidemque Dei simulacra: sua cuique veneratio, suum nomen: quibusdam verò etiam fontes. Nam præter illum, quasi parentem cæterorum, sunt minores capite discreti; sed flumini miscentur, quod ponte transmittitur. Is terminus sacri profanique. In superiore parte navigare tantùm, infrà etiam natare concessum — Nec desunt villæ, quæ secutæ fluminis amœnitatem, margini insistunt. In summa, nihil erit, ex quo non capias voluptatem, &c.* 'Adjoining to it is an old and awful
'temple, in which the god Clitumnus stands, cloathed and adorned with
'the *prætexta*. The oracles delivered shew the god propitious and pro-
'phetic. There are little temples scattered up and down in these parts,
'in every one of which is the statue of the deity: each has a distinct wor-
'ship, and a particular name. Some of them have also springs consecrated
'to them: for besides the original spring, which seems, as it were, the
'parent of the rest, there are several smaller streams, divided from the
'chief source. They mix with the river, over which a bridge terminates
'the sacred, and divides them from the profane places. Above the bridge
'you are permitted only to go in boats; below it you are allowed to
'swim, &c.'

by

From ROME to LORETTO.

by too long an indulgence of his curiosity; especially when alone, and in a solitary place.

The ancients erroneously imagined that the great number of horned cattle brought from Umbria owed their white colour to the river Clitumnus. Hence Propertius says : *Of the breed of white cattle in this country.*

*Quà formosa suo Clitumnus flumina luco
Integit ; & niveos abluit unda boves.*
            Prop. lib. ii. *Eleg.* 19. *v.* 25.

'Shaded with trees, Clitumnus' waters glide,
'And milk-white oxen drink its beauteous tide.'
                                                        ADDISON.

Claudian, speaking of the journey of Honorius to Rome, says:

*Quin & Clitumni sacras victoribus undas,
Candida quæ Latiis præbent armenta triumphis,
Visere cura fuit.* - - - -
            CLAUDIAN. *de Sexto Conf. Hon.*

——————————' Next he came,
'Where fair Clitumnus rolls his sacred stream,
'Whence hecatombs of milk-white oxen come,
'To grace the triumphs of imperial Rome.'

*Et lavet ingentem perfusum flumine sacro
Clitumnus taurum, Narque albescentibus undis
In Tibrim properans, Tineæque inglorius humor.*
                                            Sil. Ital. lib. viii.

'Clitumnus, that presents its sacred stores,
'To wash the bull: the Nar's infected tide,
'Whose sulph'rous waters into Tiber glide:
'Tinea's small stream that runs inglorious on.'
                                                        ADDISON.

*Hinc albi, Clitumne, greges, & maxima taurus
Victima, sæpe tuo perfusi flumine sacro
Romanos ad templa Deûm duxere triumphos.*
                            Virg. Georg. ii. *v.* 468.

' There

'There flows Clitumnus through the flow'ry plain;
'Whose waves, for triumphs after prosp'rous war,
'The victim ox and snowy sheep prepare.
ADDISON.

Servius, in his commentary upon these words, says: *Clitumnus autem fluvius est in Mevania, quæ pars est Umbriæ, partis Tusciæ, de quo fluvio, ut dicit Plinius in Historia naturali, animalia, quæ potaverint, albos fœtus creant.* 'Now Clitum-
' nus is a river in Mevania, a part of Umbria, which is a
' province of Tuscany. And Pliny, in his natural history,
' says, that the cattle which drinks its waters produce a
' white breed.' Possibly Servius has an eye to the passage of Pliny, (*Hist. Nat. lib.* ii. *c.* 103.) which in the common editions runs thus: *In Falisco omnis aqua pota candidos boves facit.* Some Editions, instead of *omnis* have *amnis*; and others, though but few, read *Clitumnus*; so that Servius's copy must must have been one of the latter. But, should this reading be admitted, it is hard to conceive how Pliny should commit such a geographical error relating to a country so near Rome, as to place the Clitumnus in the province of the Falisci, which belonged to Hetruria: whereas nothing can be more certain than that it is in Umbria, betwixt Spoletto and Tacarena; or more precisely in the country formerly called Mevania, as is evident from Pliny, Suetonius, &c. That the Hispellates had a public bath and house of entertainment near the Clitumnus, is mentioned by the younger Pliny. Now Hispellum is certainly the modern Spello, lying northwards, beyond the Topino, betwixt Foligno and Assisi, and famous for the many antiquities daily discovered there. As to the particular nature of the cattle of this country, their whiteness is by no means owing to the water of the Clitumno, the same species being seen in all the northern parts of Italy; especially in the Bolognese, whither the Clitumno does not direct its course. Neither does this river alter the colour of the swine bred near it, which in its neighbourhood and all over Italy are generally black, or of a dark brownish colour.

The Clitumno joins the Tacarena, the Rucciano, and the Tinia, which discharge themselves into the Topino, and under that name mingle with the Chiascio, through which at last it loses itself in the Tiber.

Not

From Rome to Loretto.

Not far from the above-mentioned temple of Clitumnus lies the village Pesignano, or Pissignano, on the right-hand of the road towards Foligno. The ancient name of it was Piscina Jani; so that some have been induced to believe, that the ruins which pass for a temple of Clitumnus, are rather the remains of a temple of Janus: but this conjecture wants father support for its confirmation. *Pissignano.*

Trevi stands also on the right-hand on an eminence; and the road all the way betwixt La Vene and Foligno is upon the level, and exceeding pleasant. *Trevi.*

Foligno (in Latin *Fulginus*) has a greater trade in cloth, silk, and spices than any of the neighbouring cities; and the magnificent altar and paintings in *fresco* in the episcopal church are worth observing. *Foligno.*

On the left, at the next stage beyond Foligno, lies Assisi, the native place of St. Francis, and very famous for the beautiful church belonging to the order instituted by that saint, in which some say he is buried; and also for the great number of pilgrims resorting to it. Those who are not drawn hither by devotion, will meet with such entertainment among the fine paintings in this church, by Giotto, Giottino, Giovanni Cimabue, Pietro Cavallino Romano, Frederico Barocci, &c. that they cannot be displeased with the journey. The convent of Franciscan nuns, called the nuns of St. Clare, is likewise worth seeing. To the south of Assisi, at the distance of an Italian mile, lies another beautiful church, called S. Maria Portiuncula, which is also much visited by pilgrims. *Assisi.*

Near a hill, just without Foligno, in the way to Tolentino, it is worth while to go up to Castro Pales, where, besides a famous paper-mill, is to be seen the palace of the bishop of Orvietano, marquis of Elisei, to whom this place belongs. Here is a very remarkable grotto, where the lapideous exsudations have formed all kinds of ornaments, as pillars, bunches of grapes, pears, and other fruit, which hang down from the top. This grotto consists of several passages and apartments, and has a communication with the house. In the court are several inscriptions, indicating the time when Christina queen of Sweden, Violanta hereditary princess of Florence, count Daun the vice-roy of Naples, and other persons of distinction, visited this place, &c. *CastroPales. Grotto.*

The road from hence to Tolentino lies over the Appennine mountains; but in these parts the roads are kept in exceeding good repair; and in several places stone monuments are erected in praise of the several popes, or surveyors by whom the *Tolentino.*

the roads have been made or repaired. I cannot here forbear wishing, that, in several parts of Germany, the sovereigns would affect to perpetuate their names in this useful manner; it must be owned, however, that the house of Austria has set them a very laudable example in its hereditary dominions.

The villages and inns on this road are so mean, that it is advisable for a traveller to carry cold provisions with him; and especially some wine, as that of the country (which is always boiled for keeping) is not agreeable to every one's taste.

Macerata.

From Tolentino the road leads again into a level, fruitful, and well cultivated country. The prospect near Macerata over the vallies on each side of the road is extremely delightful. The chief gate of Macerata is built after the manner of a triumphal arch, with three arches; and over it on the country side stands a brass statue of cardinal Pio. The town affords nothing remarkable, and the clock-work, which the inhabitants so much boast of, is but a mere bauble. When the clock strikes, the three eastern *magi* makes their appearance, attended by an angel, and passing before an image of the virgin Mary make a reverential bow, the crowns on their heads being lifted up. Over them a star is suspended, which ascends whilst the images are passing under it. The figures are but a foot high, and perform their adoration in a very aukward manner.

Ruins of Helvia Ricina.

Betwixt Macerata and Recanati are to be seen the ruins of the ancient town of Helvia Ricina, built by the emperor Septimius Severus. After its destruction by the Goths, the inhabitants of Recanati and Macerata found a good supply of stones for building, among its ruins. At the last mentioned town the following ancient inscription hath been found:

Imp. Cæsari L. Veri. Avg. fil. divi. Pii. Nep. Divi Hadriani. Pron. Divi. Trajan. Parth. Abnep. Divi. Nervæ. Adnepoti. L. Septimio. Severo. Pio. Pertinaci. Augusto. Arabico. Adiabenico. Parthico. Maximo. P. M. Tribunit. Potest. XIII. Imp. XI. Cos. III. P. P. Colonia. Helvia. Ricina. Conditori. suo.

Recanati.

From Seravalle to Macerata the road runs along the bank of the river Chiento; and betwixt Macerata and Recanati crosses the Potenza. Recanati stands on a hill within three miles of Loretto; and, after passing through the gate of this town, one has a glorious prospect towards the Adriatic sea and adjacent valleys. The aqueduct, which, according to the infcription on it, was built by Paul V, is nothing extraordinary. But fuch is the fertility of this country, that the Macerata artichokes are frequently known to weigh above twenty pounds. The Recanati celery and the Loretto fennel are alfo highly efteemed; but the latter is yet inferior to that which grows in Sicily. {Large artichokes.}

LORETTO.   I ever remain, &c.

LETTER LXII.

Defcription of LORETTO.

SIR,

THE Cafa Santa, or the houfe in which the virgin Mary is faid to have lived in Nazareth, has rendered Loretto famous all over Chriftendom. It is pretended to have been carried in the month of May, 1291, through the air from Galilee to Terfato in Dalmatia by angels; and four years and a half afterwards to have been carried to Italy, where about midnight on the 10th of December, 1294, it was fet down in a wood in the diftrict of Recanati, about a thoufand paces from the fea. If Turfellini may be credited, on the alighting of this facred houfe from its aerial journey, all the trees and fhrubs in the wood bowed with the greateft reverence, and continued in that pofture till at laft they withered and decayed. It feems the remains of this pious wood, by the brutal irreverence of the peafants, were dug up in the year 1575 in order to improve the land*.

A rich and pious lady whofe name was Laureta, being at that time lady of the manor, the holy houfe was from her name called the houfe of Laureta. The road leading to this facred houfe becoming dangerous by the cruelties of robbers, which deterred the pilgrims from reforting thither to perform their devotions, at the end of a few months the angels took it up again and removed it to a hill about a thoufand paces nearer to Recanati. The place where it was then fituated belonged to two brothers, who at firft received the {Derivation of the name of Loretto.}

* Vide Horatii Turfellini Hiftoria Lauretana, edit. Venet. 1727, 8vo, p. 27 & feq.

present

present with becoming joy and gratitude: but it was not long before the vast profits accruing from the resort of pilgrims to the holy house, and the rich offerings they made, kindled such feuds betwixt them as terminated in a duel, in which both the brothers lost their lives.

To prevent any farther misfortunes, and as a punishment to the unworthy possessors of such a treasure, it is pretended the holy virgin again directed the angels to remove the house a bow-shot further up the country, to an eminence about two thousand geometrical paces from the sea; and this is the place where it now stands. This happened a few months after it had been placed on the estate of those bloody-minded brothers; and it is received as a matter of fact, that the Casa Santa, within a year after its first arrival in Italy from Dalmatia, shifted its place three times in the district of Recanati.

The popish writers are at a loss for an answer to the objection, that the Casa Santa had been near two hundred years in Italy before any author of that country took any notice of it*. But what greatly contributed to bring the *Madona di Lorretto* in vogue was the offering of a golden cup by pope Pius II. in person, on which is to be seen the following inscription:

Pia Dei Genitrix,

Quamvis tua potestas nullis coarctetur finibus, ac totum impleat Orbem miraculis; quia tamen pro voluntate sæpius uno loco magis quàm alio delectaris, & Laureti tibi placitam sedem per singulos dies innumeris signis & miraculis exornas; ego infelix peccator, mente & animo ad Te recurro supplex orans, ut mihi ardentem febrim molestissimaque tussim auferas, læsisque membris sanitatem restituas, Reipublicæ, ut credimus, salutarem. Interim hoc munus accipito meæ servitutis signum.

Pius Papa II. Ann. hum. Sal.
MCCCCLXIV.

‘ Propitious Mother of God!
‘ Though thy unlimited power fills the whole world with
‘ miracles; yet as thou art often pleased to shew thyself
‘ more delighted with some places than others, and continuest
‘ daily by innumerable signs and wonders to distinguish this
‘ thy favourite seat at Lorretto; I, who am a miserable

---

* The author's confutation of this and other miracles of the same kind I have omitted, since the bare mention of them is enough to shew the ridiculous absurdity of such fables, which would hardly gain credit among Hottentots.

‘ sinner,

'sinner, run to thee for succour, and from the bottom of my
heart implore thy assistance; humbly intreating thee to relieve me from a burning fever and a violent cough, and
likewise to restore the use of my feeble limbs, as I am persuaded that my recovery will be a public benefit to Christendom. In the mean time gracioussly accept of this offering
from thy devoted servant, Pius II. pope, 1464.'

This offering and the omnipotence ascribed to the virgin Mary in the above-mentioned address were however of little effect; for his holiness died that very year at Ancona, and of the same complication of distempers against which he was for procuring the virgin's assistance, by means of this splendid offering. But Tursellini roundly affirms, that the pope was cured at Loretto immediately after he had finished his prayer.

As to the dimensions of the Casa Santa, it is about forty feet in length, not quite twenty in breadth, and about twenty-five in height, according to Tursellini; but this author is even here very inaccurate: the house being properly forty-three Roman *palmi* wanting two inches in length within the edifice, eighteen *palmi* four inches broad, and twenty-six *palmi* in height. Hence it appears that the length is thirty-one feet and three quarters, the breadth thirteen feet and near three inches, and the height eighteen feet and three quarters English measure, reckoning a *palmi* and a half equal to thirteen inches. In the center of the roof it is five *palmi* higher than on the sides. Formerly this house had only a timber cieling; but, left by a great number of lights continually burning here it should happen to take fire, Clement VII. caused a vaulted roof to be made. For that end, and to strengthen the foundation as well as to prevent any damage by making this alteration, it was strongly compacted with rafters, boards, and ropes, and supported by machines till the new foundation was carried up, so as to be joined with the old walls of the house. At the same time also the door was altered: for there being only one entrance towards the north, which was in the front; to remedy this inconvenience, on account of the vast concourse of people coming in and going out, it was thought advisable to wall this up and make three other doors; two for the people, and a third opening into the holiest part of the chapel for the clergy. These breaches for the doors, by order of the pope, were not entered upon till after a proper course of

[margin:] Description of the holy house.

fasting,

LORETTO.

fasting, &c. For it is pretended that Nerucio the architect, going about it without the proper preparations, as if it had been a common work, was seized with a sudden illness which was very near proving fatal to him. The west window opposite to the image of the virgin was also enlarged and secured with a gilt iron-work. The rafters, boards, tiles, and other materials that were taken away when these alterations were made, are deposited under the floor of the Casa Santa, that they might not be set up as reliques in other places, which might prove prejudicial to Loretto. With this view also the people are made to believe, and numberless instances are alledged, that those who presume clandestinely to carry away so much as a bit of stone or mortar belonging to this sacred house, are punished with diseases and other misfortunes, and become extremely wretched, having no peace of mind till they bring back what they have pilfered. This is farther confirmed by shewing a stone fastened with two iron braces in the wall, which John Soarius bishop of Conimbria, in the year 1562, sent back from Trent, that his health which had been impaired for taking away that stone might be restored; though he had pope Pius the Fourth's permission for so doing, and the stone was intended to be preserved as a relique in a new-built church in Portugal. The people therefore must be satisfied, and even account it no small favour to be permitted to kifs or lick the walls of the Casa Santa. This celebrated edifice is manifestly built of bricks of unequal sizes, though the popish writers labour labour hard to prove it a kind of stone*, at present, no where to be found. These bricks indeed are not placed in the most regular order: however, should curiosity or devotion prompt a person to carry off the least fragment, he would find it difficult to avoid discovery; the cement, as is observed in all old buildings, being very hard to break off. On the cieling is painted the assumption of the virgin Mary; but at present it is almost obscured by the smoke of the great number of lamps continually burning in this house.

On the top of the Casa Santa is a little tower, which the Roman-catholics cannot deny to have been the work of Christians; since it is contrary to all probability to imagine, that the virgin Mary had such a tower erected upon her

---

* It would be no difficult matter to make the people believe this, when they have swallowed the fable recited above concerning this house.

mean-

mean habitation. In violent tempests of thunder and lightning, they ring two little bells which are hung in the tower, not doubting but their sound will disperse any tempest, and prevent any ill effects from it.

There is one part of the Casa Santa, which may be looked upon as the holy of holies; for it is separated from the other part by a silver balustrade and a gate of the same metal. This is said to be the spot where the virgin was sitting when the angel Gabriel appeared to her at the time of the annunciation. The silver balustrade was a gift of cardinal Portacarrero, and the gate of the same metal of cardinal Magalotti.

The window through which the angel came into the house, is shewn on the west side of the Casa Santa. The image of the virgin Mary, which stands facing it, is made of cedar, and is five feet in height. The evangelist St. Luke (who from the number of portraits of our Saviour and his mother, said to be done by him, must have had little time to spare for any thing else) has in this piece given us a specimen of his skill in sculpture*. The divine infant in her right arm is not quite two *palmi* high, and of the same wood; in her left-hand she has a globe, and two fingers on the right-hand are erect, as if she was giving the blessing. The faces of both images have been overlaid with a kind of silver lacker, which is now become quite black with the continual smoke of the lamps; so that the virgin Mary wants only a thick upper lip to make her a perfect negro †. The infant Jesus is dressed in a flame-coloured habit, and the virgin Mary in an azure robe, with which she is so modestly covered; that

Remarkable window. The image of the virgin.
Of Christ.
Dress.

---

* All the pieces shewn as St. Luke's works would make a very large collection; but it happens that the whole pretence of the evangelist's skill in painting relies upon the slender foundation of Nicephorus's testimony, and some other stories no less suspicious. The probability of it, however, vanishes, by considering that the ancient Jews and primitive Christians, according to the accounts of Josephus and Clemens Alexandrinus, exploded painting, as highly pernicious both to the state and religion. This is farther confirmed by the silence of the most ancient writers; and merits the more attention, as the fathers of the second council of Nice make no mention of St. Luke's painting; whereas it would have made very strongly for their zeal in support of images. It is very probable that St. Luke's descriptive account of the virgin's virtues, &c. have given rise to this fiction of his being a painter.

† The apocryphal book of Baruch, ch. vi. v. 21, likewise mentions the faces of idols grown quite black with the smoke of the lamps burning before them. See also Arnobius, *lib. vi. adversus gentes, p.* 202.

nothing

nothing is to be seen of the statue but its face and the toes. The mantle hanging down her shoulders is of the same colour, powdered with golden stars; her hair hangs on her shoulders and part of her back. On her head is a triple crown of gold, enriched with pearls and diamonds, and another on that of the child Jesus; both were the gift of Lewis XIII. king of France, and valued at seventy-five thousand *scudi*, or crowns. On the former are these words engraven:

Crown.

> *Tu caput ante meum cinxisti Virgo coronâ,*
> *Nunc caput ecce teget nostra corona tuum.*

‘ In return for the crown which thou, O holy virgin, didst bestow on me, accept of this which I have placed on thy head.’

On the latter:
> *Christus dedit Mihi,*
> *Christo reddo coronam.*

‘ Christ gave me a crown, and I restore it again.’

Jewels.

The gold-chains, rings, and jewels with which this image of the virgin Mary is loaded, though they make a most splendid appearance, I pass over, as they cannot be very entertaining in a description. They are also sometimes varied, in order to strike the eye with such alterations; and the jewels which are taken off at such times are laid up in the treasury. Her apparel also is not always the same; for on the seven days of passion-week she is dressed in deep mourning, and complimented with a fresh suit every day. When they take off or put on any part of the virgin's apparel, they use a great deal of ceremony, and low inclinations of the body; whilst the crouding spectators lay their distresses before the saint with loud invocations, the violence of which increases as the priests proceed in undressing the image; as if the cries of the suppliants could sooner touch the heart of the virgin when naked, than when she is dressed in her robes. The sculptor has taken care that the modesty of the priests should not be offended with the sight of a naked female statue, by adding a proper covering. An account of some of the ornaments which are generally to be seen on this pompous pious image may not be displeasing to the reader. 1. A jewel consisting of thirteen rubies, sixty-six emeralds, and three hundred and fifty-one diamonds, which was an offering of Anne, a princess of Neuburg, and consort of Charles II. of Spain. 2. A golden crucifix, with very large and beautiful emeralds, the gift of cardinal Paolo Sfondrata. 3. Two large pearls set in gold, hanging at the divine infant's hand, presented by a princess of Darmstadt. 4. A crucifix set with diamonds of great value, given by cardinal Marescotto. 5. and 6. Two other crucifixes set with rubies and diamonds, offered by the cardinals Barberini and Corsi. 7. The badge of the golden-fleece, with a collar set with large sapphires, rubies, emeralds, and topazes, the gift of Catharine wife of Gabriel Bethlen Gabor, prince of Transylvania. 8. A large golden heart hanging at a gold chain set with rubies and diamonds, offered by Maximilian I. elector of Bavaria. 9. A cluster of diamonds, rubies, and emeralds set in gold, on which is a pelican feeding her young-ones with her blood, represented by a very large ruby at her breast, an offering of the dutchess d'Ucceda, 10. A large emerald, set round with diamonds and rubies, which hangs on one of the infant's hands, the gift of the dutchess de Salviati. 11. Three admirable emeralds set in gold, and surrounded by diamonds and other emeralds, presented by Violanta Beatrix, a princess of the house of Bavaria, and widow of Ferdinand hereditary prince of Florence. The niche in which the image stands is adorned with seventy-one large Bohemian topazes, the offering of the cavalier Capra.

On the right-side of the image is an angel of cast gold, profusely enriched with diamonds and other gems, with one knee inclined, offering a golden heart embellished with large diamonds and terminating in a flame of rubies and pearls, with a lamp burning continually over it. This piece, which is said to have cost 50,000 ducats, was offered by Maria Beatrix Eleanora, of the house of Este, queen of King James II. of England, that by the intercession of the virgin Mary she might conceive a son. Accordingly, soon after, as it is said, she had a son; who has since made so much noise in Europe, under the name of the pretender to the British crown.

Offering on the birth of the pretender.

On the left-side of the virgin's image is a silver angel, in the same reverential posture offering her a golden heart crowned, and glittering with pearls, emeralds, and diamonds, likewise terminating in a flame. This was the gift of Laura Martinozzia,

LORETTO.

tinozzia, widow of Alphonso IV. duke of Modena, and mother to the above-mentioned queen of England.

On the right-hand of the virgin is a silver angel, weighing three hundred and fifty-one pounds, and offering, on a cushion of the same metal, an infant of massy gold, which weighs twenty-four pounds*. This was the gift of Lewis XIII. king of France for the birth of the dauphin, afterwards Lewis XIV. who made a much greater stir in Europe than the Pretender mentioned above. Many other gold and silver images of children I omit; though some of the former exceed twelve pounds in weight. Here one also sees an infinite number of other costly votive pieces, the enumeration of which would engage me in a tedious detail.

The robe which this famous image had on, when it was brought from Dalmatia into Italy, is of red camlet, and kept in a glass shrine. The dish out of which it is pretended the virgin and her divine infant used to eat, is shaped like a shallow bowl, and of glazed earthen-ware; but its outside is now plated over with silver. This utensil is not only kissed; but rosaries, medals, *agnus Dei*'s, crucifixes, and paper caps painted with the image of the Madonna of Loretto are rubbed against it, from a firm persuasion that they thus become an infallible remedy against the head-ach and other disorders. An ague is said to have been perfectly cured only by drinking a little cold water out of this dish: even the oil and wax of the lamps and candles burning before the image, are not without their medicinal virtues. Besides the dish, here are other pieces of furniture, the meanness of which shews the virgin's humility or low condition. Under the image image is the hearth, or fire-place, where she used to dress her victuals, which is now stiled *sacrosanctus caminus*.

Seven golden lamps are continually burning before the image, one of which, presented by the republic of Venice on account of the ceasing of an epidemical distemper, weighs

---

* Dion, in his seventy-second book, says, that the emperor Commodus was possessed of a golden statue weighing a thousand pounds; but this still falls very short of the pieces which Ptolemy Philadelphus once exhibited to the people, as a display of his riches and power. Among these, according to Callixenes of Rhodes, cited in Athenæus's first book, were two golden eagles, each of them fifteen cubits long; one hundred golden couches, three thousand two hundred golden crowns; and likewise a crown eighty cubits in height, which was placed over the entrance of the temple of Berenice; not to mention some other particulars almost incredible.

thirty-seven pounds and a half. Under this hangs another, richly set with jewels, offered a few years since by duke Elia di Palma, who declared that it cost fifteen thousand ducats. The lamp that stands next the virgin's face, which is held by three angels, weighs nine pounds, and is a memorial of the devotion and skill of Francis Maria duke d' Urbino, who is said to have made this admirable piece with his own hands. Another golden lamp, weighing twenty pounds, to be seen here, passes for the work of Sigismund king of Poland. That which Francis II. duke of Modena offered to the virgin, weighs eighteen pounds and a half. Among the thirty-seven silver lamps, with which the other part of the Casa Santa is illuminated, several weigh fifty, eighty, a hundred, and four of them a hundred and twenty-eight pounds. For the supplying of all these lamps with oil, such legacies have been left, or funds settled by the persons who presented them, that that they are so far from being a charge to the Casa Santa, as to yield a confiderable profit to it; some thousands of dollars being the least legacy left for each lamp.

The altar stands in the middle of the partition betwixt Altar. the *sanctum sanctorum* and the other part of the chapel. It does not intercept the full view of the image, which stands pretty high in the sanctuary behind the altar. The credulous papists affirm, that this altar was made by the apostles themselves, and brought hither from Galilee along with the sacred house.

On this altar is a square stone, on which St. Peter is said to have celebrated the first mass. The splendid *palliotto*, enriched with jasper, *lapis lazuli*, and agate, was the gift of Cosmo II. great duke of Tuscany.

Over the window, through which the angel Gabriel came into the virgin's house at the annunciation, stands a picture of the crucifixion, pretended to be brought by the apostles into this house, and to have been by St. Luke.

The present new floor of the Casa Santa consists of square pieces of red and white marble. The walls seem to have been formerly plastered with mortar; part of which, with the protrait of the virgin Mary, and a groupe of angels painted on it, is still remaining.

Notwithstanding the mean appearance of the walls within, the outside of the Casa Santa is most elegantly adorned with the finest marble; but it is so contrived, that the marble structure serves only as a case for it, leaving a small interval betwixt it and the brick walls of the Casa Santa. This is partly to
be

LORETTO.

be attributed to the veneration entertained for those sacred materials, and partly from an apprehension that they would not have suffered the new and unhallowed marble to be in contact with them; but would have repelled it with such violence, as to endanger the lives of the workmen. This (according to tradition) formerly happened to some builders, who, out of an indiscreet zeal, were going about to strengthen these sacred walls by some new additions.

The above-mentioned marble case was begun in the year 1514, in the pontificate of pope Leo X. and consecrated in the year 1538, by Paul III. The expence of it at that time, when labour was cheap, amounted to twenty-two thousand ducats, exclusive of twenty marble statues, and four brass doors of curious workmanship, which have been since added, and must have cost an immense sum*. The most celebrated sculptors of that age, as Andrea Sansovino, Francesco Sangalli, Domenico Lamia, Nicolo de Pericoli, Biagio Bandinelli, Giovanni della Porta and his brother Tamaso, Girolamo Lombardi with his brother Aurelio, Rafaëlle da Monte Lupone, il Mosca Fiorentino, Nic. Tribulo, Contucci, &c. seem to have emulated each other in this noble structure. It is about fifty feet in length, thirty broad, and about the same height. No meaner materials than the whitest Carrara marble have been employed in this building. The two longer sides are adorned with twelve Corinthian pillars, and the other two sides with eight. The intervals between the

Fine basso-relievo'a.

pillars, are filled with basso-relievo's finely executed, representing the most remarkable incidents in the life of the blessed virgin, ten statues of the prophets, and above these the ten sibyls. Among the prophets on the southside, David, with the head of Goliah at his feet, is greatly admired by all connoisseurs; and on the northside, in a groupe representing the espousals of the virgin Mary, a boy playing with a dog, whilst his mother, with a child in her arms, looks at him with a countenance full of maternal tenderness and complacency, cannot be viewed without pleasure. This piece was designed and begun by Contucci, and finished by Raphael da Monte Lupone and Nicolo Tribulo. In the basso-relievo that exhibits the extraordinary conveyance of the Casa Santa

* The Casa Santa has indeed four doors, but one of them is a false door; for there are but three entrances cut through the wall. The brass-work is said to be done by Girolamo Lombardi.

through

LORETTO.

through the air, the expreffion in a peafant driving his afs before him is ftrong and natural. This is the joint work of Tribulo and Sangalli. Under this piece is the following infcription:

Chriftiane Hofpes, qui pietatis causâ huc advenifti, facram Lauretani ædem vides divinis myfteriis & miraculorum gloriâ toto Orbe terrarum venerabilem. Hic fanctiffima Dei Genitrix Maria in Lucem edita. Hic ab angelo falutata. Hic æterni Dei Verbum Caro factum eft. Hanc Angeli primùm à Paleftina ad Illyrium adduxere ad Terfanctum Oppidum anno falutis MCCXCI. Nicolao IV. fummo Pontifice. Poftea initio Pontificatûs Bonifacii VIII. in Picenum tranflata prope Recinetam urbem in hujus collis nemore eâdem angelorum operâ collocata; ubi loco intra anni fpatium ter commutato, hic poftremo fedem divinitùs fixit anno abhinc CCC. Ex eo tempore tantæ ftupendæ rei novitate vicinis populis ad admirationem commotis, tum deinceps miraculorum famâ longè latèque propagatâ, Sancta hæc domus magnâ apud omnes gentes veneratione habita, cujus parietes nullis fundamentis fubnixi, poft tot feculorum ætates integri ftabilefque permanent. Clemens VIII. Pontifex Maximus in hoc marmoreo lapide infcribi juffit. Anno Domini MDXCV.

' Chriftian ftranger, whom devotion has brought hither,
' thou feeft here the facred houfe of Loretto, which by its
' divine myfteries, and the fame of its miracles, claims the
' veneration of the whole world. In this houfe the moft
' holy Mary, mother of God, was born; here fhe was vi-
' fited by the angel; here the WORD of the eternal God
' was made FLESH. This facred houfe was firft brought
' by angels from Paleftine to the town of Terfati in Illyria,
' in the year of the Chriftian Æra 1291, and in the ponti-
' ficate of Nicholas IV. Afterwards in the beginning of
' the pontificate of Boniface VIII. it was removed by angels
' a fecond time acrofs the feas, and placed in a wood near
' Recanati: and laftly, after changing its fituation three
' times within the fpace of a year, it was at length, by di-
' vine appointment, fixed on this hill, about three hundred
' years fince. From that time the reputation of this facred
' houfe has been continually increafing by the univerfal won-
' der raifed among the neighbouring ftates by fo remarkable
' an event, and likewife by the fame of its miracles, which
' have attracted the veneration of the whole world. Its
' walls, though without any foundation, after fuch a fuc-
' ceffion

'ceſſion of ages, ſtill remain found and intire. This inſcription was cut in marble, and put up by order of his holineſs Clement VIII. in the year of Chriſt 1595.'

The Caſa Santa could not be truly ſaid to ſtand without a foundation in the time of pope Clement VIII. which (according to Turſellini, p. 138.) had been laid by pope Clement VII.

Caſe of the holy houſe. The edifice which incloſes the holy houſe was deſigned by Bramante. Sanſovino, Tribulo, and Andrea Contucci deſigned the ſculpture, and alſo executed the greateſt part. It was at laſt compleated in the year 1579, and Gregory XIII. had the honour of putting the finiſhing hand to this ſuperb work. It ſtands in the middle of a beautiful and ſpacious church, which preſerves it from the injuries of the weather. The pilgrims, in their firſt proceſſion, generally walk round the Caſa Santa on their knees, though they are under no particular injunctions to do this; for the manner of their performing their devotions here is left to the dictates of their blind zeal.

No perſon to enter the Caſa Santa with arms. No perſon is permitted to enter the houſe with a ſword, or any other weapon, which muſt be delivered to an eccleſiaſtic, who ſits over-againſt the door of the ſanctuary, and receives the little pecuniary preſents which are made for the benefit of the church. A *ſcudi* is a ſufficient gratuity for a company of two or three perſons, and the like ſum muſt be given at ſeeing the treaſury: but the offerings of the pilgrims are very conſiderable, and may without exaggeration be computed at many thouſands of ducats annually.

The extraordinary worſhip paid by the Romaniſts to the virgin Mary is ſufficiently known: and as the veneration for reliques has been, in the laſt century, carried to the higheſt pitch, it may eaſily be conceived what a concourſe of people muſt be continually reſorting to a houſe in which the virgin Mary was born, brought up, eſpouſed, and lived after marriage; in which alſo the incarnation of Chriſt was made known to her, where ſhe was overſhadowed by the Holy Ghoſt, and laſtly, where our Saviour himſelf paſſed a great part of his life. From this laſt circumſtance, ſome Romaniſts, when aſked why this relique only, preferably to any other memorial of the evangelical hiſtory, eſpecially the holy ſepulchre, was brought away from the infidels by the miniſtry of angels, and removed into Europe? alledge for anſwer, that, among other reaſons, it was owing to that natural rural fondness which our Saviour retained for the house in which he had passed many pleasant hours in his childhood, &c.

The number of pilgrims who visited this place in a year has formerly amounted to two hundred thousand; but the reformation has given a severe blow to the sale of indulgences; and even among those who still adhere to the Romish church the zeal for tiresome pilgrimages has cooled, or run into other channels; so that at present the number of pilgrims repairing hither annually, for devotion, seldom exceeds forty or fifty thousand. It is not many years since nine thousand happened to be at Loretto at one time; and what a confusion such a number must occasion in this little town, may easily be conceived. Some pilgrims come afoot, some ride on asses or horses. The female pilgrims who can afford it, generally travel to Loretto in a carriage; and, as large companies often journey together, many droll incidents happen on the road. As soon as they enter the suburbs, at the foot of the hill, they set up a singing, which continues till they reach the church. If the company be too large, the ceremony of going round the Casa Santa on their knees is omitted; and they are obliged to express their devotion in some other manner. The poorer sort of pilgrims are received into an hospital, where they are provided with beds, and bread and wine every morning and evening for three days. The greatest concourse is seen here in May, June, and part of July, and likewise in September; for it seems Paulus à Sylva was informed in a vision that the virgin Mary was born on the eighth day of that month.

The large church, in which the case of the Casa Santa stands, as if it was under a tent, is built of Istrian stone, which resembles the Travertino stone used at Rome. The front is entirely of marble, and embellished with very fine sculpture; and over the portal is a statue of the holy virgin, by the ingenious Lombardi. The three doors on this side of the church are of bronze with beautiful basso-relievo's, representing different histories of the Old Testament; these are likewise the work of Lombardi. Over the middle door are these words:

Domus Deiparæ, in quâ Verbum Caro factum est.

'The house of the mother of God in which the word
'was made flesh.'

Besides

LORETTO.

Altars and fine paintings.

Befides the altar of the annunciation which ftands on the weft fide of the church without the Cafa Santa, there are reckoned in the church about nineteen other altars and chapels, in which Peregrino Tibaldo, Annibal Caracci, Frederico Barocci, Frederico Zuccari, Gafparino, Giovanni Baglioni, Simon Vouet, Girolamo Mutiani, Francefco Orvieta, Lorenzo Loth, Filippo Bellini d'Urbino, Giovanni Battifta de Montenuovo, Francefco Minichio di Forli, and other celebrated artifts, have given fpecimens of their uncommon fkill.

The fetters of four thoufand Chriftians, who, by the naval victory at Lepanto in the time of pope Pius V. in 1571, were releafed from Turkifh flavery, afforded materials to make the iron grates at the front of the feveral chapels in this church. The great cupola is fupported by eight large pilafters; and in it is painted the affumption and glorification of the virgin Mary, painted by Chriftopher Roncalli, otherwife called il Cavaliere Pomarancio. This cupola is covered on the outfide with a hundred and thirteen thoufand pounds of lead *.

Font.

The font ftands in a feparate chapel and coft fixteen thoufand *fcudi*. It is of bronze and embellifhed with beautiful baffo-relievo's, reprefenting fcriptural hiftories. The bafon ftands on four angels, and over it is the baptifm of our Saviour by John the Baptift. It is the work of Verzelli da Camerino.

Cardinal Gaetani's monument.

On the beautiful marble monument of cardinal Gaetani is the following infcription:

NICOLAVS GAETANVS, Cardinalis Sermonetæ, Gentilis Papæ Bonif. VIII. cum fub id tempus, quo ille Pontificatum iniit, fanctam hanc domum hic tandem divinitús confediffe, & multa fe a Deo Opt. Max. B. Virg. Deiparæ precibus obtinuiffe meminiffet, fperans ejufdem opem morienti non defuturam, monumentum hoc marmoreum vivens & incolumis fibi faciendum curavit, atque in eo, ubi mortalitatem exuiffet, corpus fuum recondi voluit, ann. agens LIV. Obiit annos natus ferme LX. Ann. Sal. hum. MDLXXXV. Menfe Majo.

' Nicholas Gaetini, cardinal Sermoneta, domeftic chaplain to pope Boniface VIII, calling to mind, that about the

---

* *Vide Le Glorie maeftofe del Santuario di Loretto*, publifhed in octavo at Macerata by Baltafar Bartolini.

' time

LORETTO.

'time in which he entered into holy orders, this sacred house
'had by divine appointment been fixed on this spot; and
'that he had received many favours from the Almighty by
'the intercession of the blessed virgin mother of God; in
'hopes that her assistance would not be wanting to him in
'his last moments, whilst alive and in his health, caused
'this marble monument to be erected, in the 54th year of
'his age, for the receptacle of his body, when he should
'put off mortality. He died in the month of May 1585,
'when he had almost reached the sixtieth year of his age.'

The remains of this cardinal were brought hither from Rome, where he died, and on his tomb-stone is this inscription:

Hic habitabo, quoniam elegi eam:

'Here will I dwell, because I have chosen her.'

The pavement of the church consists of square pieces of white and red marble.

Here are several confessionals with superscriptions over them, signifying in what language strangers may confess at any of them, and receive absolution. Upwards of twenty Jesuits are appointed as constant confessors; and among these a person of any European nation at least may find one who understands his native language. Formerly the Carmelite monks had the care of the Casa Santa, and it was promised them by pope Innocent VIII, as they alledged, that they had, for a long time before, been in possession of it, whilst the house stood in Galilee. This allegation was further confirmed by the deposition of a female demoniac*. But these fathers having for the space of nine years quitted not only their function, but the town of Loretto also, on account of its unhealthfulness, pope Leo X. instituted canons in their stead, with a cardinal as president over them; and at last pope Sixtus V. settled a bishop here. The air of this place owes its present salubrity to pope Clement VII. who caused several little eminences to be levelled, woods to be cut down, and the morasses to be drained.

Confessio-nals.

Canons.

---

* Turselllin. p. 104. This demoniac was a native of Grenoble, from whom information was received concerning the spot on which the virgin Mary and the angel stood at the annunciation.

LORETTO.

Chaplains. On account of the many masses partly founded for ever, and partly well paid for and said here daily on particular occasions, the Casa Santa maintains near eighty chaplains, who, with the canons, beneficiaries, and ecclesiastics that came to Loretto out of devotion, constantly perform this essential part of the Romish religion. The number of masses, daily said in the Casa Santa and in the great church where it stands, amount to a hundred and twenty-three, and in the whole year to forty-four thousand eight hundred and ninety-five.

Eunuch priests. The eunuchs, who sing the offices in the choir of the Holy Chapel, likewise say masses here; and on such occasions carry their testicles about them in a little box, wisely concluding, according to mathematical calculation, that the fractions $\frac{9}{100}$ and $\frac{6}{100}$ are always equal to an integer. No such practice however is known at Rome; but in the northern parts of Italy it is very common.

The priests of Cybele the mother of the gods, according to Lucian *de Dea Syria*, were eunuchs; and the indispensable qualification for performing the rites of the said goddess was,

Per triste vulnus, perque sectum dedecus;

' A grievous wound and an infamous castration,'

as Prudentius expresses it.

Mutilated persons excluded from holy orders. Eunuchs saying mass, however, is not contrary to the papal laws, which exclude from the priesthood only such mutilated persons as have voluntarily and deliberately deprived themselves of their virility, a finger, a foot, or an eye*. But if any such thing has happened to a person in his childhood, or involuntarily, or by the direction of physicians, it shall not disqualify him for holy orders †. As to the loss of the left eye, which is called *oculus canonis*, the reason assigned for rejecting a candidate on that account is, that a priest who wants that eye when he reads mass, is obliged, at saying *Dominus vobiscum*, the Lord be with you,' to turn his head‡. Those who are deprived of any member, either by their

---

* *c. pœnitentes* 3, *c. si quis abscidit* 4, *c. qui partem* 6, *c. lator.* 11, *c. si Evangelica* 13, *dist.* 55.

† *Dist. c. si quis abscidit c.* 1, 3, & 5, *corp. vitiat. ord. c. si quis a medicis* 7, *dist.* 55 : *Nisi fit elusçatus c. fin. dist.* 55 : *quia talis nunquam ordinari potest.*

‡ A certain ignorant priest, who had lost one eye, looking round, and observing only a single person present at mass, thought he had done mighty well in saying *Dominus tibiscum*.

own

own hand, defire, or fault, muft have a difpenfation previoufly to their admittance into holy orders. Where the *minutiæ* of the canon law are fo cautioufly obferved, it were to be wifhed that fome attention were paid to more important precepts, founded both in natural and revealed religion; and that the Italian clergy could more ferioufly confider and put in execution the canons *de vita & honeflate cleric.* as alfo *de excef. prelat.* which deprive incumbents of their benefices *ob mafculam Venerem*.

Formerly the walls of the church at Loretto were covered with multitudes of pictures and votive pieces; fome of wood, others of wax or brafs: but, befides the coarfenefs of the performance and meannefs of many of them, they very much darkened the church; and therefore, in 1673, the far greater part of them were removed, and the filver and gold tablets employed to better ufes. Near the Cafa Santa in this church is ftill to be feen the picture of a prieft offering his entrails to the virgin Mary. The occafion of putting up this picture, according to the infcription under it, is as follows: This prieft, by birth a Dalmatian, lived at the beginning of the fixteenth century, and had always entertained the higheft veneration for the Madonna di Loretto; being taken prifoner by the Turks, and ftrongly folicited to abjure the Chriftian religion, he not only withftood their menaces and promifes, but to vex the infidels never ceafed calling upon the name of Chrift and the virgin Mary, till he was afked the reafon of fuch loud and continual invocations. His anfwer was, that, thofe names being engraven in the inmoft receffes of his heart, he could not forbear it. And when they threatened to tear his heart and entrails out of his body, if he did not immediately renounce Chrift and Mary, he replied, that the firft was in their power, but that it was impoffible to take away Chrift and Mary from him. Upon this, the Turks immediately put their threatenings in execution. The Dalmatian prieft in the midft of his torture ftill perfifted in calling upon Mary with a loud voice, and promifing a pilgrimage to Loretto. As he lay expiring, they put his heart and entrails, which they had torn out of him, into his hands, farcaftically telling him, that he might now go and perform his promife, and carry that offering to Loretto.

They had no fooner fpoke but the martyr immediately fet out with his heart and entrails in his hand, and at length arrived at Loretto; where having fhewed his empty thorax,

Ridiculous fable.

and offered his entrails, &c. and after relating the whole affair, and receiving the facrament, he died in an ecftacy of joy. The Jefuit Terfellini, in his *Hiftoria Lauretana*, lib. ii. c. 18, adds, that thefe entrails hung a long time in the church as memorials of the miracle; but, that decaying by length of time, a reprefentation of them cut in wood was put in their place. Thefe wooden entrails however were afterwards removed by order of Paul III, becaufe the common people began to entertain a greater veneration for them than even for the virgin Mary herfelf. Terfellini's words are, *Quia rufticani homines Lauretanum templum ingreffi, animis tali fpectaculo occupatis, Deiparam fegniore colebant curâ, tandem ea* [exta] *tolli placuit.*

Of the many fabulous ftories related herewith the greateft air of truth, many of which are made public in printed narratives, I fhall only mention one more, concerning a votive piece fent hither from the Netherlands in the year 1586. This was a wax taper weighing three hundred pounds. The donor of this remarkable gift was a Flemifh officer in the duke of Parma's troops, who, being once fent with eight others of the cavalry to reconnoitre the enemy, fell into an ambufcade, and was attacked by a body of three hundred men, horfe and foot. Under fo vaft a difparity, the Flemifh officer addreffed himfelf to the holy virgin, who infpired him and his handful of men with fuch courage and vigour, that they not only maintained a fharp action for two hours, till relief came; but at laft entirely routed the enemy. In this hot action not one of the nine heroes, nor even of their horfes, received any wound. The votary fent the abovementioned taper to Loretto to burn there on certain days before the Cafa Santa; and likewife a fum of money, the intereft of which was to procure fuch another candle when this fhould be burnt out, without fo much as mentioning his name; which piece of humility may to fome appear no lefs extraordinary than his victory *.

Veftry. On the fouth fide of the great church ftands the veftry, which is peculiarly appointed for thofe priefts who officiate
Paintings. in the holy houfe. The paintings in it are by Raphael, Andrea del Sarto, Parmegiano, Frederico Barocci, Guido Rheni, Mutiano, Tintoretto, Paolo Veronefe, Tearini,
Treafury. Schidoni, Cantarino, and Fanelli. Adjoining to this veftry is a large faloon, the cieling of which was painted by Po-

* Turfellini, *lib.* v. c. 18.

merancio,

LORETTO.

merancio, and the pavement is inlaid with marble of various colours. This apartment contains a treasure worth many millions, consisting of the most valuable jewels and offerings made to the virgin Mary, which are not used in decking out her image. It is remarkable, that this prodigious treasure has been accumulated within these three centuries; for all the gifts and donations belonging to the Casa Santa, in the year 1470, amounted to no more than six thousand ducats. These jewels, &c. are kept in shrines within the wall, which are secured with close grates, and cannot be viewed without astonishment. In the middle of each grate is the figure of a cock. The ecclesiastics who attend on strangers here, have a wand with which they point to every piece as they give an account of it: the same method is also observed in the sanctuary of the holy house. To enumerate every particular piece of this immense treasure would be almost impossible; and I believe it will be more to your satisfaction that I confine myself to the most remarkable curiosities to be seen here, which are as follows:

1. The crown and sceptre enriched with jewels, which queen Christina, after her abdication of the throne of Sweden, brought hither and offered to the virgin Mary.

<small>Most remarkable curiosities at Loretto.</small>

2. A golden crown set with rubies, pearls, and diamonds, presented by a princess of Ragotzi.
3. Two branches of coral near a foot and a half high.
4. A crown of *lapis-lazuli*.
5. A crown of agate.
6. A robe which Isabella a princess of the house of Bourbon, and queen to Philip IV. king of Spain, brought hither, and had fitted for the Madonna di Loretto. It is enriched with six thousand six hundred and eighty-four diamonds.
7. An emerald four times as big as a man's head, in which, as in a matrix, are to be seen a great many smaller emeralds inclosed. For this valuable natural curiosity, which was offered to the virgin by Philip IV, king of Spain, an English gentleman offered ninety thousand *scudi*, or crowns.
8. In another shrine is a very large amethyst set in gold, but not so big as the emerald before-mentioned.
9. A chain of the golden fleece presented by the same king Philip, which is set with so many fine rubies, pearls, and diamonds, that it deserves to be reckoned one of the most valuable pieces in this treasury.

10. A golden candlestic set with rubies, opals, emeralds, pearls, and diamonds, weighing twenty-three pounds, and of very curious workmanship, offered by prince Camillo Pamfili.

11. A crown set with pearls and rubies, presented by the above-mentioned princess of Ragotzi.

12. A missal, the cover of which is adorned with twelve large topazes, given by Ferdinand II, great duke of Florence.

13. A pearl looked upon as invaluable, and the most extraordinary jewel in this treasury; nature itself (as is pretended) having delineated on it the holy virgin, sitting on a cloud, and holding the infant Jesus in her arms. To this art has contributed nothing, as pearls will not admit of it; but it must also be allowed, that imagination must strongly assist the eye to make out any distinct figure on it. However, this pearl (the donor of which has out of humility concealed his name) is, by reason of its extraordinary size, very valuable. Sir Hans Sloan of London is possessed of a fine pearl, to which several others are concreted in the form of a bunch of grapes *. Pieces of marble plainly representing Apollo and the Muses have been discovered by the ancients. Pliny (*Hist. Nat. lib.* xxxvi. *c.* 5.) mentions a representation of Silenus found in a block of Parian marble.

14. A pearl of the bigness of a pigeon's egg, presented by the marquis del Vasto, one of the chief commanders under Charles V.

15. A piece of virgin gold, as it came out of the mine, weighing eleven ounces.

16. A set of altar-furniture of amber, with a *palliotto*, &c. set with between six and seven thousand pearls, besides diamonds and rubies, and valued at two hundred thousand crowns. This was sent as an offering, in the year 1639, by Catharine Zamoiscia, dutchess of Ostrog, the high chancellor of Poland's lady.

---

* This is not the first time our author has made mention of Sir Hans Sloan's *Museum*: and indeed the value and magnificency of it is so great, that for some time past the learned world has been in expectation that an act of parliament would pass, to prevent the curiosities in it from being dispersed, after the decease of its worthy possessor. [This *museum*, after the death of Sir Hans Sloan has been purchased by the public, according to act of parliament, and is now called the *British Museum*.]

17. Another

LORETTO.

17. Another complete set of altar-furniture, with a crucifix, the canopy, vestments, &c. all set with coral, and presented a few years ago by prince Avellini of Naples.

18. The imperial eagle set with diamonds.

19. The same entirely made of diamonds, with a brilliant of an uncommon size and lustre on the breast, which is of the finest water in the whole treasure. This work, with the golden fleece appendant to it, which is likewise enriched with valuable diamonds, is one of the finest pieces in the whole treasury, and was the offering of the empress Mary, mother to the emperor Leopold I.

20. A ship of gold, being a votive piece of a princess of Mansfeldt, who imagined, that, by the assistance of the virgin Mary, she was saved in a shipwrec.

21. The virgin's statue of amber, on a pedestal of gold.

22. A diamond weighing seventy-three grains, offered by prince Carlo Doria.

23. Two silver candlestics, one weighing a hundred and nine, the other a hundred and twelve pounds, presented by cardinal Paulusi d'Altieri.

24. The imperial eagle, of gold, flying into the virgin Mary's lap, enriched with diamonds and pearls, presented in the year 1700 by prince Vasto.

25. Two golden candlestics, inlaid with agate, chrysolite, *lapis-lazuli*, hyacinths, and topazes, of excellent workmanship, presented two years ago by Violanta Beatrix, hereditary princess-dowager of Florence, of the house of Bavaria, on her coming to Loretto.

26. A silver *ostensorium*, so weighty as scarce to be carried by a single man, the gift of the same princess.

27. A large golden crucifix, enriched with six sapphires of an extraordinary size, and a great number of diamonds, the offering of cardinal d'Acugna of Portugal.

28. The pretender to the crown of Great-Britain, coming to Loretto some years since with his lady, offered a golden angel about a foot in height; which the virgin should look upon as an instance of extraordinary devotion, as he could but ill afford such costly presents.

Pretender's offering.

29, 30. Two regal crowns, one enriched with pearls, the other larger, and richly set with diamonds, both tokens of the great respect which the above-mentioned princess Ragotzi bore to the virgin Mary.

31. A beautiful goblet of *lapis-lazuli* on an emerald stand, embellished with three golden sywns, eight diamonds, ten pearls,

pearls, and twelve rubies: the cover is of rock-cryftal fet with large rubies and diamonds. This was the gift of Henry III. of France, with a view of obtaining from the mother of God an heir to his crown, as is expreffed in thefe words on the pedeftal of the cup:

Ut quæ prole tuâ Mundum Regina beâſti,
Et Regnum & Regem prole beare velis.
Henricus III. Franc. & Polon. Rex Chriſtianiſſ.
Anno MDLXXXIV.

‘ That thou, O adorable queen, who haft bleffed the
‘ world by thy offspring, wilt be pleafed to blefs the king
‘ and kingdom with royal iffue, this is offered by his moſt
‘ Chriſtian majeſty Henry III, king of France and Poland.
‘ 1584.’

This rich offering, however, did not procure the defired effect.

32. A filver ftatue, weighing a hundred and fifty-three pounds, given by Adelaide electrefs of Bavaria.

33. A gold ring, fet with a moft beautiful emerald, put into the offering-box by a perfon unknown, with this billet faſtened to it:

Virgo Singularis,
Mites fac & caſtos,
O Amor, qui femper ardes,
Et nunquam extingueris,
Accende me,
Sufcipe me fervum tuum B.

‘ O thou, of virgins the moft extraordinàry, render them
‘ mild and chafte; and thou, Love, whofe bright flames
‘ are never extinguifhed, inflame me, and accept thy
‘ fervant B.’

The meaning of this petition I leave to be unriddled by others.

34. A large golden heart, enriched with diamonds, in which is a reprefentation of two diamond eyes of curious workmanſhip. Thefe were the offerings of Chriſtina dutchefs of Savoy.

The number of fuch votive pieces fet with jewels is above three hundred, exclufive of the fingle jewels often fent

or

or put into the box, without mentioning the votary's name.

35. A large silver altar.

36. The city and citadel of Nancy in Lorrain, of silver chafed, three spans and a half in breadth, and betwixt five and six in length.

37. The Baftile, in silver, sent hither by the prince of Conde; likewise a representation of the cities of Milan, Ferrara, Bologna, Ascoli, Fermo, Recanati, Ancona, Monte Santo, Sarnano, Saverne, &c. also the entire lordship of Montalto, all of silver, which I think may be called the most valuable geographical collection in the world.

Some part of it has been put into three other veftries, where are also kept the twelve apoftles in silver, altogether weighing four hundred and twenty-five pounds, or eight hundred and fifty marks, with an incredible number of other silver and gold statues, &c. The silver pieces are not usually shewn to strangers, as they make too mean an appearance among the more costly and valuable jewels; although the prodigious number of such pieces makes some amends for the basenefs of the metal, when compared to the rest.

It is, however, not improbable that a great number of tablets and votive pieces, that make no great shew, are continually melted down and sent to the mint. The superfluous jewels also, which are not employed in ornaments, are converted into money, for a better use; especially if they have been offered by persons long since dead; or, if from other circumstances, no further enquiry after them is to be apprehended. This I know, that foreign jewellers find their account in visiting the convents in Italy, and get many a valuable jewel for a small sum of ready money, which the monks are very fond of; secrecy being strictly enjoined on both sides. Possibly in many convents, &c. the number of jewels is kept up, and only an exchange is made of a fine stone for a less valuable one, with some allowance. This is a kind of embezzlement which a short space of time puts beyond the possibility of a detection.

Votive pieces melted down.

Church jewels clandestinely sold and changed by monks, &c.

In the above-mentioned Sara del Teforo, on a stone in the pavement is inscribed the date 1626, as a memorial of a thief, who, in that year, found means to convey himself into this place, so proper for him to exercise his trade in; but the pavement, as it is said, immediately opened, and swallowed him up to his waift, so that, being unable to stir, he was taken, and suffered the punishment of his intended sacrilege.

Miraculous discovery of a thief.

Others

LORETTO.

Others relate this story with some additional circumstances: however, the design of them all is to deter people from any future attempt, by citing such dreadful examples of judgments inflicted on the sacrilegious.

The people of Loretto, whatever reason they may have to depend on the invisible protection of the virgin Mary, especially as to what concerns the treasury consecrated to her, do not think it advisable to put it to the trial: for the window of the treasury is not only secured with a strong grate, but the city is also fortified. These fortifications, according to an inscription on one of the bastions, were built in the year 1521, in the pontificate of pope Leo X, and are indeed a sufficient security against any sudden attack of pirates, but otherwise of little importance; for in many places the houses supply the place of walls.

Fortifications.

Loretto is generally without a garrison, so that it seems something strange the Turks have not made greater efforts for getting into their hands the precious booty kept there than they have hitherto done. It can hardly be their reverence to the virgin that restrains them; though the people of Loretto pretend, that even the Turks, in any extremity at sea, have often recourse to her, and express their acknowledgments of her assistance by sending to Loretto very valuable presents. The Roman-catholics, indeed, affirm, that, in all the attempts which the Turks have hitherto made against Loretto, they have either been repelled by some extraordinary miracle, or miscarried by a supernatural panic. But all these miracles have not produced such a confidence in the inhabitants as to put the affair upon such an issue; the treasure being, upon the least appearance of danger, sent away to Ancona, or some other place of security. General Langallerie and the count de Linange are highly censured, that, among all their enterprizes, which mostly turned upon chimera's and impossibilities, they never thought of attacking Loretto. But the reason why the Turks do not make any formal attempt upon this place may probably be owing to the shallowness of the Adriatic, which in these parts has not a sufficient depth of water for large ships to approach the shore. Besides, Loretto being three Italian miles from the sea, and in an open country, no descent can be made with such secrecy and expedition as not to alarm the whole neighbourhood, who are ready to venture life and fortune in defence of their virgin, and would be soon in arms. The burghers of Loretto amount to above three hundred, and the inhabitants in the town and the two suburbs are reckoned

The Turks do not endeavour to make themselves masters of Loretto.

The reason of it.

to exceed seven thousand; and a Turkish squadron is no sooner known to be at sea, than a strong garrison is immediately sent hither.

In going out of the church, on the right-hand, is a statue of Sixtus V, sitting on a pedestal decorated on every side with basso-relievo's, all of bronze, by Antonio Calcagni. In the great area before the church is a beautiful marble fountain, made at the expence of Paul V, to whom the town owes the fine water it receives, by means of an aqueduct from a neighbouring hill. In the palace, which stands in this area, the clergy, the officers of the holy house, and the governor of the town have apartments, besides those appointed for persons of distinction, who come hither upon pilgrimages. Here are also the wine-vaults belonging to the Casa Santa, which are a hundred and fifty-eight common paces in length, consisting of twelve apartments. In these vaults are generally kept a hundred and forty large casks of wines, one of which holds above four hundred and twenty barrels, allowing ninety Paris *chopines* to a barrel. Another cask contains three hundred and sixty-five barrels; and out of it three sorts of wine are drawn through one cock, *viz.* white, claret, and a deep red wine. Over the wine-cellar are the kitchens, offices, and dispensary. In the latter are three hundred and sixty-eight gallipots, most of them very large and with covers, which are extremely valued on account of the paintings on them, said to be the work of the great Raphael. The subject of these paintings is a medley of stories taken from the scriptures, Roman history, and Ovid's Metamorphosis, *&c.* These pots were presented by one of the dukes of Urbino, Raphael's birth-place, and are a collection which the Italians never mention but with raptures: they would also fain make us believe, that one of the great dukes of Florence offered to exchange them for silver pots of the same bigness. For the four evangelists and St. Paul, Lewis XIV. of France is said to have offered their weight in gold. Queen Christina of Sweden offered six thousand *scudi* for five others; her majesty, as the story goes, preferring this collection to all the other curiosities of Loretto, because the richest jewels, silver, gold, *&c.* may be equalled, and consequently the loss of them may in some measure be repaired; whereas pots so exquisitely painted were not to be matched. That princess is said, on the refusal of her offer, to have borrowed a very fine piece of porcelain; but never had the honour to return it.

Statue of Sixtus V.

Gallipots painted by Raphael.

If

LORETTO.

Whether they were really painted by Raphael.

If all those earthen vessels shewn in different places, to which Raphael's name gives a very considerable value, were actually painted by that master, he must have had little else to do. But probably there is not a single piece of that kind, done by him, extant; unless perhaps a few, which he painted by way of amusement in his younger years. Possibly Battista Franco, an ingenious Venetian painter, who, according to Vasari, when he designed for such porcelain vessels, drew from copper-plates of the works of Raphael and other celebrated masters, gave rise to this mistake. Something of that kind, however, may have been done by Raphael himself; for baron Tallis of Venice has in his hands a letter from that eminent artist, wherein he acquaints the dutchess of Urbino, that he had finished the designs which that princess had desired for a side-board of porcelain *.

Arsenal.

The arsenal is in one of the upper stories, and is pretty well furnished. Among other votive pieces offered by pilgrims, here are several arms; among which is a short pistol made by one of the dukes of Urbino. Here is another pistol, presented about two years since by a foreigner, which is hardly four inches long; it is of most curious workmanship, and carries a ball about the size of a pepper-corn. Two small field-pieces, said to be taken, about two hundred years since, from the Turks, who had landed to pillage Loretto, are likewise shewn here; and a large bomb charged.

Story of a wax flambeaux.

It is said that the latter was concealed in a large wax taper sent by the Turks as an offering to the virgin for some pretended deliverance, and that, if it had burnt to the bomb, the whole Casa Santa would have been blown up; but that by the miraculous foresight of the virgin Mary this dreadful mischief was prevented. One closet is full of prohibited weapons which have been offered to the virgin.

Bel's.

From the arsenal you ascend to the apartment where the bells given by several popes are hung. The largest of these is called Loretto, and weighs ten tons: it was the gift of Leo X.

The revenues and expences of the holy house.

The clergy here allow, that the annual revenue of the Casa Santa, from lands and other settled funds, amounts to twenty-nine or thirty thousand *scudi*, exclusive of presents and offerings, which, from the resort of many thousands of

---

* *Vide D. Vincenzo Vittoria's Offervazioni sopra il Libro della Felsina Pittrice, Rom.* 1703.

votaries,

LORETTO.

votaries, muſt be very conſiderable. However, that the ſuperſtitious may not be wanting in their liberality, all kinds of arguments are uſed by the clergy, both verbally and in print, to make ſtrangers believe, that their neceſſary annual expences exceed the ſettled yearly income by ten thouſand *ſcudi*; at the ſame time intimating, that it is the indiſpenſable duty of every pious Chriſtian to contribute. According to their computation, no leſs than fourteen thouſand pounds of wax is every year conſumed in the holy houſe and the church, which quantity is valued at three thouſand two hundred and twenty *ſcudi*. I ſhall not examine into the truth of this article, no more than that of four hundred and twenty *ſcudi* expended for lamp oil: but other articles are ſtill more exaggerated, *viz.* the annual expence of maintaining the twenty Jeſuits, and other prieſts, is ſaid to exceed the ſum of five thouſand *ſcudi*; the twelve canons ſix thouſand; and the other officers about ſixteen thouſand *ſcudi*. The *Collegium Illyricum*, founded by Gregory XIII, for the education of thirty Sclavonian youths in philoſophy and divinity, was, by order of Clement VIII, removed from hence to Rome.

The trade carried on by the inhabitants of Loretto, beſides what they get by entertaining of ſtrangers, conſiſts in making and ſelling medals, crucifixes, images of the virgin Mary, painted paper caps, ribbons, roſaries, &c. which are bought by the credulous papiſts as amulets.

Trade of the inhabitants of Loretto.

The walls of Loretto are about half an Italian mile in circumference, and yield a delightful proſpect on one ſide of the ſea, and a beautiful vale finely cultivated; and, on the other, of its elegant ſuburbs, which extend to Monte Reale along a ſtraight broad road. About ſun-ſet in clear weather the mountains of Croatia may be diſcerned, though they are a hundred and fifty Italian miles diſtant from Loretto.

Deſcription of the town of Loretto.

The vaſt concourſe of foreigners neceſſarily occaſions a great conſumption of proviſions at Loretto. The innkeepers are for impoſing as much as they can upon ſtrangers; but the entertainment is here generally very good. The inhabitants behave civilly to travellers; and at the poſt-houſes from Rome to Bologna a perſon has a much better ſort of people to deal with than on the rout from Florence to Rome; for their frequent converſation with ſtrangers probably contributes to mend their manners. It is alſo obſerved, that the lower claſs of people are much more reaſonable in their demands, &c. from thoſe travellers who return from Rome, than from ſuch as travel towards that city; for they conclude
that

Entertainment at Loretto.

that the latter are strangers to the customs of the road, and therefore think it allowable to take all advantages they can of the unexperienced.

The country about Loretto as well as the town itself swarms with beggars; with whom it is customary in spring to strew flowers in the road when strangers approach, who cannot see such an honour paid them without giving a small gratuity in return for it.

Cirolo or Scirolo.— At the distance of a few Italian miles from Loretto towards Ancona, lies the little town of Cirolo or Sciroloy famous for the resort of pilgrims on account of a miraculous crucifix. It is a common saying here, *Chi è andato à Loreto, e non à Cirolo, ha visto la madre, e ha lasciato il figliolo*; i. e. 'Whoever goes to Loretto and not to Cirolo visits the mother, and takes no notice of the son.' But in reality this is only another invention to drain the pilgrims purses. The votive pieces to be seen here are very inconsiderable; and a traveller who goes to Cirolo only out of curiosity, will find that he has quitted the road to little purpose. The wine of this country is very good; and possibly may be that which Pliny (*Hist. Nat. lib.* xiv. *c.* 6.) classes among the best Italian wines under the name of *vinum Anconitanum*; but the wine now made at Ancona and in the neighbourhood of it is but very indifferent.

Globular stones.— Before I close my account of Loretto, I must observe, that, at certain times of the year, the sea throws up globular stones here, the origin of which I cannot venture to account for, though possibly the roundness of them may be owing to the agitation of the waves: it must however be acknowledged, that there are several *strata* of the earth, remote from the sea, in which an infinite number of round stones are to be found; particularly about half a mile from Helmstadt, near the convent of St. Marienthal in the iron mines in the country of Wirtemberg, and according to Agricola, near Polenza in the kingdom of Naples, where there are many such stones to be seen of the size of a cannon-ball.

LORETTO, April 1730.   I am, &c.

LETTER LXIII.

Account of ANCONA, and several Kinds of Fishes in the Adriatic Sea; of SENIGALLIA, FANO, PESARO, RIMINI, the River RUBICON; also of the Towns of CESENA and CERVIA.

SIR,

THE distance from Loretto to Ancona is fifteen Italian miles; and the road lies through a charming plain intersected by the rivers Musone and Aspido. Here I cannot but observe, that in no other chain of mountains so many sources of brooks and rivers are to be found as on the east side of the Appenines.

Ancona is badly built on an uneven situation, from which it derives its name, which is of Greek original. Over one of the gates are these words:

Alma Fides, Proceres, vestram quæ condidit Urbem,
  Gaudet in hoc socia vivere Pace loco.

' Fair Probity, which built this city, delights to associate with Peace on this happy spot.'

The cathedral stands on an eminence, and affords a delightful prospect of the town, and along the sea-coast. In the portico before the church are two remarkable pillars resting on two marble lions. This church wants light extremely.

This city besides its out-works is also fortified with a citadel; but neither of them is sufficient to hold out against an army. The harbour is very commodicus*; but the trade is inconsiderable, which is generally the case in every part of the papal dominions: persons of all religions are on an equal footing here, only they are not allowed the public exercise

---

* There is a common saying in praise of the harbour, *viz. Unus Petrus est in Roma; una Turris in Cremona; unus Portus in Ancona;* i. e. ' The only Peter is at Rome; the only tower is at Cremona, and the only harbour at Ancona.'

of

ANCONA.

Jews. of their religion. The Jews are very numerous in Ancona; however they live in a particular quarter, and are obliged by way of distinction to wear a bit of red cloth in their hats. Their synagogue is an oblong edifice with an arched roof, **Exchange.** and is illuminated with several lamps. The exchange has a beautiful front, and over the entrance is an equestrian statue, &c. Within it is a lofty spacious apartment, in which, among other statues, are those of Faith, Hope, Charity, and Religion. The harbour is secured by a strong mole; **Triumphal arch.** and near it is a triumphal arch, erected by the Roman senate to the emperor Trajan, Plotina his consort, and Marciana his sister, in gratitude for the great improvement made in this harbour by that emperor, at his own expence. This arch was formerly ornamented with great numbers of brass statues, trophies, and inscriptions, and consequently must have made a quite different appearance from what it does at present. The sculpture, being cut on the large pieces of marble with which the arch is built, was not so liable to be demolished, and could not be carried away; so that this arch was more magnificent, and calculated for a longer duration than most other monuments of antiquity of this kind. The marble for building this arch was brought from the island of Paros, and is so closely compacted, that the whole seems to consist only of one block. On both sides are four fluted pillars of the Corinthian order; and over the front towards the city is this ancient inscription:

Ancient inscription.

Imp. Cæsari. Divi. Nervæ. F. Nervæ
Trajano. Optimo. Aug. Germanic.
Dacico. Pont. Max. Tr. Pot. XVIIII. Imp. IX.
Cos. VI. P. P. Providentissimo. Principi.
Senatus. P. Q. R. quod. accessum.
Italiæ. hoc. etiam. addito. ex. pecunia. sua.
Portu. tutiorem. navigantibus. reddiderit.

Betwixt the pillars on the front opposite to the city, and on the right side of the arch, are these words:

Plotinæ.
Aug.
Conjugi. Aug.

And on the left:

Divæ.

ANCONA.

Divæ.
Marcianæ.
Sorori Aug.

The head of the mole is fortified, and eight or ten guns are generally mounted on it. There is a kind of wooden cover over it, supported in the center by a long pole fixt in the ground. The inhabitants of Ancona, especially the female sex, so far excel those of the other parts of Italy in shape and complexion, that they seem to be quite a different race of men. The same may be observed of the inhabitants beyond Senegallia, Fano, and Pescaro as far as Rimini. If it be true that the resort of young gentlemen to the universities, and the numerous retinue of a court, greatly contribute to render Leipsic, Hall, and Dresden, as it were, the nurseries of fine women; the superior beauty of the female sex at Fano, Ancona, &c. may likewise be attributed to the great number of strangers and pilgrims continually travelling through those cities. _{Beauty of the inhabitants of Ancona and to what owing.}

The eastern part of Italy is much more fertile and pleasant than most parts on the west side, especially if the coast from Genoa to Leghorn be included. The whole Adriatic sea abounds in testaceous and other kinds of fish. A singular species of the former are the Ballani or Ballari found alive in large stones. The shell of this fish is thin, rough, and of an oblong figure: it is not unlike a date; hence they are called Dattili del Mare, or sea-dates. They are chiefly found in the shallows near Monte Comero or Conaro, about ten Italian miles from Ancona. There is also a kind of clay found there very much resembling brown earthen ware, and likewise several kinds of porous stones. Within the small interstices or pores of these stones and clay-clods, the spawn or fry of these Ballani are lodged. Here they are provided both with air and water, whilst by their motion they gradually abrade the stone in which they are inclosed, and thus make themselves room for their growth. The clay is hard within; but, as it is continually moistened by the sea-water, the outside is soft. Since the inhabitants of Ancona have observed that the Ballari, taken up in their harbour, were larger than those of the Monte Conaro, they generally fetch them in boats from thence, and lay them within the mole; where, by the rest and nutriment they enjoy from the depth and sliminess of the bottom, they soon come to perfection. In fishing

VOL. III. P

ANCONA.

fishing for Ballari, such stones are chiefly picked up as have the surface full of little holes; that being a certain sign these fishes have insinuated themselves into them. Sometimes the aperture through which the spawn of the fish penetrated into the stone happens to be afterwards stopped up or covered with slime, so that it is not discernible, and yet the fish thrives very well. In breaking some of these stones taken up in the harbour, I have found twenty or thirty live fish in a stone, though not the least fissure or opening was to be observed on the outside; they always lie in a little cavity, which allows them no more room than is just necessary for opening their shell a little way, probably to take in the air and moisture or nourishment. The only way of getting them out of the stone is by breaking it; for the passage through which they entered, is much too small, even for the young fry to come out at. If two or more of these shells by their growth happen to come in contact with each other in the same stone, only one fish is found alive. Their propagation and increase may in some measure be explained by observing how butterflies, spiders, &c. lay their eggs in galls, or excrescences of oak leaves. As to the position of the Ballani, it is not always exactly in the middle of the stone; however the thickest part of their body which attracts most nutriment is generally farthest from the surface. The inside of the shell is white, but the outside is of an ash colour: the largest of those found at Ancona are not much above a finger in length. When they are taken out of the stone, a gut resembling a worm, of the length of one's finger, hangs to them, like that of the Solenes or Cappe longhe, as they are called at Venice. This is entirely white and full of clear water, which it squirts out when pressed. Those persons that find a particular delicacy of taste in them, say, that the Ballani do not feed on the gross parts of the sea-water, but as it were on the subtile dew that penetrates through the stone, and thus undergoes a kind of filtration. Both the fish and the juices of it are so luminous in the dark that one may see to read by it; and even water in which this fish has been squeezed, when put in a glass, emits an effulgence which lasts from eight to twelve hours. But this phænomenon is nothing extraordinary, as fresh oysters when opened, and whitings, have also something of a lucid appearance in the dark.

It must be in a great measure owing to custom, that the Ballani are reckoned so palatable: however great quantities of them are sent to Rome, where they are reckoned *beccone di Cardinale*, or dainties fit for a cardinal. There is also a species of this fish found near Civita Vecchia, and likewise near Narbonne in France. Some naturalists call them *Pholides* or *Pholæ*, from a Greek word signifying a thing concealed*. In the district of Ancona, the stones in which they are found are called *Saffi del ballaro*.

Oysters are preserved here, alive in sea-water for several years. At Ancona they are indeed very large, but flabby, and far from being palatable. Here is also a kind of sea craw-fish, called Nocchia, in appearance like those called lobsters in England; but of a more delicate flavour. Their claws are less than those of craw-fish, and the head and tail of a very uncommon shape. The largest of this species is about four inches long: this fish is by some called *Squilla arenaria*.

Among other remarkable sea-animals found in the harbour of Ancona and the Adriatic, is a fish called the Sepit†, which has a longish white shell on its head. These shells are often found along the shore, and, when pulverized, are used for cleaning of plate.

Here is also the univalve shell-fish, which in Latin is called Patella, and adheres to the rocks. Through the small aperture in its convex shell it expels its excrements.

The name of Patella major is by some given to those shells, which, on account of their variegated lustre resembling that of mother-of-pearl, are very much used in the decoration of grotto's and water-works: but their more common name here is Orecchia marina, and they are found not only in the Adriatic, but Neapolitan seas. The spiral tubes observed in these shells serve for imbibing the water.

Another small species of shell-fish are thrown in great quantities upon this shore, which seem to be inscribed with Arabic characters. There is such an infinite variety in this species, that I am apt to think two of these Bavarazzi del Mare, as they are called, could not be found that are perfectly alike.

The Solenes, Fistulæ, Canales, or Ungues, as they are called in Latin, from the colour or shape of the shell, resemble the handle of a razor; and at Venice are known by the name of Cappe longhe; but at Ancona they are called Cannolichii,

---

* The Greek word φωλις, in the plural number φωλιδες, signifies the scale of a fish; so that there is a mistake in the etymology above.
† Probably a species of the Sepia, or Cuttle-fish.

ANCONA.

or Pesci Canelle. These are also found in many parts of the Mediterranean.

Arca Noæ. The Concha Rhomboides, or Musculus striatus, Mitulus, also called Arca Noæ, is a shell covered with filaments like hair or wool.

PolypoMoscardino. The Nautilus subtilis, which is distinguished by the name of Polypo Moscardino, is as white as the finest writing paper.

Noce di Mare. The Noce gentili di Mare, or Nuces Marinæ, are of the bivalve kind, striated, and have a brown border. The finest of these species are found on the coasts of Africa.

Chiocciola celata. The Chiocciola celata is a shell resembling mother-of-pearl. It is rough within, and is secured with a cartilaginous cover adhering to it, like the nail of a man's finger. This is common almost to all the Turbinatæ, which, on this account, may be reckoned among the Testacea Bivalvia. The surface is smooth and variegated with red and brown, and marked with a spiral line. The above-mentioned cartilaginous cover is called, at Puzzuolo, Occhi di pesce, fishes

Occhi di S. Luca. eyes; and, in other places, Occhi di S. Luca, Umblici, Belliculi, and Pietre di Margarita.

Turbinatæ. The Testacea Tubinata likewise abound in the Adriatic.
Purpureæ. To this class belong the Purpureæ Echinatæ, or Turbinatæ, Vermiculatæ, and Chermisinæ, &c. The last name is said to be derived from Chermi, an ancient town in Sardinia, where wool is said to have been first dyed of a *cramoisi*, or crimson colour, with the red juice or blood of this fish.

Extensive meaning of the word *purpureus* among the anceents. The word *purpureus* among the ancients was of a very comprehensive meaning, and denoted any vivid and bright colour; so that it has been applied even to snow *. One species of the above-mentioned Turbinatæ is not only guarded with *aculei*, or prickles, at the opening; but even the intervals betwixt its volutations are so full of them, that this

Purpura aculeata. kind is very properly called *purpura aculeata*, which answers to the name Sconciglio spinoso, as it is called by the Neapolitans.

Jacob's shells. In the Adriatic are likewise found the species called Jacob's shells, or Pectines, Ctenites and Conchites striati: one half of the shell is almost plain and smooth, and the other

---

* *Albinovanus ad Liviam.-- purpurea sub nive terra latet.* ' The dazzling snow conceals the earth.' Horace gives swans the epithet of *purpurei*, as Catullus does the oaken branches; and Anacreon calls Venus πορφυρα 'Αφροδίτη, i. e. ' effulgent Venus.'

convex;

ANCONA.

convex; this is used in Holland, and other places for stewing oysters.

The Tubulara Purpurea, Spongia rubra, or the Alcyonium Milesium, is found here in very large pieces at a great depth in the sea. It is of a beautiful colour, and resembles red coral; which has induced some naturalists, though improperly, to class it among corals. This mass is properly nothing but a congeries of several thousands of fine tubes, which serve for nests and receptacles to a certain species of small worms. Tubulara Purpurea.

Here are several shells covered with filaments of a dark brown colour, not unlike coarse hair. This is called Fucus Capillaris, and is frequently a foot or a foot and a half in length, when taken off the shell. Fucus Capillaris.

The Pilæ marinæ lie also very thick along this shore. These seem to be only a mass composed of slime, &c. Pilæ marinæ.

Among the smaller kinds of shells found here, are several of such a singular, and, as it were, grotesque figure, that they cannot properly be ranged among the common classes; and therefore the Italians give them the name of Capricciose. Capricciose.

The largest shell-fish found on this coast are the Pinnæ, or Pernæ, so called from the resemblance they bear to a gammon of bacon. The outside of their shell is red, and at the acute angle of it generally grows a *byssus marinus* to the length of five or six inches. The shell itself is two feet in length; and, from its largeness and shape, it might be of service to those Indian nations who are said to cover their houses with the shells of fish *. Pinnæ.
Use of some shells.

The sea near Ancona is observed to ebb and flow about a foot, or a foot and a half; which phænomenon gradually abates as the Adriatic approaches to its junction with the Me- Ebb and flood in the Adriatic.

---

* Peter Martyr, *lib.* iv. *Dec.* 3, relates, that some nations in India make the same use of the shells of fish as Adam and Eve did of fig leaves, as represented in the common pictures. Others polish them from the coarse opaque crust, and make transparent panes for windows of them, as may be seen in Sir Hans Sloane's museum at London. At the house in the wood, near the Hague, is an oyster-shell of such a large size, as to serve as a bason for a fountain. At Goa an oyster of prodigious size was once accidentally drawn up with an anchor; and the fish, exclusive of the shell, weighed above a hundred pounds. The two shells of it are now in the royal museum at Copenhagen, each of which weighs about two hundred and twenty-four pounds. The circumference of them is about eight feet and a half, and the longest diameter near five. In the above-mentioned museum of Sir Hans Sloane is a prickly oyster-shell, which is seven common spans in its greatest diameter.

FANO.

diterranean, and increases in its northern part towards the city of Venice.

Senegaglia. The town of Senegaglia, so called from the founders of it the Galli Senones, lies on the sea-coast, about sixteen Italian miles from Ancona; but has nothing worth the observation of a traveller of taste. Betwixt the river Misa, which runs through this town, and the little stream of Cesano, are *Roman* some ancient ditches marking the limits of the Roman camp; *camp.* and on the other side of the Cesano some antiquarians imagine they have discovered the traces of the Carthaginian camp. So far, however, it is certain, that Asdrubal (whose *Asdrubal,* name a neighbouring mountain still bears) brother to the re-*where slain.* nowned Hannibal, lost both his army and life in a battle fought in these parts *.

Fano. The distance from Senegaglia to Fano is two posts, or sixteen Italian miles. Those who would persuade the world that the country about the latter is the finest spot in Italy, certainly do a great injury to many other parts of it. Fano derives its name from a Fanum, or temple of Fortune, which anciently stood here. In commemoration of this, the image of Fortune is not only erected on the fountain in the market-place, but has also a place in the coat of arms of the town. *Triumphal* The greatest curiosity here is a triumphal arch built of mar-*arch.* ble, which, after having withstood the injuries of time, &c. till the year 1458, was then very much damaged by the cannon during the siege of this town. This arch had formerly three gates; but the smallest on the left-hand in coming from the town has been pulled down, to make room for St. Michael's church, and the other is stopped by a mean house; so that the middle gate is now the only one open, and over the arch of this not so much as the ox-head, which was formerly placed there, is left standing. Some of the inscriptions are over-run with weeds, and others effaced by time. However, they are copied under a sketch of the triumphal arch itself, which is cut in the wall of the above-mentioned church of St. Michael.

Over this representation of the arch are these words;

Effigies
Inscriptions. *Arcûs ab Augusto erecti, posteaque tormentis ex parte diruti bello*
Pii II. contra Fanen. Ann. M.CCCC LXIII.

* *Vide Livii Hist. ad f.nem.*

' A rc-

FANO.

'A representation of the triumphal arch erected by Augustus, part of which was afterwards demolished by cannon in the war of Pius II. against the inhabitants of Fano, in the year 1463.'

On the upper part, where seven windows or doors are to be seen, is this ancient inscription:

Divo Augusto Pio Constantino Patri Domino. 2.

And underneath:

Imp. Cæsar. Divi. F. Augustus. Pontifex. Maximus. Cos. XIII. Tribunitia. Potest. XXXII. Imp. XXVI. Pater. Patriæ. Murum. dedit.

Curante. L. Turcio. Secundo. Aproniani. Præf. Urb. Fil. Asterio. V. C. Corr. Flam. & Piceni.

Vitruvius says, that this city took the name of *Julia Fanestris*, in memory of Augustus, who built the walls of it; whereas before, according to Pomponius Mela, it was called *Colonia Fanestris*.

In the cathedral of Fano are to be seen some admirable paintings representing the annunciation, the Lord's-supper, and the gathering of manna, by Quercini; likewise the assumption of the virgin Mary, by Caraccioli. In the chapel of the virgin Mary are the fifteen mysteries of the rosary, painted by Domenichino. {Cathedral.}

St. Peter's church likewise deserves notice, for its fine paintings, sculpture, and cupola. On the high altar are two angels of white Carrara marble, by an eminent hand. The picture of Christ delivering the keys to St. Peter is by Guido Rheni. On each side of it are the raising of Tabitha from the dead by a Fleming; and St. Peter curing the lame man, by Simone Cantarini, who was called Pesarese. {St. Peter's church.}

A nobleman, of the name of Torelli, built on the market-place at Fano a very elegant theatre for exhibiting comedies and opera's, which is made use of in carnival-time. {Theatre.}

Pesaro lies about eight Italian miles from Fano. Here is a fountain of mineral waters which, though its *jet d'eau* is nothing extraordinary, is very convenient for the inhabitants, and ornamented in a good taste. In its upper bason, which is in the form of a drinking-glass, are several sea-goddesses {Pesaro. Medicinal waters.}

and sea-horses, which spout water out from above thirty different apertures. On one side of it are these words:

Pisauri Patritii ære publico.

'By the contribution of the nobility of Pesaro.'

And, on the other, the names of those under whose direction the work was completed.

Statue of Urban VIII. On the great market-place is a statue of pope Urban VIII. in a sitting attitude, with the following inscription on one side of the pedestal:

VRBANO VIII. P. O. M.
Civitas Pisaurensis
Per egregia ejus prudentiæ consilia
Cum universa ad Metaurum ditione,
Inter plurimas difficultates, sine strepitu armorum,
Ad Sedis Apostolicæ dominationem revocata,
Præclaro constantiæ ac moderationis exemplo
Sanctas Prædecessorum leges confirmante ;
Mox præter alia plurima beneficia
Liberali condonatione
Sexaginta millium aureorum obstricta,
Grati animi monumentum.

'This was erected as a monument of gratitude to Urban VIII. the greatest and best of popes, by whose wisdom and prudence the city of Pesaro, together with the whole country as far as the river Metaro, was again recovered without the violence of war, though amidst many difficulties, to the dominion of the apostolic see. The same gracious sovereign, by an illustrious example, both of firmness and moderation, confirmed the sacred laws enacted by his predecessors, and, among several other acts of munificence, remitted a tribute of sixty thousand crowns of gold that was due to him from the inhabitants of this city.'

On the other three sides are inscriptions in honour of cardinal Barberini the pope's legate, &c.

Fortifications. Pesaro is a large well-built city; but its fortifications are but very inconsiderable, though set forth with such pomp of expression in the following inscription over the Rimini gate:

GUIDUS

PESARO.

GUIDUS UBALDUS DUX URBINI IIII. hoftium pallori ac pavori, oppidanorum & fuorum faluti atque ornamento Pifauri amplificatâ circummunitione, quam à fe prius excogitatam Francifcus Maria Pater ob vitæ brevitatem vix inchoatam reliquit, paternis vefligiis prudentiffimè inhærens admirabili ftudio ac diligentiâ perfecit. M.D.LXIV.

' Guido Ubaldi, fourth duke of Urbino, having, to the
' dread and terror of his enemies, the fafety of his fubjects,
' and the ornament of Pefaro, enlarged its fortifications,
' and compleated with admirable diligence and fkill the plan
' laid by his glorious father Francefco Maria, whofe untime-
' ly death fcarce permitted him to fee the beginning of this
' public work. 1564.'

The Pefaro figs are accounted the beft in all Italy, and even preferred to thofe of Sclavonia.

Poggio Imperiale, an ancient pleafure-houfe of the dukes of Urbino, ftands on a hill about an Italian mile from Pefaro, and is furnifhed with fome good paintings by Genga. Here is alfo a fine orangery.

Along the coaft as far as Pefaro, the country wears an agreeable afpect; but the foil and road are none of the beft, the latter being very fandy for the laft ftage.

From Pefaro you enter into a fine corn country, divided into fquare inclofures by rows of trees interwoven with vines. This whole tract of land belongs to the dukedom of Urbino, which the popes, on the demife of the laft duke Francefco Maria di Rovere in 1631, without male iffue, have found means to get it into their hands. The faid duke, by his will figned in 1626, had confirmed the papal claim, and in effect previoufly renounced his own title. But Victoria, daughter to his fon Frederico Ubaldi, who died before him, and wife to Ferdinand II. great duke of Tufcany (to whom fhe was married in the year 1631, when fhe was but eight years of age) obtained the allodial part of the dutchy, whence it comes to pafs that Poggio Imperiale and fome other places in thefe parts belong to the ducal family of Florence.

About an Italian mile from Catholica, which is feven miles diftant from Pefaro, the road croffes a canal by means of a bridge of one arch; however in dry weather there is not a drop of water to be feen under this bridge, though there is a

moft

most ostentatious inscription cut in marble on it in honour of cardinal Altieri. It begins as follows:

Clemente X. P. O. M.
Torrenti crebris alluvionibus tumido,
Auctu ingentibus prædis,
Claudibus editis formidabili,
Pontem hunc opere magnifico juxta & commodo viatoribus
Pietate proximi Jubilæi Romam advocandis
Palutius Cardinalis Alterius S. R. E. Camer.us
Imponendum ære suo curavit. Ann. Dom.
MDCLXXIV.

' Over this torrent, swelling with frequent floods, driv-
' ing heaps of ruins along its rapid stream, and formidable
' for its numberless devastations, Paluti, cardinal Altieri, &c,
' has, at his own expence, built this bridge; a work, which
' besides its grandeur affords convenience and safety to those
' whom devotion shall incite to visit Rome at the approach-
' ing jubilee. 1674.'

Catholica council against the Arians.

Catholica is a village so called from the orthodox bishops, who in the year 359 withdrew to this place from the council of Rimini, where they had been out-voted by the Arians. This remarkable transaction is commemorated in the following inscription on the wall, and not far from the entrance of the church:

Anno reparatæ Salutis CCCLIX,
Liberio Pont. Max. Constantio Imp.
Cum Hæreticorum fraudibus ingemiscens Orbis terarum
Se Arianum esse miratus est,
Ex quadringentis Episcopis ad Synodum Ariminensem convocatis.
Perpauci orthodoxi in hunc locum ventitantes,
Ut seorsim ab Arianis sacra facerent,
Et Catholica communione Catholicos impertirent,
Occasionem præbuerunt, ut vicus ipse Catholica nuncuparetur.
Cujus nominis rationem ac totius rei gestæ memoriam
Cæsar Cardinalis Baronius Annalibus Ecclesiasticis inseruit,
Bernardinus Cardinalis Spada
Ad peregrinantium pietatem erudiendam
Amoremque suum erga patriam provinciam testandum
Hoc posito marmore indicavit. Ann. Dom.
M. DC. XXXVII.

' In

RIMINI.

'In the year of the Christian Æra 395, in the reign of the emperor Constantius, and the pontificate of Liberius, when the whole world, with grief and surprize, saw itself, through the craft of heresy, infected with the errors of Arianism; out of four hundred bishops assembled at the council of Rimini, very few were found orthodox, who, by frequently resorting hither to perform the divine offices apart from the Arians, and administer to catholics a catholic communion, gave this village the name of Catholica. The origin of this name and the particulars of the whole transaction cardinal Cæsar Baronius has inserted in his annals of the church; and cardinal Bernardine Spada, in order to testify his affection to his native country, has exhibited it on this marble, for the information of devout pilgrims, in the year 1637.'

A few Italian miles from Catholica towards Rimini, are to be seen the ruins of the ancient city of Concha in the sea; and farther on towards the left lies the republic of St. Marino. The freedom of this little commonwealth is more owing to the poverty of the individuals than the abilities of the governors.

Rimini or Ariminum was formerly a city of note, but is now extremely decayed, especially since it received a fatal blow by an earthquake in 1671: however it is still venerable for the many monuments of its ancient splendor. A little without the town town towards Pesaro is a triumphal arch, on each front of which are two beautiful Corinthian pillars and two busts. On that towards the country is this imperfect inscription:

Coss. Sept. designat. Oct. Aug. M. V. Celeberrimeis Italiæ vieis consilio Senatus Pop. ---- lleis ---

On a pyramid on the other side:

Cos Ariminen. poss. id. Mart. M.DLXVII.

'Erected by the consuls of Rimini, March 15, 1567.'

In the market-place is the following inscription cut in stone:

C. Cæsar

RIMINI.

Monument of Julius Cæsar.

    C. Cæsar
    Dict.
    Rubicone
    Superato
    Civili bell.
    Commilit.
    Suos hic
    In foro Ar.
    Adlocut.

'Caius Cæsar the dictator, after passing the Rubicon,
'here in this area of Ariminum harangued his army to pre-
'pare them for a civil war.'

On the other side:

Suggestum hunc vetustate collapsum Coss. Arim. mensium No-
vembris & Decemb. MDLV. restit.

' This ancient Suggestum, decayed by length of time, was
' repaired by the consuls of Rimini in the months of Novem-
' ber and December, 1555.'

On the wall of the council-house is a stone with the following ancient inscription:

  C. Cæsari August. Cos. vias omnes a Rimin. 5 tern.

Underneath it is also this inscription:

Japanese ambassadors at Rimini.

  Mantii Franci Regis Bungi, Michaëlis Protasii Arimanorum
Regis, ac Bartolomæi Omuræ Principis, Juliani, Martinique
Comitum, ab Japaner. remotiss. insulis ad D. Gregorium XIII.
legatorum, ut jam susceptam Christi fidem profiterentur, optatiss.
Ariminum adventui XVI. Kl. Julii publico sumptu, maximâque
lætitiâ hosp. MDLXXXV. Sixto V. P. O. M. seden. S. P. Q.
Ar. D.

' Manti Franco king of Bungo, Michael Protasi king
' of Arima, and Bartholomew prince of Omur, sent the no-
' ble Julian and Martin ambassadors from the remote islands
' of Japan to pope Gregory XIII. in order to make a public
' profession of the Christian faith, which they had already
               ' embraced,

RIMINI.

'embraced; who arrived at Rimini June 16, 1585, where
'they were entertained with the greatest festivity and mag-
'nificence at the public charge. In memory of this remark-
'able transaction, the senate and people of Rimini have set
'up this monument in the pontificate of Sixtus V.'

Here are other inscriptions relating to such natives of this city as have deserved well of the state, by contributing to its prosperity after the plague, and by other signal services. *Other inscriptions.*

Behind the Capuchin convent are shewn some ruins, said to have been an amphitheatre. These being in a garden, and consequently not very obvious to the public view, an index is cut on the outside of the convent-wall, pointing with its finger to those ruins, and over it are these words: *Amphitheatre.*

Amphitheatri olim P. Sempronio Cos. excitati reliquias indigitat Sen. Ar.

'This points to the remains of the amphitheatre built in the consulship of P. Sempronius.'

On that side of the city which lies towards Ravenna, near a bridge over the Ariminum, now called Marecchia, is an inscription, denoting that it was either built or repaired by Augustus and Tiberius. This bridge is two hundred feet in length, fifteen in breadth, and consists of five arches. *Ancient bridge.*

In the middle of the area before the council-house is a magnificent fountain, on which stands a small bronze statue of St. Paul. Not far from this is likewise a bust of pope Paul V. of brass. *Fountain.*

The Franciscan church was built, in the year 1450, by Sigismund Pandulfo, of the family of Malatesta, who for a long time were lords of Rimini, as is expressed in an inscription over the main entrance. This Sigismund Pandulfo was two years commander in chief of the Venetian troops against the Turks in the Morea; and, having made himself master of the city of Sparta, brought back with him the bones of Themistius, a celebrated philosopher of Constantinople, and one of the best commentators upon Aristotle. These bones he deposited in a marble tomb without this church, with the following inscription: *Franciscan church. Malatesta family. Tomb of the celebrated Themistius.*

Themistii

Themistii Byzantini
Philosophorum suâ tempestate Principis reliquum
Sigismundus Pandulphus Malatesta Pand. F.
Belli Pelopon. adversus Turcarum Regem Imperator,
Ob ingentem eruditorum, quo flagrat, amorem
Huc adferendum introque mittendum
Curavit. M.CCCC.LXV.

' These remains of Themistius, a native of Constantinople, the most eminent philosopher of his time, were brought over by Sigismund Pandulfo Malatesta, son of Pandulfo, general in the Morean war against the Turks, who, being a friend and patron to learned men, deposited them here, *A. D.* 1465.

<small>Tombs of Vanti and Valturi.</small>
Near this tomb are also six others in the church-yard, containing the remains of persons eminent for their learning; among these are the civilian Sebastiano Vanti, and Robert Valturi who wrote twelve books on the art of war, which he dedicated to the above-mentioned Malatesta.

In one of the chapels in this church is also a marble bust of the former.

<small>Statue of Sigismund Pandulfo.</small>
A statue of Sigismund Pandulfo, in complete armour, was set up in the famous armory at Ambras in Tirol by the archduke Ferdinand, with a large book in his hand, as an emblem of his affection to men of learning. He died in the year 1468; and, on the right-hand within the church, a monument is erected to his memory, with the following epitaph; in which the dipthong *æ*, according to the custom of those times, is expressed by a single *e*:

<small>Epitaph on him.</small>
Sum Sigismundus Malateste e sanguine gentis,
Pandulfus genitor Patria Flaminia est.
Vitam obiit VII. Id. Oct. etatis sue ann.
I. & L. mens. III. D. XX. M. CCCC. LXVIII.

' I am Sigismund, of the family of Malatesta; Pandulfo was my father, and Rimini my native place. He died on the ninth of October, 1468, aged fifty-one years, three months, and twenty days.'

Near this monument hang some old standards, and at a little distance a helmet with two horns; but the distich annexed

RIMINI.

flexed to them, in which Malatefta claffes himfelf among the cornuted, is not very proper for a Chriftian church:

Porto le corna ch'ogn'uno le vede;
Et tal le porta che non fe lo crede.

‘ All the world is welcome to fee my horns; it is no more
‘ than the fate of many a one who little thinks of it.’

These lines, according Francesco Sansovini *, allude to his unfortunate marriages; who adds, that, if he did wear horns, he knew how to rid himself of the authors of his difgrace; for he caused his two firft wives to be poisoned, and his third to be ftrangled. His second wife was a daughter of Nicholas margrave of Efte and Ferrara; and the father of his third wife was no lefs a person than Francefco Sforza duke of Milan.

On both fides of the church are several tombs belonging to the Malatefta family. The church, as yet, is not roofed, but only covered with planks laid acrofs.

Travellers who have a tafte for letters should not omit visiting count Gambalonga's library at Rimini, which, pursuant to a deed of truft, is kept in good order, and daily augmented. The building also in which the books are depofited is elegant and well contrived. [Count Gambalonga's library.]

Rimini had formerly a good harbour; but it is now fo choaked up with fand, as scarce to afford depth of water sufficient for paffage-boats. The above-mentioned Sigifmund Pandulfo Malatefta, feeing the marble with which the harbour was faced could be of no farther use there, removed it, in order to build the Francifcan church with it. The fea at that time had withdrawn half an Italian mile from its ancient limits; and at prefent the brick tower, which formerly ferved for a Faro, or light-houfe, is furrounded with gardens. However, they ftill fhew on the coaft the fpot on which St. Anthony is faid to have ftood when he preached to the fifhes. [Ancient harbour. Light-houfe. Place where St. Anthony preached to fifhes.]

A few Italian miles from Rimini you pafs by a bridge over the river Lufa, which by Clementini, Giacomo Villani, and other learned men, has been erroneoufly taken for the ancient Rubicon. Two miles on this fide Cefenatico the road croffes the river Fiumefino, and, scarce fifty or fixty paces from thence, the Pifatello, which likewife difembogues itfelf here- [The river Lufa. Fiumefino. Pifatello.]

* *Dell' Origine delle Cafe Illuftri d' Italia, p. 368, edit. Venet. 1674.*

abouts

abouts into the Fiumesino. The Pisatello, though it appears so shallow and small in any continuance of dry weather, was the river celebrated in the Roman history under the name of the Rubicon, as the limit betwixt the Italian provinces and Cisalpine Gaul*. For this reason the hostile views of Julius Cæsar plainly appeared by his passing this river with his army; for by the Roman laws no General could march the legions under his command out of the territories of his province into another, without an order from the senate and people of Rome. Likewise, in returning from an expedition, the army was not permitted to cross this river, and come into the *Regiones suburbicariæ*, without laying down their arms, on pain of being adjudged enemies to their country. Cæsar, being resolved to break through this law, frankly said, *Jacta est alea*; i. e. ' Now the die is cast;' since, after that, no amicable accommodation was to be expected. Lucan speaks of passage of the Rubicon in the following manner:

<blockquote>

Jam gelidas Cæsar cursu superaverat Alpes,
Ingentesque animo motus, bellumque futurum
Ceperat: ut ventum est parvi Rubiconis ad undas,
Ingens visa duci patriæ trepidantis imago
Clara per obscuram vultu mæstissima noctem,
Turrigero canos effundens vertice crines;
Cæsarie lacerâ nudisque adstare lacertis,
Et gemitu permista loqui: quò tenditis ultra?
Quò fertis mea signa viri? si jure venitis,
Si cives; huc usque licet. - - -

- - - - - - - - - - - -

Fonte cadit modico, parvisque impellitur undis
Puniceus Rubicon, cùm fervida canduit æstas:
Perque imas serpit valles, & Gallica certus
Limes ab Ausoniis disterminat arva colonis.

- - - - - - - - - - -

Cæsar ut adversam superato gurgite ripam
Attigit, Hesperiæ vetitis & constitit arvis;
Hic ait, hic pacem temerataque jura relinquo;
Te, Fortuna, sequor: procul hinc jam fœdera sunto.
Credidimus fatis, utendum est judice bello.

PHARSAL. *lib.* i.
</blockquote>

' Now

---

* *Plin. Hist. Nat. lib.* iij. *c.* 15. *Octava regio determinatur Arimino, Pa-do, Apennino. In ora fluvius Crustumium, Ariminum colonia cum amnibus Arimino*

RIMINI.

' Now Cæsar marching swift, with winged haste,
' The summits of the frozen Alps had past,
' With vast events and enterprizes fraught,
' And future wars revolving in his thought.
' Now near the banks of Rubicon he stood;
' When lo! as he survey'd the narrow flood,
' Amidst the dusky horrors of the night,
' A wond'rous vision stood, confess'd to sight.
' Her awful head Rome's rev'rend image rear'd,
' Trembling and sad the matron form appear'd:
' A tow'ry crown her hoary temples bound,
' And her torn tresses rudely hung around;
' Her naked arms uplifted e're she spoke,
' Then groaning, thus her painful silence broke;
' Presumptuous man! Oh whither do you run!
' Oh whither bear you these my ensigns on!
' If friends to right, if citizens of Rome,
' Here to your utmost barrier are you come. ———
' - - - - - - - - - - - - - - - -
' While with hot skies the parching summer glows,
' The Rubicon in narrow currents flows:
' Through shallow vales it slowly winds its way,
' Losing its ruddy waters in the sea.
' Its bank on either side a limit stands
' Between the Gallic and Ausonian lands.———
' The leader now had pass'd the torrent o'er,
' And reach'd fair Italy's forbidden shore.
' Then rearing on the hostile bank his head:
' Here farewell peace and injur'd laws he said:
' Snce faith is broke, and compact set aside,
' Henceforth thou, goddess Fortune, art my guide,
' Let fate and war the great event decide.'

}

Rowe.

Suetonius, in the life of Julius Cæsar, writes thus: *Cæsar - - consecutus cohortes ad Rubiconem flumen, qui Provinciæ ejus finis erat, paullum constitit: ac reputans, quantum moliretur, conversus ad proximos, Etiamnum, inquit, regredi possumus: quodsi ponti-*

Arimino & Aprusa. Fluvius hinc Rubico, quondam finis Italiæ. Vid. Sidon. Apollinar. lib. i. *epist.* 5. 'The eighth district is bounded by Ariminum, ' the Po, and the Apennine mountains. On the confines, are the river ' Crustrumium, the colony of Ariminum, together with the river of that ' name, and the Aprusa. The river Rubicon was formerly the bounda-
' ry of Italy on this side.'

Vol. III. Q *culum*

culum transierimus, omnia armis agenda erunt. - - cap. 32. *Tunc Cæsar, Eatur, inquit, quo Deorum ostenta & inimicorum iniquitas vocat. Jacta alea est, inquit.* ' Cæsar, coming with his
' troops to the bank of the Rubicon, which was the bounda-
' ry of his province, stood musing for some time on the im-
' portance of his design; and then, turning to those about
' him, said: " We may still retreat; but, if we once pass
" this little bridge, a war is the certain consequence." Then
Cæsar called out, " Let us march whither the omens of the
" Gods and the perverseness of our enemies call us. The
" die is now cast."

<small>The Pisatello, an ancient boundary.</small>   Scipio Claramonti of Cesena has in a particular treatise shewn, that the Pisatello, and not the Lusa, was the ancient Rubicon; and even at this day the neighbouring country people call it Rugon. What seems to put this beyond all doubt,
<small>Ancient monument and inscription.</small> in an ancient stone monument dug up on the banks of the Pisatello, and, at the desire of the inhabitants of Cesena, erected by cardinal Bivarola, late legate of Romagna. It is to be seen on the road leading from Rimini to Cesena, not far from the latter, and is commonly called *la Colonna di Rubicone.* Near the top of this pyramid are the following words:

S. P. Q. R. Sanctio ad Rubiconis pontem.

Underneath, on a large marble table, is this inscription:

Jussu mandatuve Pop. Rom. Cos. Imp. Trib. Miles, Tyro, Commilito, armate quisquis es, manipulariæve centurio, turmæve Legionariæ, hic sistito, vexillum sinito, arma deponito, nec citra hunc amnem Rubiconem signa, ductum exercitum, commeatumve traducito. Si quis ergo hujusce jussionis adversus præcepta ierit, feceritve, adjudicatus esto hostis S. P. Q. R. ac si contra Patriam arma tulerit Penatesque è sacris penetralibus asportaverit.
S. P. Q. R. Sanctio Plebisciti S. Ve C.

On the base are engraven these words:

Ultra hos fines arma proferre liceat nemini.

To these is added the following modern inscription:

Rubiconem

CESENA.

Rubiconem ponti subjectum transis, Viator,
Romano interdicto, Cæsaris ausu
Et adagio JACTÆ ALEÆ celebratum.
Flumini huic stabilem imponere trajectum
Ethnica diu vetuit pavida superstitio,
Catholica nunc suasit secura Religio,
Innocent. X. Summo Pont.
Card. Donghio Legato
Anno MDCLIV.

' Traveller, thou passest the Rubicon, over which this
' bridge is built; a river famous for the ancient Roman pro-
' hibition, the bold attempt of Cæsar, and the adage of *Jac-*
' *ta est alea.* Superstition had long deterred the pagans from
' building a bridge over this river; but the Catholic religi-
' on, less fearful, resolved upon and performed this useful
' work in the pontificate of Innocent X. and the legateship
' of cardinal Donghi, in the year 1654.'

Cesena lies wide on the left-hand, in the road from Ri- *Cesena.*
mini to Ravenna. Over-against it lies Cesenatico, which *Cesenatico,*
has an excellent harbour and a commodious canal. Upon
the bridge, on the Rimini side, stand two fine marble pillars of the Corinthian order. On one of these pillars is a
representation of a dragon, and under it are these words:

Jo. Petrus Ghist.   Inscriptions
Præses P. C.   on two pil-
    lars.

On the pedestal is the following inscription:
Ut maris intumescentis
Undas occluderent
In hujus postea canalis ac portûs
Custodiam & munditiem
Iterum ad fluendum quotidie relaxandas,
Veteri ponte jam penè ætate
Confecto,
Novum hunc ære publico a fundamentis
Erexere
S. P. Q. C.
Anno Domini MDCCXVI.

' In order to shut up the waters of the sea during the flood,
' and afterwards to let them out again when it ebbs, for the
' security and cleansing this canal and harbour, the old
                                          ' bridge

'bridge having been almost ruined through length of time,
'the senate and people of Cesenatico erected this new one,
'in the year 1716.'

On the other pillar are the pope's arms, and the following words:

Gregorio XIII. *Pont. Max.*

'In the pontificate of pope Gregory XIII.'

Removal of the town of Cervia on account of the bad air. About half-way betwixt Cesenatico and Savio lies the episcopal city of Cervia, which at the beginning of this century entirely changed its situation, having formerly stood a quarter of a mile distant from the sea. The inhabitants removed on account of the unhealthful air, from which, in its present situation, the town is entirely free. This new city is built with beautiful broad streets, which for the most part are under covering. On that side of the city opposite to Savio, or Ravenna, over one of the gates is the following inscription:

Cerviæ Urbem insalubri damnatam cælo,
Ad solitudinem jam diu redactam
In hujus apricam Adriatici plagam,
Clementiori perflandam aurâ,
Propinquo spectandam mari,
Nunquam antea tentato opere
Innocentius XII. & Clemens XI. Rom. Pontifces
Fulvii S. R. E. Cardinalis Astalii
Solicitudine allaborante,
Laurentii Corsini Ecclesiastici ærarii generalis Præfecti
Adspirante studio,
Michaëlis Angeli Comitis Mafæi Æmiliæ Questoris
Votis exposcentibus,
Traduxerunt
Ann. Dom. MDCCIII.

'Popes Innocent XII. and Clement XI. by the indefatigable care of cardinal Fluvio Astali, the great diligence of Laurenzo Corsini, &c. removed the city of Cervia, which, being infested with an unwholesome air, had long been reduced to a desolate condition, into this high situation on
'the

'the coast of the Adriatic, that it might enjoy a more sa-
'lubrious air, &c. in the year 1703.'

One would scarce believe there could be such a difference in the nature of the air within so small a distance, did not experience in many instances shew it, especially in hot climates.

Without the above-mentioned gate is a beautiful and broad canal, through which, in June, July, and August (namely, when the season is hottest and driest) the water is let out into a low piece of ground covered with rushes and weeds, about half a mile in length, and in some places as broad. Here the heat of the sun totally exhales the water, and the salt remains at the bottom and sides, to the great profit of the court of Rome. The papal provinces Urbino, Ferrara, Ancona, Bologna, and Romagna, that lie near the Apennine mountains, have the greatest part of the salt they use from these salt-works. {.sidenote: Salt-works.}

In the country beyond Rimini there is a visible alteration for the worse; but the soil is no where so barren as between Cervia and Ravenna; the sea-shore being very sandy, and the country full of morasses and fens. {.sidenote: Barren country.}

About three or four miles on this side of Ravenna, the road lies through a wood of *pigni**; a tree perfectly like the pine, or rather the fir-tree, only it spreads into a broad crown at the top, and has something of an aromatic smell. The fruit called *pigna* is larger than the pine-apple, and, when laid upon the fire, opens, so that the kernel may be taken out, and eaten without any farther preparation, or else put into soop. This fruit is no inconsiderable branch of trade here, and the husks make a clear and excellent fire; but they are chiefly burnt in stoves. {.sidenote: Pigni wood.}

About two Italian miles on this side Ravenna lies the monastery of La Classe, which was founded in honour of St. Apollinaris, in the year 534, finished in 548, and in 1721 rebuilt by pope Innocent XIII, and cardinal Cornelius Bentivolo, his legate (as appears by an inscription on the right-hand of the portico at the entrance of the church.) The fathers call themselves Monachi Classenses, and also Camaldulenses. The church doors stood open when I was there; but not a soul was to be met with either in the church, or in the convent; for the monks, on account of the unhealthful {.sidenote: Convent of La Classe.}

---
* *Jornandes de rebus Gothicis* mentions this wood.

air in these parts, as soon as the summer heats commence, quit the monastery in order to spend that season at Ravenna. On each side of the church are twelve very beautiful pillars of a lightish-grey marble. Here are also ten large stone coffins, being the repositories of so many bishops of Ravenna; and some of them, in their epitaphs, are called *sanctissimi* and *ter beatissimi*. Within the church, over the main door, is an inscription, signifying, that in 1653 the body of St. Apollinaris was brought hither from Ravenna. On the right-hand in going up to the high altar, is shewn, within a grate near the wall, the print of a foot, which is pretended to be an impression made by Gregory the Great in his ecstasy when he was struck with the sanctity of this place; but, by the direction of the foot that made this impression, the saint seems to have been rather leaving the church than coming into it. The door through which Gregory entered the church is at present walled up, and over it is to be seen the following inscription:

Quite deserted in summer. Church.

The print of St. Gregory's foot.

D. O. M. Sanctum
Gregorium M.
Pontificem ter maximum
Per januam hanc
Templum ingredientem,
Ob loci sanctitatem & majestatem
In exstasin raptum,
Vestigium nudi pedis limini infixisse,
Quod antiquâ populi veneratione
Craticulâ ferreâ   -
coopertum est
In Urbe Ravennâ
Traditio & Fama
Viget.

' To God the greatest and best of beings.
' A tradition is still fresh at Ravenna, that Gregory the
' greatest of popes, entering the church through this door,
' and being struck with the awfulness and sanctity of this place,
' was rapt into an ecstasy, and left the print of his naked
' foot at the entrance; which the people, out of veneration
' to the saint, have long since inclosed within an iron grate.'

The high altar is insulated or detached from the wall, and of yellow marble: it is adorned with four beautiful Corinthian

thian pillars made of a kind of marble with white and black veins. About the altar is a good old mosaic work, representing several saints, with their names inscribed near them. On the left-hand in coming into the church, is the following inscription on the wall:

* *Otho III. Rom. Imp. Germ. ob patrata crimina austeriori disciplinæ Sancti Romualdi obtemperans, emenso nudis pedibus ab Urbe Româ ad Garganum montem itinere, Basilicam hanc & Cœnobium Classense XXXX. dies pœnitens inhabitavit, & hic cilicio ac voluntariis castigationibus peccata sua expians, augustum dedit humilitatis exemplum, & Imperator sibi Templum hoc & pœnitentiam suam nobilitat. Anno P. C. M.* Penance of the emperor Otho.

'The emperor Otho III, having, in compliance with the
' severe discipline which St. Romuald enjoined him for his
' sins, travelled barefoot from Rome to mount Garganus; to
' complete his penance, resided in this church and the con-
' vent of la Classe, for forty days, expiating his sins with
' hair-cloth and voluntary castigations. By this means the
' emperor made this church and his own repentance famous,
' in the year of Christ 1000.

LETTER LXIV.

Account of RAVENNA, FERRARA, FAENZA, and IMOLA.

SIR,

RAVENNA, absurdly supposed by some learned men to have been founded by Esau, was, not only during the grandeur of ancient Rome, but a considerable time afterwards, very famous for the exarchate*, of which it was the seat. It contains at present scarce fifteen thousand inhabitants, which bears such a disproportion to the convents, being no less than four-and-twenty, that the city must sensibly feel the weight of this useless load. Its former unhealthfulness has in a great measure been remedied by diverting the

Ravenna.

Number of inhabitants and convents.

* The *exarchus* was the emperor's vice-roy in Italy, whose residence was at Ravenna. *Vid. Hist. Med. Ævi.*

Q 4 course

RAVENNA.

course of the rivers Montone and Ronco from their ancient channels, and causing them to run close by the city; and by draining the stagnating putrid water from the marshy land about it.

In coming from Rimini you enter Ravenna through the Porta Pamfili, so called from the papal family of that name; and, as Innocent X. was of that house, the inscription on the gate begins thus:

Porta Pamfili.

Imperante columbâ Pamphiliâ, &c.

' Under the auspices of the Pamphilian dove, &c.

The Porta Cibo likewise derives its name from the cardinal under whose administration it was built.

Porta d'Oro.

On the Porta d'Oro is the following ancient inscription:

Ancient inscription.

Ti. Claudius. Drusi. F. Cæsar. Aug.
Germanicus. Pont. Max. Tr. Pot.
Cos. II. DES. III. Imp. III. P. P. dedit.

Palace of a Gothic king.

Among the antiquities of this city are shewn the remains of the palace of Theodoric king of the Ostro-Goths; and several superb pillars are to be seen in the upper part of it.

His tomb.

In the lower part is a large porphyry vessel, or sarcophagus, closed up, where formerly the remains of that monarch were deposited. It is decorated with sculpture, representing circles and lions heads. This sarcophagus is indeed something smaller than those at Rome, which I have already taken notice of: however, it is very well worth seeing, being no less than eight feet in length, four in breadth, and cut out of one block*. Near it is the following inscription:

Vas hoc Porphyriacum ol, Theodorici Gothorum Imp. cineres in Rotundæ apice recondens huc Petro Donato Cæsio Naruien. Præsule favente translatum ad perennem memoriam Sapientes Reip. Rav. P. P. C. MDLXIIII.

' This porphyry vase, formerly placed on the top of the
' Rotonda, and containing the ashes of Theodoric king of

---

* Besides this piece of antiquity, Ravenna boasts of another not less venerable; I mean the silver bowl made by Peter Chrysologus bishop of Ravenna, and preserved amidst all the ravages of the Barbarians.

the

' the Goths, was, with the confent of Pietro Donato Cæfi
' bifhop of Narni, and by order of the wife magiftracy of
' the commonwealth of Ravenna, removed hither, for the
' better prefervation of this valuable piece of antiquity.'

The church called the Rotonda lies without the city, and **Rotonda.**
on the right-hand in going from the Porta Cibo. At prefent
it looks like a ruined cupola, or chapel. Its diameter is a-
bout fixteen common paces; and its pavement, excepting
in the dry fummer months, is always under water. It is
fuppofed to have been built by Amalafunta, king Theodo-
ric's daughter, in the year 526. The moft remarkable part **Remarkable**
of it is the roof, which is in the form of an inverted difh, **roof of a**
and confifts of one fingle ftone, which, many years after **fingle flint.**
this church was built, was fplit by lightning: it is as hard as
a flint, and, according to an account written on vellum and
kept on the altar of the chapel, was brought out of Egypt.
The thicknefs of this ftone is four geometrical feet, the circumference a hundred and fourteen, and the diameter one-
and-thirty feet and two inches.

It is difficult to conceive in what manner, at a time when
the modern machines were in a great meafure unknown, this
huge mafs, the weight of which cannot be lefs than an hun- **Its weight.**
dred tons, was raifed to the top of this edifice. Indeed a
perfon who has feen the ftupendous obelifk at Rome, will the
lefs wonder at this. Miffon, *tom.* I. *p.* 293, makes this ftone
thirty-eight feet in diameter, and fifteen thick; but the
laft article is a grofs miftake, the thicknefs at moft not exceeding five Englifh feet.' I am furprifed that any writer,
who pretends to have been at Ravenna, fhould fay, that this
ftone roof has an aperture in the center, like that in the Rotonda at Rome; for it is very certain that there is no fuch
thing in the roof of the Ravenna Rotonda; and, though it
be a little convex on the outfide, a perfon may walk over e-
very part of it.

' Round this ftone formerly ftood the ftatues of the twelve
apoftles, as appears from their names ftill to be feen on the
pedeftals, which project a little way out from the ftone
roof.

On the top of this roof, near the center, was formerly **King Theo-**
placed the porphyry farcophagus mentioned above, with the **doric's**
remains of king Theodoric. According to a narrative writ- **tomb.**
ten on vellum, and kept on the altar of the chapel, this
farcophagus, in the fifteenth century, was beat down by a
cannon-

cannon-ball; but others will have it that this happened in the sixteenth century, in the year 1512, when the French under Lewis XII. made themselves masters of Ravenna, and committed the most violent outrages, without any regard to the sanctity of churches, &c. Those authors who say, that in this expedition Lewis XII. made use of bombs, do not reflect, that, according to Blondel, in his *Art de jetter des bombes*, those dreadful instruments of war were first made use of in the year 1588, at the siege of Wachtendonk: others are of opinion that they were not invented till the year 1639, and that their dreadful effects were first felt by the castle of La Motte. They seem to have the greatest probability on their side, who think that the French soldiers threw down this sarcophagus without the help of cannon; however, they destroyed the cover of it, which was made of gilt Corinthian brass, and finely ornamented with basso-relievo's.

On the right-hand without the Porta Cibo are some remains of the towers of the old castle. On the left-hand, where formerly the sea beat against the city-walls, as is evident from the iron rings for making fast the ships still to be seen in them, is a large tract of land, finely cultivated; for Ravenna at present lies three Italian miles from the sea. As Misenum was the ancient port of the Roman fleet in the Mediterranean, designed to keep Gaul, Spain, Mauritania, Egypt, Sardinia, and Sicily in awe; Ravenna was the rendezvous of the other Roman fleet, appointed for the same purpose with regard to Epirus, Macedonia, Achaia, Propontis, Pontus, Crete, and Cyprus, as appears from Vegetius, *lib.* iv. and Suetonius, in the life of Augustus [*]. And it is not improbable that the convent of la Classe derives its name from the *classiarii* or marines, who used to encamp on that spot. Strabo describes Ravenna as a city built on piles among morasses and shallows, and subject to frequent inundations; and adds, that it had a great many bridges, and that boats were used in going from one part of it to the other. But it is almost incredible to think how much things are now altered; for it is certain that the city stands on the same place as it formerly did, as appears from the old walls and other re-

---

[*] *Cap.* 49. *Classem Miseni, & alteram Ravennæ, ad tutelam superi & inferi maris, collocavit.* ' For the defence of the upper and lower sea, he ' stationed a fleet at Misenum, and another at Ravenna.' *Tacit. Annal.* iv. *cap.* 5. *Italiam utroque mari duæ classes, Misenum apud & Ravennam præsidebant.* ' Two fleets, one at Misenum, and the other at Ravenna, ' protected Italy in both seas.'

mains

RAVENNA.

mains of antiquity. To this place what Ovid says on another occasion is applicable:

> - - - *vidi factas ex æquore terras,*
> *Et procul à pelago conchæ jacuere marinæ.*

'I saw dry land where once the billows roll'd, &c.

This alteration is not of late date; for Jornandes, who lived in the middle of the sixth century, relates, that in his time the harbour was turned into delightful gardens*.

The ancient pharos†, or light-house, stands about half a mile from the city; it is at present in a ruinous condition, and of no manner of service. The pharos must be distinguished from the watch-tower within the walls, near the Palazzo de Spetti. The former is a square tower not entirely straight or perpendicular, but leans to one side. When any danger is apprehended from pirates, the inhabitants on the coast have notice of it by signals from this tower by lamps, or a fire made in it.

_{Pharos.}

The large market-place of the city is adorned with two lofty pillars of granate, upon which stand at present the statues of St. Victor and St. Apollinaris; but formerly, when

_{Pillars in the market-place.}

---

* *A meridie Padus, qui & Eridanus, ab Augusto Imp. altissimâ fossâ demissus, qui septima sui alvei parte mediam influit civitatem: ad ostia sua amœnissimum portum habens, qui classem ducentarum quinquaginta navium, Dione referente, tutissimâ dudum credebatur recipere statione. Qui nunc, ut Fabius ait, quod aliquando portus fuerat, spatiosissimos hortos ostendit, arboris plenos, verum de quibus pendeant non vela, sed poma.* 'Towards the south the Po, otherwise called the Eridanus, Augustus conveyed into the city through a very deep canal, at the mouth of which was a delightful and spacious harbour, where, according to Dio, two hundred and fifty ships could lie in safety. Whereas now, to use the words of Fabius, the harbour is turned into spacious gardens, planted with trees, where fruit hangs instead of sails.' The quotation from Dio, that the harbour of Ravenna could contain two hundred and fifty ships, must have been in some piece of that author that is now lost, for it is not to be found in any of his works that are now extant. But it is impossible that the Po should ever run southward of the city, as that branch of this river running from Ferraro, called *Pò di Primaro* or *Pò d' Argenta*, is seven miles distant from Ravenna, to the north of that city.

† *Plinius, Hist. Nat. lib.* xxxvi. c. 12. *Usus Phari (Alexandrini) nocturno navium cursui ignes ostendere, ad prænuncianda vada portusque introitum: sicuti compluribus jam locis flagrant, ut Puteolis & RAVENNÆ.* The use of the Pharos (of Alexandria) is to hang ought lights, for the benefit of ships sailing in the night, that they may avoid shelves, or know they are near the entrance of a harbour. This is done in many other places, namely, at Puteoli and Ravenna.'

this

this city remained under the jurisdiction of Venice, the arms and the patron saints of that republic were to be seen on them. In this area is also erected a brass statue of pope Alexander VII. sitting, which is the usual attitude in public monuments erected to the vicars of Christ. Behind this statue is a monumental inscription on the wall of a house, by which Ravenna testifies her gratitude to the holy virgin for averting the plague in 1631, when it raged all over the neighbourhood.

Statue of pope Alexander.
Memorial in honour of the virgin Mary.

Farther on, under an arcade in the market-place, are eight small iron grates, which are said to have been gates taken from the city of Pavia, and set up as trophies of the valour of the inhabitants of Ravenna. The common people are persuaded that these gates were brought from the Holy Land, and that they were those which Samson carried away from Gaza: if this were true, he had no extraordinary load to carry.

Gates of Gaza.

In the council-house are to be seen several inscriptions set up in honour of the pope's legates who presided here. Such a vice-gerent ordinarily presides here only three years; after the expiration of which time, a new patent is requisite to continue him in his office.

Statue of Hercules Horarius.

On a fountain in the area before the pope's palace is to be seen an ancient statue of Hercules, bearing on his shoulder an hemisphere that serves for a sun-dial, which is called *Hercules Astrologus*, or *Horarius*. Those who believe, with Vossius (*de Idololatria*) that the sun was worshipped under the name of Hercules, may easily comprehend why this hero was chosen as a support for a sun-dial*. The club on which this statue leans distinguishes him from Atlas, for whom he might otherwise be taken. According to Pighi (in his *Hercules Prodicius p.* 257.) just such another statue, with a celestial sphere, was formerly to be seen in Stephano Bubali's *villa* at Rome.

How scarce good spring water, fit for drinking, was anciently at Ravenna, appears from Martial, who says, in his fifth book:

---

* Some learned persons before Vossius have, in the worship paid to the sun and moon, traced out all the deities of antiquity, and their conjecture is favoured by Macrobius, *Saturn. lib.* i. *c.* 17. who says, *Omnia numina masculini generis ad unum solem: feminini generis ad lunam referri.* ' That ' all the male deities are included in that of the sun alone, and the female ' in that of the moon.'

Sit

RAVENNA.

*Sit Cisterna mihi quàm Vinea malo Ravennæ,
Cum possim multo vendere pluris aquam.*

'I would rather be possessed of a cistern than a vineyard at Ravenna, where water is sold at a dearer rate than wine.'

On the area before the cathedral stands the statue of the virgin Mary, on the top of a pillar erected to her in the year 1659, *ob reparatam* (perhaps it should be *præservatam*) *pluries à peste Civitatem*, 'because she preserved the city more than once from the plague,' according to the inscription upon it. The great door of the church is made of rough boards, without any ornaments; but the most remarkable thing is, that these boards are sawed out of vines, and some of them are twelve feet long, and two spans in breadth*. In the cathedral are fifty-two large marble pillars arranged in four rows. In the choir is some very old mosaic work; and in the chapel of the holy sacrament is a representation of the children of Israel gathering manna in the wilderness, with some other paintings, by Guido Rheni.

Statue of the virgin Mary.
Broad boards of vines.
Cathedral.

In the Theatine church is shewn the window through which it is pretended the Holy Ghost came twelve different times in the shape of a dove, after the death of St. Apollinaris, at the election of the bishops his successors, and settled upon those who were to be elected. St. Severus's pulpit of white marble, &c. is kept here with great veneration.

Theatine church. Frequent appearance of the Holy Ghost in the form of a dove. St. Severus's pulpit.

On the left-hand near the main entrance of the church of St. Apollinaris, in the cloister, is to be seen the following ancient inscription on a stone fixed in the wall:

Ancient monument.

---

* Plin. lib. xiv. c. 1. init. *Jovis simulacrum in Urbe Populonia ex una (vite) conspicimus tot ævis incorruptum: item Massiliæ pateram. Metaponti templum Junonis vitigineis columnis stetit. Etiamnunc scalis tectum Ephesiæ Dianæ scanditur vite unâCypriâ, ut ferunt --- Verum ista ex silvestribus facta crediderim.* 'The image of Jupiter in the city of Populonia, cut out of 'a single vine, we see undecayed for so many ages; as likewise the dish 'at Marseilles. The pillars in the temple of Juno at Metapontum were 'of vine-tree: and even the steps to the temple of Diana at Ephesus are 'said to be made of one Cyprian vine---- but I take them to be made 'of the wild vine.'

Propa-

*Propagatori. Roma-
ni. Imperii. fundato.
quietis. publicæ. D.
Fl. Conftantino.
Semper. Aug. Divi.
Conftanti. Filio
Setorius Sillanus
V. P. Præpofitus
Fabricæ. Devotu.
N. M. Q. E.*

The letters at the end of this infcription fignify *Numini Majeftatique Ejus.*

Near this is a grave-ftone, with the following ancient infcription:

Epitaph of MarcusCocceius.

*M. Cocceio. M. Pollionis. Nepoti
Trib. Pleb. Defi.
Leg. Pr. Pr. Prov. in
Siciliæ. Quæft.
Trib. Mil. Leg. XI. Cl.
Se Viro Eq. R. XVI. R. St.
Primitivos. Lib.
VI. Vir.*

St. Apollinaris's church.

The church of St. Apollinaris deferves a traveller's notice. On each fide of it are twelve marble pillars; and the cieling is an old, but beautiful mofaic work, reprefenting the three eaftern kings worfhipping the infant Jefus; and alfo feveral faints, with their names infcribed over them. In the center is to be feen the head of the emperor Juftinian; and from the gold and filver ornaments in the mofaic work this church is commonly called *il Ciele d'Oro,* or the golden ciel-

CardinalRagio's tomb. Great altar.

ing. Cardinal Ragio, who died in 1687, has a fine monument here of white and black marble, embellifhed with fome excellent ftatues. The high altar is infulated, and both the fculpture and marble about it are exceeding beautiful.

St. Antony's chapel.

In St. Antony's chapel are feveral fine marble ftatues: the altar is ornamented with black marble pillars; and near the entrance are two pillars of quince-coloured alabafter, which on that account are very remarkable. The altar of the chapel *delle Reliquie* is decorated with four beautiful pillars of red porphyry. All the other altars in this church are likewife of marble, and adorned with many excellent pieces

of

of painting. Great devotion is paid to the body of St. Apol- *Paintings.*
linaris; and on his coffin are three silver tablets, on which *Corpse of St.*
is engraven a long account of his life and martyrdom. Near *Apollinaris.*
the entrance of the church, on the roof, are two mosaic *Mosaic*
pieces, one representing Theodoric's palace, and the other *work.*
over-against it the old harbour of Ravenna.

In the wall of the convent of St. Vitalis is an antique *St. Vitalis's*
monument, on one side of which is a representation of a *convent.*
man, and on the other a woman, with the following inscription:

Oliæ P. F.   Ancient
Tertullæ   epitaph.
V. Ann. XV. M. VIIII. D. X.
Olius Tertullianus
Filiæ pientissimæ & sibi.

Near the door is the marble monument of Isaac, one of the exarchs, with a Greek inscription.

This convent belongs to the Benedictines, and the annual revenues of it amount to upwards of thirteen thousand *scudi*.

The pavement of St Vitalis's church is very beautiful, *Church.*
and the mosaic work in the choir is extremely curious; Ci- *Curious mo-*
ampini has inserted a copper-plate of it in his treatise *de Ope-* *saic work.*
ribus Musivis. It seems to represent the consecration of this church. The emperor Justinian, the archbishop Maximilian, and several other assistants, are to be seen on one side; and the empress Theodora, with her retinue, on the other. The cieling of this church is painted in *fresco*. On the pavement is shewn the spot on which St. Ursicinus was beheaded. Near it are some beautiful pieces of painting, one of which, *Paintings.*
by Federico Boracio, a native of Ravenna, represents the martyrdom of St. Vitalis. It was painted in the year 1583; and the connoisseurs are particularly pleased with the representation of a woman suckling her infant, in this piece.

The chapel of St. Ursicinus is called *Sancta Sanctorum*; *Sancta*
and, on account of the extraordinary sanctity of this place, *Sanctorum.*
no woman is permitted to enter it.

On the altar della Madonna stand three beautiful white marble statues of the virgin Mary, and two angels. Over another altar, which is also of white marble, is an excellent Pietà betwixt two angels, copied from an original piece in the church of St. Justina at Padua.

The

RAVENNA.

An Æsculapius.

The altar of St Vitalis has also some curious pieces of sculpture in white marble. Behind it is shewn the well, into which the body of that saint was thrown. Near the choir is Æsculapius, represented under the figure of a dragon, and two marble basso-relievo's standing over-against each other. This church having frequently been damaged by inundations, the following inscription on a pilaster is addressed to every pious traveller:

Inscription against inundations.

De Die XXVIII. Maji MDCXXXVI.
Nec sacris parcens ruit unda huc usque, Viator,
Molliter ut jaceant flumina nostra, roga.

'On the 28th day of May, 1636, the raging flood, without regard to the sacredness of the place, penetrated even thus far. O traveller, kindly pray that our river may keep quietly within its bed.'

Representation of a sacrifice.

Fault in it.

Near the entrance of the church is a basso-relievo, representing four persons in a Roman dress, to whom four others are bringing an ox. It may possibly represent a sacrifice, though no idol is to be seen; and, contrary to the rules of perspective, the farthest figure of the groupe seems to be the largest.

Tomb of the emperor Honorius, &c.

In the garden of the convent of St. Vitalis is a chapel consecrated to St. Celsus and St. Nazarius, built by Galla Placidia daughter of Theodosius the Great, sister of the emperors Arcadius and Honorius, and mother to Valentinian II. This chapel, which is paved with marble, seems to have been intended for a family burial-place; for there are three tombs in it, and on the altar is the following inscription:

Viator, qui antiqua invisis, hic tergemino clausi marmore jacent Galla Placidia, Honorius Theodosii Senioris Imperatoris Filii*, Constantius Placidiæ Conjux, ac Valentinianus Tertius eorum Filius, mundanæ Celsitudinis reliquiæ & terrenæ caducitatis argumentum.

'Traveller, who comest in search of monuments of antiquity, behold the poor remains of worldly grandeur, and an instance of the transitoriness of sublunary glory! with in these three marble repositories lie inclosed Galla Placi-

---

* It should be *filius*, and not *filii*: for Constantius, Placidia's husband, was not descended of the imperial family, but only of a Roman patrician house. [*Filii* seems to refer to Placidia and Honorius, who were both the children of Theodosius, the masculine gender being used here for both.]

'dia,

RAVENNA.

'dia, Honorius son of the emperor Theodosius the elder,
'Constantius the husband of Placidia, and Valentinian III.
'their son.'

Close by is an Italian inscription, signifying that Placidia lies in the large white marble repository behind the altar, with her brother Honorius on her right-hand, and her husband Constantius, together with their son Valentinian III, in a mausoleum on the left.

Placidia is said likewise to have founded the church of St. John at Ravenna, if the inscription quoted by Gruter, p. 1048. but not to be seen in that city, deserves any credit. For it cannot be denied that the vow made to St. John the evangelist, when she was in peril of being shipwrecked, renders it very suspicious. The inscription runs thus: *Whether Placidia built St. John's church.*

> Sanctissim. ac. Beatissimo
> Apostolo. Johanni. Evangelistæ
> Galla. Placidia. Augusta
> Cum. suo. Filio
> Plac. Valentiniano. Aug.
> Et Filio. suo
> Justa. Grata. Honoria. Aug.
> Liberationis. maris
> Vot. solvit.

From this it may be inferred, that the vow might not include the building of the church, but only the erecting of this monument, or votive table.

At one corner of the Franciscan convent in the public street is to be seen the tomb of the celebrated Florentine poet, Dante Alighieri, under cover, and inclosed within iron rails; and over his bust the following words are inscribed within a laurel wreath: *Dante's tomb.*

VIRTVTI
ET
HONORI

' To Virtue and Honour.'

Vol. III.   R   And

RAVENNA.

And near it, on the left side:

Op.
Petri
Lombardi.

'The work of Pietro Lombardi.'

On the right side of the poet are the following Latin verses in rhyme, which, as appears by the letters *S. V. F.* i. e. *Sibi Vivens Fecit*, over them, were composed by Dante himself:

His epitaph.

Jura Monarchiæ Superos, Phlegethonta Lacusque
Lustrando cecini, voluerunt fata quosque.
Sed quia pars cessit melioribus hospita castris,
Factoremque suum petiit felicior astris.
Hic claudor Dantes patriis extorris ab oris,
Quem genuit parvi Florentia mater amoris.

'Of monarchs rights I sung, and tun'd my lay
'To hell's dark regions, and the realms of day.
'My better part now soars above the stars,
'In perfect bliss, free from intestine jars;
'My body lies within this narrow tomb,
'For ever exil'd from its native home *.'

On the left is the following inscription cut in marble:

Exulem à Florentia Dantem liberatissimè excepit Ravenna vivo fruens, mortuum colens. Magnis cineribus, licet in parvo, magnificè parentarunt Polentani Principes erigendo, Bembus Prætor luculentius extruendo pretiosum Musis & Apollini Mausolæum, quod injuriâ temporum penè squalens Emin. Dominico Maria Curfio Leg. Johanne Salviato Prolegato, magni Civis cineres patriæ reconciliare cultus perpetuitate curantibus, S. P. Q. R. jure ac ære suo tanquam thesaurum suum munivit, instauravit, ornavit.
Anno Domini M. DC. XCII.

Ravenna having very kindly received Dante, when he was
' exiled from Florence, enjoyed him when living, and re-
' veres his memory when dead. The funeral honours paid
' to his venerable ashes were great, though they are con-

* Florence:.

' fined

RAVENNA.

'fined in a narrow tomb, first erected by the princes *Pole-
'tani; but the prætor Bembo raised this more splendid mau-
'soleum, sacred to Apollo and the Muses. When this had
'suffered by the injury of time, the most illustrious Dome-
'nico Maria Cursi being legate, and Giovanni Salviati vice-
'legate, &c. the senate and people of Ravenna, by their
'own authority, and at their own expence, repaired, embel-
'lished, and fenced this monument with iron palisadoes as
'their most valuable treasure *A. D.* 1692.

Under some Latin verses by Bernardo Bembo, on his embellishing this tomb with a marble arch, &c. is the following
inscription:

An. Sal. M. CCCC. LXXXIII. VI. Kal. Jun.
Bernardus Bembus aere suo posuit.

'Erected by Bernardo Bembo at his own expence, in the
'year of our Redemption 1483.'

Misson and others ascribe the repairing of this monument
to the famous cardinal Pietro Bembo; but the subscription
and the year both shew, that the honour is due to his father
Bernardo Bembo, a nobleman of Venice; with which likewise agrees the testimony of *Pocciantius de Script. Florent. p.*
45. But that author is mistaken in placing this transaction
in the year 1433; whereas it should be 1483, as appears by
the inscription above. Dante was born in 1265, and died in 1321. The animosities of the Bianchi and Neri factions drove him from Florence, his native country; for the former, with which Dante sided, being worsted, were driven
out of the city. This poet's proper name was Durantes, which, during his childhood, was contracted into Dante, the
name he was ever after known by †. Buonanni affirms, that
Alighieri was only the name of his father; but that his
right family name was Bello ‡. As the poetical genius of
Petrarch was first kindled by his passion for his beloved Laura,
so Dantes's genius for poetry appeared very early in passio-
nate addresses to the object of his love §. Beatrix Pontinaria

Some account of Dante.

His proper name.

---

* Guido Poletani, to whom Dante fled for protection, was at that
time prince and lord of Ravenna. See *Volaterr. Comm. Urb. lib.* xxi.
p. 771.   † *Volaterr. lib.* xxi. p. 770.'   ‡ *Discorso sopra*
l'Inferno de Dante, p. 2, 3, 184.   § Propertius says,
Ingenium nobis sola puella dedit.
'Beauty alone inspir'd my infant muse.'

R 2   and

His mis-   and Gentucca were the two nymphs whose names he has
tresses.   conveyed down to posterity; and Dante, in a particular po-
              em, introduces Theology under the name of his beloved
Why hated   Beatrix, then lately deceased. His treatise *de Monarchia*, in
by the court which he defends the emperor's power in secular affairs against
of Rome,   the usurpation of the pope, caused him to be declared a he-
and declared retic by the court of Rome.
a heretic.

About three Italian miles from Ravenna, on the road to
Forli, and near the river Ronco, is shewn the spot on which
the French, in the year 1512, obtained a signal victory over
Gaston de the papal and Spanish army; but with the loss of their brave
Foix killed. general Gaston de Foix duke of Nemours. This nobleman
who was then only twenty-four years of age, was celebrated
for his valour and conduct, and lost his life in the pursuit of
the enemy, which very much damped the joy of the French
army. In memory of this battle Pietro Donato Casi, bishop
of Narni, and governor of this province under Paul III,
erected a square pillar here, with the following inscriptions:
On the west side, near the pedestal:

Monument   *Videbis hospes hûc parùm attollens caput, inscriptus iste quid*
of the battle
in which   *velit lapis tibi. Recenset illam nempe cladem maximam Galli atque*
he was kil- *Iberi exercitûs, Æmiliam quæ penè totam maculavit sanguine.*
led.

    ' Stranger, look up, and thou wilt see what the inscripti-
    ' on on this stone means; it gives thee an account of that
    ' very great slaughter of the French and Spanish armies, by
    ' which almost the whole territory of Romagna was deluged
    ' with blood.'

The word *clades* does not relate to the slaughter of the
French, but to the pope's troops, which the bishop conceals
under the general name of Spaniards; probably from a tenderness for the honour of the pope, being willing, as far as
possible, to suppress the memory of the victory gained by the
Most Christian King, Lewis XII. when he made war upon
the Vicar of Christ. Ferdinand the Catholic king was indeed at that time in alliance with the pope; but his auxilia-
ries did not make up the greatest part of the papal army.
On the north side of the pillar are these words:

Paulo

From RAVENNA to IMOLA.

Paulo III. Pont. Max. sedente Petrus Donatus Cæsius Episc. Narn. Utr. Sign. Refer. dum Æmiliæ præsideret locumque hunc conflictûs Ravennatis celebritate clarum diligenter explorâsset, ne tantæ rei memoriam vetustas temporum aboleret, hoc erecto marmore conservandum curavit.

' In the pontificate of Paul III, Pietro Donato Cesi bi-
' shop of Narni, &c. after a careful survey of this place, fa-
' mous for the bloody battle of Ravenna, erected this mar-
' ble, that the memory of that signal action might not be
' lost by the injuries of time *.'

The effusion of blood, however, was not so terrible as these inscriptions represent it, though supported by the authorities of Platina and Ciaconi; for both armies put together hardly exceeded thirty thousand men. And Guicciardini, *lib.* x, says, that, though there was no exact account taken of the slain in this battle, they amounted at least to ten thousand, and only one third of that number on the side of the French. Justiniani, *Hist. Venet. lib.* xi. *p.* 237, affirms, that the French lost six thousand foot, and seven hundred horse; and the Spaniards eight hundred horse, and above eight thousand foot. This memorable battle, which does great honour to both parties, was fought on the 12th day of April, 1512, which in that year happened to be Easterday.

On the south side of the above-mentioned pilaster are these words:

Acta sunt hæc pridiè Idus Aprilis Anno a partu Virginis supra sesqui millesimum duodecimo, Julio II. Pont. Max. Christianorum Rempublicam Gubernante.

' This battle was fought on the 12th day of April, in the
' year of Christ 1512, in the pontificate of *Julius* II. &c.'

And over this:

* Some other inscriptions to the same purpose, signifying that twenty thousand men were killed on each side, are omitted. This circumstance, as well as the natural construction of the first inscription mentioned above, shews that *clades* may be very justly applied to the French as well as the Spanish army.

FAENZA.

Hinc post, cruenta Gallorum victoria Gastone perempto, Hispanorum reliquiæ evaserunt. Postremo capitur Ravenna à victoribus ac diripitur.

Abi.

'This way fled the remains of the Spaniards defeated by the French, whose bloody victory cost them their commander Gaston; and afterwards Ravenna was taken and plundered by the victorious enemy.

'Farewel.'

As we were desirous of reaching Piacenza at the time of its yearly fair, and as a contagious distemper raged for some weeks at Ferrara, we were deterred from visiting this last city.* The roads are likewise so bad, that, though Ferrara is but five stages from Ravenna, it is a whole day's journey; and, unless it be in very dry weather, there is no traveling the nearest way.

Country from Ravenna to Bologna. The distance from Ravenna to Bologna is five stages, and the road lies through Faenza, Imola, and S. Nicolo. This road, especially after heavy rains, is something dangerous, as it runs close to the river L'Amoni; but this is but a small part of the road, and is afterwards compensated by the pleasure of travelling between delightful rows of trees, and a fertile country on each side, divided into square inclosures by ditches and hedges interwoven with vines. The soil, though it be fruitful, is more clayey, and not so black and rich as in the southern parts of Italy. Just on the other side of Ravenna I perceived that the common people pronounced the letter *s* like the German *sch*; so that instead of *subito*, they say *schubito*, or, as the French would write the latter, *choubito*. This pronunciation prevails as far as Bologna; and the inhabitants of this tract of land may not improperly be called the Italian Swabians.

Swabian dialect of this country.

Faenza. Fine earthen ware made there. Faenza is famous all over Italy for its fine earthen ware, few places affording such good clay for that purpose as the neighbourhood of this city. The name of *majolica* given to this ware is a compliment paid to the inventor of it.

The

---

* The bloody-flux has this spring been very fatal all over Italy, sweeping away old and young. Some days there is no going into a church at Rome but one sees (according to the shocking custom of the country) corpses

BOLOGNA.

The palace, or council-house, the fountain on the market-place, the cathedral (in which are some good basso-relievo's, tombs, and six beautiful statues in the Capella di S. Pietro) are the most remarkable objects at Faenza.

Imola, anciently called Forum Cornelii, lies on the Via *Imola.* Æmilia, which leads from Bologna to Rimini; but affords nothing worth seeing, except the cathedral, in which is a fine monument of cardinal Gozzadini, and three fine *sarcophagi* of fine marble, adorned with good statues.

BOLOGNA, April 16, 1730.

LETTER LXV.

Description of the City of BOLOGNA.

SIR,

BOLOGNA, on account of its extent, the number of *Bologna, its* its nobility and other inhabitants, and the importance *extent and* of its trade, is, next to Rome, unquestionably the finest and *situation.* most wealthy city in the whole ecclesiastical state. Its circuit is between five and six Italian miles; but the length of it greatly exceeds the breadth, and is supposed to resemble a ship, the tower of Asinelli being the mast. The number *Number of* of inhabitants in this city is said to be near ninety thousand; *inhabitants.* but the whole district, which includes three hundred and eight cities, towns, and villages, contains three hundred and eight thousand souls. The ancient name of this city was *Its name.* Felsina, from Felsinus, a Tuscan king, who is supposed to have built it twenty-five years before the foundation of Rome. The name of Bononia is, by some, derived from a successor of Felsinus, called Bonus; but others derive it from the Boji. This city had for a long succession of years retained a kind of liberty under the emperors of Germany, namely, till the year 1278, when it was resigned, with the reserve of some privileges, to pope Nicholas III. But from intestine *How it came into the pope's* corpses lying in open coffins from morning to night. Possibly this custom *hands.* of exposing the dead was originally intended to remove all suspicion of poison, or a violent death.

commotions,

BOLOGNA.

commotions, and wars with the neighbouring states, it continued in a fluctuating condition till the pontificate of pope Julius II, who, taking advantage of the Venetian war, made himself absolute master of it, and annexed it to the papal dominions, by expelling the family of the Bentevoglio's: however, some of that family are the leading men of the city even to this day. On account of their voluntary submission, it was at first stipulated, that the Bolognese should have the privilege of keeping a nuncio at the court of Rome, and an auditor in the Rota; that no citadel should be built; and that the effects of the citizens should not be liable to confiscation on any pretence whatsoever. This compact has hitherto been punctually observed; so that it is said of Bologna, as an extraordinary circumstance, that it is a city *senza fisco e citadella*. Ecclesiastical affairs are decided by the archbishop, and civil matters by a cardinal, with the title of *Legatus à latere*, assisted by a prelate as vice-legate. The legate is either changed or confirmed every three years. The president of the council, which consists of fifty senators, is the *gonfaloniere*, who is at the head of the police and revenue.

Its government.

Genius of the inhabitants.

The Bolognese are famous for their vivacity and wit; and particularly for the satirical poignancy of their jests. However, a stranger no where meets with more civility than at Bologna. But their assiduous application to their several trades and manufactures is a much more valuable quality than the former. This city carries on a large trade in silk; and the little river Reno, a branch of which runs through Bologna, is extremely convenient for their silk-mills, in which a single wheel often runs round four or five thousand little cylinders or smaller wheels with surprising velocity, and, especially if the silk be good and strong, does more work than so many thousand hands in winding it. The motion of this wheel is so regulated, as to be easily stopped, and then the whole machine stands still, as in the silk-mill at Utrecht; for the lifting up of a weight of a single pound only, that hangs in the water, does it.

Silk manufactures.

Silk-mills.

Its trade.

The Bologna damasks, sattins, taffeties, and velvets, are in great repute. This city also carries on a considerable trade in flax and hemp, and great quantities of the latter are exported to Venice, for sails and cordage. It likewise supplies the neighbouring provinces with its oil and wine. The wine made about Bologna is so strong, that when it first comes

Wine.

BOLOGNA.

comes from the prefs it is generally diluted with a fourth part of water, except that appointed for the facrament, which is made by itfelf, and without any mixture: this net wine is to be purchafed at the convents.

Many ingenious works are here made of walnut-tree; for the country abounds with thofe trees. The quinces which grow here are alfo very large, and of an exquifite flavour. Bologna is likewife celebrated for effences, *aqua-vitæ*, foap, and fnuff, but more particularly for its *theriaca*, which is openly, and with no fmall folemnity, prepared in the public elaboratory; and another *alexipharmic*, highly efteemed, which is called *Elettuario di Martino*. Near the river Setta is found good rock cryftal, which at Bologna is wrought into fnuff-boxes, luftres, &c. *Effences.*
Medicines, &c.

The nuns of this city are very ingenious in making moft beautiful artificial flowers of filver, filk, muflin, enamel, ifinglafs, &c. And, though the beft fort of flowers are made only for prefents, yet abundance of them are to be met with in the fhops, where travellers may buy them at a moderate price. Fruits of all kinds are alfo imitated in wax, fo as fcarcely to be difcerned at firft fight from the products of nature. *Artificial flowers.*

Formerly little dogs of the Bologna breed brought no inconfiderable fums to this city; but at prefent the ridiculous paffion for thofe animals is fo far exploded, that even in Bologna itfelf, by the decreafe of the breed, they are become fo fcarce, that one of any tolerable beauty is valued at four or five guineas. Some people tell us, the means ufed for checking the growth of thefe creatures is, to rub their legs and back as foon as they are brought forth with fpirits of wine, and afterwards frequently repeating the operation. If this be true, the effect muft arife from the heat of the liquor, which dries up the vital juices; and poffibly this recipe may be better grounded than what is afferted in the *Mifcellanea Curiofa Medico-Phyfica*, publifhed at Leipfick in 1670, *viz.* If you anoint the back-bone of a new-born infant with the fat of rats, moles, and bats, they will never exceed the ftatue of a fmall dwarf. *Bologna dogs.*

This country alfo abounds in honey and wax, great quantities of which are exported; and all kinds of provifions are here exceeding good, and in great plenty. St. Marco and il Pelegrino have for fome years paft been famous for being the beft inns in all Italy. Fowls of all kinds in thefe parts are *Inns.*
Excellent fowls and pigeons.

BOLOGNA.

are very large, and of a particular fine flavour; especially the pigeons, as they are all over Lombardy. The Bologna *cervellat*, and its other dried sausages, tongues, &c. are famous not only throughout Europe, but are well known in the East and West Indies.

The Bolognese affirm, that their cheese is not inferior to that of Parma, and they sell a great quantity of it under the name of Parmesan cheese. From all these circumstances it may be easily conceived how Bologna came to be stiled *la Grassa*, or the fat. The small branch of the Reno, which runs through their city, has been improved, and rendered extremely commodious for trade; a canal of communication having been cut from it to the lake Valle di Marara, from whence they send their merchandizes to Ferrara and other places situated on the Po.

Dress of the women. The Bolognese dress entirely in the French fashion. The women of the middle class generally appear in a black gown, with a black silk veil over their heads: but the female sex here in general enjoy a greater freedom than in most cities in Italy. I was surprized to see so great a number of blind people in this city, and have not received any satisfactory account of the cause. One also meets with not a few persons walking the streets with spectacles on, who are yet so far from labouring under any weakness of sight, that they roll their eyes about on all sides without once looking through their glasses. This fashion is of Spanish origin, and is supposed to be a sign of greater gravity than ordinary: this has recommended it to the generality of the monks and clergy.

Portico's. The houses in most of the principal streets have before them a kind of portico, which supports the second story. These must be allowed to be very convenient in windy or rainy weather, and in shading the houses from the sun; but they deprive them of that ornament which they would receive from a fine front, or an elegant entrance. As the pillars of these portico's are very irregular before different houses, some being high, others low; some round, others square or octangular; some of stone, and others again of wood; they are no great ornaments to the city. These portico's or galleries serve only for walking; and that part of the streets where the carriages pass is considerably lower*. The roofs

---

* These portico's are somewhat like what they call the Rows at Chester.

of

of the houses are of tiles but flat, with a kind of parapet towards the streets.

The tower degli Afinelli is by some, but erroneously, said to be the highest in all Italy; for the cupola of St. Peter's at Rome far exceeds it. The height of it is but three hundred and seventy-one feet, and it is ascended by four hundred and sixty-four steps; of which four hundred and forty-nine bring you to the gallery, and fifteen more to the very top, where the bells hang. The report of a hamper of gilt iron hanging out of this tower, *in terrorem* to confessors, is without foundation: A monk, for divulging some particulars confessed to him, having, as the story goes, been put in this hamper, and left to perish. This tower is square, and the steps by which it is ascended are only of wood. It derives its name from Gerardo Afinelli, who built it at his own charge in 1109. It is a common saying here, that from the tower of Afinelli one has a view of *Cento e cinque Città*, i. e. a hundred and five cities. But this is no more than a pun upon the word Cento, the name of a small town a little to the northward of Bologna; and, to make up the five, they bring in Bologna with Imola, Butrio, Ferrara, and Modena. A like piece of wit one hears in France concerning the prospect from a mountain near the village of Trente, between Beziers and Narbonne, viz. *J'ai vû d'une montagne Trente & deux villes*; i. e. 'I have seen from the top of a mountain two-and-thirty cities;' but it means no more than, I have seen the village Trente and two cities; *Trente* being the French word for thirty.

Near the Afinelli tower is another square tower, called Garisenda, which name some derive from the name of the person who built it, to emulate the above-mentioned Gerardo Afinelli; and others from the name of the architect. Its height is now reduced to a hundred and thirty feet, the foundation having so far given way, that a great part of it fell, or was taken down. The inclination of this tower on one side is such, that a plumb-line, let down from the top, falls seven feet from the wall at the bottom. It is ridiculous to imagine that this tower was originally built in this manner, as it would have been the height of folly to have laid out so much money, only to shew that such a thing as a leaning tower might be built. This may be demonstrated at a much less expence with the men of a draught-board, or a thousand other ways; and consequently no great skill was required to

raise

raise such a structure. But that this is not the only leaning tower in Italy is well known to those who have been at Pisa, Ravenna, Mantua, or Venice.

The tower of Garisenda is quite covered in at the top; and the city-council, in whose hands the keys are kept, seldom indulge any person with the use of them to go up the tower, by which it is manifest that they have no great confidence in the strength of this pretended master-piece of architecture; and, as far as possible, endeavour to prevent any motion in it. In the walls of this tower, as in that of Asinelli, are holes six or seven feet above one another, for the conveniency of fixing scaffolds for necessary repairs.

Legate's palace. The palace in which the vice-legate, the *gonfaloniere*, and other officers of state have their apartments, and the several boards and courts of justice are held, stands on the great market-place. The front is two hundred and eighteen common paces in length, which, in *A Journey to Italy*, published under the name of one de Seine, is increased to one thousand four hundred and twenty feet. This, however, is but a small exaggeration, in comparison of the many hundred palpable untruths with which that book is stuffed.

Statue of Gregory XIII. Over the entrance stands a brass statue of pope Gregory XIII, who was a native of Bologna; the weight of it is eleven thousand three hundred pounds, and the workmanship does great honour to Minganti, the artist who made it.

Of Boniface VIII. On the left-hand as one enters the door, is the statue of pope Boniface VIII.

The interview between the emperor Charles V. and pope Clement VII. in 1529, when that prince submitted to be crowned by the pope, is commemorated here by the following inscription on a copper-plate:

CLEMENS

BOLOGNA.

CLEMENS VII. PONT. MAX.
Ut Chriſtianæ Reip. ſtatum formaret, cum Carolo V. Imper.
Bononiæ congreſſus eſt: In hanc Urbem Cæſar Non. Novemb. a
Chriſti Natali 1529 introiit, pro Templi foribus de More Pont.
Max. adoravit. Ejus hortatus conſilio cùm reſtituto in Mediolani
avitum Regnum Franciſco Sfortia ac Venetis Pace datâ cunctæ
Italiæ otium ac tranquillitatem diu optatam reddidiſſet, Imperii
coronam hoc pompæ ordine accepit. Feneſtra hæc ad dextram fuit
Porta Prætoria, eâ greſſus Cæſar per pontem ſublicium in ædem
D. Petronii deductus, Sacris ritè peractis a Pont. Max. Auream
Coronam Imperii cæteraque inſignia accepit; inde cum eo trium-
phans, exercitu ornatiſſimo præeunte, urbem perluſtravit. Cum
ambo in eodem Prætorio totam hyemem conjunctiſſ. de ſumma de-
liberantes egiſſent, Cæſar poſt ſuum adventum Menſe V. in Ger-
maniam ad tumultus impiorum civium ſedandos, & Bellum Tur-
cicum cum Ferdinando Fratre Pannoniæ Rege apparandum pro-
fectus eſt. Hujus rei monumentum hoc Innocentio Cibo Card.
Legato auctore, Uberto Gambara Urbis Præf. referente,
S. P. Q. B. extare voluit.
Non. Nov. MDXXX.

‘ His holineſs pope Clement VII, for the tranquillity of
‘ the Chriſtian commonwealth, had an interview at Bologna
‘ with the emperor Charles V. in this city on the fifth day
‘ of November, in the year 1529 from the birth of Chriſt,
‘ who paid the cuſtomary veneration to his holineſs before
‘ the gate of the cathedral; and having, at the pope's ex-
‘ hortation, given the long-wiſhed-for tranquillity to all
‘ Italy, by reſtoring Franceſco Sforza to his hereditary do-
‘ minions the dutchy of Milan, and by granting peace to
‘ the Venetians, he received from the hands of his holineſs
‘ the imperial crown, with the following ceremony: the
‘ window on the right was the prætorian-gate through which
‘ the emperor entered, and was conducted over a wooden
‘ bridge to St. Petronius's church, where, after divine ſervice
‘ had been ſolemnly performed, he received from the pope's
‘ hands the golden imperial crown, and all the other rega-
‘ lia; and when this ceremony was over, theſe illuſtrious
‘ perſons went in a triumphant proceſſion through the city,
‘ preceded by a fine army. They ſpent the whole winter in
‘ the ſame palace, concerting deſigns of the higheſt impor-
‘ tance, and emulating each other in reciprocal tokens of
‘ regard and affection; and the emperor, about five months
‘ after

'after his arrival in this city, set out for Germany, to quell
'the seditions of his rebellious subjects, and, together with
'Ferdinand his brother, king of Hungary, to make prepa-
'rations for a war against the Turks. In memory of such
'a glorious transaction, this monument was erected by car-
'dinal Cibo, legate, and the senate and people of Bologna,
'on the fifth day of November, in the year 1530.'

How far Charles V. humbled himself to the pope.

This inscription says, that Charles V. paid the usual veneration to the pope, without mentioning what that ceremony was. According to Jovius Masenius and Frundsberg's history, the emperor kissed the pope's foot: but Burnet, in his History of the Reformation, says, that the pope, whom the reformation, already begun in Germany, had probably inspired with sentiments of moderation, drew back his foot, and cordially embraced the emperor. Even Jovius observes, that the pope, after the emperor was crowned, had the discretion not to suffer Charles V. to hold his stirrup; which probably, however, was far from the emperor's intention, who had brought a powerful army along with him, and had already given pope Clement VII. to understand, that his filial obedience to his holiness knew its proper bounds, when any unbecoming condescensions were required of him [*]: and, even when he was at Bologna, Charles V, in a public assembly of the pope and cardinals, insisted on a free council. When the pope interrupted the imperial secretary of state (who in a Latin speech was urging the fitness of such a measure) with the following reprimand: *Quare Tu mihi sic contradicere audes, & dominum contra me incitas?* i. e. How dare you thus contradict me, and set your master against me?' Charles took up the cudgels, and in the same language boldly delivered with his own mouth what he had before recommended to his secretary [†].

Former pride of the popes.

Nothing can be more haughty and arrogant than the compliment that the *servi servorum*, as they were pleased to call themselves, expected should be paid them by crowned-heads, namely, that of holding the stirrup; which they formerly

---

[*] The pope was obliged to permit several very express limitations of his authority, and confirmations of all the imperial rights, before Charles V. would take the formulary oath. The coronation was performed on two different days, the Roman succeeding the Lombardian. Guicciardini and Jovius have examined the reasons of the city of Bologna's being chosen for this solemnity preferably to Rome.

[†] See Muller's History of the Augsburg Confession, p. 409.

had

had so much at heart, that they would not suffer themselves to be attended in any other manner by the Roman emperors, than as if they were equerries or grooms of the holy see.

At first, indeed, princes might, partly out of complaisance, and partly out of a blind religious zeal, have been drawn in to perform such an unbecoming office; but it was not long before the popes claimed it as an established right. It is surprising to find the emperor Frederic I, after the obstinate refusal of the princes and great men attending him, stooping, in conformity to this old custom, to the indignity of holding pope Adrian the Fourth's stirrup. Before the emperor could be brought to such an abasement, the pope suffered him to kiss his foot; but refused him the *osculum pacis*, i. e. 'kiss of peace *.' After that time, the like demands, with farther incroachments, were inserted in the Roman ceremonial † as a settled point of right; to which, however, several secular princes, who zealously adhere to the papal see, will scarce conform in this article: for the reformation has, in many particulars, opened the eyes of the Roman-catholic laity. We are told, in Matthew, ch. xx. v. 26. 'That 'whosoever will be the greatest among Christ's disciples, 'shall be the servant or minister of the rest.' And probably the popes had an eye to this text, when they assumed the appellation of *servi servorum*, or the 'servants of servants ‡.'

Frederic I. holds the stirrup.

Never

---

* *Vid. Acta Adriani IV. MS. ex Codice Vaticano ap. Baronium tom.* xii. *ad ann.* 1155. *n.* 8. *p.* 403. the last words of which run thus: *Rex Fredericus præcessit aliquantulum, & appropinquante Papa tentorio Regis, per aliam viam transiens descendit, & occurrens Rex ei, quantum jactus est lapidis, in conspectu exercitûs* officium stratonis cum jucunditate implevit, ET STREGUAM FORTITER TENUIT. *Tum verò Pontifex eundem Regem ad pacis osculum primo recepit.* ' King Frederic went a little ' before, and, as the pope drew near to the king's pavilion, his majesty, ' passing another way, alighted; and, running up to him about a stone's ' throw, before the whole army *with pleasure performed the office of a* ' *groom, AND HELD THE STIRRUP TIGHT.* Then it was that the ' pope first admitted the said king to the kiss of peace.'

† *Ceremoniale Rom. lib.* i. *s.* 3. *c.* 3. *Quando Papa per scalam ascendit equum, major Princeps, qui præsens adest, etiamsi Rex esset aut Imperator, Stapham equi Papalis tenere debet, & deinde ducere equum per frenum aliquantum, &c.* ' When the pope mounts his horse, the greatest prince ' who is present, though he be a king or emperor, ought to hold his ' stirrup, and, after that, to lead the horse a little way by the bridle, &c.'

‡ Pope Gregory the Great was the first who, by assuming this hypocritical title, set the example to his successors. Johannes Jejunator, formerly patriarch of Constantinople, assumed to himself the name of universal bishop;

BOLOGNA.

Never was any yoke fo galling as that which thefe fervants have laid on the necks of their fellow-fervants, being watchful to feize every opportunity of increafing their wealth and power. *Prætextu cæli captant terras.* 'While they feem 'intent on heaven only, they endeavour to engrofs the whole 'earth.'

Memorial of a plague in 1650. An infcription is to be feen on the front of this papal palace, giving an account of the peftilence with which this place was fo vifited, that within the city twenty-three thoufand four hundred and eighty-eight perfons died of it; and, in the diftrict belonging to it, eighteen thoufand. The ceffation of it is folely afcribed to the omnipotence of the virgin Mary, and this infcription was put up in memory of that deliverance.

Among the apartments fhewn to ftrangers, there is one called il Salone d'Ercole, where is to be feen a noble ftatue of Hercules, of an uncommon fize; it is of *terra cotta*, and by *Life and imprifonment of king Henci.* the fkilful hand of Lombardi. In another little faloon are reprefented in *frefco* the moft confiderable atchievements of the Bolognefe, infcribed with Latin verfes, in which the victory over Henci king of Sardinia is not forgotten; and under the triumphal proceffion are thefe words:

Felfina Sardiniæ Regem fibi vincla minantem
Victrix captivum Confule ovante trahit.
Nec patris imperio cedit, nec flectitur auro,
Sed putat hoc magnum, detinuiffe, decus.
Excitat auguftam regalis carceris aulam,
Sic noftri victis confuluere Patres.

'Victorious Bologna, amidft the pomp of a triumph, fees 'the king of Sardinia, who had threatened to enflave it, 'dragged as a captive; and difdaining the offers, and fear-'lefs of the power of his father, detained him prifoner, but 'in a grand palace built for that purpofe. Such is the treat-'ment our anceftors gave their prifoners of war.'

bifhop: this arrogancy the artful pope Gregory wanted to difcredit by his pretended humility. Baronius, in very pompous terms, extols this condefcenfion; and obferves, that the bifhops of Rome exhibit a very ftriking refemblance of Chrift's humiliation. It is a great pity that the popes fhewed this appearance of humility in name only; and that Boniface III. has fince, out of the fame ambition with the patriarch, affumed the title of univerfal bifhop.

The

BOLOGNA.

The first three lines are written in black, with the letter *N* near them. The three following are in red, and on one side of them *PÆ*.

Henci was a natural son of the emperor * Frederic II, who opposing the pope's grant of the island of Sardinia to the Pisans, sent his son, who was married to Adela, a Sardinian princess, with an army, which at first gained great advantages over the pope and Pisans; and afterwards, with the like success, assisted the Modenese. It is commonly reported here, and the Bononian historiographers also relate, that Frederic II. offered for his son's ransom a gold-ring as large as the circumference of the city. Probably some equivocation was apprehended in the offer, as the thickness of the ring was not specified; and consequently it might have proved only a piece of gold wire of such a length as to inclose the city. The long imprisonment of Henci might also be owing to the death of the emperor, which happened soon after, *viz.* in 1250; this unfortunate prince being forgot amongst the disturbances of the interregnum. So far is certain, that he remained a prisoner at Bologna from the year 1249 till his death, which happened in 1272. To say that this palace, at present the residence of the legate and other great officers, was built merely for the reception of that captive prince, is an idle piece of ostentation, the falsity of which appears at first sight, as such a vast edifice would require more years in building than a prisoner could naturally be expected to remain among them. Besides, Sigoni, in his *Historia Bononiensis*, lib. iv. p. 78. and lib. vi. p. 115, says, that one of the public palaces, called il Palazzo vecchio del Commune, or del Podestà, was begun in the year 1200, and the other distinguished by the name of Palazzo Maggiore in the year 1245. Now the latter is the palace in question, and, as appears by this date, was built before Henci was taken prisoner. However, Malespini does the Bolognese great injustice, by saying, in *cap.* cxi. p. 97, that they locked up this prince in an iron cage, and confined him in it as long as he lived.

Over the Salone d'Ercole is the Sala Farnese, so called from a marble statue of pope Paul III, who was of the Farnese family. The cieling and walls of this apartment were painted by the best masters in Bologna, at the expence of

---

* *Vid. Continuator Martini Poloni, p.* 1417. *Riccobaldus Ferrariensis in Historia Imperator, f.* 1174.

BOLOGNA.

cardinal Farnese. Among others, Emilio Taruffi and Carlo Cignani have united their skill in a piece, representing Francis I, king of France, touching for the evil at Bologna, in the presence of pope Leo X, by virtue of the miraculous power of healing assumed by his predecessors the kings of France. As to any one miracle performed by Leo X, historians are entirely silent: and the protestants possibly exceed the truth, in asserting that he was an atheist *. However, Jovius, a zealous popish historian, in his Life of Leo X, acknowledges this pope to have been suspected of being given to unnatural lusts, and makes no secret of his sensuality and voluptuousness; to which vices other authors †, of unsuspected veracity, add his excessive love of hunting, fowling, music, spectacles, and feasting. That he chiefly delighted in the frivolous mirth of sycophants, buffoons, and jesters, is affirmed by Matthieu's *Hist. de Henry IV. lib.* vii. *t.* ii. *p.* 716. And, on the contrary, the little esteem he had for divines, and his preference of poetry, mythology, and other profane sciences to those of his profession, appears even from Pallavicini's History of the Council of Trent. With such dispositions it may well be supposed, that Leo X, when he saw Francis I, a libertine young king, assume to himself a power of working miracles, thought, as Cato the censor

Marginal note: Suspicions concerning Leo X.

---

* The great confidence which our fathers reposed in this pope inclines us Germans to a tenderness for his character; and it must be owned he was not without some eminent qualities: but they extremely deviated from German sincerity, or had too good an opinion of him, when at the renewal of the *concordat. nat. German.* they termed him a zealous patron of religion, and a shining example of sanctity. It is alleged, in extenuation of his irregularities, that he was very early exalted to the papal see. Luther, who in this pope's time restored the truths of the gospel to their primitive purity, prostrates himself before him with the most implicit veneration. *tom.* I. *epist. p.* 71. *an.* 1518. *Quare, Beatissime Pater, prostratum me pedibus tuæ beatitudinis offero cum omnibus, quæ sum & habeo; vivifica, occide, voca, revoca, adproba, reproba ut placuerit, vocem tuam Christi vocem in te præsidentis & loquentis agnoscam. Si mortem merui, mori non recusabo.* 'Wherefore, most holy father, I prostrate myself at thy 'sacred feet, offering myself and all that I have: come life, come death, 'call me, reject me, approve me, condemn me, as it seemeth good to 'thee. In thy voice I hear that of Christ speaking through thee his vice-'gerent. If thou thinkest I deserve death, I shall willingly submit.' And Leo himself does Luther the justice to say: *Che fra Martino Luthere haveva un bellissimo ingegno, e che cotefte erano invidie fratefche.* 'Brother Martin Luther is a person of an extraordinary genius, and these 'are only monastic bickerings.'

† *Onuphrius in vita p.* 396. *Ciacon. in vit. p.* 327. *Natalis Alex. tom.* VIII. *p.* 34.

did

BOLOGNA.

did of the *aruspices*, (which he is said indeed not to have concealed) ' That one could not look upon the other without laughing *.'

Another fine piece of painting in the Sala Farnese represents the public entry of Paul III. into Bologna. The aqueduct by which cardinal Albornò has immortalized his name in this city, is represented in this piece by a plan of it laid before him. The coronation of Charles V. is by Luigi Scaramuccia di Perusa. Lastly, among the remarkable transactions of the republic is also classed the acquisition of a portrait of the virgin Mary, said to be painted by St. Luke.

Other fine paintings in the Sala Farnese.

The Aldrovandi museum, which is kept in this place with such care, that it is never opened but in the presence of a senator, consists, among other curiosities, of a hundred and eighty-seven folio's, and above two hundred bags full of single leaves, all written by the hand of that indefatigable person. Here is also shewn the portrait of a woman, with a beard as long as that of a Capuchin monk, whom Aldrovandi affirms to have seen. This collection has been enriched with the cabinet of the marquis Cospi, which contains a great number of valuable medals, as may be seen in the printed catalogue of them. On the stairs, and over the doors of the apartments, are the busts of several popes, as Urban VIII, Innocent X, &c.

The Aldrovandi museum.

Bearded woman.

The military stores and artillery, with arms for six thousand men, are also kept in this place. The physic-garden in the court of it is very small, and has nothing remarkable in it. The area before the palace is three hundred and seventy feet long, and three hundred broad. The fountain in this area, together with the leaden pipes, &c. are said to have cost seventy thousand *scudi d'oro*; or golden crowns; and it is indeed a very noble ornament to it. The brass statues erected here are by Giovanni di Bologna; the others are by Antonio Lupi; but the disposition of the whole work was left to Lauretti. The statue of Neptune on the top is eleven feet high. Within the bason are a great number of dolphins ejecting water, and four women with three streams issuing out at each breast. The only exception to this superb work is, that the *jetteaus* are not proportional to the size of the figures.

Arsenal.

Physic-garden.

Fountain.

---

* *Cicero, lib. ii. de Divinat. Cato mirari se ajebat, quod non rideret aruspex aruspicem cum vidisset.*

BOLOGNA.

Mint. The mint affords nothing remarkable. The balancer, or press used for coining, moves like the pendulum of a clock, and in a minute stamps fifteen or sixteen pieces. The privilege of coining was first conferred on this city, in the year 1291, by the emperor Henry V; and on the large pieces coined here is the following legend alluding to the university of Bologna, which formerly was in such reputation: *Bononia docet*. And on the smaller pieces, the important word *Libertas*; but both at present are used with little propriety.

A connoisseur in painting will meet with a great deal of entertainment in the private palaces of this city.

Paintings in Bonfiglioli palace. In the Palazzo Bonfiglioli, besides several beautiful pieces by the Caracci's, are about fifty drawings by the most celebrated masters; among which are the massacre of the Innocents, by Raphael; Veturia and Coriolanus, by Baptista Franco *, &c. All these pieces are elegantly framed and glazed with ground glass, which not only preserves them from the dust and the fingers of the beholders, but gives no little addition to their beauty.

Campeggi palace. The Palazzo de' Campeggi is built with free-stone of a diamond cut, and was once the residence of the emperor Charles V. Here also, in the time of James III. and Paul III; the bishops and prelates, appointed to assist at the council of Trent, held their meetings in the year 1547, when the unhealthfulness of the air had obliged them to leave Trent. In the garden is a lion of white marble, formerly erected at Ravenna by the Venetians; but, when that city fell under the papal yoke, it was brought hither.

Bentivoglio palace. The spacious superb palace, which formerly the family of the Bentivogli had in Bologna, was, upon their expulsion out of the city in the year 1507, totally demolished and razed: however, they have since built a very fine house in another part of the city.

Caprara palace. But the palace which most gratifies a traveller's curiosity is that of Caprara; where he cannot but admire the double stair-case, the large looking-glasses (which are seldom seen in the Italian palaces, and what they have are generally but very mean) the tapestry hangings, and the richness of the other furniture. Here are particularly a great many small

---

* Livy, *lib.* ii. *c.* 40, calls Coriolanus's mother Veturia, and his wife Volumnia; which names are used *vice versâ* in Plutarch; but Aurelius Victor, *de viris illustribus*, follows Livy.

BOLOGNA.

coffers of admirable Florentine work; one of raised mother-of-pearl, another with six large, and as many small, pillars of rock-cryftal; several curious works in ivory and wood, and general Caprara's brass statue on a pedestal of red porphyry, supported by a Turk. At the corners of a splendid gallery are closets filled with shells and other marine productions; but both the sides of it are taken up with four large tables, covered with Turkish utensils, belts, money, furniture, &c. count Tekeli and prince Ragotzi's cabinets; two swords set with diamonds, presented to general Caprara, one by the emperor Leopold, and the other by Auguftus king of Poland; the golden-fleece, and several other curiosities within glass-cases, and little brass statues on the top of them. The walls are hung with Turkish arms in the form of trophies. In this gallery are likewise some fine paintings; among which is the death of Brangandini, who was flead by the Turks, painted on wood. Here are also two beautiful tables of Florentine work, and several large silver vases. The last male heir of the Caprara family died in the year 1724; and his daughter, on her marriage with a gentleman of the name of Montecuculi, insisted, that he should take upon him the name of Caprara; which he agreed to, rather than lose her fortune of eighty thousand *scudi* a year: however, the Caprara family is not the richest Bologna; for those of Magnani, Pepoli, and Ranucci are possessed of a hundred thousand *scudi* or crowns sterling a year. Rich families in Bologna.

On the cieling of a saloon of the Palazzo de' Favi are the adventures of Jason in eighteen pieces painted in *fresco* by the two brothers Augustino and Annibal Caracci, under the inspection of their uncle Luigi. In another apartment are painted on the frize twelve passages of the Æneid painted in *fresco* by Luigi Caracci, copper-plates of which are to be had at Rossi's in Rome for two *scudi*, under the following title: *Galleria dipinta in Bologna in casa de' Signori Favi, colle favole di Enea, secondo la descrizione di Virgilio, colorite da tutti trè i Caracci, Annibale, Agostino e Ludovico, intagliata in acqua forte da Giuseppe Maria Mitelli, libro in XVII. fogli reali per traverso.* The rest of the adventures of Æneas are painted in ten pieces by Albani, under the direction of Luigi Caracci, and his other disciples have finished the remainder; but the latter are in a different apartment, and under every picture is a Latin verse out of the Æneid, explaining the subject. On the frize of one apartment are several landscapes in *fresco*, by the cavalier Creti; by whom are two
other

BOLOGNA.

other pieces, representing painting and music by two women. Several other fine pieces of painting are likewise to be seen in this palace, and particularly some very delicate drawings with a pen.

Paintings in honour of Julius III. On a wall in the Palazzo de' Legnani are some imperfect remains of a piece of painting in praise of pope Julius III, by Nicolo del Abbate. Under the papal crown are these words: *Innocentes manibus & mundi corde.* A motto little applicable to Julius III.

Magnani palace. The Palazzo Magnani is finely furnished; but the most remarkable thing here is the history of Romulus, painted in *fresco* by the three Caracci's. Count Carlo Cesare Malvasia, in the third part of his *Felsina Pittrice*, and other connoisseurs give the preference to the piece representing Romulus's victory over Numitor's shepherds, which was done by Augustino Caracci; but it is a great disadvantage to all these master-pieces, that the beauty of the colouring is faded, and on that account they are not beheld with the same pleasure and admiration as the noble works of those artists in the Farnesian palace at Rome.

Palazzo Marescotti. In the Marescotti palace are several fine pieces of painting, and a very superb double stair-case.

Palazzo de' Molari. The Palazzo de' Molari exhibits a good collection of paintings; but is chiefly remarkable for a meridian-line drawn by Dr. Montanari.

Palazzo de' Monti. Humour of the Italian nobility. The Palazzo de' Monti shews the genius of the Italian nobility for decorating their palaces with collections of paintings and other curiosities; who often abridge themselves of a great many of the conveniencies of life, in order to be possessed of something which attracts the admiration of other people, and especially of foreigners. The first floor of this grand edifice, consisting of above thirty apartments, which are by far the best, is never, or at least very seldom, inhabited, and then only for the reception of some person of distinction; the general use of them being only to display an amazing collection of paintings and other curiosities. Besides the great number of pieces by Albani and the Caracci's, here is a gallery painted by young Cignani; together with a very large piece of painting representing the raising of the siege of Turin, by Antonio Casa. In another apartment is to be seen a woman asleep, with a wanton boy laughing, whilst he lets down a mouse hanging by a thread upon her breast. In this piece the expression is very strong, and the mouse is admirably done. This palace is well furnished, and the apartments

BOLOGNA.

ments are lofty and magnificent. The Bolognese family of Monti claims kindred with pope Julius III, who was a Florentine.

The Palazzo di Pepoli is a fine edifice, and is remarkable for its superb stair-case, spacious hall, fine tapestry and other rich furniture. Here is to be seen a silver triumphal car, with two ladies sitting it, which moves by clock-work about the room, as if it was drawn by two lions. The best paintings in this palace are the cieling-pieces. *Palazzi di Pepoli.*

The palace of Ranucci is likewise built in a grand taste, with a noble stair-case, and spacious lofty rooms. Here is some beautiful tapestry made at the Gobelins, and several closets full of Florentine work, silver vases, and other furniture; particularly a clock of raised inlaid work of gems on a ground of *lapis-lazuli*. The height of the chapel takes up three stories of the house. Among the paintings in this palace are a fine piece of perspective, by Agostino Mitelli; St. Jerom, and Joseph flying from Potiphar's wife, by Guido; the fall of Haman, by Antonio Gionima (a new piece, where the beautiful figure of Esther is particularly admired;) and the portraits of the great dukes of the Medicis family. In the upper saloon is an indifferent piece of the reception of the king of Denmark at this palace, with these words under it: *Palazzo Ranucci. Paintings.*

> *Fridericus IV. Daniæ, Norvegiæ,*
> *Gothiæ ac Vandaliæ Rex,*
> *Ranutiæ Domûs bis hospes*
> *MDCCIX.*

‘ In this palace of Ranucci, Frederic IV, king of Den-
‘ mark, Norway, the Goths and Vandals, was twice en-
‘ tertained in the year 1709.'

Facing it is a piece representing the coronation of the emperor Charles V, as performed by the pope at Bologna in the year 1530.

The family of Ranucci have also a charming villa, of which, together with the Dominican convent, one has a fine view from the Monte della Guardia. *The Ranucci villa.*

In the Palazzo Sampieri are several pieces, by the three Caracci's; and one of the best that was ever done by Albani, representing Cupid kissing his mother Venus, and, with an air of triumph, as it were to shew his power, pointing at the *Sampieri palace. Admirable picture by Albani.*

rape

rape of Proserpine by Pluto: and near him is a groupe of sportive loves joining in a dance.

Palazzo di Volta. Not far from the church of Madonna di Galiera, Gieronimo Trevisano has painted in *chiaro oscuro,* on the outside of the wall of the Palazzo di Volta, several remarkable transactions of the Roman commonwealth; but it is almost defaced by length of time. In the apartments are to be seen the works of Mitelli, and several other painters. Besides another palace in this city, the family of the Volta have a seat at Casaralta, where the following ænigmatical epitaph, on which so many of the literati have already exercised their wits, is to be seen:

Seat of the di Volta family.

A Enigmatical epitaph.

D. M.
Ælia Lælia Crispis
Nec Vir, nec Mulier, nec Androgyna,
Nec Puella, nec Juvenis, nec Anus,
Nec Casta, nec Meretrix, nec Pudica,
Sed omnia.
Sublata
Neque Fame, neque Ferro, neque Veneno,
Sed omnibus.
Nec Cælo, nec Aquis, nec Terris,
Sed Ubique jacet.
LVCIVS AGATHO PRISCIVS
Nec Maritus, nec Amator, nec Necessarius
Neque Mœrens, neque Gaudens, neque Flens
Hanc
Nec Molem, nec Pyramidem, nec Sepulchrum,
Sed omnia,
Scit & Nescit Cui Posuerit.

' Ælia Lælia Crispis, who was neither male, female, nor
' hermaphrodite; neither a girl, a youth, nor an old woman;
' neither chaste, a whore, nor a modest woman; but was
' all these. She died neither by famine, sword, nor poison;
' but by all three. She lies neither in the air, nor in the
' waters, nor in the earth; but every-where. Lucius Aga-
' tho Priscius, who was neither her husband, nor gallant,
' nor relation; neither weeping, rejoicing, nor mourning,
' erected this, which is neither a fabric, a pyramid, nor a
' tomb, but all three; but to whom, he knows, and yet
' knoweth not.'

Under

BOLOGNA.

Under this ænigma are the following words:

> *Ænigma*
> *Quod peperit gloriæ*
> *Antiquitas,*
> *Ne periret inglorium*
> *Ex antiquato marmore*
> *Hic in novo reparavit*
> *Achilles Volta Senator.*

' That this ænigma, the invention of ingenious anti-
' quity, might not be loſt by the decay of the ancient mar-
' ble on which it was firſt engraven, it ſtands here cut in
' freſh characters, by order of Achilles Voltes, a ſenator.'

On the four ſides of the ſame ſtone are twelve different explanations of this epitaph, with the names of their ſagacious authors. Mario Michael Angelo will have it to be rain: Fortunius Licetus, the beginning and ending of friendſhip; John Caſper Gevartius interprets it to be love; Zachary Pontinus ſays it was deſigned for the remains of three different perſons; Johannes Turrius is of opinion that it is the *Materia Prima*; Nicholas Barnaud, that it is an eunuch, or the philoſopher's ſtone; Agathias Scholaſticus (if that was his name) affirms it to be Niobe; Richardus Vitus will have it to be the rational ſoul, or the *Idea Platonis*; and Ovidius Montalbanus, hemp. Count Malvaſia, in a particular treatiſe intitled *Ælia Lælia Criſpis non nata reſurgens*, interprets it of a daughter promiſed to a perſon in marriage, who died pregnant with a male child before the celebration of her nuptials *.

Beſides theſe learned perſons, M. de Cigogne Ingrande has diſcovered pope Joan in it; the celebrated Boxhorn † ſays it is a ſhadow; and a ludicrous hand has taken the liberty

to

---

* Whether this be our author's meaning, I cannot ſay, it being ſomething obſcure in this paſſage; but it is ſomething applicable to the ænigma, though I know not whether it be agreeable to Malvaſia's interpretation, having never ſeen it.

† In the *Acta Eruditorum Lipſienſ. menſ. Mart. ann.* 1732, is an anonymous letter, in which the author interprets this riddle of a monument erected by one of the Ælian family to his own ſoul, where he puts the letters *A. M. P. P. D.* at the beginning of the epitaph, denoting *Animæ Meæ Propriæ Dico*. This interpretation he ſupports as grounded on the old

inſcription

BOLOGNA.

to scratch on the stone under the above-mentioned illustrations *un petto*, or a f---t. The original epitaph is said to have been broken to pieces in the last century, and the fragments were made use of in laying the foundation of this house; and, what seems not a little surprising, all the explanations hitherto given of this inscription have their difficulties. And though Malvasia's has the most probability on its side; yet the particulars are grounded on so many historical circumstances, that an ingenious pen would not be much at a loss to cook up a romance out of them. Give me leave to subjoin another ænigmatical inscription, though it be something satirical, made on a woman at Basil, who lived fifteen years in the matrimonial state with an eunuch:

Another ænigma of the same kind.

> Palladiæ Veneris, vel Veneriæ Palladis
> Thalamum Sepulchro similem cernis.
> Ubi Virgo simul & Matrona, Nupta & Innupta,
> Nec Sterilis, nec Fœcunda: nec Uxor, nec Pellex:
> Conjux sine conjuge: Cœlebs sine cœlibatu.
> Annos quindecim, sine querela,
> Cum Viro jacuit semiviro.
> Mirante naturâ, tamdiu potuisse fœminam
> Sic jacere, vel tacere *.

' Behold a marriage-bed, or rather a grave, of a lady en-
' dowed with the beauty of Venus, joined with the prudence
' of a Pallas; who was at once a virgin and a matron, mar-
' ried and unmarried; neither barren nor prolific, neither
' wife nor concubine; a wife without a husband; single,

inscription; but adduces no proof. Not to mention that those letters are not on the Bologna epitaph, but only on an old copy at Milan, supposed by Malvasia to be spurious; and to the end of which is taked the following addition, not to be found in the editaph of Bologna:

> Hoc est sepulchrum intus cadaver non habens,
> Hoc est cadaver sepulchrum extra non habens,
> Sed cadaver idem est & sepulchrum sibi.

' Here is a sepulchre without a corpse; here is a corpse without a se-
' pulchre: the corpse and sepulchre are one.'

[A correspondent of the *Mercure de France* will have this epitaph to be designed for Lot's wife.]
* *Vid. Comes Emanuel Thesaurus, in Idea argutæ & ingeniosæ dictionis, p. 455.*

' and

'and yet not in a state of celibacy. Here she lay fifteen years without any complaints, with a man who was but half a man, while nature itself admired that a woman could lie or be silent for so long a time under such circumstances.'

I shall not take upon me to decide, whether the silence of the abovementioned Pallas be more wonderful than her patience; or than the ignorance of another wife, who lived some years with an impotent husband, without being sensible of his deficiency; for she imagined that the rest of the world had no further commerce together than she and her husband. Hilarion de Coste, in his *Eloges des Dames illustres*, tom. I. p. 697, relates this story of Isabella di Gonzagua, the wife of Guido Ubaldi duke of Urbino, who died in 1508: but now, since women are better acquainted with the secrets of nature, their knowledge renders them less patient under such disapointments. To what a degree of immodesty not a few are arrived, appears from their processes for divorces *ex capite impotentiæ*.

The Giardino de Poëti at Bologna, so extolled by some travellers, is in reality but meanly laid out. It derives its name from the family of the Poëti, to which it belongs. [Poëti garden]

A little without the Porta S. Mamala is a passage through a garden into a grotto, in which is a statue of Venus, some shell-work on the walls, and several small basons filled with water for baths. This work generally passes for a bathing-place of the ancient Roman emperors; but I am of opinion, that the chief design of this work was to find out a good spring of water: for many passages are hewn in the rock, in which are several springs, at last meeting in a deep reservoir; and from thence the water is conveyed by an aqueduct, which is to be seen behind the church dell' Annonziata, to the large fountain in the area before the Palazzo Publico. The lapideous concretions that hang on the bricks with which the above-mentioned subterraneons passages are lined, perfectly resemble the incrustations on the pillars in the *Piscina Mirabilis* at Baiæ, and are so hard and tenacious, as not to be separated without damaging the brick-work. In some places these strong concretions are of such a thickness, that an altar has lately been made of them at Bologna. [Grotto out of the Porta S. Mamala. Aqueduct.]

I come now to the ecclesiastical edifices at Bologna, and shall begin with St. Agnes's church, which belongs to the Dominican nuns. This church is finely gilt and painted; among [St. Agnes. Fine painting.]

among the latter the martyrdom of St. Agnes over the high altar is one of Domenichino's beſt pieces.

St. Antony. In St. Antony's church, over the great altar, is an admirable piece, by Luigi Caracci, repreſenting the preaching of the primitive hermits. On another altar is a picture of the virgin Mary with her divine infant, with a groupe of angels hovering over her; St. Francis' and St. Carlo in a devout poſture, &c. In the oratory or ſmall chapel near this church is a moſt beautiful piece, repreſenting the annunciation, by *Abſurd repreſentation of the Holy Ghoſt.* Tiarini; but with this preſumptuous abſurdity, viz. God the Father is repreſented above, in heaven, holding a dove in both his hands, juſt as if he was going to let it fly. The *Montalto college.* convent near this church is called *Collegio di Montalto*; for it was converted by pope Sixtus V. from an hoſpital into a convent. Here is a good library, which is prettily painted in *Miraculous Image of St. Antony.* *freſco*, by Geſſi. On the wall without the college is a miraculous image of St. Antony, before which a perjured man being once brought, all his fleſh, as the fable goes, was inſtantly reduced to aſhes, and fell off his bones. On the feſtival of that ſaint thoſe aſhes and bones are publicly expoſed to the devotion of the credulous people.

Statue of St. Petronius. St. Bartholomew's church. Before St. Bartholomew's church ſtands a marble ſtatue of St. Petronius, by Brunelli. This church is divided into three iſles, and that in the middle is of a remarkable height. All the three make a fine appearance, and are excellently painted, particularly that on the ſouth ſide. Angelo Michael Colonna, as is mentioned in an inſcription, from a motive of devotion, performed this grand piece, and ſome others, without any reward. The high altar is of beautiful marble, with ſome figures inlaid. An annunciation, by Albani, to be ſeen here, is accounted an incomparable piece; and indeed nothing can ſurpaſs the expreſſion of the virgin's admiration; though, in my opinion, it is not accompanied with that humility, and, as it were, bluſhing modeſty, which are expreſſed in ſome of the beſt pieces on this ſubject. The two other pieces, repreſenting the nativity, and the flight into Egypt, are alſo by the ſame maſter. On the outſide of the cloiſter which faces the ſtreet, and conſiſts of ten arches, are ſome fine baſſo-relievo's, by Formigini; with the life of St. Gaetano, painted from Cignani's deſigns.

A maſterpiece by Guido. In the veſtry of the Capuchins church is a crucifixion, by Guido Rheni, which is extremely admired as a real maſterpiece.

The

BOLOGNA.

The Certosini, or Carthusians, whose convent is without the city, are in possession of that celebrated piece of Agostini Caracci, in which St. Jerome is represented receiving the sacrament at the point of death, and taking leave of his friends. This picture stands on the great altar; and in a chapel on one side of it is St. John preaching in the wilderness, painted by Luigi Caracci, who in this piece strove to emulate Agostini Caracci in that mentioned above. By the same master is also the scourging of Christ. Here is also a capital piece, representing the baptism of Christ, by Elizabeth Sirani; and the feast where Mary Magdalene anoints our Saviour's feet by her father Giov. Antonio Sirani. St. Bruno kneeling before the holy virgin is by Guercino; the ascension of Christ, by Bibiena; the descent from the cross, by Gessi; St. Catharine of Sienna, by Tiarini; and Christ led to the place of execution, a capital piece, is by Massari.

Fine painting at the Certosini.

The church *ad Corpus Domini*, belonging to the nuns of St. Clare, has been newly rebuilt, and suitably ornamented; the roof was painted by Franceschino. On the right-hand, near the entrance, is a beautiful altar, adorned with red and white marble pillars. Here are also two fine pieces by Luigi Caracci; one represents Christ descending into the *limbus patrum*, and the other the interment of the virgin Mary. The undecayed body of Catharine de' Vigri, a Bolognese, the foundress of this convent, who died in the year 1463, is preserved by the nuns as a relique of singular value. The body is sitting in a chair, and looks like a dried mummy. As to the fragrant odour emitted by this corpse, that may be effected without any difficulty; but that its nails and hair are continually growing and often cut, is what, out of meer complaisance to the fair nuns, one would not chuse to dispute. We are indeed informed by historians, that the beard of the brave Gustavus Adolphus grew considerably after he had been laid in his grave *; and this is no more than can easily be cre-

Ad Corpus Domini church.

Superstition about the corpse of Catarini de' Vigri.

---

* The possibility of the beard, and consequently of the hair, growing on dead bodies, has been maintained by Aristotle, in *hist. anim. l.* iii. *c.* 11. who says, ' In persons afflicted with some distempers, especially in con-
' sumptive persons, the hair grows more than ordinary. In aged persons,
' and even after death it continues to grow, and is very hard like bristles.'
D. *Joh. Christ. Stock in diff. phys. de cadaveribus sanguisugis.* §. 5. *Jen.* 1732. has shewn the possibility of this from the natural causes; but in the same year was opposed by M. *Joh. Christoph. Pohl, in diff. de hominibus post mortem sanguisugis,* in a treatise printed at Leipsic. Whoever is willing to be convinced by historical accounts, may read *Christ. Frid. Garmann. de miraculis mortuorum, l.* i. *tit.* 1. *de capillorum in cadaveribus augmento,* §. 19. & *seq.*

dited.

dited of a body full of blood and juices. But whether this be poffible in a corpfe totally dried up, is much to be queftioned, or rather may be faid to be impoffible. In this convent is given to devout perfons a kind of holy water, which is faid to derive particular virtue by being ufed to wafh the body of St. Catharine, and likewife the wool with which it is dried at thofe times.

S. Chriftina della Fundaca. Cathedral.
S. Chriftina della Fundaca belongs to a convent of nuns, and is adorned with a great number of fine pieces of painting. The cathedral is dedicated to St. Peter, and exhibits a great many monuments, among which is that of Tancred, a celebrated civilian. On each fide of the main entrance is a large lion, couchant, of red marble, on which are placed the holy-water bafons. On the center-arch, near the Tribuna, is a marble ftatue of pope Gregory XV. who was a native of Bologna, with an eagle on one fide of him, which was the arms of the Ludovifio family, from which he was defcended. On the cieling of the chapter-room is a fine piece of painting, by Luigi Caracci, reprefenting St. Peter on his knees before the virgin Mary: here is alfo the annunciation, by the fame hand, which was the laft piece he painted. In the choir are feveral good baffo-relievo's.

Dominican church.
St. Dominic's tomb.
The church of the Dominicans is at prefent totally altered by repairs and new ornaments begun by the late pope, who was of that order. St. Dominico, who died at Bologna in the year 1221, lies buried here in a magnificent chapel. His monument is of white marble, adorned with beautiful baffo-relievo's, by Michael Angelo; and the altar, together with the large candlefticks which ftand upon it, are of filver. In the choir is a beautiful inlaid work, reprefenting fcriptural hiftories; and in the veftry is a very confiderable trea-

Manufcript of the Old Teftament by Ezra.
fure of jewels and rich church furniture, with the Old Teftament, faid to be written by Ezra himfelf; it is a large folio, inclofed within a glafs-cafe, fo that only one fide of it can be feen. Here are alfo feveral reliques, fet in gold at the expence of the city; on which account the fenate or council keep one of the keys of this place; fo that there is no feeing it without their permiffion. This is attended with fo much trouble and folicitation, that I rather chofe to deprive myfelf of the pleafure of taking a more exact view of this extraordinary manufcript; and the rather as Montfaucon, in his *Diarium Italicum*, fays, that it contains only the Pentateuch, and that it is by no means of Ezra's writing, though it be very ancient: for the Jews, even at the beginning of the fourteenth century, prefented it to this convent, as a

manufcript

BOLOGNA.

manuscript of great antiquity. In the other vestry also, which serves for the ordinary uses, are several fine paintings.

Henci king of Sardinia, and son of the emperor Frederic II, whose imprisonment has been mentioned above, lies near the choir in this church.

Henci died in the year 1272, after an imprisonment of twenty-three years. The Bolognese, who imagine that they have gained immortal honour by their victory over him, and their firmness in detaining him prisoner, have taken care to give a particular account of the whole affair in the following inscription cut in marble:

Epitaph on the imprisoned king Henci.

Viator, quisquis es,
Siste gradum, & quod scriptum est, perlege,
Ubi perlegeris, pensita.
Hoc is, cujus causâ hoc scriptum est, fieri rogat.
Orto inter Bononienses & Mutinenses bello,
Cæsar Fredericus II. Rom. Imperator
Filium HENTIVM,
Sardiniæ & Corsicæ Insularum Regem
Mutinensibus suppetias ferre jubet,
Qui
Inito apud D. Ambrosii pontem certamine
A Bononiensibus capitur,
Nullâque re, ut dimittatur, impetrat,
Licèt Pater minis, deinde precibus, & pretio
Deprecatoribus uteretur,
Cum tantum auri pro redimendo filio polliceretur,
Quantum ad mœnia Bononiæ circulo aureo cingenda
sufficeret.
Sic captivus annos XXII. menses IX. dies XVI. tenetur,
Aliturque Regio more publicâ Bononiensium impensâ.
Sic defunctus magnificentiss. ac pientiss. funeratus
Hic tumulatur.
Præterea simulacrum hoc in perpetuum monumentum
Et hosti & captivo
S. P. Q. B. P.
Anno Sal. MCCLXXII. II. Id Mart.
Hoc volebam, ut scires.
Abi & Vale.

Monumentum hocce vetustate collapsum
Senatûs Bononiensis jussu
Instauratum fuit MDLXXVI.

' Traveller,

'Traveller, whoe'er thou art, stop and read this inscription; when thou hast read it, consider what it contains:
this is the request of him on whose account it was written.
In a war between the states of Bologna and Modena, the
emperor Frederic II. ordered his son Henci king of Sardinia and Corsica to come to the assistance of the Modenese;
but in a battle fought near St. Ambrose's bridge, this prince
was taken prisoner by the victorious Bolognese, who would
by no means suffer him to be set at liberty, notwithstanding the threats and intreaties of his father, who, finding
his power disregarded, offered for his son's ransom as
much gold as would make a ring large enough to compass
the walls of Bologna: however, he remained prisoner
twenty-two years, nine months, and sixteen days; during
which time he was entertained in a manner becoming his
dignity at the expence of the city. When he died, the
Bolognese crowned this generosity with bestowing on him
a pompous funeral, and this magnificent tomb March 13,
1272. STRANGER, FAREWEL!
'This monument, being much decayed, was, by order
of the senate of Bologna, repaired in the year 1576.'

Underneath are the following words:

Senatûs Bononiensis
Pietate ac Liberalitate
Ossa REGIS HENTII
Et hostis & captivi
Hic jacent.
Humanæ sortis memor
Piis manibus benè precare.
Instaurat. iterum A. D. MDCLXXXX.

'By the humanity and generosity of the senate of Bologna, here are deposited the bones of king Henci, their enemy and prisoner of war. Be mindful of the vicissitudes of
human life, and pray for the repose of his soul. This
monument was repaired a second time in the year 1690.

Riches of the chapel del Rosario. In this church lie Luigi Caracci, the celebrated painter, and several famous civilians. The Capella del Rosario is at all times embellished with a great quantity of plate, pursuant to a clause in the will of the founder, enjoining that the silver ornaments should never be removed upon any pretence whatever.

BOLOGNA.

whatever. This treasure is guarded in the night by a man well armed, and several large mastiffs.

In the Dominican convent, to which this church belongs, are about a hundred and forty monks. On the walls of the refectory are several inscriptions, commemorating the most remarkable transactions of pope Pius V. An anti-chamber, divided into three isles by two rows of pillars, leads to the library. On each side are statues and paintings in honour of the Dominican order and pope Pius V. Over the entrance of the library is an inscription, signifying that this treasure of books was completed *Dei & Patriarchæ Dominici peculiari patrocinante providentia*; 'Under the patronage of the providence of God and of St. Dominic.' The books are very numerous, and judiciously arranged. In the lower cloister of the convent is a small chapel, said to have been the apartment in which St. Dominic, in the year 1221, departed this life. In one piece of painting in this chapel an angel is represented going up a ladder into heaven with St. Dominic on his back; but the angel ascends the ladder backwards, that he and St. Dominic may not turn their backs on the spectators. Another circumstance equally absurd in this piece is that our Saviour and the virgin Mary are represented standing above holding the ladder. In the passage leading to the church lies the celebrated civilian Socinus, who in his epitaph is called Zozinus. On a green plot behind this convent is shewn an old cypress-tree, said to have been planted by St. Dominic, and consequently not less valued than the orange-tree in the Dominican convent at Fondi, affirmed to have been planted by Thomas Aquinas. On the area before the Dominican church the brass images of the virgin and St. Dominic are erected on two pillars. Betwixt these statues is a large stone tomb, supported by nine pillars, and adorned with basso-relievo's representing several persons writing while one dictates to them. The inscription on this tomb is inexplicable, and is as follows; but I could get no certain account of it:

Dominican convent.

Library.

S. Dominic's chamber.

Picture of an angel carrying St. Dominic to heaven.

Tomb of Socinus a civilian.

Cypress planted by St. Dominic.

† *Autore magno nature lege vocabo*
Patre Rolandino cetus pro consule primo
Nunc hic scribe locant Octobris tertia deri
Mille trecentenis celestis prolis ab annis
Restauratum MDCIII. iterum MDCCXII.

Jealousy between the Franciscans and Dominicans.

A continual emulation reigns betwixt the Franciscans and Dominicans, especially at Bologna; for each of these orders strive to surpass the other in buildings and other external magnificence, in order to increase their revenues and authority. The Dominicans have the advantage in the splendor of their churches; but in wine-cellars they have hitherto been exceeded by the Franciscans. The high altar of the Franciscan church is in the Gothic taste, or, as it is called in Italy, *alla Tedesca*. Among the paintings in this church are some highly-finished pieces, by Facini, Luigi Caracci, Brizio, Guido, and Tiarini. Pope Alexander V, some old civilians and glossographers, as Franciscus Accursius, Ortofredus and Romanzo, the philosopher Boccaferri, and other celebrated men in the republic of letters, are interred here. Under the marble bust of the civilian Hannibal Monterenci, who died in 1586, and lies on the left-hand of the main entrance, are these distichs:

Franciscan church.

Epitaph of Monterenci.

Docta per ora Virûm volitas, clarissime Doctor,
Æternusque tui nominis exstat honos.

‘ Thy memory shall live, consign'd to fame,
‘ And every tongue shall celebrate thy name.’

And lower down are these lines:

Vivida cui virtus, cui summa scientia juris,
Dum vixit, fuerat, nunc brevis urna tenet.

‘ Within this little urn, alas ! he lies
‘ Whose better part exults above the skies;
‘ His virtue lives, his knowledge never dies.’

Accursi tomb.

Accursi, who lies on the right hand as you go towards the convent, has only these words for his epitaph:

Sepulchrum Accursii Glossatoris Legum.

‘ The tomb of Accursi, a commentator on the law.’

On the same side is the following epitaph:

‘ Barbara

BOLOGNA.

Barbaræ Pretæ Blanchinæ
Pietate & moribus irſigni,
Quæ Prætorum Familiam,
Per quingentos annos belli & pacis muneribus
Bononiæ illuſtrem,
Noviſſimis Hieronymi Preti Muſis Italiæ conſpicuam,
Immaturâ morte concluſit,
Co. Cæſar Blanchinus Senator
Juſſis chariſſ. Conjugis obſequentiſſimus
Inſtauravit & poſuit Anno Dom. MDCLIII.

'To the memory of Barbara Preti Blanchini, a lady emi-
'nent for her piety and ſweetneſs of manners, the laſt ſurviv-
'ing perſon of the family of the Preti, which, in a ſucceſſion
'of five hundred years, had diſcharged at Bologna the high-
'eſt civil and military poſts with honour and reputation;
'and of which illuſtrious houſe the late Gieronimo Preti,
'whoſe poetry does honour to Italy, was deſcended. Count
'Cæſar Blanchini, a ſenator, in compliance with the re-
'queſt of his beloved conſort, erected this monument in the
'year 1653.'

On each ſide of this convent are fine arched cloiſters, or galleries, one of which is a hundred and thirty-three, and the other two hundred common paces in length. In the ſtreet before the convent is a pillar, on the top of which is a braſs ſtatue of the virgin Mary ſtanding on a creſcent.

S. Giacomo Maggiore, which belongs to the Auguſtine monks, is well furniſhed with good paintings; and, among other reliques, here is ſhewn a thorn, as is pretended, of the crown worn by our Saviour at his crucifixion. *S. Giaco-mo Maggi-ore.*

The Jeſuits church is dedicated to St. Lucia, and is adorn-ed with ſome fine marble altars; but the front is a very in-different one (the defect of moſt of the churches of Bologna) and has nothing of the riches and ſplendor by which the Jeſuits in other cities affect to diſtinguiſh their churches. In a chapel near the entrance is repreſented the proceſſion of St. Gregory in order to put a ſtop to the plague, painted by Frederico Zuccaro; St. Lucia and St. Agatha, to be ſeen over the high altar, are by Procaccino; here are alſo ſome pieces of painting by Cignani and Brizio. In the college is ſhewn the chamber or cell of St. Francis Xavier. *Jeſuits church.*

T 2   The

BOLOGNA.

Chiefa del buono Giesù. The church called Chiefa del buono Giesù is of an oval figure, and is adorned with paintings in *frefco* by Pianori, a difciple of Albani, and other hands. Here is a very good ftatue of our Saviour, or an *Ecce homo*, by Brunelli; and by the fame mafter, is alfo S. Antonio di Padua, to be feen on the altar of the chapel dedicated to that faint. St. Apollonia of marble, and St. Bernardine of *terra cotta*, are admirable fpecimens of Lombardi's fkill in fculpture: but nothing can exceed the baffo-relievo of the circumcifion, on the high altar, by the celebrated Brunelli.

Paintings in S. Giorgio. A connoiffeur in painting will not omit feeing S. Giorgio's church, were it only on account of four celebrated pieces of painting: the firft reprefents the nativity of Chrift, in *frefco*, by Cignani; the fecond, the annunciation, by Luigi Caracci; the third is the virgin Mary with her divine infant, by Annibal Caracci; and the fourth is the baptifm of Chrift, by Albani.

S. Giovanni Battifta. The church of S. Giovanni Battifta de' Celeftini is everywhere ornamented with fine paintings. The high altar-piece is a picture of the virgin with the infant Jefus, as is pretended, by St. Luke. The appearance of Chrift to Mary Magdalene, in the difguife of a gardener, is by Maffari. Clofe by this piece lies Alexander Fibula, who died in 1541, aged forty-nine; and in his epitaph he is ftiled *Eques Cafareus*, and *Juris Utriufque Candidatus*.

Monument of Fibula.

S. Giovanni in Monte. Picture of St. Cecilia, by Raphael. S. Giovanni in Monte is famous for an admirable picture of St. Cecilia, by Raphael. The faint, inraptured with the harmony of a choir of angels, dafhes all her mufical inftruments againft the ground. In this piece are alfo feen St. John, St. Paul, Mary Magdalene, and St. Auftin. Count Malvafia, in his lives of the celebrated Bolognefe painters publifhed in two volumes in quarto in the year 1678, under the title of *Felfina Pittrice*, cenfures the ftiffnefs and want of expreffion both in this and many other pieces by Raphael; and fupports his opinion with the authority of Annibal Caracci. And though Vincenzo Vittoria, in his *Offervazioni fopra il Libro della Felfina Pittrice*, printed in 8vo. at Rome in the year 1703, labours hard to vindicate Raphael's pencil from fuch an imputation; yet it is not done to the fatisfaction of impartial judges. However, this piece is greatly valued, and the painter's mafterly ftrokes at a certain diftance give it fuch a charming appearance, that the ftiffnefs of the defign is not obferved. Befides, Raphael's laft pieces fhew, that he had pretty well got the better of this defect. Vafari relates,

Cenfured.

that

that Francesco Francia, one of the best painters of that time, being desirous to get acquainted with Raphael, whose fame had then begun to spread, wrote a letter to him; and the friends of both these masters endeavoured to bring them to an intimacy. Raphael accepted the offer with the greatest civility, and sent Francia the picture of St. Cecilia, which was designed for a church in Bologna, requesting him to mend what faults he might observe in it, and afterwards get it placed where it was designed for. Francia, being extremely elevated at such a confidence reposed in him by Raphael, was resolved to hang up the piece himself; and, by that means, the longer he now viewed it, the more beauties he perceived in it, so that he was quite lost in admiration: it was, however, accompanied with such a mortifying conviction of his being so vastly inferior to Raphael, that it threw him into a deep melancholy, which soon proved fatal to him. *Cause of a painter's death.*

In the Capella del Rosario in this church, is a fine piece of painting, by Domenichino, representing the fifteeen mysteries of the Rosary. In another chapel is a good picture of the martyrdom of St. Laurence, by Facini. In an apartment near the vestry are several paintings by Ercole di Ferrara. On the vestry altar is a picture of St. Patricius, preaching, by Spifanelli. In the refectory is a representation of the marriage-feast made by a king for his son, according to the parable in the gospel, at which he finds one of the guests without the wedding-garment: this piece is painted in *fresco* by Gesi.

In the church of St. Gregory is a capital piece, by Luigi Caracci, representing St. George delivering a lady by killing a dragon. The baptism of Christ is one of Annibal Caracci's first pieces, and in which he had some assistance from his master Luigi Caracci. The large picture of St. William is by Guercino. *S. Gregorio.*

In the church of S. Maria del Baracano is shewn an image of the virgin Mary, which, as it is pretended, on being wounded with a musket-ball, shed tears, while the blood was seen to issue from the wound, and the offender was immediately struck dead with lightning. But one miracle performed by this image is not sufficient; they tell you, that in the year 1512, when Bologna was besieged, a mine blew up the whole wall of the chapel in which this same image stood, to such a height, that both armies being drawn up, though it was night, could plainly see one another through the breach; *S. Maria del Baracano. Miraculous image. Miracle of springing a mine.*

breach; however, that the wall fell again into its place and was joined as exact as if it had never been separated. A Latin inscription near it says:

Mœnium pars ubi picta Virginis imago cernitur, pervia utriusque exercitús oculis facta, & mirabiliter in eundem locum restituta.

'That part of the wall where the painted image of the
'virgin is seen, was laid open to the view of both armies,
'and miraculously restored to the same place.

The Italian account concerning this church says of the wall, *Si levò tant' in alto, che per quello spazio rimasto tra il terreno e 'l muro gittato in alto, ambo gli esserciti si videro l'un l'altro.* 'It was carried up to such a height, that, through
'the intermediate space betwixt the earth and the wall which
'was blown up, both armies plainly saw each other.' The monks who invented this story must have no idea of the dust and rubbish of the earth, sand, and stone which are always thrown up at the springing of a mine. That Jovius, in his second book of the life of Leo X, should follow the common report, is not to be wondered at; but one would little expect to meet with such an absurdity in Guicciardini's judicious history. Sigoni, in his fifth book *de episcopis Bononienfibus*, only says, that by the particular intervention of the virgin Mary the walls received no other damage from springing the mine than a gentle concussion. But the zealots for the see of Rome in this story must needs find a stumbling-block, which certainly they cannot easily get over; for, according to the story, a miracle must have been performed in favour of pope Julius the Second's enemies.

S. Maria di Galiera. S. Maria di Galiera is a beautiful church, and belongs to the fathers of the oratory. The stucco-work in this church is greatly admired; and likewise the paintings by Guido Rheni, Guercini, Albani, and Caracci.

Annual miracle of ants in the church of S. Maria di Genna. I shall just mention the church of S. Maria di Genna on the Monte delle Formiche, on account of the annual miracle exhibited in it on the 8th of September, which is the anniversary of the virgin Mary's birth-day. They tell you, that multitudes of winged emmets rendezvous near this church, and that this whole swarm direct their flight on that day to an old altar in the church, where they immediately expire. These dead emmets the monks distribute as infallible

BOLOGNA.

ble remedy againſt a diſeaſe called *il male di Formica*, which is occaſioned by a worm or inward ulcer. But, that the papiſts may not complain that this is a fiction fathered upon them by hereticks, I refer them to the pamphlet intitled *Informatione per i Foraſtieri curioſi di vedere le coſe più notabili di Bologna*, which has ſeveral times been printed with the approbation of Franceſco Aloſi Barelli, who is ſtiled *Clerici Regul. Congreg. S. Pauli, Sanctiſſimæ Inquiſitionis Conſultor, & in Ecclefia Metropolitana Bononiæ Pœnitentiarius*; as alſo of *Fr. J. M. Mazzani Vicarius Generalis Sancti Officii Bononiæ.* The church of S. Maria di Genna is ſtill dependent on Bologna, though it be ſituated thirteen Itallian miles from that city, beyond Pianoro, towards the river Idice.

Madonna di S. Luca, on the Monte della Guardia, is a Dominican nunnery, about four Italian miles from Bologna, and is much reſorted to on account of a picture of the virgin Mary pretended to have been painted by the hand of St. Luke. According to Sigoni, it was brought by a hermit from the church of Sancta Sophia at Conſtantinople in the year 1160; and ſince that time its power has ſeveral times been manifeſted to the great benefit of the country; on which account it is every year, in the month of May, brought into the city of Bologna in a ſolemn proceſſion, and ſaluted by firing of guns. For the greater conveniency of the pilgrims, an arched colonade has been built from the city to the top of the mountain, which, on account of its great length, may be accounted the moſt remarkable building of that kind in Italy. In the contribution of the neceſſary ſums for this colonade, all the handicraft-men, &c. ſeemed to vie with each other in the erection of a perpetual monument of their zeal for the bleſſed virgin; even the very lackeys of the city were at the expence of building fifteen of the arches. On every one of the other arches are the names and even the arms of the benefactors. One ſide of the arcade is walked; but, in that towards the road, every arch reſts upon its reſpective pillars. Every arch is five common paces, or twelve feet wide, which is alſo the breadth of the walk. The height is about ſixteen feet. This arcade does not run in a ſtraight line; but its direction is now and then interrupted with ſmall windings: however, in many parts of it there are very long viſta's, particularly at the grand portico near the city; from which one has a view of nintey-three arches in a direct line, which, taken together, are ſeven hundred and fifty common paces in length. There are thirty-three flights of ſteps to aſcend the acclivity of the mountain; theſe flights

Madonna di S. Luca.

Picture painted by S. Luke.

Remarkable colonade.

T 4

flights consist of a few steps, and the space between is level, and paved with flat stones.

Della Guardia wine. On the road to Madonna di S. Luca one has a view both of the Carthusian convent, and S. Michele in Bosco, or St. Michael in the wood. This little hill is called della Guardia, and produces a very good sort of wine.

S. Maria de' Servi. S. Maria de' Servi, or the church of the Servites, has a spacious portico, adorned with thirty-seven red and white marble pillars, and painted in *fresco*. In the church are to be seen some fine paintings, and no less than thirty-four altars. The high altar is remarkable for the statues and other sculptures with which it is embellished. In the choir are two epitaphs, highly esteemed by the Italians for their *concetti*, or playing on words: but, as this false beauty cannot be well preserved in a translation, these *concetti* may be concluded to be no part of true wit *.

Martino Maggiore. In S. Martino Maggiore, among other good paintings is St. Jerom, by Luigi Caracci.

S. Michele in Bosco. The convent of S. Michele in Bosco lies on an eminence without the city, and belongs to the Olivetan monks. Just within the entrance is a marble monument of Capt. Ramazzotti, by the celebrated Lombardo. On the altar of the choir is a curious tabernacle of inlaid gems. On one side of the altar is a piece of painting, which was probably first done by Guido Rheni, and retouched in the year 1689, as the following distich seems to intimate:

Hoc jussit Pratus fecitque colore Vianus
Vt Rhenio & Rheno reddat uterque decus.
A. D. MDCLXXXIX.

The stalls in the choir are embellished with inlaid work, by Raphael da Bressia, an Olivetan monk; and on the left-hand near the entrance to the church is a crucifix of the natural size, of one piece, cut out of a fig-tree.

Paintings. This convent was formerly accounted a treasury of fine paintings. Luigi Caracci has here distinguished his skill by several pieces representing the life of St. Benedict; but that piece which exhibits the saint in the wilderness, and the neighbouring peasants bringing to him fruit, eggs, sheep, &c. was painted by Guido. The figure that chiefly attracts the admiration of the beholder in this piece, is a beautiful young woman, with a turban on her head, and a basket of

* These epitaphs, and several others, which are nothing but a string of puns, are omitted in this translation.

eggs

BOLOGNA.

eggs under her arm; so that from her the whole picture is called *La Turbantina*. Here were also some valuable pieces of painting by Tiarino, Brisio, Massari, Cavedoni, and other disciples of Luigi Caracci; but by the injuries of the weather to which these paintings in *fresco* were exposed, and the carelesness of the monks, who little concern themselves about the real beauty of fine paintings, many of the pieces are almost effaced, the plaster being fallen off in some places, &c. Some of the pieces are indeed retouched by such unskilful hands, that they have spoiled what they endeavoured to mend.

La Turbantina.

This convent has a very elegant library, the cieling of which is painted by Asner and Canuti. Besides the books, here is a very good collection of mathematical instruments, optical glasses, &c. The small bronze image of the archangel Michael, shewn here, is the work of the cavalier Algardi. The terrass belonging to this convent yields a most delightful prospect towards the east (as far as the eye can reach) of an extensive plain, beautifully diversified with corn-fields, meadows, vineyards, villa's, and summer-houses; and the city of Bologna, which is but two Italian miles from it, lying as it were just under it, is a great addition to the prospect.

Library.

Prospect.

The Mons Pietatis, or the Charitable-corporation-office, near the cathedral, is a handsome building; and in the portico of it several persons attend to advance money to the necessitous on very moderate terms. Over the entrance is a *Pietà* or the virgin Mary lamenting over Christ's dead body, well executed in *terra cotta*, with this inscription:

Mons Pietatis.

Mons Pietatis
Adversus pravas Judæorum usuras erectus
M.DLXXVI.

' The charitable society instituted against the extravagant
' usuries of the Jews in the year 1576.'

The church of S. Paolo de' Padri Bernabiti is remarkable for the two marble statues of St. Peter and St. Paul, by Cæsare Coventi, erected on the front; and of St. Carlo and St. Philippo Neri, in plaster, by Ercole Fichi, placed above them. The state of bliss in heaven is admirably well painted in the cupola of this church, by Luigi Caracci. The nativity of Christ, the adoration of the eastern *magi*, and some

S. Paolo de' Bernabiti.

some other pieces, are by Cavedoni: a reprefentation of purgatory, and S. Carlo bearing a crofs in a public proceffion at Milan in the time of a peftilence, are by Guercini. On the high altar are three pieces of perfpective, confifting of beautiful fmall pillars. The baffo-relievo, reprefenting the martyrdom of St. Paul, is the work of Algardi, a Bolognefe.

S. Paolo de' Padri Minori.

The church of S. Paolo, called *l'Offervanza de' Padri Minori Offervanti, Reformati di S. Francefco*, lies without the city, and affords nothing remarkable; but in the convent is

St. Anthony's cell. Cypreffes fet by St. Bernard.

shewn the cell where St. Anthony lived; and in the garden are fome cyprefs-trees, faid to be planted by St. Bernard. The monks difpofe of a kind of white ftone, which they call *latte delle Madonna*, or our Lady's milk, for money, and

What the fuppofed milk of the virgin Mary is in reality.

recommend it as a fpecific to procure milk in women. I believe I have before obferved, that the relique which paffes under the name of the virgin's milk, is no more than a kind of *terra lemnia*, or a medicinal foffile, of an alkaline quality, which is a fweetener of the blood and juices; and confequently, from its natural property, it may be of fervice in fuch cafes.

St. Petronius's church. Coronation of Charles V.

The church of St. Petronius is the largeft in all Bologna, on which account the coronation of the emperor Charles V. was performed there in the year 1530. The length of this church is three hundred and fixty, and the breadth a hundred and fifty-four feet. The large piece of painting, reprefenting that memorable tranfaction, is by Brizio. The high altar, which is infulated or detached from the wall, refts on four beautiful pillars of grey marble. On the right-hand near the entrance of the church is the tomb of cardinal La-

Miraculous image.

zari, who died in the year 1677: and in the firft chapel on that fide is the image of a foldier with a dagger in his hand, as a memorial of that wretch's impiety, who, as the ftory goes, in the year 1405, being enraged at an ill run in gaming, ftabbed an image of the virgin Mary with his dagger, and broke off one of the toes of the infant in her arms. Upon this he fell down immediately deprived of his ftrength, and was fentenced to die: but the virgin, moved by his repentance, at once reftored him to his health; and this miracle alfo procured him a full pardon.

Ancient picture of the clergy, &c. in hell.

In a chapel on the left-hand fide of the church is a piece of painting, reprefenting hell, where a great number of red hats, mitres, and crowned heads are to be feen among the damned; but, this piece being almoft effaced by length of time,

time, one cannot rightly diftinguifh whether the artift went fo far as to put a pope in this wretched groupe.

The greateft curiofity in this church is the brafs meridian-line drawn by Caffini, the celebrated aftronomer. It confifts of pieces of red and white marble inlaid, of a hand's breadth; but thofe pieces in which the figns of the zodiac are cut, are a foot fquare. All the reft of this church is paved with brick. This line is above half the length of the church, but does not run parallel with the church-wall. At the beginning is this infcription: *Meridian-line by Caffini.*

Meridianæ hujus femitæ tota longitudo, auƈta titulis, eft fexcenti-millefima pars circuitûs univerfæ terræ.

'The whole length of this meridian-line, diftinguifhed by
' the figns, &c. is the fix hundred thoufandth part of the
' circumference of the terraqueous globe.'

The length of this meridian-line is faid to be a hundred and eighty feet, twenty thoufand of which feet are equal to a German mile; and the circumference of the earth is computed to be 5400 fuch miles, reckoning 15 to a degree. I cannot conceive by what meafure Miffon makes the length of the line to be two hundred and twenty feet.

On the pavement, at the end of the line, is this infcription in white marble:

*Linea Meridiana
A vertice
Ad Tropicum Capricorni.*

'The meridian line from the zenith to the tropic of Ca-
' pricorn.'

The divifions are marked with the following words along the line:

Maximi terræ circuli II. & III. Gradus diftantiæ a vertice. Perpendiculi partes centefimæ. Horæ ab occafu ad orientem. Signa Zodiaci defcendentia. Signa Zodiaci afcendentia, &c. Oppofite to the vertical point is the date MDCLII.

A fmall round aperture has been made in the roof of the church, towards the fouth, through which the rays of the
sun

BOLOGNA.

sun form a circular luminous spot about eight inches in diameter, on the pavement, which shews the proper meridional point on the line every day. On the wall, at the end of the meridian line, is to be seen the following inscription cut in white marble:

D. O. M.
Autoritate illustrissimorum Senatorum
Præsidis & Fabricensium
Meridiana hæc linea Horizontalis
Solem in meridie è templi fornice
Ad inscripta cœlestium locorum signa toto anno excipiens,
Ante XL. annos per intercolumnium obliquè occurrens
Reperto augustissimo tramite perducta
Ecclesiasticis. Astronomicis,
Geographicisque usibus accommodata
A. JOH. DOMINICO CASSINO
Bononiensis Archigymnasii Astronomo primario
Et Mathematico Pontificio.
Ab eodem in Italico itinere è Regia astronomica Parisiensi
Regiaque Scientiarum Academia
Quò ad Christianiss. Regem Ludovicum Magnum,
Annuente Clemente IX. Summ. Pont. concesserat,
Ad Solem iterùm diligentissimè expansa
Cœlesti meridiano adhuc mirè congruere inventa est,
Et sexcenti-millesimam terræ circuitûs partem
Ab initio ad speciei solis hibernæ ipsam finientis medium
Accipere;
Horizontali autem positioni, unde exiguo templi motu
Inæqualique soli attritu recesserat, accuratè restituta,
Instante anno maximæ æquinoctiorum in Kalendario Gregoriano
Præcessionis
Hic potissimùm observandæ
Labente anno Salutis MDCLXXXV.

' To God the greatest and best of beings.'
' By order of the most illustrious senators, the president
' and surveyors of the works, this horizontal meridian-line
' on which the rays of the sun during the whole year fall at
' noon through the roof of this church, and which forty
' years ago passed obliquely betwixt the pillars, was, for the
' benefit of the clergy and all mathematicians, drawn by
' Giovanni Domenico Cassini, chief astronomer in the uni-
' versity of Bologna, &c. in a more magnificent manner.

' The

BOLOGNA.

'The same celebrated astronomer in his return to Italy
'from the royal academy of Paris, whither he had gone at
'the invitation of his most Christian majesty Lewis the
'Great, and with the permission of his holiness Clement
'IX, accurately examined this line, and found it still to
'correspond exactly with the celestial meridian; and that,
'from the beginning to the tropic of Capricorn where it
'terminates, it was equal to the six hundred thousandth part
'of the circuit of the earth. It was likewise with the most
'exact punctuality, in the year of the greatest precession of
'the equinox, according to the Gregorian calendar, observed
'in this place, restored to its horizontal position, from
'which by a small concussion of the church and the une-
'qual attrition of the pavement it had a little deviated.
'*A. D.* 1695.'

Under this inscription is a brass line not above a span and
a half in length, divided into a thousand parts, the divisions
being marked out by hundreds, with this inscription near it:

Centesima pars altitudinis fornicis millies subdivisa.

'The hundredth part of the height of this arched roof
'subdivided into a thousand parts.'

The following epitaph on the outside of the wall of the S. Proculo.
church of S. Proculo, is another complete specimen of the
genius of the Italians for *concetti*, i. e. puns, or playing upon
words:

Si procul a Proculo Proculi campana fuisset,
Jam procul a Proculo Proculus ipse foret.
A. D. 1393.

But the wit of this piece, if any, as has been before observed, would be quite lost in a translation.

Whether this Proculus, who was buried here, was a student who shortened his life by rising every morning to his
books, when the bell of this church rung for mattins; or
whether according to the other account, he was killed by a
bell belonging to this church that fell on him, is a matter of
no great importance.

In the convent to which this church belongs is shewn the Gratian's
cell where Gratian the monk drew up the *Decretum.* In the cell.
refectory is a picture of St. Peter, fishing, painted by Leo-
nello

nello Spada. St. Proculo, a nobleman of Bologna, is said to have suffered martyrdom without the city, oppofite the Porta di S. Mamolo. The place where his head was ftruck off is marked by a crofs erected on the fpot; but it feems the faint carried his head in his hands, from this crofs, to the place where the church dedicated to him now ftands. This miracle is commemorated in the following infcription under the crofs:

St. Proculo after his decollation carries his head into the city.

Hic S. Proculus Miles, Bonon. facro Martyrio coronatus exftitit abfciffo capite, quod iftuc ubi nunc illius Templum confpicitur manibus propriis detulit. Anno. Dom. D. XIX.

' Here St. Proculo, a noble knight of Bononia, was
' crowned with martyrdom by the lofs of his head, which
' with his own hands he afterwards carried to the fpot where
' his church is now built.'

The church di S. Salvatore belongs to a religious fraternity who ftyle themfelves, *Canonici Regolari della Congregatione Renana del Santiffimo Salvatore,* or canons regular, &c. and have been in poffeffion of this church and convent ever fince the year 1100. The former has been rebuilt from a defign of P. Magenta, a Barnabite monk of Milan, and is ornamented with fine ftucco work and paintings. On feveral feftivals, the cornifhes within the church are fet all round with fmall orange-trees in filver flower-pots. Here are feveral fine pieces of painting by Luigi Caracci; of which, the moft admired are the affumption of the virgin Mary, and a picture of our Saviour. Girolami Carpi, Guido, Benevenuto Tifio, Samachino, and Cavedoni have likewife difplayed their fkill in this church. The convent is fpacious and elegant: it confifts of four courts. The perfpective pieces in *frefco,* at the end of the cloifters, are by Mitelli; and the marble ftatue of Chrift, an excellent piece, is the work of the celebrated Brunelli. Thirty-three canons always refide in the convent, exclufive of the noviciates, who ftudy divinity and philofophy, under two profeffors. In the library are a great number of curious manufcripts; particularly, one of the hiftory of queen Efther, written on yellow coarfe leather, which is done up in a roll, or volume, according to the original fignification of the word. It is written in large Hebrew characters, which the canons would have one believe to have been written by Ezra.

S. Salvatore.

Orangery in a church.

Convent.

Library.
Manufcript of the book of Efther.

When

BOLOGNA.

When I took the liberty to object, on account of the points or vowels, against the great antiquity of this manuscript, their answer was, That these points had been added by some officious modern hand; and indeed it must be acknowledged, that the ink with which the text was written, is much blacker than that of the vowels under it.

Here is also shewn a Hebrew Pentatech, or rather all the books of the Old Testament, written on vellum, in three volumes in folio, said to have been written in the year 953. At the beginning of one of the volumes is inserted the following account in Italian: *Isaac filiolo de Jacob scrisse questo Libro con tutto il corpo di questa Biblia, e Manuel filiolo de uno chiamato Solthedar, e fu furnita el Martedi a di 26. del mise di Marzo del 953. in tre Volumini.* i. e. Isaac the son of Jacob ‘ wrote this book, and almost this whole Bible, assisted by E- ‘ manuel the son of one called Solthedar (or rather Soleedar). ‘ It was finished on Tuesday the twenty-sixth day of March, ‘ 953, in three volumes.' This manuscript is written with the points or vowels.

<small>Hebrew manuscript of the Old Testament.</small>

Among the other manuscripts, which are about three hundred in number, are the following. 1. The Pentateuch, with the comments of the rabbi's, in Hebrew. 2. A medicinal treatise in Hebrew. 3. *Meurophanes de Spiritu Sancto* in Greek, and bound in silk. 4. Several of the Greek homilies of St. Chrysostom. 5. Ten discourses by the same author, in Greek, upon that text in Isaiah, ‘ I saw the ‘ Lord,' supposed to have been written in the tenth century. 6. A Greek version of the Psalms of David, by the same, father. 7. The New Testament, said to be of the eleventh century, full of abbreviations; among which ΘΘΣ is commonly written ΘC. 8. A Greek version of the minor prophets, and Daniel, supposed to be of the tenth century. 9. A Greek manuscript of St. Basil's exposition of the psalms, and his homilies on fasting, of the same date. 10. A Greek fragment of the history of Byzantium, or Constantinople, by an anonymous author, said by Montfaucon to be of no ancienter date than the thirteenth century. 11. Lactantius's works, which the canons, on account of some marginal corrections, will have to be the original manuscript.

<small>Other manuscripts.</small>

Among the most ancient printed books, in this library, are Cicero's works, published by Alexander Manutius at Milan, in the year 1498, in four volumes, folio; likewise a Latin Bible in folio, at the end of which the following account is printed:

<small>Old edition of Cicero.</small>

*Pñi hoc opusculum artificiosâ adinventione imprimendi seu ca-
racterizandi absque calami exaratione in civitate Moguntii sic
effigiatum, & ad Eusebiam Dei industrie per Joh'ez Fust civem,
& Petrum Schoiffher de Gernsheym Clericum dioces ejusdem est
consummatum. Anno Domini MCCCCLXII. in Vigilia assum-
tionis Virg. Marie.*

' This work is a specimen of the invention of printing,
' or expressing characters without the assistance of the pen,
' and was completed at Mentz, for the benefit of religion,
' by the industry of John Fust a layman, and Peter Schoiffer
' of Gernsheim, a priest of the diocese of Mentz, in the
' year 1462, on the eve of the assumption of the virgin
' Mary.'

S. Stefano.   St. Stephen's church belongs to the Cælestine monks, and properly consists of seven churches built together; but in such an irregular disposition, that a person may soon lose himself in it *.

University.   The archigymnasium, or university, according to some writers, was founded by the emperor Theodosius in the year 433. Others with more probability attribute it to Charles the Great. Here are professors for oratory, philosophy, the oriental languages, geometry, astronomy, anatomy, physic, the civil and canon law, civil and ecclesiastical history, and divinity; and all of them have handsome salaries. Both the civil and canon law have been taught at Bologna with very great reputation by Ireneri, Gratiani, Burgari, Alberico da Porta, Accursi, Bartoli, Baldi, and Uzo. The last mentioned is said to have had, at one time, ten thousand students for his pupils. At present, the foreign students are in all about four hundred. The public college, or university,

Il Studio.   which is also called *il Studio*, is seven hundred and forty palms, or two hundred and thirteen common paces in length, and was built by Giacomo Barocci, an architect of Vignola. Near the entrance of this structure, on the right-hand, is a grand stair-case, adorned with some good paint-ings in *fresco*, by Valesio, represening the noble actions of S. Carlo Borromeo. On the left side of the stair case, Le-onarda Spada has painted a monument in honour of Wence-

---

* A great number of reliques mentioned by the author are here omitted.

slaus

BOLOGNA. 289

flaus Lazarus, a philosopher and physician, with such masterly strokes of the pencil, that it appears to be a beautiful basso-relievo. Gaetano Creti has given a noble proof of his skill on another monument painted in *fresco*, to Giovanni Gieronimo Sbarabeo, M. D. who died in the year 1710. Of Sbarabeo. The inscription on that of the celebrated Malpighi is as follows: Malpighi.

Virtuti & Famæ
In ævum mansuræ
Inclyti Viri
MARCELLI MALPIGHII,
Medicinæ Professoris celeberrimi,
Utraque Artistarum Universitas
Anno Salutis
MDCLXXXIII.

Miraris breve Lemma?
Nomen ingens
Ornari negat: est
Satis referri
Jussum cætera cur
Tacere marmor:
Omnis MALPIGHIUM loquetur ætas.

' To the eminent virtues and immortal fame of the great
' Marcello Malpighi, professor of physic, the two academies
' have erected this monument, in the year of our redemp-
' tion 1683.'

' Reader, if thou art surprized at the brevity of this epi-
' taph, know, that an illustrious name needs no panegy-
' rics. It is sufficient to tell thee why the marble is thus
' silent in his praise: Fame thro' every age will resound
' MALPIGHI's name.'

But among the multitude of learned persons to whose memory, as in the college at Padua, monuments are raised, here are several obscure names to be seen, whose reputation never extended itself beyond the limits of their own country *.

Theatrum anatomicum. The anatomical theatre is ornamented with wooden statues of the most celebrated anatomists, and the floor is boarded with cypress; but it wants a proper light. Not far from it is a monument of Francescus and Achilles de Moratoriis, which has been repaired and embellished with good painting by Theresia de Moratoriis, a relation of the deceased.

Privileges of German students. The German students at Bologna are under particular regulations of their own forming, and have a distinct register, with several other privileges.

Fees for doctors students. The fees, paid by a German student for the degree of doctor in the civil law, amount to two hundred and ninety-two *lire* †, or about forty-three rix-dollars.

Count Marsigli's new academy of sciences. Luigi Ferdinando, count de Marsigli, instituted at Bologna an academy of sciences, in the year 1712, for the improvement of natural history, mathematics, natural philosophy, chemistry, anatomy, and physic. M. de Limiers published an account of this academy at Amsterdam, in the year 1723. With this, the *academia Clementina bonarum artium*, founded at Bologna not long before by pope Clement IX, for architecture and painting, was incorporated. For the farther advancement of this institution, the city purchased

L'Instituto. and gave the Palazzo Celesi to the academy, that the library, the museum, the observatory, the schools, and professors apartments might be under the same roof. Over the entrance of this magnificent edifice is the following truly catholic inscription:

Bononiense
Scientiarum & Artium
Institutum
Ad publicum
Totius Orbis
Usum.

' The Bononian academy of arts and sciences for the pub-
' lic use of the whole world.'

* Several epitaphs of such obscure persons, where there was nothing remarkable in the sentiment, language, &c. are omitted in the translation in this and other parts of these volumes.

† 19 *l.* 12 *s.* A *lire* at Bologna is equal to a shilling, the author must therefore mean the Hamburgh rix-dollars, at 4 *s.* 6 *d.*

In

BOLOGNA.

In ascending the tower belonging to this structure, you first come to the astronomical school, where is to be seen a model of the Copernican system. Here is also a perpendicular meridian-line, cut through a wall a foot thick, which was altered above eight times before it could be made to correspond with the meridian of this place. Manfredo had the direction of this work. On each side hang telescopes, compasses, quadrants, &c. so that, as the stars cross the meridian, proper observations may be the more conveniently made. For which end also the shutters of the line, or aperture in the wall, may be removed at pleasure *. On the walls of the astronomical school hung several drawings and paintings relating to the observations taken of the sun, moon, comets, and other celestial bodies. *[margin: Schola astronomica. Linea meridionalis.]*

Higher up in this tower is the observatory, which on every side has shutters to be opened or shut as required, and a gallery on the outside. Though this observatory, with its apparatus, has already cost the city twenty-six thousand scudi or crowns, it is not yet completed. This tower is ascended by two hundred and seventy steps; and the top of it also serves for astronomical observations; through an aperture in which, just over the middle of the spiral stair-case, the stars may be seen in the day-time from the vault under the tower, when it is finished. Such a phænomenon was formerly seen from the royal observatory at Paris, before an alteration was made there on account of a new meridian-line. *[margin: Observatory. Expences of it. Stars seen by day-light.]*

The library belonging to the college is in the second story, and chiefly consists of count Marsigli's books, who founded the academy, as mentioned above. It contains several Turkish, Arabic, and other oriental manuscripts, which were part of the Corvini library; for Marsigli was present at the taking of Buda. Before this nobleman incurred his imperial majesty's displeasure by the affair of old Brisac, the emperor Leopold offered him four thousand ducats for this collection of manuscripts. Here is a great variety of other books relating to philosophy, mathematics, and antiquities. An *[margin: College library. Collection of antiquities.]*

---

* The Italians in general, and the Bolognese in particular, were the first who gave their sanction to Copernicus's system; who was instructed in the first rudiments of astronomy at Bologna, under Domenico Maria. The first of the German literati, who espoused his opinion, was cardinal Nicholas Schonberg, at whose recommendation pope Paul III. made him professor of mathematics at Rome, which was the first preferment that famous astronomer had.

BOLOGNA.

Vasa lacrymatoria. apartment adjoining to this library is full of ancient weights, urns, *vasa lacrymatoria*, or lacrymatories, in which the ancients collected the tears shed over their deceased friends, and afterwards set them by the urn *. Here are also sacrificing instruments, Roman, Grecian, and Egyptian idols; Roman votive pieces, and a tablet inlaid with Egyptian hieroglyphics, after the manner of the *tabula Isiaca* at Turin; but it is not so large.

School for experimental philosophy. In another apartment is taught experimental philosophy. The paintings and designs with which it is decorated, represent remarkable particulars on several parts of the globe, as volcano's, and other mountains of a singular quality; large islands of ice, frequent in the north seas; the cataracts of the Nile and other great rivers; the formation of the rainbow, of clouds, &c.

Loadstones. In a closet adjoining to this school several loadstones are kept; among which there is one, scarce so big as a man's fist, and weighing only nine ounces without the cap, that lifts up two hundred and thirty ounces. This put me in of the Hartsoker magnet to be seen in the landgrave of Hesse-Cassel's musæum, which takes up a pound and a half, though it weighs not much above a drachm. The attractive power of this stone greatly depends on the capping, by which it has been observed to be surprisingly augmented.

Marine productions. Another apartment exhibits a variety of shells and other marine productions. Adjoining to this is a closet containing a collection of semi-pellucid stones. In this class are comprehended agate, jasper, turquoise, chalcedony, onyx, and lapis-lazuli. The transparent stones are kept in another closet; and among them are several uncommon kinds of crystal, amethyst, &c. with the name affixed to each piece.

Collections of jasper, agate, &c.

Crystal, amethyst, &c.

Marble. Here are also many hundred species of marble and other stones in separate repositories, which being well polished, and all arranged according to their different colours, make a beautiful appearance. Here is a great number of pieces of porphyry, and near a fine stone marbled with green and blue, is the following inscription:

Lapis ad Smaragdi Pramam accedens, nonnullis lapidis Lazuli portiunculis elegantissimè interspersus.

---

* The abbé Bencini of Turin assured me that he and Fabretti had found several of these lachrymatories of glass in the catacombs of Rome; and that the mouth of those vases was contrived to be held so close to the eye that not a tear could be lost.

i. e.

BOLOGNA. 293

i. e. ' A stone resembling a kind of emerald, beautifully
'variegated with small veins of *lapis-lazuli*.'

No mention is made from whence this curious stone was
brought.

A kind of marble known by the name of *verde antico*, so
often mentioned in my letters from Rome, is called *ophites
viridis & luteus* in this collection. The finest among the
assortment of alabaster was brought from the island of Paros.
Those pieces of marble in which shells are inclosed form a particular class, to which the *lumachella* belongs. <small>Marble petrifactions.</small>

The Saxon fossiles are put together in the shape of a mountain. These were a present from king Augustus, and are kept in a particular closet; in which are also to be seen all kinds of glebes, earths, sulphur, allum, vitriol, fossile salts, spars, plaster, Bononian stones, sand, free-stones, marcasites, blood-stones, magnets, cinnabar, antimony, and other ores of quicksilver, iron, lead, tin, copper, silver, gold, &c. <small>Saxon fossiles.</small>

In another room are kept several kinds of sea-weeds, as *keratophyta marina*, *alcyonia*, *vegetabilia marina libidea*, corals, spunge, &c. <small>Marine plants.</small>

The next apartment exhibits all kinds of exotic fruits, woods, leaves of plants, roots, and barks of trees, (among which are thirteen species of the Peruvian cortex) gums, resins, balsams, *fungi*, with the seeds of all kinds of vegetables. <small>Exotics.</small>

One large room is distinguished by the appellation of *museum animalium*, and contains a very great variety of all kinds of animals, as *stellæ marinæ*, or star-fishes, shell and squamose fishes, serpents, crocodiles, lizards, chameleons, birds, locusts, &c. <small>*Museum animalium*.</small>

The stone in which a kind of shell-fish grows, and mentioned above in my account of Ancona, has also a place in this collection with the following inscription: <small>Shell-fish in stone.</small>

*Lapides, in quibus Pholades seu Balani Bonn. ingenti numero
nidulantur ex littore Anconitano.*

i. e. '. The stones in which the *pholades* or *balani* are in-
' closed in great numbers, brought from the coast of An-
' cona.'

U 3 Near

BOLOGNA.

Pearls extracted from an animal. Near a cluster of some hundreds of small pearls, in the form, and about the bigness of half a walnut, are these words:

Unionum congeries elegantissima ex animali extracta.

' A most beautiful congeries of pearls taken out of an animal.'

Method of preserving butterflies, birds, &c. Butterflies are here preserved, which, being dipt in a balsamic liquor, retain all their original beauty for several years. An abbé at Florence is said to be possessed of a secret for preserving birds against all corruption or damage by worms; but he is so very fond of this *nostrum*, that it is likely to die with him; at least he has hitherto obstinately rejected all overtures made to him for communicating this secret.

Closet of warlike instruments. Fortifications, &c.. The warlike instruments, as models of cannon, mortars, &c. take up a particular apartment, in which also is seen the model of the citadel of old Brisac, and likewise of other fortifications, after the different methods practised by Vauban, Sturm, Rusenstein, Malleti, Bellini, Floriani, Molder, Werthmuller, Cohorn, Grotta, Bombelli, and several other engineers.

Weights and scales. Another room contains a collection of all sorts of weights and scales.

Turnery-room. In the turnery-room are all kinds of lathes and instruments for turning; portraits, and other master-pieces; and likewise all the instruments used in making clock-work.

A school for geography and navigation. A superb gallery designed for the library is just finished, which leads into a room appropriated for curiosities relating to geography and navigation. In the centre of it hangs a small galley; and the walls of it are covered with just and elegant drawings and models for ship-building. The chemical apartment is on the ground-floor; but, the necessary funds for teaching this science and ship-building not being yet settled, no colleges are yet assigned for those useful arts: However, the other professors are obliged, once a week, to read a public lecture in this school.

Academy for painting. The painting academy stands also on the ground-floor, and is ornamented in a manner becoming such a place. The cieling is beautifully painted by Pellegrino di Baldi, where Polyphemus, seeking out Ulysses and his companions, after the loss of his eye, cannot be sufficiently admired. In winter, the disciples who are instructed in painting, meet in a

particular

BOLOGNA.

particular room, built in the form of an amphitheatre and well illuminated with lamps, where above a hundred and fifty of them may conveniently sit in three or four rows and draw from the life.

In the academy of sculpture are to be seen wooden models of the ancient obelisks at Rome, with drawings and copper-plates of several mechanical machines. In a room adjoining to it are statues, and copies of the most famous pieces, as the Venus of Medicis, the Farnesian Hercules, the Vatican Apollo, gladiators, Flora, &c. in plaster. *School for sculpture.*

In the cloister round the court are several stones inscribed with Hebrew characters; the thumb of a Colossus, and a great number of ancient Roman inscriptions and statues. *Hebrew and Roman inscriptions and statues.*

Count Marsigli was born in the year 1650, and deserves to have the pleasure of spending the close of his life at Bologna, with more tranquillity and comfort than is actually the case, on account of the learned foundation mentioned above; on which he has expended the greatest part of his fortune, and bestowed all the fruits of his labour and application. It seems the city has given him no small vexation by crossing him in several particulars relating to his favourite academy, and has laid an unreasonable restraint upon him to prevent his regulating it according to his own judgment. It is true, that as his public donations to the academy, and his manner of applying them, are ratified by the pope's bull, it is no longer in his power to make any alterations. And this, perhaps, has induced the city to think that there is no farther need of carrying it fair with him, and that the season of flattery and respect is now over. But, were not gratitude utterly extinct among the Bolognese, certainly the magistrates of the city would avoid thwarting and contemning a nobleman of such a public spirit, which was so signally exerted for the advantage of Bologna. Even supposing it true, that count Marsigli were whimsical and obstinate, and that, if a full scope was given to his will, he would launch out into many indiscretions in regulating an affair to which the city has already contributed no small sum: Yet does it not deserve some consideration, whether it were not better to connive at the caprice of an old man, than to exasperate him with the mortification of thinking his liberality ill-bestowed? This behaviour at the same time gives the commonalty room to suspect, that the harsh treatment of Marsigli proceeds rather from private views than any concern for the right management of the academy, &c. It is known that *Some account of count Marsigli. His particular disquietude.*

BOLOGNA.

Marsigli obtained a grant from the pope of the reversion of several benefices, to the yearly amount of some thousands of scudi, which on the decease of the present incumbents (who, *The cause of his being hated.* being left in the quiet enjoyment of them, have no cause to complain) are to devolve to his academy. This, in the opinion of many people, is the source of all the animosity and rancour against Marsigli; several families in Bologna being incensed to find themselves deprived of these places, which in their imaginations they had made themselves sure of. On this account Marsigli resides but seldom at Bologna; and thus the far greater part of his time is spent at a distance from the academy on which his heart has ever been set. He returned hither yesterday for the first time after he had left the city, but with all the weakness and infirmities to which old age is incident*. How highly this gentleman has deserved of the republic of letters is well known, and his natural histories of the Mediterranean and the Danube are *His reserve.* lasting proofs of it. His reserve and extreme modesty appeared conspicuous in several particulars relating to this foundation; especially in the strict orders he gave that his name should not be inscribed on any part of the building, either within or on the outside, nor on any of the curiosities *Printing-house.* which are deposited in it. The noble printing-house, which he added to this foundation, is well furnished not only with Latin, Greek, and Hebrew, but also with Arabic, and other oriental types. He ordered it to be called the printing-house of St. Thomas Aquinas, and appointed the Dominican *Medals of the academy.* monks to be trustees of it†. The medals struck, when this academy was founded, have on one side the head of pope Clement XI. and on the reverse the edifice appropriated to this institution, with the following legend:

Bonarum Artium cultui & incremento.

* He died in November 1730, in the eightieth year of his age. Some make him two years older, and say that he was born in the year 1648.
† All the deeds of gift, contracts, &c. that passed betwixt count Marsigli and the senate of Bologna, and likewise betwixt the said count and the Dominican monks, were published at Bologna in the year 1728, with the following title: *Atti Legali per la Fondazione dell' Instituto delle Scienze ed Arti liberali per memoria degli Ordini Ecclesiastici e Secolari che compongono lu Città di Bologna.* Here it must be farther observed that the academy,·once known by the appellation of *Academia degl' Inquieti,* is also annexed to Marsigli's foundation. Vide *De Bononiensi Scientiarum & Artium Instituto atque Academia Commentar. Bonon. ann.* 1731, 4to.

' For

BOLOGNA.

'For the cultivation and improvement of arts and sci-
'ences.'

On the exergue are these words:

Institut. Scient. Bonon.

'The academy of sciences at Bologna.'

But not the least mention is made of count Marsigli on these medals.

Though Marsigli was so eminent for his knowledge and learning, and was deservedly esteemed as an encourager and promoter of arts and sciences, he makes but an indifferent figure when viewed in a military light: For in the affair of old Brisac, in the year 1703, he brought an indelible blemish upon his reputation. Count Arco was the governor of that place, and count Marsigli and colonel Von Egg were lieutenants under him; and tho' the emperor had sent positive orders to defend the place against the French, to the very last extremity, yet it was surrendered without making the least resistance; and Marsigli was the first who voted for a capitulation. At the council of war held on account of this miscarriage, on the fourth day of February 1704, at which general Von Thungen presided, count Arco was condemned to lose his head; which sentence was accordingly executed [*], tho' he had before served the emperor with distinguished honour, and could shew the scars of eighteen wounds.

The indifferent figure which Marsigli made with regard to old Brisac.

Count Arco's condemnation.

The French marshal de———, who had been employed by his master in conducting this siege, told M. Forstner, one of the ministers of state in Lorain, That count Arco did not deserve to die as a traitor; but that his disobedience to the orders of his sovereign required an exemplary punishment. However, one may see, in count Arco's fate, the secret hand of divine justice, as he had several times immediately before the siege treated with the French about the surrender of this fortress.

As to colonel Von Egg, the third commanding officer in Brisac, tho' he was deprived of all his employments, yet the emperor was pleased to bestow him a yearly pension of a thousand *guldens* [†], on which he lived privately with his family at Rodenburg on the Neckar, where I was several times

Von Egg's sentence.

[*] *Vid. Rink, &c.*   [†] About 116 *l.* 13 *s.* 4 *d.* sterling.

in his company last year. The other officers, who signed the capitulation, were cashiered and fined; however they were all afterwards received into other regiments, excepting Von Egg. Prince Lewis of Baden affirmed, 'That 'what chagrined him most, was, to find all the officers 'were so unanimous for a capitulation; for (continued he) 'had there been but a single ensign who had opposed it, I 'would have given him a regiment.'

What happened upon this to Marsigli. Marsigli was never accused of want of courage; but he is thought to have the foible of too many of the Italians, and to have been influenced by envy; so that he used many indirect means and artifices to form cabals, and prevent a good understanding betwixt count Arco and the garrison; by which means several good measures, that might otherwise have taken place, miscarried. The sentence passed by the court martial on Marsigli, was, that his sword should be broken as a mark of infamy, which was immediately executed. But what some have advanced, namely, that the count had the alternative granted him either to lose his head, or his reputation; and that with great joy he preferred his life to his honour; is a groundless aspersion *. In the year 1704, he he published a vindication of himself, in which he does not deny his being acquainted with the order for defending the place to the last extremity; but alledges, that this order was founded on a false report made to prince Lewis of Baden, namely, that the town was sufficiently provided with men, and stores; whereas it was in such a condition that resistance would have been contrary to all the rules of war, as it would be only deliberately throwing away the lives of the

* Such another report prevails about general Heiderfdorff, and with no better foundation; it being certain, when he was informed of the emperor's order to change his sentence of death into a deprivation of his honours, he answered, 'This is what I have not deserved.' What was laid to his charge, was, that he had not properly defended Heidelberg against the French in the year 1692. After he was stript of the *insignia* of the Teutonic order, he was carried on a hurdle, which was driven by the executioner, thro' the whole army, while he continually cried out, 'Rather death than this!' After undergoing this ignominy, his sword was broken by the common hangman, who struck him on the head with the pieces of it, and then he was banished the country. He died not many years since, at a convent at Hildesham, and left a very amiable character behind him. General Schnebelin was also tried on the same charge; but he cleared himself, by proving that he was ignorant of the orders which had been sent for the defence of the place. Concerning Schnebelin, I shall only add, that he was the author of the famous entertaining and moral piece called *Tabula Utopiæ*.

men

BOLOGNA. 299

men in garrison. This assertion he supports by several authorities and examples, as may be seen in the extract of his defence in the *Esprit des Cours de 'L' Europe*, under that year. How far a commanding officer may deviate from the orders he receives, according to the circumstances of his army, or those of the place in which he commands, and what severity may be used by way of example, I shall not take upon me to determine. The Italians, to this very day, treat the memory of the prince of Baden with great acrimony. But he sufficiently cleared himself of the imputation of severity by shewing the necessity of such a proceeding; for he was even obliged to break his own regiment, tho' the men were afterwards admitted into other corps. This, however, is certain, that Marsigli's reputation will always suffer by it; and that such a stain is not effaced by the post which afterwards pope Clement XI. conferred on him, by appointing him general of those wretched troops which he had picked up to act against the emperor Joseph, in the dispute concerning Comacchio. For, by the consequence, it appeared, that the command of such an army did no great honour to the general, nor was such a commander any credit to the papal see *.

Marsigli, was a papal general.

But to return to my observations on the present state of learning at Bologna. Giuseppe Monti, professor of botany in the university, and of anatomy in the Marsiglian academy, is now engaged in writing a natural history of this country; which is the more impatiently expected by the public on account of the proofs he has already given of his accurate knowledge in the sciences, &c. †.

Monti, professor of botany.

Zanoni, an apothecary at Bologna, who has published a curious herbalist, embellished with several copper-plates, is possessed of a large collection of natural curiosities. The above-mentioned professor Monti has a great variety of petrifactions collected in the neighbourhood of this city: he has also published a small but elaborate dissertation on the

Zanoni, apothecary.

Petrifactions.

---

* A sarcastical anagram on Marsigli's name is here omitted, as such kind of wit is exploded in England, tho' it still prevails in Germany.

† Among other pieces of his are *Catalogi Stirpium agri Bononiensis Prodromus, gramina ac hujusmodi affinia complectens, in quo ipsorum Etymologiæ, Notæ characteristicæ, peculiares usus Medici, Synonyma selectiora summatim exhibentur, ac insuper propriis observationibus exoticisque graminibus eadem dispersè locupletantur à Josepho Monti, ap. Constantinum Bisarri*, 1719. Likewise *Plantarum varii indices ad usum demonstrationum Bononiæ studiorum*, published in 1724, in which is a plate of the physic garden.

head

BOLOGNA.

Sea-horse's head. head of a sea-horse, or sea-cow, dug out of the adjacent mountains, in which the *dentes molares* are still to be seen *.

Dentales. Among other petrifactions found in the little river Martignone, not far from Castello Crespellano, as also in a brook near Cottibo, are several *siphunculi marini*, which some take to be the teeth of a kind of fish; whereas in reality they have neither the smoothness nor the hardness of a tooth, but rather consist of a testaceous substance which was once the receptacle of a worm or snail. Those commonly called the large Dentales are white, streaked longitudinally, and somewhat crooked; the smaller teeth, which terminate in a slender point, and are of a reddish colour, are called *antales*. Both these species are worn by the common people next their skin, by way of amulet or preservative against a disease called in Italian la Schiranzia or Squinanzia and Angina *i. e.* a quinsey or sore-throat. These are also found near Verona, Vicenza, &c. near Lunenburg in Germany, and at Achim in the duchy of Bremen.

Pinna. On the summit of mount Blancano, in a stratum of marle, is found a species of shells commonly called in Latin *Pinnæ*, and by the French *Nacres*, i. e. mother of pearl shells, or *Moules*, i. e. mussels, which, from their shape resembling a gammon of bacon, have also the name of *Perna*. While the fish is alive, the lower shell strongly adheres to the bottom **Large shells.** of the sea. Some other large shells are also dug up near Madonna del Sasso, which lies about eleven Italian miles **Dentes laminæ.** from Bologna; and several of the *Dentes laminæ* are found near Poggivoli Rossi, or the Red hills.

Petrified fish, and other animals In and near the Martignone are also found petrified fish, *Fungi* and *Pectinites*, which, on account of their thin shell, are also called *Membranuli*; *Conchites Pectinites, Pectunculitæ striati, Tubulitæ vermiculares recti, & intorti, majores & minores, &c.*

In the brook dell' Inferno, as it is called, are found *Conchitæ leviter per longum striati, Conchitæ majores, Pectunculitæ leviter striati, &c.*

The rivulet Mercati exhibits congeries of *Conchitæ, Tellinitæ, &c.*

On the mountain, called Monte delle Grotte, are found *Turbinatæ, Conchitæ, Echinitæ, Spinulæ Pectinites, &c.*

* *De monumento diluviano nuper in agro Bononiensi detecto Dissertatio, in qua permultæ ipsius inundationis vindiciæ à statu terræ antediluvianæ & postdiluvianæ desumtæ exponuntur a Josepho Monti, Bononiæ, 1719, apud Rossi & sociis.*

In

BOLOGNA.

In other parts of the territory of Bologna are found fragments of the *Ostreitæ Polyleptoginglymi*, the *Ostreum imbricatum & sulcatum* of different sizes, ash-coloured oyster-shells; *Conchitæ bivalves*; *Conchitæ turbinati*, *Pectines bivalves*, *Pectinites striati*, *Pectunculi*, *Pectunculitæ*; *Chamæ leves, bivalves Glychcimerides*; *Chamæ ingentes margaritiferæ polyginglymæ bivalves*, as Lister in his history of shells terms them; *Chamæ oblongæ leves et leviter striatæ*; *Dendritæ, Lignum fossile et petrifactum*, or fossile petrified wood; and *Gagates* or *Gangetes*, which is also called *Lapis Thracius*. Among petrified fishes the Sarda * is frequently found here. In the yellow sand, which abounds in the territories of Bologna, and derives its colour from a yellow kind of earth, are found great numbers of Cornua Ammonis, and other shells, many of which are so small as hardly to be distinguished without the help of a microscope.

I must not here omit the well known *Lapis Bononiensis*. This is a small stone of a light grey colour, and irregular shape. It is full of sulphureous particles, and of a lax texture, yet heavier than would be conceived from its size, and sparkles like talc. It is found in several parts of Italy, but especially in the district of Bologna, towards the Appenine mountains, and on mount Paderno which stands about five Italian miles from Bologna. They are most commonly found after heavy rains among the earth washed off from the neighbouring mountains. This stone is of the size of a walnut, and has no lucid-appearance in the dark until it undergoes a particular calcination, by which it acquires the property of imbibing, when exposed for a few minutes to the sun-beams, such a quantity of light, that it afterwards shines in the dark from eight to fifteen minutes like a glowing coal, but without any sensible heat. This experiment may be repeated at pleasure; and it is sufficient, if the stone be laid only in the open air in the day-time where the sun does not shine; for the heat of the sun is apt to make it crumble to pieces. If the stone be well prepared, the light of a candle is sufficient to give it this luminous quality; but it is not affected by moon-shine. It retains its lustre, even tho' it be put into water, and preserves this property for three or four years; and then it may be calcined anew, but it never perfectly recovers the same refulgency that it acquired at the first calcination.

The fish Sarda.

Of the Bononian stone, a kind of phosphorus.

---

* This is a small fish well known in the Mediterranean, and called by the French *Sardine*. It is not unlike a sprat, but something larger.

BOLOGNA.

In the fourth article of the Philosophical Transactions of the Royal Society at London for the month of January 1666, it is said, that only a certain ecclesiastic had the art of preparing this stone, and that the secret died with him. But this supposed loss was happily retrieved by M. Homberg, a celebrated German naturalist, who, on his return from his travels in Italy, brought with him a great many of these stones, and calcined two hundred of them so many different ways, that at last he found out the secret. His method was as follows: He first scraped the stone all over till it appeared exactly like talc; then having soaked it thoroughly in brandy, and inclosed it in a paste or crust made of other stones of the same kind pulverized, he calcined it in the fire, or a small furnace. After this, all the powder of the crust in which the stone was inclosed is taken off. Both the powder and the stone, when brought into the dark from the open air, make a luminous appearance; and the former, if kept in a strong and well stopt phial, when exposed to the air, imbibes the light, and, if sprinkled on pictures and letters, illuminates them in the dark. In preparing the paste the stone must be pulverized in a brass mortar; for a glass or marble mortar is very detrimental to the virtue of this kind of Phosphorus; an iron mortar particularly is worse than any other. For this information we are obliged to Lemery, who, in his *Cours de Chymie*, describes at large the whole process of preparing this stone, which, he candidly acknowledges, he learned from Homberg himself. I have been assured, that in calcining this stone over a fire, as it must be frequently turned, the operator must take care not to hang his head over the effluvia arising from it. The uncalcined *Lapis Bononiensis* is sold at Bologna at a *Paolo* * per pound; but a prepared piece of the bigness of a dried fig costs two or three *Paoli*, or more. This phænomenon is generally attributed to the sulphur with which the *Lapis Bononiensis* abounds; for when it is fresh calcined the smell of it is an evident proof of this. Besides, its evaporations are known to tinge silver: However, sulphur cannot be productive of any light or effulgence, unless it be previously purged from all heterogenous particles; and this is done by fire. Day-light, which is nothing but the finest rays of the igneous matter emitted by the sun, kindles the sulphur on the surface of the stone, when exposed to the open air, as fire does common fuel.

Its preparation.

---

* Six-pence sterling.

BOLOGNA.

Upon this supposition, Lemery directs that this stone be calcined in a moderate fire, and observes, that, if the heat be too slow, the sulphur is not carried to the surface of the stone; and on the contrary, if it be too intense, the sulphur is too much dissipated and evaporates.

The Phosphorus Balduinus, invented by Baudovin, a Frenchman, who published an account of it in 1675, under the title of *Phosphorus Hermetius*, without acquainting the world with the secret of preparing it, was nothing else but an imitation of the *Lapis Bononiensis*. Baudovin's magnet of light, as he pompously styled it, was nothing but a compound made of English chalk and *aqua fortis*, or spirit of nitre. *[Phosphorus Balduinus.]*

Not long after, in the year 1677, one Brand, a German chemist at Hamburgh, found out the secret of making burning Phosphorus, and that by chance (to which we owe many curious inventions) whilst he was endeavouring to extract a liquid from human urine in order to transmute silver into gold. *[Burning Phosphorus.]*

Runkel carried the invention still farther, and at length it was brought to such perfection, that at present a burning or incendible Phosphorus may be made from vegetable or animal substances, when calcined with allum. This is best kept in water, and emits light when exposed for a little while to the open air. I myself have seen experiments of this kind exhibited by Homberg, and Lemery, the son.

Besides this *Phosphorus fulgurans*, several other similar discoveries have been made, as for example: By mixing two cold fluids, as the acid spirits of a mineral and an oil extracted from vegetables, flame has been produced. I shall on another occasion speak of the luminous barometer, and a kind of *Phosphorus*, which may be called *Smaragdinus*. *[Flame from two liquors mixt. Phosphorus Smaragdinus.]*

I have already given an account of some sea-animals that emit an effulgence in the dark, in describing the Datali del Mare of Arcona: And I would recommend it to the inquiries of naturalists, whether this shining be owing to the seasalt, or to the resinous and sulphureous particles with which the sea-water is impregnated; I have often observed at sea in a dark night coruscations not unlike ignited sparks, caused by the collision of the waves, the motion of the ship, and especially of the oars: and, if a person makes water from the deck of a ship into the sea in a dark night, a multitude of luminous sparks are seen to rebound, as it were, from the surface *[Sea-animals which shine in the dark. Radiancy in sea-water.]*

face of the water. But both these scintillations are observed only in dry weather; and possibly the cause is to be looked for in the motion of the saline spirits.

Luciola, or glow-worm, a natural phosphorus. The *luciolæ*, or glow-worms, common in Italy and other countries, is to be classed among the natural *phosphori*. These insects appear most luminous in rainy weather; as rotten wood, which is another kind of natural phosphorus, is known to emit light in the dark, if it be moist.

BOLOGNA, April 21, 1730.

LETTER LXVI.

Account of MODENA and REGGIO.

SIR,

THE country betwixt Bologna and Modena is very pleasant, fertile, and well cultivated, and abounds in vineyards. The inhabitants have a method of preserving ripe grapes, from the vintage-time till the month of August in the following year, by keeping them in little rooms well secured against the external air and the light of the sun; and they never go into these store-rooms but with one small candle, and that as seldom as possible. The bunches are not laid upon the floor, but hang separate, being tied to a great number of small sticks; and, when a single grape has the least appearance of decay or rottenness, it is plucked off, to prevent the rest from the infection.

How grapes are preserved.

The horned cattle of this country are very large, and generally white. Six or eight oxen are here put to a carriage, with a great number of bells hanging about them, which make no disagreeable noise. The design of this music, as I am informed, is to chear the creatures under their labour, and to give notice at a distance on the road that such a carriage is coming.

White-horned cattle with bells.

Not far from the city of Bologna the river Reno * crosses the road. Though this river, during the greatest part of the year, has but a small current; yet there is a bridge consisting of two-and-twenty arches, which is four

Bridge over the Reno.

* *Sil. Ital. lib.* viii.———*Parvique Bononia Rheni.*

hundred

MODENA.

hundred and feventy paces long, and feven broad, built over it. In the year 1530, when Charles V. paffed it in great folemnity juft before his coronation, it broke under the multitude of people who attended in the proceffion, which occafioned great damage, befides the lofs of many lives. This misfortune fome prophetic genius's of that time looked upon as a certain omen that Charles V. was to be the laft emperor who would receive his crown from the hands of the pope.

It was not far from Bologna that the Triumviri, M. Lepidus, M. Antonius, and C. Octavius, formed that alliance which afterwards proved fo bloody in its confequences. Plutarch, in his Life of Cicero, c. 67, and in that of Antony, c. 24, fays, that the Trumviri had this interview on a fmall ifland; to which Dio, *lib.* xlvi. adds, that the ifland was formed by a little river (probably the Reno) near Bologna. However, there is no river in the neighbourhood of this city that forms an ifland exactly agreeable to the defcription given us by this hiftorian; for by an ifland is now always underftood a place which is generally furrounded with water. But whether this ifland was near Bagneto, at the conflux of the Lavino and the Reno; or at Bagno, where the little ftream Dofio empties itfelf into the Reno; or laftly, whether it was in the neighbourhood of the village called Trebo di S. Giovanni, it is not eafy to determine. *Place where Lepidus, Antony, and Octavius entered into an alliance.*

About fourteen Italian miles from Bologna, near this road, lies Fort Urbano, which confifts of five baftions, and was built by pope Urban VIII. as a key to the ecclefiaftical ftate on this fide. A little farther on we ferried over the little river Panaro, about five Italian miles on this fide Modena. This river ferves as a boundary to divide the dutchy of Modena from the Bolognefe. On a pillar erected in this place is the following infcription, which would better become a warlike monarch, than the head of the church of Chrift, who faid to his difciples, 'The princes of the Gen-
' tiles exercife dominion;———but it fhall not be fo among
' you.' Matt. xx. 25, 26. *Fort Urbano. Martial infcription.*

Vol. III. *Viator,*

Viator,
Hic eſt limes agri Bononienſis
Et Ecclesiaſticæ ditionis initium,
Quod, ut
Urbanus VIII. Pont. Max.
Tectum ſartumque redderet,
Arce munitiſſimâ, ut mox videbis, excitatâ
Sic Pontificiæ Majeſtati, ſic ſubditorum ſecuritati conſuluit,
Ut exinde clavibus imperterritè
Ovilis Dominici gereret curam,
Et gladio truculento arceret luporum rabiem.

'Traveller, here thou ſeeſt the boundary of the Bolog-
'neſe territories, and the entrance into the eccleſiaſtical
'ſtate; for the defence and ſecurity of which his holineſs
'pope Urban VIII. has built, as thou ſhalt preſently ſee, a
'very ſtrong fortreſs; who thus at once conſulted the dig-
'nity of the papal majeſty and the tranquillity of his ſub-
'jects, that he may henceforth intrepidly protect the ſheep-
'fold of the Lord with the keys committed to him, and
'drive away the ravenous wolves from the flock with the de-
'ſtroying ſword.'

Modena.

Meſſages carried by pigeons.

Modena is a very ancient city, and frequently mentioned in the Roman hiſtory. When Decimus Brutus was beſieged in this city, Hirtius made uſe of tame pigeons (which by hunger he had trained up for ſuch a ſervice) as meſſengers *, to give the beſieged advice of his intentions, and to receive intelligence from Decimus Brutus on their return. The memory of this device is perpetuated even to this very day at Modena, where pigeons are taught to carry letters to a place appointed, and bring back anſwers. According to the relations of travellers, the ſame is practiſed at Aleppo, and other cities in the Levant †. Of what benefit theſe letter-carriers

---

* Plin. Hiſt. Nat. c. 73. *Magnis in rebus fuere internuntiæ* (columbæ) -- *Quid vallum & vigil obſidio, atque etiam retia amne prætenta profuere Antonio per cælum eunte nuntio?* 'In affairs of great importance (pigeons)
'were made uſe of for meſſengers. - - - What did the trenches, the centi-
'nels, and even the ſnares laid acroſs the river avail Antony, while a
'courier made his way through the air?'

† That Mahomet alſo made pigeons ſubſervient to his impoſtures, appears from the ſeveral hiſtories of his life; as alſo from Ximenes, *in hiſt. Arab. Elmacen. in hiſt. Sarac. &c.*

proved

MODENA.

proved to the city of Leyden *, when hard preſſed by the Spaniards, is ſufficiently known from the hiſtory of the ſixteenth century.

The city of Modena boaſts of having given birth to ſeveral eminent perſons, among whom they reckon Sigoni the civilian and hiſtorian, Fallopi the phyſician, from whom certain tubes † in the human body derive their name; Corregio the painter; the poets Aleſſandro Taſſoni and Teſti; Gicopo Barocci da Vignola the architect; cardinal Sadoleti, and the imperial general Monteculi. *Eminent perſons natives of Modena.*

In the cathedral of Modena they ſhew a very uncommon trophy of the valour of the inhabitants, namely, a wooden bucket with iron hoops, which the Modeneſe, for what purpoſe I know not, brought away from Bologna, and kept as a memorial of their expedition to the capital city of their enemies. The war was originally occaſioned by the Bologneſe refuſing to reſtore the towns of San-Ceſario and Nonantola according to the deciſion of the emperor Frederic II. who had been appointed arbitrator of the difference: upon this, the emperor, out of reſentment for the indignity offered, ſent his natural ſon Henci, king of Sardinia, to the aſſiſtance of the Modeneſe, whoſe unhappy fate has been already taken notice of. As Geminianus was the patron ſaint of Modena, and Petronius that of Bologna, the contending parties were called Geminiani and Petroniani. Aleſſandro Taſſoni has ludicrouſly deſcribed the whole courſe of this war, in his moſt ingenious poem intitled *La Secchia rapita*; and, to heighten the burleſque, he makes the Modeneſe give riſe to that bloody war by ſtealing this bucket. *Taſſoni's poem. La Secchia rapita, or the rape of the bucket.*

It was from this Modeneſe poet that the celebrated Boileau took the hint for the *Lutrin*. The only fault in Taſſoni's burleſque poem is a want of delicacy in ſome of his expreſſions, which are ſometimes ſo groſs as to offend a chaſte ear. The bucket that has been thus immortalized hangs in one of the towers of the cathedral by an iron chain; to come at it, a perſon muſt go through no leſs than ſix doors, and give a handſome gratuity.

---

* Theſe pigeons, on account of their good ſervices, when they died, were ſtuffed, and are ſtill kept in the council-houſe at Leyden. Janus Douza's pigeon, which was one of theſe winged expreſſes, has further been honoured with two poetical panegyrics in Latin and Greek by the famous Daniel Helnſius. The great ſervice done by pigeons at Haerlem in the year 1573, at Zirickſee in 1575, and Gertrudenberg in 1593, are related by Strada, Meterano, and other hiſtorians of thoſe times.

† *Tubæ Fallopianæ.*

Cathedral. In this church the remains of St. Geminianus are deposited. Here is also a piece of painting by Guido, representing Christ in the temple, which well deserves a traveller's notice. Before the church are several low and slender pillars belonging to the building, which are supported by large figures of lions, &c.

Jesuits church. The Jesuits church is extremely beautiful, and the roof of it is painted from a design of father Boffi. The altars are very elegant, and behind the high altar is the history of St. Bartholomew, painted in several capital pictures by Procaccini.

Theatine church. The Theatine church is remarkable for its high altar, which is finely decorated with columns and statues. The choir is painted with fine pieces in *fresco*, representing the life and martyrdom of St. Vincentius, by Galati.

St. Dominic's church. They are now rebuilding St. Dominic's church; and, by what may be conjectured from the Capello del Rosario, a masterly white marble statue of the Madonna, and the great number of pillars of white and blue marble to be seen there, it will be a splendid and magnificent edifice.

St. Margaret's church. St. Margaret's church belongs to the Dominicans. It exhibits some good statues of *terra cotta* by Begarelli, representing our Saviour, two usurers, and some of the apostles. A much greater object of curiosity is that of the virgin standing at the crucifixion, and supported by the two other Mary's, of the same materials with the rest, but far exceeds them in expression, &c. being made and painted by Corregio.

College of St. Charles Borromeo. In the college of St. Carlo Borromeo, between seventy and eighty young noblemen are maintained, and instructed in the sciences and academical exercises. In the hall are the portraits of celebrated persons who received their education at this college.

Ducal palace. The ducal palace will be an elegant structure; but at present it is not above half finished. In the passage leading to the palace-church are painted all the saints who were of the ducal family; and among the rest the history of St.

Prediction of the death of any of the ducal family. Beatrix is to be seen there, who is said always to predict the death of every one of the ducal family by stamping with the foot on the floor. The cielings of most of the apartments are finely painted in *fresco*. Here are also other valuable paintings, particularly the following, viz. a capital piece, representing a pestilence; Titian with his wife and son paying their devotions to the virgin Mary; a Madonna sitting, attended by four saints, all as big as the life,

Fine paintings.

by

MODENA.

by Antonio Corregio; the virgin Mary, with St. George, and a groupe of little boys, by the same hand; the virgin Mary attended by several saints, and her assumption, both by Luigi Caracci; Paolo Veronese and his family prostrate before the virgin Mary and her divine infant; a capital piece representing Abraham's intended sacrifice of his son, by Del Sarto; ten pictures by Giulio Romano; the adoration of the eastern *magi*, and the marriage at Cana, by Paolo Veronese; a most beautiful landscape painted on copper, and a night-piece, by Corregio, representing Mary Magdalen lying on the ground in the wilderness and reading in a book. The frame of this piece is set with rubies, amethysts, turquoises, and other gems. St. Roch distributing alms is by Annibal Caracci, and formerly stood in the Scola di S. Rocco at Reggio; but was given the duke of Modena in exchange for a good copy. Here also is a picture of St. George, by Dosso da Ferrara. I have often observed pictures placed together on account of the equality of their size, though the subjects of them were extremely improper, which is the case here; a large piece representing Bacchanals is placed near another of our Saviour's crucifixion. But that piece, which for its excellence I should have mentioned first, is La Notte di Corregio, or Corregio's incomparable night-piece, representing the infant Jesus lying in his mother's lap. As Corregio's excellence was more conspicuous in the colouring and *chiaro oscuro*, than in designing, it must be allowed that in this piece he has shewn the utmost effort of his skill. The infant's body is represented as it were semi-pellucid, and emits such a radiancy, as to throw a proper light on the objects that are near it; and indeed this incomparable piece is never viewed without the highest admiration and pleasure. It was painted in the year 1522, and at first was sold for no more than two hundred Reggio *lire*, or livres*, which, according to the present course of money, are not much more than eight louis-d'ors †.

Metelli has published a copper-plate of this picture on a sheet of royal paper, which Rossi sells at Rome for ten *bajochi* ‡. Corregio's paintings are the more valued, because he has not left a great number of pieces behind him; for he be-

margin notes: Corregio's night-piece. La Notte di Corregio.

---
* About eight guineas.
† See Richardson's treatise on painting and sculpture.
‡ Seven-pence halfpenny.

stowed

MODENA.

stowed a great deal of time on his works, and died in the forty-second year of his age.

Looking-glass closet. The looking-glass closet is filled with the portraits of the ducal family. A connoisseur sees with concern the fine cieling-pieces in this and several other rooms here damaged by cracks and fissures.

Garden. The garden is at some distance from the palace. It has an orangery, but exhibits nothing very remarkable or cu-
Stables. rious, no more than the stables that stand near it.

In this part of the city likewise the duke's state-coaches are kept; some of which are ornamented with fine sculpture; others are of a wonderful largeness, being made a great many years since.

Library. The ducal library is under the care of Muratori, who was formerly Ambrosian library-keeper at Milan, and is well known in the republic of letters by his *Antichità Estensi ed Italiane*, the first part of which was published in folio at Modena in the year 1717; and for his large collection of the *Scriptores Italici**. The manuscripts of the Modena library are enumerated by Montfaucon, in his *Diarium Italicum*, p. 31.

How Mirandola came to the duke of Modena. The duke of Modena has been in possession of the principality of Mirandola ever since the year 1710; Francesco Maria Pica, the last prince, having forfeited it by being guilty of felony. An offer indeed was made this unhappy prince that he should be restored to his principality, on paying a fine of a hundred thousand ducats, and on condition that he should marry a daughter of Charles Maximilian Von Thurn, steward of the houshold to the empress-dowager Eleanora. As this lady was maid of honour to the empress, her majesty zealously promoted such an advantageous match; but by delaying the affair, and some failure in the immediate payment of the hundred thousand ducats, the imperial exchequer, in the year 1710, receded from these conditions, and at once sold the principality of Mirandola for a million

---

* The life of this great man has been written not only by several Italians, but by Mr. Rathlef and Mr. Brucker, two German writers. His *Scriptores rer. Ital.* in twenty-seven volumes, and his *Thesaurus veterum inscriptionum* in four, are lasting monuments of his judgment and application, as is his invaluable work of the history of Italy. By the last accounts from Modena we are informed, that Muratori, being in a very advanced age, has lost his sight, of which he had made such an excellent use.

MODENA.

of *guldens* * to the duke of Modena, who was invested with it by the emperor on the 12th of March, 1711. On this occasion the duke of Modena, in order to raise money for such a large purchase, proposed to some persons in Germany a loan of two hundred thousand *guldens* on a mortgage of the territory of Mirandola. That he might carry his point, his agents were for making the people believe, that the annual revenues of Mirandola were no less than a hundred thousand Spanish Spanish pistoles †; but I question whether Modena and Mirandola both together, after the necessary deductions, amount to more; though it is certain that the duke draws very considerable sums from the tax on mills, monopolies, and farms, with other imposts. John Frederic, the second son of Rinaldo the present duke, lived some years at Vienna, and during that time endeavoured to create a suspicion of his brother the hereditary prince Francesco Maria, on account of his marriage with Charlotta, the duke regent's daughter, in hopes of gaining the emperor's consent for dismembering the principality of Mirandola from the dutchy of Modena. This prince, especially in the year 1722, pushed the affair with all possible vigour; and, to hasten the accomplishment of his desire, is said to have proposed a marriage with a princess of the Sobieski family, who is related to the emperor; but all his measures were frustrated, and he ended his days in the year 1727, in the twenty-seventh year of his age. The former deposed prince of the house of Pica betook himself to Spain, where, in regard to his birth, personal accomplishments, and zeal for that crown, he was made master of the horse.

The duke's revenues.

Difference betwixt the two princes.

The animosity betwixt the two brothers, as related above, is not the only disturbance that happened in the ducal family. The father's rigid treatment of the hereditary prince, which was imputed to the violent counsels of Salvatico a Paduan, his prime minister, has been the occasion of great feuds. The same person is also charged with oppressing the subjects, and other iniquitous measures, which raised great murmurs and complaints. At last such high words passed betwixt the hereditary prince and Salvatico, that the latter thought it adviseable to make the best of his way to his own country. Since this minister has withdrawn, frequent endeavours have been used for restoring a harmony betwixt the duke and his son; and an outward reconciliation has been effected; but

As also between the duke and hereditary prince.

---
* 100,016 *l.* 13 *s.*   † 89,583 *l.* 7 *s.* sterling.

the

MODENA.

the inward miſtruſt, uſual in ſuch caſes, after an open rupture, ſtill ſubſiſts; the father keeping his court at Modena, and the ſon living with his princeſs at Reggio.

Intereſt of France with regard to the Italian ſtates.
France is unwilling that Italy ſhould be parcelled out into petty ſovereignties, but rather wiſhes that it were gradually united again; imagining, that by the ſub-diviſion of the ſeveral principalities the emperor has an opportunity of enlarging his power there. This is certain, that, in the wars of Italy, the emperor knows very well how to draw conſiderable ſuccours from the Italian princes, and never fails putting them in mind of the ſervices they owe to the Roman empire, by virtue of their fiefs.

High pretenſions of the Italian princes.
But this is alſo highly neceſſary, and without ſuch memento's they might poſſibly think that they were independent ſovereigns, and on a level with the German electors. The ceremonial which they think to procure for themſelves and their envoys at ſeveral foreign courts, does not a little favour their ambitious views. This brings to my mind what happened to M. Huldenberg, envoy from the elector of Brunſwic Lunenburg to the imperial court in the year 1698, when he was at the courts of Modena, and of ſome of ſome other Italian princes, to treat about the marriage of the empreſs Wilhelmina Amelia. The duke of ———, ſpeaking of the Italian princes, obſerved, that the

Pretended right of non appeal.
German electors and princes were indeed poſſeſſed of great power and large revenues; but that the Italian princes, were more abſolute in their dominions. In proof of which aſſertion he alledged, that an appeal lay from the German electors and princes to the emperor, whereas it was not ſo with the Italian princes, who judged without appeal. To this M. Huldenberg replied, That his highneſs was miſinformed in this affair, with regard to the German electors, and mentioned ſeveral inferior princes of the empire who are inveſted with the *Jus de non adpellando* in caſes that do not exceed a certain ſum; adding, he could not apprehend why an appeal might not be lodged from the decree of an Italian prince to the Aulic council, or his imperial majeſty. The duke inſiſted that no inſtance of this kind could be produced. After dinner M. Huldenberg took occaſion to reſume the ſubject with the prime miniſter, with whom he was very intimate, and to aſk him whether there was not an example of ſuch an appeal to the emperor? Upon the miniſter's anſwering in the negative, M. Huldenberg farther aſked him, if the Italian princes had found means to hinder complaints from being brought againſt them by way of appeal, as no law, in this caſe, could tie up the

hands

MODENA.

hands of the imperial court? The minister was silent for some time; but at last, upon M. Huldenberg's urging him farther, he gave him the wink, and whispered him, *Facciamo tic tac, tic tac,* intimating, that they caused those persons who threatened to make such appeals to be assassinated. Upon which M. Huldenberg smiled, and said, ' That this was an extraordi-
' nary privilege, indeed, and for which the Italian princes
' had little reason to value themselves above the electors of
' Germany,' &c.

But to return to Modena. This city is supposed to contain thirty-five thousand inhabitants: but this computation seems to exceed the truth; and, indeed, it is not at all credible. Before most of the houses there are portico's or cloisters, as in Bologna, under which a person may walk secure from rain and the heat of the sun: however, on account of their unequal height and breadth, they are no great ornament to the city. Here is but little trade stirring; and though a great number of masks (in making of which Modena excels) be exported to Venice and other places, yet so inconsiderable an article can contribute but little to the prosperity of the city.

The soil of the country about Modena is of a singular constitution, and well deserves the notice of the curious naturalist. It gives no small weight to the opinion that petrifactions are chiefly owing to the universal deluge. In every part, not only of the city, but of the adjacent country, plenty of good water is to be found; only, before it can be attained, the ground must be dug to the depth of sixty-three feet. For the first fourteen feet are found large stones, which seem to be the remains of paved streets, or roads, and buildings; and from hence there is sufficient reason to conclude that the foundation of this city was anciently much lower than it is at present. In the next place is found a stratum of hard and compact earth proper to build upon. This seems to be a kind of *terra virginea,* or virgin mould, which has never been disturbed by digging, though such kind of earth is looked upon as the best foundation for the largest structures. Under this is a stratum of black marshy earth, in which are found a great many sea-weeds, the leaves, branches, and trunks of trees in great abundance; and, at the depth of twenty-four feet, undecayed ears of corn have been dug up. The next is a stratum of chalk, which begins at the depth of twenty-eight feet. As soon as the labourers find this, they are sure of being no longer molested with the muddy

Particular property of the soil.

water

water breaking in upon them. This chalky stratum is about eleven feet deep, and very full of shells. It terminates at the depth of thirty-nine feet, after which follows a moorish or muddy soil two feet deep, in which are found rushes, leaves of plants, and branches of trees. Next to this is a cretaceous stratum, which is eleven feet deep, and consequently terminates at the depth of fifty-two feet from the surface of the earth. This is succeeded by a marshy or muddy soil, resembling the former, of two feet in depth; and then follows a stratum of chalky earth, but not so deep. The next to this is another stratum of marshy soil, or turf, under which is found a soft sand intermixt with gravel. This appears to be the original stratum laid by nature; in which are found sea-shells and other indications of an inundation or deluge. This stratum is very firm; and, by only boring a little way into it, a great plenty of good water immediately springs up, and soon fills the well to a proper height. No trunks of trees are found in the chalky strata; but they are met with only in the marshy or turfy soil *. It will not be amiss to subjoin here the different strata of the earth, and their arrangement, as found in digging a well two hundred and thirty-six feet deep, about the beginning of the last century, at Amsterdam, by order of the magistrates. This well is still to be seen at the Oudemannshause, betwixt the Doelestreet and Russland, where is stuck up a printed account of the order in which the strata lay, which is as follows:

Strata, or constitution of the soil at Amsterdam.

	Feet
1. A stratum of garden-mould in depth	7
2. Black turf, or peat	9
3. Soft clay	9
4. Sand	8
5. Earth	4
6. Clay	10
7. Earth	4
8. Paving-sand, upon which, as good a foundation, most of the houses in Amsterdam are built, piles being first driven into it	10
9. Clay	2
10. White sand	4
11. Dry earth	5
12. Marshy or muddy earth	1
13. Sand	14
14. A sandy clay	3
15. Sand	

* Vide Bernardinus Ramazzini *de fontium Mutinensium admiranda scaturigine, Mutinæ,* 1691. and Montfaucon's *Diar. Italic.*

MODENA.

		Feet
15. Sand intermixt with clay	—	5
16. Sea-sand in which are a great many shells		4
17. Clay — —		102
18. Sand where they left of digging	—	31
		232 feet

It is well known, that ashes, coals, bones, potsherds, trees, &c. are frequently found in the turf-lands or marshes in Holland and Friesland: but that these were overwhelmed and buried by some inundation or deluge may be concluded from the similarity of their position, the branches and tops always lying towards the N. E. and the roots in the opposite direction. *Position of trees in turf-lands.*

In the Modenese, especially near St. Polo, which is not far from Reggio, an excellent alkaline earth, which the Italians call *terra vergine aurea*, is dug up. Sometimes it is found in a kind of powder, and sometimes it resembles a fat and oleaginous *tophus*, or friable stone. It is first pounded fine, and then made into a soft, white, and insipid paste. This is in great repute, and reckoned of equal virtue with Terra Samia; the Bolo bianco and Terra Silesiaca are used as alexipharmics, and found very beneficial in fevers, dysenteries, and hypochondriac disorders *. *Terra vergine aurea. Medicinal use.*

Near the castle on Monte Baranzone, and in a place called Fiumetto, wells or pits are dug thirty or forty ells, and more, in depth, in which a kind of oil is seen floating on the surface of the water: this is what the Italians call Oglio di Naptha, or the Olio di Sasso, but more commonly known by the name of Petroleum, or oil of Peter. It is found in greatest plenty in autumn and spring, and is skimmed off the water once in a fortnight; but the wells are kept shut up close. It is of a reddish colour; and, when one of these wells becomes dry, they either dig deeper, or make a new one. Besides these, near Castello di Monte Gibbio are three other such springs, which are perennial. The oil which these last yield is of a yellowish colour, and is accounted the best in this country. Petroleum is used for embalming the dead, varnishing, painting, and in pharmacy, and is found not only here, but likewise in the neighbourhood of Parma and Naples, in Sicily, several of the islands of the Archipelago, India, the southern parts of France, and in other places †. *Oglio di Naptha, or rock oil.*

---

* *Vide Boccon. Observat. Phyfic.* vi. xxx, xxxi.   † *Boccon. Observat. Phyfic.* v,

Some

Of the origin of amber.

Some naturalists will have this to be a species of Succinum liquidum, which after its induration is distinguished by the name of amber; and this opinion is founded on Bocconi's observations, who tells us that he found some drops of Petroleum inclosed in the middle of a piece of amber; and that amber is to be met with on the coast of Sicily only in those places where Petroleum is found, and in no other. How well grounded the assertion of Oligerius Jacobæus, a Dane, who has writ a particular treatise on this oil, may be, namely, that it will grow hard and solid if it be boiled with spirit of nitre, I cannot say, as I have hitherto had no opportunity of trying the experiment. This, however, is certain, that sea-water is not necessary to the production of amber, which is often found in parts very remote from the sea. That it is not generated from the resin of pine or fir-trees, appears evident, because, in the countries about Foligno, Ancona, and Sessa, in the papal dominions, amber, sulphur, and resinous fossils of several kinds are dug up, though there is not a wood of pines or firs to be seen all over the country. Near Quercola and la Sasso, in the Modenese, amber is likewise not uncommon; and is there found in a soil which has yielded a great quantity of Petroleum. In the district of Luneburg, and in places which are so far from having any communication with the sea, that they are at the distance of ten German miles from it, I myself have gathered large pieces of amber, which had both the proper hardness, and, when rubbed, the electric quality of attracting light substances. Also in a marshy ground, on an estate called Gartow, belonging to baron Bernstorf, very good amber has been found. This was of several kinds; some pieces were yellow and transparent, some white and opaque or cloudy, and others black, which indeed are properly a kind of agate. These pieces of amber lie single in a turfy soil within a concretion of grey sand, and intermixt with filaments of roots; they are also found in the same manner in the mountains of Prussia. It is also no uncommon thing to find there, and in other places, pieces of wood impregnated with sulphur and resin, which have infinuated themselves into the pores and interstices.

The Elbe throws up fine pieces of amber on its banks in several places. Amber is also dug up in a mountain called Bugarach, in the province of Languedoc, in France; but it has not the hardness of the Prussian; and perhaps the inhabitants make their lamps of it on that account.

But

MODENA.

But to obviate the objection, That possibly the first formation or perfection of amber has been occasioned by the sea-water, which by some extraordinary inundation may have overwhelmed those countries that are, at present, at a great distance from the sea, I shall observe, that amber is daily formed in the earth, and, from a liquid or soft substance, is gradually indurated, and becomes a hard body. An instance of this I met with in a piece which, a few years ago, was dug up in the abovementioned estate of Gartow, and is now in Sir Hans Sloane's museum at London. On the surface of that piece of amber is seen a withered birch-leaf, the fibres and indented edges of which are imprinted in the most accurate manner on the amber. This must have been done while the latter was in its liquid state. Now this leaf cannot be supposed to have continued there whole ages, without corruption or decay; especially as the strata in which the Gartow amber is found, do not lie above the depth of three or four feet from the surface of the earth.

The animals that I have seen inclosed in amber, as far as I can recollect, are only of the terrestrial kind, as gnats, spiders, pismires, locusts, and the like. Minerals have also been found inclosed in amber; which is a plain proof that the former could not be in liquid amber in the sea, tho' such pieces of amber may have been washed away from their strata by the sea, and be again thrown by the tides on the shore, or accidentally drawn up in nets.

They who attribute the origin of amber to gum or resin of trees, forget that amber remains indissoluble in water, contrary to the nature of gums; and that there never was any vegetable found, from which a resinous oil and volatile acid can be extracted, as may be done from amber and other fossils. Amber loses its hardness and transparency after fusion; but retains its electric or attractive quality, which the modern philosophers, who are for exploding all occult qualities, attribute to the subtile saline and sulphureous particles of which amber is composed. For, say they, these, being detached and emitted by the friction, rarefy the air near the the amber, so that light substances, as straw, pieces of paper, &c. being propelled by the denser air, move towards the amber, where the air is rarefied more or less in proportion to its proximity, or distance from the latter.

Two Italian miles from Saffuolo in the Modenese is to be seen a chasm in the earth, called la Salsa, which often ejects smoke, flames, ashes, and stones of a sulphureous smell;

Fire emitted from Salsa.

and

REGGIO.

and throws many of them to the height of thirty yards. These eructations generally fall out in spring and autumn, and are sometimes attended with very great noises under ground. The mountain in which this aperture appears, has been rendered quite barren by the ashes, stones, &c. ejected out of the chasm; and during its eruptions the Petroleum or oil of Peter-wells, at Sasso and Monte Gibbio, is extremely turbid. Bocconi, in his *Museo di Fisca & di Esperienze*, published in quarto at Venice in 1697, pretends to have found out that la Salsa agrees not only as to its effects, but also the time of its eruptions, with mount Ætna in Sicily, and that this agreement was particularly remarkable on the 10th, 11th, and 12th of May 1693.

Petrifactions. The country about la Salsa affords petrifactions of several kinds, *Cochleitæ, Turbinitæ, Dentales, Tubuliti varii, recti & intorti*; but at what depth they are found I have not been informed.

In the little river Salsa, near Sassuolo, are found the teeth of *Hippopotami* and *Tubulitæ vermiculares*; and farther towards Sassuolo, *Buccinitæ, Caryophylla marina fossilia Scheuchzeri, Turbinitæ fasciculati, læves & striati, Turbinitæ cylindroidei*, &c. On Monte delle Meraviglie, are found large *Chamæ ventricosæ*. The other most remarkable *petrifacta* in the territories of Modena are *Conchitæ valvis æqualibus lævibus & rotundis; Conchitæ oblongi & læves; Conchitæ striati, transversim rugosi; Conchitæ in longum & transversim minutissime striati; Cochleitæ cælati; Cochleitæ trochiformes; Chamæ; Chamæ læves, rhomboideæ; Chamæ ventricosæ; Pectines auriti; Pectunculitæ tam in longum quam transversim striati; Tellinitæ subrotundi minutissime striati; Pectunculi læves; Ostreitæ imbricati; Ostreitarum opercula; Ostreitæ rugosi; Murices auriti, oris recurvi; Turbinitæ muricati* of several kinds; *Turbinites auriti, oris dentati; Umbilici fossiles,* alias *opercula cochlearum cælatarum,* &c.

Floating island. Lastly, I must here observe, that Pliny (*lib.* ii. *c.* 95.) mentions a floating island in the Modenese; but at present no such phænomenon is to be seen in these parts.

Reggio. Betwixt Modena and Rubiera, you cross the little river Secchia over a very long bridge: Rubiera is one post-stage from Modena, and about half-way to Reggio. This last mentioned city is better built, and has more regular streets than Modena; it also appears but little inferior to it in extent.

The street, in which the famous fair is yearly kept, is particularly remarkable both for its length and breadth; and

REGGIO.

and the only defect is, that it is not laid out in a direct line. In the cathedral of Reggio is to be seen, over the high altar, the assumption of the virgin Mary, painted by Vincenzo Gotti, and four marble statues by Clemente da Reggio; and by the same hand are also those of Adam and Eve, which stand before the front of the church. Among the sepulchral monuments in this church are several belonging to the family of Maleguzi; particularly that of Horatio Maleguzi, count of Monte Obizi, who was ambassador to Philip II. king of Spain, and also wrote the life of pope Pius V. He died in the year 1583. The monument of Ugo Rangoni, legate of Paul V. to several princes, is extremely beautiful. On the right side of the Tribuna are six fine marble statues, and in an adjoining chapel the images of St. Fabian and St. Sebastian.

The Chiesa della Madonna is a very lightsome building; and the cieling is elegantly painted. *Church of the Madonna.*

Before St. Prospero's church stand six lions which formerly served for pedestals to some structure. The roof is painted by Camillo Procaccino, and, among other things, exhibits the last judgment. In the vestry is to be seen a descent from the cross, together with the three Mary's, by Luigi Caracci, which consequently deserve notice. *St. Prospero.*

The road betwixt Modena and Parma is a part of the ancient Via Æmilia, and is very pleasant to travel. It lies all along through gardens, and is planted on both sides with rows of white mulberry-trees, interwoven with vines which form a kind of natural festoons. The whole plain consists of plantations and inclosures, every-where separated by rows of fruit-trees and vines, so that few countries can form a richer scene, or yield a more beautiful landscape to the eye. *Via Æmilia. Delightfulness of the road and prospect.*

On the road about five miles from Reggio, a very long bridge is built over the river Lenza, which is the boundary betwixt the dutchies of Modena and Parma. *River Lenza, boundary betwixt Modena and Parma.*

On the Modenese side, and on the left-hand, lies the castle of Canossa, which belongs at present to a family of the same name, and is famous in the history of the middle-ages, being the residence given by the powerful countess Mathilda to pope Hildebrand or Gregory VII. Here the emperor Henry IV. was obliged, in very severe cold weather, to stand for three days in the court-yard clad in sack-cloth, and bare-footed, without either meat or drink, and with tears to beg for pardon, before the pope could be prevailed on to receive him *Canossa castle. Ignominious penance of the emperor Henry IV.*

him again into the bosom of the church *. Concerning the suspicion of a criminal commerce between this pope and Mathilda, see *Lambertus Schaffnaburgensis ad ann.* 1077, *p.* 809; and the author of *Apologia pro Henrico* IV. *p.* 219. †

Several protestants make use of the testimony of these historians in order to complete the scandalous history of the court of Rome; and when it is objected that pope Hildebrand was old and emaciated, and that Mathilda was not very young, they answer, That old men are often concerned in such intrigues. But if, from the histories of those times, we enquire into the character of pope Gregory VII, they will inform us that ambition and avarice had the predominance over that pontiff; so that lust could make but little opposition against those reigning passions. A person of such a cast of mind is seldom known to indulge himself in sensual pleasures; and if he happens to be surprized by a strong temptation, so as to make a false step, he is ashamed of it, and his former ambition and avarice soon resume the ascendant over him, and put him upon projects which the world look upon as grand and enterprising.

LETTER LXVII.

Observations on Parma and Placentia.

SIR,

Parma.

PARMA is a large and populous city, and has broad regular streets and a great number of handsome houses, which the Italians here, according to the custom of other

---

* *Vide Baron. Annal. Tom.* xi. *ad ann.* 1077, *n* xviii. *p.* 524. *Donnizo, in vita Matbildis, lib.* xi. *c.* 1 & 7. *Arnulphus Mediolanensis, lib.* iv. *Gestorum Mediolanens. c.* viii. *p.* 746. The sovereign princes of Europe are not sensible how much they are indebted to Luther's reformation, were it only in respect of the temporal prosperity and outward security of their several dominions. See also on this head *Balth. Bebel. de beneficiis magistratui politico à Luthero exhibitis, Georg. Hern. Götze, de beneficiis œconomicis Lutheri ministerio exhibitis,* & *Joh. Hermann. Fürstenau, de meritis Lutheri in œconomiam publicam & privatam, Rintel.* 1749.

† To the historians who charge pope Gregory with carrying on amorous intrigues, may be added *Leo Ostiens. in chron. Cassin. lib.* iii. *c.* 49. *Sigbert. Gemblac.* and *Alberic. ad an.* 1085, who relate that Gregory on his death-bed heartily repented of this cruel treatment of the unhappy emperor Henry IV. but to these may be opposed the silence of other credible historians on this head.

parts

PARMA.

parts of Italy, dignify with the name of *palazzi*, or palaces. The little river Parma divides the city into two parts, which have a communication with each other by three stone bridges. Its circuit is about four Italian miles; and the citadel very much resembles that of Antwerp. The number of inhabitants is supposed to be from forty-five to fifty thousand; but this computation certainly exceeds the truth.

<small>River of the same name.

Circuit.
Citadel.
Number of inhabitants.</small>

Among the ancient writers who speak of this city, are the following: Strabo, *lib*. v. Livy, *lib*. xxxix. *c*. 55. Pliny, *lib*. iii. *c*. 15. Cicero ad Famil. *lib*. x. *ep*. 33. *n*. 8. Ptolemy, Columella, and others. In an ancient inscription it is stiled *Colonia Julia Augusta Parma*.

<small>Antiquity of the city.</small>

The ducal palace is not yet completed: however, in the duke's apartment, a great number of fine paintings are to be seen; among these, the pieces which Annibal Carracci has copied in oil colours from the paintings in *fresco* in the cupola of St. John's church, by Corregio, are eminently distinguished from the rest. A night-piece of Peter denying Christ, and another piece, representing Abraham entertaining three angels, deserve a particular attention. Here are two very large pieces by the cavalier Malogio, representing the glories of heaven, and fall of Lucifer into hell, who, to gain the favour of the ecclesiastics, has taken care to fill the former with bishops and friars.

<small>Ducal palace.
Its paintings.</small>

Adjoining to the dutchess's apartment is a looking-glass closet; but it has no very large glasses. Most of the principal rooms are hung with red velvet laced with gold, with the richness of which the brick flooring little agrees.

The vast theatre at Parma, so famous throughout all Europe, was built by Rainutius I. in the year 1618. The *parterre*, or pit, is sixty-five, and the stage sixty-two common paces, in length. In Parma, the length of the whole building is generally computed at a hundred and ninety ells, and the height about forty-nine or fifty. On each side of the stage stands an equestrian statue of one of the former dukes, and several other statues on each side of the pit. The latter consists of twelve rows, rising gradually one above another, as in the ancient Roman amphitheatres; and over it is a double gallery. Some, indeed, will have it that it will conveniently hold eight or nine thousand spectators; but this is an assertion which the eye manifestly contradicts at first sight. On occasion of the marriage of prince Edward, brother to the present duke, with Dorothea Sophia, daughter of Philip William elector Palatine, in the year 1670,

<small>Noble theatre.</small>

Vol. III.   Y

1670, it was most splendidly illuminated; and, during the opera, the *parterre*, or pit, was laid three or four feet under water, in order to represent a naval engagement betwixt two gondola's. For this purpose two large rooms on each side of the theatre were filled with water, the entrances to the pit were stopt, and as the flooring and seats of the amphitheatre * are of stone (the latter being only covered with wood) there was no great difficulty in exhibiting such a *naumachia*. But the gondola's must certainly have been very much confined in their motions, as the pit could not be enlarged; for in extent it is far short of that of the Aliberti theatre at Rome. The most remarkable thing, in the construction of this edifice, is, that a word spoken ever so low on the stage is distinctly heard in every part of the pit, (which saves the actors no small trouble) and the greatest elevation of the voice causes no echo. It is said, that, when Lewis XIV. designed to build an opera-house in the palace of the Thuilleries at Paris, he sent the celebrated architect Vigarani to Parma, in order to examine into the cause of this extraordinary effect; but to no purpose. The Paris opera-house is indeed supposed to be large enough to contain seven or eight thousand people; but I question whether this be not an exaggeration little short of that mentioned above; at least I am certain that the opera-house at Hanover exceeds it both in largeness and elegance.

Naval engagement exhibited in it.

Extraordinary construction of the theatre.

Observation about the opera-house at Paris.

Theatre for common use.

The illumination of the large theatre at Parma being very expensive, a smaller theatre has been erected for common use in a saloon adjoining to it; and this has a pit large enough to contain two thousand spectators. On the sides of it are three rows of seats, and eight more rising one above another, in the manner of an amphitheatre in front, and over these are three galleries.

Library.

The duke's library makes a very grand appearance; the books are all in French binding, and elegant pillars are placed at certain distances along the shelves. The number of books does not exceed seventeen or eighteen thousand volumes; and all the care taken to preserve them from worms and moths is, only by shaking and beating them a little at certain times.

The manuscripts are likewise bound in the same pompous manner. The printed books are for the most part in folio, and chiefly relate to history. At the end of the library is this inscription:

---

* The amphitheatre, as it is called, in the foreign theatres answers to the front boxes in our play-houses, and consists of several rows of seats raised above the pit with a gradual ascent.

Theatrum.

Theatrum Orbis miraculum   Inscription.
Ne suspicito,
Majus hic sibi vindicat
Sapientia,
Maximum Farnesia
Serenissimi Francisci
Ducis VII.
Magnificentia.

'Ceafe to admire the theatre of Parma, which is the
' wonder of the world; for wifdom here exhibits a greater:
' but the greateft wonder of all is the magnificence of his
' moft ferene highnefs duke Francefco VII. of the illuftri-
' ous houfe of Farnefe.'

The cabinet of medals confifts of eighteen thoufand Cabinet of
pieces, all of different dies, though there are no lefs than medals.
five hundred of the emperor Adrian. Over every medal is
a little ticket, with black letters on a gold ground, fhewing
on what occafion it was ftruck, &c. Thefe medals are inferted in copper-plates glazed, fo that by turning them you
have a view of the reverfes of the medals, without taking
them out of the fockets. This collection comes no lower
down than the reign of Heraclius; but the feries is continued in gold, filver, and copper pieces, each affortment of
which is kept in a feparate cafe.

The rareft piece in this collection is a medallion of Pif- Rareft piece.
cennius Niger, which was ftruck at Antioch, with *Dea fa-*
lutis or the goddefs of health, on the reverfe. The three
copper medals of Otho are of the *medius modulus*, or mid-
dling fize; one of which is a Latin medal, and the other
two Greek. But the genuinenefs of thefe pieces is much
difputed by feveral learned antiquarians. Petrufi, a Jefuit,
in the year 1694, began the publication of a catalogue of Catalogue of
this mufeum, the eighth part of which, confifting of a thin
volume in folio, was publifhed at Parma in the year 1717.
After his death the continuation of the work was undertaken by Pioveno, another Jefuit of Placentia, and fon to a
Venetian nobleman; but he is fo fparing of his labour, that
he has publifhed nothing yet.

The medal-tables are placed on both fides of a long gallery, where the eye is farther entertained with the fight of
feveral admirable pictures. The moft efteemed amongft the Paintings.
latter

latter are the following pieces, *viz.* a naked Venus asleep, by Annibal Caracci; under which is a looking-glass in a frame of white Carrara marble, beautifully carved with five angels and a variety of flowers in *relievo*, by Giuliano Mozani; the last judgment, by Michael Angelo; a *Pietà* by Annibal Caracci; the espousals of St. Catharine, by Corregio; and the celebrated Zingana, or gipsey, by the same master. This figure was accidentally so called from the brown complexion it had when first painted; but it is a picture of the virgin Mary in a wild, desert, country on her flight to Egypt. Here are also Lucretia, by Parmeggiano, and a remarkable copy of a protrait of pope Leo X. executed in such a masterly manner by Andrea del Sarto, that it is preferred by the Parmesans to the original, which is in the possession of the great duke of Tuscany. This copy is said not only to have deceived Vasari, but even Giulio Romano himself, who, though he worked on the drapery of the original by Raphael, when, some time after, he saw this copy at Parma, took it for Raphael's piece, and imagined he could distinguish in it some strokes of his own pencil, as Felibien tells us, in his Lives of celebrated painters. Pope Clement VII, who was of the house of Medicis, promised the original picture to one of the dukes of Mantua; who paid his holiness a visit, and asked him for it. But the cunning Florentine, being very unwilling, upon second thoughts, to part with such an exquisite piece, contrived to put the duke off with a copy of it (which is that we are speaking of) and kept the original still at Florence. This instance renders something dubious that infallible certainty, which many connoisseurs pretend to, of immediately telling us, upon seeing any celebrated picture, the name of the artist that painted it.

Remarkable copy of a picture.

Near the picture gallery is a smaller apartment, which, as it contains many costly and valuable curiosities, may be called a museum, or treasury. Here are several cabinets, tables, and clocks of plain and raised Florentine work, and one embellished with admirable sculpture, and set with gems; two tables of rock-crystal, adorned with figures, one of which has a silver border gilt, and the other is embellished with flowers of enamel and gold; several marble and agate vases; a fine hanger set with very valuable jewels, among which is a chrysolite of the bigness of a large bean; several caskets ornamented with enamel and gems; paintings on *lapis lazuli*, and curious works in ivory. Among the last are several crucifixes, where the whole body of our Saviour, the arms

Museum.

arms excepted, is made of a single piece. Here is an assortment of mother-of-pearl, curiously wrought; another of amber, and a closet full of pieces of rock crystal, most of which were brought from the country of the Grisons. Some of these pieces are near the bigness of a man's head; and in this closet is an intire set of altar furniture of crystal, with a casket of crystal, several crystal pillars, and a remarkable piece of the same, resembling a mountain dividing itself into two forked tops, which weighs near a thousand pounds. It has not indeed the finest lustre; but, as to its largeness, I question whether its equal can be produced in any part of the world. The largest piece of crystal known in Pliny's time weighed no more than fifty pounds, and was presented by Livia to the capitol as a very extraordinary curiosity *. *Extraordinary large pieces of crystal.*

Adjoining to this museum is an apartment filled with shells, ancient inscriptions, busts, and lamps; Egyptian, Greek, and Roman idols. Not long since the paintings in *fresco* discovered at Rome in the Farnesian gardens, and supposed to have belonged to Nero's apartments, were also brought hither. The figures of men represented in these paintings are not designed in the best manner; the faces are scarce distinguishable, and the colours at present quite faded. In my opinion it would be doing injustice to the ancients to form an idea of their skill in painting from such pieces; for though, probably, antiquity produced no paintings which can rival the works of Raphael and some other modern artists; yet their painters could not but draw great advantages from the flourishing state of sculpture, in which the ancients deserve the highest applause. *Antiquities. Paintings in fresco belonging to Nero's apartments.*

In a cabinet in this room is kept a missal curiously illuminated and painted, at the end of which is an altar painted in miniature, and inscribed with these words:

Julius Clovius Monumenta hæc Alexandro Farnesio Domino suo faciebat M.D.XL.VI.

' Julius Clovius painted these memorials for Alessandro Farnese, his patron, in the year 1546.'

Concerning the works of this Clovius mention has already been made in my account of the Vatican library. These

* Plin. Hist. Nat. lib. xxxvii. cap. 2.

paintings have been also retouched by P. Ramelli, who died very lately.

Righino the painter. As to the theatrical and perspective paintings, Parma may may now boast of a masterly hand in Righino, a native of that city.

Stables. The duke's stables consist of several separate buildings; and near them are also kept the state coaches, &c. both of ancient and modern times, many of which are very superb.

Disposition of the academy de' Nobili. Duke Rainutius I, besides the university erected in 1599, also founded an academy in 1601 for persons of noble families, in which young students from their childhood are instructed not only in grammar, the classics, rhetoric, philosophy, mathematics, geography, history, divinity, the civil, feodal, and canon law; but likewise in the German, French, and Spanish languages; in music, painting, fortification, dancing, fencing, vaulting, and riding. This academy is under the direction of the Jesuits; and the annual allowance to every student for board, lodging, washing, fire and candle, attendance, and instruction is about a hundred *filippi* *, one of which is equal to nine *paoli* and a half. The riding-school is furnished with horses from the duke's stables, to the number of twenty or thirty; and only a *ducatoon*, or *scudo* †, is given every month to the head groom. For other arts, as painting, fortification, &c. they pay about four *paoli* ‡ a month; and the gratuities to servants, contributions to the chapel, feasts, comedies, and the carnival diversions may amount to about four *ducatoons* ‖ a year.

The morning lectures generally take up two hours and a half, and those of the afternoon about three. The students are divided into *camerate*, or classes, of ten or thirteen; and every *camerata* has a servant and monitor, which must be an ecclesiastic. There are at present a hundred and thirty young noblemen, either counts or barons, in this college; but the foundation admits of two hundred and fifty students. Youth of all nations are received here indiscriminately; but with regard to birth they must be noble, and such as are capable of being admitted among the knights of Malta. When they walk about the city, the students are dressed in black; but in hunting, and during the festivities in autumn, they are allowed to wear cloaths of any colour. That student

---

* A *filip* is about four shillings and ninepence sterling. † A crown. ‡ Two shillings. ‖ About a guinea.

who

PARMA.

who fignalizes himfelf moft by his exercifes, &c. is ftiled *principe*, and has a particular refpect paid him by the reft. He likewife wears a medal hanging at a purple ribbon with a filver border, on his breaft.

There are two elegant theatres in the college, in one of which the ftudents act plays during the carnival; at other times they allow the players to perform in them. The autumn vacation they fpend at one of the duke's country-feats in fifhing, hunting, and other innocent paftimes; but under the care of proper directors: nor are their ftudies quite laid afide during this feafon. The duke and the principal nobility of the city lend their coaches and horfes to carry the ftudents into the country; and, at the expiration of the time allowed them, they are brought back in the fame manner.

The cupola of the cathedral is admirably painted by Correggio, and reprefents the affumption of the virgin Mary. In this piece the noble invention of the painter, the delicacy of the ftrokes of his pencil, and the beauty of the colouring cannot be fufficiently extolled. Copper-plates of this cupola are fold at Rome by Roffi for two *fcudi* and a half. This work is intitled *La Cupola di Parma, cioè la virgine affunta in gloria con cori d' Angeli e Santi fra le nubi e fplendori celefti, gli Apoftoli, i Santi Dottori cogli altri Angeli e Putti, con candelieri e odori, difegnata e intagliata in acqua forte da Giov. Battifta Vanni*, and is comprifed in fifteen fheets of imperial paper. *Cathedral cupola painted by Correggio.*

In the large fubterraneous vault under this church is feen the ftately monument of S. Bernardo degli Uberti, a native of Florence, and bifhop of Parma. In the area before the church, as before many other churches in this part of Italy, ftand the figures of feveral lions, which fupport the pillars of the portico. The baptiftery, or particular chapel for adminiftering baptifm, ftands clofe by the cathedral. It is an octangular, lofty, fpacious ftructure, and refembles the baptiftery at Pifa. The font is of one intire piece of white marble, and the baluftrade round it is of yellow marble. In this chapel are to be feen feveral ancient pieces of painting, which are very much valued. *Monument of Bern. degli Uberti. Chapel for baptifm.*

Not far from the cathedral ftands the Chiefa di S. Giovanni which has an elegant front, a tribuna decorated with fculpture and gilding, and two fine organs erected oppofite to each other. The cupola of this church, as well as that of the cathedral, was painted by Corregio, and reprefents the *Church of St. Giovanni.*

virgin

virgin Mary crowned by God the Father and the Son. But when the Benedictiae monks, to whom this church belongs, thought proper to widen the choir, the cupola was broken down: however, before that happened, copies were taken of the paintings with which it was adorned by Annibal and Auguſtino Caracci; and from thoſe copies the preſent cupola was painted by Ceſare Aretuſi. The copies painted by the two Caracci's are kept in the duke's palace. Corregio worked on the original paintings in the old cupola from the year 1520 to 1524 *.

Proper name of Parmeggiano the painter. The aſcenſion or aſſumption of the virgin Mary over the high altar is the work of Parmeggiano, whoſe proper name was Franceſco (or, as others will have it, Giacomo) Mazzuoli; and by that name he is diſtinguiſhed from his uncle Girolamo Mazzuoli, who was alſo an eminent painter.

His misfortune. According to Vaſſari's account, Franceſco Mazzuoli, or Parmeggiano, was unhappily ſeduced by alchymiſtical chimera's, ſo that he neglected his proper art, and at laſt he loſt his reputation, his eaſe, and his life.

The above-mentioned high altar is inſulated or detached from the wall, and ſet with *lapis lazuli*, agate, and curious ſorts of fine marble. The ſtalls in the choir are of wood beautifully inlaid. In the Capella della Madonna are to be ſeen two original paintings by Corregio, and two copies of his famous night-piece and Madonna, which are in the ducal palace at Modena.

Church del Sepolcro. In the church del Sepolcro is likewiſe to be ſeen, in a chapel near the entrance on the right hand, the virgin Mary with her divine infant, and Joſeph. Oppoſite to this is a picture of Joſeph exhorting Mary to eſcape to Egypt; both by Corregio.

S. Antonio l'Abbate. In the church of S. Antonio l' Abbate is a fine piece by the ſame maſter, repreſenting St. Jerome and the virgin Mary, with the infant Jeſus, and St. Mary Magdalene worſhipping him.

Madonna della Steccata. The church of Madonna della Steccata is elegantly built, and is adorned with four ſmall cupola's, painted in *freſco* by Parmeggiano.

Capuchin church. The monuments of ſeveral princes of the houſe of Farneſe are to be ſeen in the Capuchin church. Under the arch or vault where the ſarcophagus of the celebrated hero Aleſſandro Farneſe lies, is the following inſcription:

* See Richardſon's treatiſe on painting and ſculpture.

* *Pro*

PARMA.

'* *Pro partis Victoriis in Belgio clarus,*   Alex. Far-
Pro Christianis virtutibus in cœlo clarior,   nese's epi-
Et Sereniſſima ejus Uxor Maria Luſitana,   taph.
Quomodo in vitâ suâ dilexerunt ſe,
Ita et in morte non ſunt ſeparati.
Hæc ambos urna capit;
Et quos pietas fecerat ſimiles,
Sepulchrum facit æquales.
Obiit Ille anno MDXCII. Hæc autem M. D. LXXVII.

' In this urn lies a prince famous for his victories in the
' Low-countries, but more illuſtrious in heaven for his
' Chriſtian virtues, together with his moſt ſerene conſort
' Mary, a princeſs of Portugal; who, as in life they loved
' each other, in death are not divided; for thoſe who re-
' ſembled each other in piety, are equally commemorated by
' theſe monumental honours. He died in the year 1592;
' and his conſort 1577.

On the pavement of the church near the door, juſt over the grave, are theſe words:

D. O. M.
Alexander Farneſius,
Belgis devictis,
Francifque obſidione levatis,
Ut
Humili hoc loco
Ejus cadaver reponeretur
Mandavit.
III. Non. Decemb. MDXCII.
Et
Ut ſecum Mariæ Luſitanæ
Conjugis optimæ oſſa
Jungerentur, illius
Teſtamentum ſecutus,
Annuit.

' To God the greateſt and beſt of beings.'
' Aleſſandro Farneſe, after defeating the Flemings and

' relieving

---

* I ſuppoſe Alexander Farneſius muſt be inſerted here to make the ſenſe complete, though it is omitted in the German edition.

'relieving the French who were besieged, ordered his body to be laid in this humble place on the third of December 1592. And, in compliance with her last will, consented that the remains of his dear wife Mary of Portugal should be deposited in the same grave.'

Here are likewise some good paintings by Guercino, Annibal Caracci, and Augustino Carracci; the last of these artists lies buried in this church.

Duke's revenues. Salt-works. The yearly revenues of the duke of Parma are computed at five hundred and fifty thousand *scudi* or crowns sterling. It is said, the salt-works alone, all charges deducted, yield above fifty thousand *scudi*. They are carried on at Salso, about twenty-four Italian miles from Parma; where there are twelve wells or pits of salt-water, which are two hundred ells in depth. The water being drawn out of the wells is boiled in large caldrons till it evaporates, and begins to coagulate or break so as to produce salt. After this it is mixed with putrified bullocks blood; and that of other animals, and the whole is boiled together for about an hour, and carefully skimmed all the while. By this process a pure and white salt is obtained. The mixture of blood with the salt-water I had seen practised at Hall in Saxony, and some other parts of Germany; but did not think it was used for refining salt in any other country in Europe, as this method is intirely unknown at Luneburg and other salt-works. It is indeed pretended, that the volatile salts with which the blood of animals is replete, purify the salt-water drawn from wells, and help to precipitate the heterogeneous particles; however, this may be effected by many other ingredients, without making use of blood.

For which blood is used.

Mineral springs. At Lisignano, which lies twelve Italian miles from Parma, are two medicinal springs of mineral water.

Petroleum. Petroleum is found in several places in the Parmesan territories; sometimes without water, as at Miano and Vizzole; sometimes floating on the surface of the water in wells, as at Ozzono, St. Andrea, Fornovo, Ribiano, Lisignano, Torre, Saffo, and Calestano.

Crystals. In some veins of loam and chalk near Bardi, sexangular crystals are frequently found, and also a few petrifactions.

Parmesan cheese. The excellency of the Parmesan cheese, so celebrated at all the elegant tables in Europe, proceeds from the excellent pastures in this country; particularly those about Placentia, where the meadows during the whole summer may be watered at pleasure, by means of small sluices which convey

vey water from the Po. Besides, the waters of that river are impregnated with a slimy subſtance, which proves a very good manure to the grounds which they overflow. The cows here yield an uncommon quantity of milk, so that in a good season the milk of fifty cows will make a rich cheese of a hundred weight every day. But within a few miles of this fertile tract of land, which does not extend above ten Italian miles in length, the cows do not yield such plenty of milk as they do in the Parmesan; nor is it so rich. But as in Germany great quantities of Dutch cheeses are sold, which never were in Holland, so likewise many thousands of pounds of cheese made in Lodi, Trino, Bologna, &c. pass under the name of Parmesan; especially as the peasants about Lodi, in the Milanese, have the like advantage of watering their meadows, so as to mow them four or five times a year. There are three kinds of Parmesan cheese: 1. Formaggio di Forma, which is commonly two palms in diameter and about eight inches thick. 2. Formaggio di Robiole, and 3. Formaggio di Robiolini. Sometimes saffron is used for colouring these cheeses, and half an ounce suffices for a hundred of them. Parmesan cheese is in great perfection when it is three or four years old; and that which crumbles in cutting is reckoned the best.

At Vianino, near the Appenine mountains, a very palatable cheese is made of sheeps-milk.

The distance from Parma to Placentia is about thirty-three Italian miles, and about five miles from the former there is a ferry over the river Taro. A little way farther, on the left-hand, lies Castello Guelfo, which is still inhabited: not far from it stands Castello Gibellino. Both these castles derive their names from the two factions by which Germany and Italy were for a long time made a scene of slaughter and confusion *. Caſtello Guelfo and Caſtello Gibellino.

Borgo S. Donnino which is the next poſt-ſtage, though it be a very mean place, is an epiſcopal ſee. The country about this town abounds in truffles. The road here is very good and exceeding pleaſant all the way, like that from Fa- Borgo S. Donnino.

* Concerning the origin of the names of Guelphs and Gibellines, the Italians have publiſhed ſeveral ridiculous fictions, *vide Sigon. de regn. Ital. c. 13. Philipp. Bergam. ad an.* 1234. *Trithem. chron. Hirſaug. ad an.* 1140. The true epocha of theſe appellations is to be dated from the year 1140, when, at the battle near Wicſberg, the oppoſite parties of duke Guelph and Conrad diſtinguiſhed themſelves by the military words *Hye Welff* and *Hye Gibelingen*. See *Andr. Presbyter. chron. Buvar. p.* 25. *Adlzweiter annal. Boi. P. I. lib.* 21. and *Eccard. de uſu & praeſt. etymol.* § 5.

enza

Rainutio Farnefio
Placentiæ, Parmæ, &c. Duci IIII.
S. R. E. Gonfalonerio perpetuo
Cuſtodi juſtitiæ,
Cultori æquitatis,
Ob
Opifices allectos,
Populum auctum,
Patriam illuſtratam,
Placentia Civitas
Principi Optimo
Equeſtrem Statuam
D. D.

' To Rainucel Farneſe, fourth duke of Placentia, Parma,
' &c. the beſt of princes, the patron of juſtice and equity,
' the city of Placentia, in gratitude for his care in procuring
' the moſt ingenious artificers, in promoting the glory of his
' country, and increaſing the number of his ſubjects, has
' erected and dedicated this equeſtrian ſtatue.'

Theſe inſcriptions, with ſeveral others, ſhew that the Placentians give themſelves the preference to the Parmeſans. The Scots, in the title of thoſe kings, who, at the ſame time were kings of England, were guilty, but in a greater degree, of the ſame arrogance.

The caſtle of Placentia is but improperly ſo called, and the city is not capable of making any defence. The river Po runs at the diſtance of five or ſix hundred paces from Placentia; and the whole diſtrict, on account of which the city is very juſtly called Piacenza, *i. e.* pleaſantneſs, exhibits a delightful proſpect from the top of one of the towers in the city. The high-ſtreet, called Stradone, is five and twenty common paces broad, and three thouſand feet long in a direct line; but the buildings are not anſwerable.

In St. Sixtus's church, which belongs to the Benedictines, is to be ſeen a fine picture in which Raphael has repreſented the virgin Mary with St. Sixtus and St. Barba. The ſtalls in the choir are of wood finely inlaid, and it is furniſhed with two fine organs, erected oppoſite to each other. On one ſide of the high altar this inſcription is cut in marble, *Engilberga Auguſta Hludovici Germ. Reg. F. Hludovici Pii Aug. Neptis, Karoli M. Aug. Proneptis, Hludovici II. Aug. Conjux*; ſignifying,

nifying, 'That Engilberga Augusta, the daughter of Ludo-
'vic king of Germany, grand-daughter of Ludovic the pi-
'ous and august, great-grandaughter of Charles the great
'and august, and wife to Ludovic II. the august, founded
'this church.' Near this altar is to be seen a large sepul- Monument
chral monument of white and black marble, on which are of M...et
two lions, two statues of women, and two of men, all of of Austria.
white marble, together with the Austrian and Farnese arms.
There is no inscription on the monument itself; but, probably, it was erected in honour of Margaret of Austria, the
wife of duke Ottavio Farnese, and mother to the celebrated
hero Alessandro Farnese. Close by it on the left hand, as
you go towards the altar, are the following words:

Margaretæ Austriacæ
Caroli V. Aug. F.
Octavii Farn. Plac. & Parm. Ducis II.
Uxori
Alexandri Max. Ducis III. Matri,
Rainutii Ducis IV. Aviæ,
Majoribus, Viro, & Sobole felicissimæ,
Rarissimi exempli fœminæ,
Rebusque in Belgio gestis
Insigni,
Quòd in Samnio decedens ossa sua
In hanc ædem transferri jussit,
Quódque eidem pretiosam supellectilem
Et cœnobio in pios usus pecuniam
Legavit,
Abbas & Monachi pos.
MDCXVII.

'To Margaret of Austria, daughter of Charles V. the
'august, wife of Ottavio Farnese, second duke of Placentia
'and Parma, mother of Alessandro the great, third duke,
'and grandmother of Rainucci, the fourth duke, who was
'remarkably happy in her ancestors, her husband, and her
'descendants; a woman whose exemplary piety was equalled
'by few, and famous for her noble actions in the Nether-
'lands, &c. who left her rich furniture and a large sum of
'money to this convent for pious uses; the abbots and
'monks erected this monument in 1617.

This lady was a natural daughter of the emperor Charles Account of
V. and in her fourteenth year was married to the first duke of her.
Florence,

enza and Bologna. It runs in a straight line with fine inclosures on both sides, which are divided by rows of fruit-trees interwoven with vines; particularly the part that leads from Reggio (which has been already described) to Placentia, where the country is so delightfully cultivated, that it has the appearance of a large garden or orchard. In such a charming fertile country, it may be supposed, that the clergy have not neglected to procure fat benefices and large endowments. Accordingly I have been assured, that, of the twenty-eight thousand inhabitants of the territories of Placentia, two thousand are ecclesiastics, monks, nuns, &c. On the fifth day of April the great yearly fair commences, and lasts a fortnight. Placentia fair is accounted the largest in all Italy; but it is not to be compared with the fairs held in Germany. The stands and booths take up a very large area near the ducal palace, which is laid out in regular lanes or passages, which are covered with canvas, as a shelter both against rain and the heat of the sun. The best entertainment in Placentia, during the fair, was the opera, where three of the best singers in Italy performed the vocal part, namely, Carlo Broschi, detto Farinelli, Giovanni Carestini, and Francesca Cuzzoni Sandoni. A person is admitted into the pit for a *paolo* *. One inconveniency that attended this diversion was, that the opera did not begin till ten o'clock at night, and was not over till near four in the morning. The duke and dutchess of Parma, with a very numerous retinue, were present. The duke, as to his person, is very corpulent, though he has formerly used a great deal of exercise, as riding and hunting, &c. to bring down his fat. But, as at present his corpulency will not bear any violent motion, he passes most of his time in reading and conversation †. He is very affable to strangers, and during the opera several persons were admitted into his box. The dutchess is of the duke of Modena's family. They live very happily together, and their only concern is the want of a male heir ‡. The court generally resides at Parma, the air of that city being reckoned more salubrious than that of Placentia. The ducal palace at the former is also larger and more commodious than that of Placentia.

Great number of ecclesiastics in Placentia.
Annual fair.
The present duke of Parma.

* Sixpence.
† Since this author wrote, the dutchy of Parma is become subject to a prince of the house of Bourbon.
‡ Duke Antonio, who succeeded his brother Francesco in the year 1727, died on the 20th of January 1731.

On

PLACENTIA.

On the area before the town-houfe are two bronze eque- Equeftrian
ftrian ftatues, and on each of the pedeftals, which are of ftatue of
ftone, two bronze baffo relievo's with an infcription in brafs Alexander Farnefe.
under each of them. One ftatue, which is much fuperior
to the other, reprefents duke Aleffandro Farnefe, and the
baffo relievo's on the pedeftal exhibit the fiege of Antwerp,
and the raifing of that of Paris, with the following infcription on two fides of it :

Alexandro Farnefio
Placentiæ, Parmæ, &c. Duci III.
S. R. E.
Gonfalonerio perpetuo
Belgis devictis Belgico,
Gallis obfidione levatis Gallico,
Placentia Civitas,
Ob ampliffima accepta beneficia,
Ob Placentinum nomen
Sui nominis gloriâ
Ad ultimas ufque gentes
Propagatum,
Invicto Domino fuo
Equeftri hâc ftatuâ
Sempiternum voluit extare monimentum.

' To Aleffandro Farnefe, third duke of Placentia, Parma,
' &c. the conqueror of the Netherlands, to whom Paris the
' capital of France owed its relief, the city of Placentia in
' gratitude for the many great benefits received from him,
' and for his propagating the honour of Placentia by his il-
' luftrious name to the remoteft part of the globe, have erec-
' ted this equeftrian ftatue, as to their invincible fovereign,
' and as a perpetual monument of his glory.'

Under the other ftatue which is that of Rainucci I. are Rainutius
the following words : the Firft,

Rainutio

PLACENTIA.

Florence, Aleffandro de Medicis, who was a natural fon of Lorenzo de Medicis duke of Urbino, or, according to others, of pope Clement VII. But he being foon after murdered, in the year 1538, fhe was again married to the duke of Parma; her fecond hufband being hardly fourteen years of age, and fhe fcarce entered into her feventeenth year. After the death of Charles V. fhe was appointed governefs of the Netherlands, in the year 1559; which high ftation fhe difcharged with fo much prudence, for the fpace of eight years, that probably the Spanifh affairs in that country would have taken a better turn, had her advice been followed by the miniftry. She was not only remarkable for her firmnefs and refolution, but was alfo famous for her bodily ftrength, and is faid to have had a beard like that of a man. She died, in the year 1586, at Ortona in the kingdom of Naples, as appears by the infcription quoted above, which fays that Margaret died at Samnium, the ancient name of that city.

St. Auguftine's church. The church of St. Auguftine is remarkable for its fine nave and fpacious ifles. Here are alfo feveral pieces in ftucco-work, and, in the veftry, the crucifixion finely cut in wood.

S. Maria in Campagna. S. Maria in Campagna is one of the beft churches in the city, and is adorned with a great many pieces of painting by Georgione, Paolo Veronefe, Aleffandro Tiarini, and Pordenone.

S. Sabino. S. Sabino's church is remarkable for its fine organ, and for a certain feftival, at which feafon the church is for fome days ornamented with a furprifing quantity of rich furniture and plate: And on the middle of the great altar, which then looks like a magnificent fide-board, is a kind of pyramid of large filver difhes, &c.

Salt-works. Vitriol. Iron. There are in the dutchy of Placentia a great number of falt-works. A confiderable quantity of vitriol is alfo gathered and refined there; and fome iron forges have likewife been fet on foot in this country near the Appenines, where they have alfo begun to work in copper.

Petrifactions. Among the petrifactions of this country the Dentales are remarkably beautiful, and well preferved.

LETTER

LETTER LXVIII.

Journey to CREMONA and MANTUA.

SIR,

FROM Placentia to Cremona is a journey of eighteen Italian miles, along a fruitful well cultivated country; but the road is not so pleasant, nor kept in such good repair as the Via Æmilia leading to Placentia.

Road to Cremona.

In the way to Cremona the Po is ferried over; there being no bridge over this river below Turin. It is here about the breadth of the Rhine at Manheim; but a little lower it grows much wider. According to Burnet's computation, in his theory of the earth, the Po hourly discharges into the gulph of Venice eighteen millions of cubic feet of water; which, however, I shall not dispute with him.

River Po.

Cremona is an university, which was founded by the emperor Sigismund; but is now in a very declining condition. The fortifications of this city are at present of no importance; and it owes a great part of its reputation to the attempt made on this place by prince Eugene, in the year 1702. By means of a correspondence carried on betwixt the Imperialists and some of the townsmen, and particularly with an ecclesiastic of the name of Cosoli, who was curate of S. Maria Nuovo, a church that stood near the ramparts, he got possession of the Porta Santa and Palazzo Publico, or town-house, where marshal Villeroy resided; and on the first of February entered the city by a canal or aqueduct, through which formerly the French had also surprised this place. But unfortunately the troops which were to support this bold enterprize, having lost their way by the darkness of the night and a fog, came up too late; and gave the French (to whom the Irish brigades, by furiously attacking the Germans, performed signal service) time to recover from their panic, and put themselves in a posture of defence: so that the Imperialists were obliged to retreat; contenting themselves with the honour of carrying off Villeroy prisoner from a garrison of six thousand men. The French, in the first transport of their rage against Cosoli, pulled down the church of S. Maria Nuova to the ground; so that nothing of it is now to be seen. But near the place where the church stood, not far from the Porta Santa, is shewn the subterraneous

Cremona. University. Fortification.

Prince Eugene's attempt in 1702.

Bravery of the Irish.

neous passage through which the Germans entered the city; it is now secured with a strong iron gate.

There are in Cremona a great many towers and steeples; but the highest of them does not deserve the encomiums commonly bestowed on it; for Italy affords a great many towers which not only equal, but surpass it in height. There goes a story that the emperor Sigismund and pope John XXII. once ascended this tower, attended by Gabrino Fundolia, the sovereign of the city; and that the latter afterwards said, 'He repented of nothing so much as that he had not thrown down the civil and temporal heads of Christendom from the top of it, and by that means immortalized his name, in imitation of Erostratus, who set fire to the famous temple of Diana at Ephesus.'

A remarkable instance of false ambition.

Cathedral. In the cathedral is a handsome monument erected to the memory of cardinal Francesco Sfondrato, adorned with fine basso-relievo's; and likewise some paintings by celebrated masters. Before the entrance of the church are two lions, each supporting a pillar. The like also is to be seen before the baptistery, which is a large, lofty, octangular building, with two galleries round the upper part of it.

Dominican church. The Dominican church is adorned with some good paintings, and a superb altar made of *lapis lazuli*, agate, and beautiful marble. On the cieling is seen a picture of the Madonna, who, in token of her peculiar protection, lays her mantle over three monks, and as many nuns, of the Dominican order. In the area before the church is a statue of St. Dominic holding a cross in his right-hand, and in his left a dog with a lighted torch in his mouth. Under it is the following inscription:

Image of St. Dominic.

S. Dominico.
Ord. Præd.ᵐ SS. Ros.ⁱ ac S. Inq.ⁱˢ Instit.
Fidei Reparatori ac Orbis,
Viro
Pietate eximio, Charitate optimo, Religione maximo,
Patri
Devotissimus filius posuit
M.DCCXXII.

'To St. Dominic, founder of the order of the predicants of the most sacred rosary, and of the holy inquisition; the restorer both of the faith, and reformer of the world; a man eminently distinguished for his extraordina-

'ry piety, extensive charity, and zeal for religion, one of
'his most dutiful sons, as to the father of his order, erected
'this statue in the year 1722.'

St. Peter's church, which belongs to the canons regular, *St. Peter's*
is a beautiful structure, adorned with elegant paintings. *church.*
Here is kept the body of St. Mary of Egypt, who, after *Body of S. Maria*
she had spent a dissolute life in her youth, became a perfect *Ægyptiaca.*
pattern of repentance and mortification. Her picture over
the altar is not black; and they are very much mistaken
who do not distinguish this saint from the virgin Mary, because in some places she is represented of a black complexion: the latter is particularly called Madonna di Loretto.

The Augustines have a good library in their convent, and *Augustines*
their church also exhibits several good pieces of painting. *church.*

The distance from Cremona to Mantua is forty Italian
miles; and about the midway between these two cities lies
a pretty little town called Bozzolo. It is fortified with a *Bozzolo.*
castle, and is the chief place of a small principality of that
name. Three miles from thence we passed near S. Martino
di Marcaria over the Oglio, which is a considerable river. *The Oglio.*
In winter, after great rains, the road between Cremona and
Mantua is almost impassable, because of the softness and *Bad roads.*
depth of the soil; as when we travelled there after a long
drought it was but very indifferent. This inconveniency *Delightful*
is fully compensated by the exuberant fertility of the whole *country.*
country; and a person cannot sufficiently admire the ver-
dure of the fields and meadows, which are divided by beautiful rows of trees, with abundance of vines twining round
their trunks and branches. The great number of nightin-
gales that frequent this tract of land, by their plaintive
warblings at this season of the year, make the charming
scene still more delightful. Indeed a person who makes any *Satiety of*
stay in Italy is so accustomed to fine prospects and enchant- *fine pros-*
ing landscapes, that in time they grow familiar to the eye, *pects.*
and are less regarded than when they first presented themselves to his view. I am certain, however, that a native of
the mountainous parts of Franconia, Tirol, Saltzburg, the
forest of Hartz, the hilly parts of Saxony, or those who
have always lived in the woods of Thuringen and Pomera-
nia, the sandy parts of Silesia, the margraviate of Brandenburg and Mecklenberg, or on the wild uncultivated heaths
of Luneburg and Westphalia, must feel an uncommon emo-
tion,

MANTUA.

tion, and be enraptured with a kind of vernal delight, when the enchanting scenes of Italy first strike their admiring eyes.

Mantua. Mantua lies in a lake or morass, caused by the overflowing of the river Mincio. On the side towards Cremona this morass is not above two or three hundred paces wide; but on the opposite side of the city it is about an Italian mile in breadth. The river Mincio runs through Mantua, which is fortified with a good citadel, but otherwise is more indebted to nature than art for its strength. Claudian, in *Sexto Conf. Hon.* not improperly, calls the river Mincio,

The river Mincio.

———— *tardusque meatu*
Mincius ————

' The slow-winding Mincius *;'

Unhealthy air. And the vapours arising in the summer from the stagnant putrid waters about this city render the air so unhealthful, that no-body would stay in Mantua during that season, who could go any where else. This city contains eighteen parish churches, and fourteen convents, which are undoubtedly too many for a place that, exclusive of the imperial garrison (consisting at present of three or four thousand men) has not above ten thousand inhabitants. The number of Jews at Mantua is supposed to be four or five thousand; who have their Ghetto or particular quarter, the gate of which is shut every evening. They have also four or five synagogues here; and the principal synagogue is well built, and has a sky-light, or large aperture in the roof.

Number of churches and convents.

Christian inhabitants.

Jews.

Decay of trade. No court is kept here at present; and since the last war the place is very much fallen to decay; for a considerable trade was formerly carried on here, and the silk manufacture particularly brought large sums into the country. Of the flourishing condition and origin of Mantua in ancient times, Virgil speaks thus in his tenth Æneid:

* Virgil describes the Mincio in the same manner:

———— *Tardis ingens ubi flexibus errat*
Mincius, & tenerâ prætexit arundine ripas,

' Where the slow Mincio thro' the valley stray'd ;
' Where cooling streams invite the flocks to drink,
' And reeds defend the winding waters brink.'

DRYDEN.

Ille

MANTUA.

Ille etiam patriis agmen ciet Ocnus ab oris
Fatidicæ Mantûs, & Thusci filius amnis;
Qui muros, matrisque dedit tibi, Mantua, nomen:
Mantua dives avis, sed non genus omnibus unum.
Gens illi triplex, populi sub gente quaterni;
Ipsa caput populis, Thusco de sanguine vires.

Æn. x. v. 198.

' Ocnus was next, who led his native train
' Of hardy warriors thro' the wat'ry plain;
' The son of Manto, by the Tuscan stream,
' From whence the Mantuan town derives the name:
' An ancient city, but of mixt descent,
' Three sev'ral tribes compose the government.
' Four towns are under each; but all obey
' The Mantuan laws, and own the Tuscan sway.

DRYDEN.

The treasury and curious museum, founded here by the duke, made this city very famous in the last century; but, as the imperial general Colalto took the city by storm, and plundered it on the 18th of July, 1630, all the curiosities, which were worth some millions, fell into the hands of the soldiers, by whom they were partly destroyed, and partly dissipated, or sold to persons who knew little of the value of such things. At that time a common soldier was so lucky as to get a booty of eighty thousand ducats; but he was so bad an œconomist as to game it all away in one night, for which Colalto hanged him the next day. The few curiosities collected here since that time have fallen a prey to the public tumults that happened in the present century; the best part of them having fallen to the share of the French by way of plunder. However, some apartments in the castle are worth seeing, the cieling being painted by Giulio Romano, and in which are some tortoise-shell cabinets, several tables of Florentine work, inlaid with very beautiful pieces of *lapis lazuli* and agate; some marble statues and busts; a Moor's head on a pedestal of white marble, with a turban curiously inlaid, so as exactly to imitate a kind of Indian stuff; two large pieces of painting by Palma; two others by Costa; four large pictures, representing battles between the Turks and Christians; a female saint in a chapel, painted by Annibal Caracci. Here are also two galleries

Famous museum.

Punishment of prodigality.

Its present condition.

ries of protraits; three saloons, which are something dark, but well painted in fresco; however, but little care is taken to preserve them. The large gallery that was formerly full of all sorts of curiosities, contains nothing curious at present but four large globes, with two of a smaller size; the skin of a sea-ox stuffed, and an old picture of one of the Roman emperors, painted on wood, by Titian. The twelve Cæsars must have been of an inestimable value; but eleven of them are gone, and this is the only one left: the board on which it is painted is also split. Besides this flaw, the piece has been designedly damaged by some spiteful or ignorant person. In a closet are likewise kept the skeletons of several animals. The ducal palace is large and spacious; but old, and built without any symmetry or regularity. The grotto's in the garden are intirely gone to ruin. The best thing here is the academy, which indeed, for the grotto-work, pillars, sculpture, galleries, and height, has not its equal of the kind. The riding-course belonging to it is extremely well contrived.

Fine academy.

The palace church contains a rich treasury of reliques, gold and silver crucifixes, statues, and other altar-furniture. In it are also two large pictures, one of the baptism of Constantine the Great, and the other of the martyrdom of St. Andrew, both by Costa, otherwise called il Vecchio; and it is said that a thousand *Louis-d'ors* * have been offered for each of these pieces.

Palace church.
Paintings.

Mantua is an episcopal see immediately dependent on the pope. Giulio Romano was the architect of the cathedral, who also painted the Tribuna, and a part of the cieling. Here are also several pieces of painting by other celebrated masters, as the calling of Peter and Andrew to the apostleship; the martyrdom of a female saint, whose breasts are torn off with pincers; but the finest of all is a night-piece of S. Antonio del Fuoco by Paolo Veronese. This picture is in the upper vestry, and cannot be viewed without admiration. Among the figures in this piece, a fat comely woman is represented, such as Paolo Veronese seems to have been particularly fond of; as in his other pictures, and especially those of the marriage of Cana, all his figures are very plump, and of a florid complexion, and not one pale or meagre object is to be seen among them. Paul Rubens and Van Dyke, who generally looked upon Paolo Veronese as

Cathedral.

Masterly piece by P. Veronese.

* About 1000*l.* sterling.

MANTUA.

their pattern, have alſo imitated him in this particular. The cathedral is very ſpacious, and divided by rows of pillars into five iſles.

In the church of St. Agnes is to be ſeen a moſt beautiful *Ecce homo*, by Dolci. The tower of this church is obſerved to lean a little from the perpendicular. {St. Agnes's church. Its leaning tower.}

St. Andrew's church is accounted the principal in all Mantua for a large collection of reliques *. {St. Andrew's church.}

In a chapel on the left-hand in going into this church is a ſtatue of the famous painter Andrea Mantegna, in which ſmall diamonds once ſupplied the place of the pupils of the eyes; but they have been ſtolen away long ſince. The inſcription under it is as follows:

Eſſe parem noris, ſi non præponis, Apelli, {Epitaph on Andrea Mantegna.}
Ænea MANTINIÆ qui ſimulacra vides.

' Reader, if thou haſt ſeen the copper-plates engraved
' by Mantegna, thou wilt own that he was equal, if not
' ſuperior, to Apelles.'

On the pavement the following words are cut in ſtone:

Oſſa Andreæ Mantiniæ famoſiſſimi pictoris cum duobus filiis in ſepulchro per Andream Mantiniam nepotem ex filio conſtructo repoſita. MDLX.

' The bones of Andrea Mantegna, a moſt celebrated
' painter, with thoſe of his two ſons, were depoſited in this
' tomb, built by Andrea Mantegna his grandſon. 1560.'

Over the altar is a piece of painting by Mantegna, repreſenting the birth of John the Baptiſt. Andrea Mantegna, who was born in the year 1451, and died in 1517, is by ſome writers ſaid to have been the inventor of engraving on copper-plates; or rather, of the method of repreſenting paintings by prints: but this admits of ſome doubt. For when Valturi's treatiſe of the art of war, which was printed at Verona in the year 1472, and embelliſhed with a great number of plates, repreſenting arms, military machines, fortifications, &c. Andrea Mantegna was but a youth. From {Whether Mantegna invented copper-plates.}

---

* Some obſervations on a relique kept here are omitted in the tranſlation, as ſcholaſtic and trifling.

this and several other circumstances, it may be concluded, that Matteo Pasti was the engraver and printer of the figures in that work. It does not indeed appear that Mantegna had any share in the impression of Æsop's fables, which was published in verse in the year 1479: not to mention the book published by Coster at Haerlem in 1440; though it seems that the art which he invented rather consisted in taking an impression from a piece of wood, containing all the letters of one page (which is the invention we are speaking of) than any thing like our present printing, by which single letters or types are put together, and afterwards separated again. It must, however, be owned, that, if Mantegna was not the inventor, he at least made great improvements in this art.

Perforated bell. Near one of the side-doors of this church is a very large bell of brass, but not of a proportionate thickness, in which there are eight oblong holes, each of them being one foot broad, and three feet in length. The design of this whimsical piece is not known; for the fabulous story that formerly its sound was so long, as to throw pregnant women into labour, and contribute to their delivery, is too absurd to gain much credit.

Broad and lofty roof. St. Andrew's church is old, and contains no ornaments besides what I have taken notice of. The nave is of an extraordinary height, and is twenty-seven paces in breadth. The main door is ornamented with some fine marble basso-relievo's, representing flowers, &c.

St. Giles's church. In St. Giles's church lies Bernardo Tasso, father of Torquato Tasso, the celebrated Italian poet: of the monument of the latter I have spoken elsewhere.

Tomb of Battista of Mantua. Battista of Mantua, a celebrated divine, philosopher, and poet of the fifteenth century, who was general of the Carmelite order, lies in the Capella della Madonna, on the left-hand as you enter the church. I was surprised to find, that a person who had done so much credit both to the city, and to the order of which he was the head, was not honoured with a monument.

On the opposite side of the church, facing this chapel, is a marble basso-relievo, representing a kind of trophy consisting of a lute, a violin, a lyre, a trumpet, and other musical instruments; and in the center of it is the following epitaph on a female singer:

Inspice,

Inspice, Lege, Defle!
Catharina Martinella Romana,
Quæ vocis modulatione & flexu
Sirenum cantus facilè
Orbiumque cœlestium melos præcellebat,
Insigni ea virtute, morum suavitate,
Formâ, Lepore, ac Venustate
Ser. Vinc. Duci Mant.
Apprimè cara,
Acerbâ eheu morte sublata
Hoc tumulo
Beneficentissimi Principis jussu,
Repentino adhuc casu mærentis,
Æternum quiescit.
Nomen mundo, Deo vivat anima;
Obiit adolescentiæ suæ anno XVIII.
Die VIII. Mart.
MDCVIII.

Epitaph on a female singer.

' Behold this monument, read, and weep!
' Catharina Martinella, a native of Rome, who, by the
' sweetness and exquisite modulations of her voice, greatly
' surpassed the syrens, or even the harmony of the spheres,
' and by her extraordinary virtues, and sweetness of man-
' ners, her graceful mien, beauty, and wit endeared herself
' to his serene highness Vincenzo duke of Mantua, being
' snatched away in her early bloom, here enjoys an eternal
' rest. This tomb was erected by the above-mentioned be-
' neficent prince, whilst his grief was fresh for the loss of
' this amiable young lady. She died on the eighth day of
' March, 1608, in the eighteenth year of her age: may her
' fame live in this world, and her soul with God!'

No mention is made in this epitaph of the lady's chastity; for, as to the panegyric that she was *insigni virtuti*, many who know in what an extensive sense the words *virtù* and *virtuoso* are taken, will be apt to imagine that this incomparable lady was a favourite mistress of the duke, and that it was not the loss of a fine voice only which so extremely affected his highness.

In this church is also a marble monument of a person called Andreasio, which very well deserves a traveller's notice.

Andreasio's monument.

Giulio

MANTUA.

St. Barnabas's church. Guilio Romano lies in St. Barnabas's church, which belongs to the Servi S. Mariæ, or Servite monks; but, on account of the many alterations and repairs of that church, the spot where that celebrated artist lies is not known. Here is an admirable piece representing the marriage of Cana, by Carlo Cignani Bolognese. Near the church, and facing the Gonzague palace stands the house where Giulio Romano lived, which is distinguished by a fine statue of Mercury over the entrance.

Giulio Romano's house.

Dominican church. At the Jacobines or Dominicans I gave myself a great deal of trouble in looking after the tomb of John de Medicis, father of Cosmo I. duke of Florence, whom some suppose to have been buried there; but without success, though the monks very obligingly assisted me in the search. But I saw there a fine marble monument of Pietro Strozzi, and some exquisite pieces of sculpture in wood, both in the choir and in the vestry. The remains of a saint called Ossana Andreassa is kept here with great devotion.

Theatine church. Its paintings. About the high altar of the Theatine church hang seven large pieces of painting by Guercino. Here is also a piece representing a martyr kneeling before the executioner, and presenting his head to be struck off, by Luigi Caracci, who also painted a duplicate of it for the cathedral; it stands between two fine pictures by Massari, a disciple of Caracci.

St. Theresia's church. The church of St. Theresia is remarkable for its altar and tabernacle of curious inlaid work of agate, and the finest sorts of marble. On each stands an angel and another statue.

Chiesa di quarante Hore. The Chiesa di quartane Hore has a beautiful front, and contains several good pieces of painting, and eight statues, representing David, Solomon, and some of the prophets, made of plaster, by the celebrated Barbarigo. On the outside of this church, over the entrance, is a basso-relievo of the annunciation, with a statue on each side of it.

Palazzo della Giustizia. In il Palazzo della Giustizia is a saloon that is remarkably large. In the wall is a statue of Virgil, sitting; but the artist was not so expert in sculpture as Virgil was in poetry.

Private palaces. Among the private edifices the principal are the palaces of count Manzelli, Valenti and Benedetto Sorti.

Suburbs. The city of Mantua has three suburbs on the other side of the lake, namely, Porta Fortessa towards the north, il Borgo di S. Giorgia towards the north-east, and il Thé towards the south. In the last suburb stands the Porta Virgiliana, over which is to be seen the bust of Virgil. Half a league from thence lies il Palazzo di Thé, so called from its

Porta Virgiliana.
Il Palazzo di Thé.

being

VERONA.

being built in the form of the letter T. The imperial cuiraſſiers are quartered on the ground-floor of of this palace at preſent, who, it may well be ſuppoſed, will not leave it better than they found it. More care has been taken of the upper apartments, on account of the fine paintings in *freſco*; for they are always locked up. Giulio Romano drew the plan and elevation of this palace; and moſt of the pictures were painted from his deſigns, and not a few of them received the finiſhing ſtrokes from his pencil. The moſt admired pieces are the fall of Phaeton, and Jupiter's victory over the giants.

In going from the Porta Virgiliana, the left-hand road leads to the dukes menagery, which lies two Italian miles from Mantua, and in the way the Mincio is ferried over. This place alſo is called Virgiliana; and there is a tradition that the poet, from whom it derives its name, uſed to ſtudy here in a grotto. But at preſent it affords nothing worth a traveller's notice. Near it lies the village Pietola, anciently called Andes, which was the birth-place of Virgil. *Virgil's birth-place.*

MANTUA, April 26, 1730.

LETTER LXIX.

Account of the City of VERONA.

SIR,

THE diſtance from Mantua to Verona is three poſt-ſtages, or four and twenty Italian miles. On this road, within ten miles of the latter, lies Villa Franca, where are ſtill to be ſeen the walls of a ſpacious old caſtle, or palace. On the left-hand, the mountains of Trent, which are covered with ſnow, begin to preſent themſelves to the view. The road is ſomething ſtony, and the ſoil ſhallow and poor; however, the rows of mulberry-trees and vines, with which it is planted, give the country a pleaſant aſpect. *Villa Franca.*

Verona has been celebrated in the following diſtich: *Praiſes of Verona.*

Urbibus Italiæ præſtat Verona ſuperbis
Ædibus, Ingeniis, Flumine, Fonte, Lacu.

' Verona

VERONA.

'Verona furpaffes all the cities of Italy for fuperb buildings, the genius of its inhabitants, its river, fountain, and lake.'

Another poet has expreffed himfelf in thefe lines:

> *Verona qui te viderit,*
> *Et non amarit protinus*
> *Amore perditiffimo,*
> *Is, credo, feipfum non amat,*
> *Caretque amandi fenfibus*
> *Et edit omnes gratias.*

'Verona, whoever fees thy beauties, and is not paffionately enamoured of thy charms, I am apt to think, does not love himfelf, and is deftitute of all fenfibility and tafte for elegance and beauty.'

Verona defcribed. However, as to its beauty, it will not bear a comparifon with moft of the large cities in the fouthern parts of Italy. Moft of the ftreets of Verona are narrow, winding, and dirty, and the houfes are meanly built; and, as it ftands in a very pleafant country, when viewed from a neighbouring eminence, it appears much more beautiful than it is really found to be upon entering it. Its fortifications are but contemptible, though they confift of three caftles, namely, Il Caftello Vecchio, S. Pietro, and San Felice. That in the middle is faid in ancient times to have been a temple of Diana. The top of this caftle affords the beft view of the city. The river Adige divides Verona almoft into two equal parts, which are joined together by four ftone bridges. All the bridges are well built; but il Ponte nuovo deferves particular notice on account of the fine profpect that it yields of the country over the river, towards the mountain of Caftello S. Felice. *Number of inhabitants.* The number of inhabitants at Verona is, at prefent, computed to be no more than forty-nine or fifty thoufand; whereas not a century ago they exceeded feventy thoufand fouls. *Il Curfo.* The beft ftreet in the city is il Curfo, where the carnival diverfions conclude with foot-races, &c. Formerly common proftitutes were permitted to enter the lifts, and to run for the prize; but this cuftom has been *Horfe-race.* juftly abolifhed, and altered to a horfe-race, which is exhibited on Shrove-Sunday, being the laft Sunday of the carnival. The prize is a piece of gold-brocade, or fome rich stuff.

VERONA. 349

stuff. The largest piazza or area in this city is la Piazza d'armi, where the two annual fairs in spring and autumn are held. On this piazza stands a marble statue representing the republic of Venice, under whose jurisdiction this city has been for some centuries past *. The family of the Scaligeri, from which the learned Julius Cæsar Scaliger would fain derive his pedigree, were formerly lords of Verona; but the arrogancy of that learned critic was smartly chastised by the poignant wit of Scioppius †. One of the Scaliger's, for his better security, and to keep the city in awe, erected within the space of three years not only the Castello Vecchio at the end of the Curso, but likewise built a bridge over the Adige, which is still in good condition, and deserves to be taken notice of; for the distance between the piers of the first arch is seventy feet, between those of the second eighty-two, and those of the third arch a hundred and forty-two feet. There is at present a governor and a small garrison in the castle. *[margin: Piazza d'armi.]* *[margin: A remarkable bridge.]*

Near the church of S. Marica antica are still to be seen some monuments of the Scaliger family, namely, three large and four small tombs. The former rest on a sexangular work of Gothic structure, adorned with six statues, and the Scaliger arms, viz. a ladder and an eagle.

On the Palazzo della ragione, or town-house, the statues of five celebrated persons, who were natives of Verona, are erected. These are the poets Catullus and Æmilius Macrus, the historian Cornelius Nepos, the famous naturalist Pliny the elder, and the architect Vitruvius, who lived in the reign of Augustus. On a high arch stands the statue of Gieronimo Fracastori, a learned physician, mathematician, and excellent poet, who flourished in the sixteenth century ‡. *[margin: Palazzo della ragione. Statues of five celebrated persons.]*

The

---

* *Maffei in Verona illustr.* P. iii. p. 20. shews, that the Venetians draw yearly from the territories of Verona above five hundred and sixty thousand ducats, which are equal to a hundred and twelve thousand *doppie*, or Spanish pistoles.

† The Veronese, indeed, acknowledge Julius Cæsar Scaliger for their countryman; but deny that he was descended from the Scaliger family, who were lords of their city. They particularly accuse his son Joseph Scaliger, that in his *Epistola de splendore gentis suæ*, as also in the *Confutatio Fabulæ Burdonum*, he has published palpable falshoods, and contrived a mere fable, only in order to support his chimerical pedigree. See *Maffei Veron. illust.* P. ii. p. 156. *seq.*

‡ The marquis *Maffei in Verona illustrata, Part* ii. p. 178, treats at large of the life and writings of Fracastori, and likewise inserts a plate of a medal that was struck for him; on one side of which is the head of Fracastori.

VERONA.

The Veronese might justly erect statues to other illustrious persons who were their countrymen; for Verona was the birth-place of Pomponius Secundus, Peter Martyr, a learned Dominican; Frà Jocondo, a great mathematician; Guarini Veronese, one of those learned men who restored the study of the Greek language in Italy; the celebrated painter Paolo Veronese, and of the learned cardinal Henry Noris.

Chief magistrates. The chief magistrates by whom the Venetians govern this province, are the *podesta*, and the *capitaneo* or general. All civil affairs are under the direction of the former, and the latter has the care of the military. Both these continue in office no longer than sixteen months. A fine house was begun for the *capitaneo* or general, but it lies unfinished.

Buildings. Among the private buildings in this city, the palace of count Maffei is the most splendid and magnificent. It stands on the Piazza de' Mercanti, and is ornamented with several statues on the roof, which is flat, like those in the south part of Italy. It is probably on account of the cold weather and great quantity of snow which falls on the high mountains in the neighbourhood, that is not usual to build the roofs flat in these parts; yet many flat roofs are to be seen at Inspruck where these inconveniencies are rather greater.

Statue of Verona. On the Piazzo de' Mercanti, or the merchants square, is a statue representing the city of Verona, or rather the republic of Venice, in a female habit, with a crown on its head. The next for magnificence, &c. to count Maffei's palace, are the houses of the counts Bevilaqua, Canossa, and the signiors Verzi, Pompeii, and Pellegrini.

Odoli palace. Formerly the most superb palace in Verona was that of the Venetian military commissary Odoli, or Lodoli; the expence of building, and the furniture, being computed at three hundred thousand *scudi*, or crowns. But all this pomp is now vanished, Odoli having been convicted of embezzling to the amount of a million of the public money; for which he was hanged at Venice in the last carnival. The splendid furniture is all sold, and a great part of it gone to Modena. A mistress of Odoli, to whom he allowed a

Fracastori; on the reverse, a burning altar, with a serpent under the base; and, on each side, a book, an armillary sphere, Apollo's lyre, and a wreath of laurel, with this inscription on the exergue:

Minervæ, Apoll. & Æsculap. sacrum.

'Sacred to Minerva, Apollo, and Æsculapius.'

grand

VERONA.

grand equipage, very feafonably eloped with forty thoufand crowns. His fon and lady, who had alfo their particular coaches (the former fpending the public money as faft as his father embezzled it) now live obfcurely in the country, on a fmall penfion allowed them by the republic of Venice.

Oppofite the unfinifhed houfe, intended for the general, is an edifice where the members of the learned Philarmonic fociety hold their meetings. In the hall, which is very large, are the protraits of the Patres, or prefidents of this academy, who are always four in number. In an apartment on the left-hand are kept the old mufical inftruments with which the nobility of Verona formerly amufed themfelves; and this gave rife to the prefent foundation. Some centuries fince, there was a literary fociety at Ancona who were termed Incatenati, which, according to an infcription in the academy, were in the year 1543 incorporated with the Philarmonici. The other apartments, which are intended for reading public lectures, are ornamented with the protraits of the moft eminent members, with the following infcription: *Philarmonic academy*

*Anno MDXLIII. cœtus Philarmonicus
Academicas leges fancit
Ac Mufis omnibus litat.*

' In the year 1543, the Philarmonic fociety eftablifhed the
' laws of this academy, and devoted themfelves to the
' mufes.'

An apartment on the right-hand is appointed for the prefidents of the Philoti, who are inftituted for the improvement of bodily exercifes, as riding, fencing, vaulting, dancing, &c. There is alfo in this building, a fine theatre for exhibiting opera's and comedies; which has five galleries, and was built from a defign of the famous Francefco Bibiena, architect to the emperor. As the nobility affemble here feveral times a week, to divert themfelves with cards, &c. this theatre may be looked upon as a kind of exchange for the Beau monde and Literati of Verona. In one room ftands the ftatue of a female of white marble, faid to have been found in the ancient amphitheatre; and fome antiquarians are of opinion that there muft have been originally feventy-two ftatues in all, though not the leaft remains, or pedeftals on which they ftood, are to be feen there. On the outfide of this edifice are to be feen a great number of infcriptions, *The Philoti fociety. Collection of ancient infcriptions.*

VERONA.

tions, and other remains of antiquity, many of which were dug up about Verona; and that they may not be expofed to any future damage, from the injuries of the weather, &c. they are inferted in a long wall, facing the fouth; the Tramontana, or north-wind, being found very detrimental to ftones. The firft in order are infcriptions confifting of characters which are at prefent unknown, as the Egyptian, Punic, and Etrurian. Next to thefe are the Greek infcriptions, to the number of fixty; and after thefe come the Roman ancient monuments. Thofe reprefenting the gods, and ancient facrifices, have the precedence; one of which is particularly taken notice of: it is a fmall idol of porphyry, with a votary proftrate before it. Another remarkable piece is a baffo-relievo reprefenting Mercury, with fomething in his hand, which he reaches to the earth under the fymbol of a woman, fitting. Over thefe two images are the Greek names of Mercury and the earth, as follows, EPMHΣ and ΓH. After thefe are placed the *infcriptiones Imperatoriæ, Militares, Confulares, Sepulchrales*, &c.

Merit of the marquis Scipio Maffei. In the proper arrangement of all thefe pieces, the marquis Scipione Maffei has been at no fmall expence or trouble, and has fpared no pains to increafe the number of them. On this account the gentlemen belonging to this academy have erected a marble ftatue of him over the entrance of the palace, with thefe words:

Monument in honour of him.

Marchioni Scipioni Maffeio
Adhuc viventi
Academia Philarmonica
Decreto & ære publico.
MDCCXXVII.

' Erected in honour of the marquis Scipione Maffei, who
' is ftill living, by the Philarmonic academy, at their own
' expence. 1727.

This honour was done him in his abfence, from a fuppofition that, had he been prefent, he would not eafily have been prevailed upon to give his confent, or at leaft have raifed fome pretended difficulties. The marquis Maffei muft be diftinguifhed both from count Maffei, whofe palace ftands on the Piazza de' Mercanti; and likewife from Paolo Aleffandro Maffei, a Patritio or nobleman of Volterra, and knight of the order of St. Stephen, who publifhed the life of

pope

pope pious V. and some other very learned treatises on antique statues, gems, inscriptions, and other antiquities, and died at Rome in the year 1716.

In the marquis Scipio Maffei's palace, are to be seen several ancient diploma's or deeds; and he has inserted copper-plates of some in his *Historia Diplomatica*; among which there is one of the year 445, which he supposes to be the most ancient original extant in Europe. He is also possessed of an original instrument containing the decrees of the council of Florence (like that famous MS. in the Florentine library, which is so much valued) and of several other manuscripts; a collection of antique intaglio's, and vases inscribed with Etruscan characters *; with great numbers of medals, gems, paintings, statues, busts, inscriptions, sacrificatory instruments and other antiquities, and several curious petrifactions. He is a very polite gentleman, and most agreeable in conversation. Formerly he entertained no great esteem for the Germans; but now he is thoroughly cured of that prejudice; and, when he mentions the Leipsic academy, he knows not how to praise it sufficiently. Possibly what may have contributed to this change was his *Systema de natalibus fulminum*, in which he maintains that thunder and lightening do not proceed from the clouds, but are generated near the earth in the atmosphere or lower regions of the air. In Italy this opinion, at first, was censured as absurd; but professor Richter of Leipsic adopted his hypothesis, and maintained it in an elaborate treatise published in the year 1725, which, as it tended to enhance Maffei's reputation in the republic of letters, could not but be highly agreeable to him.

Curiosities in his museum.

His system on the origin of lightening.

Formerly the Calceolari museum at Verona was so famous, that in the year 1622 a description of it was published with the following title: *Francisci Calceolarii Musæum a Bened. Ceruto, Medico, inceptum, & ab Andrea Chiocco perfectum, & in vi. partes divisum*. But at present it is totally dispersed, and nothing is to be seen of it under that name.

The Calceolari museum.

Misson (*Tome* I.) gives a very accurate account of the celebrated collection of count Moscardi; more curious particulars of which may be seen in *Note, overa Memorie, del Mu-*

That of count Moscardi.

---

* *Maffei, Fontani, Buanoroti*, and *Mariani*, have for for some years past applied themselves very assiduously to the old Etruscan language and antiquities; but hitherto their discoveries seem to amount to no more than very uncertain conjectures. Sir Hans Sloane, of London, has also several Etruscan inscriptions in his museum.

VOL. III. A a *seo*

VERONA.

seo del Conte Ludovico Moscardo, Veronese, published at Padua in 1656, and at Verona in 1672. For some years past that museum is not to be seen; either because a great part of it has been disposed of, or on account of the ignorance and churlishness of the present owner.

Of count Bevilaqua. Count Mario Bevilaqua has a fine collection of ancient statues; among which is a marble Venus in the attitude of the Venus de Medicis; a statue of Hermophraditus like the Borghese; Bacchus, a Bacchanalian, and a Ceres, all exquisitely done. Among the great number of busts those of Augustus, Livia, Tiberius, Trajan, Lucius Verus, Commodus, and Septimius Severus, deserve a particular attention. Among the basso-relievo's in this collection that of Jupiter Ammon is the best. Here are also several small statues of bronze, a great number of medals, and likewise a fine set of paintings; the principal among the last are a representation of paradise by Tintoretti, and a Venus half naked viewing herself in a looking-glass held by an Amorino or Cupid, by Paolo Veronese.

Capocuco's collection. A gentleman of the name of Capocuco has made a collection of several small statues of bronze, and models of all kinds of military engines, instruments, and arms; as cannons, mortars, &c. of brass. But they are now to be sold, and are valued at two thousand Spanish pistoles.

Cabinet of count Giusti. Count Gomberto Giusti is a great connoisseur in medals, of which he has a numerous and valuable collection. He is also fond of other curiosities which he has not neglected, especially paintings.

Saibanti's collection of manuscripts. Giovanni Saibanti is very curious, and succesful in collecting manuscripts; of which he is master of above thirteen hundred. The most remarkable MS. that he is possessed of, in my opinion, is the four evangelists in Greek, written about the close of the 13th century, in large round characters. The same gentleman has also a collection of antiquities and natural curiosities.

The chapter's library. The chapter-library contains a great number of curious manuscripts. *

Amphitheatre. Antiquarians may meet with a most valuable piece at Verona, which gives a clearer idea of the spectacles or public diversions of the ancient Romans than any other edifice now extant; I mean the celebrated amphitheatre,

---

* The most valuable of these, and likewise of Saibanti's collection, are taken notice of by Maffei in his *Verona illustrata*, P. iii. *p.* 244, & *seq.*

which

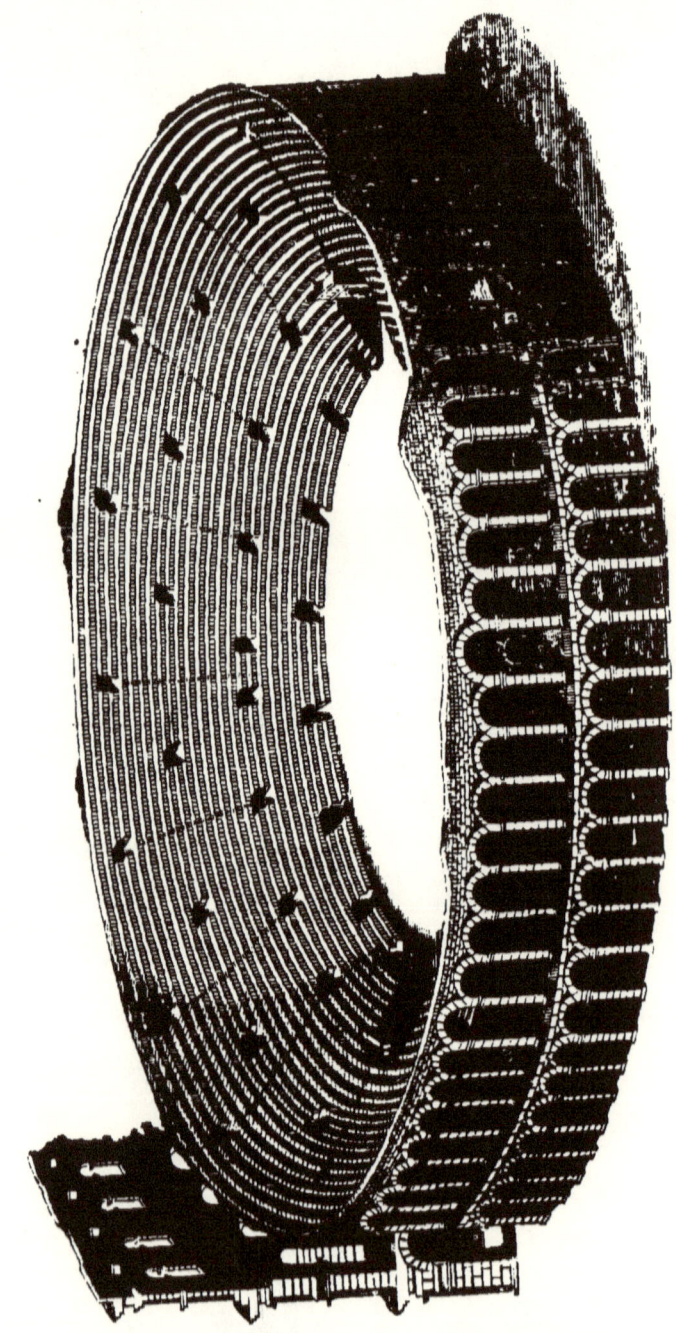

Vol. II. page 448.

VERONA.

which through a succession of so many centuries has, by the commendable care and attention of the inhabitants, been kept in such good repair, that, in this respect, it is far preferable to, though not so large as, Vespasian's amphitheatre at Rome. This noble structure, according to some, was built in the reign of Augustus: however, there is but little probability that such a superb and sumptuous edifice would be set on foot in a province of Italy before the capital of the empire, which was not adorned with any thing equal to it till Vespasian's time. To this may be added the silence of Pliny the elder, whose accuracy in the enumeration of the most celebrated edifices and artists of his time, and particularly of what concerned his native place, would not have suffered him to omit a structure of this nature, which does so much honour to Verona. A farther argument is adduced, that during the first century no such amphitheatre was to be seen at Verona; for Pliny the younger, who was alive towards the close of Trajan's reign, makes no mention of it, though, in *lib.* vi. *ep.* 34, he is so particular in describing the spectacles and shew of gladiators given at Verona by his friend Maximus, in honour of his deceased wife. On the other hand, this amphitheatre cannot be dated much later than this, as it is a structure which bears in it the marks of the flourishing state both of architecture, sculpture, and of the Roman empire.

_{Its antiquity.}

The marquis Maffei, whom I have already mentioned with the respect due to so learned a man, is at present engaged in a curious treatise which is to be intitled *Verona illustrata* *, and of which a part was published two years ago at Verona, as a specimen of this noble undertaking, and of the elegance and accuracy with which it is executed. It enters into a very accurate disquisition concerning the antiquity of amphitheatres in general, and particularly that of Verona. It were to be wished that persons of equal talents and application would also favour the world with their conjectures concerning the amphitheatres of Rome, Capua, and Nismes †.

Maffei's dissertation on amphitheatres.

According to Maffei's measurement, the longest diameter of the amphitheatre of Verona, from the first arch of the main entrance to the opposite arch, is four hundred and fifty Veronese feet, and its greatest breadth three hundred and sixty. The length of the area within the walls, according

Geometrical computation of the Verona amphitheatre.

---

* This was published at Verona, in folio, in the year 1732.

† Maffei's work is intitled *De gli Anfiteatri, e singolarmente del Veronese, libri due, in Verona*, 1728.

to his computation, is two hundred and eighteen feet, six inches; the breadth a hundred and twenty-nine; and the outward circuit of the whole edifice a thousand two hundred and ninety feet. The Verona foot is exactly one third more than the Roman *palmi*, which is used in architecture. Its present height indeed is but eighty-eight feet; but, from evident marks on the walls, it appears to have been at first a hundred and ten, or a hundred and twenty feet high. The lowest row of seats is as it were buried in dirt and rubbish; but, if we include this, the number of the rows of seats or steps, rising one above another to the highest gallery, amounts to fifty-four. This method of building amphitheatres was the most convenient for holding a vast number of spectators in such a manner, that the nearest row did not intercept the view of the Arena from those who sat at the greatest distance. If we allow a foot and a half for each person, the amphitheatre at Verona afforded room for twenty-two thousand one hundred and eighty-four spectators. The internal area of the Colyfæum at Rome does not greatly exceed it, as, according to Fontana, the length of that edifice is but five hundred and sixty-four Verona feet; its breadth four hundred and sixty-seven; the internal area two hundred and seventy-three feet long, and a hundred and seventy-three broad, and the circuit of the whole building one thousand five hundred and sixty-six Verona feet. According to this computation the Colyfæum at most contained but thirty or forty-four thousand persons. In the Colyfæum none of the seats are now remaining. The amphitheatre of Verona is much more perfect, and has no holes or chasms in the wall. However, it must be owned that the present edifice is not merely the ancient structure, but that it owes its good condition to subsequent repairs, many of which are the work of the moderns *. The new-inserted stones may be easily distinguished from

Marginalia: Number of spectators it contained. Compared with that at Rome.

---

* With this account given by the author may be compared the following description of this amphitheatre from Dr. Burnet's travels, p. 118, 119. 'The known antiquity of Verona is the amphitheatre, one of the least of
' all that the Romans built, but the best preserved; for most of the great
' stones of the outside are picked out; yet the great sloping vault, on
' which the rows of the seats are laid, is intire; the rows of the seats are
' also intire; they are four-and-twenty rows; every row is a foot and a
' half high, and as much in breadth; so that a man sits conveniently in
' them under the feet of those of the higher row; and, allowing every
' man a foot and a half, the whole amphitheatre can hold twenty-three
' thousand persons. In the vaults under the rows of seats were the stalls
' of

from the ancient work, which is much neater. The height of the feats is not the fame in all; but is generally a foot and five inches, and the common breadth two feet and two inches. Near the twenty-fixth row, reckoning from the bottom, there is one fo narrow, as to be fcarce fit for a feat, which, for this reafon, appears not to be the work of antiquity, but of the moderns who repaired it. The ancient feats are of red marble; but the modern repairs of a red friable ftone; and for greater conveniency, as the ftone feats were very cold to fit upon, they were covered with boards, and alfo with cufhions for perfons of quality. See Dio, *lib.* lix. Hence it appears, that an amphitheatre built with ftone might receive fome damage by fire. There are in this amphitheatre feparate ftone ftair-cafes, by which the fpectators afcended to their feats from the vaults below. The apertures from thefe ftair-cafes into the rows of feats, on account of the multitudes of people crowding, and as it were pouring through to fee the fpectacles, are, by Macrobius, *Saturn. lib.* vi. *cap.* 4, called Vomitoria. The number of Vomitoria within this amphitheatre are fixty-four, being difpofed in four rows.

On the outfide of this amphitheatre are twenty-feven arched entrances *, and the key-ftone of each of thefe arches is numbered; fo that, every clafs of the people being informed where they were to go in and come out of the amphitheatre, no confufion or difturbance could arife. Thefe arches are for the moft part eleven feet eight inches wide, and eighteen feet high. The lower part of the pillars is buried about four feet under the prefent furface of the ground, as appears by the ancient main entrance, where the earth has been cleared away. The baluftrades over the entrances are a modern work; two galleries over the lower arches reprefent as it were the fecond and third ftories. No pedeftals have been found either in this amphitheatre, or in that at Rome mentioned above; from which we may conclude, that it was not ornamented with ftatues in any other part but over the main entrance: and if, on any particular folemnity, ftatues were erected in thefe amphitheatres, they muft have been but fmall, and remained but a fhort time there. Thefe move-

Difpofition of the feats.

Vomitoria.

Entrances.

Whether the amphitheatres were ornamented with ftatues.

‘ of the wild beafts that were prefented to entertain the company. The
‘ thicknefs of the building, from the outward wall to the loweft row of
‘ feats, is ninety feet.’

* That at Rome has eighty, and that of Nifmes fixty arches.

VERONA.

able statues may probably be the figures still to be seen on medals that represent amphitheatres, plates of which are inserted in Maffei's work mentioned above. Indeed few or no fragments of statues have been dug up near this amphitheatre. The stones of the ancient part of this edifice are not cemented together, but only fastened with a few iron cramps or braces. The best print of this ancient structure is given us by Maffei.

Whether the amphitheatre of Verona could be laid under water. It is no wonder that such a superb theatre should be built at Verona, preferably to many other cities; for all historians agree, that, in the times of the ancient Romans, this city was very large and populous. It does not appear that this amphitheatre like that at Rome could be laid under water, as the surface of the river Adige is some feet lower than the area of it, and as no traces of any aqueducts are to be seen near it. On the other hand, some arches are shewn in the water below S. Pietro, supposed to be the remains of a Naumachia, which was not supplied from the Adige, as that river did not flow in ancient times thro' the city, but from the eminences of Montorio and Avesa, from whence it was conveyed to Verona by leaden pipes. Both these places are about two Italian miles from the city; and the leaden pipes which are still kept in repair, are laid over a bridge and furnish several private houses with fresh water.

Naumachia.

Ancient course of the Adige. On the left-hand of the road leading from Verona to Castello Vecchia the ancient course of the Adige, before it was diverted into the city, is still to be seen. There is but a very narrow stream at present in the old channel of this river*. 'Tis supposed with as little certainty that there were three triumphal arches in and near Verona. That † near Castello Vecchio is attributed to the family of the Gavii; another in the Via Leoni to Flaminius; a third in the Curso to Marius; and a fourth in the same place, consisting of two simumilar arches, to Galienus. It is too common among antiquarians to dignify the remains of old city gates with the name of triumphal arches; to which honour none of those ancient remains, which have two similar gates near each other, are in any-wise intitled. For the triumphal arches always consisted either of one large arched entrance only, or with a small one on each side.

* *Maffei in Veron. illustr. Part* I. 38. affirms, that the course of the Adige was always the same as it is at present.
† On this arch the name of the architect is still legible, *Lucius Vitruvius Cerdo,* who is thought to have been a freedman of the famous Vitruvius.

From

VERONA. 359

From the depth of the rubbish and earth about the foundations of the above-mentioned remains of antiquity, it may be concluded that the ancient situation of the city was much lower than the present. On the side of Galienus's triumphal arch, as it is called, that faces the country, there was formerly an inscription, which at present is not legible. Vignier has published a plate of it in his *Bibliotheca Historica*, as it then stood, which evidently shews that instead of a triumphal arch this structure is no more than a common gate. The words of the inscription as transcribed by that author are: *Colonia Augusta Verona Galicniana. Valeriano II. & Lucilio Coss. muri Veronensium fabricati, ex die III. Non April. dedicati prid. No. Decemb. jubente Sanctissimo Galieno Aug. N.* Over the two arches are six apertures like windows disposed in two rows. *[Alteration of the situation of the city. Triumphal arches.]*

Near the city of Verona is a fine plain, which is called by the name of Campus Martius, where the people are mustered and perform their military exercises. In the year 1712, the booths or shops, for the annual fair held on the Campus Martius till that time, were burnt down; and, for greater security and conveniency, the fair has been since that time kept in the Piazza d'armi, within the city, where the shops are curiously disposed. From the middle of the fair there are eight visto's along so many rows of shops. Besides these streets or lanes, there are four spacious areas formed by the disposition of the booths; and over the lanes between them canvass is spread to shelter the company from the rain and the sun. Scipione Maffei has prefixed a copper-plate of this fair to his miscellaneous works. The trade of this city might be put on a much better foot than it is at present. *[Campus Martius. A yearly fair. Trade and manufactures of the city.]*

The chief commodities that the Veronese trade in, are physical plants *, which are gathered on Monte Baldo; olives, (those of Verona being reckoned very good) oil, wine, with linnen, woollen, and silken manufactures. The neighbouring places indeed are no less plentifully provided with such commodities; but whether greater vent for them might not be opened at Venice, &c. is well worth their consideration.

The goodness of the Verona wine is mentioned by Pliny, *Hist. Nat. lib. XIV. c. 6. Virgil. Georg.* 2. and *Cassiodorus Var.* *[Verona wine.]*

---

* Vide *Plantæ five Simplicia, ut vocant, quæ in Baldo Monte & in Via ab Verona ad Baldum reperiuntur, per Joh. Pon. Pharmacopæum Veronensem, Basil.* 1608, 4to.

VERONA.

Lib. XII. 4. The best wines at present, produced in the neighbourhood of this city, are two sorts of white wine, one of which is called *Garganico bianco,* and the other *Vino santo.* The latter, in my opinion, is the best, and has something of the flavour of the old Hungarian wines. Some think that this is the wine which Cassiodorus calls *Vinum Acinaticum.*

Canal to Venice. There is a very commodious water-carriage from hence to Venice. The passage in a barge takes up but three days and a half; but the return is more tedious; for the barge is drawn by oxen, so that it is not performed in less than eight days.

Cathedral. In the cathedral of Verona are to be seen some good pictures by Bellini, Balestra, and Paolo Veronese. The front is large, and adorned with basso-relievo's: it is cut out of one block of marble. Lucius III, whose name before he was exalted to the papal dignity was Humbaldus Lucea, lies here with the following epitaph:

Epitaph of Lucius III.

Ossa
Lucii III. Pont. Max.
Cui Roma ob invidiam pulso Verona tutiss. ac gratissimum perfugium fuit, ubi conventu Christianorum acto, dum præclara multa molitur, è vita excessit.

‘ Here are deposited the remains of pope Lucius III. to
‘ whom, when banished thro' envy from Rome, Verona af-
‘ forded a safe and agreeable retreat, where, whilst he was
‘ concerting several great designs in a synod, he departed
‘ this life.'

He died in 1185, after he had sat in the papal chair four years, two months, and fourteen days, with much disturbance, and but an indifferent character.

Revenue of the see. The bishopric of Verona brings in four or five thousand scudi a year. On the left-hand, near the entrance of the episcopal palace, is seen a large marble statue of a woman, with the following inscription, containing the sculptor's name under it:

Alessandro Vittoria Frid. F.

Present bishop's collection of statues. The upper apartments of this palace are ornamented with marble busts of Agrippina the mother of Nero, Julia the daughter

VERONA.

daughter of Titus, Meſſalina, Matidia, Fauſtina the daughter of Antoninus, Julia the daughter of Auguſtus, and Lucilia of L. Verus; thoſe of Aurelia the mother of Julius Cæſar, Seleucus, Julius Cæſar, Marcus Brutus, Caligula, Antinous, Juba king of Mauritania, Septimius Severus, Heliogabulus, and Scipio Africanus, together with a ſtatue of Venus coming out of a bath, and many other pieces collected by the preſent biſhop of Verona, who is of the Treviſani family.

In Verona, there are convents of Carmelite monks both *calceati* and *diſcalceati*. In the church of the former is a beautiful altar of fine marble; and, in their veſtry, a fine piece of painting by one of the diſciples of the celebrated Raphael, repreſenting our Saviour, when a child, playing with John the Baptiſt; and the virgin-mother, looking, with great complacency, on their mutual fondneſs and ſportive innocence. *Carmelite church.*

In the church of the *diſcalceati*, or barefooted Carmelites, are to be ſeen three fine altars, the firſt of which is adorned with pillars of Verde antico, the ſecond with pillars of a red and white veined marble, and the third with yellow marble pillars. The high altar is likewiſe of beautiful marble, and finely executed: it is alſo embelliſhed with a picture of the annunciation, which does great honour to Antonio Baleſtra, who is ſtill living at Cremona. This artiſt is in high repute, and has painted many pieces which have been ſent into England and Germany. *Church of the diſcalceati. Baleſtra, a good painter.*

The Dominican church is dedicated to St. Anaſtaſia. Near the entrance of this church, on the right-hand, a ſuperb monument is erected to Giovanni Fregoſi, a Genoeſe officer, who raiſed himſelf by his merit to be commander in chief, by Cataneo di Carrara. I could not but take notice here of a very great impropriety, namely, the holy-water veſſels at the entrance of the church are ſupported by two grotesque figures, repreſenting harlequins or buffoons. The front of the church is partly adorned with good marble baſſo-relievo's; but that work has been diſcontinued. Before the church ſtands the tomb of count Caſtelbarro. *Dominican church. Tomb of general Fregoſi. Two harlequins ſupport the holy-water vaſe.*

St. Euphemia's church is adorned with ſome good paintings. On the high altar ſtands a curious marble tabernacle; before it are two beautiful braſs ſtatues, with eight others of plaſter. In other reſpects it is a mean edifice, neither is the cieling arched. *St. Euphemia's church.*

In

VERONA.

Jesuits church. In the Jesuits, or St. Bastiano's church, the high altar is adorned with some fine pillars of Mischia di Brentonico, a kind of marble found in this country. Here is also a white marble statue of St. Sebastian, and likewise some fine pictures, being ornaments that are common to most churches in Italy.

St. George's church. The church and convent di S. Giorgio belong to the Benedictine monks. On the outside over the church-door is this extravagant inscription:

Inscription.

*Numini Sancto propitiato
Divi Georgii
Pollentis, potentis, invicti
Piè, rite, solemnitùs
Sacrum dicatum esto.*

' Let this church which has been consecrated with so-
' lemn rites, be dedicated to the holy, powerful, strong, in-
' vincible, and propitious Deity of St. George.'

Paintings. Over the door is the baptism of Christ, painted by Tintoretto. On the high altar is a piece representing the martyrdom of St. George, by Paolo Veronese, and, on one side near it, our Saviour feeding five thousand men, by Paolo Faranati, who was seventy-nine years of age when he painted this piece. Few of this master's works are to be seen in Italy, except at Verona; most of his time having been spent in painting the Escurial in Spain. On the other side, is a very fine representation of the Israelites gathering of manna, by Felice Brusasorzi: this piece is twenty-four Veronese feet in length, and twenty-three broad. Here is another piece, by the same hand, which represents St. John's vision in the Apocalypse, of Michael with his angels protecting a woman and her child against the dragon *. Whether it be consistent with the mystery of this vision, that the child should be represented, as it were, crying out in any agony of fear, I shall not dispute. Here is also Barnabas healing the sick man, by Paul Veronese. Opposite to this piece is the virgin Mary betwixt two bishops, by Girolamo da i Libri: the carpet on which the virgin stands is justly admired. Domenico Ricci, surnamed Brusasorzi, and father to Felice, has also displayed his skill in this church, which is one of the finest in the city.

* Revelation chap. xv.

VERONA.

In the church of the hospital della Misericordia, or the in- *Chiesa della* curables, is an exquisite Pietà, or the virgin Mary viewing *Misericordia.* the dead body of Christ after he was taken down from the cross, by Alessandro Turchi. This celebrated painter, otherwise known by the name of d'Orbetto, which he had when *d' Orbetto* he was a poor boy, and used to lead about a blind man, till, *the painter.* very fortunately for him, Felice Brusaforzi, happening to see him drawing figures with charcoal on a wall, concluded that he had a genius for designing, and took him under his care *.

The Olivetan church, or Madonna in Organo, has a *Olivetan* very superb altar, and a great number of excellent paintings. *church* Among which, a Madonna Gratiosa by Antonio Balestra is *paintings.* none of the worst. The assumption of the virgin Mary and the massacre of the innocents in the Tribuna, are by Paolo Farinati. The stalls in the choir are of wood, curiously inlaid, by Giovanni Veronese, a lay-brother of the Olivetan convent. Here was also formerly kept a wooden ass, *Reliques of* within the belly of which, as some simple credulous people *an ass.* are persuaded, were kept the remains of the ass on which Christ made his entry into Jerusalem. The story of this ass, and its travels thro' various countries, till it died at Verona, where it was kept with great veneration, is related by Misson, T. I. p. 164, & seq. with several entertaining circumstances; but with such sarcasms on this and other superstitious customs which he met with in his travels, as will not easily be digested by the Roman-catholics. The Veronese particularly resent his charge against them, as he so far exposed their fondness for the relics of the Jewish ass, as to subject them to the ridicule of a nickname †. They object in their defence, that Misson must have received his information from no better authority than the chamber-maids, or boys at the inn, who had a mind to divert themselves with his credulity; adding, that all persons of sense in Verona entertain very different thoughts of the affair; and that, if this wooden ass formerly made a part of the procession on *Corpus Christi* day, it was only for the more lively representation of a part of the last scene of our Saviour's life, namely, his entrance into Jerusalem. I have also seen a wooden

---

* He died in 1648. See *Maffei Veron. illustr.* P. III. p. 165.
† Concerning the calumny with which the heathens branded the Jews, charging them with worshipping an ass, which descended to the christians, who were called *Asinarii*, on a supposition that they worshipped the head of an ass, see Tertullian *Apol. c.* 16. and also Kortholt *in Pagan obtrect. lib.* II. c. 1.

ass

afs of this kind with the image of our Saviour fitting on it, in the church of our lady at Halle near Bruffels, where it it annually carried in a proceffion for the fame purpofe; and I have been affured, that to charge all the Veronefe in general, with the ridiculous opinions held by the vulgar about this wooden afs, is doing great injuftice to feveral perfons of eminent fenfe and learning *. However, feveral particular circumftances may be adduced in fupport of Miffon's relation, efpecially his mentioning the perfon from whom he had his account, namely, one Montel, a French merchant, who had lived a confiderable time at Verona. When a perfon fpeaks ingenuoufly of the fuperftitious cuftoms of a place, it is not underftood, that thofe inhabitants who have banifhed fuch prejudices by the light of reafon, ftudy, and reflection, are not included in the lump. No city is fo defpicable but one intelligent perfon may be met with in it; yet is there no city in which fome fuperftitious cuftoms and opinions do not generally prevail. How low the vulgar may fall, with regard to fuperftition, is evident from experience and the hiftories of ancient and modern times. No nation, no fect, is free from this infection; but certainly thofe nations are more fubject to this evil, whofe fyftem of religion either too much reftrains, or utterly prohibits them the ufe of their reafon. Are there not innumerable fables concerning the afs, on which our Saviour made his entrance into Jerufalem, current alfo in other countries? And are there not fhewn on the road from Tubingen to Hildritzhaufen, feveral holes on two broad ftones, of which the vulgar of thofe parts have retained a tradition fince the popifh times, that they were the prints which the fame afs's feet made in his travels through Swabia, where the animal foon after died.

I have often confidered with myfelf whether it be not practicable for a proteftant to write an account of his travels through Italy, in fuch a manner as not to difcover what religion he is of; as it is a qualification requifite in an impartial hiftorian, not to be prejudiced in favour of any country

<small>*Particular fuperftitions of all fects and nations.</small>

---

* It cannot be unjuft to charge the Roman-catholics with thefe fuperftitious cuftoms; for what is enjoined by the clergy, and countenanced and authorifed by princes and learned men of that communion, as well as the vulgar, muft be looked upon as the general practice. Tho' the former impute fuch fuperftitions to the commonalty, when preffed on this head, yet they never refufe to attend at the moft ridiculous proceffions; nor do they ever attempt to convince the vulgar of their error. Upon the whole, the Veronefe do not deferve the apology our author makes for them.

or religion, so far as the latter implies the external difference of churches or communions: but I found, that such an impartiality would be attended with great difficulties. For instance, our Saviour's intire *præputium* which was cut off, is shewn in three or four different places. Every one of these churches, perhaps, produces a papal bull in favour of its relique: Shall a protestant historian, in such a case, pass over in silence the contradiction which must appear in such papal instruments, and the impossibility that all the three *præputia* should be genuine reliques, and in describing each of these churches tell us, that the real *præputium* is kept there? Or, shall he only mention in short, that this or that is accounted the genuine relique? The former is not consistent with the love of truth; and in the latter case, how artfully soever he may couch his expressions, it will very soon be discovered that he is no votary of the church of Rome [*].

But to return to the fable of the Verona ass. Misson's sarcastical observations, and the sneering enquiries of strangers and travellers about this extraordinary relique, and, perhaps, the superstitious abuses it caused among the vulgar, have contributed to prevent the ass from making his appearance in the procession, as usual, for these eight years past; but, on the contrary, has been concealed from the public view; and the Veronese make a great difficulty of shewing it to strangers. For my own part, I should not have been much disappointed if I had not seen it; but, by mere accident, I happened to go into a particular chapel belonging to St. Benedict's church; and there I had a full view of the ass that has made so much noise in the world. It stands upon the table behind the altar-piece, which represents St. Benedict, and may be opened like a door. The ass is a good piece of sculpture, and was carved some centuries ago by a devout monk of this convent. Our Saviour's image, which sits upon it, is likewise of wood, and holds a book in the left-hand, and with the right seems to be giving the benediction. On the wall of the same chapel is to be seen a good piece of

The ass, why no longer shewn at Verona.

---

[*] The author here makes a proper exception to the general rule, which condemns all passion in an historian, since truth is as it were the soul of history; however the position is good, that he must neither have country nor religion. A mind full of prejudices, for any particular country or religion, cannot possibly be a good historian. For this reason, Mainbury's history of Calvinism is decried by his own countrymen. On the contrary, those of opposite principles respect Thuanus as an historian. See counsellor Simonetti's character of an historian, §. 9.

painting,

painting, by Domenico Brufaforzi, reprefenting the refurrection of Lazarus.

St. Proculus's church. In the church of St. Proculus, the table of the high altar confifts of an intire piece of *verde antico*, which is fix palms in breadth, and twelve palms long. The bodies of St. Cofmus and St. Damianus are kept in a vault under this church. Whoever has a mind to fee duplicates of thefe reliques, may, according to Roffi's account in his *Roma moderna*, find them at Rome in the church dedicated to thofe faints in the Campo Vaccino. *Falfe pretence about the body of king Pepin.* In the cemitery of St Proculus at Verona, is fhewn a vault which at prefent harbours great numbers of adders, &c. where the body of king Pepin, which has been fince taken up in time of war, and carried into France, is faid to have been buried. The whole affair may be looked upon as a fable; for the grave of king Pepin is not to be fearched for at Verona, as it is certain that the French king of that name lies buried at St. Denys, where he died [*].

St. Zeno's oratory. The houfe in which St. Zeno is faid to have lived is converted into a chapel or oratory; and on a large ftone is the following diftich:

> *Hoc fuper incumbens faxo prope fluminis undam*
> *Zeno Pater tremula captabat arundine pifces.*

> 'Oft on this ftone which lay upon the ftrand
> 'The venerable Zeno took his ftand;
> 'A patient fifher, with his trembling reed
> 'Intent to captivate the fcaly breed.'

St. Zeno's church. Large porphyry vafe. The church of St. Zeno ftands not far from this chapel, where, in a particular clofet, is kept a large round porphyry veffel, twenty-fix feet in circumference, or eight Verona feet in diameter. It confifts of one piece, and refembles a fhallow goblet. The pedeftal belonging to it is cut out of another large piece. *The trouble it put the devil to.* It feems, the devil, by the commend of St. Zeno, brought both thefe hither out of Iftria. His firft day's journey with it was fomewhat unlucky, the burden being too heavy for him, fo that he let the pedeftal fall into the Adriatic fea. The excufes which Satan pleaded on this occafion were not fatisfactory to St. Zeno, who ordered

---

[*] See Eginhard, *vit. Carol. M. c.* 3. *Annales Francifci Lambeciani, Tom.* II. *Commentar. de Bibliotheca Vindobonenf. c.* V. *p.* 371. *Adelmus ad ann.* 763.

him

VERONA.

away to look out for what he had loft by his careleſſneſs. ...t I may not be charged, like Miſſon, with having my ...rmation from a ſcullion boy, or a chambermaid at an inn; ... authority is grounded upon a baſſo-relievo, which re-...ents the whole tranſaction, and is inſerted in the wall ... the porphyry vaſe, where it could hardly have come with the approbation of the ordinary and clergy belong-... to this church. This vaſe is not made uſe of at preſent. ..., if it be true, that formerly it ſerved to hold the holy ...er, it is no wonder that the devil, if he had any fore-wledge of the uſe it was deſigned for, ſhould be very ...illing to fatigue himſelf with carrying weapons to be ...loyed againſt himſelf, and provide a veſſel for that wa-... by which he and his legions may at any time be con-...ded and put to flight. However, from the largeneſs of ... vaſe, it does not ſeem probable that it was employed for ... uſe. It muſt be acknowledged to be a valuable piece, ... account of its dimenſions, and the matter of which it ...ſiſts.

...he font of St. Zeno's church is very large, and cut out ...ne block of white marble. The table of the high altar ...wiſe conſiſts of one piece of marble, thirteen feet long, ...ſix broad, which was the produce of this country. St. ...o lies in the vault under this church, which is adorned ... ſeveral pillars of yellow marble. On the church-door, ...ch is plated with bronze, are repreſented, but very rudely, ...anks and orders of eccleſiaſtics. On both ſides of the ...ance ſeveral ſcriptural ſtories are carved on ſtone; thoſe ...the Old Teſtament on the right-hand, as one enters into ... church, and thoſe of the New on the other ſide. The ...ern *magi* are here repreſented with crowns on their heads; ..., in the repreſenting the apprehending of Chriſt in the gar-..., Peter cuts off Malchus's ear, and is diſtinguiſhed by a ... hanging at his arm. The ſculpture on the outſide of ... church is ſomething remarkable, as it repreſents horſe-...n, wild beaſts, hunting matches, &c. with Latin inſcrip-...s over them, very few of which are now legible. The ...gar entertain themſelves with abundance of ſtories relat-... to theſe images. Among other things, they tell us, that ...g Theodoric and Satan entered into a compact, by virtue ... which, the latter was bound, at all times, to ſupply his ...jeſty with good horſes and hounds. The perſon on horſe-...k ſaid to repreſent Theodoric rides with ſtirrups, con-...ry to the practice of antiquity.

Baſſo-relie-
vo's on the
church-door.

painting, by Domenico Brusaforzi, representing the resurrection of Lazarus.

St. Proculus's church. In the church of St. Proculus, the table of the high altar consists of an intire piece of *verde antico*, which is six palm in breadth, and twelve palms long. The bodies of St. Comus and St. Damianus are kept in a vault under this church Whoever has a mind to see duplicates of these reliques, ma according to Rossi's account in his *Roma moderna*, find the at Rome in the church dedicated to those saints in the Can *False pretence about the body of king Pepin.* po Vaccino. In the cemitery of St Proculus at Verona, shewn a vault which at present harbours great numbers adders, &c. where the body of king Pepin, which has bee since taken up in time of war, and carried into France, said to have been buried. The whole affair may be look upon as a fable; for the grave of king Pepin is not to 1 searched for at Verona, as it is certain that the French kir of that name lies buried at St. Denys, where he died *.

St. Zeno's oratory. The house in which St. Zeno is said to have lived is col verted into a chapel or oratory; and on a large stone is tl following distich:

> *Hoc super incumbens saxo prope fluminis undam*
> *Zeno Pater tremula captabat arundine pisces.*

> ' Oft on this stone which lay upon the strand
> ' The venerable Zeno took his stand;
> ' A patient fisher, with his trembling reed
> ' Intent to captivate the scaly breed.'

St. Zeno's church. *Large porphyry vase.* *The trouble it put the devil to.* The church of St. Zeno stands not far from this chapel where, in a particular closet, is kept a large round porphyr vessel, twenty-six feet in circumference, or eight Veron: feet in diameter. It consists of one piece, and resembles : shallow goblet. The pedestal belonging to it is cut out o another large piece. It seems, the devil, by the comment of St. Zeno, brought both these hither out of Istria. Hi first day's journey with it was somewhat unlucky, the burden being too heavy for him, so that he let the pedestal fa! into the Adriatic sea. The excuses which Satan pleaded o this occasion were not satisfactory to St. Zeno, who orderet

* See Eginhard, *vit. Carol. M. c.* 3. *Annales Francisci Lambeciani, Tom.* II. *Commentar. de Bibliotheca Vindobonens. c.* V. *p.* 371. *Adelmus ad ann* 763.

him

him away to look out for what he had loft by his careleffnefs. That I may not be charged, like Miffon, with having my information from a fcullion boy, or a chambermaid at an inn; my authority is grounded upon a baffo-relievo, which reprefents the whole tranfaction, and is inferted in the wall near the porphyry vafe, where it could hardly have come but with the approbation of the ordinary and clergy belonging to this church. This vafe is not made ufe of at prefent. But, if it be true, that formerly it ferved to hold the holy water, it is no wonder that the devil, if he had any foreknowledge of the ufe it was defigned for, fhould be very unwilling to fatigue himfelf with carrying weapons to be employed againft himfelf, and provide a veffel for that water by which he and his legions may at any time be confounded and put to flight. However, from the largenefs of the vafe, it does not feem probable that it was employed for that ufe. It muft be acknowledged to be a valuable piece, on account of its dimenfions, and the matter of which it confifts.

The font of St. Zeno's church is very large, and cut out of one block of white marble. The table of the high altar likewife confifts of one piece of marble, thirteen feet long, and fix broad, which was the produce of this country. St. Zeno lies in the vault under this church, which is adorned with feveral pillars of yellow marble. On the church-door, which is plated with bronze, are reprefented, but very rudely, all ranks and orders of ecclefiaftics. On both fides of the entrance feveral fcriptural ftories are carved on ftone; thofe of the Old Teftament on the right-hand, as one enters into the church, and thofe of the New on the other fide. The eaftern *magi* are here reprefented with crowns on their heads; and, in the reprefenting the apprehending of Chrift in the garden, Peter cuts off Malchus's ear, and is diftinguifhed by a key hanging at his arm. The fculpture on the outfide of this church is fomething remarkable, as it reprefents horfemen, wild beafts, hunting matches, &c. with Latin infcriptions over them, very few of which are now legible. The vulgar entertain themfelves with abundance of ftories relating to thefe images. Among other things, they tell us, that king Theodoric and Satan entered into a compact, by virtue of which, the latter was bound, at all times, to fupply his majefty with good horfes and hounds. The perfon on horfeback faid to reprefent Theodoric rides with ftirrups, contrary to the practice of antiquity.

<small>Baffo-relievo's on the church-door.</small>

Cn-

On the wall, near the roof, two cocks are seen dragging a fox with his feet fastened to a log of wood: the like is seen of inlaid work on the pavement at St. Mark's church in Venice. The last piece, because the word *Galli* signifies both Cocks and Frenchmen, is supposed to allude to Charles VIII. and Lewis XII. kings of France, and the crafty Luigi Sforza duke of Milan. Misson also conjectures, that the Veronese figures allude to Desiderius king of Lombardy, or his son Adalgisus, and Pepin and Charles the Great. But I am inclined to think, that giving a mysterious signification to those grotesque figures with which the builders of the middle ages were fond of embellishing their works, is frequently attributing to them designs which they never thought of. As to St. Zeno's church, it is far from being of that antiquity commonly ascribed to it, as the title of *Rex Galliæ*, to be seen in a stone inscription on the porch of this church, was unknown in such a remote epocha.

Doubt concerning the antiquity of St. Zeno's church.

Connoisseurs in painting will find entertainment in the church of St. Nazario, which belongs to the Benedictines, and those of St. Stephano, Fermo, &c. The Capuchine monks have some fine pieces of painting in their church, by Farenati, in one of which, as a compliment to the fathers, St. Francis is represented taking down our Saviour from the cross.

Paintings in other churches.

The Veronese women are well shaped, and of a fresh complexion, for which, unquestionably, they are obliged to the goodness of the air. The neighbourhood of the mountains constantly refreshes this city in the heats of summer with a cool evening breeze. And tho' the orange-trees, &c. are not exposed here in winter to the open air; yet the climate produces all kinds of fruits and vegetables in perfection.

Women of Verona.

In count Giusti's garden is a very grand walk of cypress-trees, some of which exceed a hundred feet in height, and are above two hundred years old. This garden, in which there is a very curious labyrinth, is laid out on an eminence, which yields a delightful prospect of the city and the neighbouring plain. It has likewise a grotto, which is so contrived, that the least sound or whisper may be distinctly heard from one corner to another. Under a statue of Ceres erected in the garden, are these words:

Count Giusti's garden. Large cypresses.

Ne quid Veneri
Deeſſet,
Cum Bacchô Ceres
Aſſociatur.

'That nothing might be wanting to Venus, Ceres is here joined with Bacchus.'

Under the ſtatue of Venus is the following inſcription:

Sine me lætum
Nihil exoritur:
Statua in Viridario
Mihi poſita eſt
Ut in Venere Venus eſſet.

'Without me there is nothing that charms; my ſtatue is placed in this garden, becauſe a beautiful place becomes the goddeſs of beauty.'

And under the ſtatue of Bacchus:

Ambulator,
Ne trepides,
Bacchum Amatorem
Non Bellatorem
Ad Genium loci
Dominus P.

'Paſſenger, be not afraid, I am Bacchus the lover, not the warrior, and ſtationed here, as the genius of the place, by the poſſeſſor.'

The country about Verona produces good peaches, melons, figs, ſtrawberries, truffles, very large artichoaks, aſparagus, cheſnuts, apples, pears, plums, grapes, olives, and eſculent herbs.

Signior Gazzuola's garden is laid out in fine walks, planted with trees which afford an agreeable ſhade. The owner was formerly a counſellor, but has procured the title of count; and as Gazzuola, in Italian, ſignifies a magpye, that bird is his coat of arms, with this motto, LOQUENDO, *i. e.* by ſpeaking. This delightful place he owes to his ſkill in his profeſſion. The former owner of it, who, it ſeems, had ma-

VERONA.

ny law-suits on his hands, employed Gazzuola so long to plead for him till he had no other way of satisfying his demands, but by making over the house and garden to him *. As soon as Gazzuola had taken possession of the garden, he took down the arms of the former owner, and put up his own with the motto LOQUENDO, inscribed under them; which, contrary to his intention, is interpreted of the means by which he acquired this garden.

Jocular allusion to them.

I shall conclude this letter with an account of the several kinds of petrifactions which have been found about Verona, of which Bastiano Rotario, a physician, has a very large collection. The most remarkable among these, in my opinion, is a kind of sea-crabs called Paguri, which are rarely to be met with.

Petrifactions.

Sea crabs.

Betwixt Verona and Vicenza in the district of Bolco and not far from Vestene nuova are found all kinds of petrified

Fishes.

---

* A general censure from the misbehaviour of a few is extremely uncharitable. However, the lawyers, from time immemorial, have been looked upon in a disadvantageous light. Even in Augustus's time, they were become very contemptible at Rome; for they had departed from the solid eloquence by which Cicero and Hortensius did honour to their profession, instigated one party against another, and enriched themselves by chicanery and malpractices, till that emperor saw himself under a necessity of diminishing their number, and putting a check to their avarice. In the time of Lewis emperor of Germany, it was found necessary to publish a solemn edict to put a stop to their abuses. *Aventin. annal. Boj. l. IV. ad an.* 850, *p.* 244. *Diminuta sunt caussidicorum merces, quorum persidia nihil venalius. Nec est quidquam, quod Teutones, nostro ævo magis ad summam egestatem redigit quam litium calumniæ & legulejorum aurijuga turba, qui quasi Sardi vrnales fora constipant.* ' The fees of pleaders were reduced, their iniquitous venality being grown to a monstrous height: nor are the Germans more impoverished by any thing in our age than by lawsuits, and the chicanery of the venal tribe of pettifoggers, with which the courts of justice are crowded.' However, no people perhaps shewed a greater detestation of the lawyers than the ancient Germans. *Lucius Florus, Hist. Rom. l.* IV. *c.* 12. § 37, says, *Nihil illa cæde Variana cruentius: nihil insultatione barbarorum intolerantius, præcipuè tamen in caussarum patronos. Aliis oculos, aliis manus amputabant: unius os sutum, recisa prius lingua, quam in manu tenens barbarus: Tandem, inquit, vipera sibilare desiste,* i. e. ' Never was any defeat more bloody than that of Varius, nothing more savage than the insults of the barbarians; especially towards the pleaders of causes. Of some they plucked out the eyes, and cut off the hands of others: they sewed up the mouth of one of them, having first tore out his tongue, which a barbarian holding up in his hand, sarcastically said, " Now cease to hiss, viper." Among the ancients, the character of a wicked lawyer has been exposed by Ammian. Marcell. *lib.* XXX. *c.* 12. *Cicero pro Rosc. Amer. c.* 20. *Seneca de ira, l.* I. *c.* 7, *l.* III. *c.* 37. *Petron. in Satyr.* And, among the moderns, see *Ziegler in rabul. A. Fritsch in advoc. peccant.* and the famous Italian professor of law, Aurel. di Gennaro's treatise *delle viziose maniere del defender le cause nel foro,* 1745.

fish,

VERONA.

fish, most of which are of the salt-water species, in a sort of white loam. The soil contains but a small quantity of chalk. These fishes are mostly well preserved, their bones being intire, and, frequently, even their scales. They chiefly consist of the Sarda minor, pike, soals, thornbacks, the Hirundo marina, a flying fish, pearch, the scarus, and gudgeon.

Besides these, near Bolco are found crabs, large oyster-shells, and petrified leaves of the Lonchys aspera. *Other petrifactions.*

Zannichelli, a celebrated Venetian apothecary, in the year 1721, published a treatise dedicated to P. Bonanni a Jesuit, intitled *Lithographia duorum Montium Veronensium vulgò di Boricolo et di Zoppica dictorum*. The most remarkable petrifactions found in those mountains are the *Ostrea maxima rugosa, lapides lenticulares majores levigati, Conchitæ, Cochleitæ, Turbinitæ, Numismata sive Lapides frumentarii*, &c.

In the neighbourhood of Bognolo are found Coralloides, Ostrea, Numismata majora, Tubulitæ instar Cornu Ammonis in se revoluti, Cochleitæ and Buccinitæ. Petrified corallines are likewise dug up in Monte di Soave.

Near Ronca are found *Conchitæ læves, transversim minutissimè striati*, together with other species of the same, *Tellinitæ, Strombitæ læves, Strombitæ muricati & striati*, &c. *Turbinitæ fasciati, Turbinitæ fasciati & striati, Turbinitæ muricati, Turbinitæ muricati & in orbe superiore fasciati, Turbinitæ fasciati, & puncticulati, Turbinitæ fasciati & echinosi, Turbinitæ heptangulares variis striis asperati, Turbinitæ alii multangulares striati, Muricites marmoreus rostro incurvato, Muricitæ leviter striati, partim rostri curvi, partim auriti, majores & minores, Murex marmoreus auritus rufescentis coloris, ostreum bivalve rufescentis coloris, Cochleitæ læves, Buccinitæ læves, Chamæ coloris cinerei transversim striatæ, Purpuritæ echiniformes, Coralloidæ, Madreporæ, Numismata sc. Lapides frumentarii*, &c.

In several other parts of the territories of Verona are found *Conchitæ, Pectinitæ auriti, Pectinitæ sulcis latissimis insigniti, Pectines ingentes striis crassioribus rugosi, Pectunculitæ minutissimè per longum striati, Pectunculitæ Listeri, Pectunculi per longum & transversum striati, Tellinitæ, Cochleitæ leves marmorei*, together with other species of them, *Cornua Ammonis, Nautilus in marmore rufescenti, Odontopetræ, Coralloides, Lapis frumentarius sc. juxta Langium Semen fœniculi, Lapis Lyncius sc. Belemnites, Alcyonia varia, Strombi, Lapides lenticulares, Purpuræ marmoreæ, Turbines in longum undati & eleganter minutatim in transversum crispati, Turbinitæ per longum & transversim striati,*

VICENZA.

ati, Fungi, Modioli & Lapides Amygdalam referentes, Muricite ̄auriti, Chamæ dentatæ ̣̣̄̄rinitæ. Bucarditæ, which the country people call *tortelli*; these are ⸻ and nearly in the form of a heart, *musculi, ostreum bivalve muv.* ⁊. *osteocollæ cretaceæ variæ species, cancri variæ magnitudinis, Le.* ⸻ *folia*, and other petrified leaves, as also, *Echinitæ Spatagoides* nu⸻: besides *Mischio de Brentonico* and *Giallo di Torri*.

The country about Verona produces several other species of good marble besides those called Mischio di Brentonico and Giallo di Torri; and specimens of all these are to be seen in many of the churches in this city.

VERONA, May 2, 1730.

LETTER LXX.

Account of VICENZA.

SIR,

Country. THE distance from Verona to Vicenza is thirty Italian miles: The road lies through a stony but fertile and pleasant country.

The city. Vicenza contains a great many elegant and beautiful buildings, and the tops of several of them are ornamented with statues; particularly those in the piazza or area before the council-house. This piazza makes such a grand appearance that it only wants fountains to make it a Piazza di Novona in miniature. After this city fell under the Venetian yoke, they erected here, as in other conquered cities, the arms of St. Mark on a lofty pillar, which are a winged lion. On another pillar of the same kind stands the image of our Saviour.

Council-house. The council-house called il Palazzo della Ragione has a very spacious hall; but it is not kept in good order. In the criminal court is a picture representing the final judgment, painted by Titian. In another part of this palace is the story of Noah's drunkenness, &c. painted by Paris Bardone. This large edifice contains several other fine paintings; but most of them are disposed in an improper light.

Academia Olympicorum. There is in this city an academy or literary society stiled the Olympici, whose design is chiefly the improvement of the

VICENZA.

the Italian language. The academians hold their meetings ^{Curious} in a theatre built by the celebrated Palladio; which is very ^{theatre.} well worth a traveller's notice for its admirable construction. It is but very seldom used as a theatre; the opera of Sophonisba being the only one that has been exhibited in it. The perspective of the stage is admirable, and it is decorated with statues of the Roman emperors and philosophers. The parterre or pit is likewise adorned with several statues, and the seats are disposed after the manner of the ancient amphitheatres.

As for the ruins of the ancient Roman theatre, not ^{Roman} long since shewn in the Pigafetti and Gualdi gardens, nothing ^{theatre.} is now to be seen of them, an house being built on the place where it stood.

In the Campus Martius without the city is a triumphal ^{Triumphal} arch built from a design of the abovementioned Palladio, ^{arch.} in imitation of the ancient structures of that kind. Formerly the yearly fair, which lasts from the 15th day to the end of October, was held on the Campus Martius; but for some ^{Campus} years past it has been removed into the city. ^{Martius.}

In count Montenari's house is a hall finely painted, a ^{Montenari} great deal of curious stucco work, and a small gallery of ^{palace.} select pictures.

The palace of count Chiragado stands in a large area, and ^{Chiragado} is an elegant piece of architecture. ^{palace.}

In count Wale's house where Frederic king of Denmark ^{Count} lodged as he passed through Vicenza, is a good collection of ^{Wale's} fine pictures. ^{house.}

The city of Vicenza is of no extraordinary extent; ^{Number of} however there are supposed to be in it fifty-seven churches, ^{convents,} convents, and hospitals. The cathedral affords nothing ^{&c.} worth a traveller's notice.

The Dominican church deserves seeing on account of the ^{Dominican} high altar, and the inlaid Florentine work on the Palliotto, ^{church.} which represents the annunciation, the institution of the Lord's supper, and the resurrection of Christ. The other ornaments of the altar, consisting of flowers and statues, are also executed with a masterly hand. Here is a piece of painting representing the adoration of the eastern *magi* by Paolo Veronese.

On the front of St. Barbara's church the following in- ^{St. Barba-} scription is to be seen: ^{ra's church.}

Bb 3 *Senio*

VICENZA.

Senio fatiscens Ecclesia
V. Kal. Mart. A. MDCXCV. horrendis motibus
Universâ nutante Urbe
Propemodum excussa
E situ ac ruderibus elegantior exsurgit
A. MDCCII.

' This church, being almost ruinous by length of time, was, on the 25th of February 1695, when the whole city shook by the terrible concussions of an earthquake, almost demolished, but rose from its ruins with greater beauty and elegance in the year 1702.'

S. Maria in Campagnano. The cieling and several chapels in the church di S. Maria in Campagnano were painted by Pordenone.

The Theatines church has been lately rebuilt.

Mons Pietatis. The Mons Pietatis is a superb edifice, and has an excellent library opened for the use of the public.

Madonna in Monte. Without the city is the church of the Madonna in Monte, which has a good front, and is covered with votive pieces.

Remarks on a piece by Paul Veronese. There is a picture, painted by Paul Veronese, in the refectory of this convent, representing pope Gregory the Great sitting with several pilgrims at table, where our Saviour also is present. Though this piece be finely executed, the invention is very absurd; for the pope sits at the upper end without his triple crown, and next to him Christ is represented without any particular symbol or mark of distinction. The next is a cardinal, and on the other side is another cardinal with a large pair of spectacles on his nose. A page dressed in the Spanish manner waits at table with a dog under his arm. Under the table a cat, a monkey, &c. are represented. The mountain on which this church and the convent to which it belongs are built yields a very agreeable prospect, which extends as far as Padua. For the convenience of the usual processions, and of pilgrims, a large ascent by steps has been made up the acclivity of the mountain. At the beginning of the ascent in the valley, a triumphal arch is erected; and on the left-hand of it is a statue of the virgin Mary.

Situation. Fertile country. Vicenza lies between two mountains in a large plain; and the territory belonging to it on account of its fertility is generally called the garden and shambles of Venice. The meadows about Vicenza are watered by the little rivers Leogra, Loroto, Astignello, Debita, Rerone, and Tribualo: and the rivulet

VICENZA.

vulet Bachiglione runs through the middle of the city. The fineſt garden at Vicenza is that of count Valmarano, which, indeed, for its ſituation, hedges, viſta's, arbors, and beautiful walks, may be reckoned one of the nobleſt in Italy. A covered walk of cedar and orange-trees planted alternately, which is above two hundred common paces in length, is particularly admired. On one ſide of it is a broad canal well ſtocked with large barbels and other fiſh, which at the ſound of a pipe immediately appear in great numbers on the ſurface in order to be fed. Over the entrance into the garden, on the Verona ſide, is the following inſcription:

Si te ingredientem graviores fortè
Huc uſque inſecutæ ſunt curæ,
Eas velint nolint procul
Nunc ut abeant facito;
Hilaritati namque & genio
Pars hæc potiſſ, dicata eſt,

Cedros hoſce qui dempſerit
Floreſve carpſerit
Is ſacrilegus eſto,
Vertumnoque & Pomonæ,
Queis ſunt ſacri,
Pœnas luito.

Civis, Amice, Advena,
Qui loci amœnitate cupis oblectarier,
Securus huc ingredere
Teque largiter recrea,
Nullus intus canis,
Nullus Draco,
Nullus falce minaci Deus,
Omnia ſed tuta benignèque expoſita.
Sic voluit Comes LEONARDUS VALMANARA
Hortorum dominus,
Modeſtiam quòd tuam & continentiam
Cuſtodem forte fidat opportunum.
Anno MDXCII.

'If corroding cares have haply followed thee thus far, though they be loth to leave thee, diſpel and baniſh them away. This place is more particularly dedicated to genial mirth and feſtivity. Whoever ſhall damage theſe cedars,

VICENZA.

'or crop a flower, let him be accounted a sacrilegious per-
'son, and be punished to appease Vertumnus and Pomona,
'to whom they are consecrated.

'Native, friend, or stranger, who desirest to amuse thy-
'self with the rural charms of this place, thou mayest se-
'curely enter these gardens designed for pleasure and recrea-
'tion. Here is no fierce dog, no frightful dragon, no dei-
'ty, with his threatening weapon; but every thing here is
'freely and without danger exposed to thy view. Such is
'the pleasure of count Leonarda Valmanara, the owner of
'the gardens, who relies on thy modesty and good breeding,
'as sufficient to guard the place from any outrage.

Wine. This country produces plenty of excellent wine, which is particularly celebrated for its lenient quality in the pains of the gout.

Vindictive temper of the Italians, and particularly of the people of Vicenza. The inhabitants of Vicenza are charged with being of a more vindictive temper than the rest of the Italians; on which account they are commonly called Gli assassini Vicentini; i.e. 'These Vicentian assassins.' This is certain, that travellers, and especially the Germans, who have here the character of being hot and quarrelsome, should be very careful in every part of Italy to avoid disputes, and especially with the postillions, and other persons of the lower class; for the desire of revenge is such a predominant passion in them, that they have been known to follow a traveller six or eight stages to watch an opportunity of gratifying their malice and revenge.

Open violence, indeed, is little to be apprehended from them, on which account the danger is the greater.

Omne animal timidum crudele.

'Cowards are always cruel.'

Murder is looked upon in Italy in a very different light from what it is in other countries. If a robbery has been committed, either in the streets or on the market-place, in any of the towns of Italy, and the people are alarmed to stop the thief, there is always assistance at hand to pursue the criminal; but, upon crying after a murderer, no body offers to stir; and the assassin saves himself by flying unmolested to a church, convent, or other asylum, where, to the great honour of the clergy be it spoken, the villain receives all possible

VICENZA.

sible assistance that he may escape the hands of the civil power. I remember a postillion who once drove me was treacherously stabbed at the post-house of Pistoia; and, though the fact was committed in the presence of more than ten persons, not one of them stirred a foot to seize or pursue the murderer.

The meanest citizens of Vicenza, in signing contracts or other deeds, add to their name the title of Comte Vicentino, or count of Vicenza, an empty piece of pride, which they derive from an answer, as is pretended, given by Charles V. who, when he was at Vicenza, to get rid of the importunate solicitations of several of the rich citizens, to grant them the title of counts, said in jest, Todos Contes;* 'I make you all counts.'

M. della Vale, an ingenious apothecary, who lives on the Piazza, has a curious collection of petrifactions; and especially of Verona petrified fishes. Those who are fond of these natural curiosities may collect, in many places of the district of Vicenza, *Pectunculi striati, Echini* and *Chelonites*; and particularly on the chalk-hill, as it is called, are found *Conchitæ bivalves, Tellinitæ, Musculitæ, Buccinitæ, Turbinitæ per longum & transversim striati, Pectinitæ auriti, Pectinitæ cum striis latissimis distincti, Pectunculi leviter striati, Echini, Cochleites, vertebræ piscium, &c.* Beyond the Capuchine mountain, near Schium, towards the north-east and on the borders of Trent, are found the Echinitæ discoidei, Chelonites, Pectines, and Gagates.

Beyond Schium, farther north, in a mountain called il Monte Summano, medals, and other remains of antiquity, have been dug up. Some derive the name of this hill from its height; but others from a temple of Pluto, the ruins of which with the following inscription, as it is said, are still to be seen there: *Plutoni Summano aliisque Diis Stygiis*†, i. e. 'To Pluto of Summanus, and the other infernal deities.' A fragment of an altar consecrated to Pluto Summanus, placed in the church of S. Maria in Monte, is mentioned by

---

* As Charles V. did not settle any revenue on the burghers of Vicenza to maintain their imaginary dignity, the following proverb is not improperly applied to them:

Permultos Comites Vicentia nutrit egenos.

'As poor as a count of Vicenza.'

† *Vid. Fabrett. Inscript. p. 87.*

Gruter,

Gruter, *T. I. p.* 1015. *n.* 7. Macrobius and Capella *de Nupt. Philolog. lib.* ii. suppoſes that Summanus was put for *ſummus*, or *Princeps Manium*; i. e. ' The chief of the Manes.' But Summanus has not been demonſtrated to be a ſurname of Pluto; and perhaps thoſe two names may imply two different deities. Ovid, who thoroughly underſtood the heathen mythology, is himſelf at a loſs what to make of the god Summanus; for he ſays, in his *Faſti, lib.* vi. *v.* 731,

*Reddita, quiſquis is eſt, Summano templa feruntur
Tunc cum Romano, Pyrrhe, timendus eras.*

' It is ſaid, that temples were firſt erected to Summanus,
' whoever he be, when Pyrrhus grew formidable to the
' Romans.

The diſtance from Vicenza to Padua is eighteen Italian miles. The road lies through a fertile, well-cultivated plain. Paſſengers may go from one city to the other by water; but the paſſage is very tedious, being no leſs than ſixty Italian miles by reaſon of the winding of the river.

VICENZA, May 3, 1730.

LETTER LXXI.

Account of the City of PADUA.

SIR,

Padua. THE Paduans boaſt, that the republic of Venice owes its origin and riſe to their city. But it is now ſome centuries ſince Padua has been brought under the Venetian yoke, Number of which has occaſioned it greatly to decline from its former its inhabi- ſplendor; ſo that at preſent it hardly contains forty thouſand tants. inhabitants *.

Univerſity. The univerſity erected here by the emperor Frederic II, with a view of prejudicing that of Bologna, is in a very de-

* The number of inhabitants at Breſcia is computed to be thirty-five thouſand.

clining

clining state; for the number of students at present scarce amounts to four or five hundred. This is in a great measure owing to the neglect of checking the extravagant licentiousness and insolence of the students, which formerly rose to such extremities, that no one could walk the streets after dusk without being obnoxious to their insults, which they practised with impunity. The watchword of those desperadoes in their nocturnal excursions was, *Qui va li?* i.e. 'Who goes there?' Hence they came to be called *Quivalisti*. And, though their enormities are very much decreased with their numbers, yet discreet people generally take care not to be out in the night at Padua.

In the year 1722 such a tumult happened here in the day-time, that a syndic and four students were shot by the *sbirri*. As these officers exceeded their commission, several of them were hanged, or sent to the galleys, that the students might have no cause, or pretence, to forsake the university. An inscription was also set up in the place where the tumult began, as a memorial of the satisfaction given to the students on that account. It is not above two years since count la Rosa lost his life in the streets of Padua in the night.

When a protestant traveller dies at Padua, he is buried without any difficulty either in a church or a convent, if he has only taken care to be matriculated in the university. *Protestants buried in churches.*

The college is called il Palazzo degli Studii, and is adorned with great numbers of statues of the most celebrated persons educated there with proper inscriptions. The anatomy-school has six galleries round it, for the conveniency of seeing the dissections; but it is so dark, that those operations are performed in it by candle-light. Here are no skeletons to be seen; but the professors of physic have several in their respective houses. The physic-garden has very few equals; and the disposition of the plants is very elegant and convenient. It was founded by Franciscus Bonæfidei, who was the first professor of botany at Padua, and died in the year 1658. *Physic-garden.*

Over the entrance are the rules prescribed to those who frequent this garden, with the penalties for disobeying them, &c.

The superior advantages which this garden has enjoyed above most other physic-gardens is, that Guilandini, Cortuso, Alpino, Vesling, and other celebrated botanists, have successively had the superintendency of it. Vesling was a native of Minden in Westphalia, and was honoured by Ottavio Ferrari with the following epitaph:

JOANNI

*JOANNI VESLINGIO, Mindano,
Naturæ verique scrutatori solertissimo; qui sapientiæ, atque exoticarum stirpium studia Ægypto ac Syria peragrata ab Veneto Senatu rei herbariæ & corporum Sectioni præfectus, eum Latinitatis & Græcæ eruditionis cultum mutis artibus circumfudit, ut illic naturæ ludentis pompam æmularetur, hic spectaculi diritatem Orationis dulcedine deliniret, ut quantum oculi paterentur, tantum sibi aures placerent. Demum laboribus fractus dum miseræ plebi gratuitam operam præstat, noxio contactu vitam publicæ Saluti impendit. Jo. Pueppa Socero B. M. P. Anno MDCLV.*

' To the memory of John Vesling, a native of Minden,
' a most indefatigable searcher after truth, and into the works
' of nature, who, for the improvement of his knowledge,
' and his skill in botany, having travelled all over Egypt
' and Syria, was afterwards, by the senate of Venice, ap-
' pointed professor of botany and anatomy, and set forth
' those demonstrative sciences with all the ornaments of
' Greek and Roman eloquence; so that, in the former, he
' imitated the exuberance and flowery pride of nature; and,
' in the latter, he softened the horror of anatomical opera-
' tions by the harmony and sweetness of his accents, which
' pleased the ear no less than the dissections shocked the eye.
' At length broken by care, and assiduity in his profession,
' whilst he was attending the poor without fee or reward,
' he contracted a fatal disease, and thus laid down his life in
' the service of the public. John Pueppa erected this mo-
' nument as a mark of his affection to his worthy father-in-
' law, in the year 1655.'

The Morosini garden in the Brenta Vecchia deserves the notice of those who admire orangeries and exotic plants.

The Franciscan church is one of the most remarkable places at Padua. It is dedicated to S. Antonio di Padua. This celebrated patron saint was born at Lisbon in the year 1195, and died in the year 1231. Several books are published, giving an account of his life, and the great miracles performed by St. Antony, all ushered in with the licence and approbation of the superior clergy; though many passages in those books cannot be read without offence. Indeed several Roman-catholics would look upon them as the fictions of heretics, were it not manifest from their own books that nothing is falsely charged upon them with regard to this
sain-.

saint. The patronage of St. Antony is certainly worth all the endeavours that a good catholic can be at to obtain it, as it is not limited to this short life, but extends to the day of judgment, with an efficacy not inferior to that which the scripture attributes to our blessed Saviour only *. Fini, an Italian poet, has thus expressed his confidence in this saint:

> Che fo? che penso? al perentorio estremo,
> Al novissimo di mi chiama il fato,
> Con proclama di Morte io son citato
> Del' alte Rote al Tribunal supremo.
> — an punto! ò gran punto! io gelo, io tremo,
> — itar già sento il mio peccato;
> Vieni. *onio, e per me fà l' Avvocato,
> Se tu tra'. . *causa, ia più non temo.
> Io temo ben delle . . colpe il sia,
> E perche reo nel . . processo io sono
> Del' eterne Giustitia, temo il Dio.
> Mà spero al fin de la P..l. nel trono
> S'hò la lingua d' Antonio favor mio,
> Segnatura di gratia e di pen...

'Alas! what shall I do, and whither are my thoughts? Fate calls me to the last day. I am summoned by death before the supreme tribunal of heaven! O weighty crisis! O weighty concern! I shiver and tremble when I consider what pleasure I took in sin. Come, blessed Antony, and be thou my advocate; if thou wilt but plead my cause, I shall no longer fear. 'Tis true, the punishment due to my sins; I fear the divine justice, as I shall be found guilty before the throne of God: but I hope to find mercy at last if Antony's tongue be employed in my favour, as it is the seal and pledge of pardon and forgiveness.'

The chapel of this saint is almost covered with votive pieces, &c. for the cures and other favours obtained by his intercession; and among the rest is the following inscription †

---

* The devotion of the Paduans to this saint is such, that the beggars do not ask alms for God's, but for St. Antony's sake; and, among the votive tables, one of them has the following inscription: *Exaudit S. Antonius, quos non exaudit Deus;* 'Those whom God himself does not hear, St. Antony hears.'

† Vid. *Relazioni del gran Santo di Padoua Antonio, e dell' alte sue maraviglie, di Lelio Mantini. In Padoua* 1654.

Viator,

Viator, aspice novum portentum,
ne mirere,
Adsunt similia sæpe & frequentia,
At venerare.
Veneti maris unda incautum Livium
Decennem rapuit,
Inscio Patre
Alienum, non filium conquerente,
Bis horæ spatio tectum
Pietas servatum voluit.
Cur dubitas?
Ignis, Mare, Ferrum,
Cætera occurrentia mala,
Omnia Sancto cedunt.
Zacharias Pontinus Pater
Tanti muneris memor
Tanto Sancto posuit.
1645. Kal. Augusti.

'Traveller, behold a new prodigy; yet wonder not, but adore the saint who often works such miracles amongst us; Livio, a boy of ten years of age, carelessly playing on the shore of the Adriatic sea, was washed away by the waves, while his father, knowing nothing of this accident, unexpectedly found his son, whose devotion to the saint had miraculously preserved him two hours under water. Dost thou doubt of this? Even fire, water, the sword, and every disease own the power of the saint. In memory of this great mercy to his son, the father, Zachary Pontano, hung up this votive table to so great a saint on the 1st day of August, 1645.'

Rich chapel of this saint.

In this saint's chapel I saw burning above fifty large silver lamps, and one of gold, together with two very large silver candlesticks standing on white marble pedestals. The walls are embellished with admirable basso-relievo's by Tullio Lombardo, Antonio Lombardo, Giacomo Sansovino, and Gieronimo Campagna. St. Antony's sarcophagus is of serpentine, and lies under the altar. The altar is adorned with seven angels of bronze, cast by Aspetti, and likewise with some exquisite sculpture; and indeed the chapel, in every respect, has but few equals. On one side of it are shewn two wax flambeaux, eight or nine inches in diameter, which are

fixed

fixed in an iron-work; thefe are faid to have been offered by a treacherous Turk, with a defign to blow up the chapel by means of fire-works concealed in them. But it feems St. Antony prevented the calamity: for, thefe flambeaux being lighted, he cried out aloud three times from his coffin, that they fhould be put out again; which occafioned a farther examination of the flambeaux: and thus the villanous plot was difcovered. We were entertained with fuch another ftory of a powder plot at Loretto. St. Antony's remains is faid continually to emit a moft fragrant perfume, which is chiefly fmelt at a crevice behind the altar. The faint's tongue is kept with great devotion in a glafs vafe in the veftry, and very fervent prayers are offered up to it. Here is a vaft treafure of filver candlefticks, crucifixes, gold chalices, pyxes, and feveral reliques belonging to the chapel.

St. Antony's tongue.
Treafure.

Oppofite to St. Antony's chapel is that of St. Felix, in which are fome paintings in *frefco* by the famous Giotto of Florence,

St. Felix's chapel.

Under a marble buft near St. Antony's chapel is the following epitaph by Ottavio Ferrari:

CONSTANTINO DOTTORIO,

Ingentis animi juveni, qui in Dalmatia militiam aufpicatus, flagrante Cretico bello illuc tranfiit, & memorabili Urbis obfidione ftrenui & maximè pugnacis nomen implevit; nam pro vallo excubans, crebrifque in hoftem eruptionibus, non uno vulnere decorus, terrâque tormentorum impetu excuffâ penè obrutus & propè oculis captus, cum illi Senatus emeriti decoris præmium Tarvifii armorum regimen obtuliffet, honefto otio labores ac pericula præferens, dum quotidie pectus mortis capax hofti objicit, glande trajectus mortalitatem magis finivit quàm vitam. Julius Patens defolatiffimus, quod accipere debuerat, pofuit. Ann. M.DLCXX.

' To the magnanimous youth Conftantio Dottori, who,
' having ferved his firft campaign in Dalmatia, afterwards
' diftinguifhed himfelf in the Cretan war, and acquired the
' reputation of a brave and intrepid foldier at the memorable
' fiege of the city of Candia; being pofted before the trench-
' es in the frequent fallies made by the enemy, he received
' feveral honourable wounds, and almoft loft his fight, be-
' ing in a manner buried under-ground by the fpringing of a
' mine. The fenate, as the reward of his valour, offered him
' an honourable poft; but he, preferring hardfhips and dan-
' gers

'gers even to honourable leisure, continued in the army, where he intrepidly exposed himself to the fire of the enemy. He was at last shot by a musket-ball, and thus finished his mortal course rather than his life. Giulio, his afflicted father, erected this monument to his son, who ought rather to have performed this last office to his father, 1670.'

Basso-relievo's in the choir. In the choir are several brass basso-relievo's of scriptural history, executed agreeable to the subjects they represent. Among these, Sampson dying under the ruins of the idolatrous temple cannot be sufficiently admired. The artist that made them was Vellano, a native of Padua, who was a disciple of Donatello. The stalls in the choir are also worth seeing, being adorned with inlaid figures and sculpture.

Great altar. Near the high altar, on the left-hand in going up to it, is a bronze candlestick, of a very extraordinary size, and incomparable workmanship. On the altar stand six silver candlesticks, near six feet high, and in the middle a crucifix of the same metal, which is much taller. Behind the altar, which is insulated or detached from the wall, a chapel has been built, meerly as a repository for reliques.

Chapel of St. Francis. St. Francis's altar is remarkable for the delicacy of the workmanship in *pietre commesse*. It is also adorned with four black marble pillars, and two statues of white marble; one representing charity, the other grief. Among the many superb moununents in this church, that of Catterino Cornelio is one of the most remarkable: the epitaph was composed by the celebrated Ottavio Ferrari:

D. O. M. CATTERINO CORNELIO.

Andreæ Parentis summi Ducis impressa sanguine vestigia insistens, omnes honorum gradus emensus, Dalmatiæ, dein Cretæ cum summa potestate Legatus, triennium obsessa metropoli, manu, consilio, exemplo nutantia fata, & summum Urbis diem moratus est; sed dum in propugnaculo maximè hostibus infesto dies noctesque excubat, ollæ incendiariæ fulmine cœlo assertus est, Insularum nobilissimæ una in cineres collapsæ rogo funeratus. Federicus Cornelius Fratri incomparabili H. P. P. Ann. M.DC.LXXIV.

'Sacred to God the greatest and best of beings, and to Catterino Cornelio, who with hereditary courage treading in the steps of Andrew his illustrious father, having passed through all military degrees, behaved with universal ap-
'plause

PADUA.

' plaufe as commander in chief in Dalmatia; afterwards he
' defended Candia for the fpace of three years, and by his
' conduct, courage, and example; retarded the taking of
' that tottering city; but being pofted in a baftion which
' greatly annoyed the enemy, while he exerted himfelf night
' and day with indefatigable ardour, he was removed to hea-
' ven by a red-hot bomb-fhell, and buried in the ruins of
' the moft magnificent houfes, which were demolifhed at
' the fame time. To his heroic brother, Frederico Corne-
' lio erected this monument in the year 1674.'

In the chapel of the Holy Sacrament is to be feen the tomb of Erafmus Gattamelata, with an image of him in armour. The equeftrian ftatue with which the republic of Venice has honoured the memory of this general is the work of the celebrated Donatello, and ftands on the area before this church. Oppofite to Erafmus lies his John Antony Gattamelata, who, according to his epitaph, was not inferior to his father in military glory.

In St. Jofeph's chapel is a beautiful monument of two brothers, of the family of Marchetti: it is of white marble, and adorned with ftatues. The deceafed are highly celebrated in the epitaph, which is very extravagant, for their profound knowledge In phyfic and anatomy; their fkill in furgery, &c. &c. [Monument of two brothers.]

Here is alfo a beautiful tomb of Pius Capiliftius, a Venetian general, who died in 1557.

Ottavio Ferrari, a profeffor in the univerfity of Padua, and celebrated for his many learned works, lies buried between the chapels di S. Felice and del Crofififfo. His monument is fo magnificent, that few learned men can boaft of the like. His epitaph is as follows: [Tomb of Ottavio Ferrari.]

OCTAVIO FERRARIO MEDIOLANENSI in quo ornando & extollendo magni Reges & Principes certarunt. Veneta Refpublica præter alia decoramenta bis mille florenorum honorario auxit. Ludovicus Magnus, Francorum Rex, fponte aureorum quingentorum annuorum congiarium diu indulfit. Chriftina Augufta equeftri infigni extulit. Ille Regum opes ac munera animo æquans, facundiâ, fide, & confilio invidiam aut vicit, aut gloriæ incitamentum habuit. Septem & quadraginta annos cum admiratione publicè auditus eft. Quinto & feptuagefimo obticuit, quamdiu litteris honor conftabit fcriptis apud pofteros locuturus. Julius Ferrarius P. E. M. P. Anno MDCLXXXIV.

VOL. III.   C c   ' To

'To the memory of Ottavio Ferrari of Milan, whom
' great monarchs and Princes ſtrove with emulation to ho-
' nour and prefer. The republic of Venice, befides other
' honours, fettled a penfion of two thoufand florins on
' him. Lewis the Great, king of France, long favoured
' him with a yearly penfion of five hundred louis-d'ors.
' The auguſt Chriſtina, queen of Sweden, conferred on him
' the order of knighthood. His exalted foul equalled the
' wealth and munificence of kings; and by his eloquence,
' fidelity, and wifdom, he either conquered envy, or made
' it an incentive to glory. His public lectures were heard
' with admiration for forty-feven years. In the feventy-fifth
' year of his age death filenced his harmonious tongue; but
' he will fpeak in his writings to poſterity as long as learn-
' ing is honoured and eſteemed. This monument was erected
' by Giulio Ferrari, as a mark of his tender affection to the
' beſt of parents, in the year 1684.

Not far from this is the following epitaph on count Sicci's tomb.

Monument of count Sicci.

COMITI HORATIO SICCO
Patr. Pat. qui avitam gloriam fortibus geſtis æmulatus, in propugnaculo Viennæ à Turcis obſeſſæ ſagittâ transfixus, cuniculi ruinâ penè obrutus, demum plumbeâ glande trajectus Urbis, Imperii, & Religionis victima concidit, à Leopoldo Auguſto, cujus in aula adoleverat, elogio Chriſtiani Herois decoratus. Vincentius Paſchalicus Patr. Venet. H. M. P. Anno Sal. MDCLXXXVI.
Hac itur Elyſium.

' To count Horatio Sicci, a nobleman of Padua, who, in
' warlike exploits emulating the glory of his anceſtors, was
' dangerouſly wounded by an arrow in the defence of Vien-
' na, when befieged by the Turks, and was afterwards al-
' moſt buried by the fpringing of a mine; at length being
' fhot by a mufket-ball, he fell a glorious victim to the city,
' the empire, and religion, and was honoured by the empe-
' ror Leopold, in whofe court he had been educated, with
' the elogium of being a Chriſtian hero. Vincenzo Paſ-
' chali, a nobleman of Venice, erected this monument in
' the year 1686.
' By fuch brave actions patriot heroes mount
' Ætherial heights, and find the way to heav'n.'

The celebrated fculptor Auguſtino Zotto has fhewn his
fkill in the monument of Aleſſandro Contareni; under whofe
ſtatue is an infcription, fignifying that he was commander
in

in chief of the Venetian fleet againſt Adrian Barbaroſſo, the Turkiſh admiral, &c. &c.

Of Alexander Contareni.

Under the ſtatue of the celebrated cardinal Bembo, erected in his church, is the following inſcription:

PETRI BEMBI Cardinalis imaginem Hieronymus Quirinus Iſmaelii filius in publicum ponend. curavit, ut cujus in‑ genii monumenta æterna ſunt, ejus corporis quoque memoria ne à poſteris deſideretur. Vix. Ann. LXXVI. Menſ. VII. dies XXIX. Obiit XV. Cal. Febr. 1547.

Monument of cardinal Bembo.

' Gieronimo Quirini, ſon of Iſhmael, cauſed this image
' of cardinal Pietro Bembo to be publicly erected, that, as
' the monuments of his genius are eternal, the memory of
' his mortal part might alſo be perpetuated to poſterity. He
' lived ſeventy-ſix years, ſeven months, and twenty-nine
' days, and died on the 18th of January, 1547.'

The body of this famous cardinal lies at Rome in the Dominican church, called S. Maria ſopra Minerva, with the following epitaph:

Petro Bembo Patr. Ven. ob ejus ſingulares virtutes à Paulo III. Pont. Max. in Sac. Coll. cooptato Torquatus Bembus poſuit. Obiit XV. Kalend. Februar. 1547. Vixit annos 75. menſes 7. dies 28.

His epitaph.

' To the memory of Pietro Bembo, a noble Venetian, who
' for his eminent virtues, was promoted to the ſacred college
' by Paul III. this monument was erected by Torquato Bembo.
' He died January 18, 1547, aged ſeventy-five years, ſeven
' months, and twenty-eight days.'

Cardinal Bembo was a man of learning, and wrote very pure claſſic Latin; but was rather too cloſe an imitator of the ancients, for which he is cenſured by Julius Cæſar, Scaliger, Gaſper Francus, and Lipſius. It is ſaid he was ſo proud of his elegant Latin ſtile, that he would often ſay, he would not exchange it for the dutchy of Mantua. Lanzius, in his *Oratio contra Italos*, and others, charge him with hav‑ ing diſſuaded a friend from reading St. Paul's epiſtles [*], and ſays, that he himſelf would never look into the Bible or Bre‑

---

[*] He might have read the epiſtles in the original Greek without en‑ dangering his Latin ſtile. As for the Vulgate and moſt other Latin tran‑ ſlations of St. Paul's epiſtles, he might juſtly condemn them as barbarous, without any prejudice to his own character, or that of the inſpired wri‑ ter; ſo that the charge which this author mentions is no ſign of the cardi‑ nal's profaneneſs.

viary

viary for fear of corrupting the purity of his Latin ſtile. It ſeems he wrote ſome very obſcene and licentious compoſitions in his younger days.

Learned lady.

Laſtly, near the north-gate of this church is the marble ſtatue of a very learned lady of the Cornara family, with the following panegyric under it:

HELENÆ LUCRETIÆ CORNELIÆ PIS-COPIÆ, Joh. Baptiſtæ D. Marci Procuratoris Filiæ Heroinæ, animi celſitudine, pietate, caſtimonia, omni literaturâ & ſeptem linguarum peritiâ ſingulari, cum ab aliis Europæ Magnatibus, tum vel maximè ab Innocentio XI. P. M. perhonorifico diplomate, & ab Jo. III. Poloniæ Rege datis ad eam epiſtolis ſummopere commendatæ, quæ, poſthabitis Virorum Principum connubiis, ante D. Benedicti Antiſtites Deo primum virginitatem vovit, poſt ampliſſ. ædibus in aſceteria & peripatum converſis, ferreis uncis membra, divinis philoſophiciſque contemplationibus mentem acriùs exercuit. Demum in celebri Patav. Collegio unico poſt hominum memoriam exemplo Philoſophiæ Lauream adepta, Coronam prævenit, quam ipſi morum innocentiæ augurabatur in cælo. Obiit Ann. MDCLXXXIV. XXVI. Julii, Ætatis ſuæ XXXVIII.

Cujus Monumentum
Hieronymus Cornelius Frater
Graviore formâ corrigendum curavit,
Epigraphe ſervatâ
MDCCXXVII.

'To the memory of Helena Lucretia Corneliä Piſcopia, the
' illuſtrious daughter of Giovanni Battiſta procurator of St.
' Mark, who, for greatneſs of ſoul, piety, and chaſtity, her per-
' fect knowledge of ſeven languages, and every branch of
' polite literature, was honoured with letters of commenda-
' tion from ſeveral of the princes of Europe, particularly
' from John III. king of Poland, and a very honourable
' diploma from his holineſs pope Innocent XI. ſhe declined
' many advantageous offers of marriage from perſons of
' diſtinction, devoted herſelf to God at the altar of the
' Benedictines, and, having converted her ſpacious palace
' into a convent, mortified her body with great ſeverity,
' and inceſſantly employed her mind in divine and philoſo-
' phic contemplations. Laſtly, ſhe gained the palm of phi-
' loſophy at a public act in the univerſity of Padua (of which
' there never was another inſtance in the memory of man)
' and thus anticipated that crown, which her exalted virtue
' and

' and sanctity of manners seemed to promise her in heaven.
' She died in the year 1684, on the 26th day of July, aged
' thirty-eight. Her brother Gieronimo Cornelio caused
' this monument to be altered, embellished with new orna-
' ments, still preserving the former epitaph, in the year
' 1727.

This is only a memorial of this extraordinary lady's know- *Account of* ledge in divinity and philosophy, and her uncommon skill in *her.* astronomy, mathematics, and the languages; her tomb being in the church of St. Justina. She was born on the 5th day of June, in the year 1646; and, before she was eleven years of age, took the vow of perpetual chastity. On the 25th of June, 1678, she held a public philosophical disputation at Padua, where the degree of doctor of physic was conferred on her with the usual solemnity. She would likewise have been honoured with the same degree in divinity, had not cardinal Barbarigo, then bishop of Padua, prohibited it, under pretence, that by injunction of the apostle Paul, in 1 Cor. xiv. 34, no woman was allowed to teach in public. She both understood and spoke Latin, French, Spanish, and ancient and modern Greek, with fluency and elegance. The academy of the Infecondi at Rome elected her as a member, and had a medal struck in honour of her, having on one side the bust of this learned lady, with the following inscription;

Helena Lucretia Cornelia Piscopia Jo. Bap. Procurat. S.
Marci Filia.

And, on the reverse, a laurel-tree with this legend:

Etiam infœcunda perennat,

Alluding to her perpetual virginity, and her admission into the academy of the Infecondi, as likewise to the immortal fame she acquired by her extensive knowledge and learning.

Anna Maria Schurmannin, who lived in Holland, and was *Other learn-* highly celebrated for her learning, and acquaintance with a *ed women.* variety of languages, was contemporary with this lady. She was born in the year 1607, and died in the year 1678 *. I have

* When this learned lady's works were become scarce, another ingenious person of the same sex published a new edition of them, with this title, *Annæ Mariæ a Schurmannin opuscula Ebræa, Latina, Græca, Gallica,* *prosaica*

have elsewhere (in Vol. I.) taken notice of the three learned ladies at Milan *; and Charles Patin's two daughters I shall have occasion to introduce in the sequel. That women do not want capacity for literary attainments may be shewn from many unquestionable testimonies †; but the best way for such extra-

prosaica & metrica cum animadversionibus & præfatione Traugott. Christ. Dorothea Læberiæ, Lips. 1749. She was born at Cologn on the Rhine in the year 1607; but, having spent most of her time at Utrecht, the Dutch claim her as their countrywoman. With no better right has Moller, in his *Cimbria literata*, classed her among the Holstein Literati, only because she had lived for some time at Altena, where also was printed the first part of her work, intitled *Melioris partis electio* 1673. In the year 1678 she removed from Altena to Wiewert, where she died in the seventy-first year of her age. The motto she chose shews the pious disposition of her mind, *Amor meus crucifixus est*; i. e. 'My love is crucified.' The celebrated Dutch poet Jacob Cats, though she rejected his addresses, often mentions her with the highest praises.

* No longer ago than the year 1733, Laura Maria Catharina Bassis took a doctor's degree at Bologna at the age of twenty-one, and was chosen a member of the academy called *Institutum Scientiarum* in that city. In 1731 I paid a visit at a place called Warmund, about a league from Leyden, to Mr. Kænemannin, the Arminian minister there, and conversed with his daughter Sarah Maria, who, though only in her twelfth year, played a thorough bass on the harpsichord admirably, had a perfect knowledge of the Bible, was very well acquainted with the heathen mythology, spoke French, English, Spanish, High and Low Dutch, and had made a considerable progress in the Latin language. She seems to be but of a weakly constitution; and what is most remarkable in this lady is, that she has made such an extraordinary progress contrary to her inclination and the natural bent of her genius; for she was forced upon these studies by her father, only that he might have the honour of having a learned daughter. In the year 1731, I was present at Leyden at a divinity lecture on the book of Revelation, held every Sunday by an old woman of a mean condition; she quoted several passages of the Old Testament in the original language, and made some critical and grammatical remarks on those passages. She was commonly called the *Hebrew woman*, on account of her knowledge of the Hebrew language. The freedom with regard to religion allowed in Holland puts the commonalty of both sexes upon enquiries into those parts of literature, which have any affinity with religion, more than in any other country. In the year 1715, one Teuerhof, a trunk-maker of Amsterdam, used to read a lecture three times a week, for some hours, on Spinosa's philosophy; and among his audience, which mostly consisted of Plebeians and was noted for silence and attention, were several young women. The orator had indeed no great stock of learning, but he had an admirable genius, and expressed himself with great propriety and clearness. Secretary Pfaff himself, after spending some hours with this man, gave him the character of *Ingenium vastissimum*; 'A most comprehensive genius.'

† Last year Donna Maria Gaetana Agnesi, a Milanese lady, gave an illustrious proof that the fair sex are capable of attaining to the highest knowledge and skill even in those sciences which are thought to be

the

extraordinary persons is to imitate the lady of the Cornara family, mentioned above, and keep themselves single. What Juvenal, in his sixth satyr, says of a rich woman, *viz*,

Learned women bad wives.

Intolerabilius nihil est, quam fœmina dives,

i. e. ' Nothing can be more insufferable than a rich wife,'

May possibly with more justice be applied to a learned lady.

On the one hand, household affairs and the education of children demand an attention and activity incompatible with the love of books; on the other hand, St. Paul's saying, that knowledge puffeth up, is especially verified in women. A man, however learned he may be, still finds many others of his sex who can enter the lists with him, which checks the risings of pride; whereas a woman of learning, being a *rara avis*, and with whom very few of her own sex can come in competition, is infatuated with such extraordinary talents, and swells with an insupportable haughtiness and conceit.

The most abstruse. She published a treatise on Algebra with this title, *Instituzioni analitiche ad uso della Gioventa Italiana,* printed in Milan 1749, 2 vol. 4to. Laura Cereta of Brescia, and Signora Chiara Matraini of Lucca, with the late late marquis de Chatelet, and a thousand others, were glaring proofs of the vast extent of female genius. The fantastical queen Christina of Sweden might have spared her indecent manner of expressing herself, as being ashamed of her sex. In her travels she had been complimented with above two thousand harangues composed and delivered by persons celebrated for their eloquence; and yet it seems not one of them pleased her majesty. Bourdelet, her physician, took upon him to ask her the cause of this strange dislike to the orations made in praise of her; to whom she answered, ' I am tired with being always entertained with the same tune, such as, the illustrious daughter of the ' great Gustavus; the tenth muse; the Sappho of our age; the orna- ' ment of my sex.' ' These gentlemen' (continued she) ' are at a won- ' derful deal of pains in dinning my ears to put me in mind that I am a ' woman; this is what I am but too sensible of without all this pother. Such was her contempt for, and the mean opinion she had of, her own sex. Dr. Argoud of Vienna seems to have been aware of this foible of Christina; for he never made use of the word Queen throughout his whole speech. Accordingly it was the only harangue she heard with patience; and the author received substantial marks of her approbation. In drawing a comparison between her and the most distinguished heroes, he asserted that she not only equalled but surpassed them all. This piece of adulation flattered the vanity of this fantastic queen, who affected to be thought to have nothing of her own sex in her composition. See Abbe D'Artigny's *Nouveaux Memoires d'Historique, de Critique, & de Literature,* art. 26. *Paris,* 1749.

PADUA.

Oratory of the Franciscans. In the oratory of the Franciscan church, of which I am now speaking, are three large pieces of painting in *fresco* by Titian, besides several fine monuments belonging to the Corraresi family. The tower of this church is ascended by two hundred and fifty steps, and yields a charming prospect all over the adjacent large plain; but at the same time it discovers the nakedness of Padua: for it appears from the top of this high tower that a great part of it is taken up with gardens, &c.

Fine prospect.

Chiesa della Annunciata. The small church della Annunciata has little remarkable except the painting in *fresco* by Zotti. The oval area near it, called Arena, is thought to have been anciently used for exhibiting spectacles, like an amphitheatre. The palace built on it is likewise of an oval form, and belongs to the noble Venetian family of the Foscari.

Church of St. Augustine. St. Augustine's church belongs to the Dominican monks. The high altar is worth seeing on account of its fine sculpture and inlaid work; and in the choir are some tombs of eminent personages of the Carrara family, &c.

Monument of Charlotta queen of Cyprus and her mother. Not far from the altar di S. Salvatore are the monuments of Charlotta, a daughter of Jacob king of Cyprus, and of her mother Marietta. The former died in 1480, but the latter in 1503.

Vestry. The vestry-altar is a very grand piece of sculpture adorned with several exquisite white marble statues. Here also lie the Buzzacarena family, all with very extravagant epitaphs.

Library. In the convent are forty monks. Its library is well contrived but not large, and the manuscripts are kept in a separate closet.

Picture of Albertus Magnus. In the great gallery is shewn a cell said to have been that of Albertus Magnus; and under a picture of his, in this convent, is the following distich:

MAGNVS hic ALBERTVS Patavi augustissima proles
Cænobii splendor, palma, corona, decus.

‘ Behold! Albertus Magnus, the illustrious native of Pa-
‘ dua, the crown, the glory, and ornament of this convent.’

St. Bartholomew's church. In the church of St. Bartholomew, which belongs to the Benedictine nuns, are some good pieces of painting; but its other ornaments are mean, and the walls covered only with old tarnished gilt leather.

PADUA.

In the first chapel on the left-hand on entering the Capuchin church, lies the celebrated cardinal Commendon, whose life has been written by Flechier with all the judgment and elegance which recommend his other biographical pieces. He died in the year 1584, on the 7th of January, in the sixty-second year of his age: His epitaph has nothing remarkable in it. *Capuchin church. Tomb of cardinal Commendon.*

The Carmelite church, among other curious embellishments, is particularly remarkable for fine sculpture. *Carmelite church.*

In St. Andrea Corsini's chapel is the following epitaph on a lady who dropt down dead, during the celebration of her nuptials: *Epitaph on a bride.*

ELIZABETHÆ SALOMONIÆ Patritiæ Venetæ, nuptæ, innuptæ, ipso sponsalium momento extinctæ, Nicolaus Comes de Lazara Eques inter utramque fatem desolatissimus pro thalamo tumulum posuit, ut saltem cineres & ossa misceret. Ann. MDCLXXIII.

' To Elizabeth Salomonia descended from a noble Venetian family, who was neither married nor single, but died in the very instant of her espousals; this tomb was raised by Nicolas count de Lazara, her afflicted husband, instead of a nuptial bed; that at least their ashes might be mingled together. 1673.'

The cathedral is not yet finished, and the model of it is fixed against the wall at the entrance of the church. The bishop's annual revenues exceed a hundred thousand *scudi* or crowns. *Cathedral.*

In the chapel of the Zabarella family is shewn a picture of the virgin Mary, painted, as is pretended, by St. Luke; which Robert king of Naples made a present of to Petrarch the famous Italian poet, and the latter bestowed it on this church.

On the right-hand of St. Carlo's altar is the following epitaph: *Epitaph of Charles Patin.*

D. O. M.
CAROLO PATINO.
Prisc. Equ. D. M. prisc. numismat. studiis clariss. famam celeberrimi patris æmulato, è patrio in Patav. Lyceum excepto, post totam Europam lustratam, præmiis & majorum Principum grati aucto, cum calumnia feliciter luctato, ac pro fundamento virtutis fortunæ ruinis uso, ob veterem eruditionem erutam, posterorum cultum

PADUA.

cultum promerita Magdalena Ommetz Parif. uxor, Gabr. Carola Santa Paulina, & Carol. Cath. Filiæ, extremo amoris argumento, annuente Capitulo, parentant. Ob. An. MDCXCIII. X. *Oct. ætat. fuæ An.* LIX. *Menf.* VIII. D. X.

'To God the greateſt and beſt of beings.'
'And to the memory of Charles Patin, knight, and doctor
'of phyſic, of the univerſity of Paris, who, being like his
'father, famous for his knowledge of ancient coins and me-
'dals, was admitted a member of the univerſity of Padua;
'and, having travelled all over Europe, received ſignal
'marks of favour and approbation from many ſovereign
'princes; ſtruggled with envy and calumny; and ſhone
'with ſuperior luſtre in adverſity, &c. his affectionate wife
'Magdalen Ommetz a native of Paris, Gabr. Carola Santa
'Paulina and Carola Catharina, his daughters, erected this
'monument, as the laſt mark of their love, with the conſent
'of the chapter. He died on the 10th day of October,
'1693, aged 59 years eight months and ten days.'

Three learned women of the name of Patin. In this epitaph mention is made of three ladies of uncommon erudition. Magdalen Ommetz, wife of Charles Patin, publiſhed a book intitled *Recueil de Reflexions morales & Chretiennes* in 1680. Their eldeſt daughter Gabriela Carola Santa Paulina, in the ſame year, held a public diſputation on ſeveral philoſophical Theſes, her father ſitting as moderator, and wrote a diſſertation to ſhew why the figure of the phœnix was ſtruck on ſome of Caracalla's coins, which are ſtill extant. Her younger ſiſter, Carola Catharina Patin, made a public oration at Padua in the year 1683, on account of raiſing the ſiege of Vienna, which was received with great applauſe, and afterwards printed. In the year 1691 ſhe publiſhed, at Padua, *Tabellæ ſelectæ & explicatæ,* or copper-plates of the moſt celebrated paintings by the beſt hands, as Titian, Paolo Veroneſe, Leonardo da Vinci, Tintoretto, Baſſano, Holbein, &c. with explanations of them. Both theſe ſiſters were members of the academy of the Ricourati at Padua.

Inſcription on an image of Chriſt. In the church of St. Francis, at an altar over which is placed a miraculous crucifix, is the following elegant inſcription by Ottavio Ferrari:

Chriſti Servatoris imaginem, vultus placidâ majeſtate ſerenos, deciduis æternæ clementiæ radiis atque admirandis operibus humano generi beneficos ac ſalutares, ab obſcuro & ignobili loco in hanc

au-

PADUA.

augustiorem sedem transtulit Pater PAULUS A PLEBE SACCI, eamque collatitiâ piorum stipe ad fastigium perduxit, aræque suggestu & peregrino marmore excoluit. Anno MDCLXIX.

' The image of our Saviour, Christ, whose countenance,
' majestically serene, beams with rays of infinite love and
' mildness, and which has in a wonderful manner and by
' innumerable instances imparted its salutary virtues to af-
' flicted mortals, was removed into this more conspicuous
' situation from an obscure and mean place by father Paolo
' a Plebe Sacci, who, assisted by the contributions of de-
' vout persons, completed his pious design, and erected an
' altar of very costly marble in honour of it.'

In this church lies buried the celebrated civilian Gieronimo Cagnolo, who died at Padua in the year 1551. On the right-hand of the main entrance is the following florid epitaph:

Monument of Jerom Cagnolo.

JACOBO SCARABICIO Patavino, in quo Moderator temporum munerumque largitor Deus, annos simul ac virtutes contraxit; cui annum quartum supra decimum vix agenti & morum integritas, ingenii solertia, sermonisque blanditia fuit, ut Patavinis civibus foret exemplo, amori & admirationi. Nunc veluti lectissimum in terris florem, cœlo jam gratissimum, quo nonas Martii non tam veris, quàm ætheris ingressu in amœnissimum deliciarum hortum subinvidi transtulere Superi. Sebastianus Pater, in Patavino Lycæo Publicus Medicinæ Lector, acerbissimum animi dolorem hoc uno leniens, quod jucundissimo unici filii conspectu convictuque in cœlis iterùm fruiturus, flagrantis desiderii Monumentum posuit. MDCLIV.

Epitaph on Scarabicci.

' To Giacopo Scarabicci, a native of Padua, to whom
' the eternal being, who presides over time, and is the giver
' of every noble endowment, was pleased to allow a term
' of years very disproportionate to the extraordinary virtues
' and acomplishments with which he had endued him; for
' for the purity of his morals, the acuteness of his genius,
' the elegance of his language and behaviour made him, at
' the age of fourteen, the pattern, the delight, and admira-
' tion of the citizens of Padua. Now the heavenly powers,
' being enamoured of this most fragrant flower, and as it
' were envying the earth the possession of it, transplanted it
' to the celestial paradise on the ninth of March, which,
' instead of a temporary, proved to him the entrance on an
' eternal

PADUA.

'eternal spring. Under such an afflictive loss, the only comfort to Sebastino his father, professor of physic in the university of Padua, is the consideration, that he shall again one day, in heaven, see, and enjoy the conversation of, his dearly beloved son; to whom he has erected this monument of his grief and tender affection.' 1654.

Whether the expression *subinvidi Superi* becomes a Christian pen, may be questioned by some, and be absolutely condemned as profane by others.

Francesco di Paola. The church of S. Francesco di Paola is small but very elegant, and has an arched roof well painted. On the great altar are several marble statues and a very rich tabernacle.

Theatine church. The Theatines church, which is dedicated to S. Gaetano, is intirely lined with Marmo pavonazzo, or a violet-coloured marble, beautifully variegated with white; and has several other ornaments well worth seeing. The altar is adorned with eight fine pillars of black and white marble, and a representation of our Saviour in his agony on the mount of Olives, admirably cut in wood, in the middle. In the vestry are shewn two pieces representing martyrdoms, painted by Paolo Veronese. It is well known that the Theatine monks derive their name from Theati, a small episcopal see in the kingdom of Naples, where the order was first instituted in the year 1523.

Tomb of Briosci in S. Giovanni in Verdaca. On the outside of the church di S. Giovanni in Verdaca or Viridario, is a monument of Briosci, a statuary of Padua, who, if his epitaph does not run in the usual strain of those compositions, was a very extraordinary artist, and emulated the ancients.

Memorial of the siege of Padua. Over the entrance into the garden belonging to the convent adjoining to this church are to be seen two iron cannon balls, and between these a third of white stone, said to have been shot into the wall at the siege of Padua by the emperor Maximilian I. with this inscription under them alluding to the imperial standard, &c.

> *Ales Jovis ter maximi,*
> *Matris Deorum Bijuges*
> *His lusitabant sphærulis,*
> *Non ergò lucri & sanguinis,*
> *Sed imperii, sed gloriæ.*

'With

'With such little spherical balls as these, great Jove's
eagle and the lions of Cybele played, not for gain, or blood,
but for glory and empire.'

St. Justina's church is an elegant and magnificent edifice, and in many particulars resembles that of St. Paul at London. It is divided into three naves or isles, and is very well enlightened. The altars, which, exclusive of the high altar, amount to twenty-four, are embellished with the finest sculpture, and Florentine work of *lapis Lazuli*, mother of pearl, jasper, agate, &c. Even the pavement about the altar is inlaid work, and that of the church of red, white, and black marble curiously arranged. This church is adorned with nine beautiful cupola's, three of which are larger than the rest, and have galleries with a balustrade on the inside. The ornaments of this church are daily increasing; and will never be discontinued, for this prudential reason, that, whilst any work is carrying on, very large sums left by legacies, &c. accrue to the convent to which the church belongs: Besides, the stated revenue of it is computed at a hundred thousand ducats. This church is built in the form of a Latin cross, and the length of it within, the choir included, is a hundred and eighty-three common paces, and the breadth seventy-eight: The length of the cross-isle is a hundred and twenty-eight such paces.

The martyrdom of St. Justina, an admirable piece painted by Paolo Veronese, hangs over the high altar. There are two organs placed opposite to each other in the choir; and the stalls are adorned with incomparable basso-relievo's representing historical passages out of the Old and New Testament. These pieces were executed by one Riccard, a Frenchman, who spent no less than two and twenty years in carving these exquisite pieces.

Besides the remains of St. Justina and other saints, this church boasts of being possessed of the body of St. Luke the evangelist; which, however, occasioned great disputes between the Benedictines, to whom this church and convent belong, and the Franciscans of St. Job's church at Venice, who maintained that the genuine body was in their possession. But at length pope Gregory XIII. decided the point in favour of the Paduans; however the head of the same evangelist is shewn at Rome in the church of the holy Apostles. As all the ornaments of this church are new, no old inscriptions are now to be seen here, except a long narrative near

the

PADUA.

the pretended remains of St. Luke, which is inferted in Salamoni's *Infcriptiones urbis Patavinæ* *. The celebrated learned lady of the Cornara family, whom I have often mentioned before, lies in the burial-place of the monks according to her own requeft, and the monks erected a monument to her memory in the year 1684.

Eighty Benedictine monks conftantly refide in this convent. Their library is extremely well chofen, and ornamented with fine fculptures. The convent confifts of feveral courts, and in the cloifter of the largeft court the whole life of St. Benedict is painted in *frefco*, and illuftrated with Latin verfes.

Before the church of St. Juftina is a piazza or area anciently called Campus Martius, but now known by the name of Prato della Valle. On the firft Saturday of every month a market for cattle is kept in this place; and the vulgar are perfuaded that during the greateft heats of fummer no gnats or flies are to be feen in this market. As I happened to be there on a market-day, I could from ocular demonftration confute this idle tradition, which, though it be evidently falfe, paffes here for a certain truth. Between Prato della Valle and St. Juftina's church is a place feparated by a ditch to preferve it from being profaned by the cattle, becaufe a great number of martyrs are fuppofed to have been put to death there; on which account it is diftinguifhed by the name of il Campo Santo or the Holy Field.

Suppofed grave of Antenor. In the year 1273, in laying the foundation of the hofpital called La Cafa di Dio an old leaden coffin was found, and in it a fword, on which, according to Scardeoni, were the following unintelligible lines:

Obfcure infcription.

† *Cum fuper, A, fumes primum tibi Dardane gramma*
Auxilium a fuperis fubito tibi Numine clama.
Heu Patavum qui te profugus conftruxit ab igne
Multoties tali pefti fubjecte malignæ.
Mors cita, vita brevis, Patavos in Pace volentes
Vivere, non paffa eft, gens hoc fatale ferentes
Admonet, & punit nullo difcrimine Cives.

* This work was publifhed at Padua in 4to in the year 1701; but is full of typographical errors.
† This infcription muft have been the compofition of the monks, as appears by the rhymes, &c.

In

PADUA.

In order to strike out, at any rate, some elucidation of this prophetic inscription, it has been observed, that the government of all the sovereigns and lords of this city, whose name began with an A, as Attila, Acciolini, Ansedifi, Albert Scaliger, Andrea Neri, &c. were extremely tyrannical and unfortunate. This sword is said, in the year 1334, to have been delivered up to Albert Scaliger according to his command; but the above-mentioned coffin was, in the year 1283, set up on the left-hand of the main entrance into St. Laurence's church; and being supposed, for what reason I cannot conceive, to be the tomb of Antenor the Trojan, Lupatus de Lupatis, one of the magistrates of this city, and a man of learning, caused the following verses to be cut in Gothic characters on the stone case in which it is inclosed:

> C. Inclitus Antenor patria vox nisa quietem
> Transtulit huc Enedum Dardanidumque fugas,
> Expulit Euganeos Patavina condidit urbem
> Quam tenet hic humili marmore cæsa domus.

The first line of this inscription seems to convey no meaning. On the other side of the case are the following lines shewing the date 1284, when this coffin was set up here, &c.

> Cum quater alma Dei natalia viderat Orbis
> Post decies octo mille ducenta super,
> Extulit hæc Paduæ Præses, cui nomen Olive,
> Cognomen Cleri, patria Floris erat.

On the arch under which the coffin is placed are these words:

> Potestate nobili viro D. Fantone de Rubeis, de Florentia, perfectum fuit hoc opus.

'This work was completed when Fantoni de Rubeis a native of Florence was Podestà of this city.'

The abovementioned Fantoni was three times Podestà of the city, namely, in the years 1284, 1285, and 1295. Virgil, Æn. I. v. 246, & seq. says, indeed, that Antenor built a town called Patavium. And with him also agrees Seneca, Consol. ad Helviam, c. 7. But, according to the poet's description, that city must have been built on the river Timavus, which empties itself * into the sea near Aquileia, and not on the banks of the Brenta. His words are: 'Antenor

Of Antenor's Patavium.

---

* See Pliny, Hist. Nat. lib. ii. c. 103. lib. iii. 18, 19. who places the Timavus in the neighbourhood of Trieste and Aquileia. See also Livy, lib. xli.

PADUA.

Antenor potuit mediis elapsus Achivis
Illyricos penetrare sinus, atque intima tutus
Regna Liburnorum; & fontem superare Timavi:
Unde per ora novem vasto cum murmure montis
It mare præruptum & pelago premit arva sonanti.
Hic tamen ille urbem Patavi, sedesque locavit
Teucrorum ———

' Antenor, from the midst of Grecian hosts,
' Could pass secure, and pierce th' Illyrian coasts:
' Where rolling down the steep, Timavus raves,
' And thro' nine channels disembogues his waves.
' At length he founded Padua's happy seat,
' And gave his Trojans a secure retreat.'

DRYDEN.

Virgil and Claudian attribute nine mouths to the Timavus; whereas Strabo mentions only seven; with whom also Martial agrees.

Of the Euganei. The Euganei in whose country Antenor, after he had conquered them, is said to have built the ancient Patavium, according to Livy, *lib. i. c. 1*, inhabited the country that lies between the Adriatic gulph and the Alps. Hence Pliny also calls them *Graiarum Alpium incolæ*; i. e. ' The inhabitants of the Grecian Alps.' So that their country appears to have been situated towards the north-east, and at a great distance from the modern Padua. However, their colonies, in process of time, might have extended themselves towards Verona; and this conjecture is favoured by Pliny.

xli. *Strab. lib. v. P. Mela lib. ii. c. 4. Servius ad Æneid. lib. i.* But Claudian *in Sexto Cons. Honor.* seems to differ a little from these, and joins it with the Tessino, the Mincio, and the Adda. His words are:

———*Frondentibus humida ripis*
Colla levant, pulcher Ticinus, & Addua visu
Cæruleus, velox Athesis, tardusque meatu
Mincius, inque novem consurgens ora Timavus.

' Her dropping locks the silver Tessin rears;
' The blue transparent Adda next appears;
' The rapid Adige then erects her head;
' And Mincio rising slowly from his bed;
' And last Timavus, that with eager force
' From nine wide mouths comes gushing to his course.'

ADDISON.

S. Maria

PADUA.

S. Maria delle Gratie is an elegant church, and belongs to the Dominican monks. *S. Maria delle Gratie.*

S. Maria de' Servi is also called from the order of monks to which it belongs, who have assumed the name of Servi divæ Mariæ, or, as they are commonly called, Servites. A connoisseur in sculpture will be highly pleased with the altar in the middle of the church, and the exquisite basso-relievo's of bronze on the monument of the civilian Paolo de Castro, who died towards the close of the fifteenth century. *S. Maria de' Servi.*

The church of St. Philip and St. James belongs to the eremetical fathers of St. Augustine. This church and the convent to which it belongs is remarkable for being the place, where great numbers of Germans and other foreigners, have, according to their desire, been deposited. Around the genealogical tree of Luca Salvioni, a civilian, are these words: *Church of St. Philip and St. James.*

O quàm misera fortuna, quæ caret invidiâ.

'How wretched is that state of life that is not envied?'

The chapel belonging to the family of Zabarella is beautifully painted by Andrea Mantegna; and in the vestry is a picture of John the Baptist, by Guido Rheni.

In the wall on the outside of this church is to be seen a stone pulpit, in which Luther is said to have preached. The antiquary who attended us very gravely assured us, that Luther was *un gran predicatore,* i. e. 'A famous preacher;' but that being disappointed by one pope of a cardinal's hat, which another pope had promised him, he, out of resentment, gave himself up to a very strange heretical way of preaching. *Luther's pulpit.*

In the church of St. Sophia the German students of physic, or *ex ordine gratioso,* as they are styled in some inscriptions, are generally buried. On a white marble table, facing the high altar, are these words: *Church of St. Sophia.*

Serenissimi
Ferdinandi Caroli Gonzagæ
Ducis Mantuæ, Montisferr. Carolop. &c.
Clementissima viscera.
V. Jul. Ann. Sal. MDCCVIII.

A duke of Mantua's Clementissima viscera.

Vol. III.   D d   'Here

PADUA.

'Here are deposited the most compassionate bowels of the serene Ferdinand Carlo Gonzaga, Duke of Mantua, Montferrat, &c. on the fifth day of July, 1708.'

Clementissima viscera is a very common phrase, and I suppose the ingenious author alluded to the Greek word σπλαγχα, which metaphorically is often used to denote pity, compassion, &c.

Church del Spirito Santo.
In the church del Spirito Santo lies Scipio Gonemi, who, as his epitaph says, died at the age of ninety-six, on the same day and the same hour in which he was born.

St. Thomas's church.
The church of St. Thomas of Canterbury belongs to the fathers of the Oratory of S. Filippo Neri; who have assigned five separate burying-vaults for so many different classes of men, women, and children, with inscriptions over every one of them.

Town-house.
The principal among the civil edifices of Padua is il Palazzo della ragione, or the town-house, though the great hall does not answer common report. The plan of it is rhomboidal: It is a hundred and twenty-four common paces in length, and forty-three in breadth. The roof is proportionably lofty, and arched, being strengthened at the top with cross iron bars, and covered with lead on the outside. On the cieling, Giotto, assisted by some of his disciples, has allegorically represented the influences of the sun in the twelve signs of the zodiac. But, after all, this apartment has not a proper light for fine paintings, and is not kept in any tolerable order. In going up to this hall, which is in the second story, over the first door on the left-hand, is a statue of Livy the historian, with these words under it:

Inscription.
T. Livius Patavinus, Historicorum Latini nominis facile princeps, cujus doctrinum & lacteam eloquentiam ætas illa, quæ virtute pariter ac eruditione florebat, adeo admirata est, ut multi Romam non ut urbem rerum pulcherrimam, aut Urbis & Orbis Dominum Octavium, sed ut hunc virum inviserent audirentque à Gabibus profecti sint. Hic res omnes, quas Popul. Rom pace belloque gessit, quatuordecim Decadibus mirâ styli facilitate complexus, sibi ac patriæ gloriam peperit sempiternam.

'Titus Livius, a native of Padua, the chief of all the Latin historians, whose learning and flowing eloquence, even the age in which he lived, when virtue and learning
were

'were at so great a height, admired to such a degree, that
'several persons came from the remotest parts of the west,
'not to see Rome (though it was the most magnificent sight
'on earth) or the great Augustus, who was emperor of that
'city, and of the whole world, but to see and hear this
'great man. His history of all the civil and military trans-
'actions of the Roman people comprized in fourteen *decads*,
'and written with wonderful purity and elegance of stile,
'is an everlasting monument of glory to himself and his
'country.'

This statue holds a book, in which these words are legible:

Parvus ignis magnum sæpè suscitat incendium. Excessit à vita VI. Tiberii Cæsaris anno, ætatis verò suæ LXVI.

'A little fire oftens kindles a large conflagration. He de-
'parted this life in the sixth year of the reign of Tiberius,
'and the sixty-sixth of his age.'

Over the second door on this side of the town-house, stands a bust of Albertus Patavinus, with the following inscription: Albertus Patavinus.

Albertus Patavinus Heremitanæ Religionis splendor, continentissimæ vitæ, sumptâ Parisiis infulâ Magistrali, in Theologia tantum profecit, ut Paulum, Moysen, Evangelia, ac Libros Sententiarum laudatissimè exposuerit. Facundissimus eâ ætate concionator immortali memoriæ optimo jure datur.

'Albertus Patavinus, the glory of the eremitical order, a
'person of the most exemplary chastity, who, having enter-
'ed into the order of priesthood at Paris, made such progress
'in the study of divinity, that his expositions of St. Paul's
'Epistles, the Pentateuch, the Gospels, and the book of
'Proverbs, were justly received with applause. The most
'eloquent preacher of his age, as he undoubtedly was,
'well deserves a lasting monument to transmit his name to
'posterity.'

Over the door of the hall, on the other side of the build- Pietro Aponi.
ing, is a stone image of Pietro Aponi, with this inscription:

Petrus

PADUA.

Petrus Aponus Pat. Philosopiæ Medicinæque scientiss. ob idque Conciliatoris nomen adeptus, Astrologiæ verò adeò peritus, ut in Magiæ suspicicnem inciderit, falsoque de hæresi postulatus, absolutus fuit.

' Pietro Aponi of Padua, called the *Conciliator* for his profound knowledge in philosophy and physic. His skill in astrology was so great, that it caused him to be suspected of being a magician, and consequently he was charged as guilty of heresy; of which, however, he was acquitted.'

Proceedings of the Inquisition against Aponi.

On what grounds Pietro Aponi is said to have been acquitted by the Inquisition I cannot conceive. Spondanus, in his *Annal. Ecclef.* and other writers, expresly say, that Aponi died during his trial, and was privately buried; but that the Inquisition carried on the prosecution after his death, and for want of the criminal's real body burnt him in effigy. Naude, in his *Apologie des grands hommes accusés de Magie*, c. 14. Bayle, in his *Dictionaire Crit.* and M. Heuman, in his *Acta Philosoph. Art* 3. have vindicated this learned man against the charge of sorcery. But indeed in those times a small skill in the sciences was sufficient to make a man suspected of magic and dealing with the devil. Aponi owes the title of *Conciliator* to a book that he published in the year 1483, in folio, with the title of *Conciliator differentiarum Philosophorum præcipuè Medicorum*. His life has been written by Tomasini in *Elog. illust. Viror.* p. 22. and Scardeoni, *de antiq. Urbis Patavii & claris ejus civibus*. But the latter is something inaccurate: for, according to him, Pietro Aponi died in the year 1305; whereas, from other authorities and circumstances, it is evident that he lived till the year 1316, and died at the age of sixty-six.

Over the other door is the statue of Paulus Patavinus, with the following pompous encomium under it:

Inscription under Paulus Patavinus.

Paulus Patavinus Jurisconsultorum clariss. hujus nostræ urbis decus æternum, Alexandri Mammæ temporibus floruit, ad Præturam, Præsecturam, Consulatumque evectus, cujusque sapientiam tanti fecit Justinianus Imp. ut nulla non Civilis juris particula hujus legibus decoretur, qui splendore famæ immortalis, oculis posteritatis admirandus, insigni imagine hâc meritò decoratur.

' Paulus

PADUA.

' Paulus Patavinus, the moſt eminent of civilians, and
' the eternal ornament of this our city, who flouriſhed in
' the time of Alexander Mamma, and was promoted to the
' prætorſhip, præfecture, and confulate, whoſe wiſdom the
' emperor Juſtinian held in ſuch high eſteem, that he made
' great uſe of his maxims to embelliſh every part of his In-
' ſtitutes of the Roman law, and whoſe fame is immortal,
' is deſervedly honoured with this ſtatue, that he may be
' admired by poſterity.'

On the weſt ſide of the hall, under a marble ſtatue, this
inſcription is to be ſeen:

ΙΣΩ ΑΡΙΣΤΟΤΕΛΕΙ ΝΟΞΕΙΝ ΚΙΚΕΡΟΝΙ ΤΕ ΕΙΡΕΙΝ
SPERONO SPERONIO ſapientiſſimo, eloquentiſſimo, op- Inſcription
timo & Viro & Civi, Virtutem Meritaque acta vita, ſapientiam, under Spe-
eloquentiam declarant ſcripta, publico Decreto Virbis Quatuor- ronius's ſta-
Viri P. Anno a Chriſto nato M.D.XCIV. Ab urbe vero condita tue.
MM. die XI.

' To Speronus Speronius, who was equal to Ariſtotle in
' reaſoning, and to Tully in eloquence; a perſon eminent
' for wiſdom, probity, and patriotiſm; whoſe virtue and
' merit ſhone in his life; whoſe wiſdom and eloquence ap-
' pear conſpicuous in his writings, this ſtatue was erected by
' a public decree in the year 1594 of the Chriſtian æra, and
' in the two thouſandth year and eleventh day from the
' building of the city.'

A marble buſt of Livy is fixed againſt the wall; and under it, upon another ſtone, is the following inſcription:

V. F.
T. LIVIVS
LIVIAE T. F.
QVARTAE L.
HALYS
CONCORDIALIS
PATAVI
SIBI ET SVIS
OMNIBVS.

This is an ancient inſcription, and was found near the
place where a temple of Concord formerly ſtood. Others
pretend

pretend that it was dug up under the foundation of St Juſtina's church, about the middle of the fourteenth century. The head that is fixed over this inſcription is a beautiful antique: but whether the buſt and inſcription were deſigned for Livy the hiſtorian is another queſtion. Sertorius Urſatus, *in Marmor. erud. p.* 142, according to the information given him by Marquard Gudius, conjectures, with very great probability, that the latter belonged to a freedman of Titus Livius's daughter.

Livy's remains.

The Paduans are firmly perſuaded that the bones found incloſed in a leaden coffin in St. Juſtina's church, in the year 1413, muſt have been thoſe of Livy; and accordingly they were brought with great ſolemnity into the council-houſe, by order of Xiccone Polentoni, who was chancellor of Padua at that time, and may be reckoned among the chief reſtorers of learning in Italy. Under the aforeſaid ancient inſcription are the following words:

T. Livius quarto Imperii Tib.
Cæſaris anno vita exceſſit,
Ætatis vero ſuæ LXXVII.
M. D. XLVII.

' T. Livy died in the fourth year of the reign of Tiberi-
' us Cæſar, and in the ſeventy-ſeventh of his age. 1547.'

On the outſide over the door leading to the Officium Sanitatis, or Board of Health, are theſe words:

Oſſa T. Livii Patavini unius omnium mortalium judicio digni, cujus propè invicta calamo invicti populi Romani res geſtæ conſcriberentur An. 1548.

' Here lie the bones of T. Livy, a native of Padua, whoſe
' matchleſs pen alone, in the opinion of moſt men, was qua-
' lified to tranſmit to poſterity the noble atchievements of
' the invincible Romans. 1548.'

The proofs on which the opinion, that the bones found in the year 1413 did belong to Livy the hiſtorian, reſts, are ſo far from amounting to a demonſtration, that it is a dubious whether they are not the ſkeleton of a female. Indeed Xiccone Polentoni, in a letter to Nicolini Nicoli of Florence, concerning

concerning these bones, mentions the future of the skull as a proof of the sex of the person to whom it belonged; but such uncertain marks modern anatomists will not easily subscribe to.

Asinius Pollio censures Livy's stile for a sort of Patavinity or provincial dialect*; but it does not absolutely follow from thence that Livy was a native of the city now called Padua. *Statius, lib.* iv. *Silv.* 7. *ad Maximum Junium*, calls Livy, *Timavi alumnus*; but the course of the river Timavus is at a considerable distance from Padua; for it runs between Trieste and Aquileia (as has been already observed) where Antenor built his Patavium. Probably Sidonius Apollinaris *in Paneg. Anth.* points at Livy's writings in these lines: *Livy's place of nativity.*

——— *vel quidquid in ævum*
Mittunt Euganeis Patavina volumina chartis.

' Or whatever the Patavian volumes, made of Euganean
' paper, consign to immortality.'

But the Montes Euganei cannot be placed in the territories of the modern Padua (as has been said above) without greatly perplexing the ancient geography. On what authority Eusebius says, in his Chronicon, that Livy died at Padua, I know not; but that Apona was the place of his nativity Martial seems to intimate, in *lib.* i. *epigr.* 62.

Censetur Apona Livio suo tellus
Stellaque, nec Flacco minus.

This celebrated historian might be surnamed Patavinus from the neighbouring city of Patavium, as Virgil is called the Mantuan poet, though he drew his first breath at Andes, a village that is situated not far from Mantua. This conjecture would be the more plausible, were it ascertained that the Fontes Patavini mentioned by Pliny, *lib.* ii. *c.* 103. and *lib.* xxxi. *c.* 6, were the hot baths of Apona, which lie at the distance of four Italian miles and a half from Padua, and, no doubt, were well known in ancient times †. If Livy was a native of Padua, the name of Timavus must have been applied by the ancients to two different rivers.

* See *Quintil. lib.* I. *inst. Orat. c.* 9. and *lib.* viii. *cap.* 1.
* *Vid. Lucan. lib.* vii. *Claudian epig.* viii.   *Sil. Ital. lib.* xii. *Mart. lib.* vi. &c.

PADUA.

Monument and death of the marchioness d' Obizzi.

In the hall of the council-houfe at Padua is a monument, with a buft of the marchionefs d'Obizzi, who, when a gentleman of Padua, in the abfence of her hufband, had clandeftinely conveyed himfelf into her bed-chamber, chofe rather to be ftabbed by the ravifher, who was enraged at the refiftance fhe made, than violate the honour of the marriage-bed. Befides other proofs againft this execrable affaffin, one fhirt-fleeve-button, exactly refembling that which he wore in the other fleeve, was found in the lady's bed. The marchionefs's only fon, then but five years of age, whom the affaffin removed out of the bed before he made any attempt on her chaftity, was likewife produced as an evidence againft him; but, by reafon of his tender age, his depofitions were not thought fufficient to convict the villain. He ftood the torture feveral times, but his life could not be touched; and, after fifteen years imprifonment, his friends procured him his liberty; which however, he did not long enjoy: for the above-mentioned fon of the unfortunate marchionefs fhot him through the head foon after his enlargement, and thus revenged the barbarity committed againft his mother [*]. Under the marble buft of the marchionefs are thefe words:

Venerare pudicitiæ fimulacrum & victimam Lucretiam de Dondis ab Horologio, Pii Æneæ de Obizzonibus, Orciani Marchionis, uxorem. Hæc inter noctis tenebras, maritales afferens tædas, furiales recentis Tarquinii faces cafto cruore extinxit, ficque Romanam Lucretiam intemerati tori gloriâ vicit. Tantæ fuæ Heroinæ generofis Manibus hanc dicavit aram Civitas Patavina. Decreto die 31 Decembris Anni MDCLXI.

' Reader, revere this image of a noble victim to chaftity,
' namely, Lucretia de Dondis, the worthy confort of Pius
' Æneas d' Obizzi, marquis of Orciani, who, in the dark-
' nefs of the night, preferved the pure flame of conjugal
' chaftity, and with her chafte blood extinguifhed the brutal
' fire of a modern Tarquin's luft; fo that fhe furpaffed the
' glory of the Roman Lucretia, in preferving the honour of
' the marriage-bed inviolable. To the illuftrious manes of
' fo great a heroine, the city of Padua dedicated this altar
' by a public decree, December 31, 1661.'

That the heroic chaftity of the marchionefs d' Obizzi fhould be perpetuated with fuch a memorial is very proper;

[*] *Miffon. Tom.* I. *p.* 186, *& feq.*

but

but it muſt be allowed the like honour is no leſs due to a chaſte young woman, called Iſabella Ravagnina, who, when Maximilian I. had made himſelf maſter of Padua, choſe to jump off from the bridge, called il Ponte Curvo, into the water, where ſhe was drowned, rather than fall into the hands of ſome Imperial ſoldiers, who cloſely purſued her. The Roman Lucretia's heroic act is indeed highly to be commended; yet I doubt not but many other nations afford inſtances of chaſtity, which, though buried in oblivion, upon weighing all circumſtances, juſtly deſerve to be preferred to that of Lucretia *. Applicable to this is Pliny's obſervation, *lib.* iii. *Ep.* 15. *Alia clariora eſſe alia majora*; i. e. 'Some 'actions are more celebrated, whilſt others that are greater 'are buried in oblivion.' After all the panegyrics on Lucretia, the following contraſt may be drawn between her and the chaſte Suſanna:

Virtue of a country girl.

Reliques of the learned.

> *Caſta Suſanna placet*; *Lucretia, cede Suſannæ,*
> *Tu poſt, illa mori maluit ante ſcelus* †.

* In the whole behaviour of Lucretia the love of fame had a great ſhare; and Ovid alſo, in *Faſtor. lib.* ii, gives us to underſtand, that ſhe ſtabbed herſelf to avoid reproach, rather than from any principle of chaſtity, when he ſays.

> *Succubuit famæ victa puella metu.*

[Another note, by Mr. Schutz, to the ſame purport with this of the author, is here omitted; as an invidious reflection on ſuch an heroic inſtance of chaſtity ſavours of ill-nature, eſpecially ſince they both chiefly rely on the teſtimony of Ovid, who was a notorious debauchee.]

† The compariſon here drawn between the Apocryphal heroine and Lucretia is far from being juſt; for the former could not prevent the puniſhment ſhe was going to ſuffer after conviction upon the falſe evidence of the elders; whereas the latter had it not in her power to prevent Tarquin's villany, though, perhaps, ſhe might have concealed the rape, had ſhe not preferred her honour to her life. To this ſarcaſm on the Roman matron may be oppoſed the following lines:

> ' Fair Suſan did her wif-hede well menteine,
> ' Algates aſſaulted ſore by letchours tweine:
> ' Now, and I read aright that auncient ſong,
> ' Olde were the the paramours, the dame full yong.
> ' Had thilke ſame tale in other guiſe been told;
> ' Had they been yong (pardie) and ſhe been olde:
> ' That, by St. Kit, had wrought much ſorer tryal;
> ' Full marveillous, I wot, were ſwilk denyal.'
>   PRIOR, *p.* 233.
>   ' Suſanna

'Sufanna I admire, to whom Lucretia muſt yield; the latter choſe to die after ſhe had contracted the guilt which the former was reſolved to prevent by her death.'

Near the marchioneſs d'Obizzi's monument, over the door which opens into the Officium Sanitatis, is the following inſcription cut in marble:

Inſcription on account of Livy's arm.

Inclyto Alphonſo Arragonum Regi ſtudiorum Fautori, Reip. Venetæ fœderato, Antonio Panormita Poeta legato ſuo orante, & Matthæo Victurio hujus Urbis Prætore conſtantiſſimè intercedente, ex Hiſtoriarum parentis Titi Livii, oſſibus, quæ hoc tumulo conduntur, brachium Pat. Civ. in munus conceſſere, A. C. MCCCCLI. 14. Kal. Se.

'The citizens of Padua made a preſent of an arm of Titus Livius, the father of hiſtory, being part of the remains of that great man depoſited in this tomb, to the illuſtrious Alphonſo king of Arragon, encourager of learning, and ally to the republic of Venice, at the earneſt requeſt of the celebrated poet Antonio Panormita, their envoy, and the paſſionate ſollicitation of Mateo Vitturi, chief magiſtrate of this city. Auguſt 18, 1451.'

Hence it appears that there are alſo literary reliques, and that they are no leſs eagerly ſought for than the religious; but the misfortune is, that as many objections may be raiſed againſt the genuineneſs of Livy's bones, which Padua ſo much boaſts of, as againſt many of the reliques ſo devoutly worſhipped by the Romiſh church; but ſome of the latter are infinitely more profitable, and therefore more valued.

In the large hall, not far from the paſſage leading to the Poteſta's palace, is to be ſeen a ſtone ſuperſcribed with the following words:

Stone of reproach.

Lapis vituperii & ceſſionis bonorum.

'The ſtone of ignominy and bankruptcy.'

Such as become bankrupt, and are unable to pay their debts, by ſitting publicly three times with their bare buttocks upon this ſtone, and ſwearing that it is not in their power to diſcharge their debts, are cleared from any further proſecution from their creditors. This extraordinary ceremony, however, has been diſcontinued for upwards of fifty years. The

PADUA.

The chief magistrate's apartment, or il Palazzo di Potestâ, is in the council-house, where the busts, portraits, and arms of such as have been invested with the dignity of Potesta, are to be seen. Formerly, several panegyrical inscriptions were placed under the busts, &c. some of which, composed by the celebrated Ferrari, pleased me so, that I cannot forbear transcribing a few specimens of them:

Il Palazzo di Potestà.

Elogies of several Potesta's.

I.
ALOYSIO PRIOLO
Paternæ venerationis titulum promerito,
Quòd submotis peccandi causis
Levioris lapsus atque ætatis licentiam
Clementer æstimârit,
Et in pudoris notam supplicio converso
Suffundere maluerit juventutis sanguinem
Quam effundere,
Artium Studiosi
Summo regnandi artifici
Effigiem sacrârunt
Anno M. DC. LIV.

Of Aloysi Prioli.

' To Aloysi Prioli, an excellent magistrate, who well de-
' served the venerable and affectionate title of a father, for
' he wisely removed the causes of guilt, and was mild in
' overlooking the foibles and sallies of youth, by changing
' the punishment of them to some mark of shame, being de-
' sirous that the blood of young persons should rather tinge
' their cheeks with ingenuous blushes, than be shed by stripes,.
' the students have consecrated this image in the year 1654.'

II.
ANGELO CORRARIO, Prætori,
Qui Veneto cælo delapsus, populis, quoscunque adiit, beneficus ac sa-
lutaris, his etiam terris usurâ brevi commodatus, mansuetudine,
celeritate & consilii præstantiâ nominis auguriam implevit, hoc
etiam quod in ipso rerum ingentium molimine evocatus est, ut pa-
cis ac felicitatis nuntius Romanum Orbem collustraret: Litteræ
ac disciplinæ Cyllenium sidus sibi modò ostensum beneficiis præ-
sens adarant, atque erepti desiderium augustâ imagine solantur.
Anno MDCLVI.

Of Angelo Corrari.

' To Angelo Corrari, chief magistrate of Padua, who, de-
' scending from the Venetian sky, was gracious, and spread
' virtue and happiness wherever he came; though lent but
' for

'for a short time to this country, such was his mildness, his
'diligence, and wisdom, that he well deserved the name of
'Angelo; and more particularly as he was recalled from
'this scene of action, as a magistrate, to be sent as a mes-
'senger to diffuse peace and happiness through the whole
'Roman empire. Learning and the sciences adore this il-
'lustrious star (which like the planet Mercury was but just
'shewn them, but by its benign influences is still present)
'and alleviate their grief for the loss of it by his august
'image. 1656.'

III.

Of Antonio Bernardi.

Cape animos, Dalmatia mœrens,
Culti orbis limes, Italiæ mœnia,
Si totâ virium mole Ottomanus incumbit
Novusque è Thracia turbo circumtonat,
Certa Salus adest
ANTONIVS BERNARDVS,
Qui publicos hostes toto æquore cecidit,
Irruentem barbariem sistet,
Novusque Leonida
Christiani Orbis claustra tuebitur.
Facilè hostem superat
Qui se ipsum vincens
De vitiis & cupiditatibus triumphat.

'Mourning Dalmatia, thou boundary of the civilized
'world, and boundary of Italy, take courage; should the Ot-
'toman with his whole force invade, and Thrace again
'thunder from every quarter, ANTONIO BERNARDI, thy in-
'vincible protector, who slaughtered the enemies of the re-
'public in repeated engagements at sea, is present to repel
'the irruptions of the barbarians. This modern Leo-
'nidas will defend the barrier of the christian world:
'For he is sure to gain the victory over an enemy, who
'conquers himself, and triumphs over his passions and
'vices.'

IV.

Of Aloysius Mocenicus.

Hoc militari aspectu cultuque civilis imperii insignibus radiante
spectantium oculos rapiebat ALOYSIVS MOCENICVS, incer-
tum bello an pace clarior, cum à Turcicis Tropæis recens in Urbe
studiorum altrice Ottomannicas manubias Musis consecraret, ses-
sisque rebus subveniens fovendis ingeniis laudem fœneraret. Juris
publicis

PADUA.

studiosa juventus suum cuique decus rependens sacros multus quàm publicis hostibus formidatos, tam clementiæ fulgore coruscos, æternum grati animi monumentum statuit.
Ann M.DC.LVIII.

'With this military aspect, and adorned with these glorious ensigns of civil power, Aloyfi Mocenici attracted the eyes of the beholders. It is dubious whether he was more illustrious in peace than in war; for when he returned loaded with spoils, after his victories over the Turks, into this city, the nursery of the sciences, he consecrated them to the muses; and by relieving the distressed, and encouraging men of genius, acquired fresh glory. The students of the civil law, as an eternal monument of their gratitude, have unanimously set up the resemblance of that sacred face, that always struck terror into his enemies; but beamed with mildness and benevolence towards his friends.'

V.
MARCI RUZZINI Pretoris   Of Marco Ruzzini.
Sereni vultus duro marmore spirant, cujus mitissimum pectus clementia, tanquam Templum insedit, cui cùm una felicitas fuerit fecisse felices, postquam urbem annonâ, Gymnasium munificentiâ beavit, ita abscessit, ut cum nullius unquam spem frustratus sit, sui desiderium explere non potuerit. Juris studiosi B. M. P.

'This breathing marble represents the serene countenance of Marco Ruzzini. In his mild breast benevolence sat inthroned as in a temple; his sole happiness was to make others happy; and after he had relieved the city with plenty of provisions, and largely endowed the college, he by his death has occasioned a grief, which (though he never frustrated the hopes of any) it is beyond his power to allay.'

But of these and other inscriptions nothing now is to be seen: for an order was sent from Venice about five weeks ago to erase them all without exception, and afterwards to plaster them over with mortar. The real cause of such a procedure is unknown. Probably the Venetians intended, by the abolition of these panegyrical inscriptions, to put a stop to such gross flattery; or perhaps jealousy on the part of the magistrates of Venice may have occasioned such a severe order; or, lastly, they might be apprehensive that the erecting of such monuments might induce the Potesta's to connive

Why these inscriptions were defaced.

connive at the great number of irregularities too frequent among the diffolute ftudents, in order to procure themfelves the honour of fuch memorials.

Infcriptions in the Palazzo del Capitaneo erafed. Be this as it will, the precaution ufed by the Venetians has not fpared the infcriptions in the Palazzo del Capitaneo, or the governor's palace, in which Ottavio Ferrari had given noble fpecimens of his talents for this kind of writing; fo that they are no longer extant.

City library. The city library is alfo in this palace, of which Gabriel Æmo deferved fo well, that the following infcription is fet up in memory of his care and liberality :

GABRIELI ÆMO Præfecto; quod Bibliothecam ventis atque imbribus perviam, libris fitu corruptis, ipfifque parietibus vitium ducentibus, fartam tectam exegerit, & abfterfo fqualore in priftinum cultum reftitutam infigni liberalitate auxerit; Octavius Ferrarius B. M. P.

'Ottavio Ferrari erected this memorial of Gabriel Æmo, ' librarian, in acknowledgment of his great liberality in re- ' pairing this library, when in fo bad a condition, that the ' books were greatly damaged by the weather and rain, and ' grown mouldy by the dampnefs of the walls.'

Il Palazzo del Capitaneo. Il Palazzo del Capitaneo ftands on the beautiful area called Piazza de' Nobili; it is an elegant building, and the fecond ftory is adorned with a gallery fupported by seventy-three pillars of red marble. The tower is alfo a good piece of architecture, and has a clock on it which fhews the courfe both of the fun and moon.

Ezzelini palace. The ancient palace of the tyrant Ezzelini, or Acciolini, is remarkable for its fpacious vaults, and at prefent ferves both for an arfenal and granary. This old fortrefs, which was begun in the year 1237, and finifhed in the year 1242, is ornamented with two towers, on one of which the following infcription is to be feen :

Piis carcerem adfpergite lacrymis, quem majores veftri cruore, hic ætatis, sexûs, conditionis, morum, nullo difcrimine habito, quos Acciolinus Tertius de Romano inhumaniter vivos detrufit, inediâ, dolore, defperatione non nifi mortuos atque confumptos extraxit, inter tot innocentes - - - quod incredibili feritate hoc viventibus condidit fepulchrum, nocens mortuis eft. Veftram hinc agnofcite felicitatem, qui optimum Principem nacti, invidiæ, non pietati locum reliquiftis.

PADUA.

reliquiſtis. Sebaſtianus Galvanus Patavinus, annonâ & toto bel-lico apparatu à Sereniſſ. Veneta Rep. in hac arce ſuæ fidei commiſ-ſis, teterrimo carceri hæc ex hiſtoriis inſcribenda curavit. Anno. Dom. MDCXIIX.

'Shed tears of compaſſion on this priſon, where the blood
'of your anceſtors was abundantly ſhed; for thoſe, whom
'the inhuman Acciolini thruſt down alive, without any diſ-
'tinction of age, ſex, rank, or condition, into this dungeon,
'periſhed with hunger, grief, and deſpair. After ſuch
'numbers of innocent victims, who were buried alive in this
'dreadful ſepulchre, it was the juſt fate of the execrable ty-
'rant himſelf to expire in it at laſt. Hence you ought to
'be ſenſible of your preſent happineſs, in having a prince,
'who, from being objects of pity and compaſſion, has ren-
'dered you ſo happy as to be envied for your proſperity.
'This inſcription was ſet up over this dreadful dungeon by
'Sebaſtiano Galvani, a native of Padua, commiſſary of the
'proviſions and military ſtores lodged in this caſtle, in the
'year 1618.'

On a baſtion, near All-ſaints-gate, is a marble lion, with this inſcription under it:

Hoc hoſpes opus tibi indicat, an JULIANUS Gradonicus, qui Patavium ornavit atque munivit, Anci meruerit nomen; at, ſi tu legeris acta, Ariſtidem quoque dices, nam talem egit Præt. qualis quilibet eſſe deberet. Anno M.D.XVIII.

'Stranger, this monument informs thee how well Giuliano
'Gradonici, who embelliſhed and fortified Padua, deſerved
'the name of Ancus*. But, if thou wilt read the account
'of his noble exploits, thou wouldſt look upon him as ano-
'ther Ariſtides: for, when he was Podeſta, he behaved ſo as
'to deſerve univerſal applauſe. 1518.'

Over the entrance of a private gentleman's houſe not far from Ponte de' Tadi, is the following inſcription ſet up by the owner:

Domino cohoneſtanda Domus.   Inſcription
Paulus Tomaſinus Advocatus 1639.   on Tomafini's houſe.

* Alluding to Ancus Martius, fourth king of Rome, who enlarged and embelliſhed the city.

'The

'The owner's virtue reflects a lustre upon his house. Paolo Tomasini, a pleader, 1639.'

In the house is shewn the following concise form of a will by the same gentleman:

His will.

Deo vivite, Sereniss. Reip. Venctæ obsequium præstate, omnes honorate, nullum cujuscunque sortis spernite, pro nemine fideijussione vos obstringite, sic vivite, ut posteri vos vixisse intelligant. Paulus Tomasinus J. C. Filiis suis testamento reliquit.

'Live to God; be loyal subjects to the serene republic of Venice; honour all men; despise not the meanest; be sureties for no man; so live, that posterity may know you have not lived in vain. This is the legacy which Paolo Tomasini, a lawyer, left his sons by this his last will and testament.'

Near the mill-bridge are to be seen thirty mills within a small distance of each other, set in motion by the same stream.

Palazzo di Soranzo.

The finest private edifice in the whole city is the Palazzo di Soranzo, which is adorned with the portraits of a great number of princes. The garden belonging to this palace is not yet completed.

Statue of Hercules Buphiloponaus.

In the court of the Palazzo di Mantua stands a large colossus with this inscription:

Hercules Buphiloponus bestiarius, qui tristitiam depulit omnem, peramplo hoc signo Mantuæ curæ reflorescit.

Buphiloponus may possibly signify a great lover of labour *, and *bestiarii*, according to Tertullian, Vopiscus, Prudentius, and particularly Cassiodorus (*diverf. lect. lib.* v. *epist.* 42.) were those who voluntarily offered themselves to fight with wild beasts in the amphitheatres: but for what end this statue was erected I can get no information, neither do I remember that any of the ancient writers apply such an epithet or surname to Hercules.

* It seems rather, from its etymology, to denote a lover of labouring oxen, from βους, φιλος, and πονος, and probably alludes to Hercules's stealing Geryon's oxen, and driving them from Spain into Greece.

PADUA.

... the palace of count Francefco Capo di Lifta is *A large*
...n horfe fo large that it cannot ftand in the firft ftory, *wooden*
... its enormous height takes up half the fecond. It *horfe.*
... the family coat of arms is a horfe; but what gave rife
... whim of making this huge wooden horfe, no-body
... inform me. My guide affured me that it was the origi-
... rojan horfe.

...merly the cabinets of Bonaviti, Silvatico, Zabarella, *Cabinets of*
...ffini, Lazara, &c. at Padua were worth feeing; but *curiofities.*
...ave been difperfed, and nothing now remains of them.
...ver, Morgani has a good collection of curiofities. But
...oft valuable in this city is that of the celebrated phy-
... Antoni Valifnieri, who dying on the 28th of January, *Of Valifni-*
... in the five-and-twentieth year of his age, left behind *eri.*
... fon of the fame name, the prefent owner of this cu-
... ollection. It confifts of feveral petrifactions, natural
...;ies, Egyptian idols, Hetrufcan vafes, and ancient
... bufts, among which one of Junius Brutus and two
...;iter are much admired. Several animals and infects, *Methods of*
... ly kept in fpirits of wine, are here preferved without *preferving several ani-*
...;uor, in glafs bells ftopped with wax at the bottom, to *mals for a*
... them againft the air. *long time.*

...ong the pleafure-gardens of Padua, that of d'Andola, *The garden*
... le Venetian, is one of the beft, being adorned with *of Andola.*
... numbers of ftatues; but the Papafava gardens exceed *Of Papafa-*
... orange-trees, cyprefs, and other ever-greens, which *va.*
... pofed into fine walks, labyrinths, and beautiful hedges.
...; latter, fome are of box-tree, grown to the height
... rteen or fourteen feet.

...; name of Papafava is faid to be derived from Giaco- *The etymo-*
...e Carraria, to whom the monks of a convent in Car- *logy of the name of Pa-*
... where he was educated, gave that nickname, becaufe *pafava.*
...s extremely fond of beans.

...e air of Padua is accounted very healthy. Martin *Healthful-*
..., a German, father to the perfon who keeps the inn *nefs of the*
... il Rè d'Ingliterra, or the fign of the king of England, *air.*
... few years fince at the age of a hundred and fourteen.
...ver, few cities have fo many apothecaries as Padua,
...;portion to the number of inhabitants: but it muft be
...'ed, that moft of thefe venders of medicines are alfo
...;tioners. Great quantities of vipers are collected here; *Vipers.*
... of which are kept alive for various ufes, and others
...u and made into powder, which is fuppofed to be of great
...:acy in medicine. They feed the fowls with vipers and *Fowls fed*
/OL. III.   E e   meal *with them.*

'The owner's virtue reflects a luftre upon his houf
'olo Tomafini, a pleader, 1639.'

In the houfe is fhewn the following concife forn
will by the fame gentleman:

His will.
*Deo vivite, Sereniff. Reip. Venctæ obfequium præstat
nes honorate, nullum cujufcunque fortis fpernite, pro nemir.
juffione vos obftringite, fic vivite, ut pofteri vos vixiffe inte
Paulus Tomafinus J. C. Filiis fuis teftamento reliquit.*

'Live to God; be loyal fubjects to the ferene repu
'Venice; honour all men; defpife not the meaneft; t
'ties for no man; fo live, that pofterity may kn
'have not lived in vain. This is the legacy which
'Tomafini, a lawyer, left his fons by this his laft
'teftament.'

Near the mill-bridge are to be feen thirty mills v
fmall diftance of each other, fet in motion by th
ftream.

Palazzo di Soranzo.
The fineft private edifice in the whole city is the
di Soranzo, which is adorned with the portraits of
number of princes. The garden belonging to this p
not yet completed.

Statue of Hercules Buphilopo-nus.
In the court of the Palazzo di Mantua ftands a lar
loffus with this infcription:

*Hercules Buphiloponus beftiarius, qui triftitiam depulit
peramplo hoc figno Mantuæ curæ reflorefcit.*

Buphiloponus may poffibly fignify a great lover of la
and *beftiarii*, according to Tertullian, Vopifcus, Pruc
and particularly Caffiodorus (*diverf. lect. lib.* v. *epif*
were thofe who voluntarily offered themfelves to fig'
wild beafts in the amphitheatres: but for what end thi
was erected I can get no information, neither do I r
ber that any of the ancient writers apply fuch an ep;
furname to Hercules.

* It feems rather, from its etymology, to denote a lover of l
oxen, from βους, φιλος, and πονος, and probably alludes to Hercul
ing Geryon's oxen, and driving them from Spain into Greece.

PADUA.

In the palace of count Francesco Capo di Lista is a *A large* wooden horse so large that it cannot stand in the first story, *wooden horse.* but by its enormous height takes up half the second. It seems the family coat of arms is a horse; but what gave rise to the whim of making this huge wooden horse, no-body could inform me. My guide assured me that it was the original Trojan horse.

Formerly the cabinets of Bonaviti, Silvatico, Zabarella, *Cabinets of* Tomassini, Lazara, &c. at Padua were worth seeing; but *curiosities.* they have been dispersed, and nothing now remains of them. However, Morgani has a good collection of curiosities. But the most valuable in this city is that of the celebrated physician Antoni Valisnieri, who dying on the 28th of January, *Of Valisni-* 1730, in the five-and-twentieth year of his age, left behind *eri.* him a son of the same name, the present owner of this curious collection. It consists of several petrifactions, natural curiosities, Egyptian idols, Hetruscan vases, and ancient marble busts, among which one of Junius Brutus and two of Jupiter are much admired. Several animals and insects, *Methods of* formerly kept in spirits of wine, are here preserved without *preserving several ani-* any liquor, in glass bells stopped with wax at the bottom, to *mals for a* secure them against the air. *long time.*

Among the pleasure-gardens of Padua, that of d'Andola, *The garden* a noble Venetian, is one of the best, being adorned with *of Andola.* great numbers of statues; but the Papafava gardens exceed *Of Papafa-* it for orange-trees, cypress, and other ever-greens, which *va.* are disposed into fine walks, labyrinths, and beautiful hedges. Of the latter, some are of box-tree, grown to the height of thirteen or fourteen feet.

The name of Papafava is said to be derived from Giaco- *The etymo-* bino de Carraria, to whom the monks of a convent in Car- *logy of the* raria, where he was educated, gave that nickname, because *name of Papafava.* he was extremely fond of beans.

The air of Padua is accounted very healthy. Martin *Healthful-* Ichtel, a German, father to the person who keeps the inn *ness of the* called il Rè d'Ingliterra, or the sign of the king of England, *air.* died a few years since at the age of a hundred and fourteen. However, few cities have so many apothecaries as Padua, in proportion to the number of inhabitants: but it must be observed, that most of these venders of medicines are also confectioners. Great quantities of vipers are collected here; *Vipers.* some of which are kept alive for various uses, and others dried and made into powder, which is supposed to be of great efficacy in medicine. They feed the fowls with vipers and *Fowls fed* meal *with them.*

Vol. III.   E e

PADUA.

meal at Naples; where they are also administered to patients, as well as the broth made of these animals. The best way of feeding fowls is to cram them with a paste made of viper-powder and barley-meal, and then to give them milk to drink. Of these fowls the Neapolitans make a jelly, and give it to consumptive patients, and order them to continue drinking it for some weeks. This puts me in mind of Sir Kenelm Digby, an English virtuoso, who used to feast his wife, who was a very beautiful lady, with capons fattened with vipers flesh; but he did not long enjoy his pampered idol; for she died very young. Vipers are not always equal-

The best vipers. ly good; for in some years their flesh is more efficacious than in others. Those caught in the neighbourhood of Rome are accounted the best; and on that account great quantities are sent from thence to Venice, to be used as an ingredient in the Theriaca Andromachi, or Venice-treacle; though, at present, the Theriaca, made at Paris and other places, is as good as that of Venice. As all venomous creatures thrive best in a warm climate and dry soil, the vipers bred about Padua must consequently be inferior in virtue and efficacy to those of Rome.

Storms. The territory of Padua is very subject to storms, particularly those which come from the sea, which are extremely violent.

Public brothels. For the honour of the Muses, and the edification of the students in the University, it seems the Donne libere, or Done del Mondo, as they are called, are publicly tolerated at Padua. These ladies have their respective dwellings appointed them, where they live together six or eight in a class, and offer themselves to the service of the public. That so commendable an institution may not be liable to any objection, it is the peculiar office of several physicians frequently and strictly to examine these Donne, that no bad consequences may happen to those who converse with these nymphs. Of these public temples of Venus, there are two in the city of Padua; and, what seems something out of character, one joins to the Eremitical fathers convent, and the other to a nunnery of St. Blaze.

Jews place. The Jews have also their particular quarter allotted to them at Padua, out of which they are not permitted to stir. On the three gates leading thither are so many different inscriptions: that on the south-gate is as follows:

F. D.

The Country about PADUA. 419

F. D.

Ne populo cœlestis Regni hæredi usus cum exhærede esset fraudi, Judæi unum in locum hic redacti assiduo Marci Cornelii lectissimi Viri, Episcopi, Domûs Dei zelo atque studio penè universorum Sanctissimo, Dominæ Urbis Senatu auctore, facto decreto civium, Virorum amplissimorum Francisci Bernardi Prætoris, Marci Quirini Præfecti benigno auspicio, eximiâ Danielis Campesii, Sertorii Ursati Eq. Nicolai Campo San. Petri J. C. Curatorum operâ. Anno Christi M.DC. III. J. F. M.

Inscription over a gate of the Jews quarter.

' Lest any detriment might accrue to the heirs of the
' kingdom of heaven from a commerce with those who are
' disinherited, the Jews were confined to this quarter by the
' indefatigable zeal of the most excellent bishop, Marco
' Cornelio, for the house of God, and the unanimous de-
' cree of the senate, &c. in the year 1603.'

PADUA, May, 1730.

LETTER LXXII.

Description of the Country about ABANO, CATAJO, BATAGLIA, ARQUA, &c.

SIR,

NO traveller of taste will think it lost time to bestow a day on an excursion into the country that lies to the south of Padua. The village Abano, in Latin, *Aponum*, lies about four Italian miles from Padua, and is much frequented in summer on account of the warm baths which are about half a mile from it.

A house belonging to signior Cornelio, or Cornaro, in this village, is adorned with some good pictures, and two ancient monuments, one of which represents a woman sitting, with this inscription:

The village Abano.

Ancient tombs.

ΥΠΟΜΝΗΜΑ ΑΙΛΙΑΣ ΦΙΛΗ
ΜΑΤΙΟΥ.

Greek inscription.

E e 2 ' The

The Country about PADUA.

'The monument of Ælia, the wife or daughter of Phi-
lematios.'

On the other are the representations of a man and a boy, with these words under them:

Another.

ΓΛΑΥΚΟΣ ΓΛΑΥΚΟΥ
ΧΡΗΣΤΕ ΧΑΙΡΕ.

'My beloved Glaucus, the son of Glaucus, farewel!'

Over an old picture of the poet Petrarch are these words in Italian:

Inscription over Petrarch's picture.

*Vecchio penso, ardo, piango, e chi mi sfage
Sempre m'e'inanzi per mia dolce pena.*

'Old as I am, I still for Laura burn,
'And with fond tears bedew her sacred urn;
'Her pleasing form, still present to my view,
'At once my former joys and grief renew.

Opposite to Petrarch hangs Laura's picture, with the following inscription in the same language:

Over that of Laura.

*Miriam costei quand' ella parla e rie
Che sol se stessa e null' altra somiglia.*

'The beauteous Laura towers above her sex;'
'And, while we gaze, the willing soul beguiles
'With tuneful accents, or bewitching smiles.'

An admirable ancient monument, which now stands on a pillar near the college at Padua, was found at Abano. The inscription is as follows:

Ancient monument of Caia Atia.

C. ATIA C. F.
PRIMA SIBI
ET. Q. SICINIO. M. F.
VIRO SVO
V. F.
IN FRONTE
P. XX.
H. L. ET. M.
H. N. S.
DIS PENATIBVS.

i. e. *Caja*

The Country about PADUA. 421

i. e. *Caja Atia, Caji Filia, Prima sibi, & Quinto Sicinio Marci Filio Viro suo vivens fecit. In fronte pedes XX. Hunc locum & monumentum Hæres non sequitur. Diis Penatibus.* Vid. Urfati Mon. Patav. fol. 181.

The letters H. L. ET. M. H. N. S. may be read, *Hic locus & monumentum hæredem non sequuntur*; and fignify that no other person was to be buried in that place.

If Pliny by the Fontes Patavini means the baths of Abano, there is not one of them at present that does not emit a smell, which is quite contrary to what he observes of the Fontes Patavini *. In these baths are three sorts of water, of very different qualities; some of the springs are impregnated with sulphur, and have particular bathing-rooms, where, by means of steps, one may descend to any depth in the water. Others are boiling hot, and the water springs up in such quantities as to drive a mill at the distance only of about twenty paces from the source. The wooden pipes through which the water is conveyed to these baths are often incrusted with a white lapideous substance, not easily separated from the wood; and the exact impressions of the veins and knots of the wood on this concretion make it perfectly resemble petrified wood.

The warm baths of Abano.

A Sudatorium has also been built here, the effect of which is caused by the steam of the water. Some of the springs, which are tepid, are said to be impregnated with lead: and others, from their reddish sediment and other signs, appear to be ferrugineous. In those where sulphur predominates, the pipes contract a crust of whitish salt. Here is also a *bagno di fango*, or a muddy bath, where very obstinate arthritic disorders have been cured by means of the warm slime.

Sudatorium.
Minerals in the water.
Slime bath.

* Plinius *Hist. Nat. lib. xxxi. c. 6. Nec decolor species æris argentive (ut multi existimavere) medicaminum argumentum est, quando nihil eorum in Patavinis fontibus, ne odoris quidem differentia aliqua deprehenditur.* ' Nor does ' the discolouring of brass or silver prove, as many have thought, any me-' dicinal virtues to be in them; no such virtues being found in the waters ' of Padua, nor any difference in smell.' But those of Abano are not the only baths in the territory of Padua. Suetonius, in his life of Tiberius, mentions the Fons Aponus; and Martial wrote an epigram in its praise; where, among other encomiums, he says of it:

Fons Antenoreæ vitam qui porrigis urbi.

' O fountain, who bestowest life and health on Antenor's city.'

E e 3 Why

The Country about PADUA.

Why Martial, in *lib.* vi. *Ep.* 42, ſtiles theſe baths *Fontes Aponi rudes puellis,* I own I cannot conceive.

The baths of Abano belonged to two perſons of the Moroſini family, and are at preſent let for a hundred Ducati d' Argento, or ſilver ducats, a year. A very accurate account of their virtues and properties was publiſhed at Padua by Gratiani, in the year 1701. It was intitled *Thermarum Patavinarum examen,* where he alſo treats of other baths in the neighbourhood of Padua.

In ſome places betwixt this and Catajo, a ſmoke or warm exhalation is ſeen to ariſe from the water and ſoil; ſo that, if it was requiſite, the number of hot baths might be eaſily increaſed.

Palace of Inganno. On the left-hand of this road ſtands a fine palace called Inganno, *i. e.* Deceit.

Catajo. Catajo lies five Italian miles from Abano. The former belongs to a gentleman of the family of Obrizzi, the moſt remarkable actions of which are painted in *freſco* in this palace by the celebrated Paolo Veroneſe, and explained by proper inſcriptions. On the entrance of this palace are the following ingenious lines, compoſed by Paul Julian Ungar:

Ingenious Inſcription over the entrance of the palace.

Jupiter alme domum tutare, ſuperna Gigantes
 Atria ſi capiant, hic tuus orbis erit.
Heic quoque ſiderei ſunt picta palatia cœli,
 Adde notis animas, Numinis inſtar erunt.

‘ Great Jove protect this houſe. Should the giants once
‘ more ſtorm thy imperial dwelling, this may be thy reſi-
‘ dence. Here alſo are painted the palaces of the ſtarry
‘ heaven. Give life to the figures, and they will become
‘ as ſubordinate deities to thee.’

Near a ſmall ſtair-caſe in the palace is the portrait of an old woman, with theſe lines over it:

Verſes over the picture of an old woman.

Gabrina giace qui, Vecchia laſciva,
Qual dal vago Zabrin portato in groppa;
Che benche ſorda, ſtralunata, e Zoppa,
 Si traſtullò in amor, fin che fù viva.

‘ Here lies the laſcivious Gabrina, &c. who, though ſhe
‘ was deaf, old, lame, and blind, was ſtill amorous while
‘ ſhe had any life in her.’

The

The Country about PADUA.

The upper ſtory is finely furniſhed with paintings, among which hangs the portrait of the marchioneſs d' Obrizzi, in honour of whom a ſtatue was erected in the council-houſe at Padua for her chaſtity, as mentioned above. By her picture (and painters are ſeldom guilty of doing injuſtice to the ladies) ſhe appears to be no extraordinary beauty. This palace yields a beautiful proſpect, and has charming gardens, cool grotto's, a park, a theatre, a pavilion for balls, and every thing that conduces to pleaſure and magnificence. *[Portrait of the marchioneſs d' Obrizzi.]*

The village of Monſelice (in Latin, *Mons ſilicis*) lies not far from hence; and within an Italian mile from Catajo lies the little town of Bataglia, ſo called from the rapid conflux of two ſmall rivers in that place. *[Monſelice.]*

About three miles from Bataglia lies Arqua, or Arquato, famous for having been the reſidence and burial-place of Franceſco Petrarcha. This celebrated poet was born on the 20th day of July in the year 1304, at Arezzo, in the dutchy of Florence; and in his youth was forced to make his eſcape into the county of Avignon in France, where he lived chiefly at Vaucluſe (ſo called *quaſi Vallis clauſa*) near the ſource of the river Sorgue; a place he often mentions in his poems with great praiſe and affection. In the twenty-third year of his age, he happened one day to meet a young lady of about thirteen years of age without the gates of Avignon, with whoſe beauty he was immediately ſtruck; and became ſo paſſionately enamoured of her, that he not only entertained the tendereſt love for her during the courſe of one-and-twenty years, that is, as long as ſhe lived; but perſevered in his extraordinary paſſion ten years after her death, and even to the end of his days*. It does not appear that they were *[Arqua. Account of Petrarch. His amour.]*

---

* This appears from Petrarch's own words in one of his ſonnets:

Tenemi amor anni vent' uno ardendo
Lieto nel fuoco, e nel duol pien di ſpeme;
Poi che madonna, e il mio cor ſeco inſeme
Saltro al ciel, dieci altri anni piargendo.
Sonetto 313.

' For twice ten years, and more, my boſom glow'd
' With love's ſoft fires, and felt its pleaſing pangs.
' But ſince my Laura took her flight to heav'n,
' And thither carried every heart-felt joy,
' Ten years I've mourn'd her early fate, and oft
' Bedew'd her urn with unavailing tears.'

ever married*; nor is it known what could prevent these lovers from entering into the conjugal state. It is true, Petrarch once had some ecclesiastical preferment; but this was towards the latter part of his life; so that, in the first years of his passion for Laura, he was under no restraint as to marriage on that account. Possibly the want of an easy fortune might check any thoughts of entering into a condition, which is generally attended with considerable charges; for it was but few years before his death that he went to Florence, to take possession of the inheritance that his father had left him. The real name of Petrarch's mistress was Lauretta, which in his poems he always has abbreviated into Laura. Her father was Henry Chabod, lord of Cabrieres. Petrarch fell passionately in love with Laura the moment he first saw her, which was on the sixth day of April, 1327, about one of the clock in the afternoon, as he tells us in his 177th sonnet, part I. I should not have been so exact in mentioning this circumstance, had not Petrarch, in the first chapter of the Triumph of Love, and in the 291st sonnet, part II, observed, that his beloved Laura expired on the very same day of the year 1348, and in the same hour. Upon her death France became quite insupportable to him; and, after roving some time from place to place, he at length fixed upon Arquato as his place of residence, where he died in the seventy-fourth year of his age. His monument is to be seen near the church, with the following short inscription:

Frigida Francisci lapis hic tegit ossa Petrarchæ.
Suscipe, Virgo Parens, animam; Sate virgine parce,
Fessaque jam terris cæli requiescat in arce.
Moritur, Anno Dom. 1374. 18. *Julii.*

'Under this stone lie the poor cold remains of Francesco
'Petrarcha. Holy virgin, receive his soul; and thou who
'wast born of a virgin pardon his sins, and grant that he
'may rest in heaven after his weary pilgrimage on earth.'

* In the *Colloquio tertii diei, Petrarch* writes thus: *In amore meo nil unquam turpe, nil obscænum, nil denique præter magnitudinem culpabile. Adde modum, nihil pulchrius excogitari queat.* ' My love was ever free from the ' least turpitude or obscenity, and was culpable only in its excess. Had ' the ardour of my passion been less violent, nothing could be imagined ' more commendable and praise-worthy.'

Under-

The Country about PADUA.

Underneath are thefe words:

Viro infigni Franc. Petrarchæ Laureato Francifcolus de Brofano, Mediolanenfis, gener individuâ converfatione, amore, propinquitate, fucceffione, memoriâ.

' To the memory of that celebrated poet Francefco Pa-
' trarcha; Francefcolo de Brofano, of Milan, his fon-in-
' law, who was infeparably united to him by converfation,
' affinity, affection, &c. infcribes thefe lines.

And farther underneath:

Jo. Bapt. Rota Patav. amore, benevolentiâ, obfervantiâque devinctiff. tanti celebr. Vatis virtutum admirator ad pofteros. H. M. B. M. P. C.

' Giovanni Battifta Rota erected this monument as a
' mark of his fincere affection to, and admiration of the
' excellent qualities of fo great a poet, in order to perpetu-
' ate the memory of their friendfhip to pofterity.'

Under a brafs buft of Petrarch, placed over this monument, is the following infcription:

Fr. Petrarchæ Paulus Valdezucus Poëmatum ejus admirator, ædium agrique poffeffor, hanc effigiem pof. An. 1547. Idibus Sept. Manfredino Comite Vicario.

' This buft of Petrarch was fet up by Paolo Valdefuci,
' an admirer of his poems, and the poffeffor of his houfe
' and eftate, Sept. 13, 1547.'

On the north fide of the church is to be feen the following infcription on marble:

Danti Aligerio, Francifco Petrarchæ, & Joanni Bocacio, Viris ingenio eloquentiâque clariffimis, Italicæ linguæ parentibus; Ut quorum corpora mors & fortuna fejunxerant, nomina faltem fimul collecta permanerent, Joan. Brevius Canon. Cenetenfis, hujus Bafilicæ Rector, in fui erga eos amoris obfervantiæque teftimonium pofuit MDXXIIII.

'To Dante Aligieri, Francesco Petrarcha, and Giovanni Boccacio, persons celebrated for their wit and eloquence, the parents of the Italian language; that those, whose bodies death and other accidents have separated, might at least have their names perpetuated together on this marble, Giovanni Brevi, canon of Ceneda, and rector of this church, as a testimony of his regard and affection for those illustrious persons, erected this monument in the year 1524.'

Over a fountain at Arquato this distich is to be seen:

Inscription on a fountain.

Fonti Numen inest, hospes venerare liquorem,
Unde bibens cecinit digna Petrarcha Deis.

'Revere this sacred spring, whose limpid stream
Inspired Petrarch's heav'n-born muse to sing
Such lays as e'en the gods might deign to hear.'

Other memorials of this poet in his house.

The house in which Petrarch lived stands on a hill, at some distance from Arquato; and over the door leading to the garden and vineyard is the following distich, put up by order of the person who succeeded Petrarch, as proprietor of the house:

Impunè hinc Cererem sumas impunè Lyæum
Intactas habeat dum mea laurus opes.

'Traveller, thou mayest safely regale thyself with the gifts of Ceres and Bacchus; but let not thy rash hand touch my laurels.'

The memory of the poet is preserved in several of the apartments by allegorical paintings in *fresco*: copper-plates of these, and of some pieces of his furniture that still remain in this house, are to be seen in Tomasini's *Petrarcha redivivus*. Pignori has bestowed the following epigram on on the poet's chair:

Hospes

The Country about PADUA.

Hospes ades, tenuemque procax ne despice Sellam   Epigram on
Terpsichore quâ vix aurea majus habet.   his chair.
O quoties Vatum hac sedit clarissimus olim
* Dum canit ad Thuscam carmina culta lyram.*
Cum rigidæ ad numeros motare cacumina quercus
* Conspectæ, & rabiem ponere jussa fera est.*
Phœbe Pater, quid sellam axi superaddere cessas?
* Dignior haud currus instruet ulla tuos.*

    ' Stranger, approach, behold this homely chair,
    ' Which e'en Terpsichore herself might chuse,
    ' Where seated oft the bard divine attun'd
    ' His heav'nly numbers to the Tuscan lyre;
    ' While knotted oaks were seen to wave their heads,
    ' As beating time to his harmonious lays,
    ' And admiration tam'd the savage beasts.
    ' Apollo, to thy axis join this seat,
    ' For none will better suit thy radiant car.'

     Petrarch's table is also celebrated by Johannes Rhodius
a Dane:

     Limpida servavi mensis cryjtalla Petrarchæ,   His table.
     Simplicitas ævi, qui fuit, inde patet.

    ' This table held Petrarch's crystal vases, and remains
' here as a monument of the simplicity of that age.'

     That Petrarch had a daughter is evident from the in- Petrarch's
scription on his monument, Francescolo de Brossano of natural
Milan being there stiled Gener, *i. e.* his daughter's husband. daughter.
It also appears by the inscription on the tomb erected to her
memory by her husband in St. Francis's church at Treviso,
that her name was Francesca.

     Franciscæ parienti peremptæ Francisci Petrarchæ Laureati
Filiæ, Franciscolus de Brosano Mediolanensis maritus P. Obiit
anno M.CCC.LXXXIV.

    ' To Francesca the daughter of Francesco Petrarcha, the
' celebrated poet, who died in child-bed, this monument
' was erected by her husband Francescolo de Brossano of
' Milan. She died in the year 1384.'

     This

The Country about PADUA.

This daughter he is supposed to have had in his younger years at Milan. And Tomasini, in his *Petrarcha redivivus*, says, that she was, by the mother's side, of the family of the Becrarii. As it is unquestionable that this daughter of Petrarch was the fruit of stolen embraces, I cannot but wonder at Boccacio's confidence, when he says of Petrarch, *A juventute suâ cælibem vitam ducens adeo ineptè Veneris spurcitias horret, ut noscentibus illum sanctissimum sit exemplar honesti*; 'That he 'led a single life from his youth, and was so averse to lust 'and forbidden pleasures, that all who knew him looked up-'on him as a shining example of chastity.' His daughter Francesca left behind her a son, who died at Pavia, where formerly his grandfather Petrarch resided for some time *.

Wickedness of Petrarch's brother. Though I am not for making a saint of Francesco Petrarcha, yet he ought to be distinguished from his brother Gerardino, who is charged with having, in consideration of a sum of money, given up his own sister to the brutal lust of pope Benedict XII.

Laura's grave and epitaph. As for the beautiful Laura, she died in Petrarch's absence, while he was on a visit to the Scaligeri family at Verona. She lies in the Franciscan † church at Avignon, with the following epitaph :

D. O. M.

Et memoriæ æternæ D. Lauræ cum pudicitiâ tum formâ fæminæ incomparabilis, quæ ita vixit, ut ejus memoria nullo seculo extingui possit.

Restituerunt veterum monumentorum peregrini indagatores D. Christophorus de Allegre Eques Lusitanus, & D. Antonius de Prat. Prætor Parisiensis, & Gabriel Simeonius Florentinus, ευδοκιας χαριν *IV. Idus April. 1558.*

Sola manet virtus, cætera mortis erunt. 'Sacred

---

* This infant was honoured with the following elegant epitaph, which is inserted here for the sake of the learned reader :

    Vix mundi novus hospes eram, vitæque volantis
      Attigeram tenero limina dura pede :
    Franciscus genitor, genitrix Francisca, secutus
      Hos de fonte sacro nomen idem tenui.
    Infans formosus, solamen dulce parentum
      Hic dolor, hoc uno fors mea læta minùs.
    Cætera sum felix & veræ gaudia vitæ
      Nactus & æternæ, tam citò, tam facilè.
    Sol bis, Luna quater flexum peragraverat orbem,
      Obvia mors, fallor, obvia vita fuit.
    Me Venetum terris dedit Urbs, rapuitque Papia ;
      Nec queror, hic cœlo restituendus eram.
        Vid. Jac. Salomonii Inscriptiones agri Patavini, p. 580.

† Or rather the Cordeliers church, which is one of the Franciscan orders.

The Country about PADUA.

'Sacred to God the greatest and best of beings,
'And the eternal memory of Laura, a lady no less dis-
'tinguished for her chastity than her beauty; who lived in
'such a manner, that her memory will never die, but is
'consigned to immortality.

'Christopher de Allegre, a knight of Portugal; Antony
'de Prat, chief magistrate of Paris; and Gabriel Simeoni
'of Florence, searching for ancient monuments, out of re-
'spect to Laura's memory, repaired this tomb, April 10, 1558.
'Virtue alone defies the stroke of death.'

This tomb remained for many years in obscurity, till it was at last discovered by Mauritius Scæva.

Francis I, king of France, passing through Avignon in his way to Marseilles, ordered Laura's grave to be opened, and the coffin to be taken up; but nothing remained of that celebrated beauty but dust and the bones. On the breast of the skeleton lay a small leaden box, in which were some Italian verses*, and a medal of lead, on one side of which was the image of a female, and on the reverse these letters, M. L. M. I. which stands for Madonna Laura mortua jacet; *i.e.*
'My beloved Laura lies dead.'

Upon this, Francis I. erected a splendid monument to Laura's memory, with the following epitaph composed by himself:

* These verses were written on parchment by Petrarch's own hand, and are as follow:

> *Qui riposan quei caste e felici ossa*
> *Di quell' alma gentile, e sola in terra,*
> *Aspro e dor sasso hor ben teco hai sotterra,*
> *È'l vero honor, la fama, e beltà scossa.*
> *Morte hà del verde Laure suelta e mossa*
> *Fresca radice, e il premio di mia guerra*
> *Di quattro lustri e più s'ancor non erra*
> *Mio pensier tristo, e'l chuide in poca fossa.*
> *Felice pianto in borgo d' Avignone,*
> *Nacque e mori: e pui con ella giace*
> *La penna, e'l stil, l'inchiostro & la ragione*
> *O delicati membri, ò viva face,*
> *Ch'ancor mi cuoggi e struggi, in ginocchione*
> *Ciascun preghi il Signor t'accetti in pace.*
> *O Sexo.*
> *Mortal bellezza indarno si suspira,*
> *L'alma beata in ciel vivra in eterno.*
> *Pianga el pute e il futur secul priva,*
> *D'una tal luce: & io degli occhi e il tempo.*

En -

En petit lieu compris vous pouvez voir,
  Ce, qui comprend beaucoup par renommée ;
  Plume, labeur, la langue & le devoir
  Furent vaincus par l'aymant de l'aymée.
O gentill' Ame, etant tant estimée,
  Qui te pourra louer, qu'en se taisant ?
  Car la parole est tousjours reprimée,
  Quand le sujet surmonte le disant.

' Within this narrow tomb confin'd you see
  ' Her, whose fair fame the world did over-spread ;
  ' Her lover's voice, his pen, his muse conspir'd
  ' To praise her living and lament her dead.
' O gentle shade ! who can record thy worth,
  ' Since words are wanting for so high a theme ?
  ' The muse in silence droops her doubtful wing ;
  ' There need no words to eternize thy name *.

Country about Arquato.

In returning from Arquato to Padua, we passed through a very pleasant country, interspersed with many beautiful

* Giulio Camillo, after the example of the French monarch, composed the following Latin epitaph for Laura :

  Laura ego, quæ fueram Thusci olim vita Poetæ :
    Laura ego, quam in vita Thuscus alebat amor :
  Heic sine honore diu jacui non cognita, quamvis
    Cognita carminibus culte Petrarcha tuis.
  Nullus purpureis spargebat floribus urnam,
    Nullus odoratis serta dabat calathis.
  Nunc quoque Francisci, sed versu & munere Regis
    Notesco, officiis conspicienda piis.

Luigi Almanni likewise celebrated Laura in the following Italian verses :

  Qui giace il tronco di quel sacro Lauro
  Che del Tosco miglior fu dal oggetto,
  Ch' ovunque scalda il Sol n'ando l'odore :
  Hor dal Gallico Re del ciel thesauro
  (Sendo in poco terren vile e negletto)
  Et di marmi, e di stil receve honore,
  E sempre i rami hauvrà fioriti e freschi
  Sotto l'ombra immortal de duo Franceschi.

The following Latin distich was also composed on Petrarch and Laura by Golnitz, a Dane :

  Carmine laurum habui, LAVRÆ studiosus amator :
  Mors rapuit LAVRAM, carmina non potuit.
                    Vid. Golnitz Ulyss. Belg. Gall. p. 484.

The Country about PADUA.

feats of persons of distinction. The nobility of the district of Padua had formerly the criminal jurisdiction, as it is called, over their vassals. But, the Castellani of Salvazzano having ordered a woman's eyes to be put out for a theft she had committed, the republic of Padua, under pretence that such a power was liable to enormous abuses, laid hold of that opportunity to take the entire administration of justice into their own hands. This happened in the year 1120; and the loss of this privilege was confirmed by an edict in 1205, under penalty of death to such delinquents as should offer to re-assume it. After this the Paduans appointed Podesta's in several places by whom to this day justice is, or ought to be, administered; it being the common boast of the Venetians, that, in two momentous points, their subjects are happier than the rest of the world, *viz.* that they always find *Pane in piazza*; *i.e.* 'Bread in the market;' and *Giustitia in palazzo*, 'Justice in the courts.' But I would not advise any foreigner, if he can possibly avoid it, to put the second article to the trial.

How the nobility lost their criminal jurisdiction.

Administration of justice.

I am, &c.

The End of the Third VOLUME.

End of the Third Volume

TO THE THIRD VOLUME.

A

ABANO village, account of Page 419
Abbey on MonteCassino, account of 1
Academy at Parma 326
Acheron lake 143
Acquetta di li Napoli, what 37
'---antidote against it ibid.
Addison, remark on 134
Adriatic sea, its testaceous fish 209
——— ebb and flood in 213
Ætna, good effects from it 18---why called Gibello 21 N---Virgil's description of it 26---the height of it diminished 32
Agnello S. miraculous crucifix of 50---account of 51
Aldrovandi musæum, account of 259
Alphonso II, his humility and beneficence 95
Altar, incomparable 81
Amber, origin of 316
Amphitheatre il Coliseo, account of 126
——— a celebrated one at Verona 355---Dr. Burnet's account of 356 N
Amsterdam, constitution of the the soil at 314
Ancona, some account of 207, &c.---beauty of its inhabitants accounted for 209

Angelo S. a Nido, church of 52
Animals, method of preserving them 417
Antenor's supposed grave 398
——— Patavium 399
Antiquity, remains of 5
Antony, See St.
Ants, annual miracle of 278
Aponi, stone image of 403---proceedings of the inquisition against 404
Apostoli S. S. church of 52
Appia Via, account of 5
Aqueduct from Vesuvio 41
Aquinas Thomas, his statue 59, &c.---dispute about his body 60
Arco count, condemnation of 297
Arco felice, described 141
Army, Neapolitan, account of 39---coins ibid.
Arsenal at Bologna 259
Artichokes, huge ones 179
Ass, relics of one 363---reflections 364---why no longer shewn at Verona 365
Assisi, some account of 177
Astruni, royal entertainment in the feast of 120
Augustus's birth-place, where 5
——— his bust altered to that of an angel 101
Aurelius Victor, mistake of 30
Authors, flagrant mistakes of 138

Vol. III.   G g   Baiæ,

INDEX.

B

Baiæ, bay of 144, &c.
Ballani, strange manner of their breeding 209
Balle-Marine, what 154
Baptistry, uncommon mark on 66
Barbarossa, attempts to carry off Julia Gonzaga 7
Baths hot 136
Bats cave, remarkable 46
Bellemerini or Benemerini, family of 83
Bembo Cardinal, monument of 387---epitaph ibid. --- some account of ibid. &c.
Benedictine order, registers of 2
Bentivoglio palace, demolished 260
Blindness, common at Bologna 250
Bologna city, described 247
――――dogs remarkable 249
――――cervellat and sausages 250
Bomb concealed in a wax candle 204
Bonsigliosi palace, paintings in 260
Bourbon, remains of the famous Charles de 11---how preserved ibid.---inscription on 12
Bridge, ancient one, built by Augustus over the Nera 160
―――― over the Reno, accident at 304, 305
―――― over the Adige, remarkable 340
Bucket, remarkable trophy of one 307
Butterflies, birds, &c. how preserved 294

C

Calabria, famous for manna and saffron 16
Calvi, remarkable chalky bottom near 159
Campeggi palace, some account of 260
Cannon, a remarkably large one 42
Capella del Carel. Filamarino, described 52
――――de Pignatelli 53---Convent of ibid.---excellent institution at ibid.
Capella di Stigliano, some account of 59
Capella del conte di Terranuova 95
――――del Rosario, how guarded 272
Caprara, palace of, described 260 &c.---family 261
Caprea, island, where situate 122 ―account of from Claudian ibid.---Quails here whence they come ibid.
Capua, new, some acount of 14, &c.---and of the old 15, &c.
Carmelite order, the origin of 79, &c.
Casa Santa at Loretto, described 179, &c.---miracles concerning ibid.
Cassini's meridian line described 283, &c.
Castello del Uovo, some account of 43, &c.
Castello nuovo 42, &c.
Castle, remarkable, of what made 38
Catacombs of St. Gennaro, described 65
Cataract remarkable 169
Catharina S. à Formello, church of at Naples 53

Catharine

INDEX.

Catharine de Vigri, the undecayed body of 269
Cattle white, their colour whence 175
Cecilia St. admirable picture of 276
―――censured ibid. &c.
Chapel de Vico, described 68
Chapel of St. Teresa, account of 82
Chapel a remarkable one 61, &c.
―another fine one 62
Chaplains, great numbers of them at the Casa Santa 194
Charles V's behaviour towards the pope 254
Chasm emitting fire 317
Chiara S. church of, curiosities there 54
Cicero, palace of 7― where assassinated 8―last place of residence ibid. N. ― his irresolution ibid.
―――his villa 136
―――an old edition of his works 287
Clitumnus, temple of, where 173
Collegium Illyricum, account of 205
Colonade, a remarkable one 279
Communion on board gallies 40
Concezzione, the church of 57
Conradine, duke of Swabia, catastrophe of 78―80, &c.
Convent of St. Maria Maddalena for prostitutes 85
Convent at Naples, decency in 92
Copernicus's system, where first adopted 291 N
Cork-trees, a wood of, described 4 N

Cornuto illustrious 223
Coroba or Corobola, what 4
Corregio's night-piece, account of 309
Corsairs infidel, devotion to a chapel 10
Cremona, account of 337
Crucifix which spoke to Aquinas· 58
Crucifix, bows its head to avoid a cannon-ball 78
Crucifix, procures a victory at the battle of Lepanto 105
Crystal, an extraordinary large piece of 325
Cuma ancient, where situate 142
―now in ruins ibid.
Cupola, admirably painted by Corregio 327
Curta or Civita Castellana village, account of 158
Cypress planted by St. Dominic 273

D

Dante the poet, tomb of 241, 242--his epitaph 242---life of 243, &c.
Difference between the Papal and Neapolitan dominions 6
Distichs from Virgil 5---24 N 109, 140, 155--on Ætna 26 --from Ovid on Naples 37--on St. Januarius 66--over an entrance 76--on a pillar 80--surprizing one under an Annunciation 84--by Sannazario 87 --on a rural retreat by the same ibid.---on Sannazarius by cardinal Bembo 89--on the statues of Castor and Pollux 98 --on Severinus and Sosius 103 ―――from Martial 110
Distichs

INDEX.

Distichs by Sannazarius 121
———from Horace 139 N
———from Silius Italicus 147—
on a painting by Guido Rheni 280—on Verona 347—on St. Zeno's oratory 366—on the counts of Vicenza 377 N —from Ovid 378—from Juvenal 391—on Albertus Magnus 392 — on Livy's place of nativity 407—on the chaste Susanna 409—on a fountain 426---on Petrarch's table 427
Dolphin tame 139
Domenico Maggiore S. church of 58

E

Earthquakes, destruction of towns by 30 N
Earthquakes and eruptions of Vesuvio, have little effect on the inhabitants 31
Elmo St. account of the castle 44, &c.
Elysian fields, where situate 148
English gentleman, accident of one at Vesuvio 27
Epigram from Martial on Vesuvio 19—on Petrarch's house 426
Epitaph, on Charles de Bourbon 12—on Mary of France 55—on queen Joanna I. ibid.—remark on it ibid— on a young lady 56—on a monument 58 —on a wall 83 — on Pedro Navarro 85—on Lautrec 86, 90—on Sannazarius by himself 89—by Alphonso I. 96—in a chapel 97 — in a church 101—on queen Isabella 102—by Belisarius 103— of Giovanni Battista ibid.—by Sanna-

zario 104---on three brothers ibid.
———on Charles king of Naples 60—on the unfortunate king Andrea 62—by Pontano on his daughter 68—critique on ibid. N — on two excellent bishops 72—on queen Joanna II. 75—remark on ibid. N
———on Dante 242
———Enigmatical 264 — explanations of it 265, &c. N— on the imprisoned K. Henci 271—on St. Dominic 273— on Accursi 274, &c.—a punning one 285—on Andrea Mantegna 343—on a female singer 344, &c. — of Scipio Maffei 352— of Lucius III. 360— on John Vesling 380
Epitaphs by Ottavio Ferrari 383, 384 — on Ferrari 385 — on count Sicci 386—on cardinal Bembo 387—on a bride 393 —on Scarabicci 395—on Laura 428, 429, N &c.
Esther, book, manuscript of 286
Euganei, their country, where situate 400
Eugene Prince, a brave attempt of 337
Eunuchs ecclesiastical, device of theirs 194

F

Faenza, its fine earthen vessels 246
Falernum, famous for wine 14
Female singer, an epitaph on 344, &c.
Ferrari Ottavia, epitaphs by 380, 383, 384
———his tomb and epitaph 385, 386
Ferrari

INDEX.

Ferrari Ottavia, inscriptions by 411—413---why defaced 413
Figs extraordinary, where 217
Filippo Neri S. church of 100
Fini, an Italian poet, remarkable verses by 381
Fish called Cavallo marino, its use and where found 135
——— testaceous 209
Fondi, a fine prospect from to Iteri 6
Font, a remarkable one 11
Fountain, a noble one 259
Fowls fed with vipers 417—the best way of feeding them ib.
Francesco S. di Paola, church of 64
Francia, a famous painter, cause of his death, what 277
Francis St. the place where he preached to the fishes 10
Franciscan church at Padua remarkable 380
——— convent 10
Frederic I. holds the pope's stirrup 255
Frederic of Austria, catastrophe of 77, 80
Free gifts, liberal ones 74
F's, saying about three of them 38
Fulvia, her insults to Cicero's head 8 N &c.
Fungi, remarkable ones from stone 17, &c.—forwarded by warm water ibid.

G

Gaeta, account of 8
——— siege of it in 1707, an account of 13 N &c.
Gaetano S. church of 65

Gallipots valuable, account of 203
Gassendi, passage from, on an earthquake 137, &c.
Gaston de Foix, his victory and death 244, &c.
Gazzulo, count, his garden and arms 369
Gennaro S. church of 65, &c.
German students, particular privileges of at Bologna 290
Germano St. sudatories of 113
Giacome S. degli Spagnuoli, church of 67
Gianone Pietro, account of 48 N
Ginetti palace at Velletri, account of 2
Giovanni à Carbonara, church of 67
Giovanni Vangelista church 68, &c.
Giovanni Maggiore, church of 70, &c.
Giovanni Pappacodi, church of 71, &c.
Giuseppe S. church of 72
Glowworm or Lucciola, account of 304
Goats, extraordinary leap of 158
Gonzaga Julia, story of her 7
Grapes, remarkable ones 162— method of preserving ripe ones 304
Gregory VII. pope, account of 319, &c.
Grotta Traconaria, described 149
Grotto supposed to have been made by Virgil 111 N
——— del Cane, why so called 114
Grotto

INDEX.

Grotto del Cane, experiment on dogs in it ibid.—on an afs 115—account of this grotto ib. 116 and N—grotto del Cane known in Pliny's time 120
Grotto at Bologna, account of 267
Groupe, a pretty marble one 94, &c.
Guelphs and Gibellines, origin of 331 N
Guido, a mafter-piece by 268

H

Harbour, of fourteen pilafters 133
Harlequins an impropriety in a church 361
Heiderfdorf, general, fentence paffed on him 298 N
Henfi, king of Sardinia, account of 257
———epitaph on him 271, &c.
Henry IV's fevere treatment by the pope 319, &c. N
Herculaneum and Pompeii, deftruction of by eruptions of Vefuvius 30 N
Hercules, a temple of 147
Hermitage on mount Vefuvius 22
High ftreet, a fine one 334
Hiftorian, particular qualifications of 364, 365, N
Horfe, fuperftition about a brafs one 45
———a large wooden one 417
Hofpital, a wealthy one 75, 76
—bankruptcy in 77

I

James St. his church 126
Janfenifts at Naples, account of 49

Januarius St. medal of 28, 29
———the head and blood of 62
---buft of 125—his prifon 126
---ftatue of and infcription 132
Jealoufy betwixt the Francifcans and Dominicans 274
Jefuits college at Naples, account of 57
Jewellers trade with convents 201
Infcriptions on a gate 5—on an ancient maufoleum 8 — remarks on 9—Greek one on a font 11 — Spanifh one on Charles de Bourbon 12 — French one on Charles de Bourbon, ibid.—on new Capua 14—on a medal 29—on a marble ftatue, ibid.—on a fountain 41—over an entrance 42—over a gate 44—on Marino's tomb 51—on a dog 54 —on Robert king of Sicily 54—on a poet 56—on an urn 58--on Thomas Aquinas 59-- on a monument 60—on St. Januarius 64--on a ftatue 75-- on a wall 77—critique on it 78—on the emprefs Margaret 79—on a tomb-ftone 82—on the endowment of a church and convent 95—on the front of a library 97—concerning St. Peter 100—on an antique building 106—a criticifm on it 107—on a maufoleum 109 —on the warm baths at Puzzuolo 112—ancient one on marble 127—over a garden-gate 128—on marble 129—under a ftatue 130—on a pedeftal 131—on St. Januarius's ftatue

INDEX.

ſtatue 132—ancient one over a frontiſpiece 131—concerning pilaſters 134—over a gate ibid.—imperfect one 135 — fragment of one 144—on a ſtatue 150—near a rock 153—on a bridge 156—on a large ſquare ſtone 157—on a bridge 158—on a poſt-houſe 159—on a clock 162—on a pyramid 163—ancient one 164—in a cathedral ibid.—over the Spoletto gate ibid. 165—over the porta d'Annibale 171—under a piece at Loretto 189—over a gate at Ancona 207—over a triumphal arch 208—on pope Urban VIII. 216—on a catholic council againſt the Arians 218—on an ancient monument 226—over a gate 228—on the print of St. Gregory's foot 230—on Dante 242 —on Charles V. when crowned by the pope 253—about a peſtilence 256—under a triumphal proceſſion ibid.—in the palace of Ranucci 263—under an ænigma 265—another ænigmatical one 266—inexplicable 273—on a miracle in a wall 278—againſt the uſuries of the Jews 281—on Caſſini's meridian line 283,&c.—on St. Proculo's decollation 286—on an academy of ſciences 290—on a curious marble ſtone 292—on ſhell-fiſh in a ſtone 293—a martial one 306 —on the theatre at Parma 323 —on an altar in miniature 325

—on Alexander Farneſe 329, 333—on Margaret of Auſtria 335—on the image of St. Dominic 338—ancient, a collection of 351,&c.—on St. George's church 362—under ſeveral ancient ſtatues 369—on St. Barbara's church 374—on a garden at Vicenza 375—on a temple of Pluto 377—on a miracle by St. Antony 382—on cardinal Bembo 387 —on a learned lady 388, &c.—on an image of Chriſt 394—on the ſiege of Padua 396—obſcure 398,&c.—in a church of St. Sophia 401,&c.—on Titus Livius 402—under his buſt 405—on the marchioneſs d'Obizzi 408—on ſeveral poteſta's 411,&c.—on a city library 414—under a marble lion 415—on the Jews gate 419—a Greek one ibid, 420—over Petrarch's picture 420—Laura's picture, ibid.—an ingenious one 422—on Petrarch's monument 424,&c.—on ſeveral Italian poets 425—on a fountain 426—on Petrarch's natural daughter 427
Intaglia, remarkable 64
Interments over haſty, inſtances of 71 N&c.
John Don, his conſecrated ſtandard 10
Iriſh, bravery of 337
Iſchia, iſland, ſome account of 150
Italian nobility, particular humour of 262
Italian

INDEX.

Italian princes, high pretensions of 312—pretended right of non-appeal ibid.
Italy, notion of concealed treasures in 174

L

Lacus Lucrinus, some account of 139
Lacus Velini, ancient, described 166
Ladiflaus, king of Naples, his inglorious death 67
Lago d'Agnano, account of 113
Lago Averno, anciently noxious 140—Lucretius's account of it ibid.—its present state 141—its depth 141
Lamps, legacies left for lighting 187
Lapis Phrygius, account of 17 and N
Latin Bible, printed at Mentz 288
Laura, Petrarch's mistress, who 423, &c—her grave and epitaph 428—epitaphs on her 430—her grave opened by Francis I. 429—a monument and epitaph by him ibid. &c. —verses found in a leaden box 429
Lava, what 23—great quantity of it emitted from Vesuvius ibid. —and from Ætna 24
Lawyers, how in all ages treated 370N
Lazaretto near Naples 121—Lucan's account of ibid.
Learned ladies, account of 388, &c. N
—— women bad wives 391
Legates palace, account of 252

Leo X. suspicions concerning 258 N
Library of a convent at Naples 97—at Bologna 280—at Parma 322
Limbus Patrum, passage into 155
Liquefaction of St. Januarius's blood 63—how done ibid. N
Liris, account of 14
List of all the most valuable offerings at Loretto 197, &c.
Livy's remains 406—place of nativity 407
Lizards, swarm in Italy 33
Loadstones, remarkable 292
Lorenzo, S. church in Naples, account of 73
Loretto, description of 179,&c. ——trade of its inhabitants 205—entertainment at, ibid. ——globular stones there 206
Lucan, passage from, on Cuma 142
Lucretia, contrast betwixt her and Susanna 409, &c.
Luther's prostration before pope Leo X. 258 N
——his pulpit 401
Lutrec, general, disaster of 46—epitaph on 86
——account of ibid.

M

Madre di Dio, church of 81
Maffei, monument of 352
——his system of the origin of lightning 353
Magnani palace, account of 262
Malpighi, inscription on the monument of 289
Mantegra,

INDEX.

Mantegra, whether the inventor of copper plates 343
Mantua, reprefentation of, on an agate 81
────an account of 340, &c.
its fertility 339
Manufacture, a particular one, of filaments in fhell-fifh 16
Manufcripts, feveral in a library at Bologna 286, &c.
────of the Old Teftament by Ezra 270
Marble cafe of the holy houfe, when built 188
Marcellinus Comes, his account of an eruption of Vefuvio 31 N
Margaret of Auftria, account of 335, &c.
Maria delle Grazie S. church of 84
Maria del Carmine S. church of 77
Maria di donna Reina S. church of 84
Maria donna Remita S. church of 84
Maria di Piedigrotta S. church of 90
Maria del Parto S. church of 86, 89
Maria de Sangri S. church of 90
Maria della Sanita S. church of 91
Maria S. Annunclata, church of 74
Maria della Concordia, church of 82
Maria Egyptiaca S. body of 339
Marino G. Battifta, account of 50
Marfigli's new academy of fciences 290—fome account of

295, &c.—made an indifferent figure as a military man 297
─fentence paffed on him 298
vindication of himfelf ibid.
Martial's account of Vefuvio 19
────verfes concerning a bridge 101
Martino S. church of 42
Mary virgin, fome milk of 64
────miraculous image of 277
─the fuppofed milk of, what 282
Mary of France, her tomb 54, &c.
Maffaniello, where killed 80
Maufoleum ancient, account of 108
Medal of S. Januarius 28, &c.
Medals, a cabinet of 323
Medallion, a rare one ibid.
Mercato del Sabato, what 148
Mercury, temple of 145 N
Meridian line, by Manfredo, account of 291
Mincio river, defcription of 340 N
Mines, invention of 44
Mint, at Bologna, fome account of 260
Minturna, ruins of 14
Mifeno, promontory of 148—whence derived 149
Miracles, feveral 182, 186, 195, &c. 230
Miraculous image of a foldier 282
Mirandola, how it came to the duke of Modena 310
────revenues of 311
Modena, account of 304
────eminent perfons born in 307
────difference betwixt the two princes 311—and between the duke and hereditary prince ib.
Mirandola,

INDEX.

Mirandola, number of its inhabitants 313
———particular property of the soil ibid.
Mola, account of 7
Money, caution about when travelling 15
Monte Oliveto, church of 95
Monte della Pieta, its revenue and how used 98
Monte Secco, account of 123
Monte nuovo, origin of 137
Monti Giuseppe, his works 299
Monument in honour of Maffei 352
Muratori, works of 310
Murder, how looked upon in Italy 376, &c.
Museum at Parma, account of 324
———famous at Mantua 341
———curiosities in Maffei's 353
———collections of 353, &c.
Mushrooms of an extraordinary weight 18

N

Naples, why termed a paradise 16—its produce 16, &c.
———temperature of its air 32—fertility of 33—inconveniencies in ibid.—wickedness of the inhabitants 37—character of, by Ovid ibid.—Prostitutes numerous and abandoned 38 corruption of the ecclesiastics ibid. sloth of the peasants ibid.
Naples, account of the city 39 &c.—harbour of 40—number of its inhabitants ibid.—fountains ibid.—account of the viceroy's palace 41, &c.—remarks on 42—a horse the arms of 45—booksellers not restrained there 50—remarks on the churches of ibid. &c.
———cathedral at 60—by whom founded 105
Narni, account of the town of 160—why called Nequinum ibid.—birth-place of great men ibid.—extraordinary large fruit near 162
Naumachia, remains of 358
Navarro Pedro, account of 85
Neapolitan nobility, account of 38—their great numbers 39
Neapolitan clergy, attempts of, on an author 48
Neapolitans inclinable to atheism 49
Nera river, plenty of fish in 101
Nisida island, account of 120, &c.
Nobility, Neapolitan, account of 38, &c.
———their great numbers 39

O

Obizzi, marchioness, her death and monument 408
———inscription on ibid.
Obrizzi, picture of the marchioness of 423
Ocrea or Ocriculum, ruins of 159
Orbetto the painter, account of 363
Oreste St. mountain of 158, &c.
———how so called 159
Orlando, a giant, account of 160—his cavern ibid.
Otho or Otto's palace, remains of 3

P

Padua city, account of 378, &c.

Padua,

INDEX.

Padua, how its nobility loft the criminal jurifdiction 431
Painters, cuftom of, in their works 99 N
Paintings remarkable 42, 84, 85, 89, 92,
——famous one of Rheni 92, 93, 96---by Vafari 97
——the firft one in oil colours 74—account of the invention of ibid.—on an incomparable altar 81—ridiculous one 195—in the cathedral of Fano 215—at Ravenna 239—in the Sala Farnefe 257—at Bologna 268, 269, 273, 276, 277, 280, 286—at Modena 308, 309—at Parma 321, 323, 324—in frefco 325—fine in the church of St. Giovanni 327, 328—in the palace church and cathedral 342—the church of St Barnabas 346—at Verona in St. George's church 362—in other churches 368—at Vicenza, in the council-houfe 372
Palace haunted 46
Palace, a fuperb and elegant one 46
Palaces of noblemen at Naples ibid. &c.
Palazzo degli ftudii publici, account of 105, &c.
——de Monti 262
——di Pepoli 263
——Rannici ibid.
Panegyric on a learned lady 388
Paolo Maggiore S. church of 98
Papal dominions, hardfhips of 207, &c.
Parma, account of 320, &c.

Parma revenues of the duke of 330
——prefent duke of, his character 332
Parmefan cheefe, excellerce of, to what owing 330, &c.
Paffion, a curious one 68
Patin Charles, epitaph of 393, &c.
——learned women of that name 394
Patrizia S. church of 99
Paul St. the three taverns of 4
Paufilypo, mountain of 110, &c.
Pearls extracted from an animal 294
Peafants, near Vefuvio, their character 22
——their ufe for climbing up 23
Pedro Navarro, why execrated 44
Pepin, falfe pretence about his body 366
Petrarch, an account of 423, 424 and N—his amour ibid.—his natural daughter 427
Petrifactions, feveral kinds of 318
——fifhes 370, 371—other petrifactions 371, 377
Petroleum, oil of, how procured 32---for what ufed 315--where found ibid.
Petruccio, Antonio, account of 59
Pharos or light-houfe of Ravenna, its prefent ftate 235
Philarmonic academy, account of 351
Philoti fociety, what 351
Phofphorus Balduinus, what 303
——burning ibid.--fulgurans from the mixture of two liquors ibid.
Phyfic

INDEX.

Phyſic garden at Bologna 259
Picture of the virgin, by St. Luke 279—of clergy in hell 282—remarkable copy of one 324—fine ones 334—by St. Luke 393
Pieta, an exquiſite one 365
Pietra Bianca, account of 47
Pietro S. d' Ara, church of 100
Pietro S. à Majella, church of 101
Pietro S. Martire, church of ib.
Pigeons made letter-carriers 306 N—ſeveral inſtances of ibid. &c.
Pigni, fruit of the 229
Pilgrims, great number of, at Loretto 191
Piſcina mirabilis, deſcribed 150, &c.
Piſo's baths 144
Placentia, great number of ec- cleſiaſtics in 332
———fair ibid.
Pliny the elder, account of his death 30 N.
Poggio reale, a decayed palace 45
Ponte Molle, or Milvio, near Rome 156
Ponte felice 156—from what ſo called ibid.
Popes, former pride of 254
Popilius Læna's ingratitude to Cicero 8 and N
Porcaria or Portaria, charming proſpect towards 159
Porphyry veſſel, what trouble it put the devil to 366, &c.
Portello, frontier wall of Naples 9 &c.
Porto Pavone, a ſmall harbour at Naples 121

Pretender, his offering to the virgin Mary 199
Prieſt, ignorance of one 194 N
Prince, inglorious death of a martial one 67
Proceſſion remarkable 38
Procita, iſland, account of 150
Proculo St. carries his head into Bologna 286
Prodigality, remarkable inſtance of, in a common ſoldier 341
Proſtitutes, proceſſion of peni- tent ones 49
Public brothels at Padua 418
Puns on the proſpect at Bolog- na 251
Puzzuolo, where ſituate and whence named 127, &c.
———cathedral of 131
Pyrmont ſprings, an account of 117
———water, how to imitate ibid. N
Pyx, an admirable one 100

Q

Quivaliſti at Padua, who 379

R

Radiances in ſea water, what 303
Raphael paints porcelain galli- pots 203
Ravenna, account of 231, &c.
Reatini, complaint of, againſt the Interamnates, what 167— Cicero's account ſomewhat obſcure ibid.
Reggio, account of 318
Reſervoir ancient 127
———a very large one 143
Rimini or Ariminum, an anci- ent city, account of 219

Road,

INDEX.

Road, subterraneous one remarkable 110, &c.
Robert, king of Sicily, his monument 54
Rock, a remarkable fissure in 9 —to what owing 2 N--superstition concerning it 10
Rock oil, account of 314
Romish new saints, to what owing 158 N
Rubicon, account of Cæsar's passing it 224

S

Saffron, where growing, and the best 16 and N
St. Antony, place where he preached to the fishes 223
——— miraculous image of 268
——— extraordinary devotion paid to 381
St. Apollinaris, body of 239
St. Beatrix, prediction of 308
St. Justina, elegant church of 397-- reliques ibid. &c.
St. Luke, his numerous paintings 183 N
Sal ammoniacum, composition of 124
Sala Farnese, account of 257 &c.
Saltpetre, a great quantity of 126
Salt works, account of 229
——— remarkable 330
——— blood used in ibid.
Sannazario, the poet, an account of 87, &c.
——— saying of his, on the death of prince Philibert 88 N
——— his tomb 88
Saracens, account of their irruption into Naples 51, &c.
Saxon fossils, at Bologna 293

Scarabicci's epitaph 395
Schrebelin, count, author of a famous piece 298 N
Scipio Africanus's tomb, 142--- inscription on his monument ibid.
Scorpions inconveniences from 34---their bite how cured ibid.----where most dangerous ibid.----the use of, and how catched ibid.--that they sting themselves shewn to be a vulgar error ibid.
Seneca's account of Naples 144, 147 N
Senegaglia town 214
Sermoneta, its unhealthful situation 3
Servilius Vatia, his seat 143
Sessa, town of 14
Sessi, method of cooling cellars there 171
Setia, good wine of 2
Shells, large 213
Shell-fish in stone 293
Sibyl's cave 143, 154
Sicily, climate of, hot 32, &c.
——— calamities in, by earthquakes 33 N
Silk manufactures and mills 248
Skull, drinking out of Charles de Bourbon's 13
——— common among the ancients ibid. N
Sloth remarkable 39
Snow and ice, the effects of its use in liquors 31 N
Soldier, extraordinary gallantry of one 45 N
Solfatura, a volcano, account of 123
Solifuga, a spider, some account of 34
Spoletto,

INDEX.

Spoletto, where situate 171
Stanza di Venere, account of 145, &c.
Stars seen in the day-time 291
Statues, superb bronze one of Urban VIII. 3---of Charles II. of Spain 15---of St. Januarius 29---64 of the river Nile 41--of Jupiter Terminalis ibid.---of the virgin 42---on a triumphal arch ibid.&c.--of a gallant young soldier 43 N---of a brass horse 45---fine of St. Jerom, &c. 84---of Apollo and Minerva 88---of St. James and St. Nazario 89 ---of the cardinal virtues 99--antique 130---of Pandulfo 222---brass one of Gregory XIII. 252---remarkable of Hercules 256---of St. Petronius 268---of St. Peter and St. Paul 281---two bronze equestrian 333---of St. Dominic 338---of five celebrated persons 349---of Verona 350 ---a collection of 360, &c.---of St. Sebastian 362 --- of Livy 402
Stones, experiment on those of Vesuvio with the magnet 24
———red-hot ones from Vesuvio 25---heat of the soil ibid.
———globular where found 206
———a very extraordinary one 233
Stories of Julia Gonzaga 7
———of a Spaniard 12---of a waiter at Mola 16---of a physician's daughter 67---of a priest and the virgin, 195 &c.
---of a wax taper 196---of a bomb concealed in a wax flambeau 204---of Gabrino Fundolia 338
Stork, winter quarters of 122
Street, a fine one 40
Subterraneous works, remarkable 44, &c.
Suburb at Naples, delightful 46, &c.
Sudatorii di Tritoli 152, &c.
Sun and moon, comprehensiveness of the worship of 236 N
Symmachus, lines from 148

T

Tabernacle, a rich one 107---an extraordinary one 52
Tarantula, some account of 34, 35---its bite, how cured 35, 36---its haunts 37
Tarantolati, who 35
Tartans, devotion of, to a chapel 10
Tasso, the house where born 110
Tassoni's poem, la Secchia rapita, to what owing 307
Temple of the giant 141, &c.
Terni, its situation 161
———why called Interamna 162
---its trade 165
Terrenatico, his wonderful escape 169, &c.
Terracina, account of 4
Terra virgine aurea, what, and its use 315
Theatre at Parma, a noble one 321, &c.---extraordinary construction of 322
———a curious one 373
Theodoric, king of the Ostragoths, his palace 232

Tiberius,

INDEX.

Tiberius, his monument 130, &c.
Toleration in ceremonies by the clergy at Naples 48, &c.
Tomb of Marino 50---of Mary of France 54---of queen Joanna I. 55---a beautiful marble one ibid.---of three unfortunate brothers 104---remarkable characters on 71---remarks on ibid. &c.---of Scipio Africanus 142---of Agrippina 146---of Accurſi 274---of St. Dominic 270---of Jerom Cagnolo 395
Tophana, a noted prisoner, an account of her and her drops 37
Tower of Degli Aſinelli, height of 251
------of Gariſenda, a leaning one ibid.
Tranſplantation of animals and vegetables, the effects from 19 N&c.
Travelling from Rome to Naples, inconveniences of 1, &c.
Treaſury of Loretto, account of 197, &c.
Triumviri, where entered into an alliance 305
Turks, ſepulchral inſcriptions of 131
Turneps extraordinary large 162 N

U

Univerſity at Bologna, account of 288
Uva Paſſa, or Paſſarina, why ſo called 162 N
Velino, remarkable cataract of 165
Velletri, account of 2
Venus, temple of, in Naples 145
Verona, account of 347, &c.
------excellent wine of 359, &c.

Veroneſe, Paul, night-piece of 342
------remarks on a piece of his 374
Verſes, Latin, on the Bologneſe 256
------over an old woman's picture 422
------on Verona 347, 348
Veſuvio, mount, contributes to the great fertility of the country 18---wines of 19, &c.---mount, an account of 20---no pumice-ſtones on it 24---minerals in the ſtones emitted from it ibid.---the former mouth of 25---great changes in ibid. &c.---no ſeeing its cavity for ſmoke 27---communication between it and the ſea 32---effects of ibid.---freſh water ſprings in ibid---its height diminiſhed ibid.
Via Caſſia, where 156
Via Flaminia, where ibid.
Vicenza, deſcription of, 372---vindictive temper of its people 376
------the meaneſt citizen of, why a count 377
Vines, broad boards of 237
Vipers, preſerved for medicine 417
Virgil, his monument, doubts about 108
------account of ibid. N--- a verſe from, by Loyola, with a remark thereon 109 N---his ſchool 110---his deſcription of ancient Mantua 340, &c.
------buſt and birth-place of 347, &c.
Virgin Mary's image, ceremony in dreſſing it 183, &c.
Virtue

INDEX.

Virtue of a country girl 409
Vitriol made near Naples 124
Von Egg, colonel, his sentence 297
Votive pieces, great numbers of 99
———abuses of them 201
Voyage historique d' Italie, criticism on 14
Vulcano artificial 31

W

Warm baths of Abano 421—Pliny's account of ibid. N——Martial's epigram on ibid.

White horned cattle with bells, why 304
Will, a remarkable and concise form of one 416
Wine, why called Lachrymæ Christi 20
Wine cellars, effects of sulphureous vapours in 116
Wine vaults, spacious, at Loretto 203
Wood fossile 171, &c.

Z

Zanoni, an apothecary, curiosities of 299

www.ingramcontent.com/pod-product-compliance
Lightning Source LLC
Chambersburg PA
CBHW032010300426
44117CB00008B/967